EX MACHINA

BOOK THREE

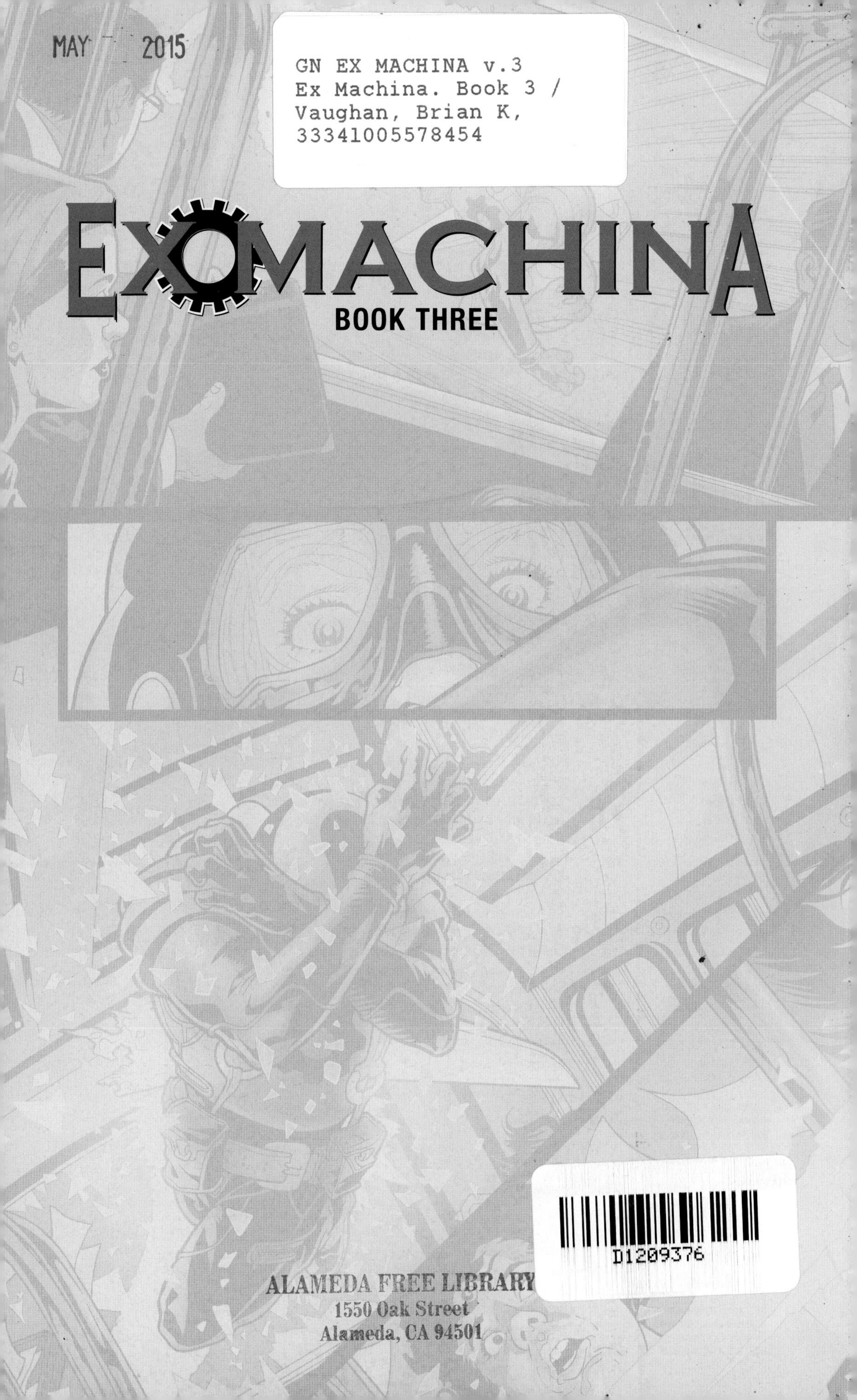

BRIAN K. VAUGHAN: WRITER
TONY HARRIS: PENCILS
TOM FEISTER & JIM CLARK: INKS

JOHN PAUL LEON: ART (MASQUERADE)

JD METTLER: COLORS
JARED K. FLETCHER: LETTERS

EX MACHINA CREATED
BY VAUGHAN & HARRIS

COLLECTED EDITION COVER
BY TONY HARRIS & JD METTLER

Ben Abernathy	Editor – Original Series
Robbin Brosterman	Design Director – Books
Hank Kanalz	Senior VP – Vertigo and Integrated Publishing
Diane Nelson	President
Dan DiDio and Jim Lee	Co-Publishers
Geoff Johns	Chief Creative Officer
Amit Desai	Senior VP – Marketing and Franchise Management
Amy Genkins	Senior VP – Business and Legal Affairs
Nairi Gardiner	Senior VP – Finance
Jeff Boison	VP – Publishing Planning
Mark Chiarello	VP – Art Direction and Design
John Cunningham	VP – Marketing
Terri Cunningham	VP – Editorial Administration
Larry Ganem	VP – Talent Relations and Services
Alison Gill	Senior VP – Manufacturing and Operations
Jay Kogan	VP – Business and Legal Affairs, Publishing
Jack Mahan	VP – Business Affairs, Talent
Nick Napolitano	VP – Manufacturing Administration
Sue Pohja	VP – Book Sales
Courtney Simmons	Senior VP – Publicity
Bob Wayne	Senior VP – Sales

EX MACHINA BOOK THREE
Published by DC Comics. Copyright © 2014 Brian K. Vaughan
and Tony Harris. All Rights Reserved.

Originally published in single magazine form by WildStorm
Productions as EX MACHINA #21-29, EX MACHINA: INSIDE THE
MACHINE, EX MACHINA SPECIAL #3 Copyright © 2006, 2007
Brian K. Vaughan and Tony Harris. All Rights Reserved. All
characters, their distinctive likenesses and related elements
featured in this publication are trademarks of Brian K. Vaughan
and Tony Harris. VERTIGO is a trademark of DC Comics. The
stories, characters and incidents featured in this publication are
entirely fictional. DC Comics does not read or accept unsolicited
ideas, stories or artwork.

DC Comics, 1700 Broadway, New York, NY 10019
A Warner Bros. Entertainment Company.
Printed by RR Donnelley, Salem, VA, USA. 8/22/14. First Printing.
ISBN 978-1-4012-5003-4

Library of Congress Cataloging-in-Publication Data

Vaughan, Brian K., author.
  Ex Machina. Book Three / Brian K. Vaughan, Tony Harris, John Paul
Leon.
    pages cm
  ISBN 978-1-4012-5003-4 (paperback)
  1. Mayors—Comic books, strips, etc. 2. Superheroes—Comic books,
strips, etc. 3. New York (N.Y.)—Comic books, strips, etc. 4. Graphic
novels. I. Harris, Tony, 1969- illustrator. II. Leon, John Paul, illustrator.
III. Title.
  PN6728.E98V354 2014
  741.5'973—dc23
                                                2014011713

SUSTAINABLE FORESTRY INITIATIVE

Certified Chain of Custody
20% Certified Forest Content,
80% Certified Sourcing
www.sfiprogram.org
SFI-01042
APPLIES TO TEXT STOCK ONLY

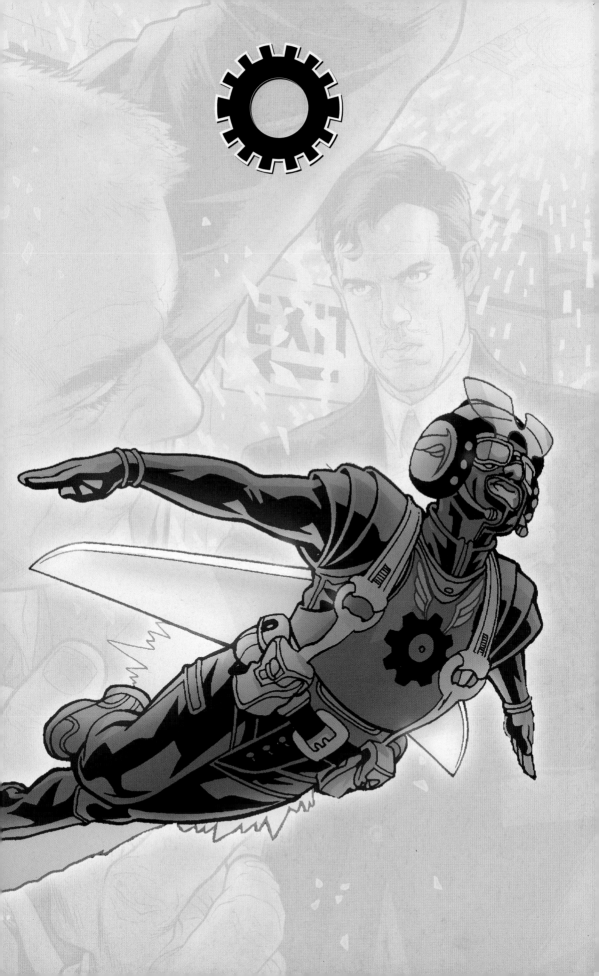

CHAPTER 1 SMOKE SMOKE

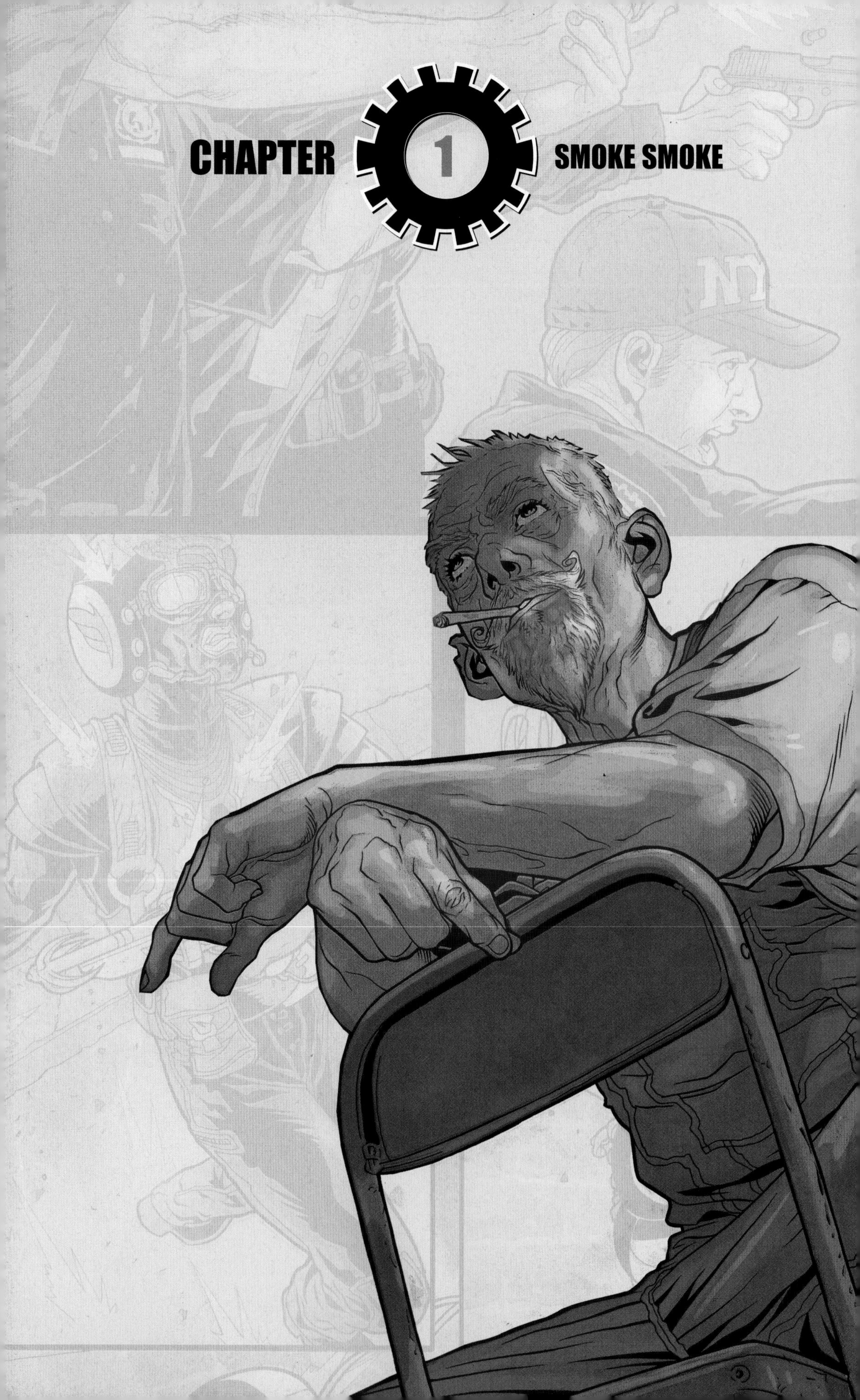

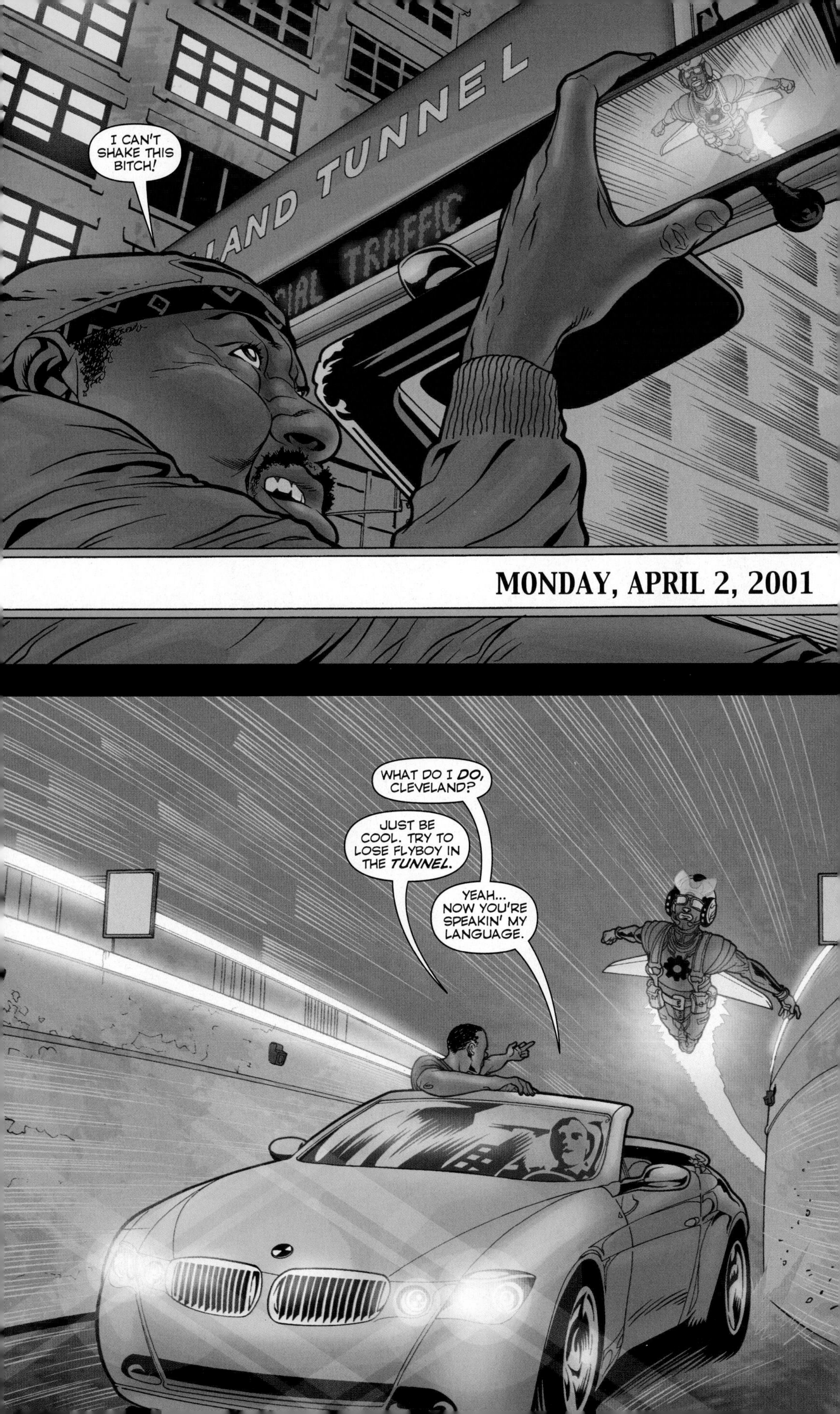

I CAN'T SHAKE THIS BITCH!
MONDAY, APRIL 2, 2001
WHAT DO I *DO*, CLEVELAND?
JUST BE COOL. TRY TO LOSE FLYBOY IN THE *TUNNEL*.
YEAH... NOW YOU'RE SPEAKIN' MY LANGUAGE.

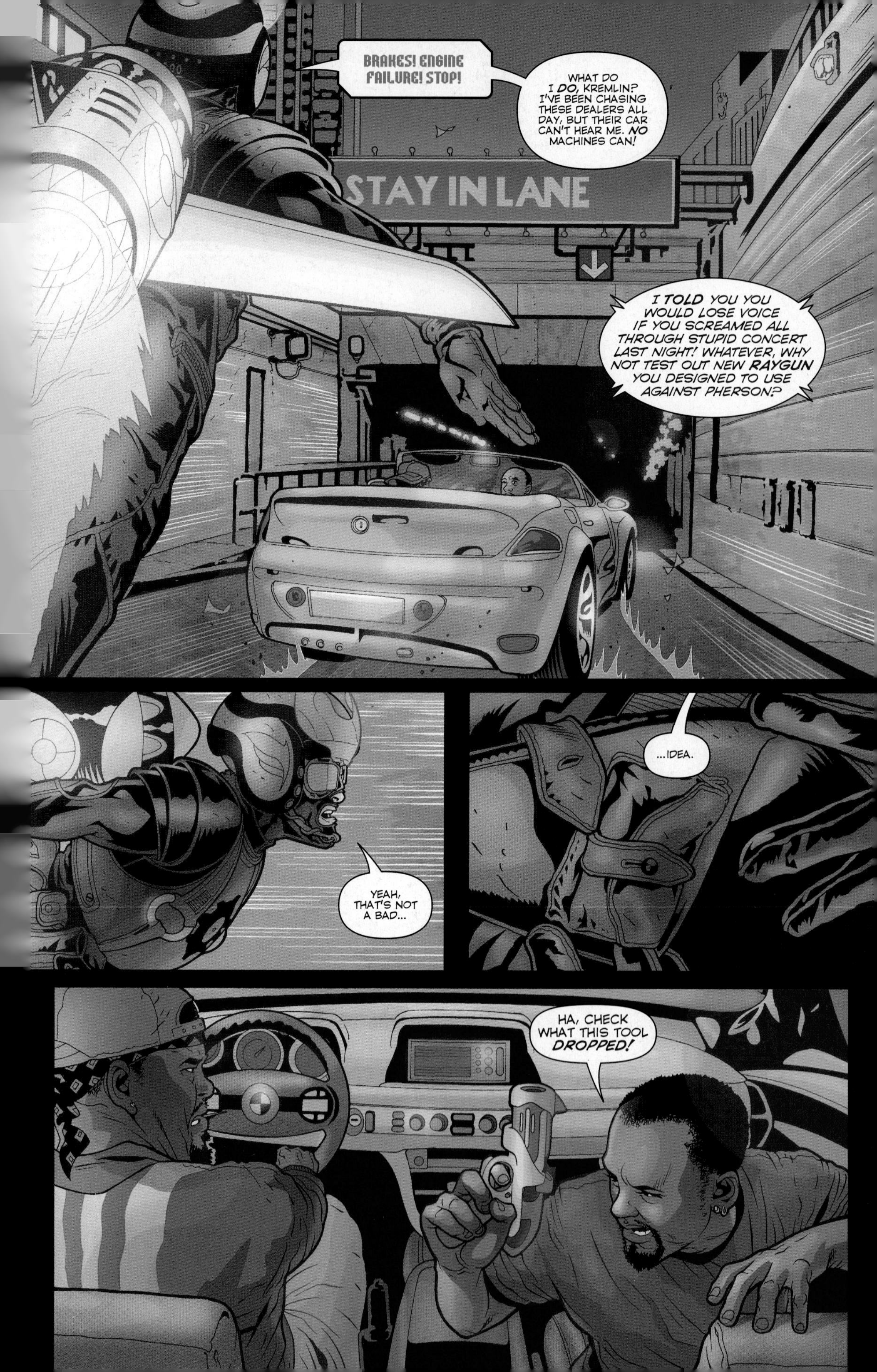
BRAKES! ENGINE FAILURE! STOP!
WHAT DO I DO, KREMLIN? I'VE BEEN CHASING THESE DEALERS ALL DAY, BUT THEIR CAR CAN'T HEAR ME. NO MACHINES CAN!
STAY IN LANE
I TOLD YOU YOU WOULD LOSE VOICE IF YOU SCREAMED ALL THROUGH STUPID CONCERT LAST NIGHT! WHATEVER, WHY NOT TEST OUT NEW RAYGUN YOU DESIGNED TO USE AGAINST PHERSON?
YEAH, THAT'S NOT A BAD...
...IDEA.
HA, CHECK WHAT THIS TOOL DROPPED!

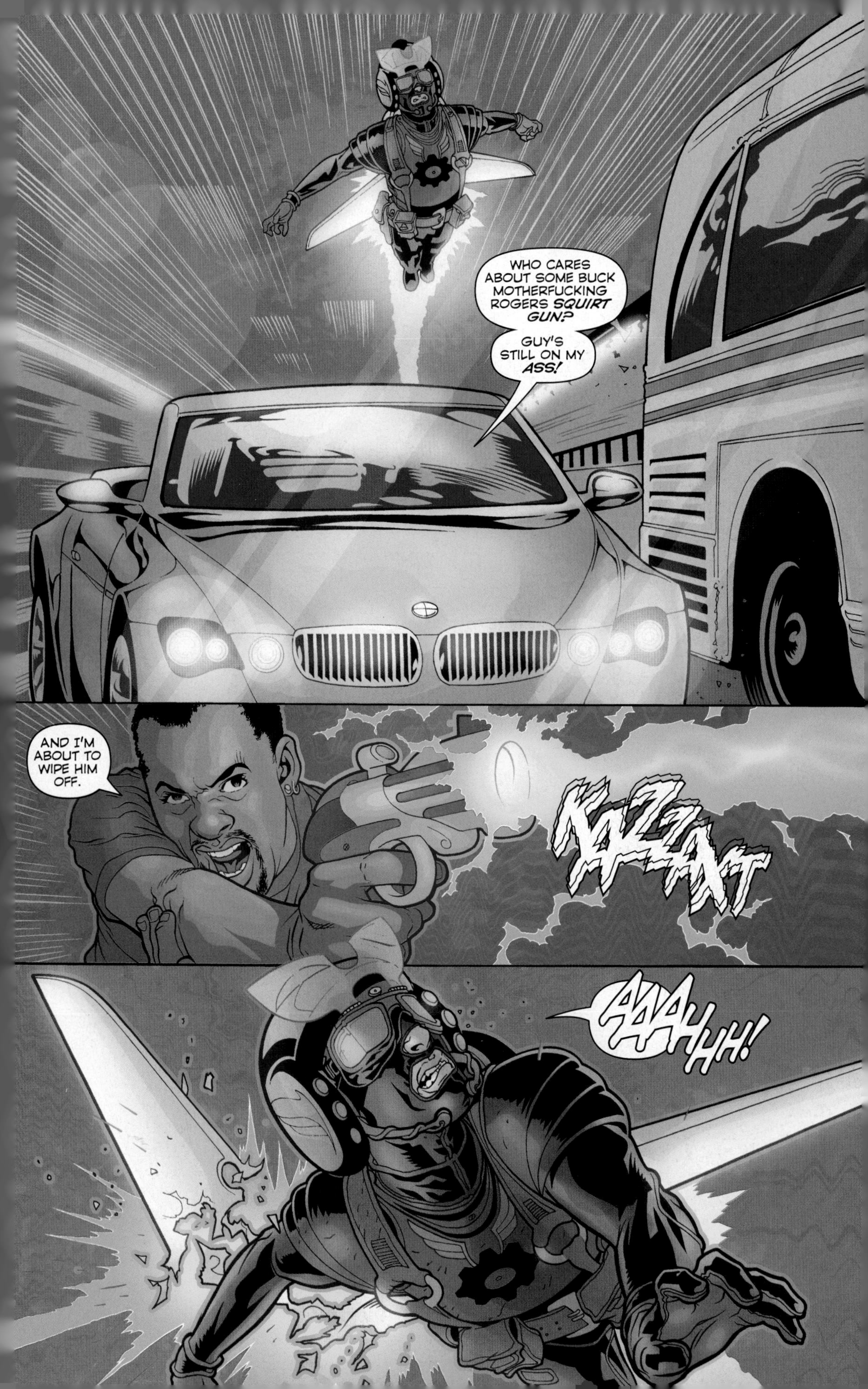
WHO CARES ABOUT SOME BUCK MOTHERFUCKING ROGERS SQUIRT GUN?
GUY'S STILL ON MY ASS!
AND I'M ABOUT TO WIPE HIM OFF.
KAZZAAT
AAAAHHH!

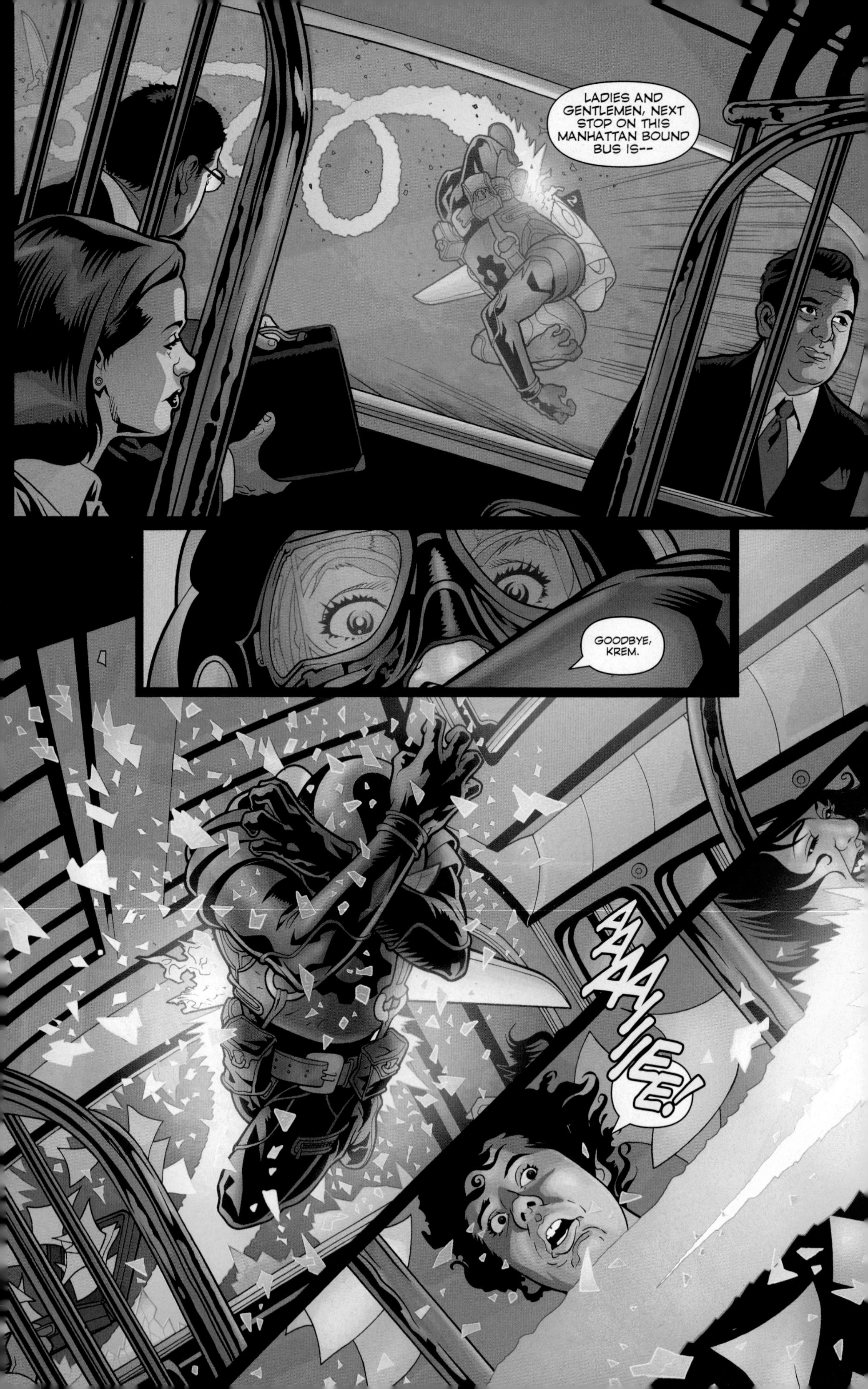
LADIES AND GENTLEMEN, NEXT STOP ON THIS MANHATTAN BOUND BUS IS--
GOODBYE, KREM.
AAAAIIEE!

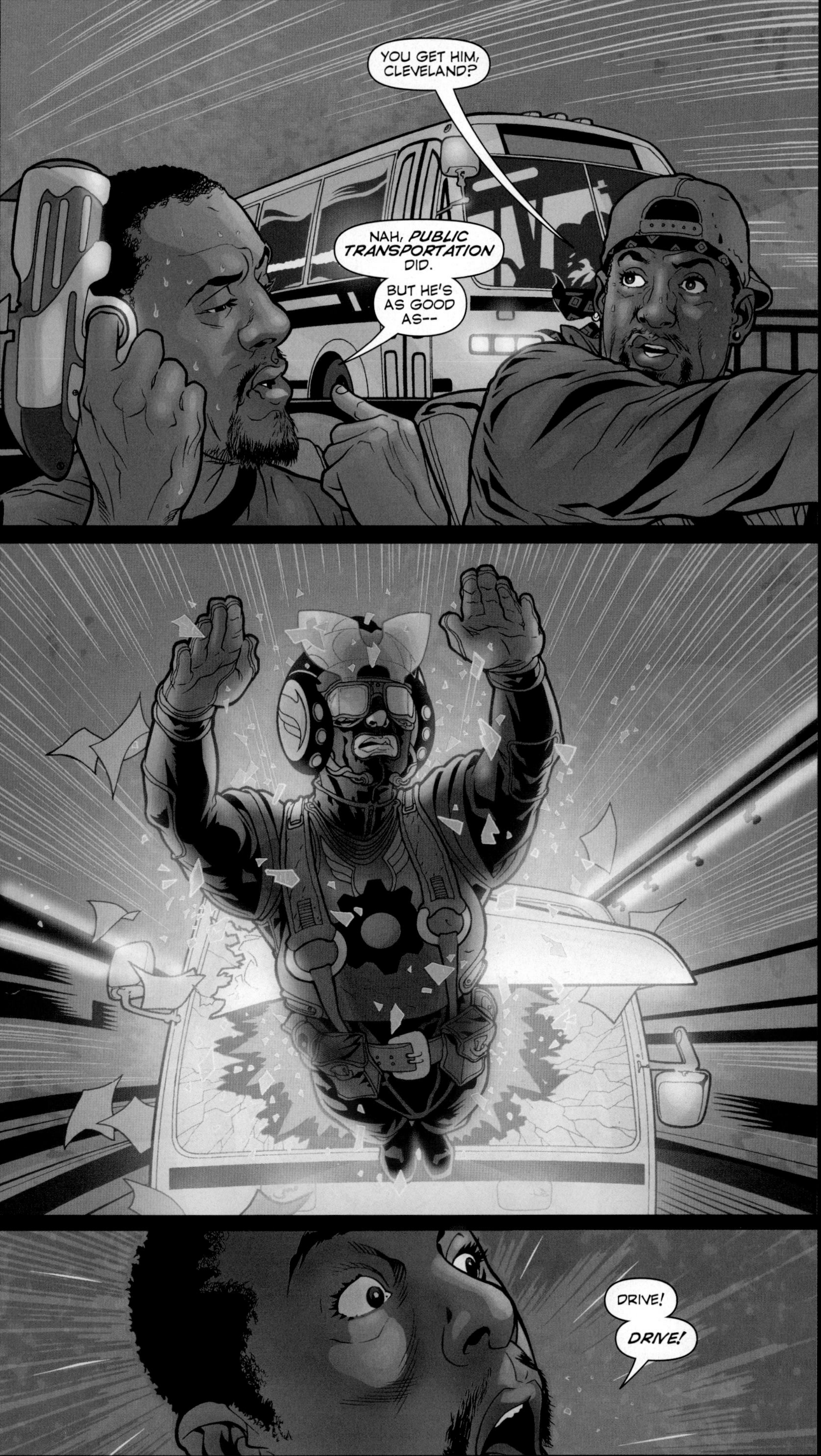
YOU GET HIM, CLEVELAND?
NAH, *PUBLIC TRANSPORTATION* DID.
BUT HE'S AS GOOD AS--
DRIVE!
DRIVE!

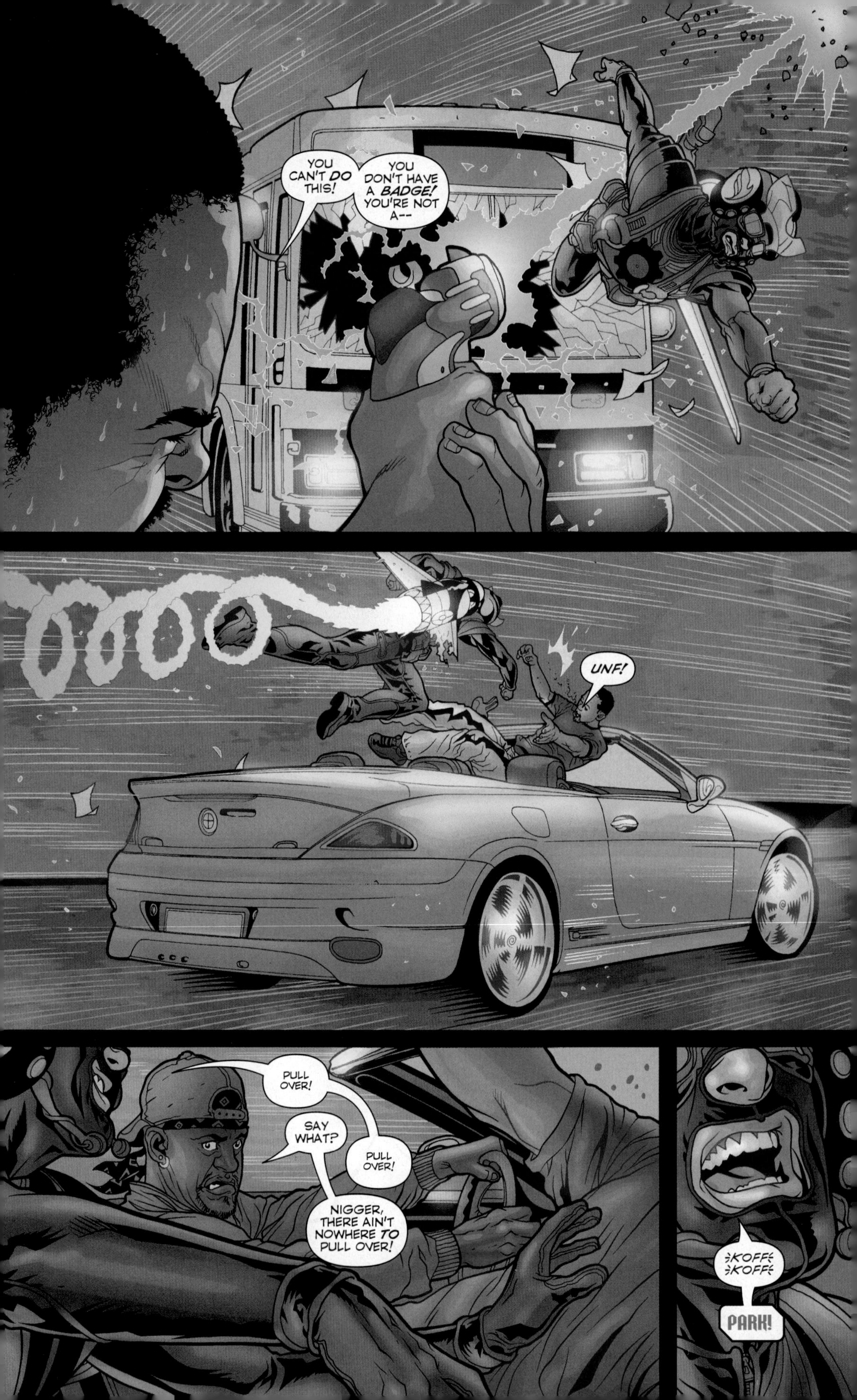

YOU CAN'T *DO* THIS!
YOU DON'T HAVE A *BADGE!* YOU'RE NOT A--
UNF!
PULL OVER!
SAY WHAT?
PULL OVER!
NIGGER, THERE AIN'T NOWHERE *TO* PULL OVER!
KOFF KOFF
PARK!

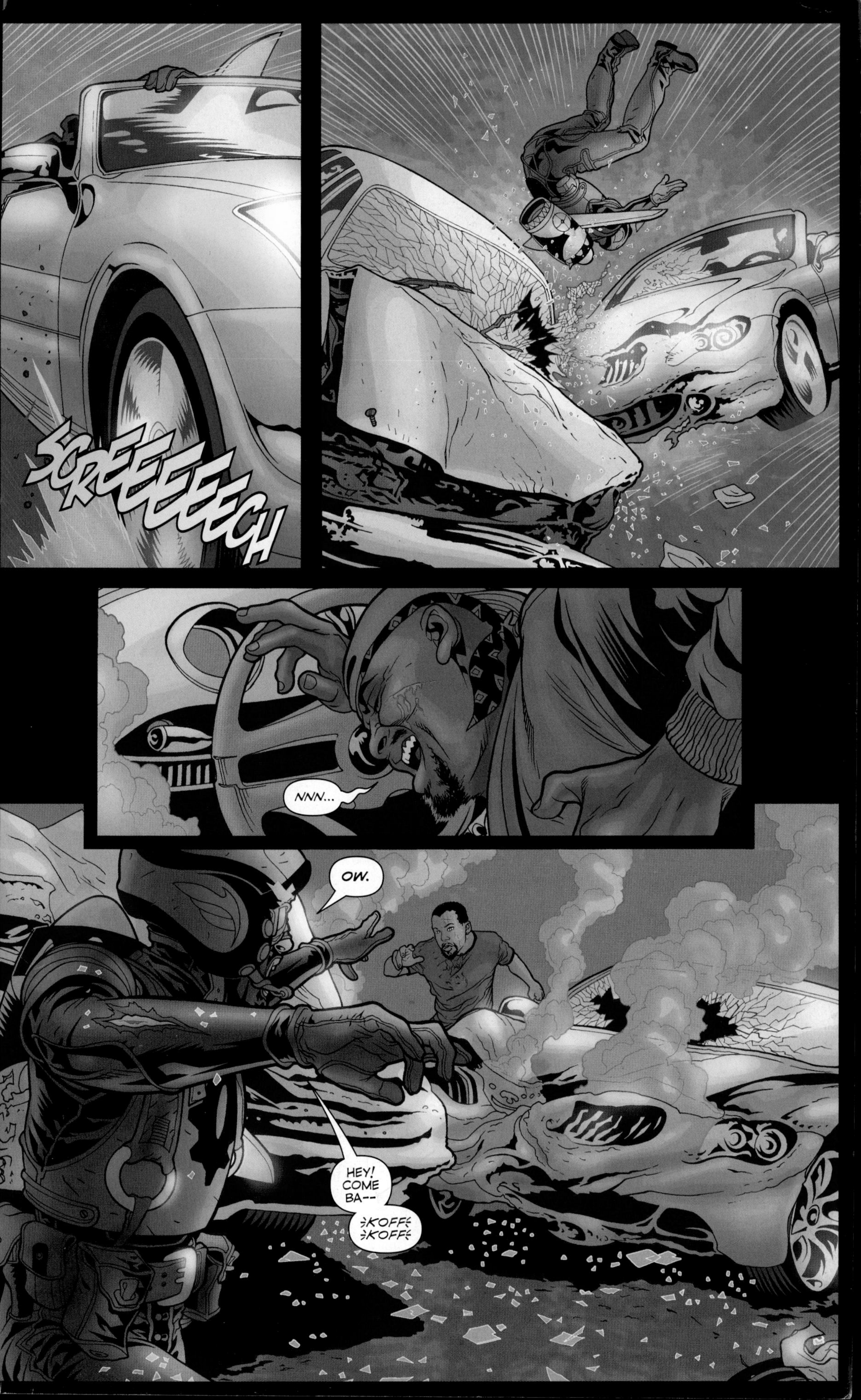
SCREEEEEEECH
NNN...
OW.
HEY! COME BA--
KOFF KOFF

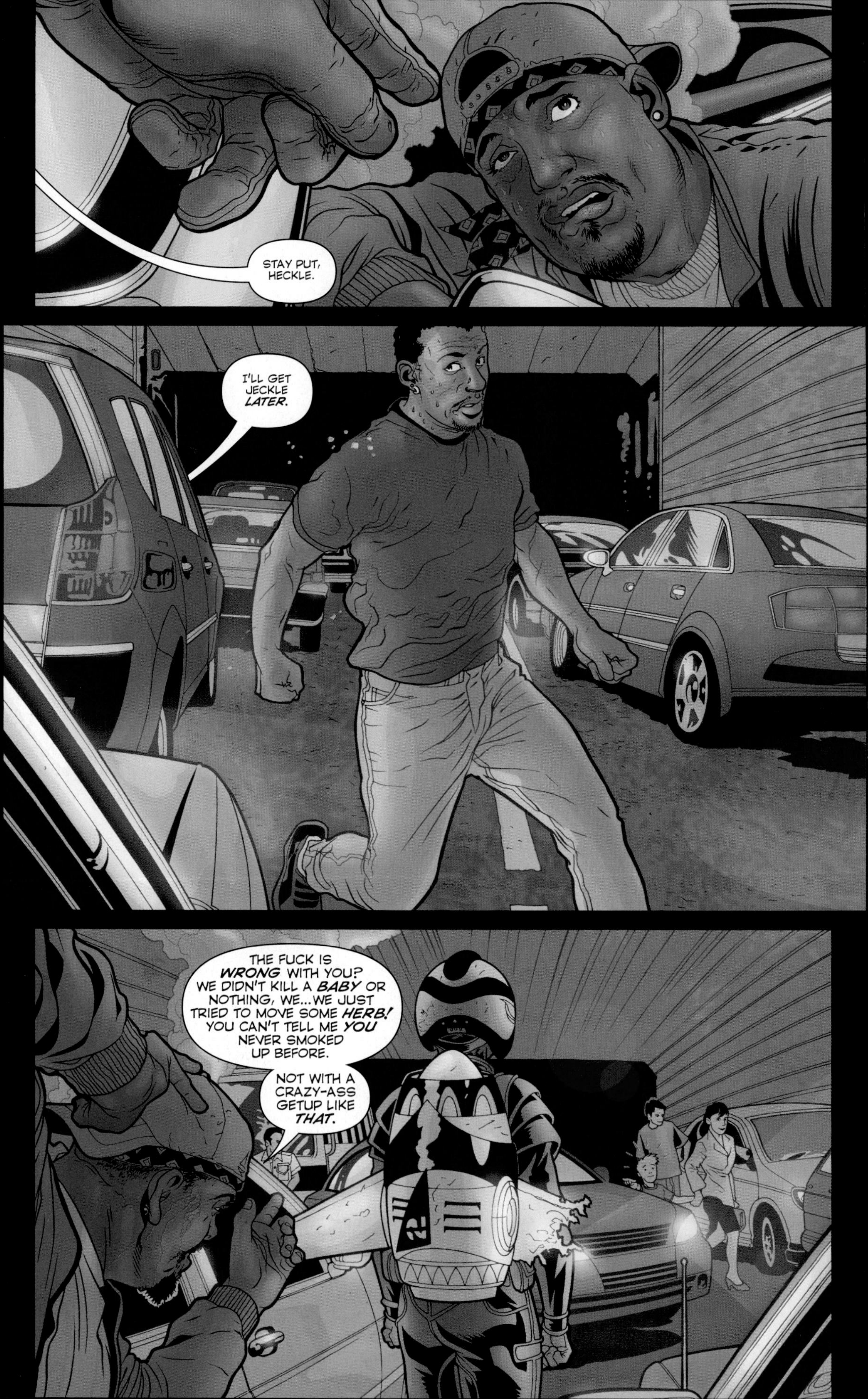
STAY PUT, HECKLE.
I'LL GET JECKLE LATER.
THE FUCK IS WRONG WITH YOU? WE DIDN'T KILL A BABY OR NOTHING, WE...WE JUST TRIED TO MOVE SOME HERB! YOU CAN'T TELL ME YOU NEVER SMOKED UP BEFORE.
NOT WITH A CRAZY-ASS GETUP LIKE THAT.

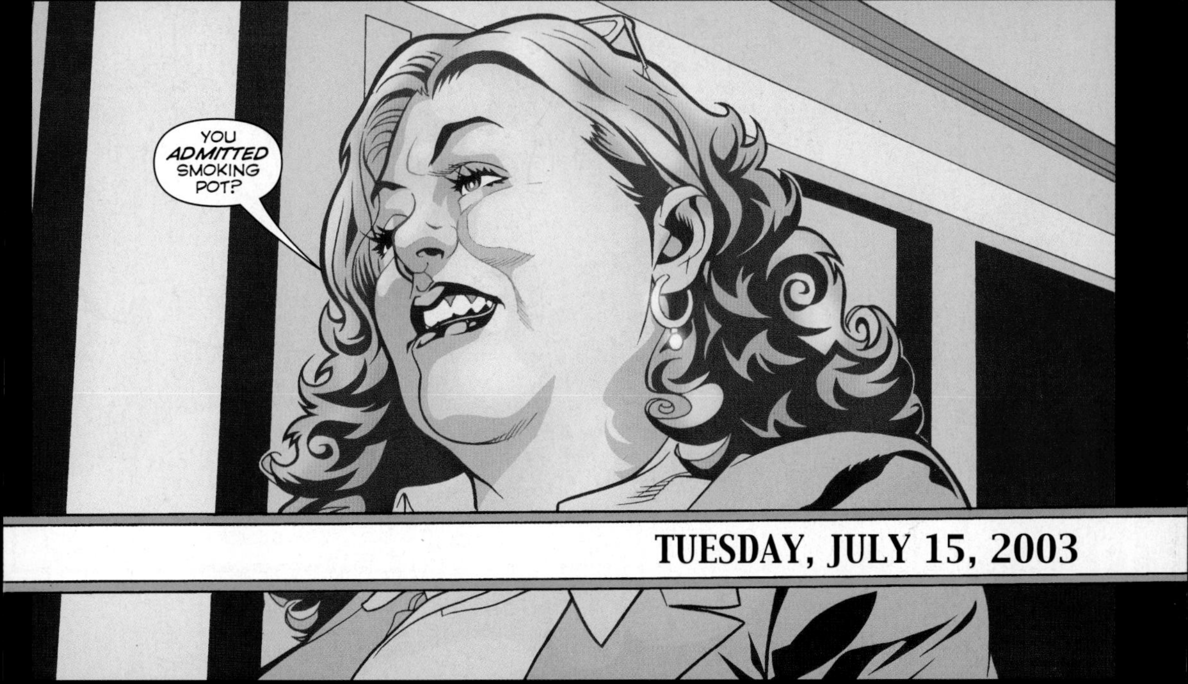
YOU *ADMITTED* SMOKING POT?
TUESDAY, JULY 15, 2003

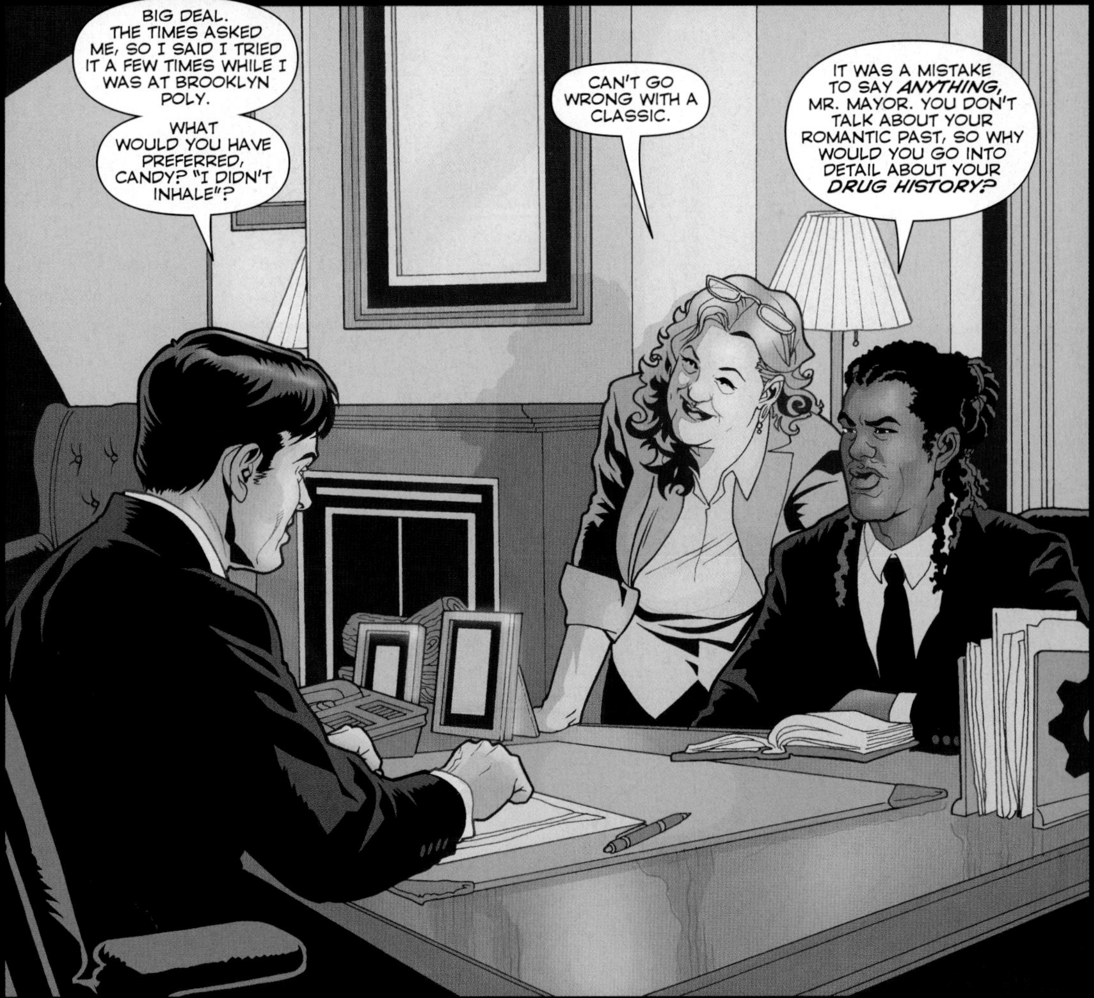
BIG DEAL. THE TIMES ASKED ME, SO I SAID I TRIED IT A FEW TIMES WHILE I WAS AT BROOKLYN POLY.
WHAT WOULD YOU HAVE PREFERRED, CANDY? "I DIDN'T INHALE"?
CAN'T GO WRONG WITH A CLASSIC.
IT WAS A MISTAKE TO SAY *ANYTHING,* MR. MAYOR. YOU DON'T TALK ABOUT YOUR ROMANTIC PAST, SO WHY WOULD YOU GO INTO DETAIL ABOUT YOUR *DRUG HISTORY?*

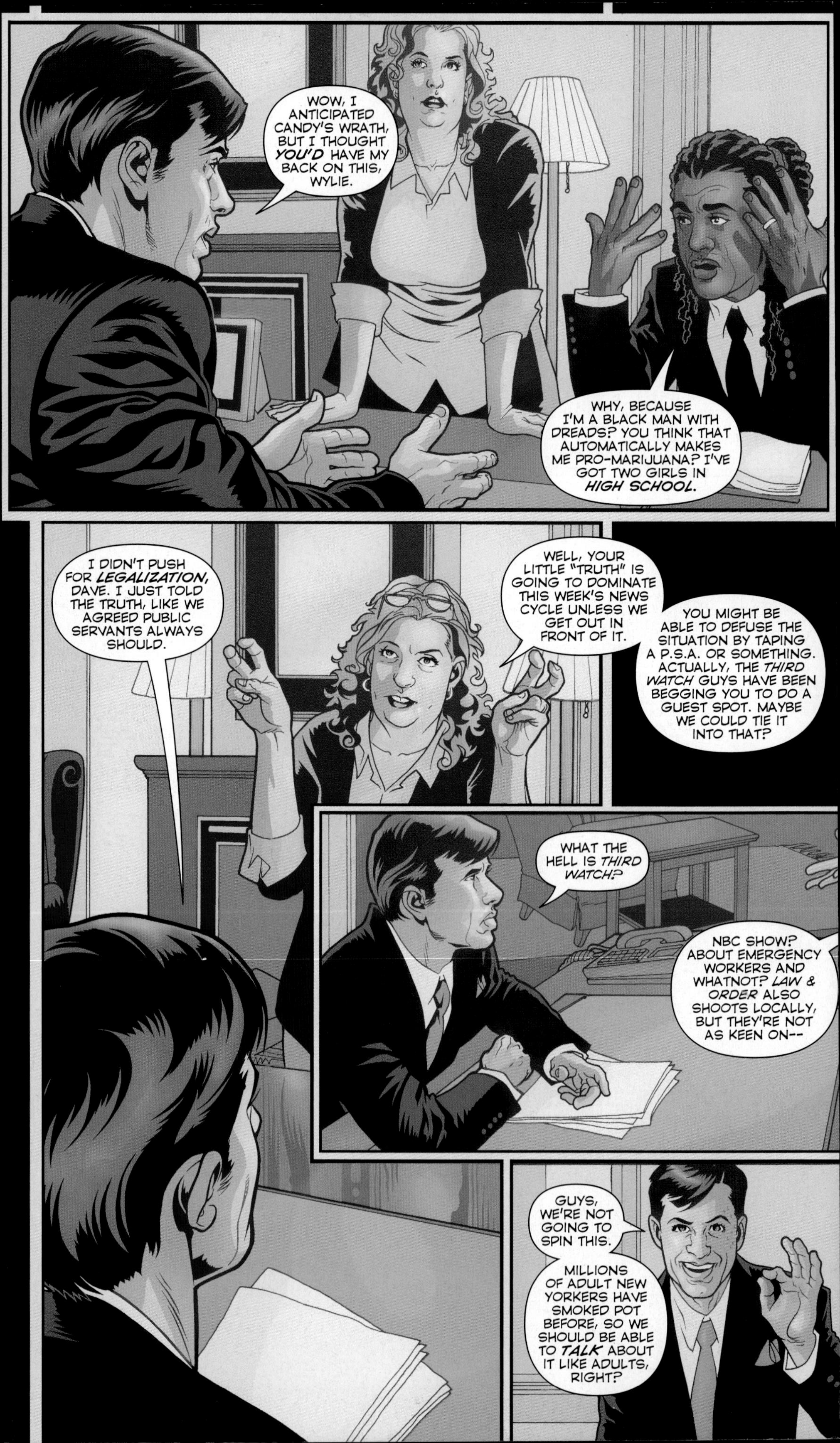
WOW, I ANTICIPATED CANDY'S WRATH, BUT I THOUGHT *YOU'D* HAVE MY BACK ON THIS, WYLIE.
WHY, BECAUSE I'M A BLACK MAN WITH DREADS? YOU THINK THAT AUTOMATICALLY MAKES ME PRO-MARIJUANA? I'VE GOT TWO GIRLS IN **HIGH SCHOOL.**
I DIDN'T PUSH FOR *LEGALIZATION,* DAVE. I JUST TOLD THE TRUTH, LIKE WE AGREED PUBLIC SERVANTS ALWAYS SHOULD.
WELL, YOUR LITTLE "TRUTH" IS GOING TO DOMINATE THIS WEEK'S NEWS CYCLE UNLESS WE GET OUT IN FRONT OF IT.
YOU MIGHT BE ABLE TO DEFUSE THE SITUATION BY TAPING A P.S.A. OR SOMETHING. ACTUALLY, THE *THIRD WATCH* GUYS HAVE BEEN BEGGING YOU TO DO A GUEST SPOT. MAYBE WE COULD TIE IT INTO THAT?
WHAT THE HELL IS *THIRD WATCH?*
NBC SHOW? ABOUT EMERGENCY WORKERS AND WHATNOT? *LAW & ORDER* ALSO SHOOTS LOCALLY, BUT THEY'RE NOT AS KEEN ON--
GUYS, WE'RE NOT GOING TO SPIN THIS.
MILLIONS OF ADULT NEW YORKERS HAVE SMOKED POT BEFORE, SO WE SHOULD BE ABLE TO *TALK* ABOUT IT LIKE ADULTS, RIGHT?

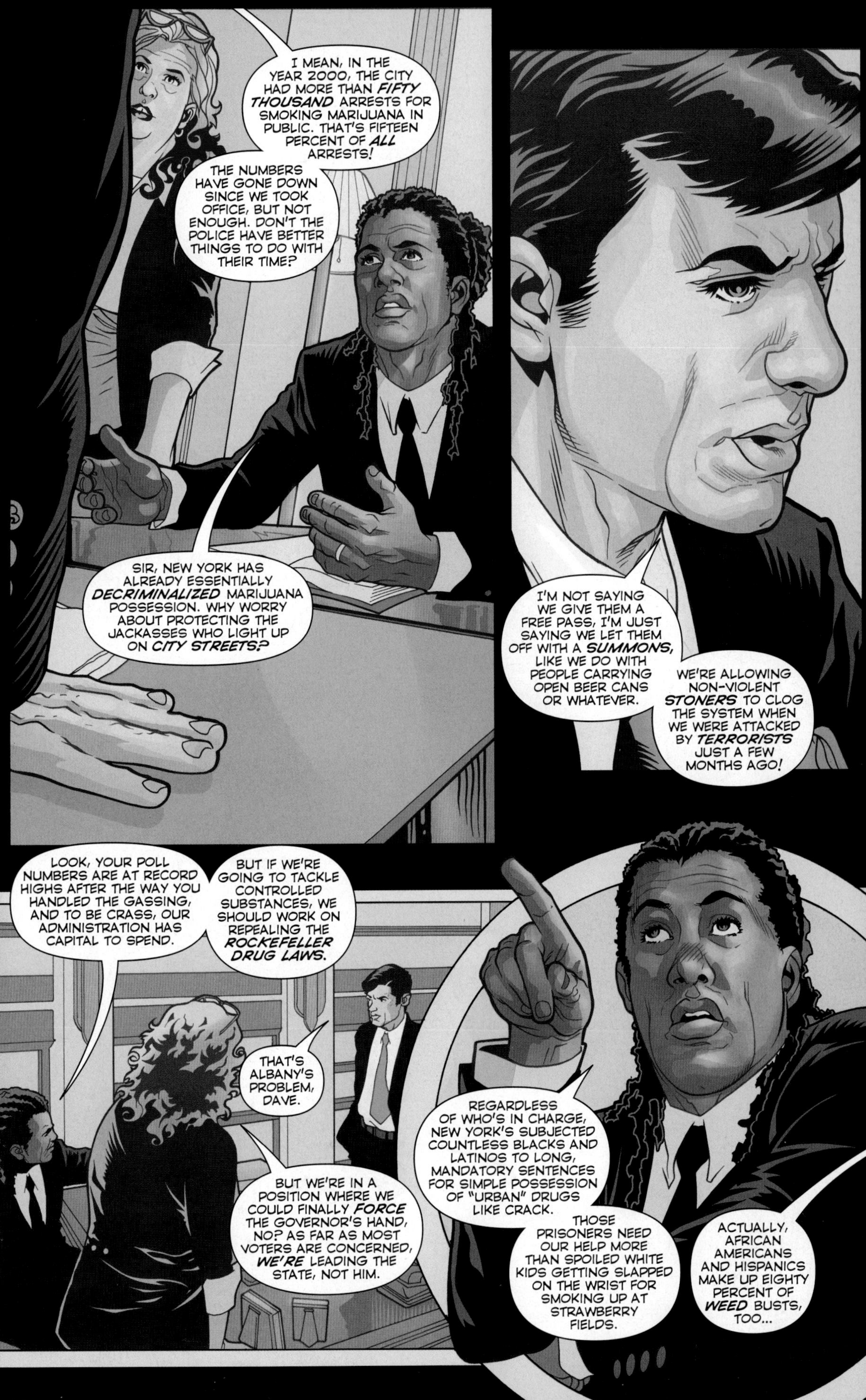
I MEAN, IN THE YEAR 2000, THE CITY HAD MORE THAN FIFTY THOUSAND ARRESTS FOR SMOKING MARIJUANA IN PUBLIC. THAT'S FIFTEEN PERCENT OF ALL ARRESTS!
THE NUMBERS HAVE GONE DOWN SINCE WE TOOK OFFICE, BUT NOT ENOUGH. DON'T THE POLICE HAVE BETTER THINGS TO DO WITH THEIR TIME?
SIR, NEW YORK HAS ALREADY ESSENTIALLY DECRIMINALIZED MARIJUANA POSSESSION. WHY WORRY ABOUT PROTECTING THE JACKASSES WHO LIGHT UP ON CITY STREETS?
I'M NOT SAYING WE GIVE THEM A FREE PASS, I'M JUST SAYING WE LET THEM OFF WITH A SUMMONS, LIKE WE DO WITH PEOPLE CARRYING OPEN BEER CANS OR WHATEVER.
WE'RE ALLOWING NON-VIOLENT STONERS TO CLOG THE SYSTEM WHEN WE WERE ATTACKED BY TERRORISTS JUST A FEW MONTHS AGO!
LOOK, YOUR POLL NUMBERS ARE AT RECORD HIGHS AFTER THE WAY YOU HANDLED THE GASSING, AND TO BE CRASS, OUR ADMINISTRATION HAS CAPITAL TO SPEND.
BUT IF WE'RE GOING TO TACKLE CONTROLLED SUBSTANCES, WE SHOULD WORK ON REPEALING THE ROCKEFELLER DRUG LAWS.
THAT'S ALBANY'S PROBLEM, DAVE.
BUT WE'RE IN A POSITION WHERE WE COULD FINALLY FORCE THE GOVERNOR'S HAND, NO? AS FAR AS MOST VOTERS ARE CONCERNED, WE'RE LEADING THE STATE, NOT HIM.
REGARDLESS OF WHO'S IN CHARGE, NEW YORK'S SUBJECTED COUNTLESS BLACKS AND LATINOS TO LONG, MANDATORY SENTENCES FOR SIMPLE POSSESSION OF "URBAN" DRUGS LIKE CRACK.
THOSE PRISONERS NEED OUR HELP MORE THAN SPOILED WHITE KIDS GETTING SLAPPED ON THE WRIST FOR SMOKING UP AT STRAWBERRY FIELDS.
ACTUALLY, AFRICAN AMERICANS AND HISPANICS MAKE UP EIGHTY PERCENT OF WEED BUSTS, TOO...

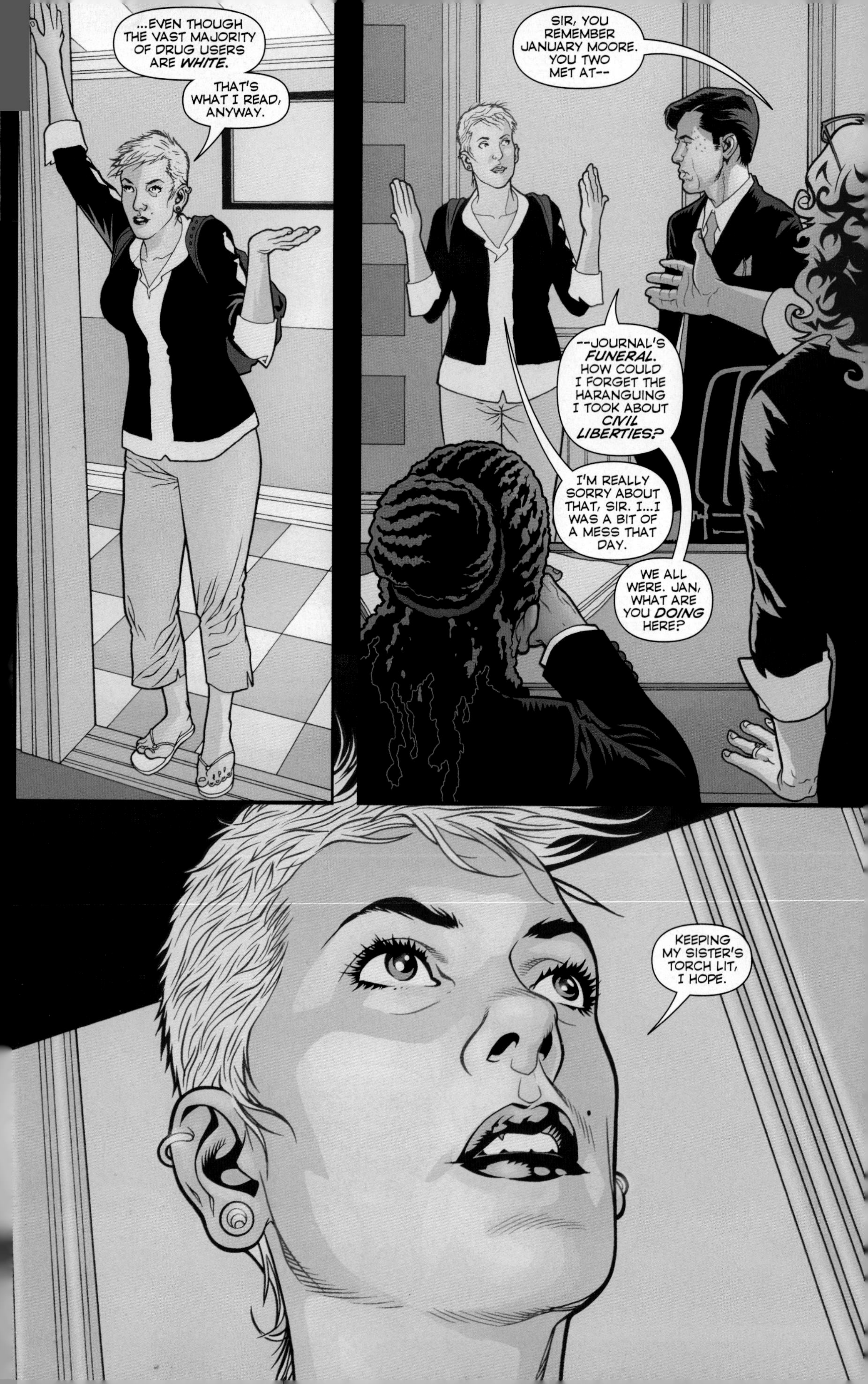
...EVEN THOUGH THE VAST MAJORITY OF DRUG USERS ARE *WHITE*.
THAT'S WHAT I READ, ANYWAY.
SIR, YOU REMEMBER JANUARY MOORE. YOU TWO MET AT--
--JOURNAL'S *FUNERAL*. HOW COULD I FORGET THE HARANGUING I TOOK ABOUT *CIVIL LIBERTIES?*
I'M REALLY SORRY ABOUT THAT, SIR. I...I WAS A BIT OF A MESS THAT DAY.
WE ALL WERE. JAN, WHAT ARE YOU *DOING* HERE?
KEEPING MY SISTER'S TORCH LIT, I HOPE.

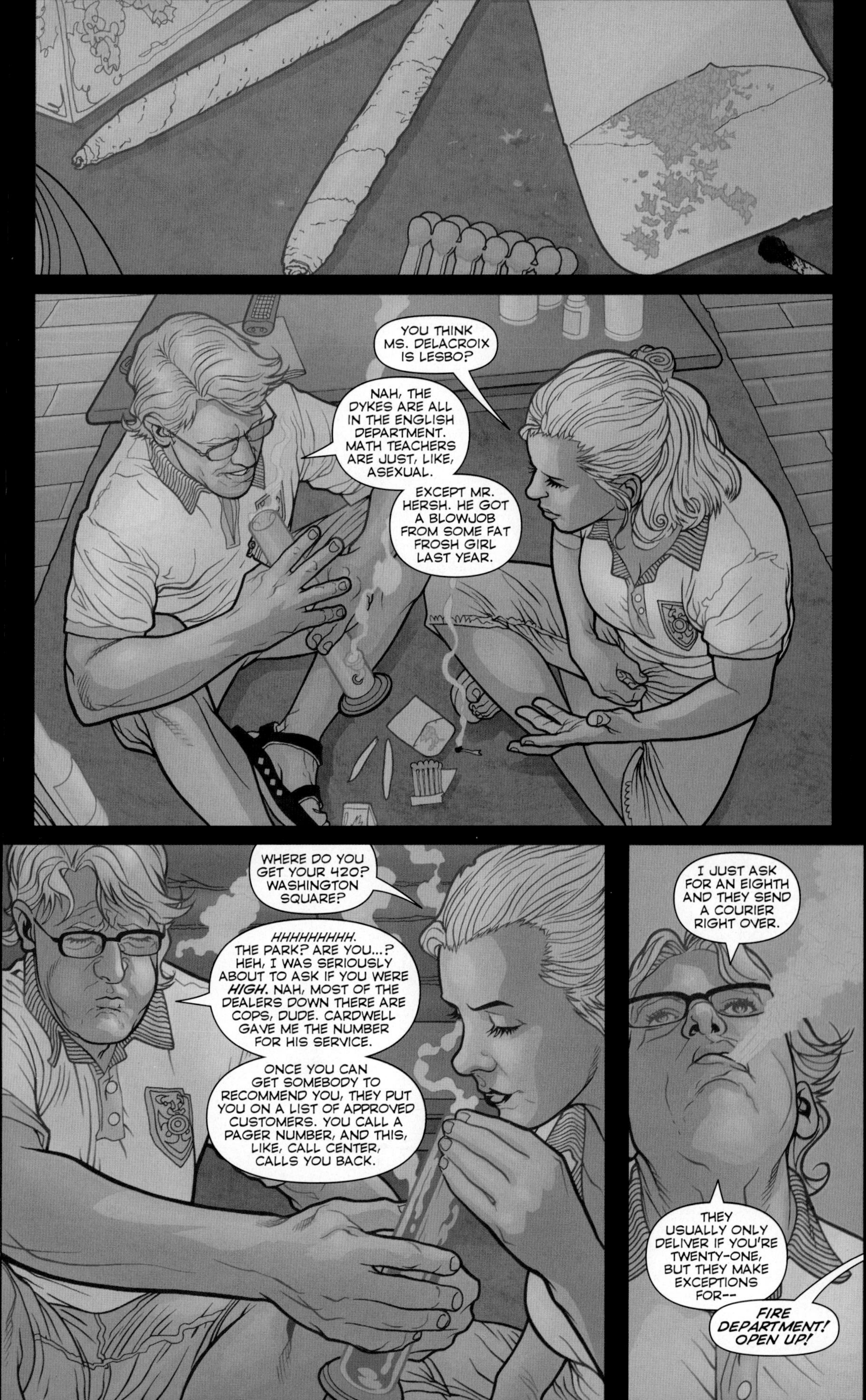
YOU THINK MS. DELACROIX IS LESBO?
NAH, THE DYKES ARE ALL IN THE ENGLISH DEPARTMENT. MATH TEACHERS ARE JUST, LIKE, ASEXUAL.
EXCEPT MR. HERSH. HE GOT A BLOWJOB FROM SOME FAT FROSH GIRL LAST YEAR.
WHERE DO YOU GET YOUR 420? WASHINGTON SQUARE?
HHHHHHHHH. THE PARK? ARE YOU...? HEH, I WAS SERIOUSLY ABOUT TO ASK IF YOU WERE HIGH. NAH, MOST OF THE DEALERS DOWN THERE ARE COPS, DUDE. CARDWELL GAVE ME THE NUMBER FOR HIS SERVICE.
ONCE YOU CAN GET SOMEBODY TO RECOMMEND YOU, THEY PUT YOU ON A LIST OF APPROVED CUSTOMERS. YOU CALL A PAGER NUMBER, AND THIS, LIKE, CALL CENTER, CALLS YOU BACK.
I JUST ASK FOR AN EIGHTH AND THEY SEND A COURIER RIGHT OVER.
THEY USUALLY ONLY DELIVER IF YOU'RE TWENTY-ONE, BUT THEY MAKE EXCEPTIONS FOR--
FIRE DEPARTMENT! OPEN UP!

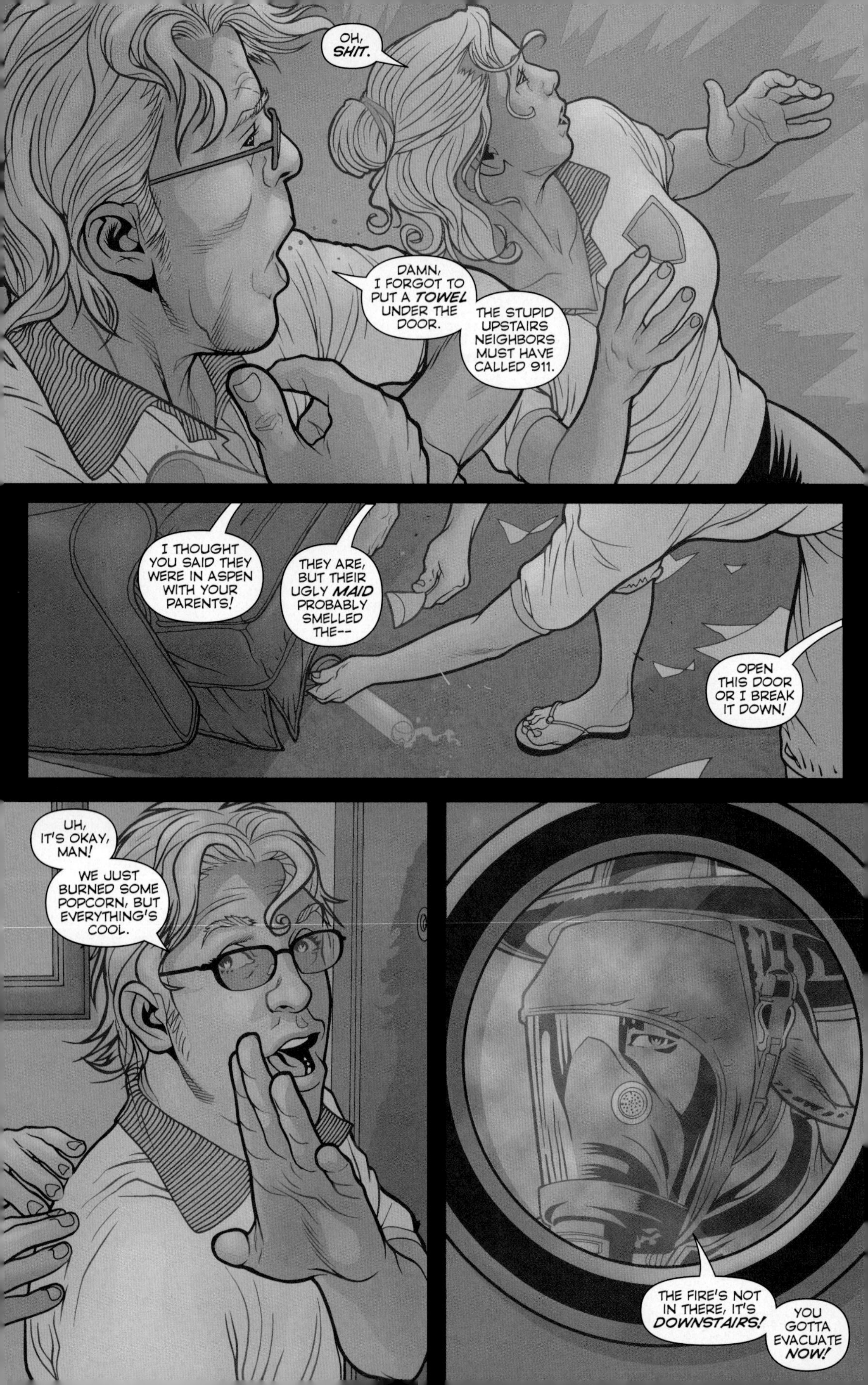

OH, SHIT.
DAMN, I FORGOT TO PUT A TOWEL UNDER THE DOOR.
THE STUPID UPSTAIRS NEIGHBORS MUST HAVE CALLED 911.
I THOUGHT YOU SAID THEY WERE IN ASPEN WITH YOUR PARENTS!
THEY ARE, BUT THEIR UGLY MAID PROBABLY SMELLED THE--
OPEN THIS DOOR OR I BREAK IT DOWN!
UH, IT'S OKAY, MAN!
WE JUST BURNED SOME POPCORN, BUT EVERYTHING'S COOL.
THE FIRE'S NOT IN THERE, IT'S DOWNSTAIRS!
YOU GOTTA EVACUATE NOW!

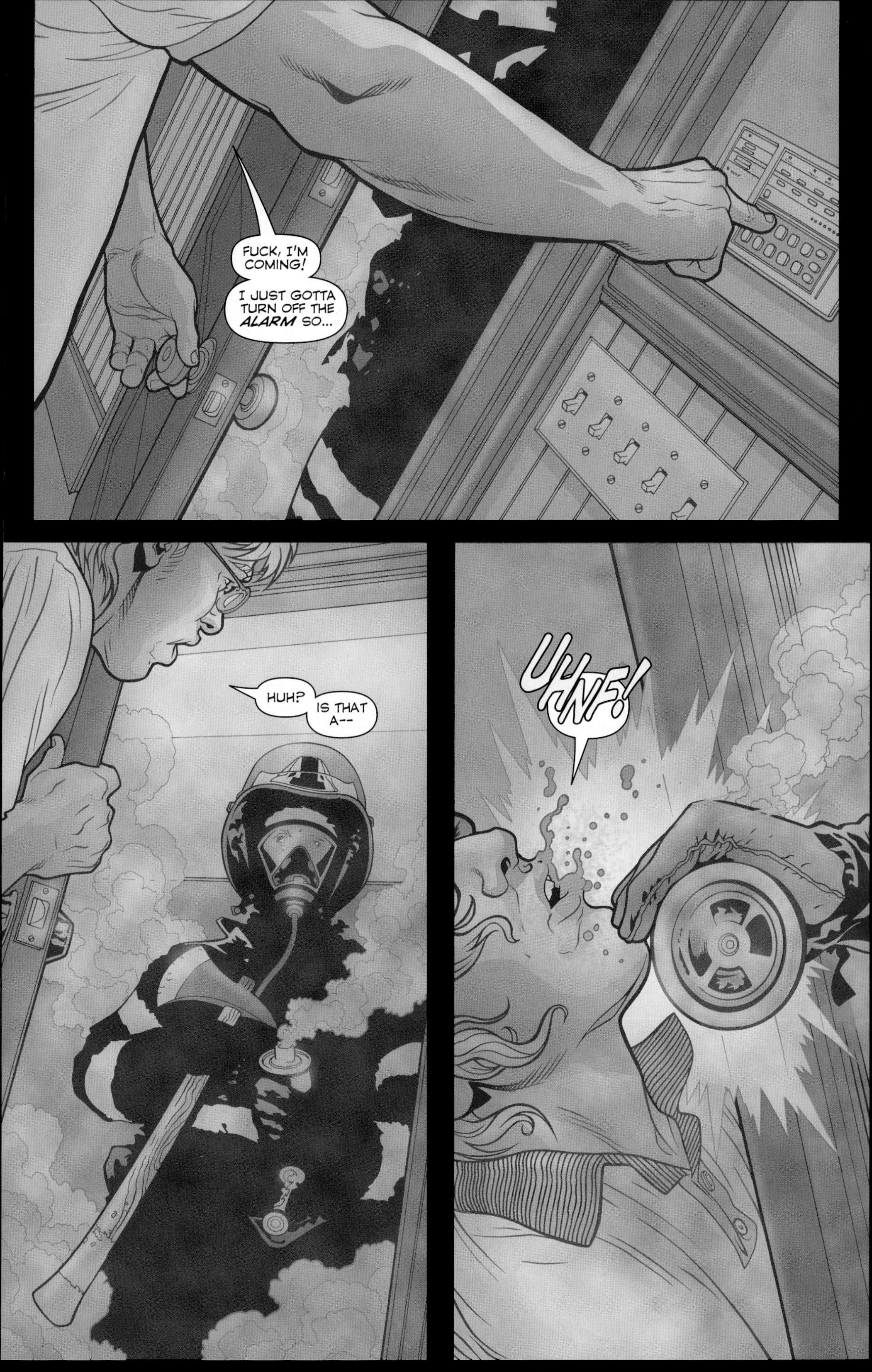
FUCK, I'M COMING!
I JUST GOTTA TURN OFF THE *ALARM* SO...
HUH?
IS THAT A--
UHNF!

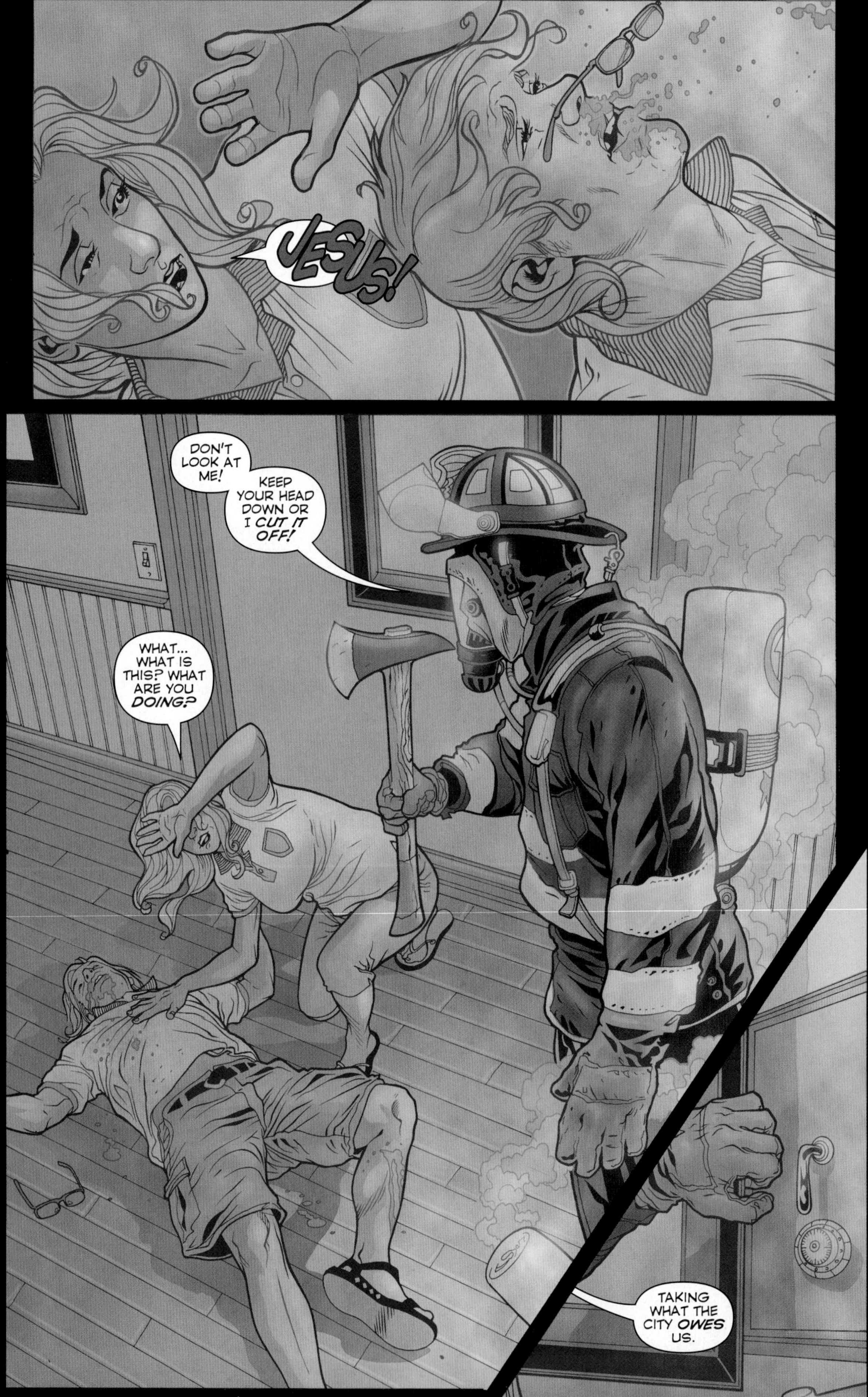
JESUS!
DON'T LOOK AT ME!
KEEP YOUR HEAD DOWN OR I *CUT IT OFF!*
WHAT... WHAT IS THIS? WHAT ARE YOU *DOING?*
TAKING WHAT THE CITY *OWES* US.

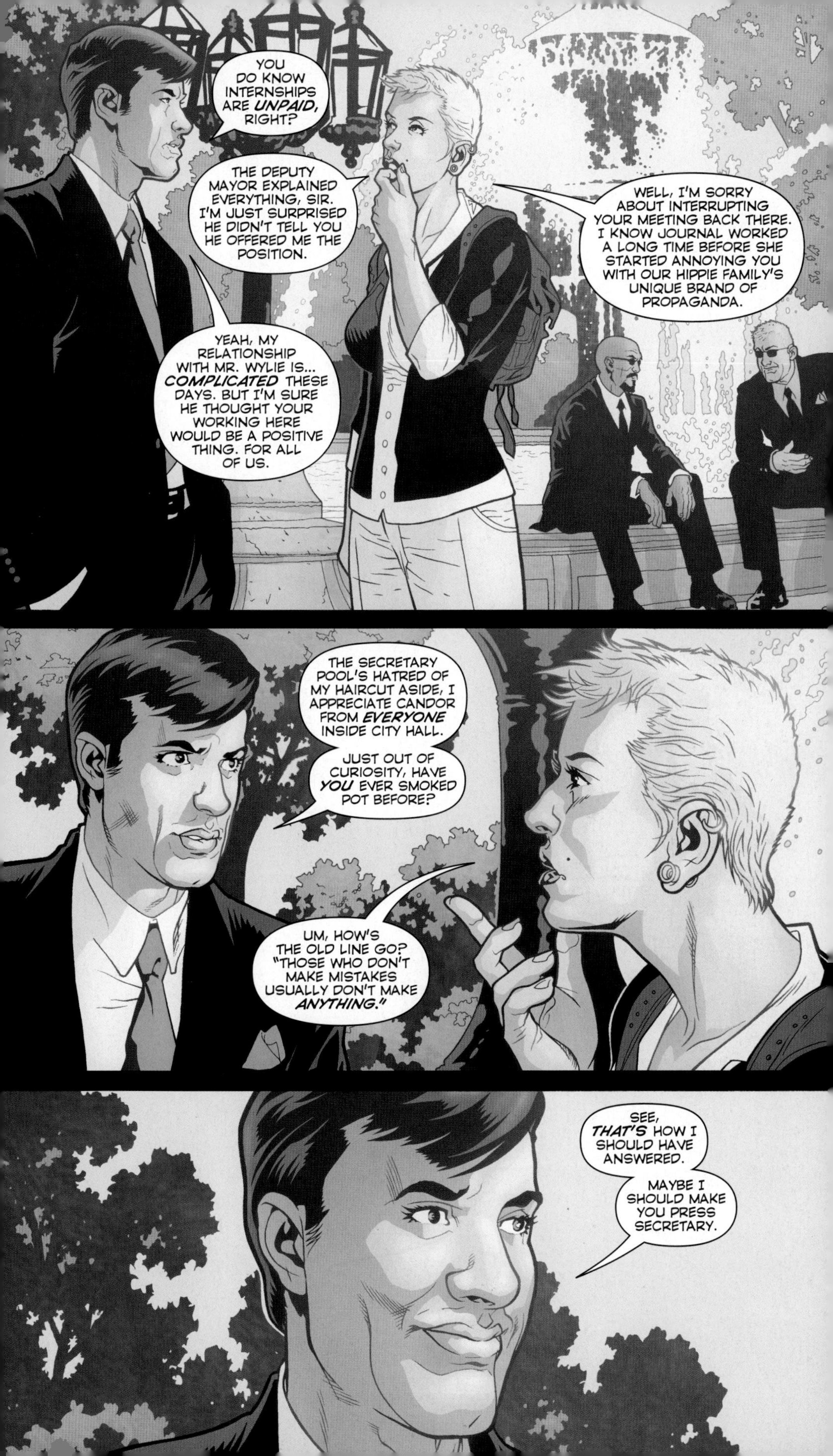
YOU DO KNOW INTERNSHIPS ARE UNPAID, RIGHT?
THE DEPUTY MAYOR EXPLAINED EVERYTHING, SIR. I'M JUST SURPRISED HE DIDN'T TELL YOU HE OFFERED ME THE POSITION.
YEAH, MY RELATIONSHIP WITH MR. WYLIE IS... COMPLICATED THESE DAYS. BUT I'M SURE HE THOUGHT YOUR WORKING HERE WOULD BE A POSITIVE THING. FOR ALL OF US.
WELL, I'M SORRY ABOUT INTERRUPTING YOUR MEETING BACK THERE. I KNOW JOURNAL WORKED A LONG TIME BEFORE SHE STARTED ANNOYING YOU WITH OUR HIPPIE FAMILY'S UNIQUE BRAND OF PROPAGANDA.
THE SECRETARY POOL'S HATRED OF MY HAIRCUT ASIDE, I APPRECIATE CANDOR FROM EVERYONE INSIDE CITY HALL.
JUST OUT OF CURIOSITY, HAVE YOU EVER SMOKED POT BEFORE?
UM, HOW'S THE OLD LINE GO? "THOSE WHO DON'T MAKE MISTAKES USUALLY DON'T MAKE ANYTHING."
SEE, THAT'S HOW I SHOULD HAVE ANSWERED.
MAYBE I SHOULD MAKE YOU PRESS SECRETARY.

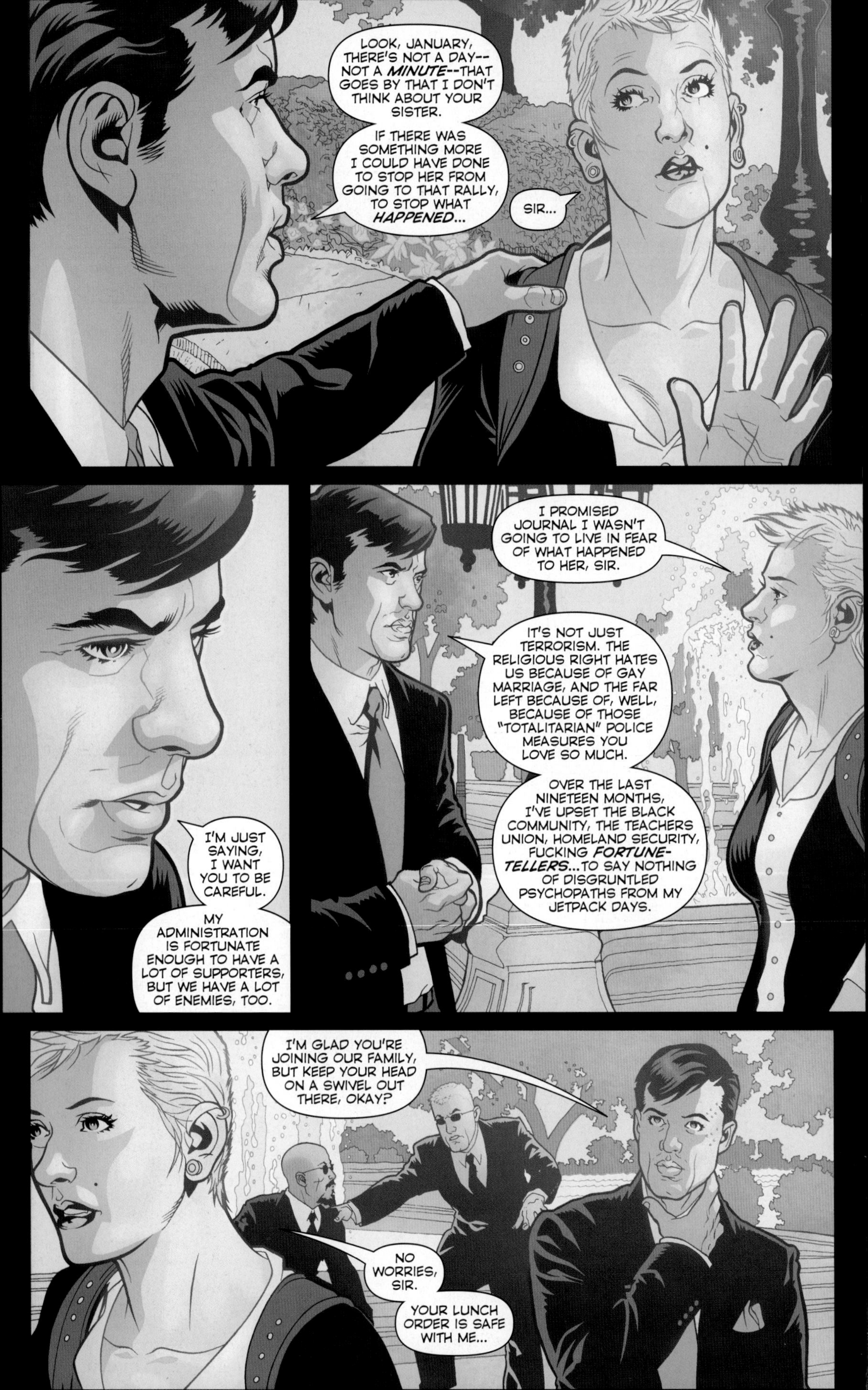
LOOK, JANUARY, THERE'S NOT A DAY-- NOT A *MINUTE*--THAT GOES BY THAT I DON'T THINK ABOUT YOUR SISTER.
IF THERE WAS SOMETHING MORE I COULD HAVE DONE TO STOP HER FROM GOING TO THAT RALLY, TO STOP WHAT ***HAPPENED***...
SIR...
I PROMISED JOURNAL I WASN'T GOING TO LIVE IN FEAR OF WHAT HAPPENED TO HER, SIR.
IT'S NOT JUST TERRORISM. THE RELIGIOUS RIGHT HATES US BECAUSE OF GAY MARRIAGE, AND THE FAR LEFT BECAUSE OF, WELL, BECAUSE OF THOSE "TOTALITARIAN" POLICE MEASURES YOU LOVE SO MUCH.
OVER THE LAST NINETEEN MONTHS, I'VE UPSET THE BLACK COMMUNITY, THE TEACHERS UNION, HOMELAND SECURITY, FUCKING ***FORTUNE-TELLERS***...TO SAY NOTHING OF DISGRUNTLED PSYCHOPATHS FROM MY JETPACK DAYS.
I'M JUST SAYING, I WANT YOU TO BE CAREFUL.
MY ADMINISTRATION IS FORTUNATE ENOUGH TO HAVE A LOT OF SUPPORTERS, BUT WE HAVE A LOT OF ENEMIES, TOO.
I'M GLAD YOU'RE JOINING OUR FAMILY, BUT KEEP YOUR HEAD ON A SWIVEL OUT THERE, OKAY?
NO WORRIES, SIR.
YOUR LUNCH ORDER IS SAFE WITH ME...

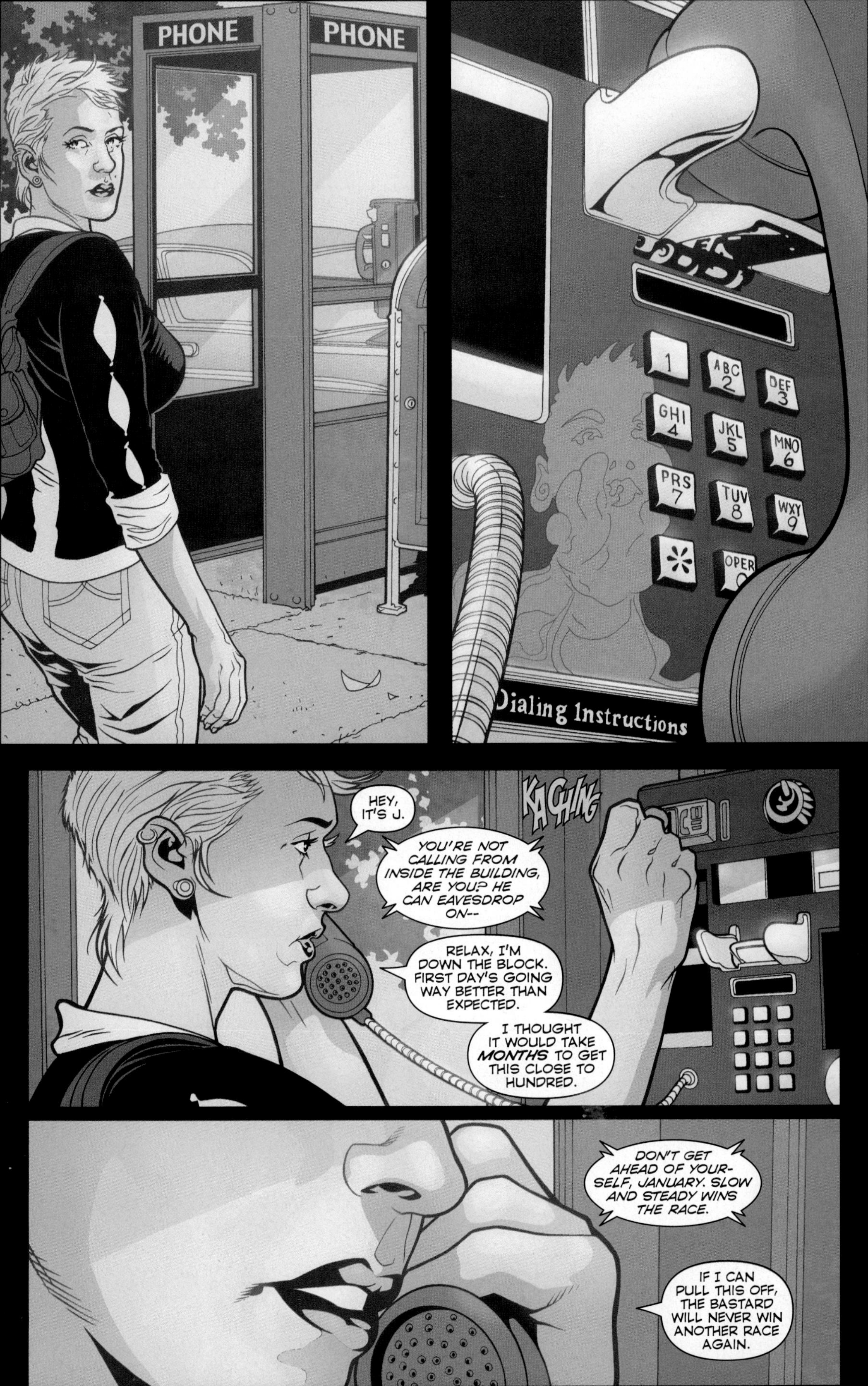
PHONE
PHONE
1
ABC 2
DEF 3
GHI 4
JKL 5
MNO 6
PRS 7
TUV 8
WXY 9
*
OPER 0
Dialing Instructions
KACHING
HEY, IT'S J.
YOU'RE NOT CALLING FROM INSIDE THE BUILDING, ARE YOU? HE CAN EAVESDROP ON--
RELAX, I'M DOWN THE BLOCK. FIRST DAY'S GOING WAY BETTER THAN EXPECTED.
I THOUGHT IT WOULD TAKE MONTHS TO GET THIS CLOSE TO HUNDRED.
DON'T GET AHEAD OF YOURSELF, JANUARY. SLOW AND STEADY WINS THE RACE.
IF I CAN PULL THIS OFF, THE BASTARD WILL NEVER WIN ANOTHER RACE AGAIN.

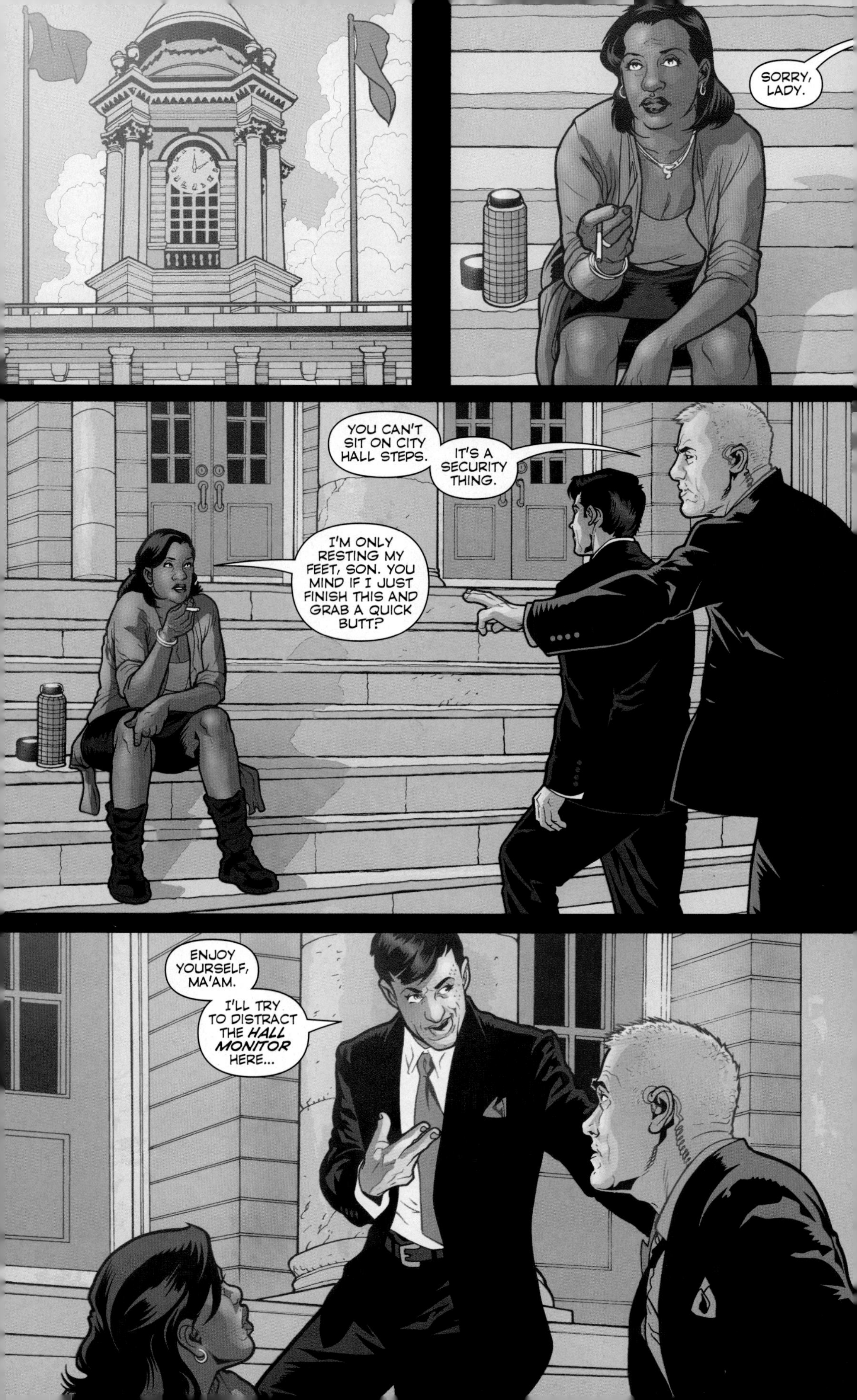
SORRY, LADY.
YOU CAN'T SIT ON CITY HALL STEPS.
IT'S A SECURITY THING.
I'M ONLY RESTING MY FEET, SON. YOU MIND IF I JUST FINISH THIS AND GRAB A QUICK BUTT?
ENJOY YOURSELF, MA'AM.
I'LL TRY TO DISTRACT THE *HALL MONITOR* HERE...

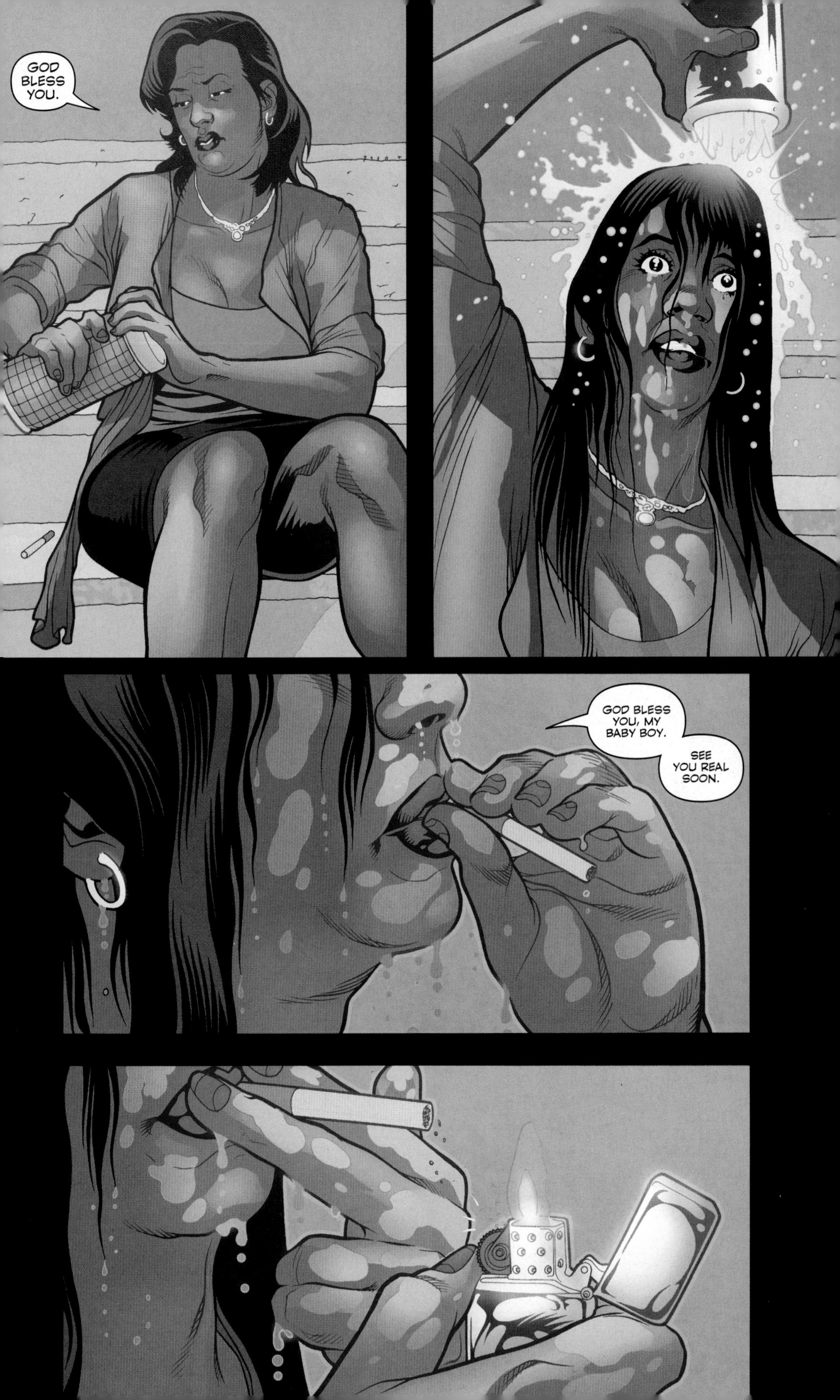
GOD BLESS YOU.
GOD BLESS YOU, MY BABY BOY.
SEE YOU REAL SOON.

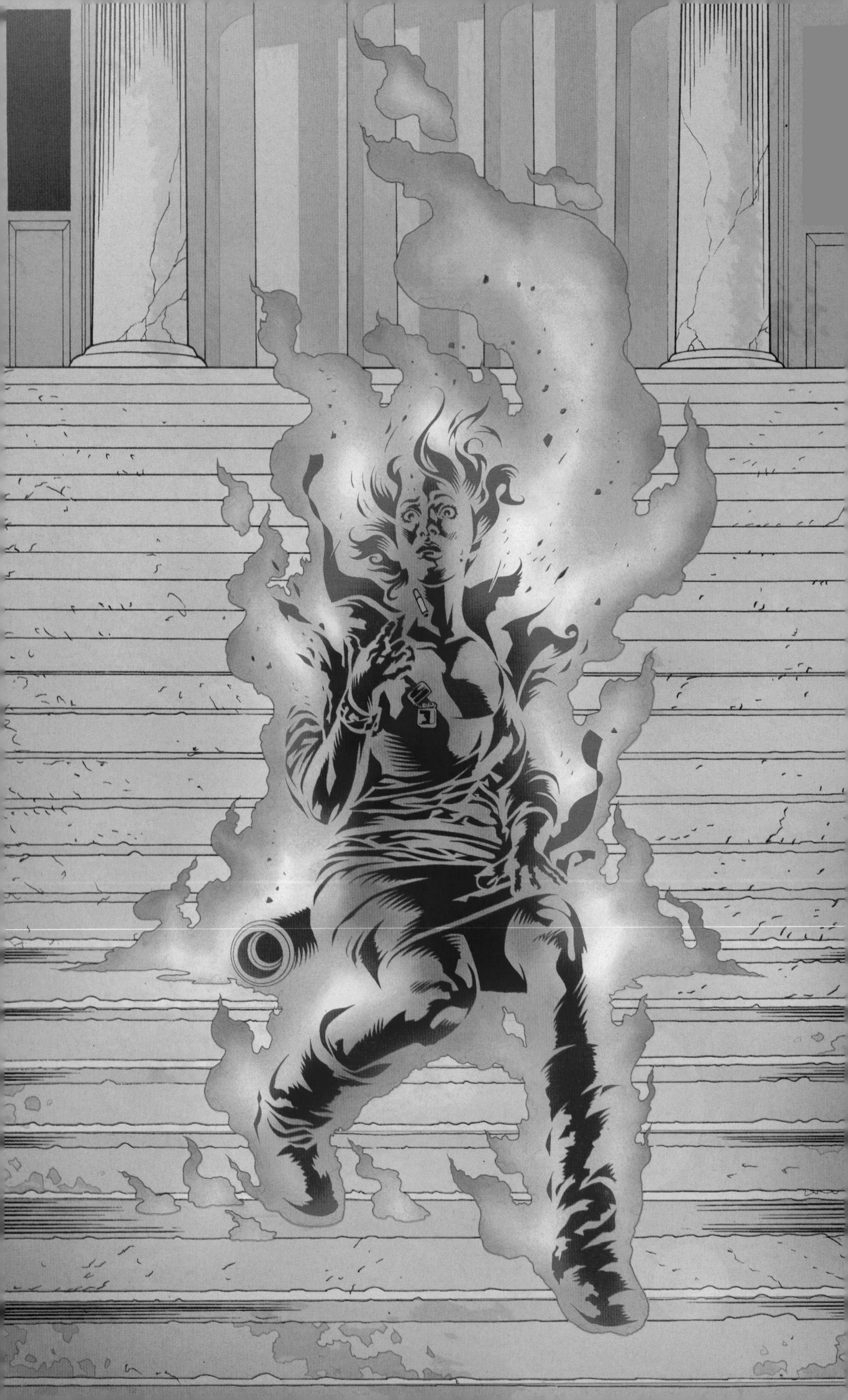

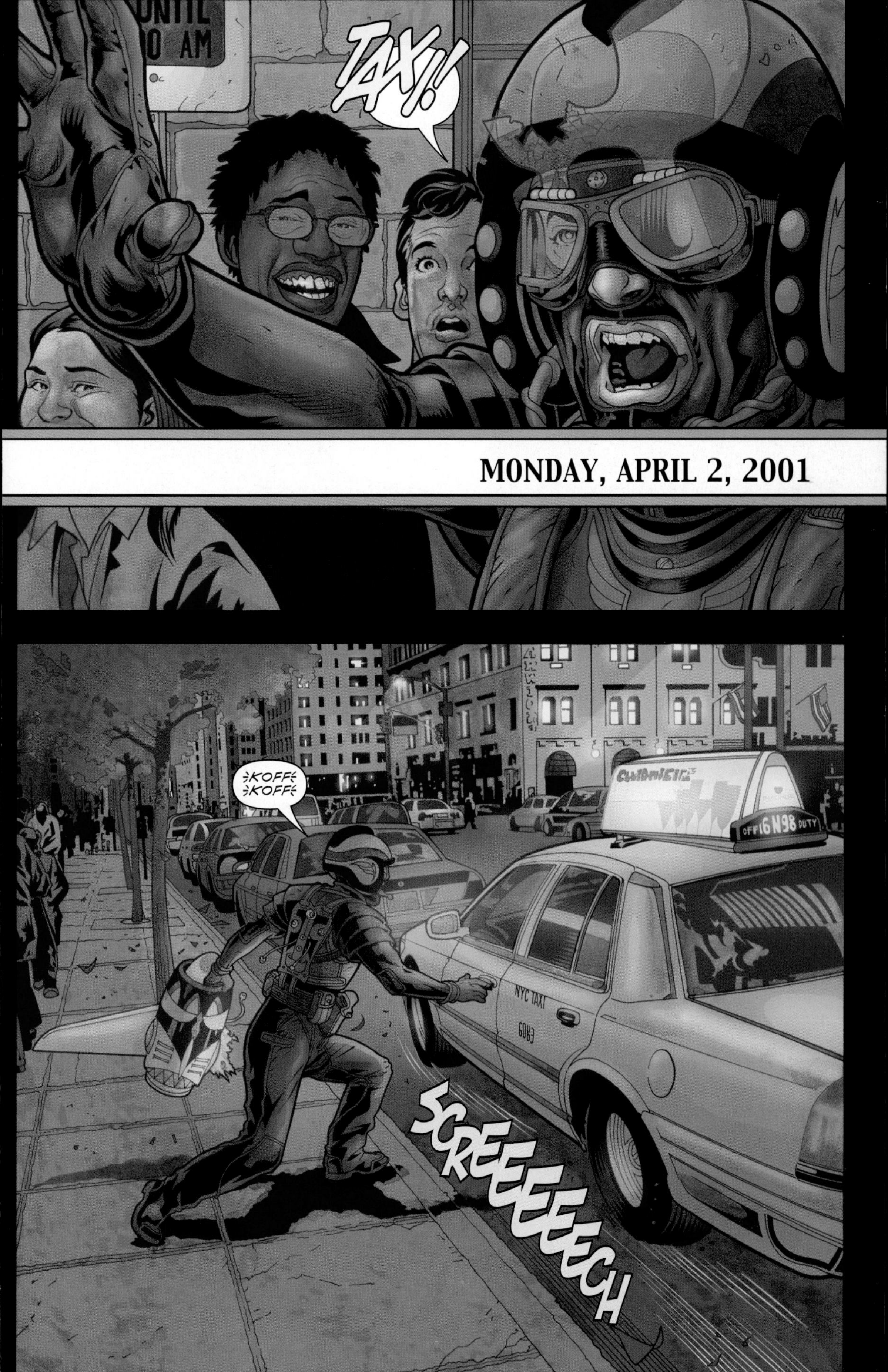
TAXI!!
MONDAY, APRIL 2, 2001
KOFF KOFF
NYC TAXI
SCREEEEEEECH

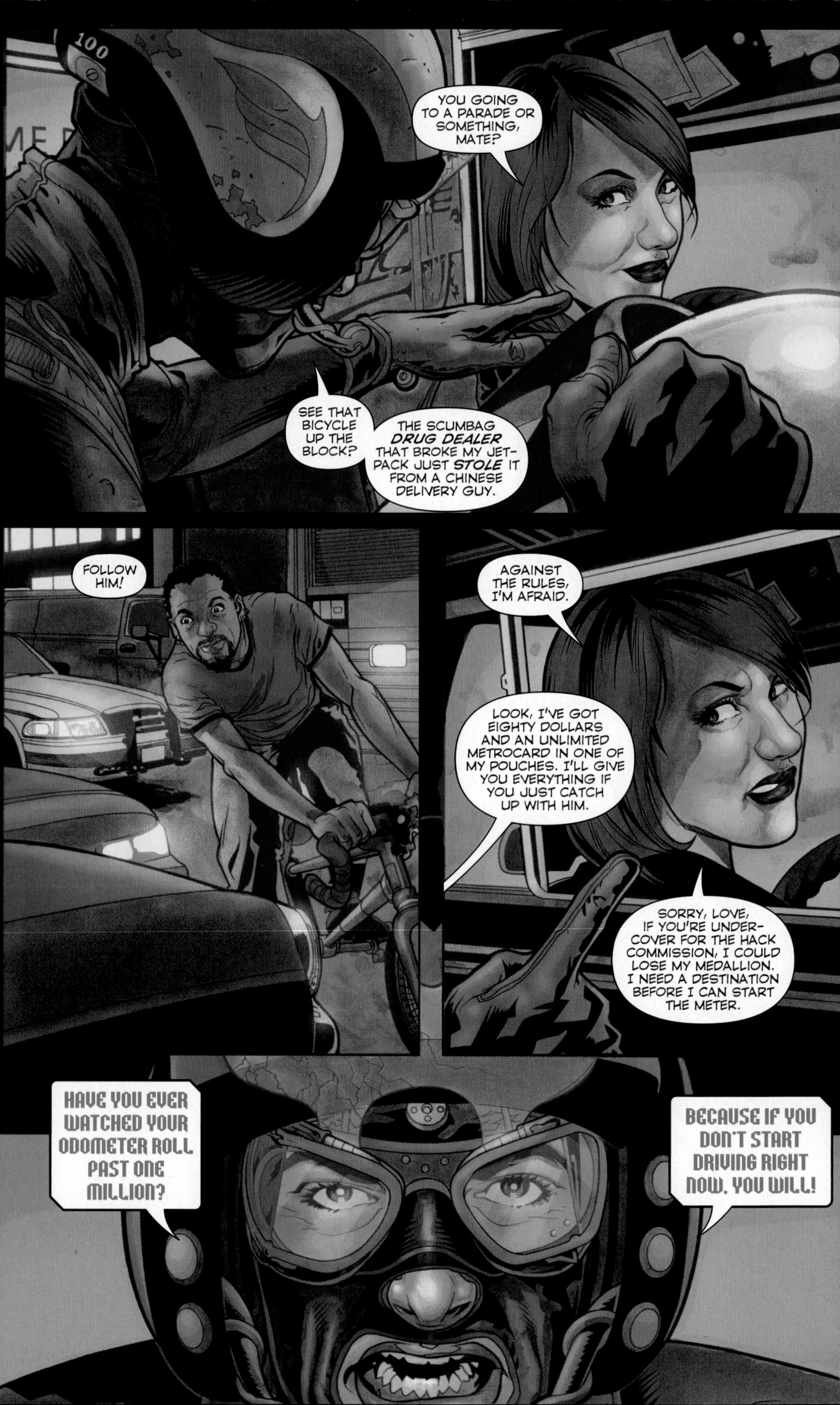

YOU GOING TO A PARADE OR SOMETHING, MATE?
SEE THAT BICYCLE UP THE BLOCK?
THE SCUMBAG DRUG DEALER THAT BROKE MY JET-PACK JUST STOLE IT FROM A CHINESE DELIVERY GUY.
FOLLOW HIM!
AGAINST THE RULES, I'M AFRAID.
LOOK, I'VE GOT EIGHTY DOLLARS AND AN UNLIMITED METROCARD IN ONE OF MY POUCHES. I'LL GIVE YOU EVERYTHING IF YOU JUST CATCH UP WITH HIM.
SORRY, LOVE, IF YOU'RE UNDER-COVER FOR THE HACK COMMISSION, I COULD LOSE MY MEDALLION. I NEED A DESTINATION BEFORE I CAN START THE METER.
HAVE YOU EVER WATCHED YOUR ODOMETER ROLL PAST ONE MILLION?
BECAUSE IF YOU DON'T START DRIVING RIGHT NOW, YOU WILL!

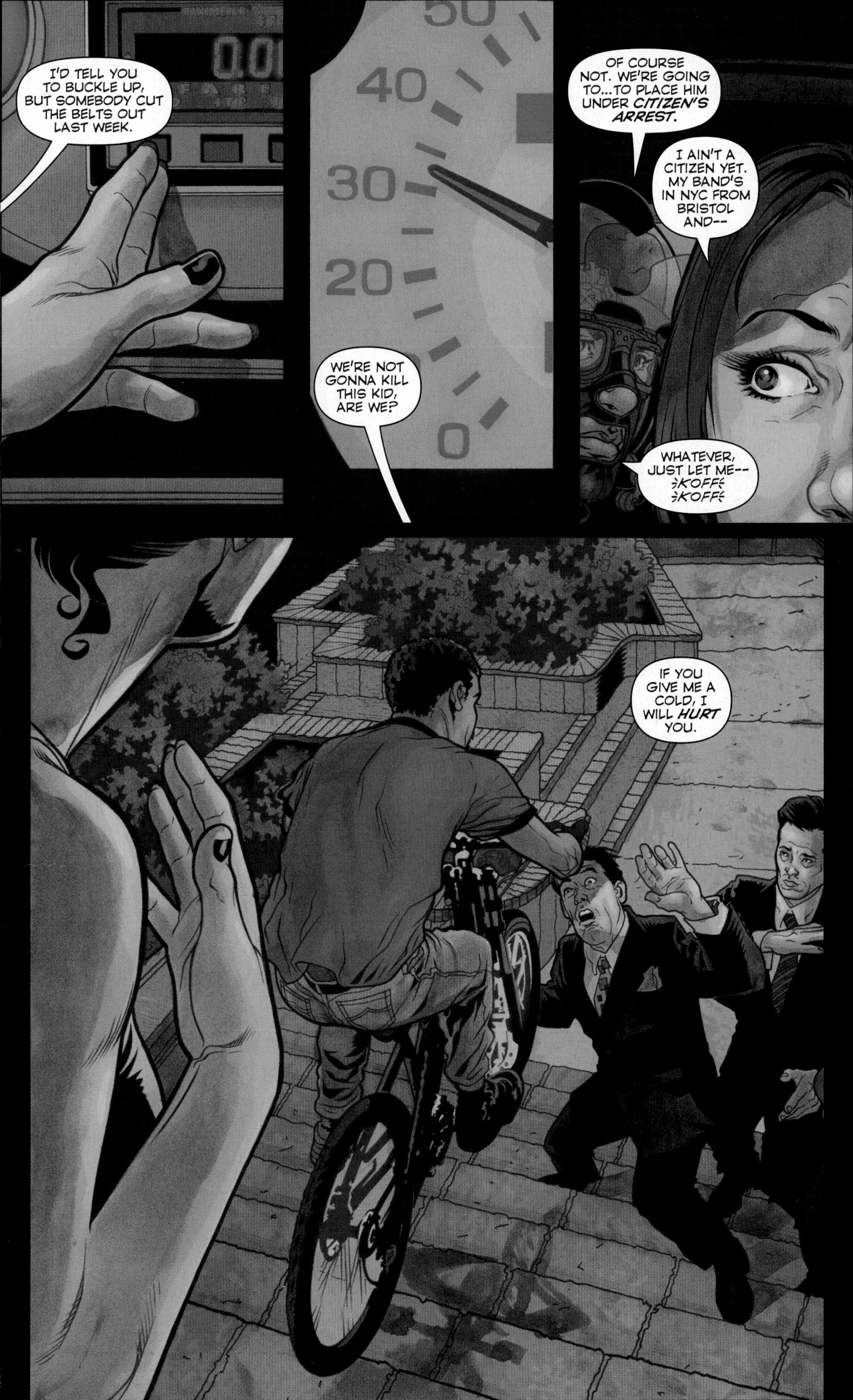
I'D TELL YOU TO BUCKLE UP, BUT SOMEBODY CUT THE BELTS OUT LAST WEEK.
WE'RE NOT GONNA KILL THIS KID, ARE WE?
OF COURSE NOT. WE'RE GOING TO...TO PLACE HIM UNDER *CITIZEN'S ARREST*.
I AIN'T A CITIZEN YET. MY BAND'S IN NYC FROM BRISTOL AND--
WHATEVER, JUST LET ME-- *KOFF* *KOFF*
IF YOU GIVE ME A COLD, I WILL *HURT* YOU.

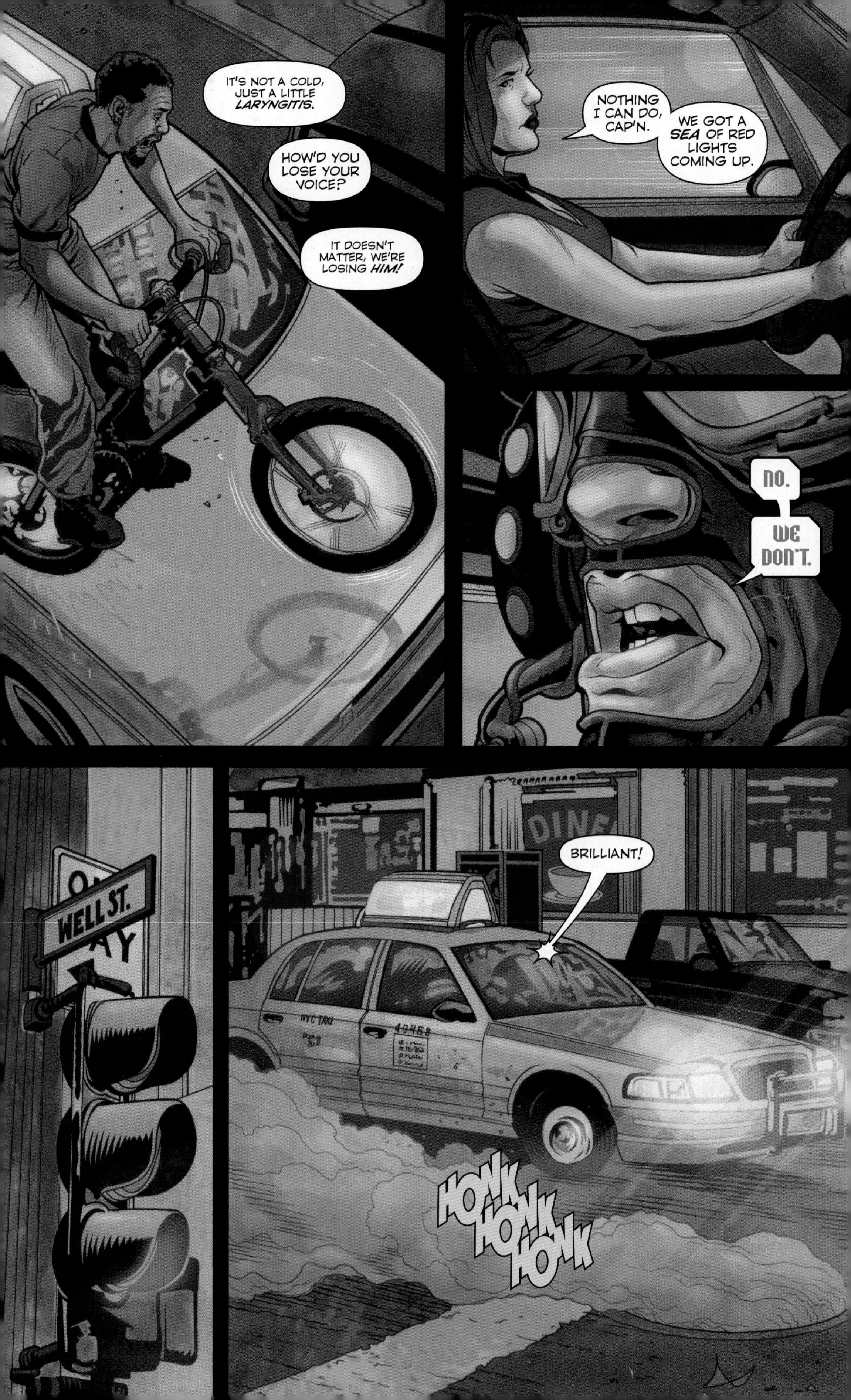
IT'S NOT A COLD, JUST A LITTLE *LARYNGITIS*.
HOW'D YOU LOSE YOUR VOICE?
IT DOESN'T MATTER, WE'RE LOSING *HIM!*
NOTHING I CAN DO, CAP'N.
WE GOT A *SEA* OF RED LIGHTS COMING UP.
NO.
WE DON'T.
WELL ST.
DINE
BRILLIANT!
NYC TAXI
HONK HONK HONK

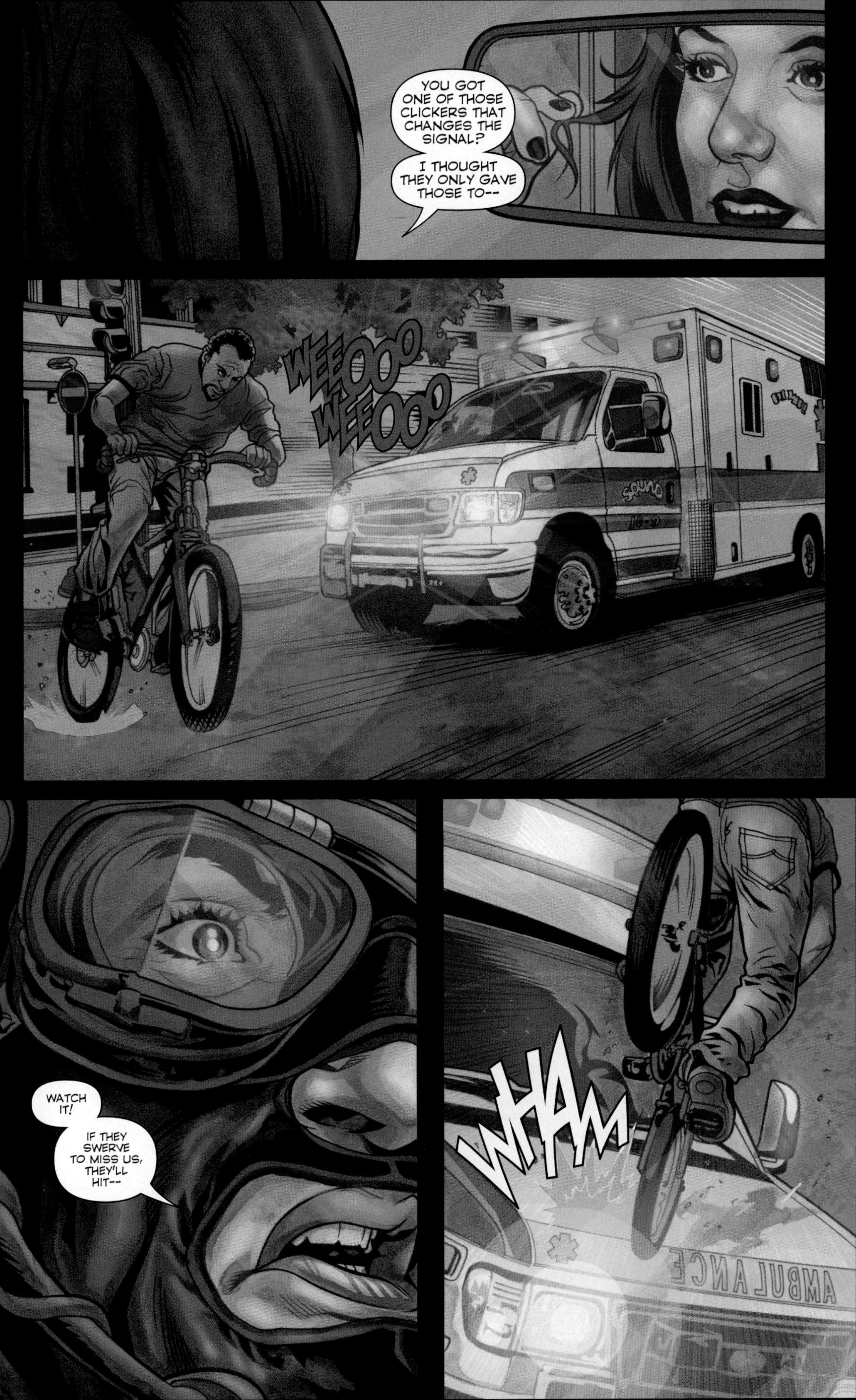
YOU GOT ONE OF THOSE CLICKERS THAT CHANGES THE SIGNAL?
I THOUGHT THEY ONLY GAVE THOSE TO--
WEEOOO WEEOOO
SQUAD
10-9
WATCH IT!
IF THEY SWERVE TO MISS US, THEY'LL HIT--
WHAM
AMBULANCE

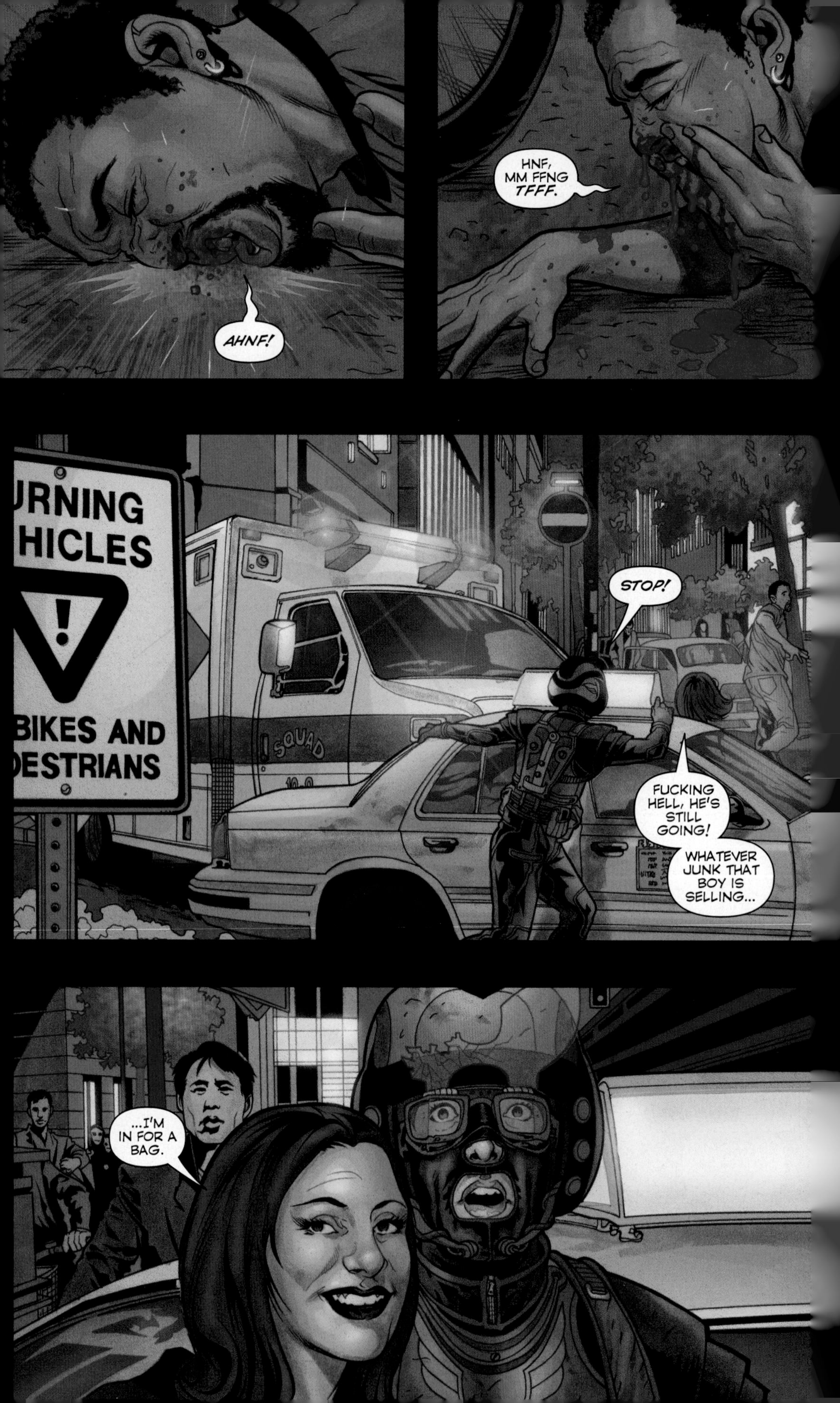
AHNF!
HNF, MM FFNG TFFF.
URNING
HICLES
BIKES AND
DESTRIANS
SQUAD
STOP!
FUCKING HELL, HE'S STILL GOING!
WHATEVER JUNK THAT BOY IS SELLING...
...I'M IN FOR A BAG.

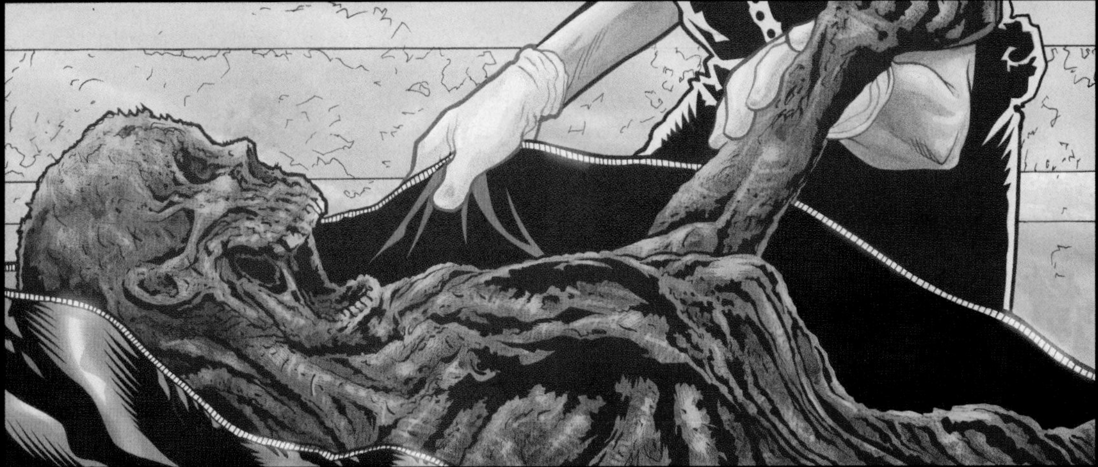

TUESDAY, JULY 15, 2003

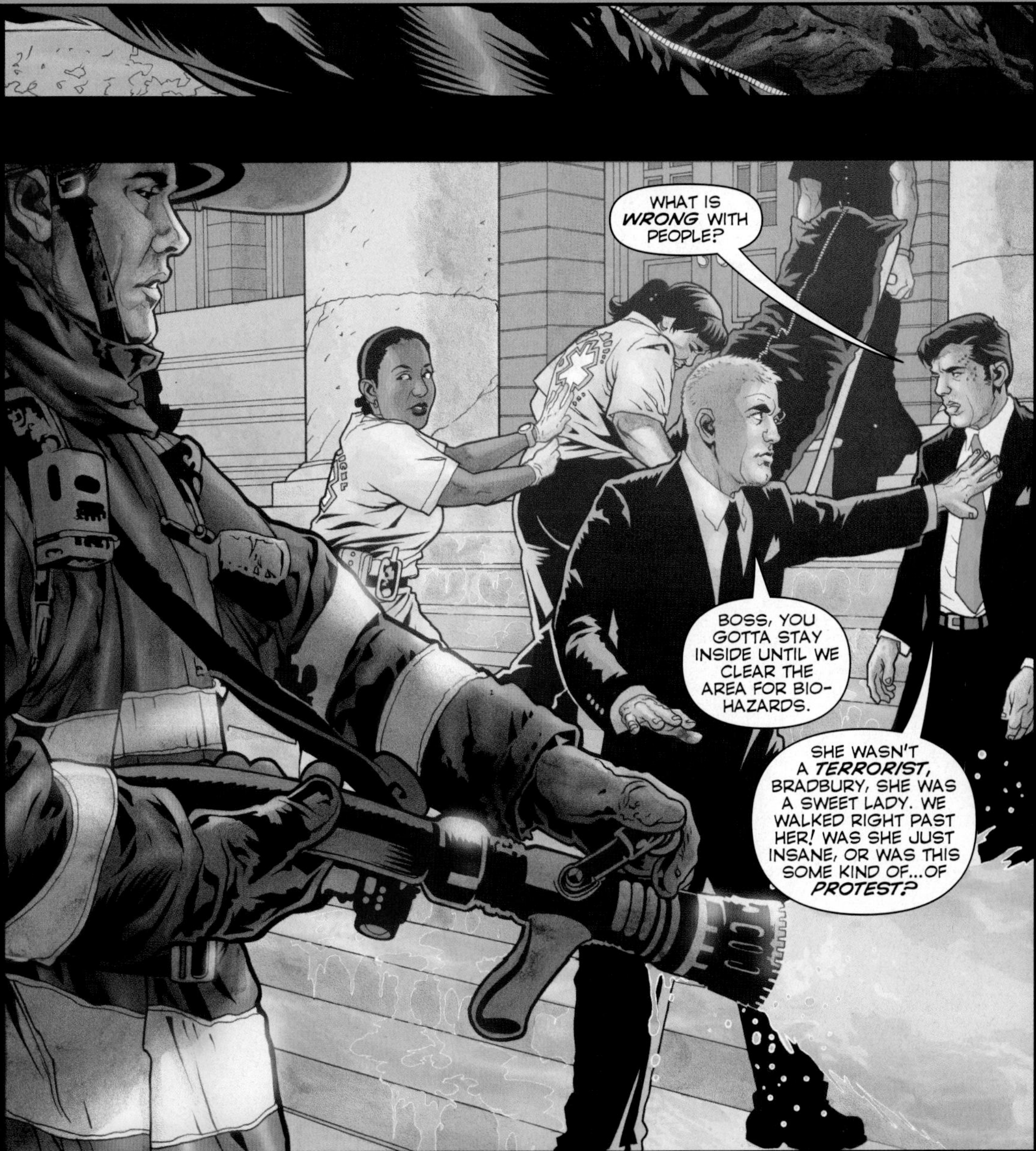
WHAT IS *WRONG* WITH PEOPLE?
BOSS, YOU GOTTA STAY INSIDE UNTIL WE CLEAR THE AREA FOR BIO-HAZARDS.
SHE WASN'T A *TERRORIST,* BRADBURY, SHE WAS A SWEET LADY. WE WALKED RIGHT PAST HER! WAS SHE JUST INSANE, OR WAS THIS SOME KIND OF...OF *PROTEST?*

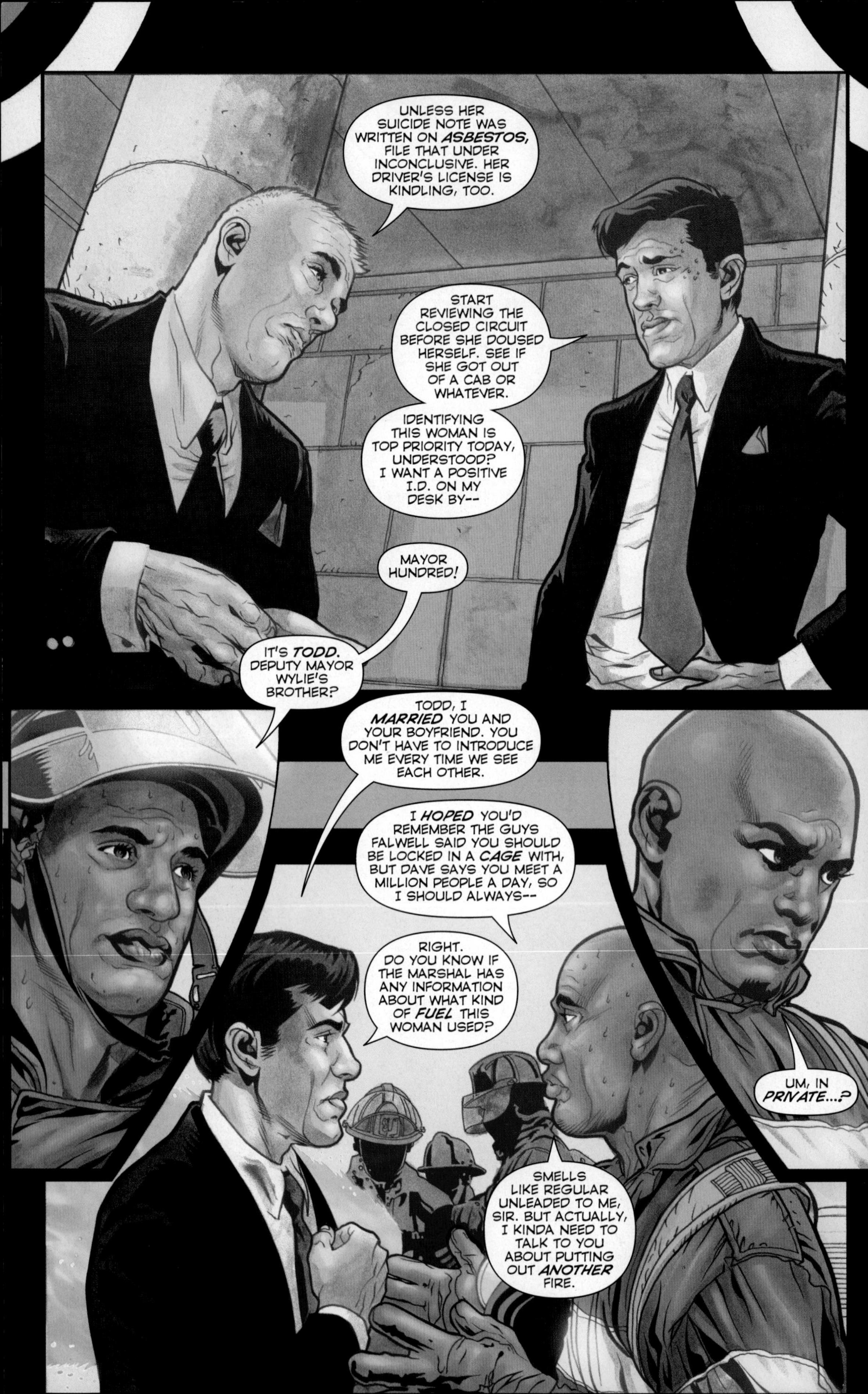
UNLESS HER SUICIDE NOTE WAS WRITTEN ON *ASBESTOS,* FILE THAT UNDER INCONCLUSIVE. HER DRIVER'S LICENSE IS KINDLING, TOO.
START REVIEWING THE CLOSED CIRCUIT BEFORE SHE DOUSED HERSELF. SEE IF SHE GOT OUT OF A CAB OR WHATEVER.
IDENTIFYING THIS WOMAN IS TOP PRIORITY TODAY, UNDERSTOOD? I WANT A POSITIVE I.D. ON MY DESK BY--
MAYOR HUNDRED!
IT'S *TODD.* DEPUTY MAYOR WYLIE'S BROTHER?
TODD, I *MARRIED* YOU AND YOUR BOYFRIEND. YOU DON'T HAVE TO INTRODUCE ME EVERY TIME WE SEE EACH OTHER.
I *HOPED* YOU'D REMEMBER THE GUYS FALWELL SAID YOU SHOULD BE LOCKED IN A *CAGE* WITH, BUT DAVE SAYS YOU MEET A MILLION PEOPLE A DAY, SO I SHOULD ALWAYS--
RIGHT. DO YOU KNOW IF THE MARSHAL HAS ANY INFORMATION ABOUT WHAT KIND OF *FUEL* THIS WOMAN USED?
UM, IN *PRIVATE...?*
SMELLS LIKE REGULAR UNLEADED TO ME, SIR. BUT ACTUALLY, I KINDA NEED TO TALK TO YOU ABOUT PUTTING OUT *ANOTHER* FIRE.

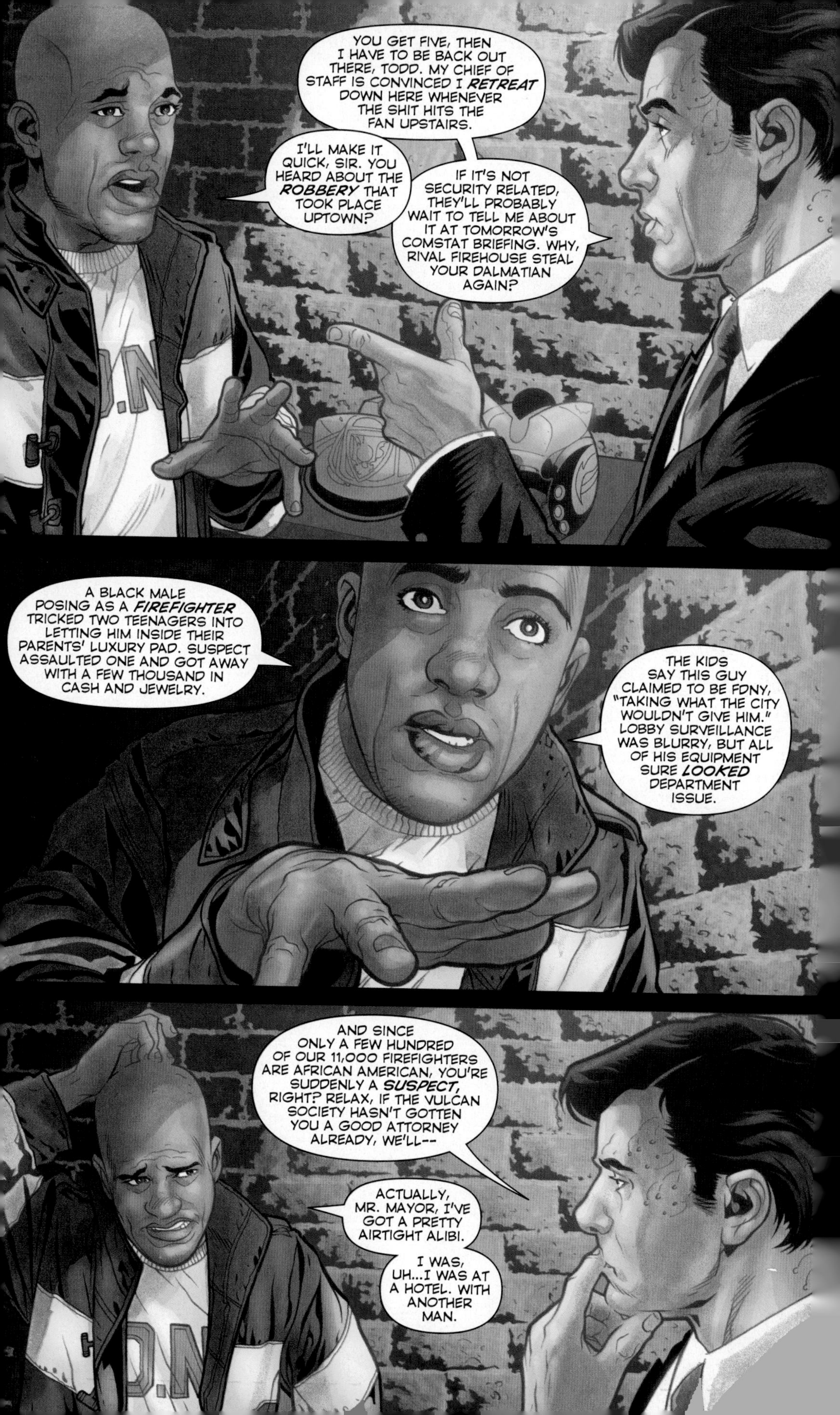
YOU GET FIVE, THEN I HAVE TO BE BACK OUT THERE, TODD. MY CHIEF OF STAFF IS CONVINCED I RETREAT DOWN HERE WHENEVER THE SHIT HITS THE FAN UPSTAIRS.
I'LL MAKE IT QUICK, SIR. YOU HEARD ABOUT THE ROBBERY THAT TOOK PLACE UPTOWN?
IF IT'S NOT SECURITY RELATED, THEY'LL PROBABLY WAIT TO TELL ME ABOUT IT AT TOMORROW'S COMSTAT BRIEFING. WHY, RIVAL FIREHOUSE STEAL YOUR DALMATIAN AGAIN?
A BLACK MALE POSING AS A FIREFIGHTER TRICKED TWO TEENAGERS INTO LETTING HIM INSIDE THEIR PARENTS' LUXURY PAD. SUSPECT ASSAULTED ONE AND GOT AWAY WITH A FEW THOUSAND IN CASH AND JEWELRY.
THE KIDS SAY THIS GUY CLAIMED TO BE FDNY, "TAKING WHAT THE CITY WOULDN'T GIVE HIM." LOBBY SURVEILLANCE WAS BLURRY, BUT ALL OF HIS EQUIPMENT SURE LOOKED DEPARTMENT ISSUE.
AND SINCE ONLY A FEW HUNDRED OF OUR 11,000 FIREFIGHTERS ARE AFRICAN AMERICAN, YOU'RE SUDDENLY A SUSPECT, RIGHT? RELAX, IF THE VULCAN SOCIETY HASN'T GOTTEN YOU A GOOD ATTORNEY ALREADY, WE'LL--
ACTUALLY, MR. MAYOR, I'VE GOT A PRETTY AIRTIGHT ALIBI.
I WAS, UH...I WAS AT A HOTEL. WITH ANOTHER MAN.

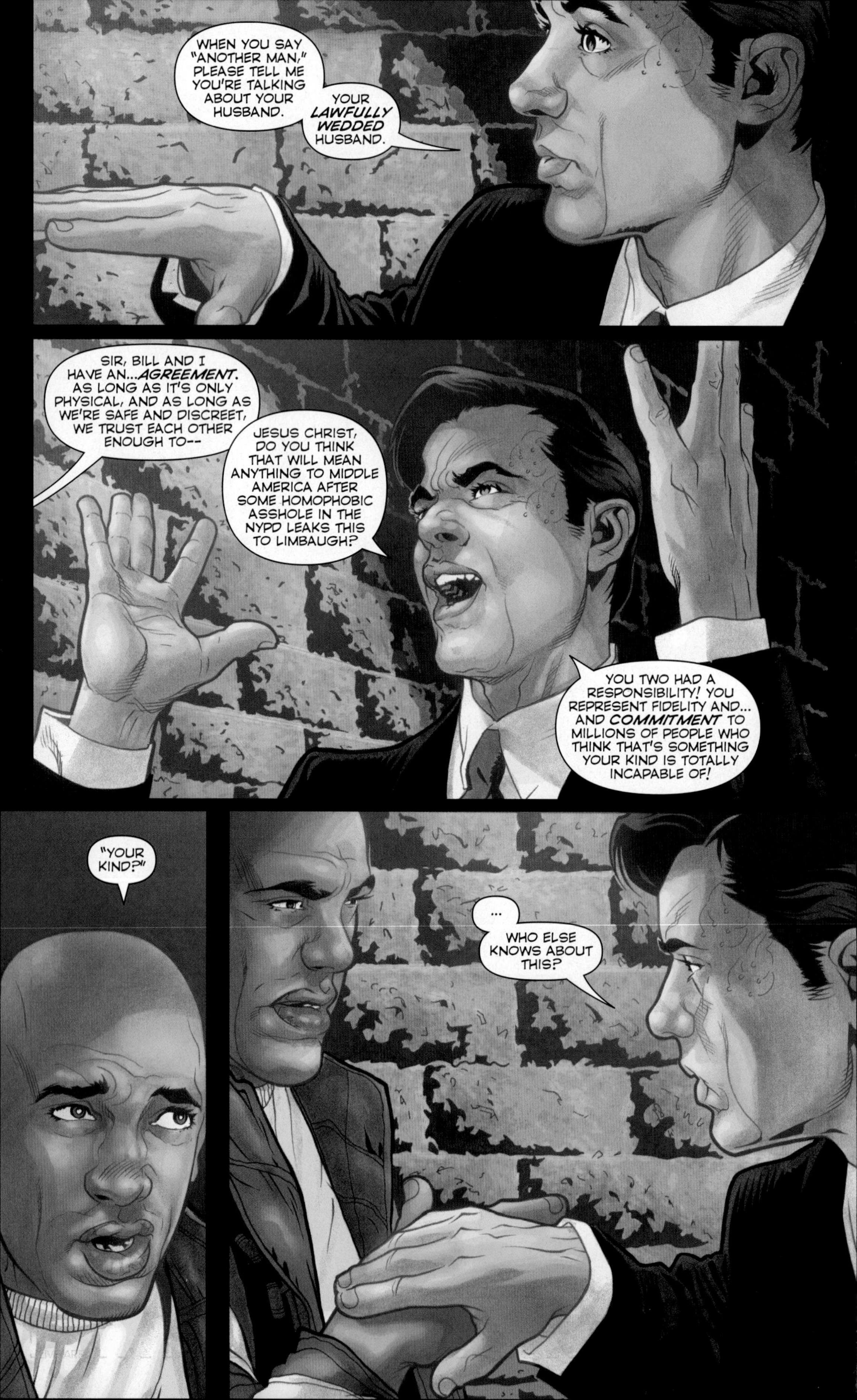
WHEN YOU SAY "ANOTHER MAN," PLEASE TELL ME YOU'RE TALKING ABOUT YOUR HUSBAND.
YOUR *LAWFULLY WEDDED* HUSBAND.
SIR, BILL AND I HAVE AN...*AGREEMENT*. AS LONG AS IT'S ONLY PHYSICAL, AND AS LONG AS WE'RE SAFE AND DISCREET, WE TRUST EACH OTHER ENOUGH TO--
JESUS CHRIST, DO YOU THINK THAT WILL MEAN ANYTHING TO MIDDLE AMERICA AFTER SOME HOMOPHOBIC ASSHOLE IN THE NYPD LEAKS THIS TO LIMBAUGH?
YOU TWO HAD A RESPONSIBILITY! YOU REPRESENT FIDELITY AND... AND *COMMITMENT* TO MILLIONS OF PEOPLE WHO THINK THAT'S SOMETHING YOUR KIND IS TOTALLY INCAPABLE OF!
"YOUR KIND?"
...
WHO ELSE KNOWS ABOUT THIS?

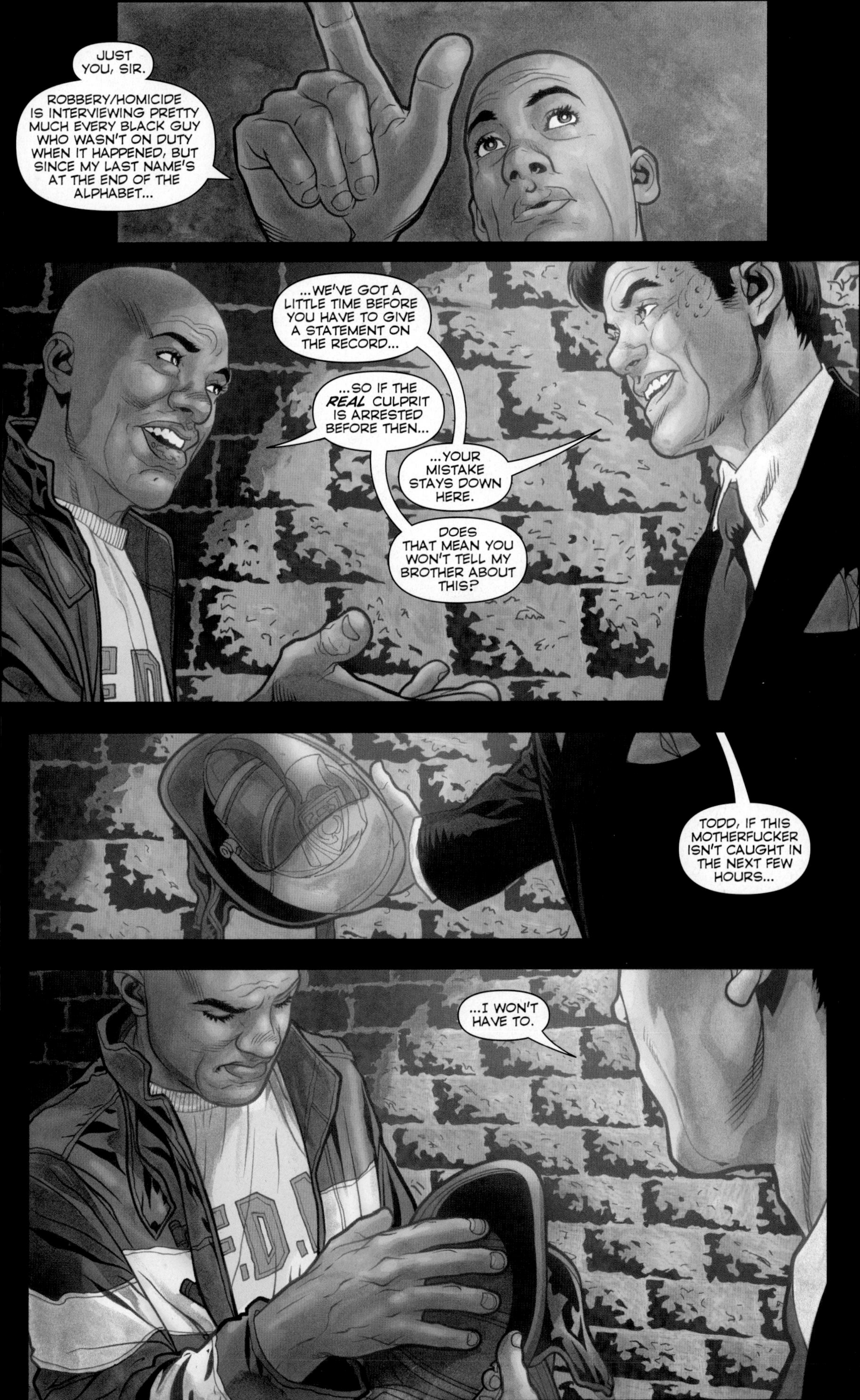
JUST YOU, SIR.
ROBBERY/HOMICIDE IS INTERVIEWING PRETTY MUCH EVERY BLACK GUY WHO WASN'T ON DUTY WHEN IT HAPPENED, BUT SINCE MY LAST NAME'S AT THE END OF THE ALPHABET...
...WE'VE GOT A LITTLE TIME BEFORE YOU HAVE TO GIVE A STATEMENT ON THE RECORD...
...SO IF THE REAL CULPRIT IS ARRESTED BEFORE THEN...
...YOUR MISTAKE STAYS DOWN HERE.
DOES THAT MEAN YOU WON'T TELL MY BROTHER ABOUT THIS?
TODD, IF THIS MOTHERFUCKER ISN'T CAUGHT IN THE NEXT FEW HOURS...
...I WON'T HAVE TO.

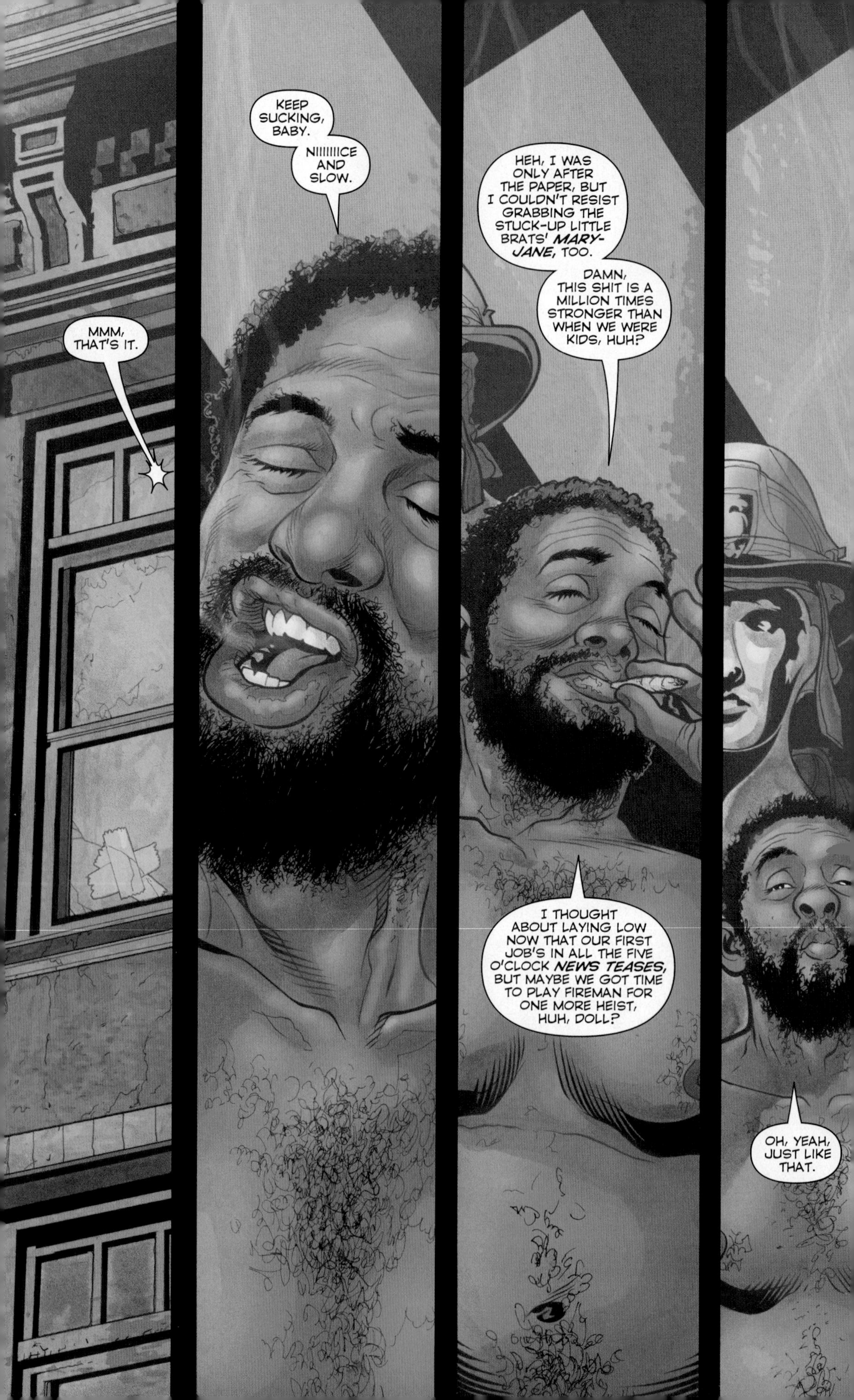
MMM, THAT'S IT.
KEEP SUCKING, BABY.
NIIIIIIICE AND SLOW.
HEH, I WAS ONLY AFTER THE PAPER, BUT I COULDN'T RESIST GRABBING THE STUCK-UP LITTLE BRATS' MARY-JANE, TOO.
DAMN, THIS SHIT IS A MILLION TIMES STRONGER THAN WHEN WE WERE KIDS, HUH?
I THOUGHT ABOUT LAYING LOW NOW THAT OUR FIRST JOB'S IN ALL THE FIVE O'CLOCK NEWS TEASES, BUT MAYBE WE GOT TIME TO PLAY FIREMAN FOR ONE MORE HEIST, HUH, DOLL?
OH, YEAH, JUST LIKE THAT.

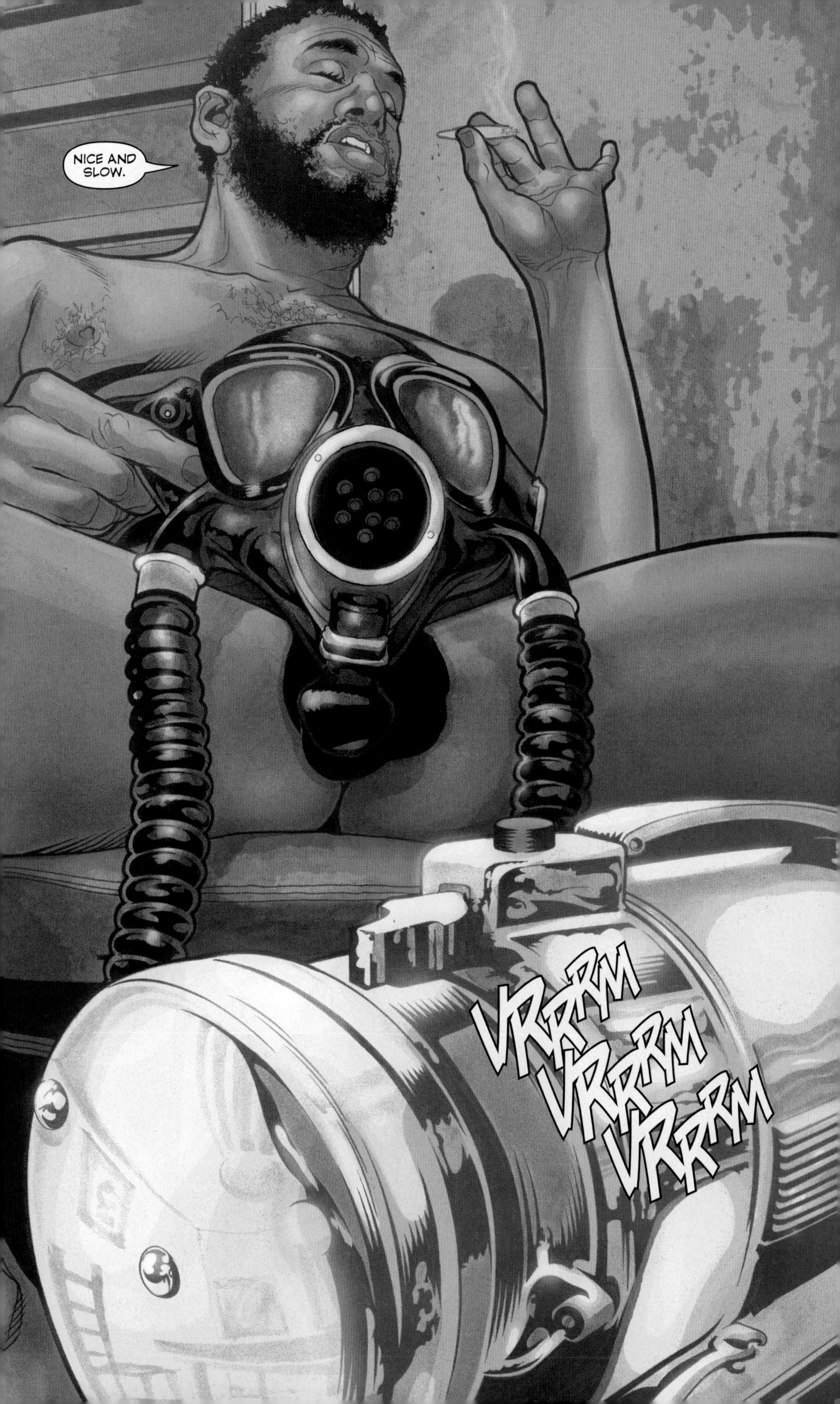
NICE AND SLOW.
VRRRM VRRRM VRRRM

WHAT WAS *THAT* ALL ABOUT?

WHAT WAS *WHAT* ALL ABOUT, DAVE?

YOUR SECURITY GUY SAID YOU WERE MEETING WITH MY *BROTHER?*

YEAH, IT'S... A LONG STORY. OR NOTHING. TAKE YOUR PICK.

SIR, I REALIZE YOU AND I HAVE SOME UNRESOLVED DIFFERENCES, BUT I'D APPRECIATE IT IF YOU WOULDN'T USE MY *FAMILY* AS LEVERAGE.

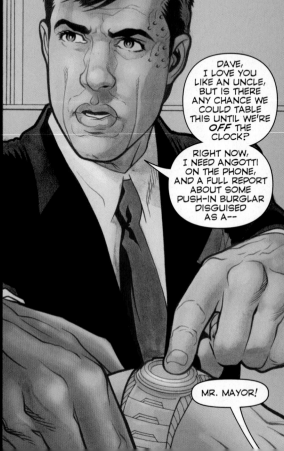

DAVE, I LOVE YOU LIKE AN UNCLE, BUT IS THERE ANY CHANCE WE COULD TABLE THIS UNTIL WE'RE *OFF* THE CLOCK?

RIGHT NOW, I NEED ANGOTT! ON THE PHONE, AND A FULL REPORT ABOUT SOME PUSH-IN BURGLAR DISGUISED AS A--

MR. MAYOR!

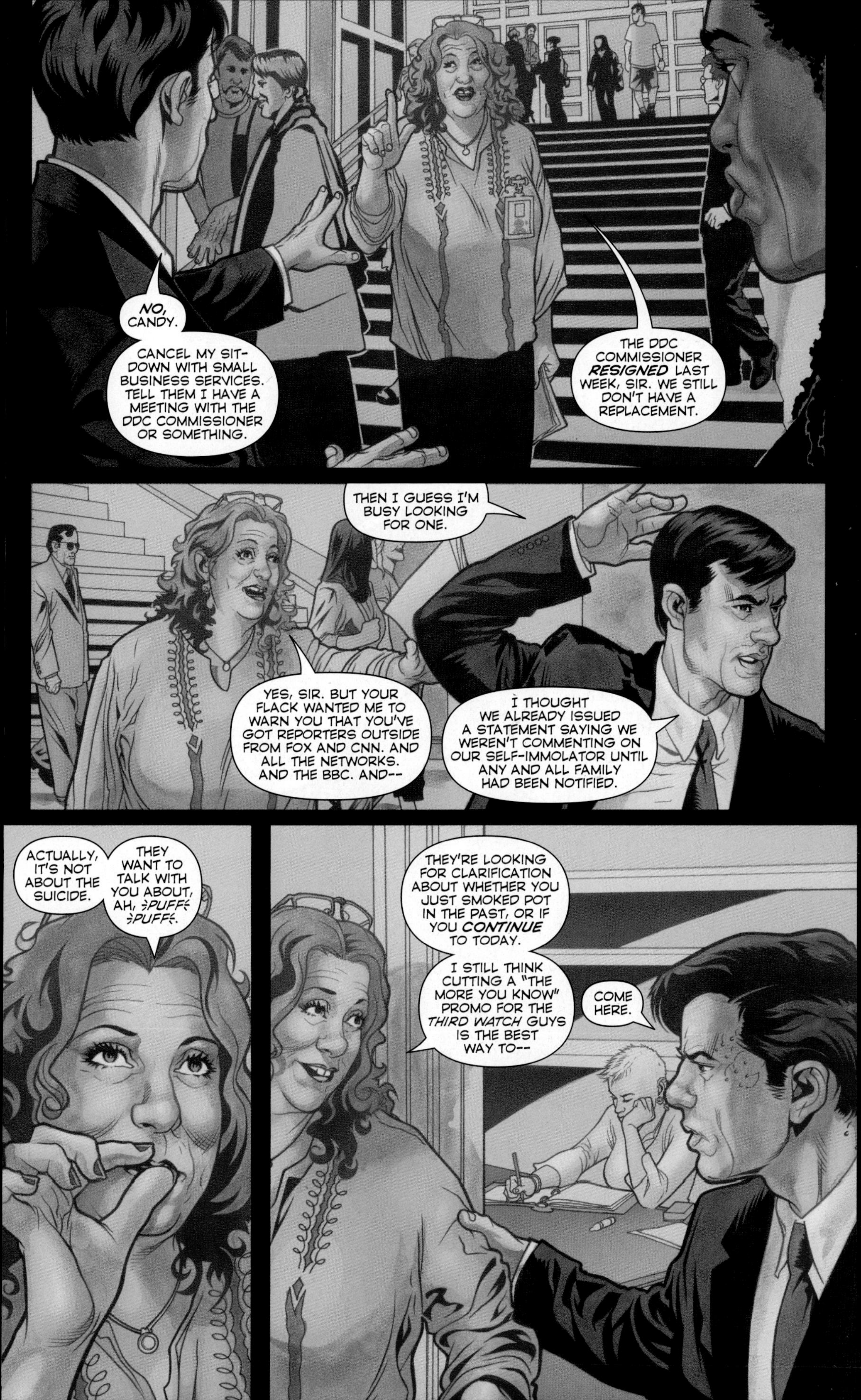

NO, CANDY.
CANCEL MY SIT-DOWN WITH SMALL BUSINESS SERVICES. TELL THEM I HAVE A MEETING WITH THE DDC COMMISSIONER OR SOMETHING.
THE DDC COMMISSIONER RESIGNED LAST WEEK, SIR. WE STILL DON'T HAVE A REPLACEMENT.
THEN I GUESS I'M BUSY LOOKING FOR ONE.
YES, SIR. BUT YOUR FLACK WANTED ME TO WARN YOU THAT YOU'VE GOT REPORTERS OUTSIDE FROM FOX AND CNN. AND ALL THE NETWORKS. AND THE BBC. AND--
I THOUGHT WE ALREADY ISSUED A STATEMENT SAYING WE WEREN'T COMMENTING ON OUR SELF-IMMOLATOR UNTIL ANY AND ALL FAMILY HAD BEEN NOTIFIED.
ACTUALLY, IT'S NOT ABOUT THE SUICIDE.
THEY WANT TO TALK WITH YOU ABOUT, AH, ≥PUFF≤ ≥PUFF≤.
THEY'RE LOOKING FOR CLARIFICATION ABOUT WHETHER YOU JUST SMOKED POT IN THE PAST, OR IF YOU CONTINUE TO TODAY.
I STILL THINK CUTTING A "THE MORE YOU KNOW" PROMO FOR THE THIRD WATCH GUYS IS THE BEST WAY TO--
COME HERE.

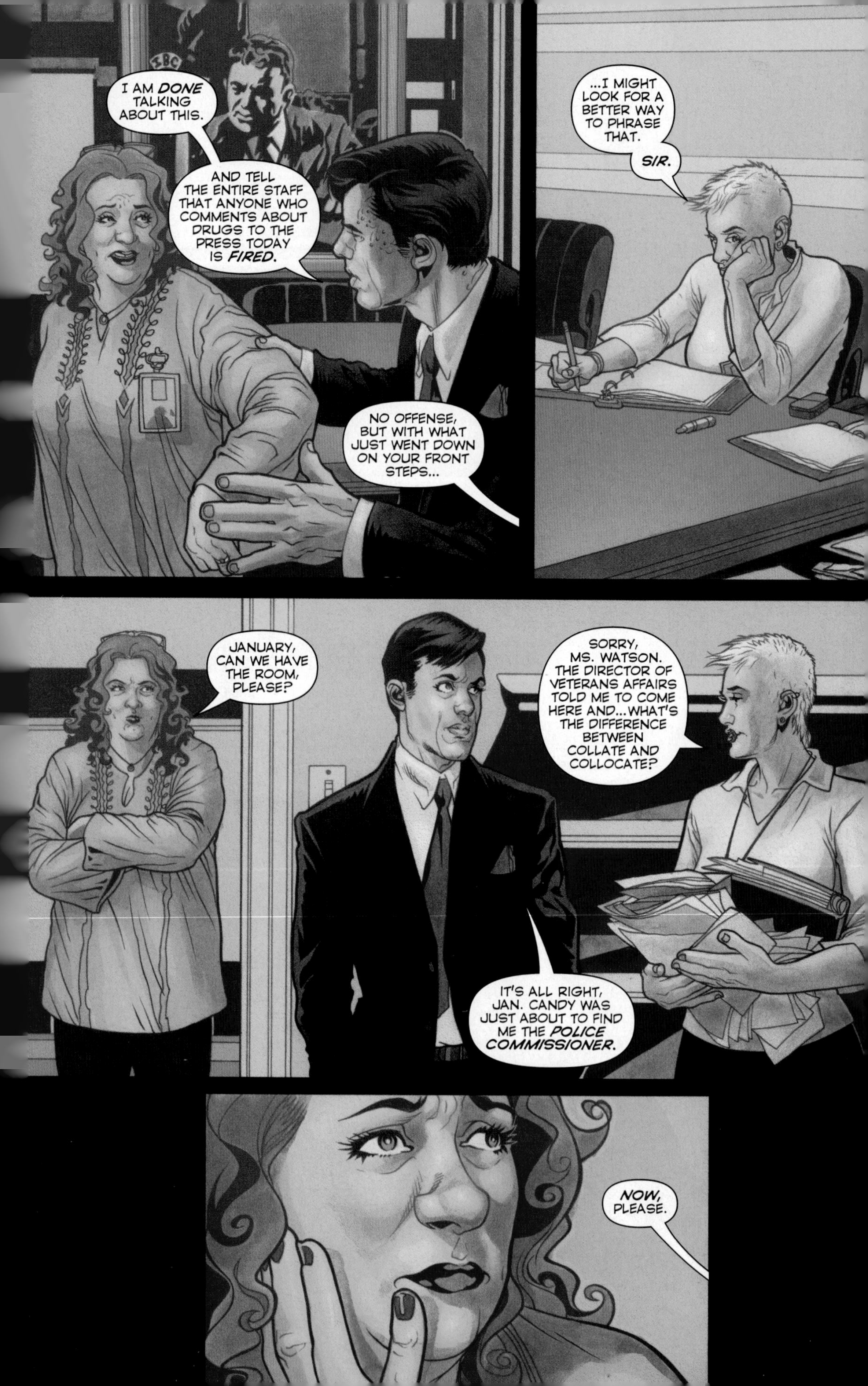
I AM *DONE* TALKING ABOUT THIS.
AND TELL THE ENTIRE STAFF THAT ANYONE WHO COMMENTS ABOUT DRUGS TO THE PRESS TODAY IS *FIRED*.
NO OFFENSE, BUT WITH WHAT JUST WENT DOWN ON YOUR FRONT STEPS...
...I MIGHT LOOK FOR A BETTER WAY TO PHRASE THAT.
SIR.
JANUARY, CAN WE HAVE THE ROOM, PLEASE?
SORRY, MS. WATSON. THE DIRECTOR OF VETERANS AFFAIRS TOLD ME TO COME HERE AND...WHAT'S THE DIFFERENCE BETWEEN COLLATE AND COLLOCATE?
IT'S ALL RIGHT, JAN. CANDY WAS JUST ABOUT TO FIND ME THE *POLICE COMMISSIONER*.
NOW, PLEASE.

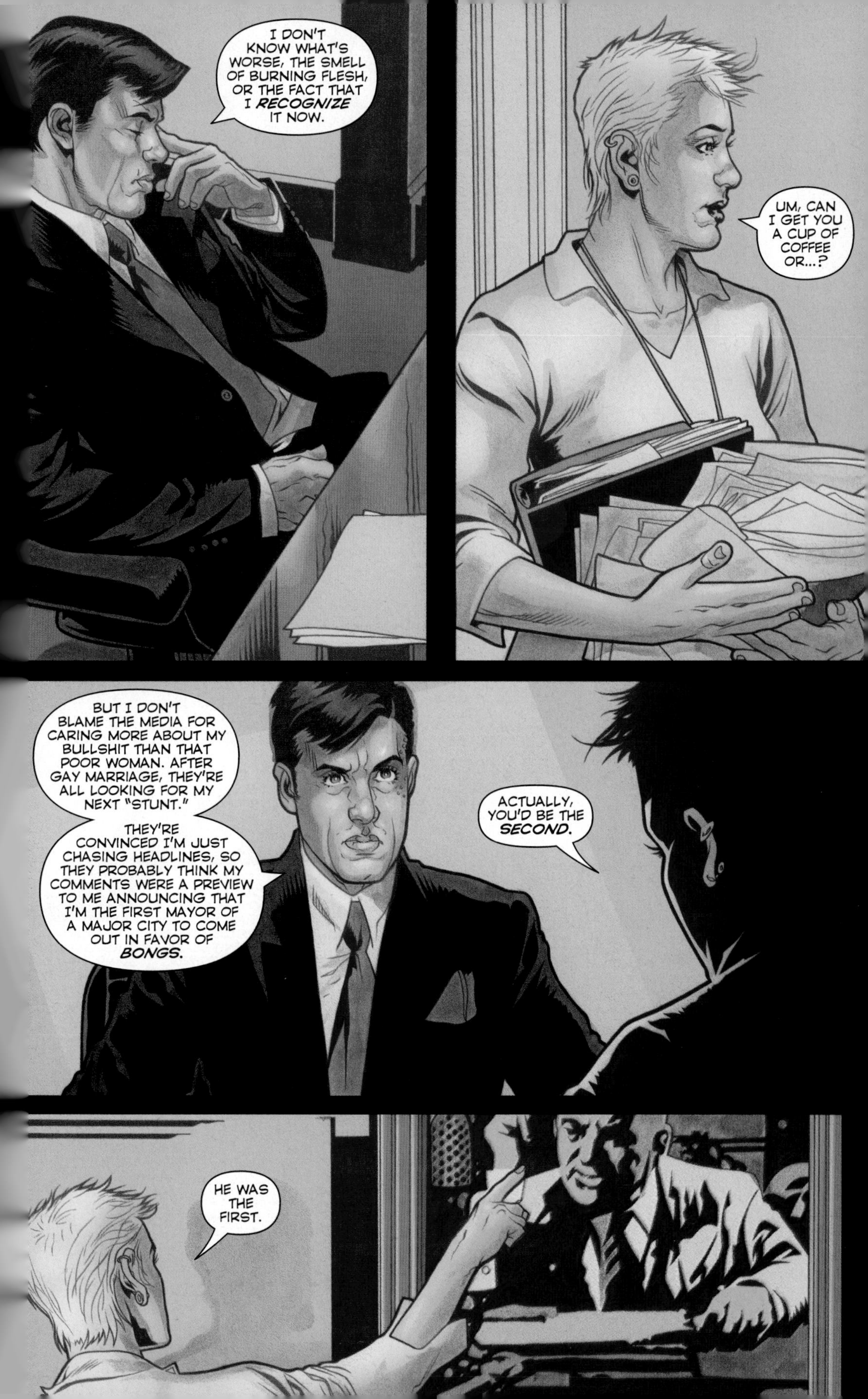
I DON'T KNOW WHAT'S WORSE, THE SMELL OF BURNING FLESH, OR THE FACT THAT I *RECOGNIZE* IT NOW.
UM, CAN I GET YOU A CUP OF COFFEE OR...?
BUT I DON'T BLAME THE MEDIA FOR CARING MORE ABOUT MY BULLSHIT THAN THAT POOR WOMAN. AFTER GAY MARRIAGE, THEY'RE ALL LOOKING FOR MY NEXT "STUNT."
THEY'RE CONVINCED I'M JUST CHASING HEADLINES, SO THEY PROBABLY THINK MY COMMENTS WERE A PREVIEW TO ME ANNOUNCING THAT I'M THE FIRST MAYOR OF A MAJOR CITY TO COME OUT IN FAVOR OF *BONGS*.
ACTUALLY, YOU'D BE THE *SECOND*.
HE WAS THE FIRST.

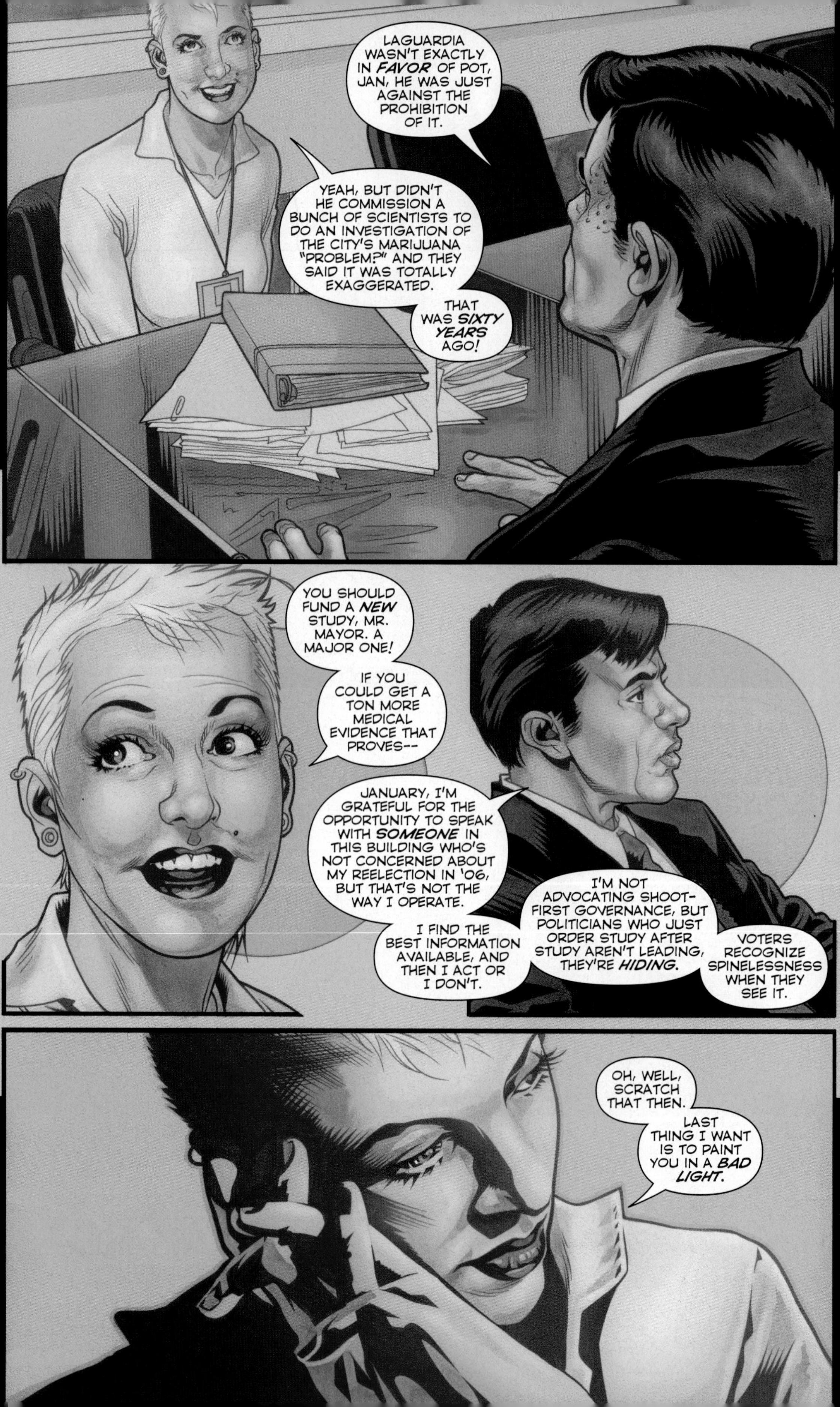
LAGUARDIA WASN'T EXACTLY IN FAVOR OF POT, JAN, HE WAS JUST AGAINST THE PROHIBITION OF IT.
YEAH, BUT DIDN'T HE COMMISSION A BUNCH OF SCIENTISTS TO DO AN INVESTIGATION OF THE CITY'S MARIJUANA "PROBLEM?" AND THEY SAID IT WAS TOTALLY EXAGGERATED.
THAT WAS SIXTY YEARS AGO!
YOU SHOULD FUND A NEW STUDY, MR. MAYOR. A MAJOR ONE!
IF YOU COULD GET A TON MORE MEDICAL EVIDENCE THAT PROVES--
JANUARY, I'M GRATEFUL FOR THE OPPORTUNITY TO SPEAK WITH SOMEONE IN THIS BUILDING WHO'S NOT CONCERNED ABOUT MY REELECTION IN '06, BUT THAT'S NOT THE WAY I OPERATE.
I FIND THE BEST INFORMATION AVAILABLE, AND THEN I ACT OR I DON'T.
I'M NOT ADVOCATING SHOOT-FIRST GOVERNANCE, BUT POLITICIANS WHO JUST ORDER STUDY AFTER STUDY AREN'T LEADING, THEY'RE HIDING.
VOTERS RECOGNIZE SPINELESSNESS WHEN THEY SEE IT.
OH, WELL, SCRATCH THAT THEN.
LAST THING I WANT IS TO PAINT YOU IN A BAD LIGHT.

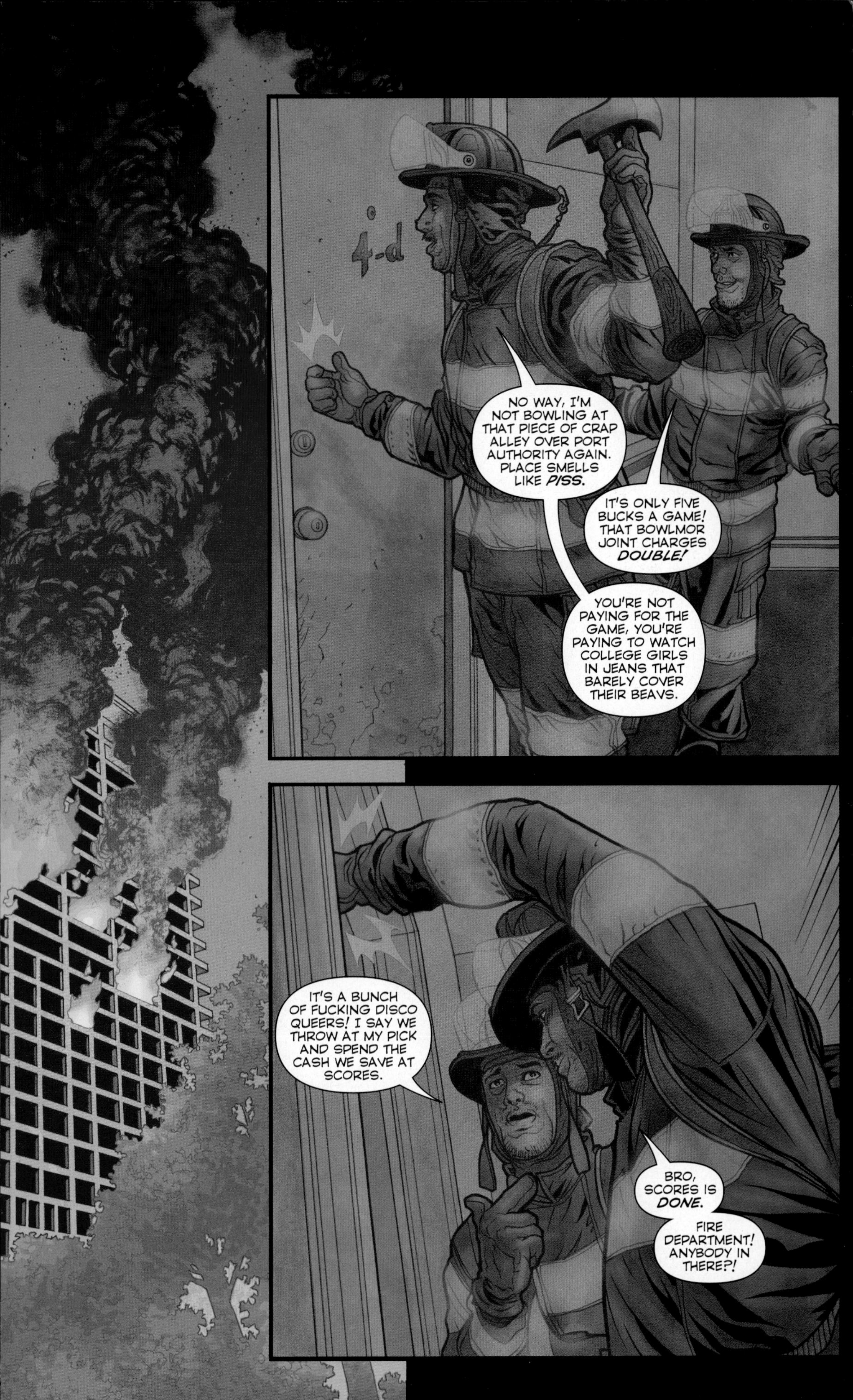
NO WAY, I'M NOT BOWLING AT THAT PIECE OF CRAP ALLEY OVER PORT AUTHORITY AGAIN. PLACE SMELLS LIKE PISS.
IT'S ONLY FIVE BUCKS A GAME! THAT BOWLMOR JOINT CHARGES DOUBLE!
YOU'RE NOT PAYING FOR THE GAME, YOU'RE PAYING TO WATCH COLLEGE GIRLS IN JEANS THAT BARELY COVER THEIR BEAVS.
IT'S A BUNCH OF FUCKING DISCO QUEERS! I SAY WE THROW AT MY PICK AND SPEND THE CASH WE SAVE AT SCORES.
BRO, SCORES IS DONE.
FIRE DEPARTMENT! ANYBODY IN THERE?!

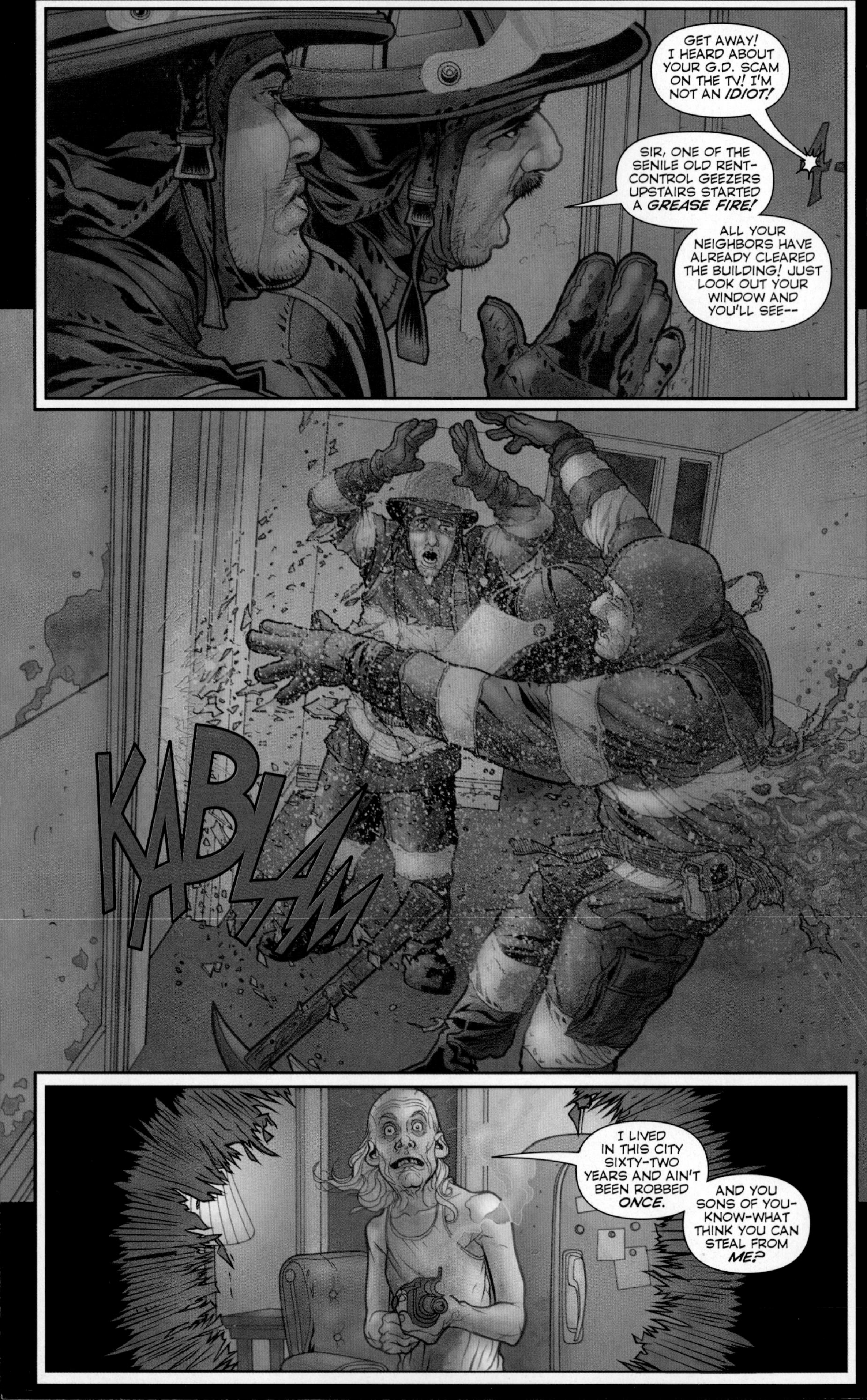
GET AWAY! I HEARD ABOUT YOUR G.D. SCAM ON THE TV! I'M NOT AN IDIOT!
SIR, ONE OF THE SENILE OLD RENT-CONTROL GEEZERS UPSTAIRS STARTED A GREASE FIRE!
ALL YOUR NEIGHBORS HAVE ALREADY CLEARED THE BUILDING! JUST LOOK OUT YOUR WINDOW AND YOU'LL SEE--
KABLAM
I LIVED IN THIS CITY SIXTY-TWO YEARS AND AIN'T BEEN ROBBED ONCE.
AND YOU SONS OF YOU-KNOW-WHAT THINK YOU CAN STEAL FROM ME?

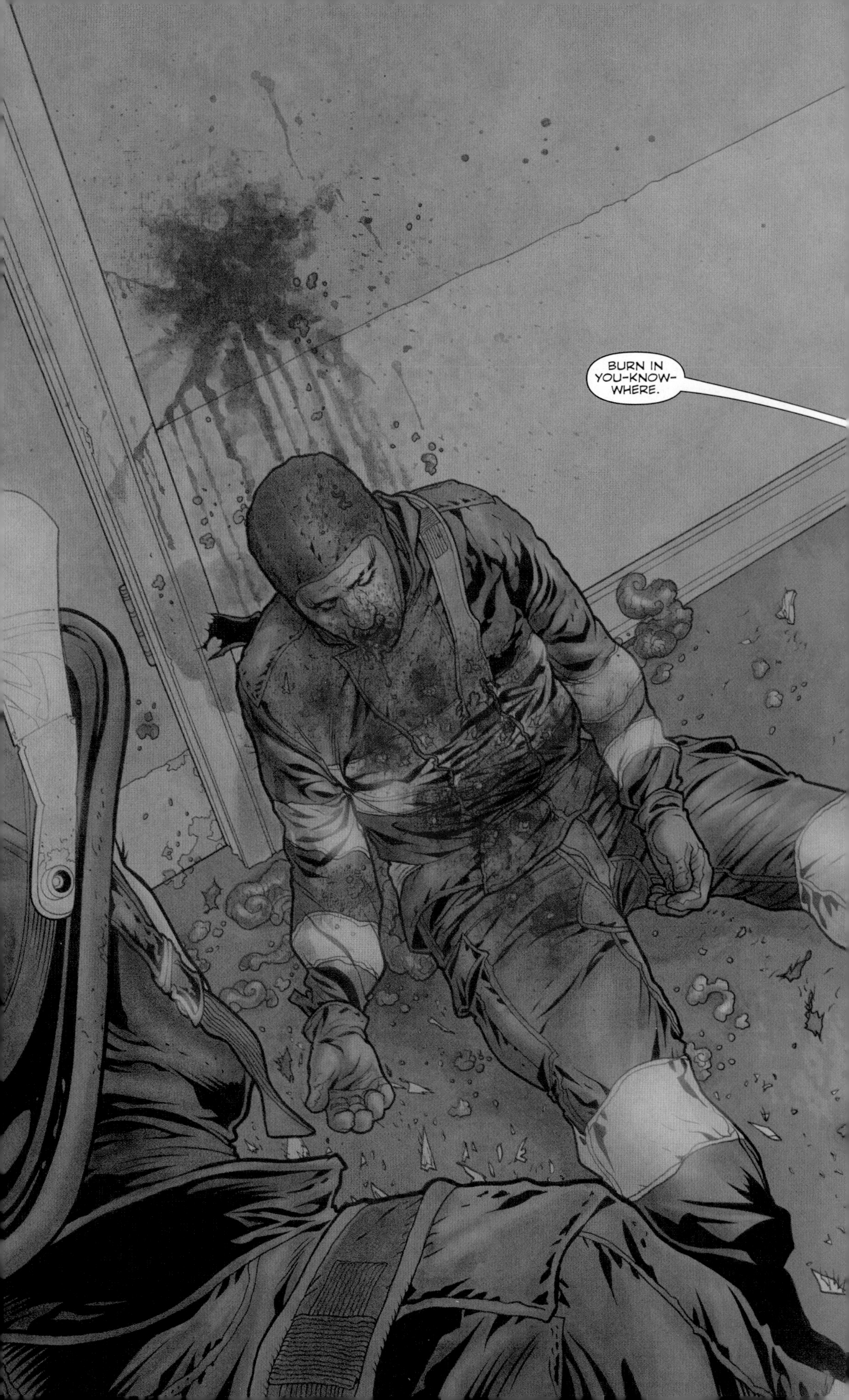
BURN IN YOU-KNOW-WHERE.

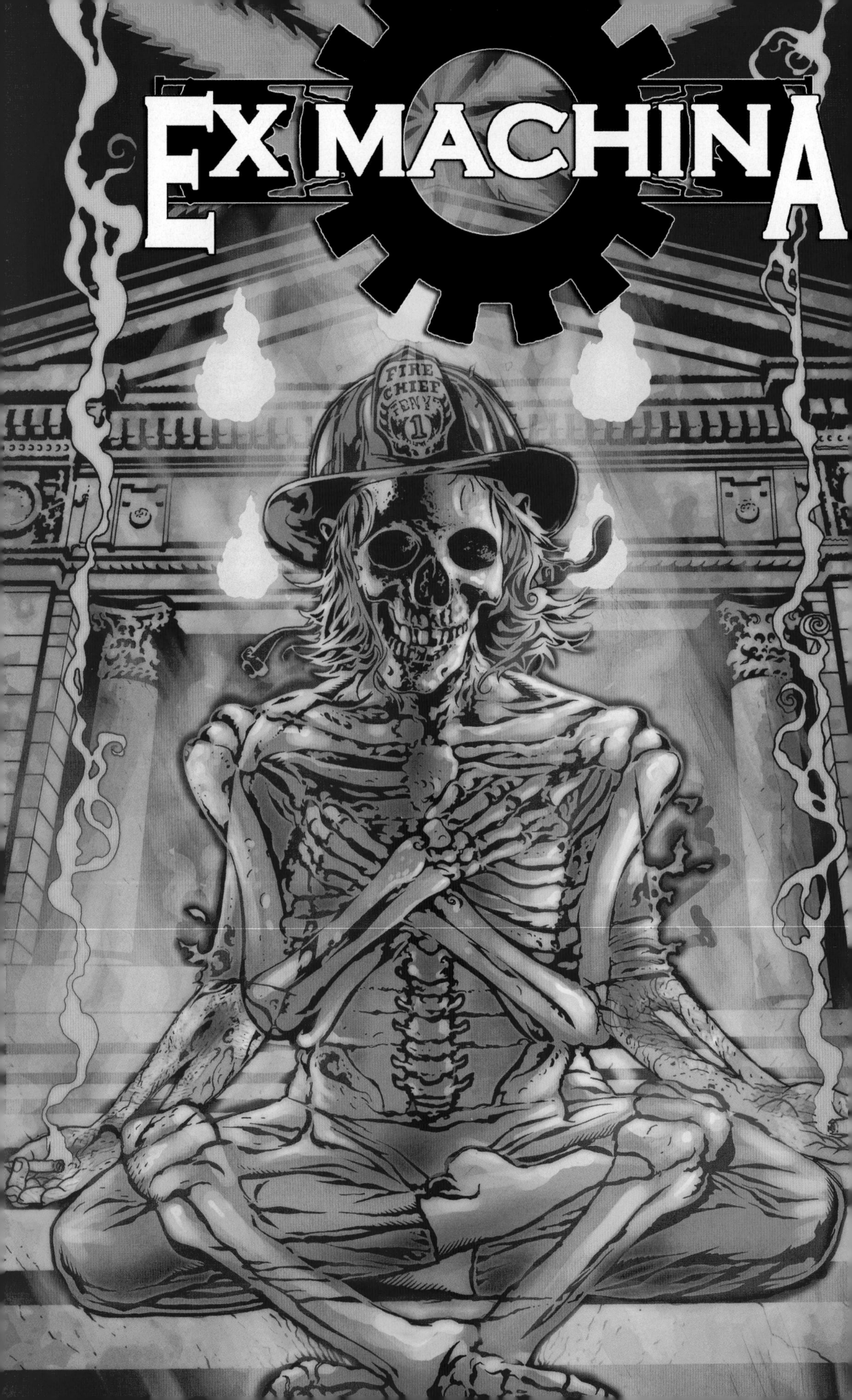

EX MACHINA
FIRE
CHIEF
FDNY
1

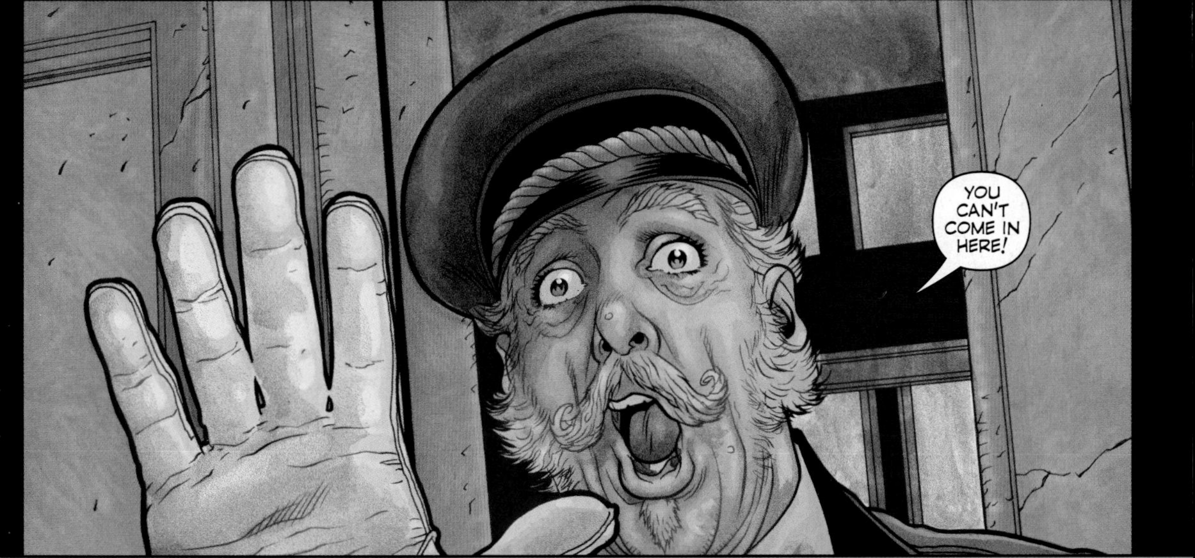
YOU CAN'T COME IN HERE!

MONDAY, APRIL 2, 2001

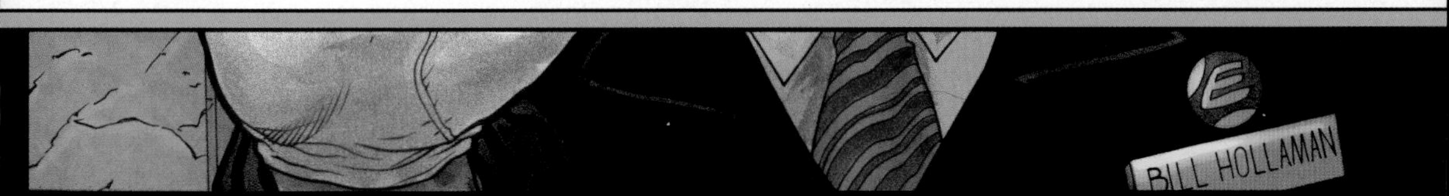
BILL HOLLAMAN

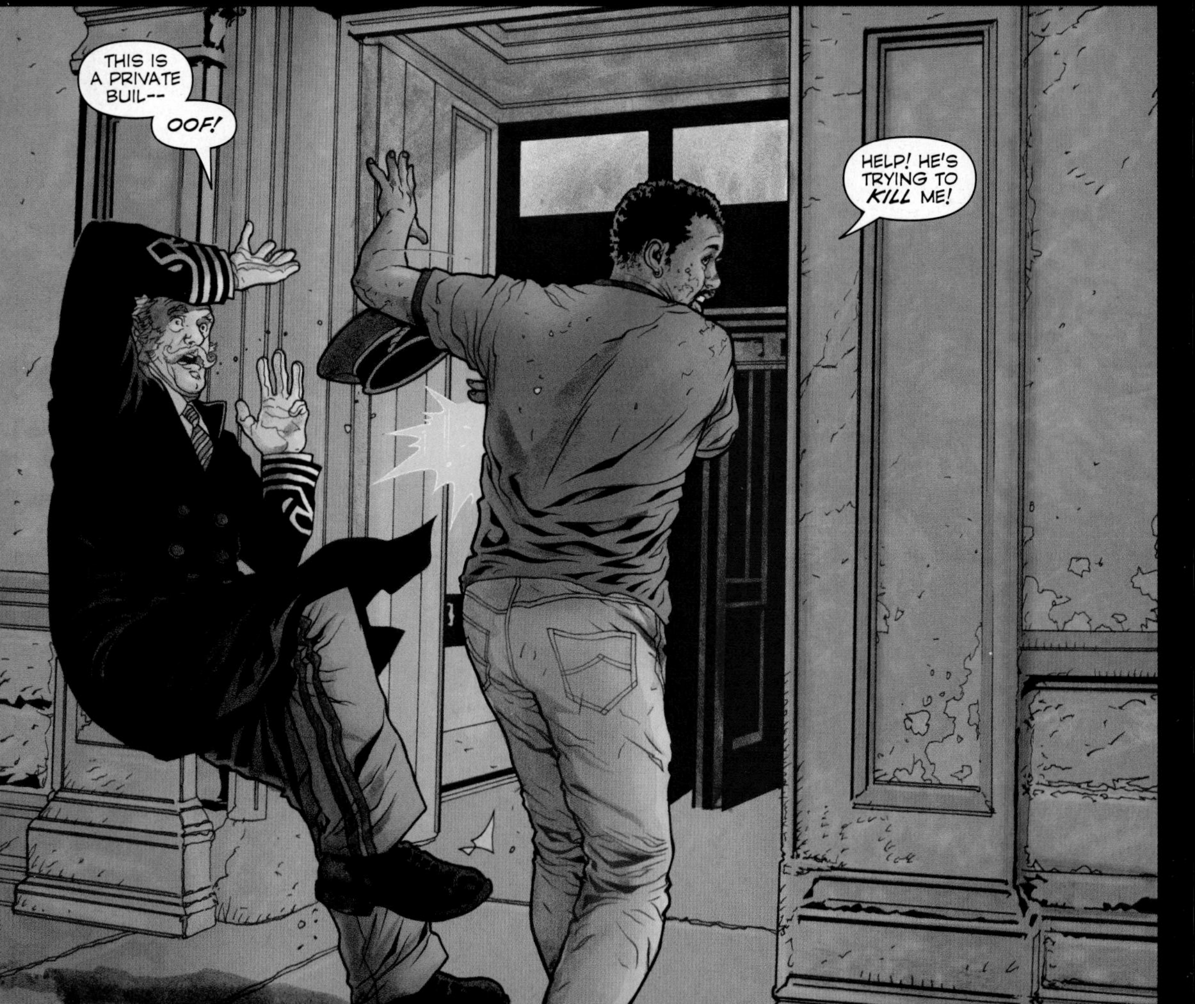
THIS IS A PRIVATE BUIL-- OOF!
HELP! HE'S TRYING TO KILL ME!

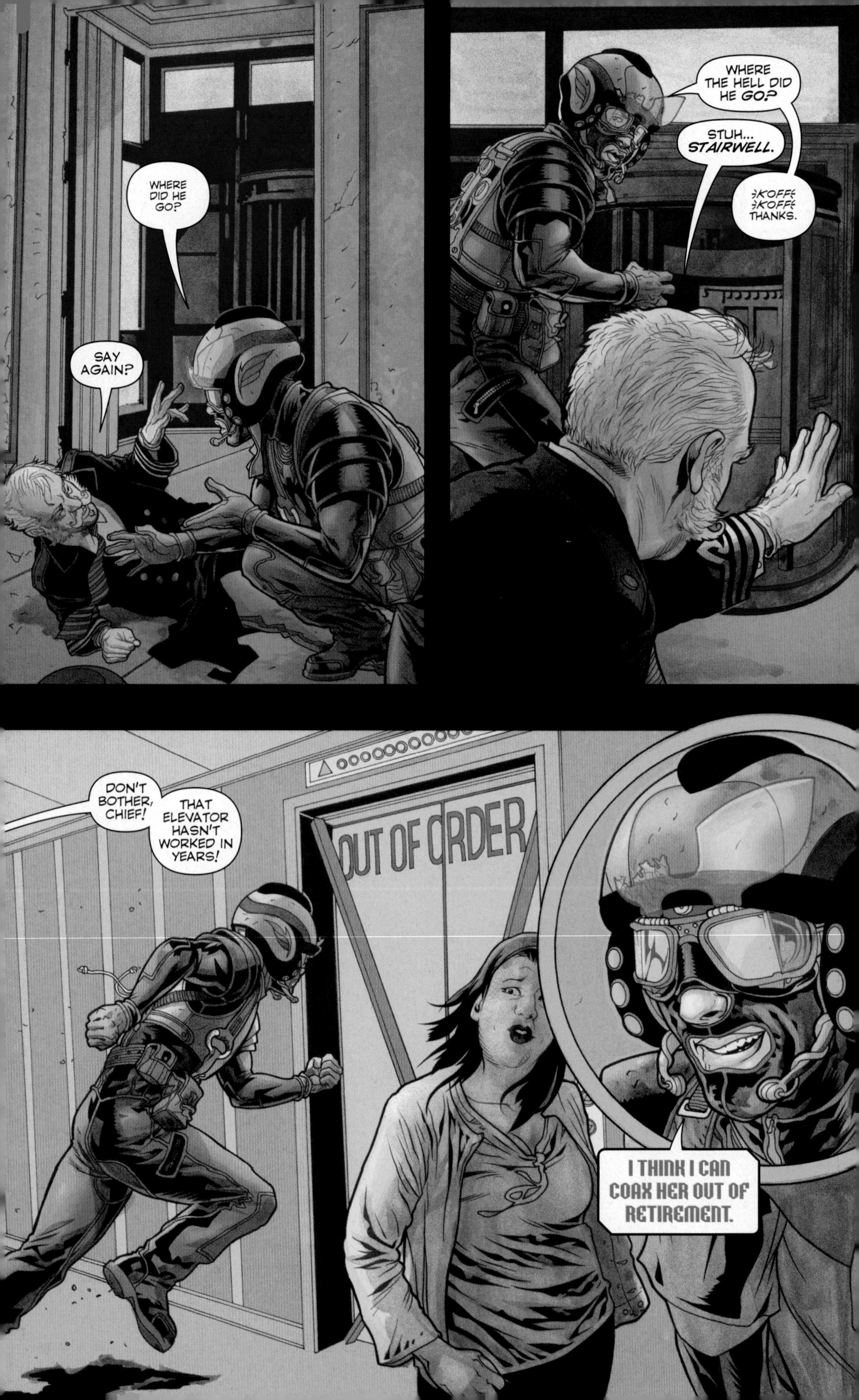
WHERE DID HE GO?
SAY AGAIN?
WHERE THE HELL DID HE GO?
STUH... STAIRWELL.
KOFF *KOFF* THANKS.
DON'T BOTHER, CHIEF!
THAT ELEVATOR HASN'T WORKED IN YEARS!
OUT OF ORDER
I THINK I CAN COAX HER OUT OF RETIREMENT.

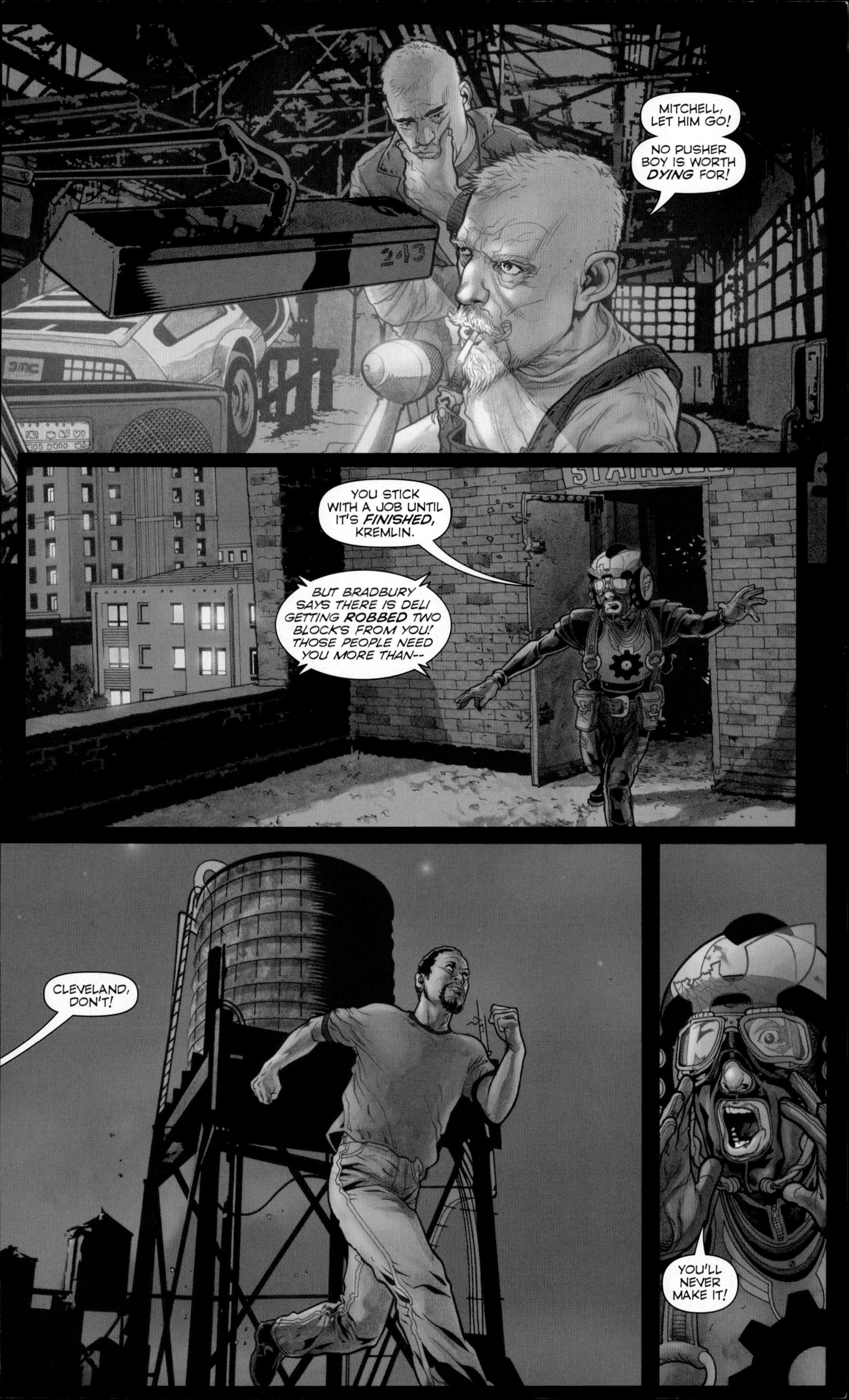
MITCHELL, LET HIM GO!
NO PUSHER BOY IS WORTH *DYING* FOR!
YOU STICK WITH A JOB UNTIL IT'S *FINISHED,* KREMLIN.
BUT BRADBURY SAYS THERE IS DELI GETTING **ROBBED** *TWO BLOCKS FROM YOU! THOSE PEOPLE NEED YOU MORE THAN--*
CLEVELAND, DON'T!
YOU'LL NEVER MAKE IT!

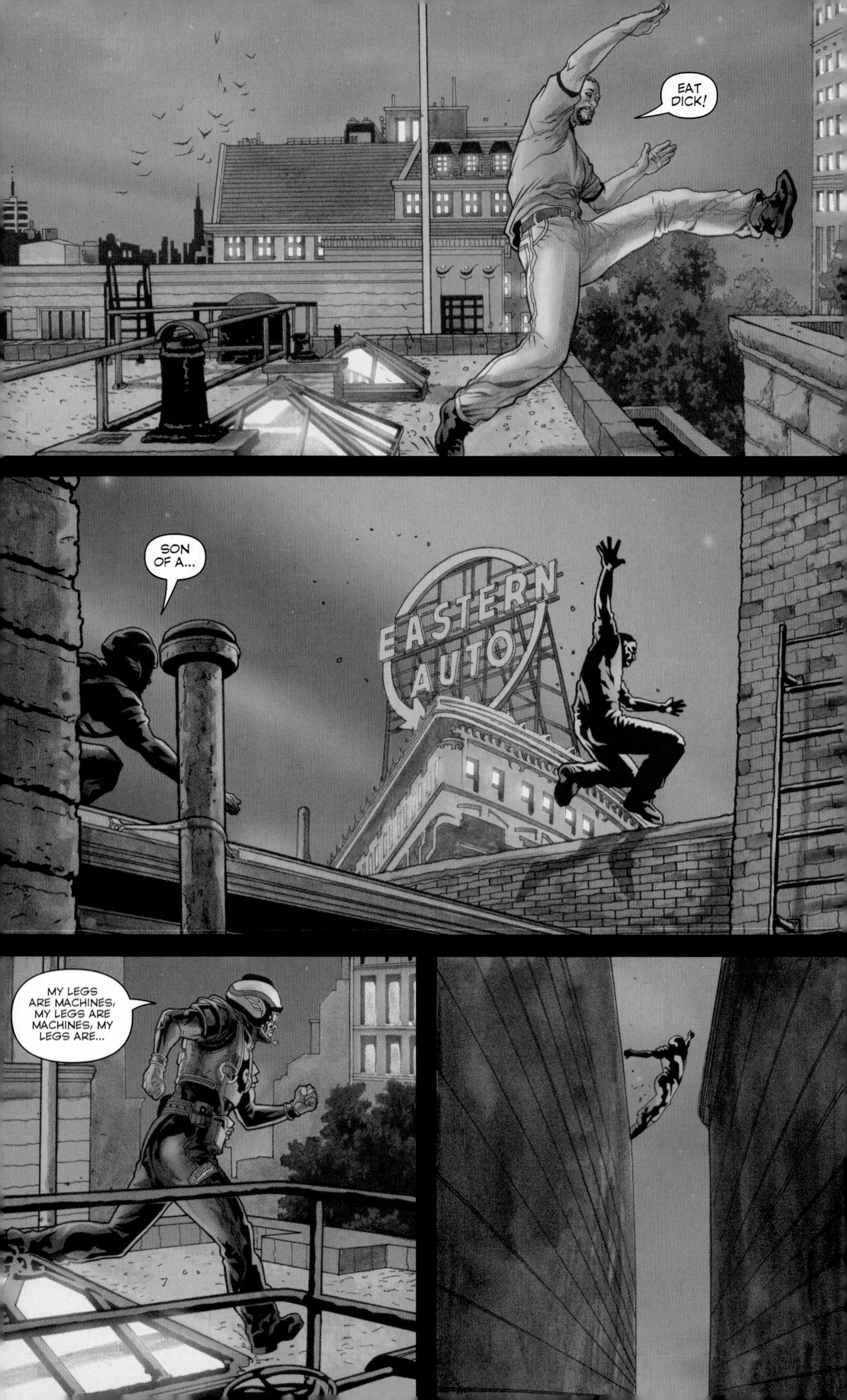
EAT DICK!
SON OF A...
EASTERN AUTO
MY LEGS ARE MACHINES, MY LEGS ARE MACHINES, MY LEGS ARE...

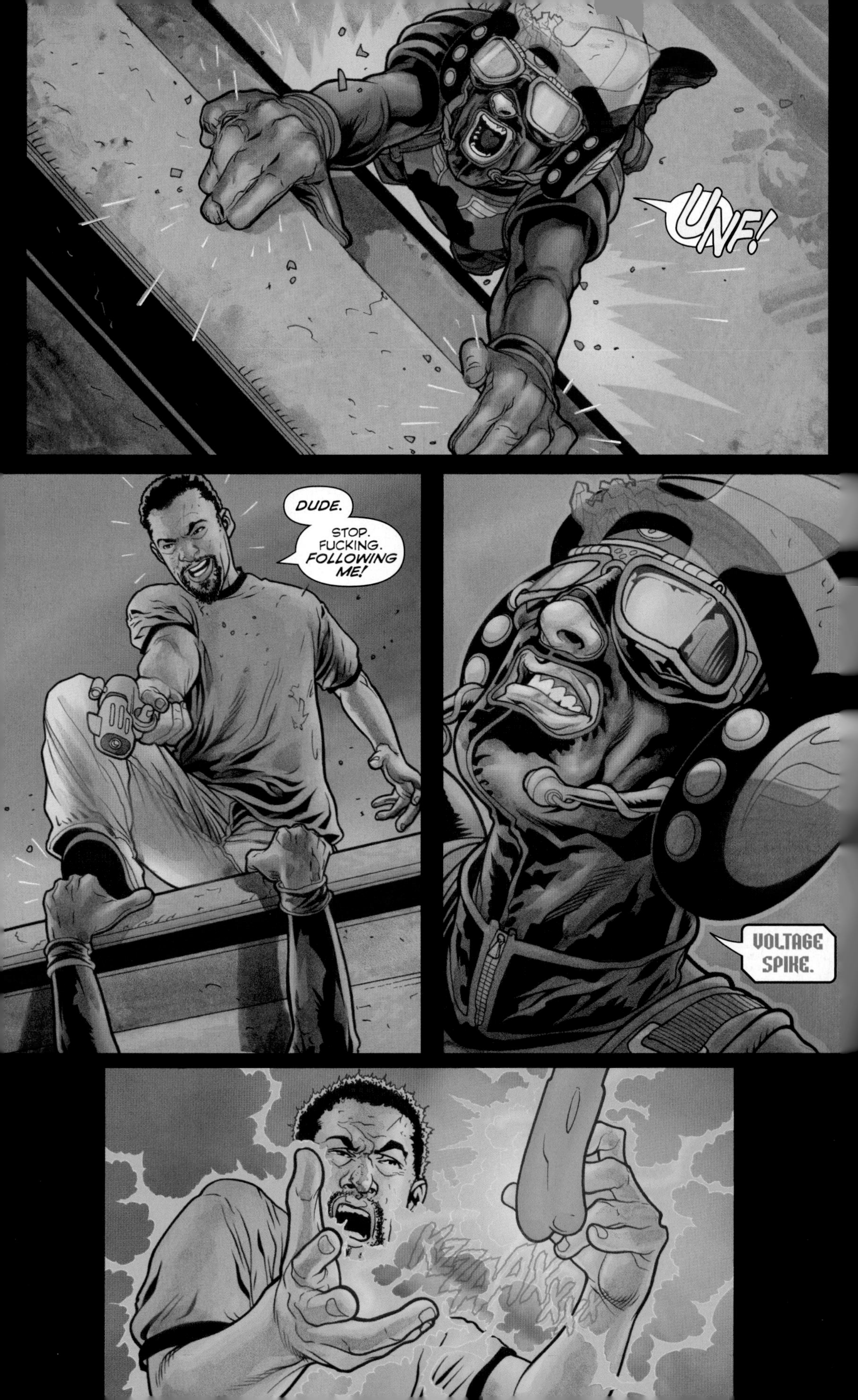
UNF!
DUDE.
STOP. FUCKING. FOLLOWING ME!
VOLTAGE SPIKE.

NGGH...
CLEVELAND SEVERTSON, I'M PLACING YOU UNDER CITIZEN'S ARREST.
ALL THIS FOR A... A LITTLE GRASS?
AN APARTMENT-FULL IS HARDLY A LITTLE. BESIDES, YOU SELL TO CHILDREN.
NO, I SELL TO RICH FOLK! I CAN'T CONTROL WHO THEY GIVE THEIR SHIT TO.
LOOK, I'M NOT A RAPIST! I'VE NEVER MURDERED ANYBODY! YOU CAN'T SEND ME TO PRISON!
I'M NOT. I'M SENDING YOU TO THE COPS.
I CAN'T CONTROL WHO THEY GIVE THEIR SHIT TO.
KOFF KOFF

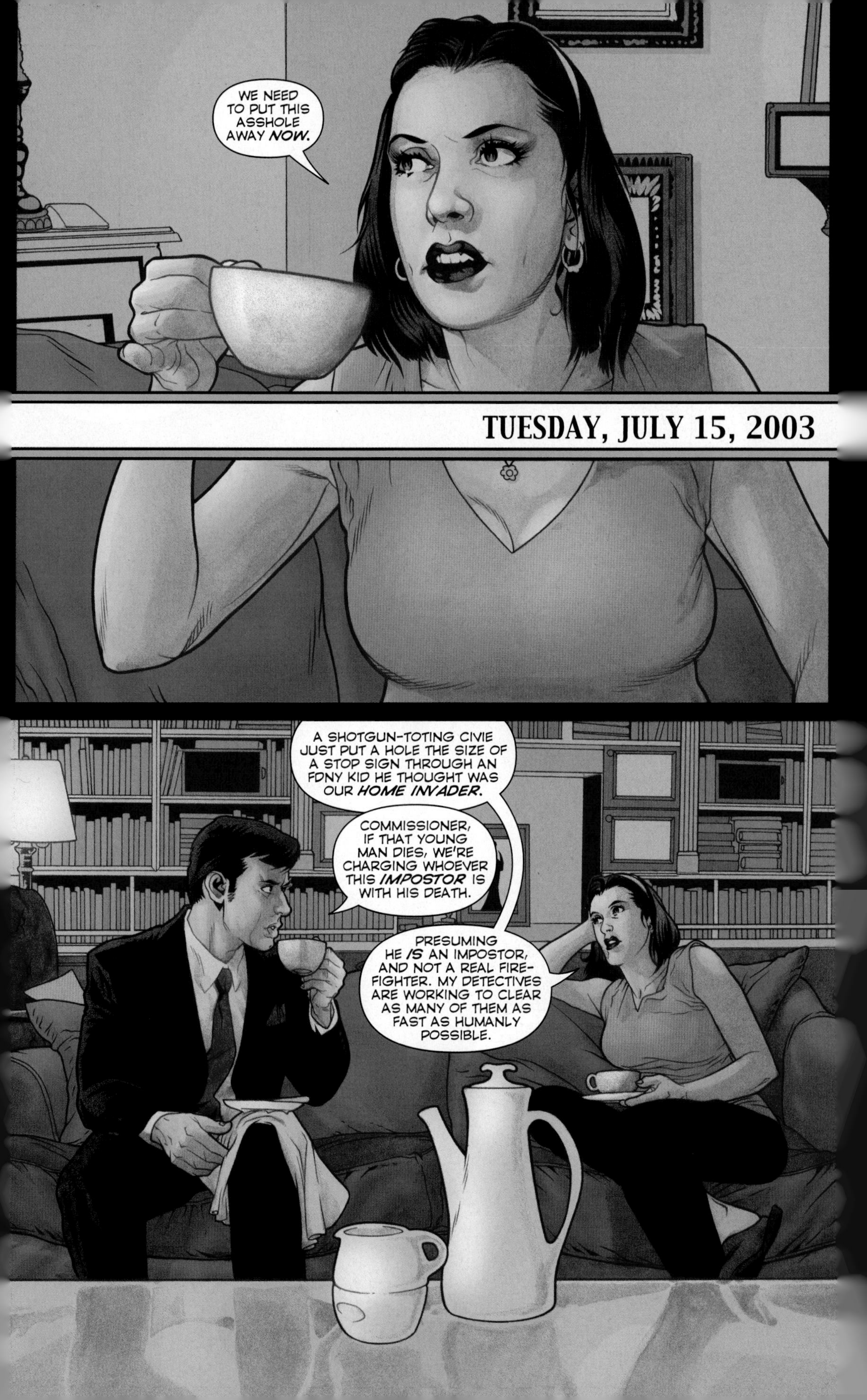
WE NEED TO PUT THIS ASSHOLE AWAY *NOW.*
TUESDAY, JULY 15, 2003
A SHOTGUN-TOTING CIVIE JUST PUT A HOLE THE SIZE OF A STOP SIGN THROUGH AN FDNY KID HE THOUGHT WAS OUR *HOME INVADER.*
COMMISSIONER, IF THAT YOUNG MAN DIES, WE'RE CHARGING WHOEVER THIS *IMPOSTOR* IS WITH HIS DEATH.
PRESUMING HE *IS* AN IMPOSTOR, AND NOT A REAL FIRE-FIGHTER. MY DETECTIVES ARE WORKING TO CLEAR AS MANY OF THEM AS FAST AS HUMANLY POSSIBLE.

IN THE MEANTIME, WOULD YOUR MEN BE ABLE TO PROVIDE POLICE BACKUP TO RESCUE CREWS RESPONDING TO CALLS?

I ALREADY MADE THE OFFER TO THE FIRE COMMISSIONER, BUT GREENE SAYS HE DOESN'T WANT MY GUYS GETTING IN THEIR WAY.

DIDN'T TAKE LONG FOR THE TURF BATTLES TO START UP AGAIN, HUH?

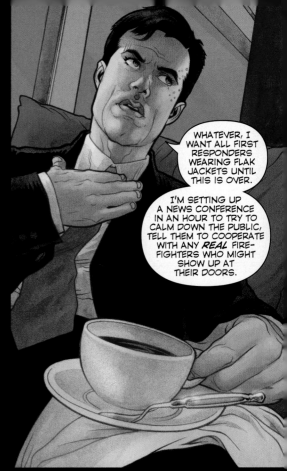

WHATEVER, I WANT ALL FIRST RESPONDERS WEARING FLAK JACKETS UNTIL THIS IS OVER.

I'M SETTING UP A NEWS CONFERENCE IN AN HOUR TO TRY TO CALM DOWN THE PUBLIC, TELL THEM TO COOPERATE WITH ANY *REAL* FIRE-FIGHTERS WHO MIGHT SHOW UP AT THEIR DOORS.

HOW WILL THEY KNOW WHO'S LEGIT AND WHO'S NOT?

OUR SUSPECT IS A LONE BLACK MALE, RIGHT?

SO WHAT, YOU'RE GOING TO TELL THEM ONLY TO OPEN THE DOOR FOR *WHITE* PEOPLE?

NO, AMY, I'M GOING TO TELL THEM ONLY TO OPEN THE DOOR FOR FIREFIGHTERS WHO SHOW UP IN *PAIRS*.

WELL, LET'S HOPE THIS BASTARD DOESN'T START WORKING WITH A *PARTNER*.

MAYOR HUNDRED?

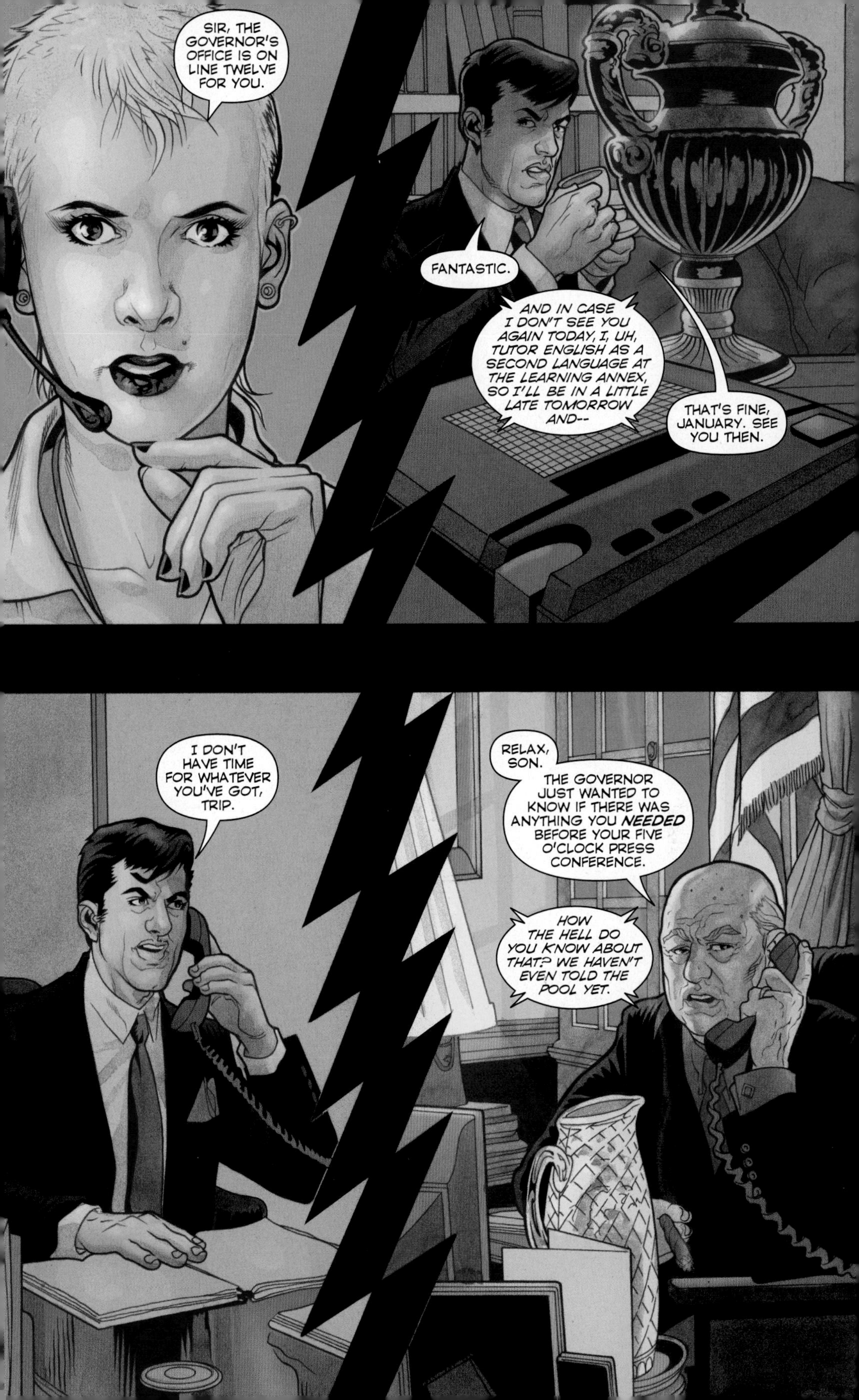
SIR, THE GOVERNOR'S OFFICE IS ON LINE TWELVE FOR YOU.
FANTASTIC.
AND IN CASE I DON'T SEE YOU AGAIN TODAY, I, UH, TUTOR ENGLISH AS A SECOND LANGUAGE AT THE LEARNING ANNEX, SO I'LL BE IN A LITTLE LATE TOMORROW AND--
THAT'S FINE, JANUARY. SEE YOU THEN.
I DON'T HAVE TIME FOR WHATEVER YOU'VE GOT, TRIP.
RELAX, SON.
THE GOVERNOR JUST WANTED TO KNOW IF THERE WAS ANYTHING YOU NEEDED BEFORE YOUR FIVE O'CLOCK PRESS CONFERENCE.
HOW THE HELL DO YOU KNOW ABOUT THAT? WE HAVEN'T EVEN TOLD THE POOL YET.

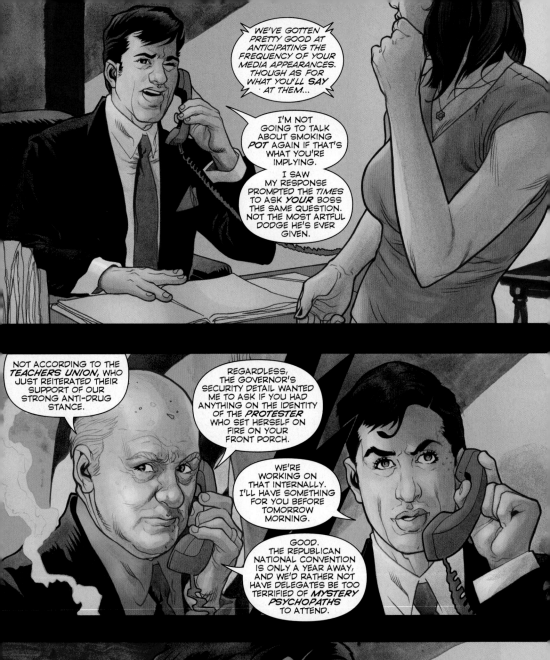

WE'VE GOTTEN PRETTY GOOD AT ANTICIPATING THE FREQUENCY OF YOUR MEDIA APPEARANCES. THOUGH AS FOR WHAT YOU'LL *SAY* AT THEM...

I'M NOT GOING TO TALK ABOUT SMOKING *POT* AGAIN IF THAT'S WHAT YOU'RE IMPLYING.

I SAW MY RESPONSE PROMPTED THE *TIMES* TO ASK *YOUR* BOSS THE SAME QUESTION. NOT THE MOST ARTFUL DODGE HE'S EVER GIVEN.

NOT ACCORDING TO THE *TEACHERS UNION*, WHO JUST REITERATED THEIR SUPPORT OF OUR STRONG ANTI-DRUG STANCE.

REGARDLESS, THE GOVERNOR'S SECURITY DETAIL WANTED ME TO ASK IF YOU HAD ANYTHING ON THE IDENTITY OF THE *PROTESTER* WHO SET HERSELF ON FIRE ON YOUR FRONT PORCH.

WE'RE WORKING ON THAT INTERNALLY. I'LL HAVE SOMETHING FOR YOU BEFORE TOMORROW MORNING.

GOOD. THE REPUBLICAN NATIONAL CONVENTION IS ONLY A YEAR AWAY, AND WE'D RATHER NOT HAVE DELEGATES BE TOO TERRIFIED OF *MYSTERY PSYCHOPATHS* TO ATTEND.

I'LL LET *YOU* WORRY ABOUT ANYONE TOO COWARDLY TO COME TO THE SAFEST BIG CITY ON THE PLANET, TRIP.

RIGHT NOW, I'M MORE CONCERNED ABOUT NEW YORK'S *BRAVEST.*

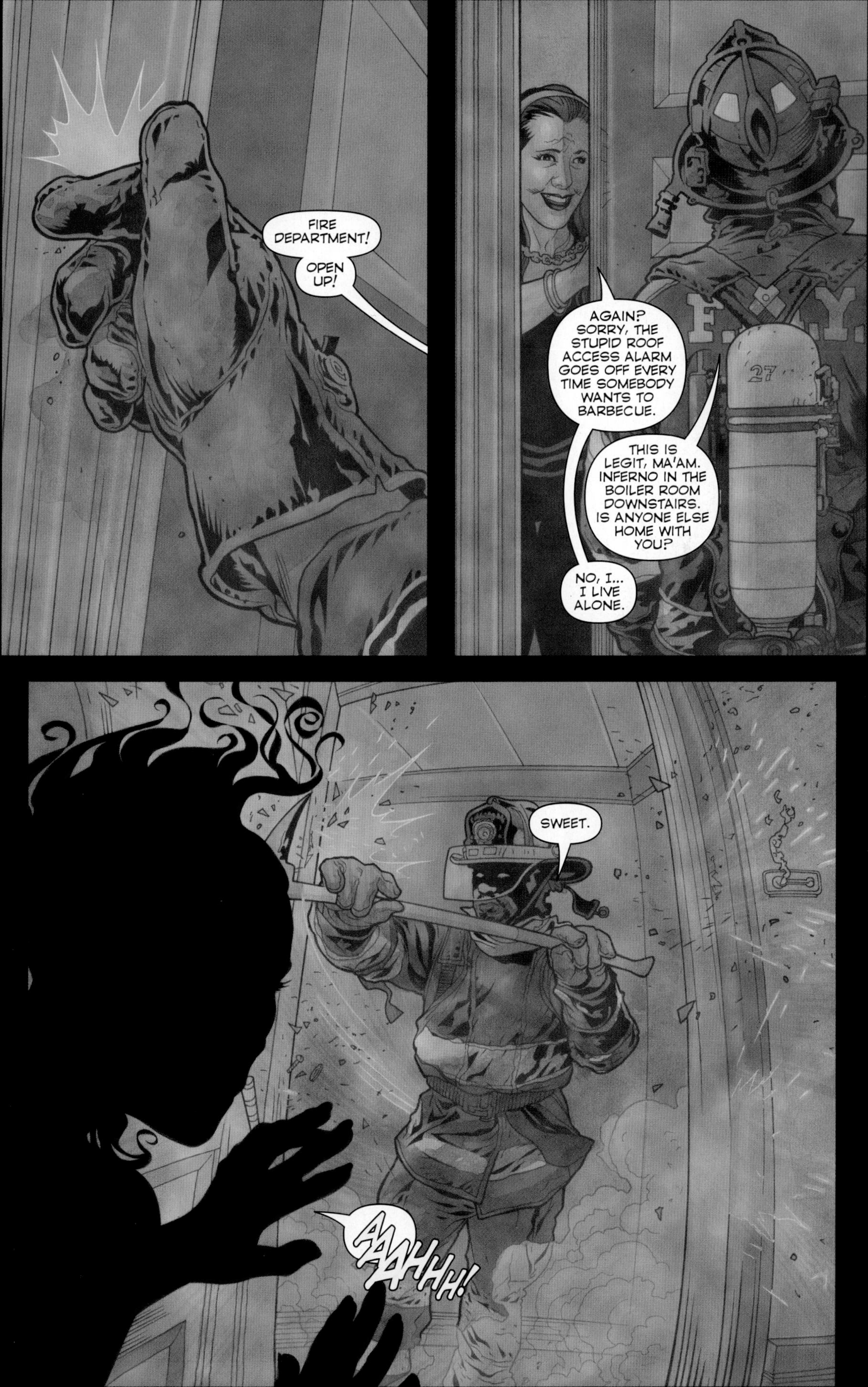
FIRE DEPARTMENT!
OPEN UP!
AGAIN? SORRY, THE STUPID ROOF ACCESS ALARM GOES OFF EVERY TIME SOMEBODY WANTS TO BARBECUE.
THIS IS LEGIT, MA'AM. INFERNO IN THE BOILER ROOM DOWNSTAIRS. IS ANYONE ELSE HOME WITH YOU?
NO, I... I LIVE ALONE.
F.D.N.Y.
27
SWEET.
AAAHHH!

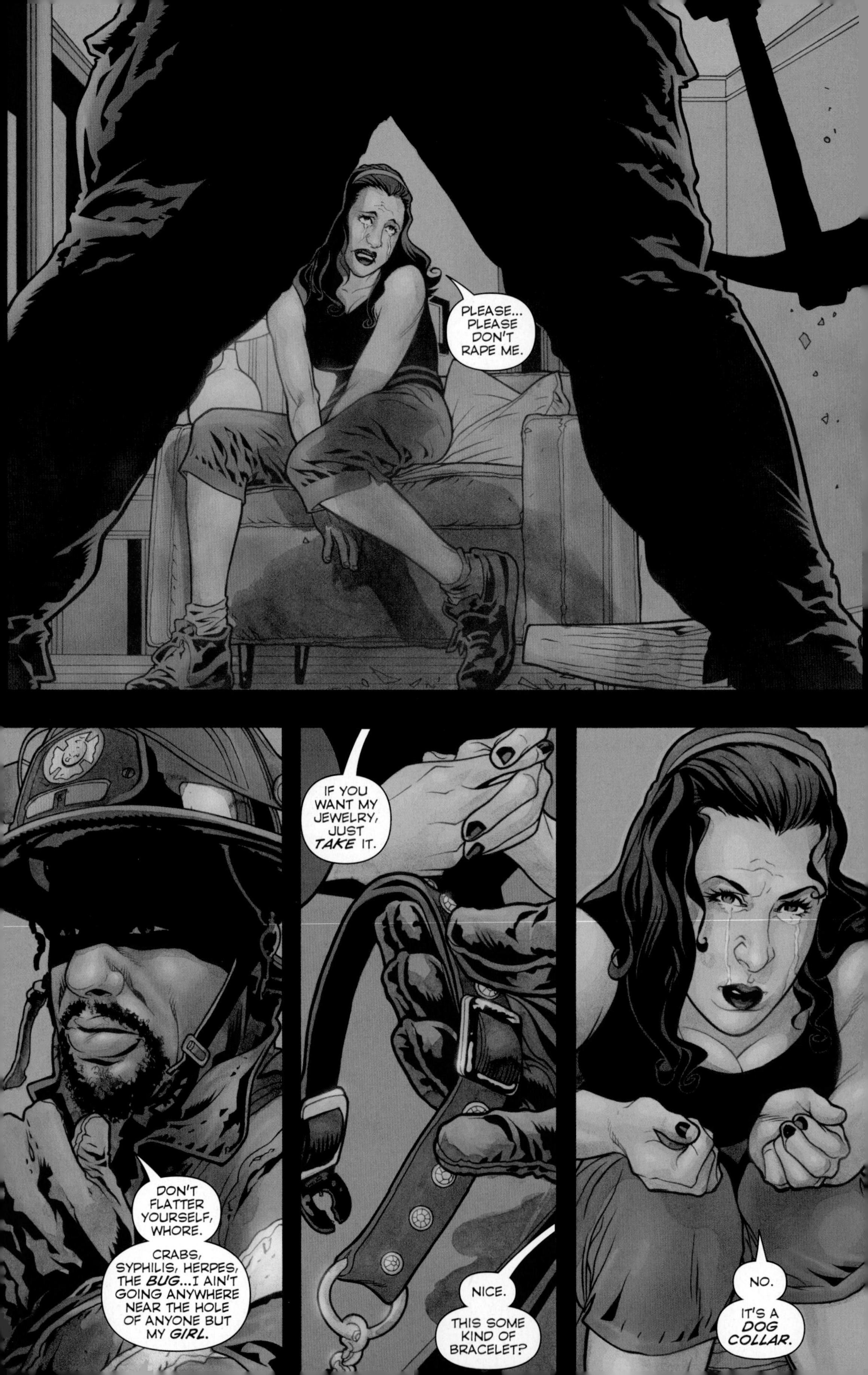
PLEASE... PLEASE DON'T RAPE ME.
DON'T FLATTER YOURSELF, WHORE.
CRABS, SYPHILIS, HERPES, THE *BUG*...I AIN'T GOING ANYWHERE NEAR THE HOLE OF ANYONE BUT MY *GIRL*.
IF YOU WANT MY JEWELRY, JUST *TAKE* IT.
NICE.
THIS SOME KIND OF BRACELET?
NO.
IT'S A *DOG COLLAR*.

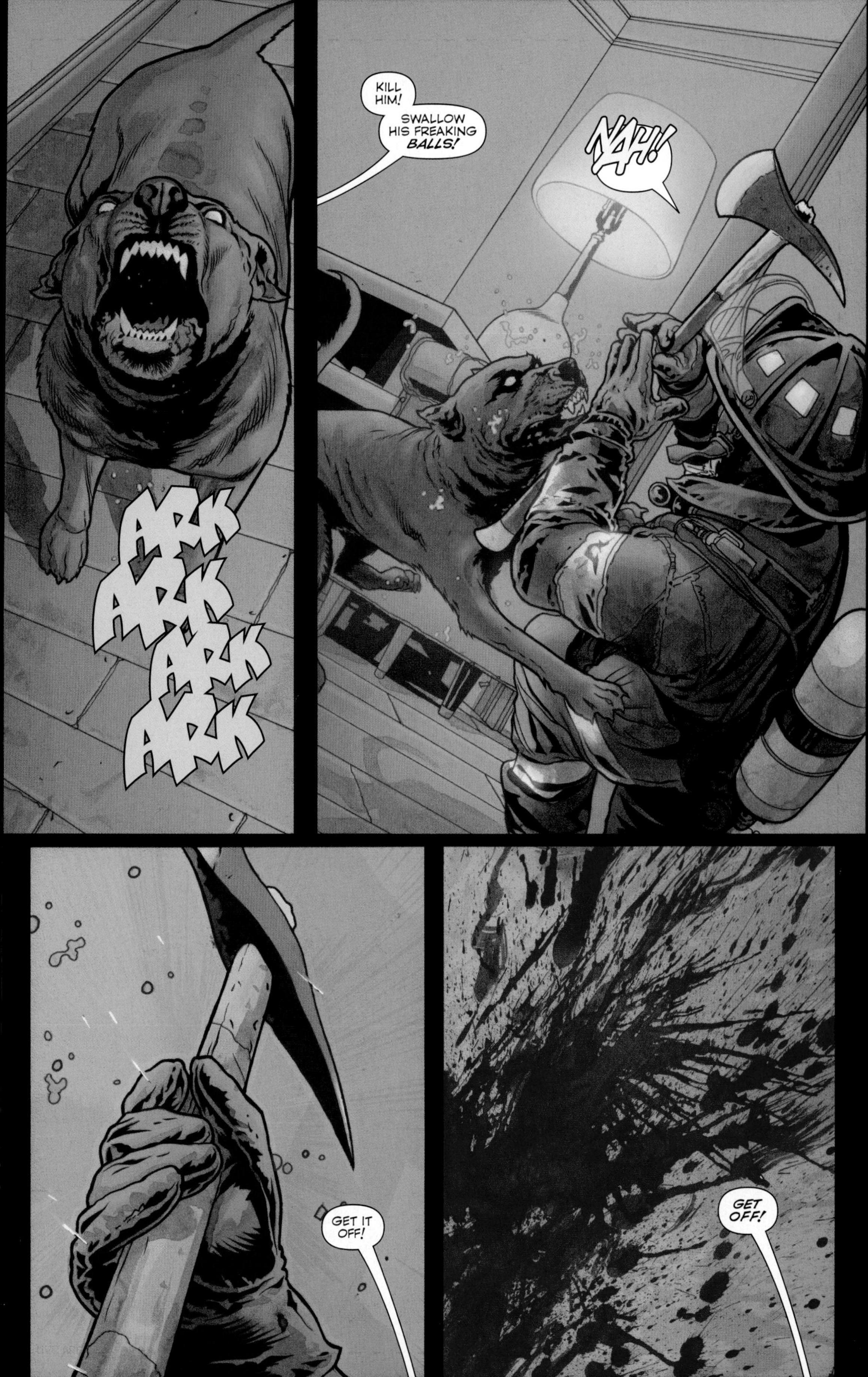
ARK ARK ARK ARK
KILL HIM!
SWALLOW HIS FREAKING BALLS!
NAH!
GET IT OFF!
GET OFF!

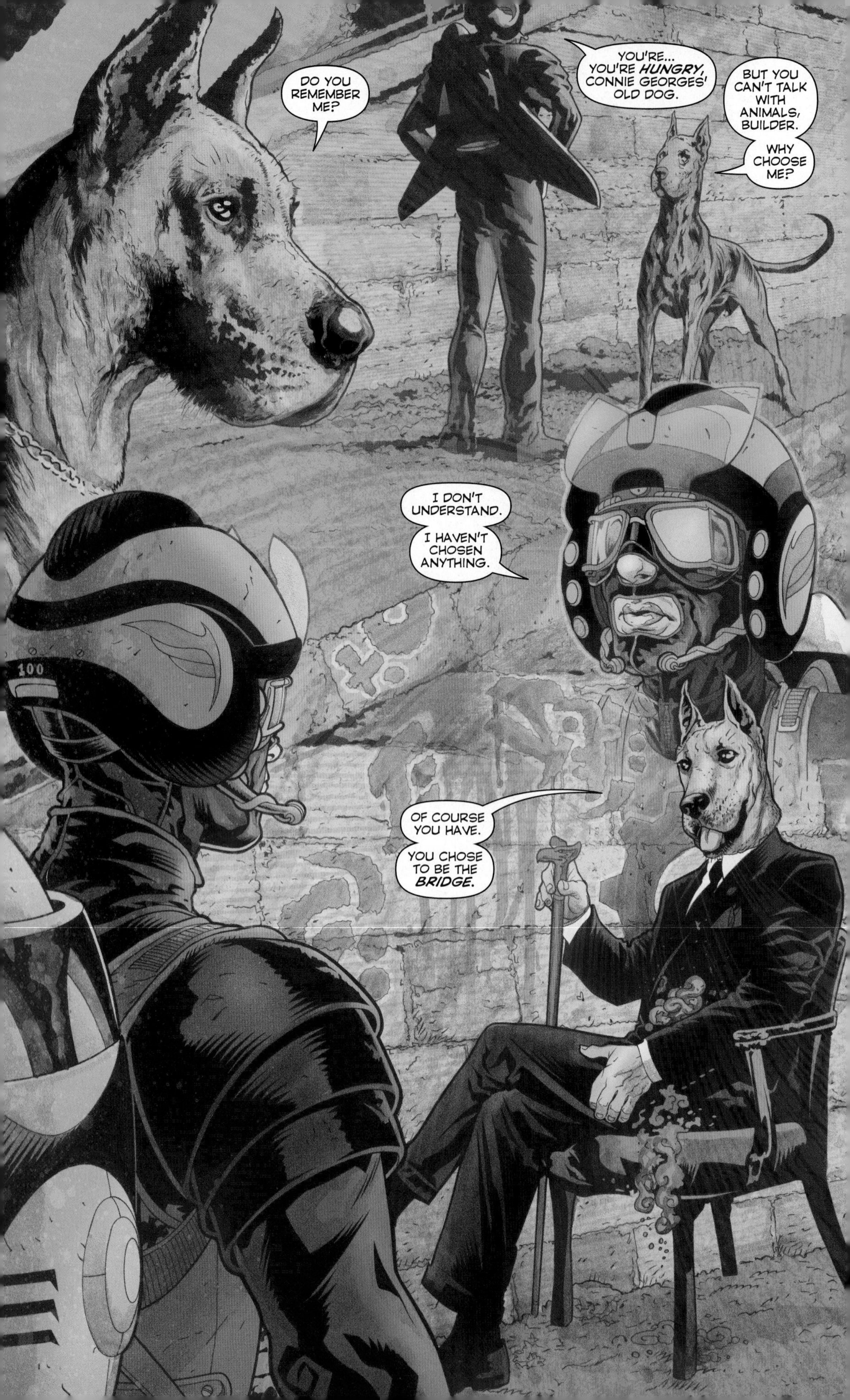
DO YOU REMEMBER ME?
YOU'RE... YOU'RE *HUNGRY*, CONNIE GEORGES' OLD DOG.
BUT YOU CAN'T TALK WITH ANIMALS, BUILDER.
WHY CHOOSE ME?
I DON'T UNDERSTAND.
I HAVEN'T CHOSEN ANYTHING.
OF COURSE YOU HAVE.
YOU CHOSE TO BE THE *BRIDGE*.

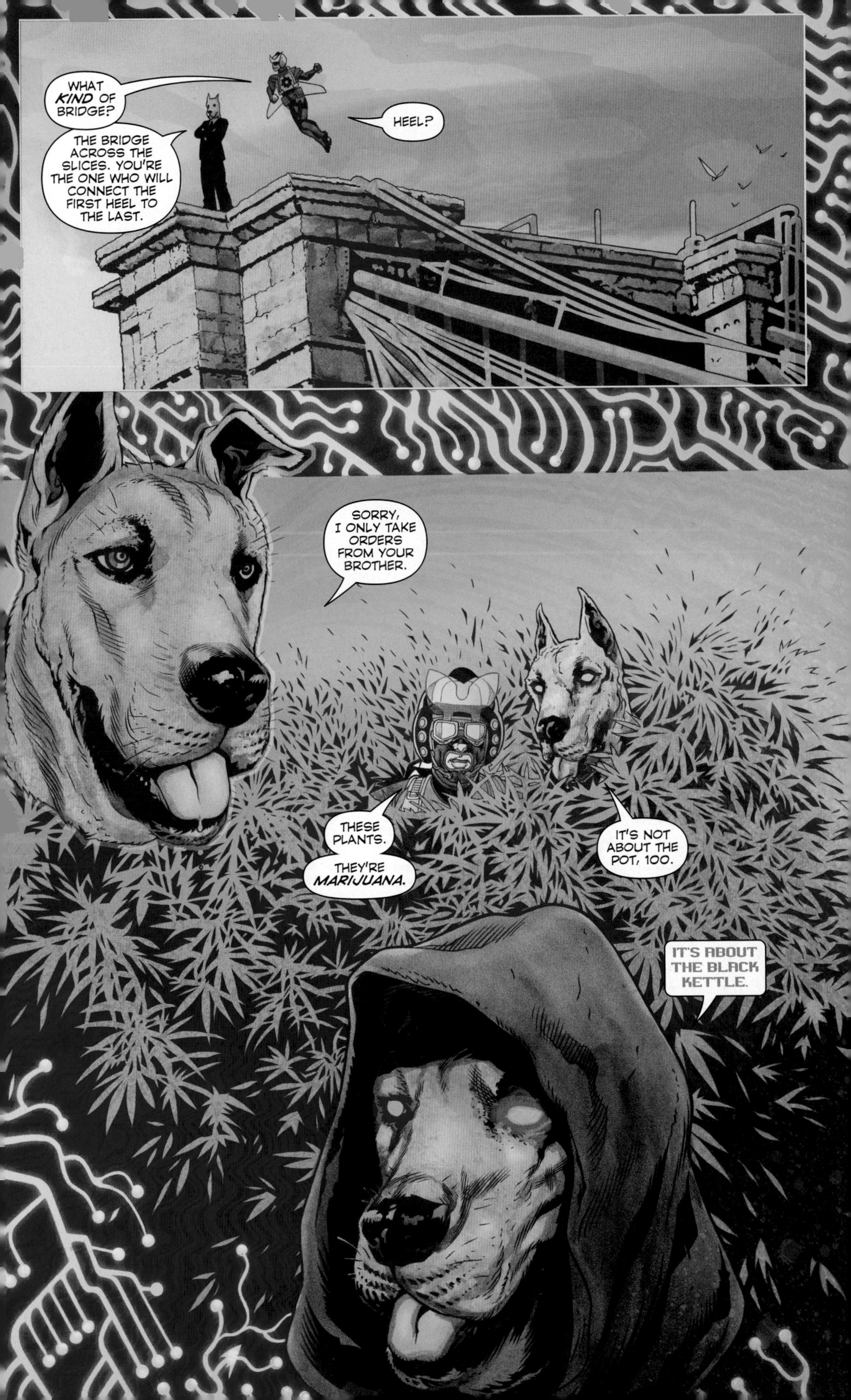
WHAT KIND OF BRIDGE?
THE BRIDGE ACROSS THE SLICES. YOU'RE THE ONE WHO WILL CONNECT THE FIRST HEEL TO THE LAST.
HEEL?
SORRY, I ONLY TAKE ORDERS FROM YOUR BROTHER.
THESE PLANTS.
THEY'RE MARIJUANA.
IT'S NOT ABOUT THE POT, 100.
IT'S ABOUT THE BLACK KETTLE.

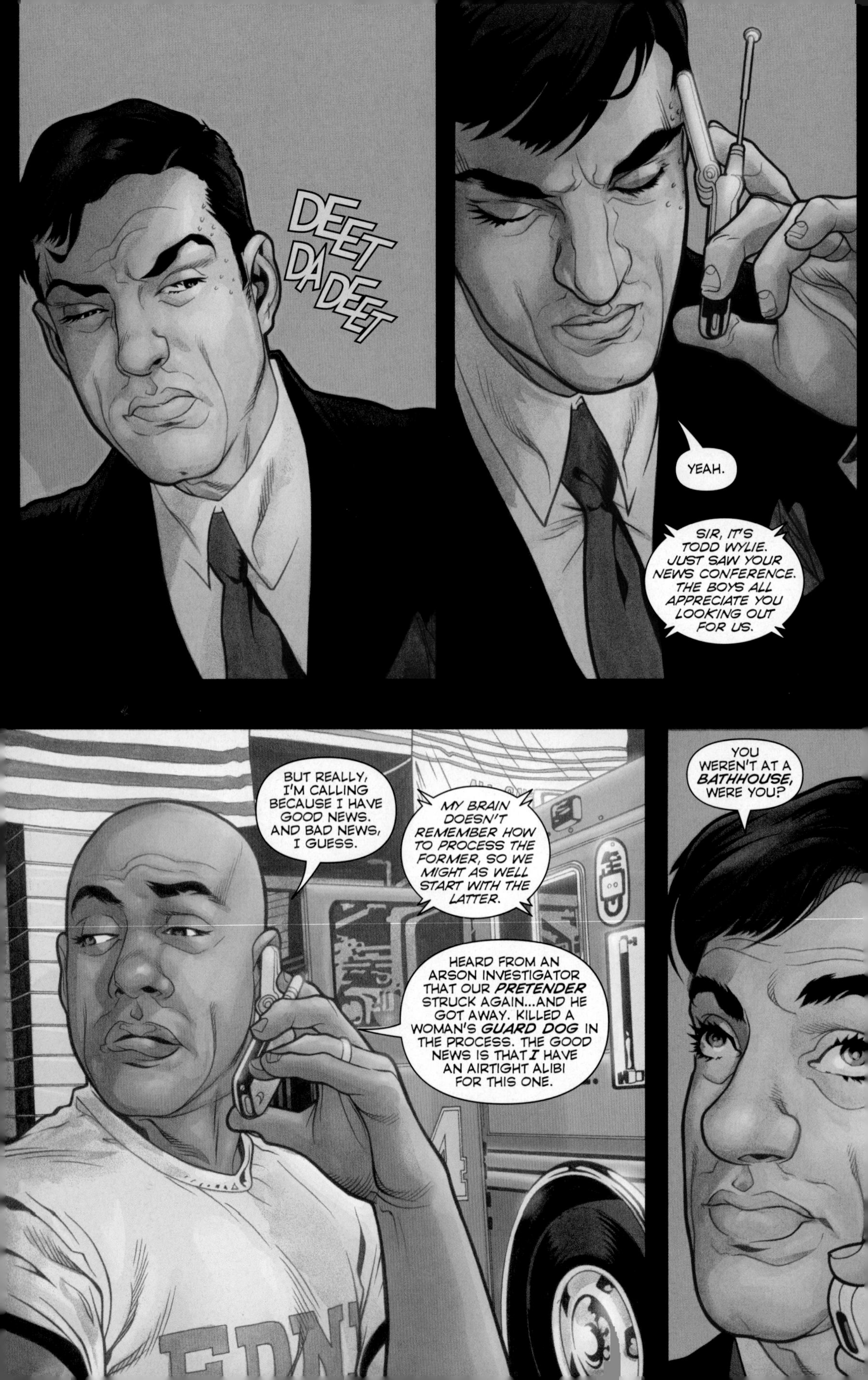
DEEET DADEEET
YEAH.
SIR, IT'S TODD WYLIE. JUST SAW YOUR NEWS CONFERENCE. THE BOYS ALL APPRECIATE YOU LOOKING OUT FOR US.
BUT REALLY, I'M CALLING BECAUSE I HAVE GOOD NEWS. AND BAD NEWS, I GUESS.
MY BRAIN DOESN'T REMEMBER HOW TO PROCESS THE FORMER, SO WE MIGHT AS WELL START WITH THE LATTER.
HEARD FROM AN ARSON INVESTIGATOR THAT OUR *PRETENDER* STRUCK AGAIN...AND HE GOT AWAY. KILLED A WOMAN'S *GUARD DOG* IN THE PROCESS. THE GOOD NEWS IS THAT *I* HAVE AN AIRTIGHT ALIBI FOR THIS ONE.
YOU WEREN'T AT A *BATHHOUSE,* WERE YOU?

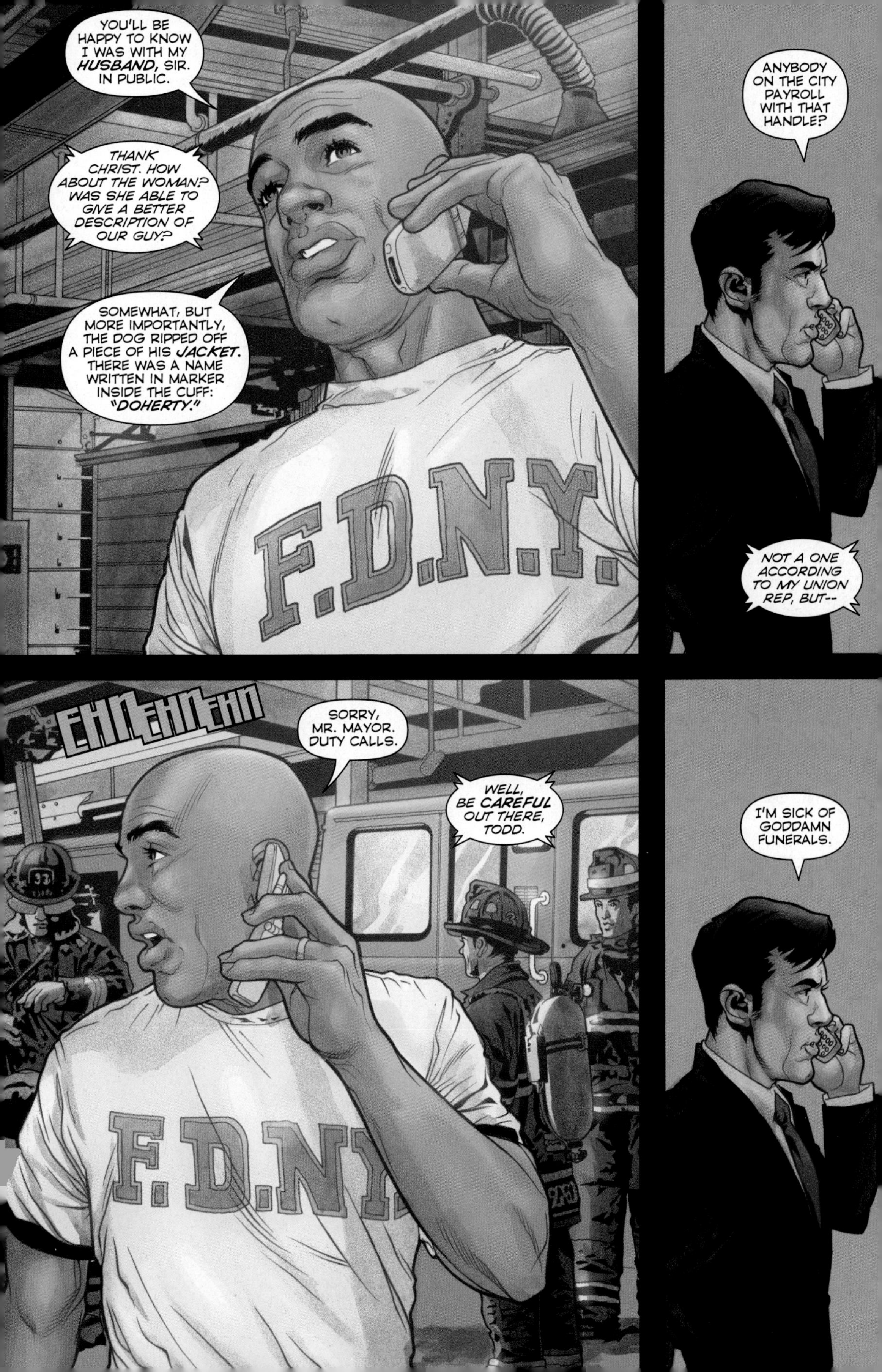
YOU'LL BE HAPPY TO KNOW I WAS WITH MY HUSBAND, SIR. IN PUBLIC.
ANYBODY ON THE CITY PAYROLL WITH THAT HANDLE?
THANK CHRIST. HOW ABOUT THE WOMAN? WAS SHE ABLE TO GIVE A BETTER DESCRIPTION OF OUR GUY?
SOMEWHAT, BUT MORE IMPORTANTLY, THE DOG RIPPED OFF A PIECE OF HIS JACKET. THERE WAS A NAME WRITTEN IN MARKER INSIDE THE CUFF: "DOHERTY."
F.D.N.Y.
NOT A ONE ACCORDING TO MY UNION REP, BUT--
EHN EHN EHN
SORRY, MR. MAYOR. DUTY CALLS.
WELL, BE CAREFUL OUT THERE, TODD.
I'M SICK OF GODDAMN FUNERALS.

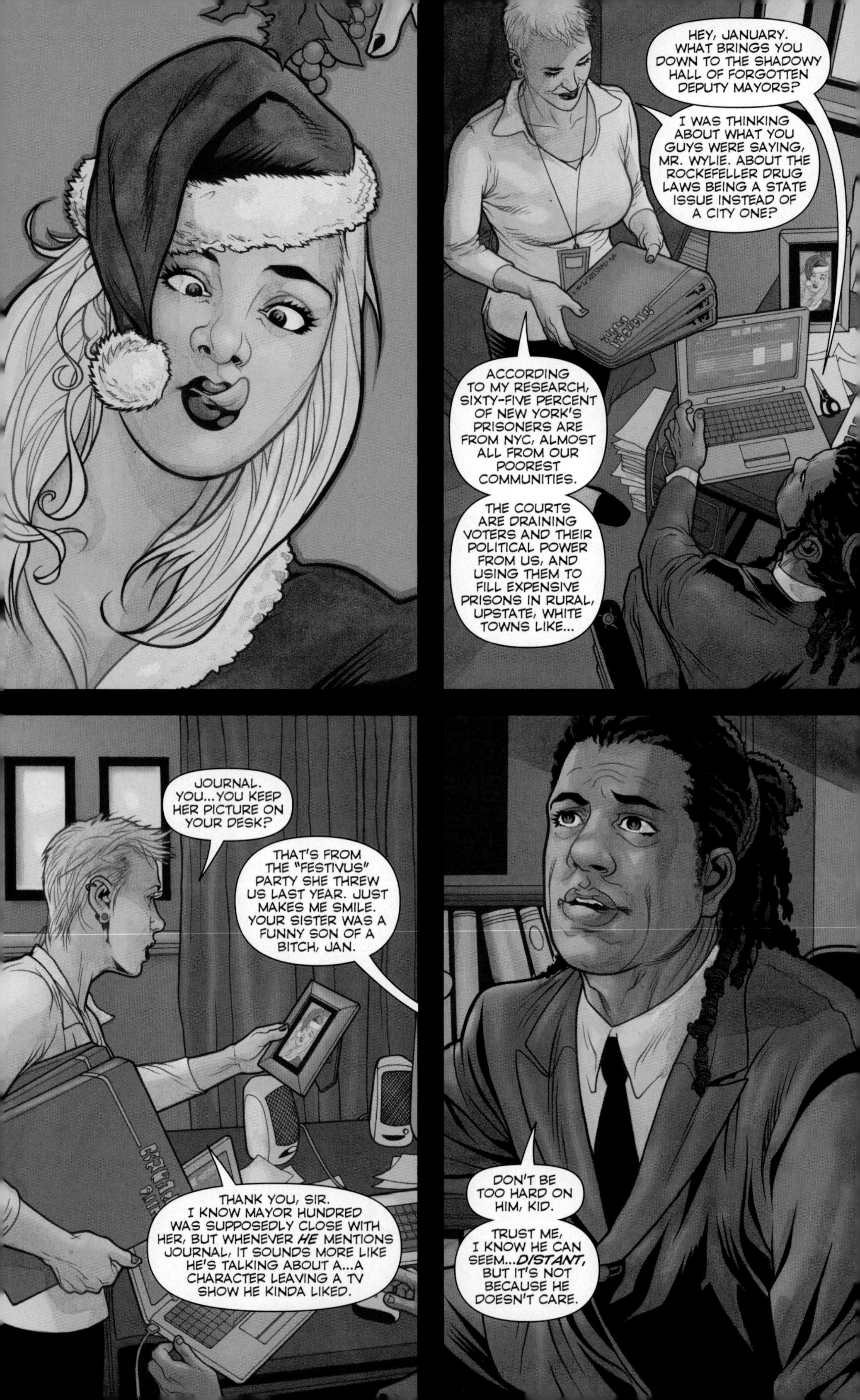
HEY, JANUARY. WHAT BRINGS YOU DOWN TO THE SHADOWY HALL OF FORGOTTEN DEPUTY MAYORS?
I WAS THINKING ABOUT WHAT YOU GUYS WERE SAYING, MR. WYLIE. ABOUT THE ROCKEFELLER DRUG LAWS BEING A STATE ISSUE INSTEAD OF A CITY ONE?
ACCORDING TO MY RESEARCH, SIXTY-FIVE PERCENT OF NEW YORK'S PRISONERS ARE FROM NYC, ALMOST ALL FROM OUR POOREST COMMUNITIES.
THE COURTS ARE DRAINING VOTERS AND THEIR POLITICAL POWER FROM US, AND USING THEM TO FILL EXPENSIVE PRISONS IN RURAL, UPSTATE, WHITE TOWNS LIKE...
JOURNAL. YOU...YOU KEEP HER PICTURE ON YOUR DESK?
THAT'S FROM THE "FESTIVUS" PARTY SHE THREW US LAST YEAR. JUST MAKES ME SMILE. YOUR SISTER WAS A FUNNY SON OF A BITCH, JAN.
THANK YOU, SIR. I KNOW MAYOR HUNDRED WAS SUPPOSEDLY CLOSE WITH HER, BUT WHENEVER *HE* MENTIONS JOURNAL, IT SOUNDS MORE LIKE HE'S TALKING ABOUT A...A CHARACTER LEAVING A TV SHOW HE KINDA LIKED.
DON'T BE TOO HARD ON HIM, KID.
TRUST ME, I KNOW HE CAN SEEM...*DISTANT,* BUT IT'S NOT BECAUSE HE DOESN'T CARE.

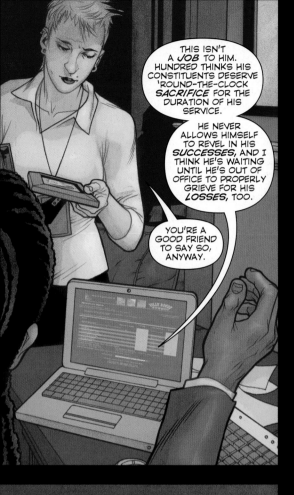

THIS ISN'T A *JOB* TO HIM. HUNDRED THINKS HIS CONSTITUENTS DESERVE 'ROUND-THE-CLOCK *SACRIFICE* FOR THE DURATION OF HIS SERVICE.

HE NEVER ALLOWS HIMSELF TO REVEL IN HIS *SUCCESSES,* AND I THINK HE'S WAITING UNTIL HE'S OUT OF OFFICE TO PROPERLY GRIEVE FOR HIS *LOSSES,* TOO.

YOU'RE A GOOD FRIEND TO SAY SO, ANYWAY.

DON'T GET ME WRONG, I STILL THINK HE'S *INSANE* MOST DAYS.

HE ALMOST NEVER SLEEPS, HAS NO HOBBIES THAT AREN'T EXCUSES TO BUTTONHOLE LEGISLATORS, AND THE ONLY VACATION HE'S TAKEN IN NINETEEN MONTHS LEFT HIM MORE STRESSED OUT THAN EVER.

BEING A "MACHINE" ISN'T ALWAYS SO GREAT.

I'M WORRIED HE'S GONNA *BURN OUT.*

YEAH, WELL, YOU KNOW WHAT KURT COBAIN SAID ABOUT THAT, RIGHT?

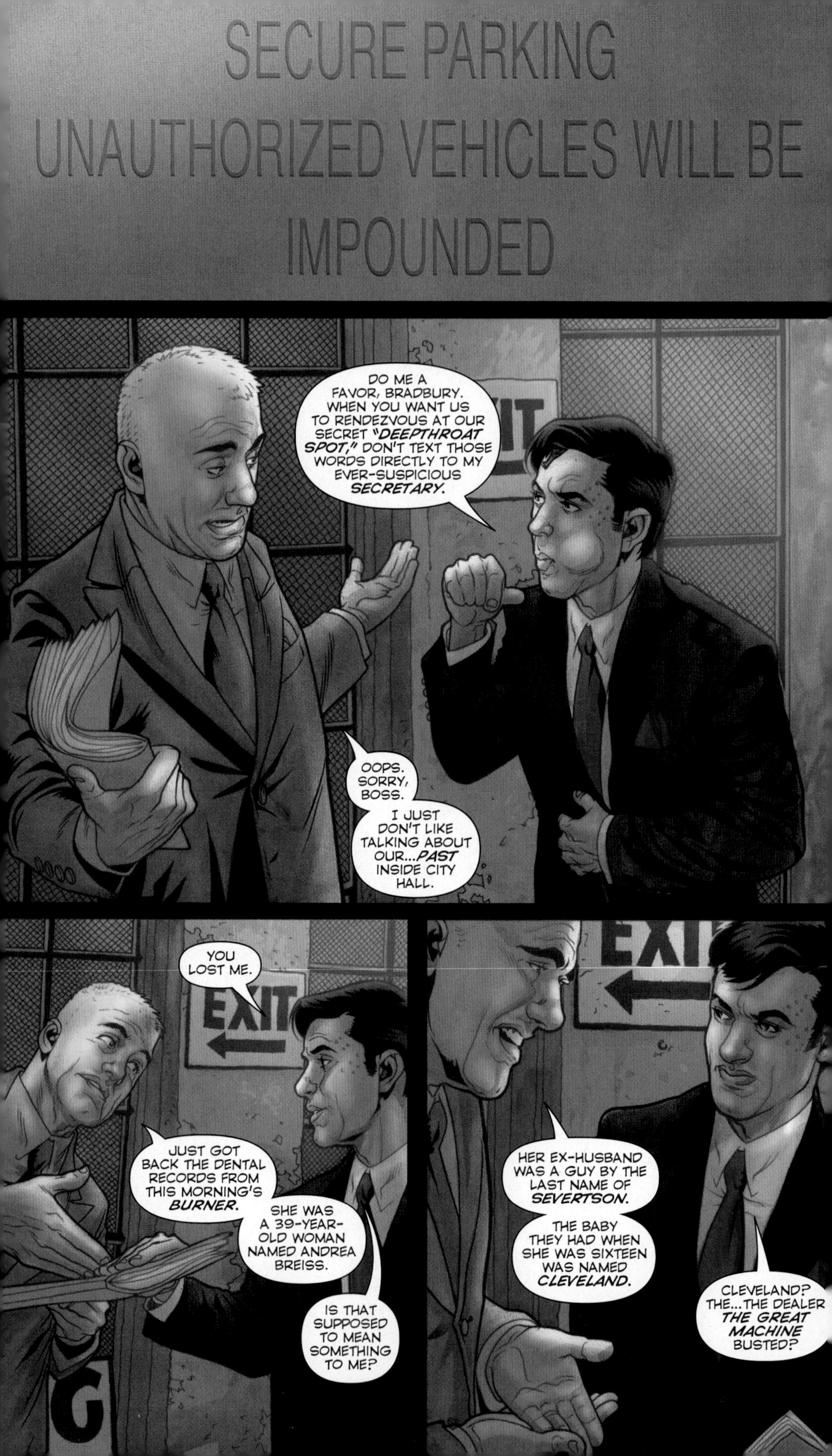
SECURE PARKING
UNAUTHORIZED VEHICLES WILL BE IMPOUNDED
DO ME A FAVOR, BRADBURY. WHEN YOU WANT US TO RENDEZVOUS AT OUR SECRET "DEEPTHROAT SPOT," DON'T TEXT THOSE WORDS DIRECTLY TO MY EVER-SUSPICIOUS SECRETARY.
EXIT
OOPS. SORRY, BOSS.
I JUST DON'T LIKE TALKING ABOUT OUR...PAST INSIDE CITY HALL.
YOU LOST ME.
EXIT
JUST GOT BACK THE DENTAL RECORDS FROM THIS MORNING'S BURNER.
SHE WAS A 39-YEAR-OLD WOMAN NAMED ANDREA BREISS.
IS THAT SUPPOSED TO MEAN SOMETHING TO ME?
EXIT
HER EX-HUSBAND WAS A GUY BY THE LAST NAME OF SEVERTSON.
THE BABY THEY HAD WHEN SHE WAS SIXTEEN WAS NAMED CLEVELAND.
CLEVELAND? THE...THE DEALER THE GREAT MACHINE BUSTED?

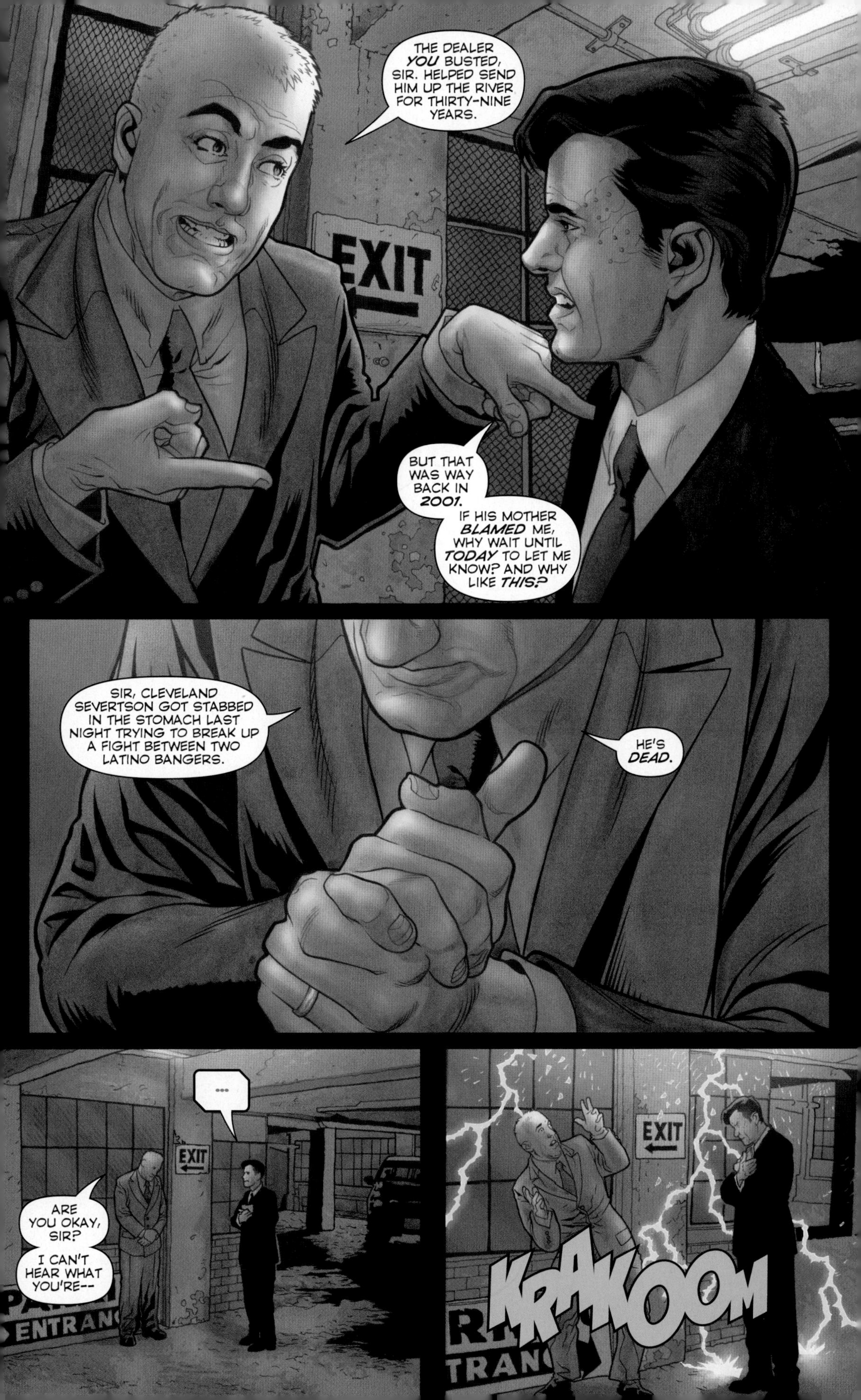
THE DEALER YOU BUSTED, SIR. HELPED SEND HIM UP THE RIVER FOR THIRTY-NINE YEARS.
EXIT
BUT THAT WAS WAY BACK IN 2001.
IF HIS MOTHER BLAMED ME, WHY WAIT UNTIL TODAY TO LET ME KNOW? AND WHY LIKE THIS?
SIR, CLEVELAND SEVERTSON GOT STABBED IN THE STOMACH LAST NIGHT TRYING TO BREAK UP A FIGHT BETWEEN TWO LATINO BANGERS.
HE'S DEAD.
...
EXIT
ARE YOU OKAY, SIR?
I CAN'T HEAR WHAT YOU'RE--
ENTRANC
EXIT
KRAKOOM
TRANC

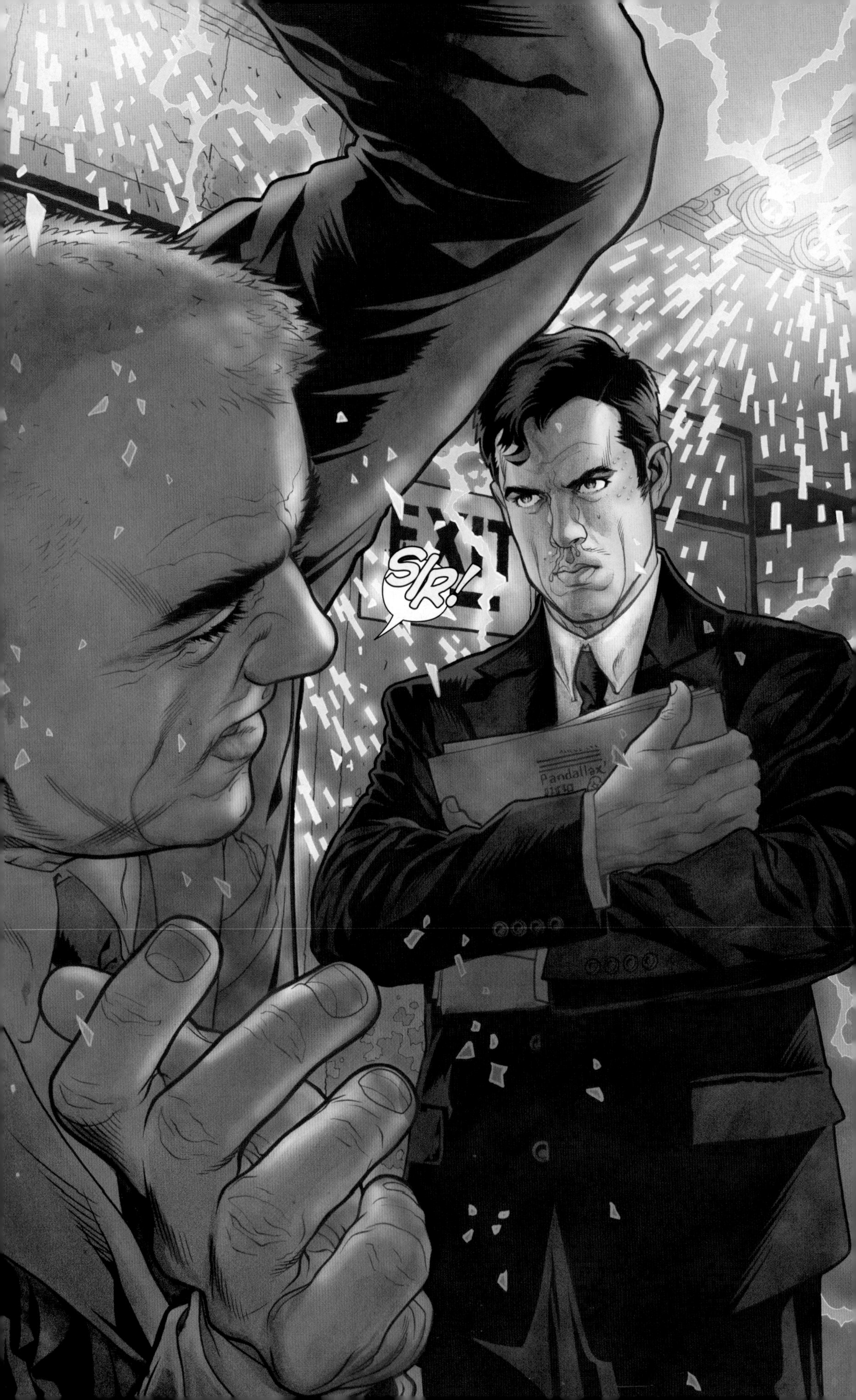
EXIT
SIR!
Pandallax

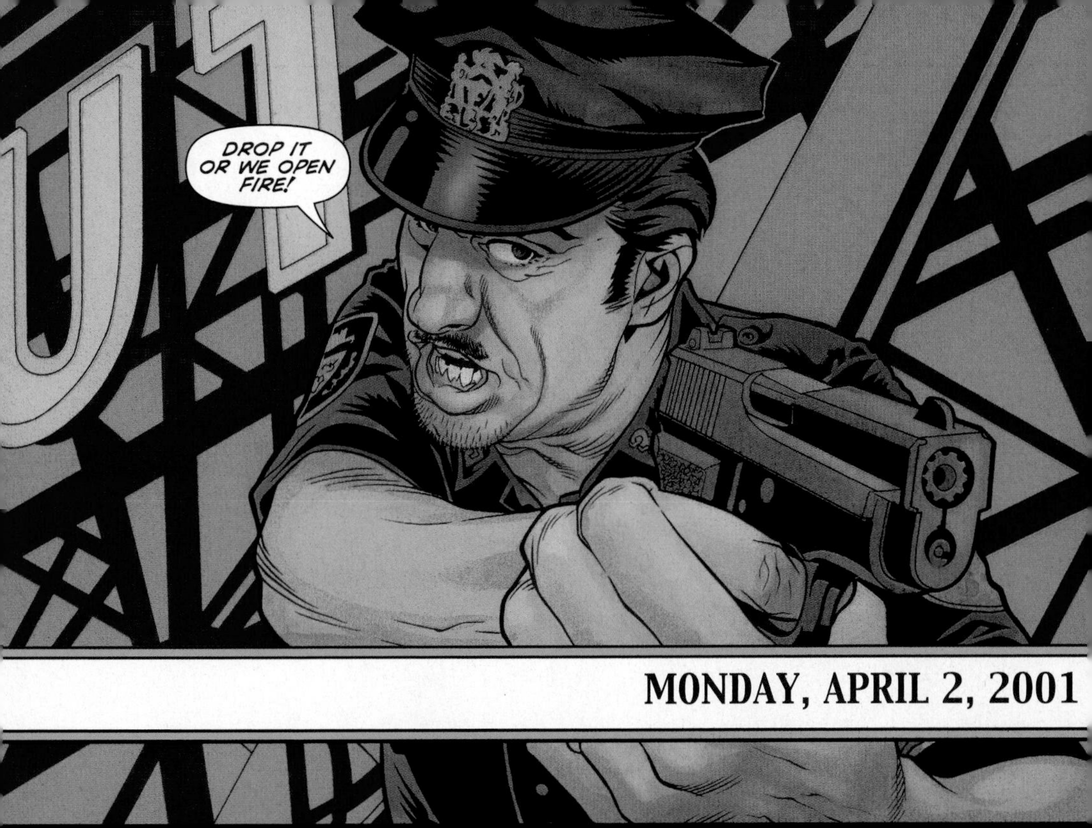
DROP IT OR WE OPEN FIRE!

MONDAY, APRIL 2, 2001

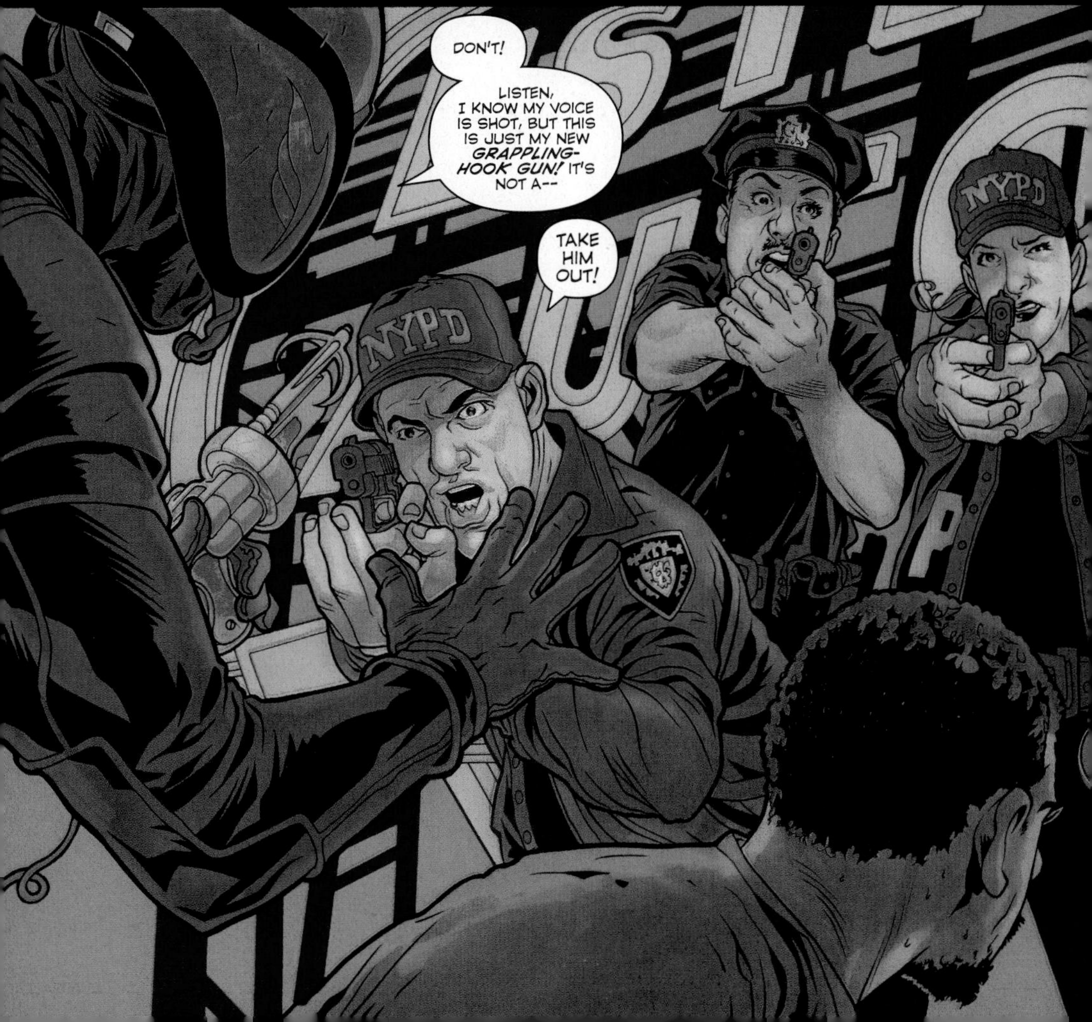
DON'T!
LISTEN, I KNOW MY VOICE IS SHOT, BUT THIS IS JUST MY NEW *GRAPPLING-HOOK GUN!* IT'S NOT A--
TAKE HIM OUT!
NYPD
NYPD

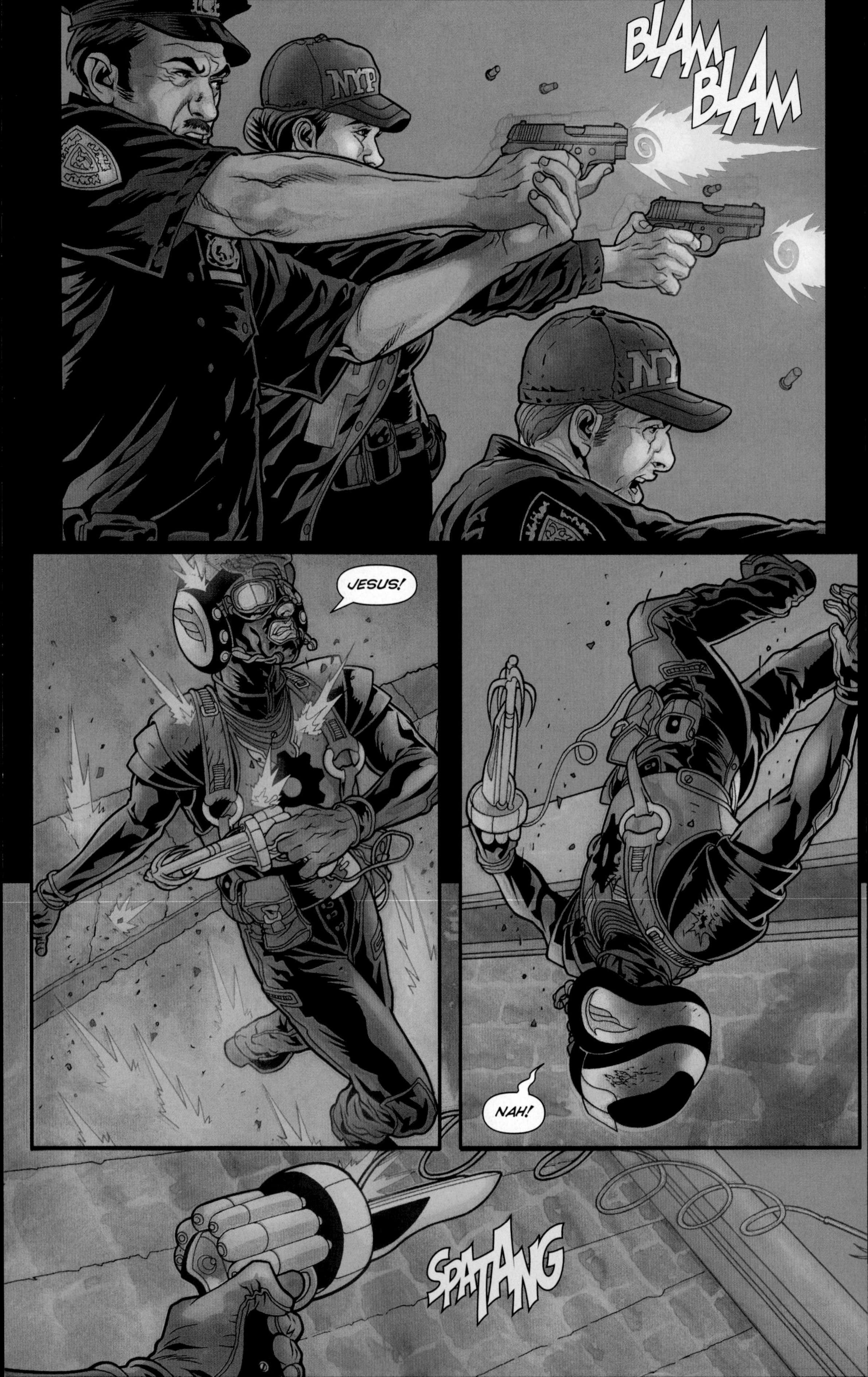
BLAM BLAM
JESUS!
NAH!
SPATANG

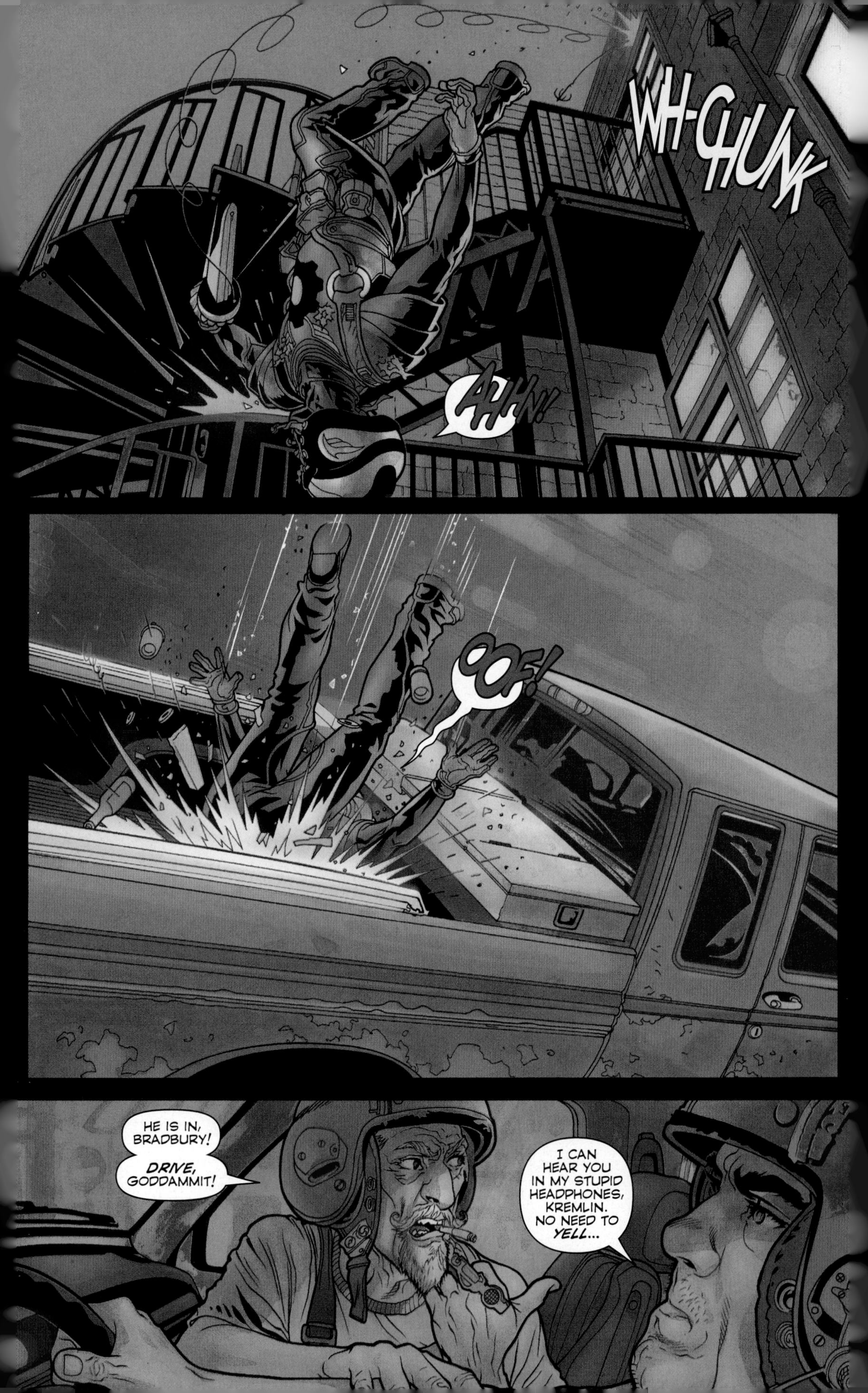
WH-CHUNK
AHHN!
OOF!
HE IS IN, BRADBURY!
DRIVE, GODDAMMIT!
I CAN HEAR YOU IN MY STUPID HEADPHONES, KREMLIN. NO NEED TO YELL...

NNN, KEVLAR STOPPED THE ROUNDS, BUT I'M LOOKING AT A FEW BUSTED RIBS HERE.

BODY ARMOR WORKED BETTER THAN MY *NEW* TOY, AT LEAST.

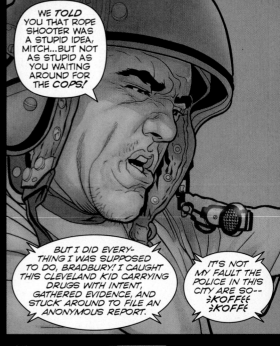

WE *TOLD* YOU THAT ROPE SHOOTER WAS A STUPID IDEA, MITCH...BUT NOT AS STUPID AS YOU WAITING AROUND FOR THE *COPS!*

BUT I DID EVERY-THING I WAS SUPPOSED TO DO, BRADBURY! I CAUGHT THIS CLEVELAND KID CARRYING DRUGS WITH INTENT, GATHERED EVIDENCE, AND STUCK AROUND TO FILE AN ANONYMOUS REPORT.

IT'S NOT MY FAULT THE POLICE IN THIS CITY ARE SO-- ≶KOFF≶ ≶KOFF≶

YOU'VE WASTED ENOUGH OF YOUR VOICE ON MEANINGLESS BULLSHIT LIKE THE MARIJUANA.

THIS CITY NEEDS YOU, BOY. SAVE YOUR WORDS FOR FIGHT THAT REALLY MATTERS.

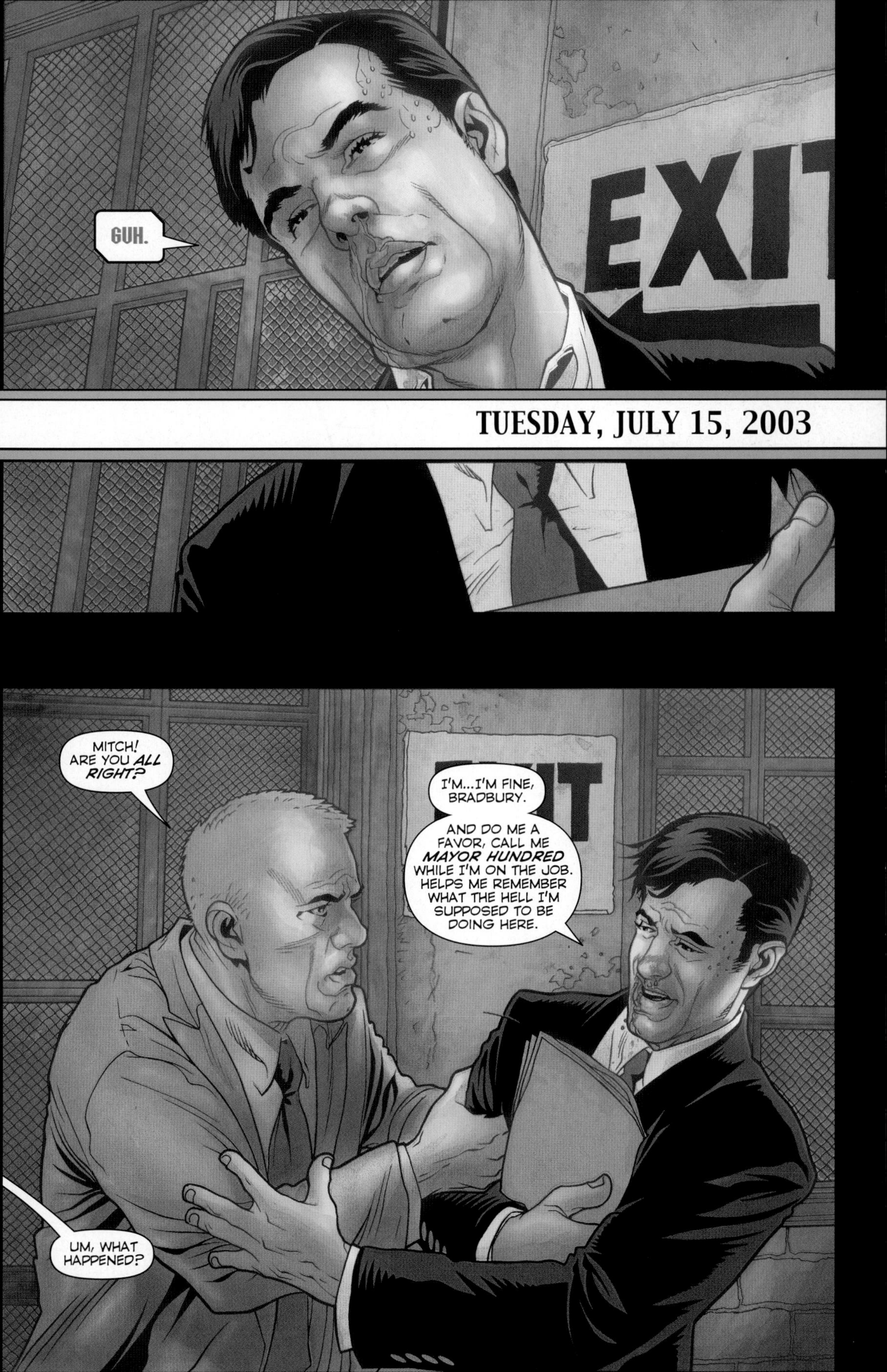
GUH.
EXIT
TUESDAY, JULY 15, 2003
MITCH! ARE YOU ALL RIGHT?
I'M...I'M FINE, BRADBURY.
AND DO ME A FAVOR, CALL ME MAYOR HUNDRED WHILE I'M ON THE JOB. HELPS ME REMEMBER WHAT THE HELL I'M SUPPOSED TO BE DOING HERE.
UM, WHAT HAPPENED?

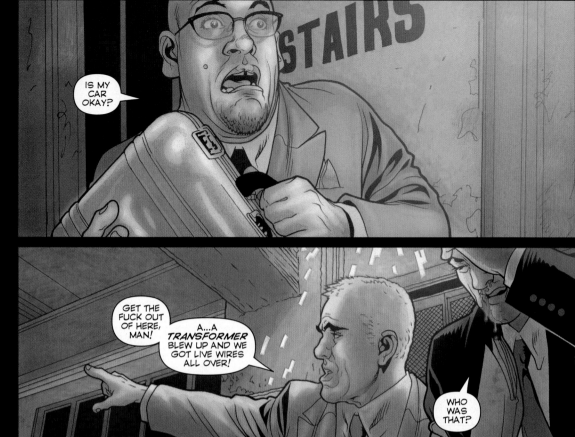

IS MY CAR OKAY?

GET THE FUCK OUT OF HERE, MAN!

A...A *TRANSFORMER* BLEW UP AND WE GOT LIVE WIRES ALL OVER!

WHO WAS THAT?

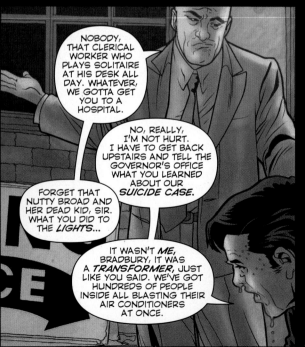

NOBODY, THAT CLERICAL WORKER WHO PLAYS SOLITAIRE AT HIS DESK ALL DAY. WHATEVER, WE GOTTA GET YOU TO A HOSPITAL.

NO, REALLY, I'M NOT HURT. I HAVE TO GET BACK UPSTAIRS AND TELL THE GOVERNOR'S OFFICE WHAT YOU LEARNED ABOUT OUR *SUICIDE CASE.*

FORGET THAT NUTTY BROAD AND HER DEAD KID, SIR. WHAT YOU DID TO THE *LIGHTS...*

IT WASN'T *ME,* BRADBURY, IT WAS A *TRANSFORMER,* JUST LIKE YOU SAID. WE'VE GOT HUNDREDS OF PEOPLE INSIDE ALL BLASTING THEIR AIR CONDITIONERS AT ONCE.

IT'S JUST STRESS ON THE SYSTEM.

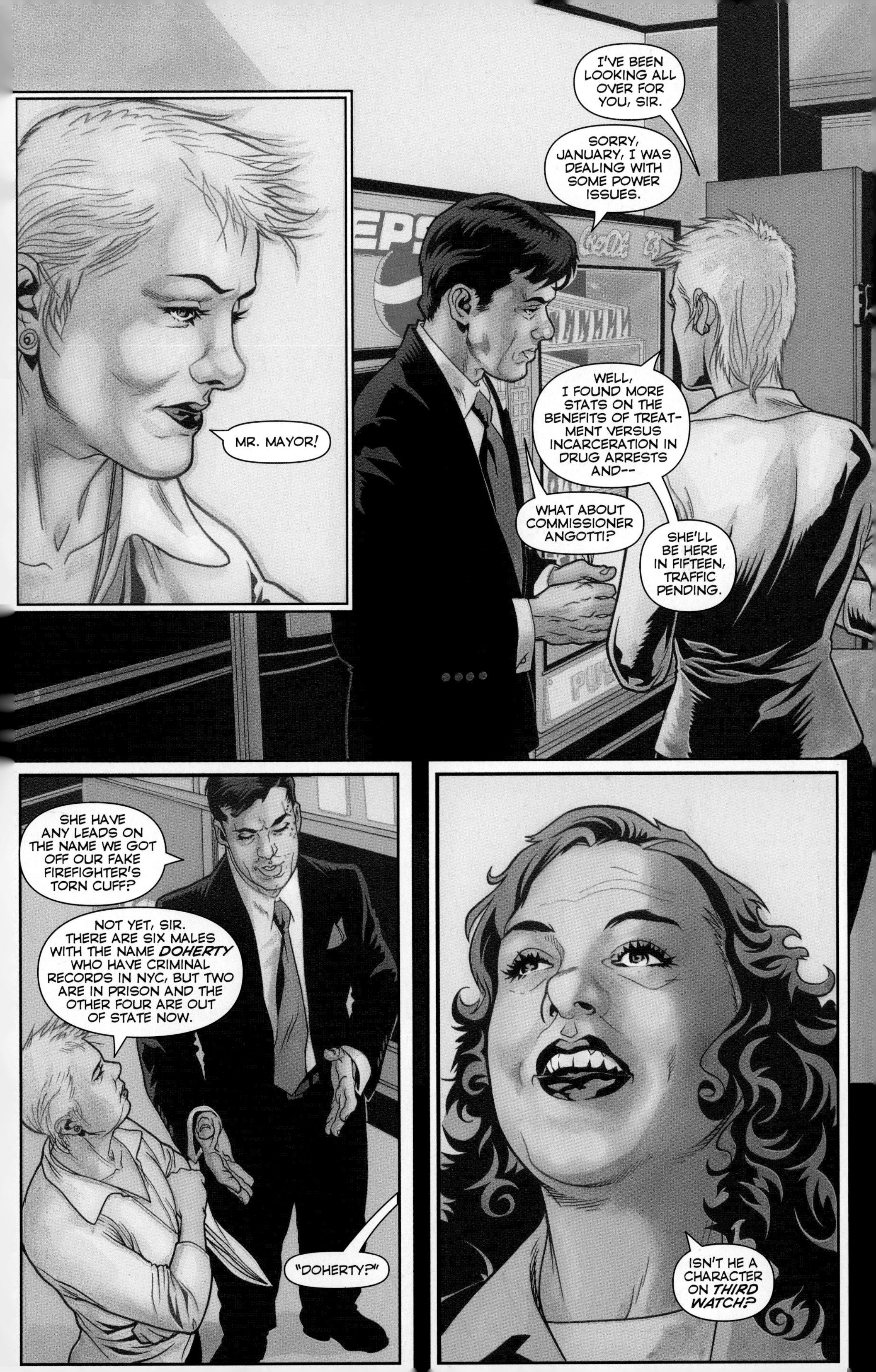
MR. MAYOR!
I'VE BEEN LOOKING ALL OVER FOR YOU, SIR.
SORRY, JANUARY, I WAS DEALING WITH SOME POWER ISSUES.
WELL, I FOUND MORE STATS ON THE BENEFITS OF TREAT-MENT VERSUS INCARCERATION IN DRUG ARRESTS AND--
WHAT ABOUT COMMISSIONER ANGOTTI?
SHE'LL BE HERE IN FIFTEEN, TRAFFIC PENDING.
SHE HAVE ANY LEADS ON THE NAME WE GOT OFF OUR FAKE FIREFIGHTER'S TORN CUFF?
NOT YET, SIR. THERE ARE SIX MALES WITH THE NAME *DOHERTY* WHO HAVE CRIMINAL RECORDS IN NYC, BUT TWO ARE IN PRISON AND THE OTHER FOUR ARE OUT OF STATE NOW.
"DOHERTY?"
ISN'T HE A CHARACTER ON *THIRD WATCH?*

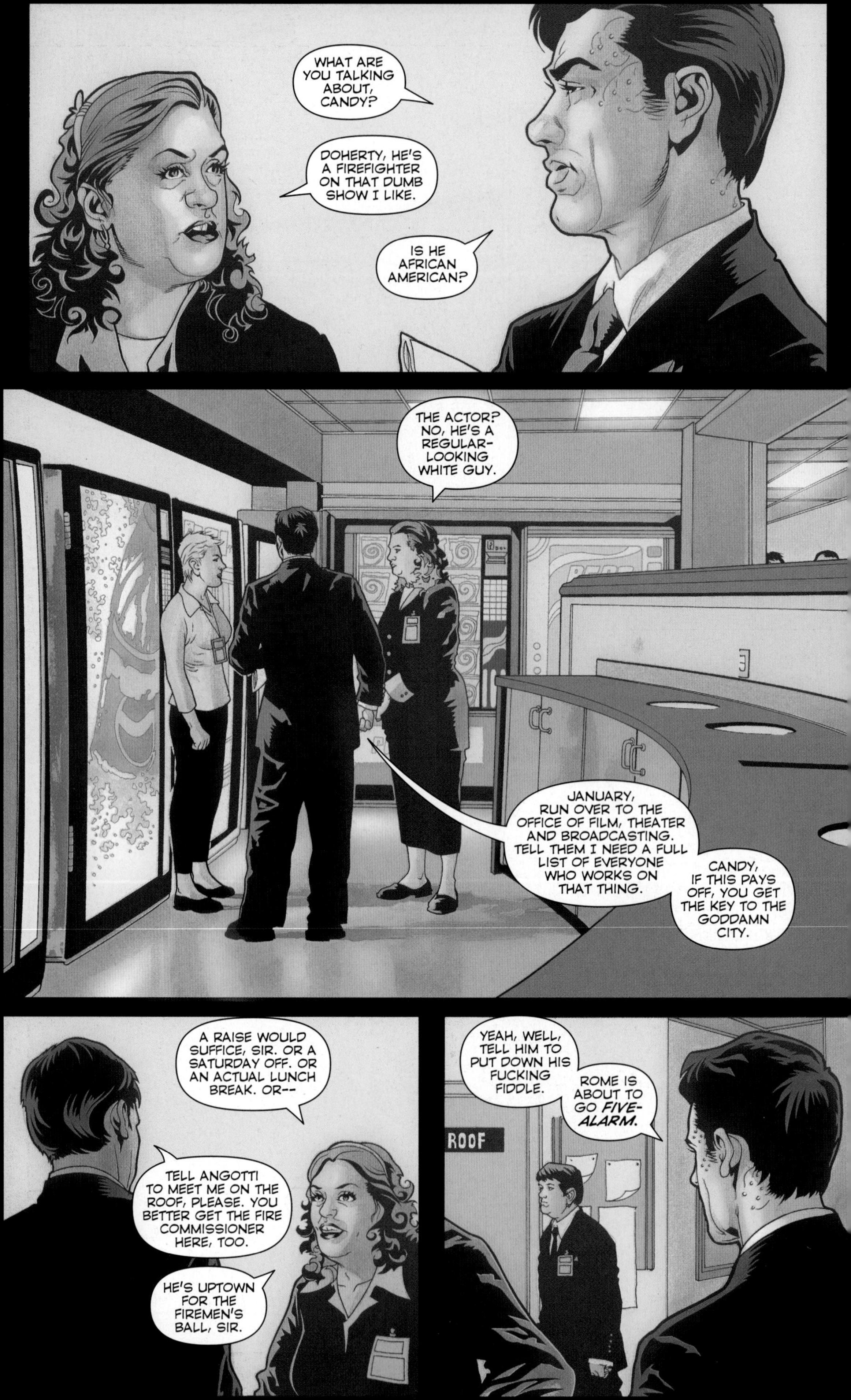
WHAT ARE YOU TALKING ABOUT, CANDY?
DOHERTY, HE'S A FIREFIGHTER ON THAT DUMB SHOW I LIKE.
IS HE AFRICAN AMERICAN?
THE ACTOR? NO, HE'S A REGULAR-LOOKING WHITE GUY.
JANUARY, RUN OVER TO THE OFFICE OF FILM, THEATER AND BROADCASTING. TELL THEM I NEED A FULL LIST OF EVERYONE WHO WORKS ON THAT THING.
CANDY, IF THIS PAYS OFF, YOU GET THE KEY TO THE GODDAMN CITY.
A RAISE WOULD SUFFICE, SIR. OR A SATURDAY OFF. OR AN ACTUAL LUNCH BREAK. OR--
TELL ANGOTTI TO MEET ME ON THE ROOF, PLEASE. YOU BETTER GET THE FIRE COMMISSIONER HERE, TOO.
HE'S UPTOWN FOR THE FIREMEN'S BALL, SIR.
YEAH, WELL, TELL HIM TO PUT DOWN HIS FUCKING FIDDLE.
ROME IS ABOUT TO GO *FIVE-ALARM.*
ROOF

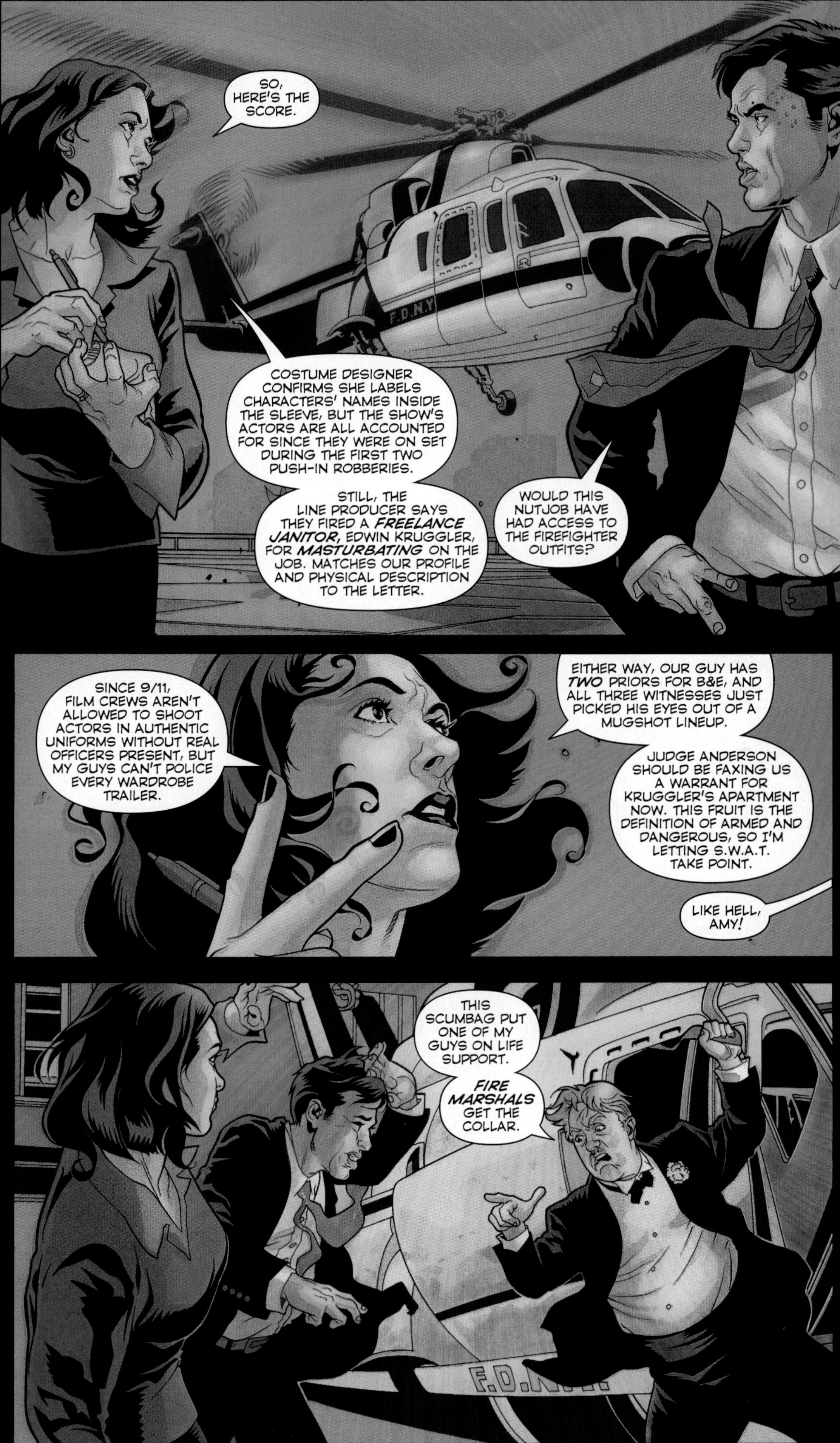
SO, HERE'S THE SCORE.
COSTUME DESIGNER CONFIRMS SHE LABELS CHARACTERS' NAMES INSIDE THE SLEEVE, BUT THE SHOW'S ACTORS ARE ALL ACCOUNTED FOR SINCE THEY WERE ON SET DURING THE FIRST TWO PUSH-IN ROBBERIES.
STILL, THE LINE PRODUCER SAYS THEY FIRED A ***FREELANCE JANITOR,*** EDWIN KRUGGLER, FOR ***MASTURBATING*** ON THE JOB. MATCHES OUR PROFILE AND PHYSICAL DESCRIPTION TO THE LETTER.
WOULD THIS NUTJOB HAVE HAD ACCESS TO THE FIREFIGHTER OUTFITS?
F.D.N.Y
SINCE 9/11, FILM CREWS AREN'T ALLOWED TO SHOOT ACTORS IN AUTHENTIC UNIFORMS WITHOUT REAL OFFICERS PRESENT, BUT MY GUYS CAN'T POLICE EVERY WARDROBE TRAILER.
EITHER WAY, OUR GUY HAS ***TWO*** PRIORS FOR B&E, AND ALL THREE WITNESSES JUST PICKED HIS EYES OUT OF A MUGSHOT LINEUP.
JUDGE ANDERSON SHOULD BE FAXING US A WARRANT FOR KRUGGLER'S APARTMENT NOW. THIS FRUIT IS THE DEFINITION OF ARMED AND DANGEROUS, SO I'M LETTING S.W.A.T. TAKE POINT.
LIKE HELL, AMY!
THIS SCUMBAG PUT ONE OF MY GUYS ON LIFE SUPPORT.
FIRE MARSHALS GET THE COLLAR.

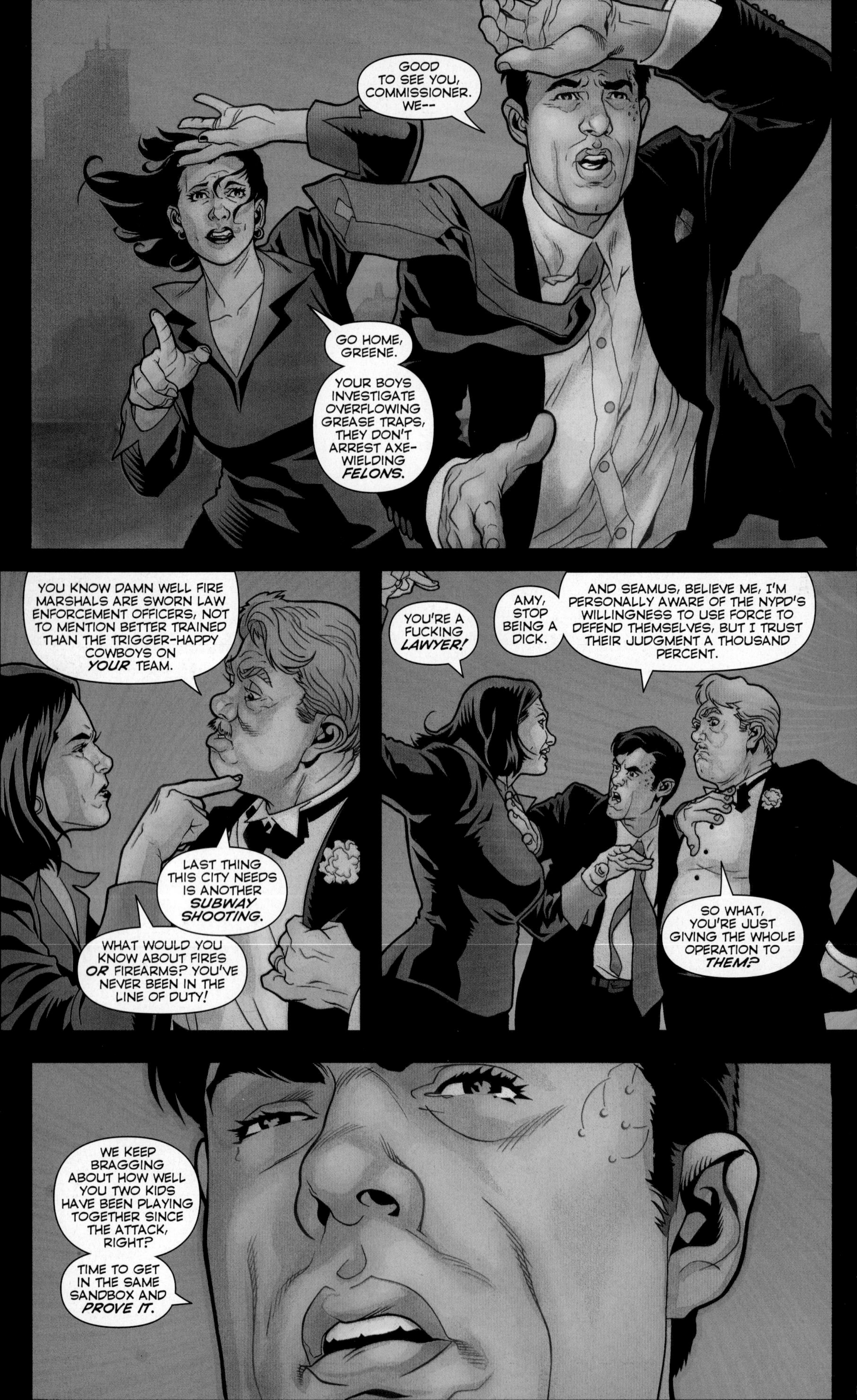
GOOD TO SEE YOU, COMMISSIONER. WE--
GO HOME, GREENE.
YOUR BOYS INVESTIGATE OVERFLOWING GREASE TRAPS, THEY DON'T ARREST AXE-WIELDING *FELONS*.
YOU KNOW DAMN WELL FIRE MARSHALS ARE SWORN LAW ENFORCEMENT OFFICERS, NOT TO MENTION BETTER TRAINED THAN THE TRIGGER-HAPPY COWBOYS ON *YOUR* TEAM.
LAST THING THIS CITY NEEDS IS ANOTHER *SUBWAY SHOOTING*.
WHAT WOULD YOU KNOW ABOUT FIRES *OR* FIREARMS? YOU'VE NEVER BEEN IN THE LINE OF DUTY!
YOU'RE A FUCKING *LAWYER!*
AMY, STOP BEING A DICK.
AND SEAMUS, BELIEVE ME, I'M PERSONALLY AWARE OF THE NYPD'S WILLINGNESS TO USE FORCE TO DEFEND THEMSELVES, BUT I TRUST THEIR JUDGMENT A THOUSAND PERCENT.
SO WHAT, YOU'RE JUST GIVING THE WHOLE OPERATION TO *THEM?*
WE KEEP BRAGGING ABOUT HOW WELL YOU TWO KIDS HAVE BEEN PLAYING TOGETHER SINCE THE ATTACK, RIGHT?
TIME TO GET IN THE SAME SANDBOX AND *PROVE IT*.

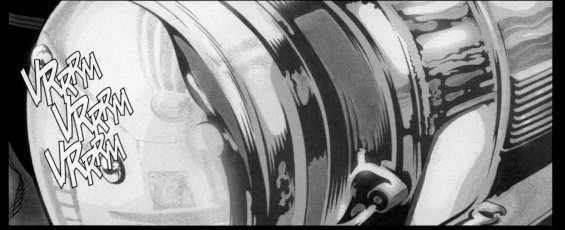

VRRRM
VRRRM
VRRRM

THAT CUNT'S BITCH DOG NEARLY TOOK MY *HAND* OFF.

LORD KNOWS WHAT THAT THING MIGHT HAVE BEEN CARRYING...RABIES, LYME DISEASE, *TYPHUS*.

I'LL NEVER FIGURE HOW PEOPLE LOVE OTHER ANIMALS.

HOW YOU *TRUST* SOMETHING WHEN IT'S JUST A BAG OF GERMS AND VIRUSES? NAH, LOVE IS *CLEAN*, RIGHT, BABY? LOVE IS--

SEARCH WARRANT, OPEN UP!

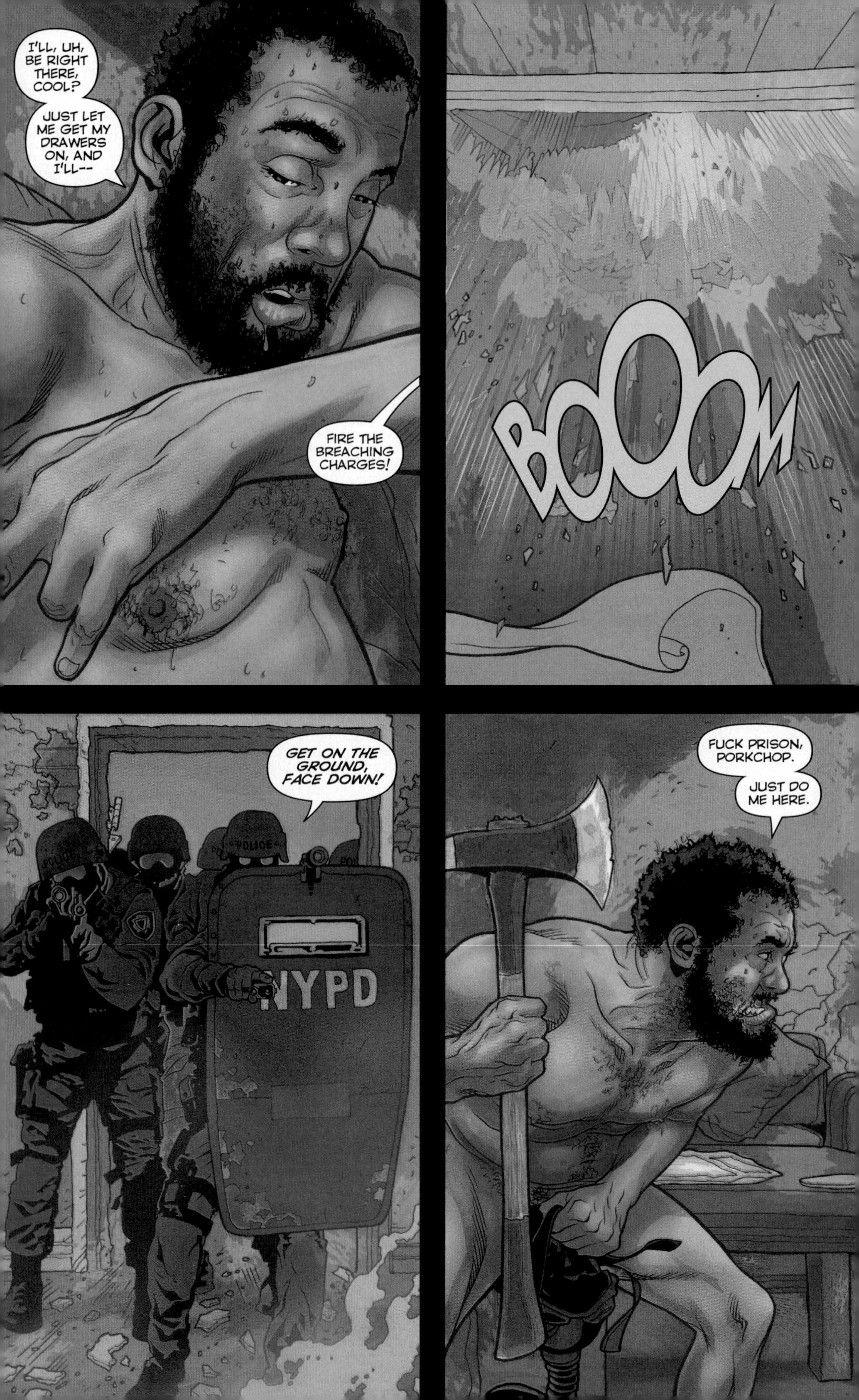
I'LL, UH, BE RIGHT THERE, COOL?
JUST LET ME GET MY DRAWERS ON, AND I'LL--
FIRE THE BREACHING CHARGES!
BOOOM
GET ON THE GROUND, FACE DOWN!
POLICE
NYPD
FUCK PRISON, PORKCHOP.
JUST DO ME HERE.

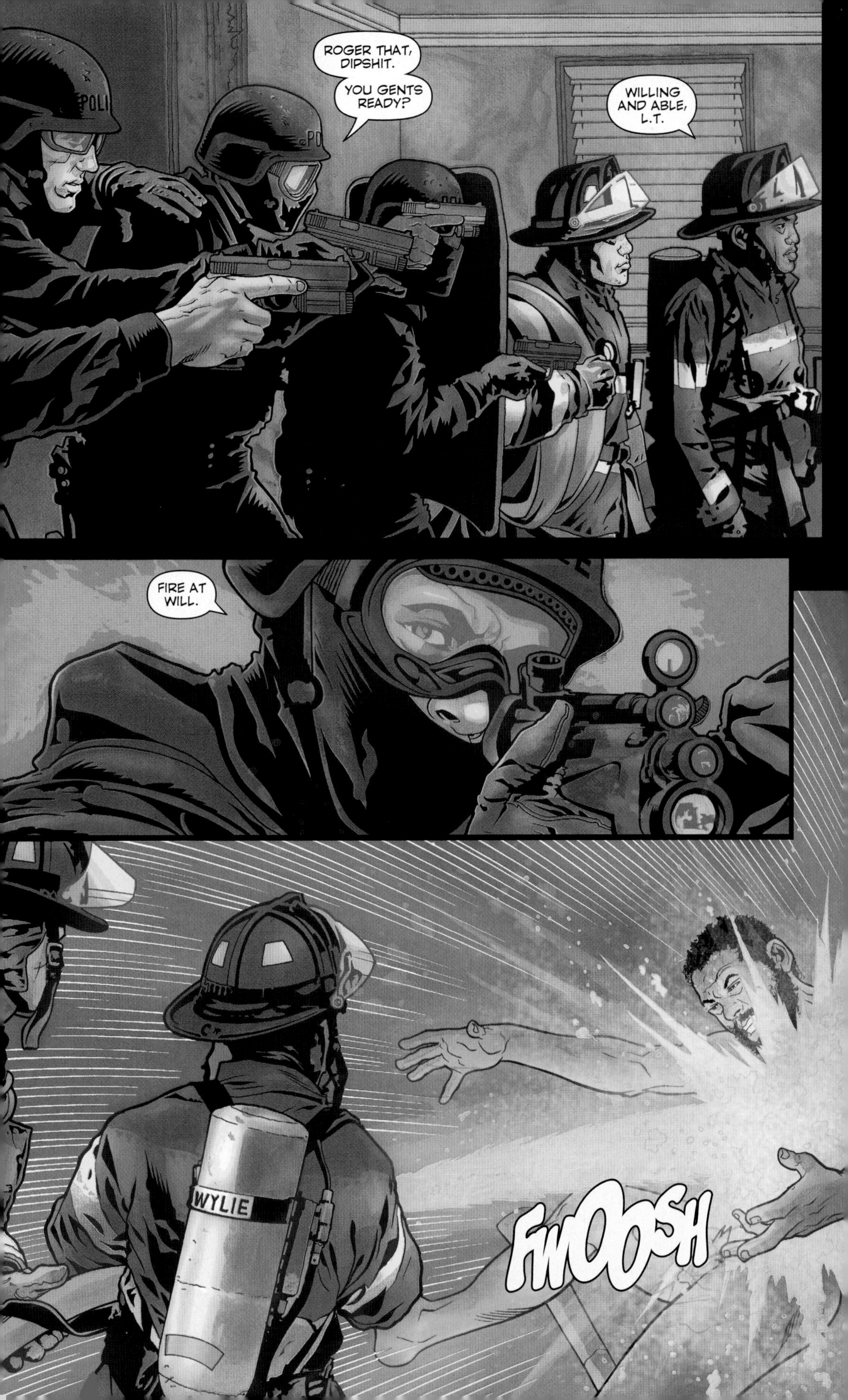
ROGER THAT, DIPSHIT.
YOU GENTS READY?
WILLING AND ABLE, L.T.
POLI
PO
FIRE AT WILL.
WYLIE
FWOOSH

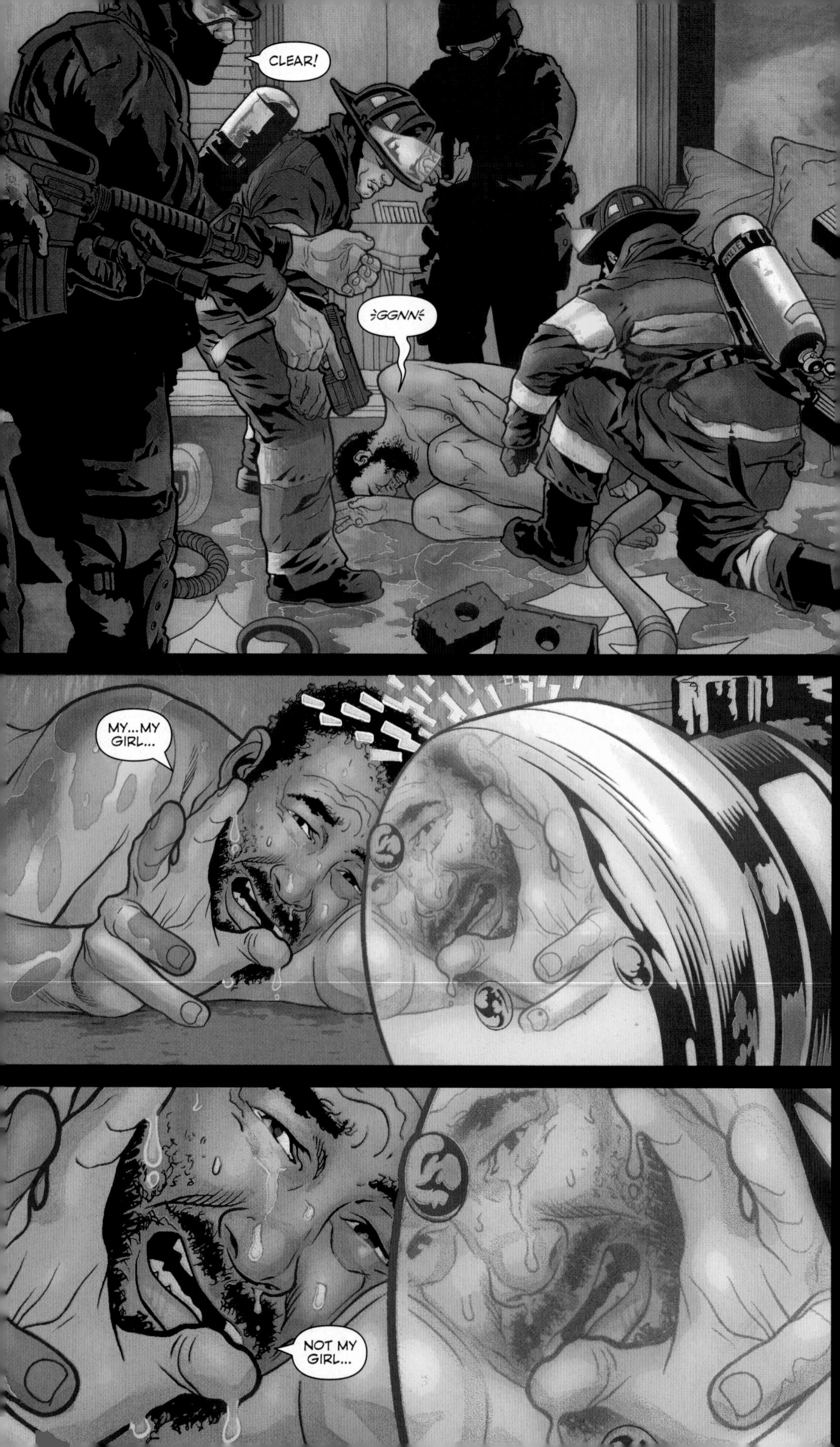
CLEAR!
GGNN
MY...MY GIRL...
NOT MY GIRL...

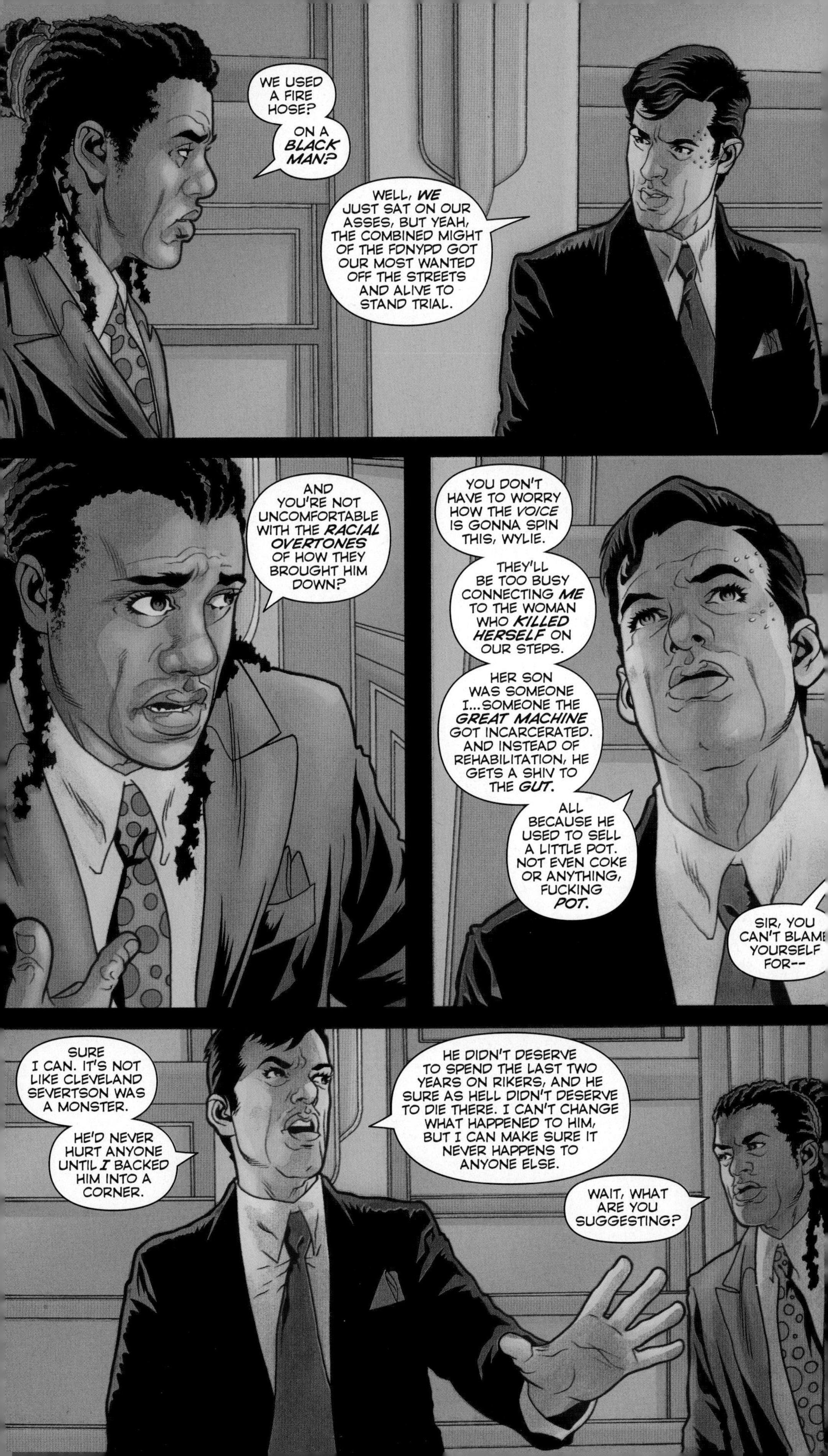
WE USED A FIRE HOSE?
ON A BLACK MAN?
WELL, WE JUST SAT ON OUR ASSES, BUT YEAH, THE COMBINED MIGHT OF THE FDNYPD GOT OUR MOST WANTED OFF THE STREETS AND ALIVE TO STAND TRIAL.
AND YOU'RE NOT UNCOMFORTABLE WITH THE RACIAL OVERTONES OF HOW THEY BROUGHT HIM DOWN?
YOU DON'T HAVE TO WORRY HOW THE VOICE IS GONNA SPIN THIS, WYLIE.
THEY'LL BE TOO BUSY CONNECTING ME TO THE WOMAN WHO KILLED HERSELF ON OUR STEPS.
HER SON WAS SOMEONE I...SOMEONE THE GREAT MACHINE GOT INCARCERATED. AND INSTEAD OF REHABILITATION, HE GETS A SHIV TO THE GUT.
ALL BECAUSE HE USED TO SELL A LITTLE POT. NOT EVEN COKE OR ANYTHING, FUCKING POT.
SIR, YOU CAN'T BLAME YOURSELF FOR--
SURE I CAN. IT'S NOT LIKE CLEVELAND SEVERTSON WAS A MONSTER.
HE'D NEVER HURT ANYONE UNTIL I BACKED HIM INTO A CORNER.
HE DIDN'T DESERVE TO SPEND THE LAST TWO YEARS ON RIKERS, AND HE SURE AS HELL DIDN'T DESERVE TO DIE THERE. I CAN'T CHANGE WHAT HAPPENED TO HIM, BUT I CAN MAKE SURE IT NEVER HAPPENS TO ANYONE ELSE.
WAIT, WHAT ARE YOU SUGGESTING?

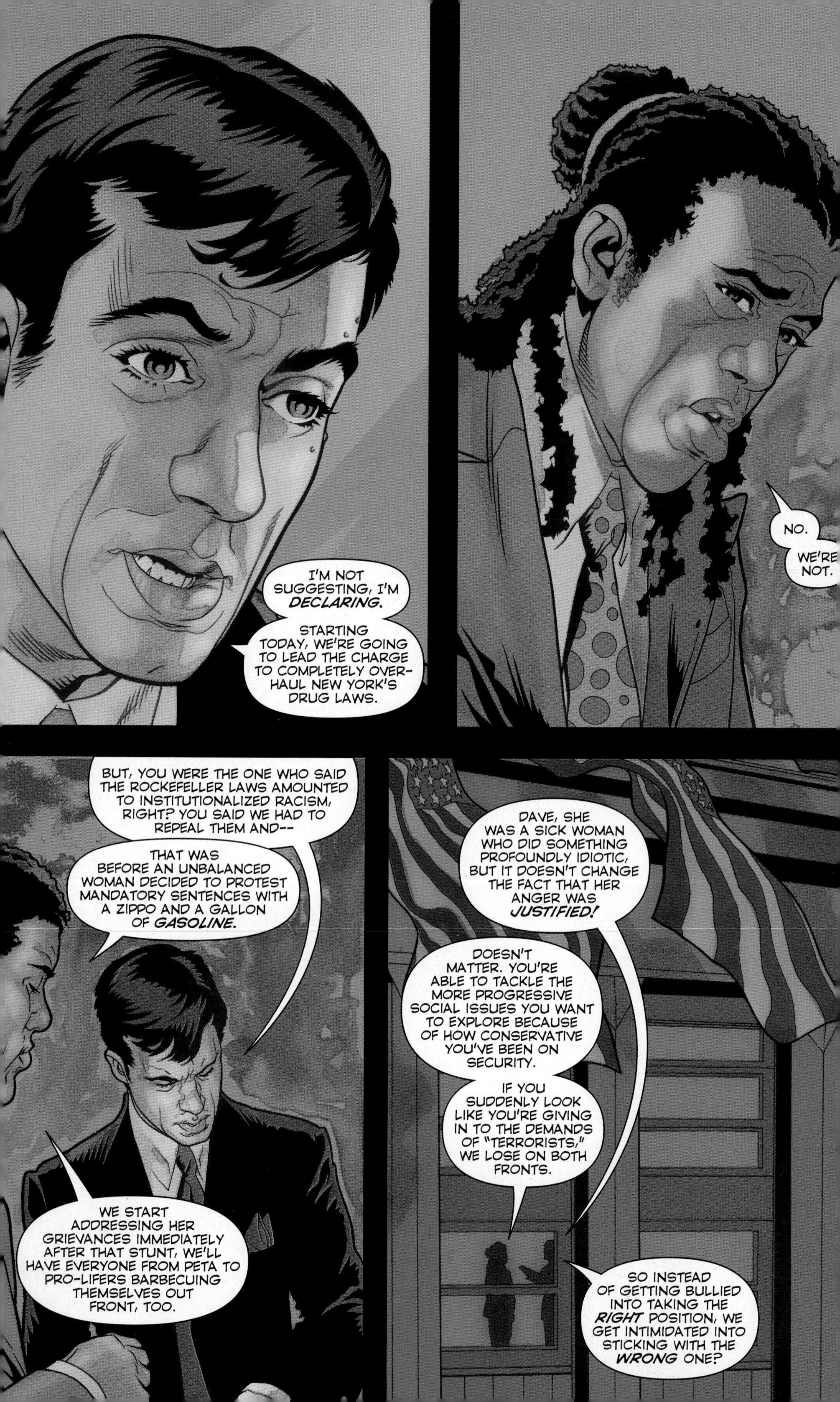

I'M NOT SUGGESTING, I'M DECLARING.
STARTING TODAY, WE'RE GOING TO LEAD THE CHARGE TO COMPLETELY OVER-HAUL NEW YORK'S DRUG LAWS.
NO.
WE'RE NOT.
BUT, YOU WERE THE ONE WHO SAID THE ROCKEFELLER LAWS AMOUNTED TO INSTITUTIONALIZED RACISM, RIGHT? YOU SAID WE HAD TO REPEAL THEM AND--
THAT WAS BEFORE AN UNBALANCED WOMAN DECIDED TO PROTEST MANDATORY SENTENCES WITH A ZIPPO AND A GALLON OF GASOLINE.
WE START ADDRESSING HER GRIEVANCES IMMEDIATELY AFTER THAT STUNT, WE'LL HAVE EVERYONE FROM PETA TO PRO-LIFERS BARBECUING THEMSELVES OUT FRONT, TOO.
DAVE, SHE WAS A SICK WOMAN WHO DID SOMETHING PROFOUNDLY IDIOTIC, BUT IT DOESN'T CHANGE THE FACT THAT HER ANGER WAS JUSTIFIED!
DOESN'T MATTER. YOU'RE ABLE TO TACKLE THE MORE PROGRESSIVE SOCIAL ISSUES YOU WANT TO EXPLORE BECAUSE OF HOW CONSERVATIVE YOU'VE BEEN ON SECURITY.
IF YOU SUDDENLY LOOK LIKE YOU'RE GIVING IN TO THE DEMANDS OF "TERRORISTS," WE LOSE ON BOTH FRONTS.
SO INSTEAD OF GETTING BULLIED INTO TAKING THE RIGHT POSITION, WE GET INTIMIDATED INTO STICKING WITH THE WRONG ONE?

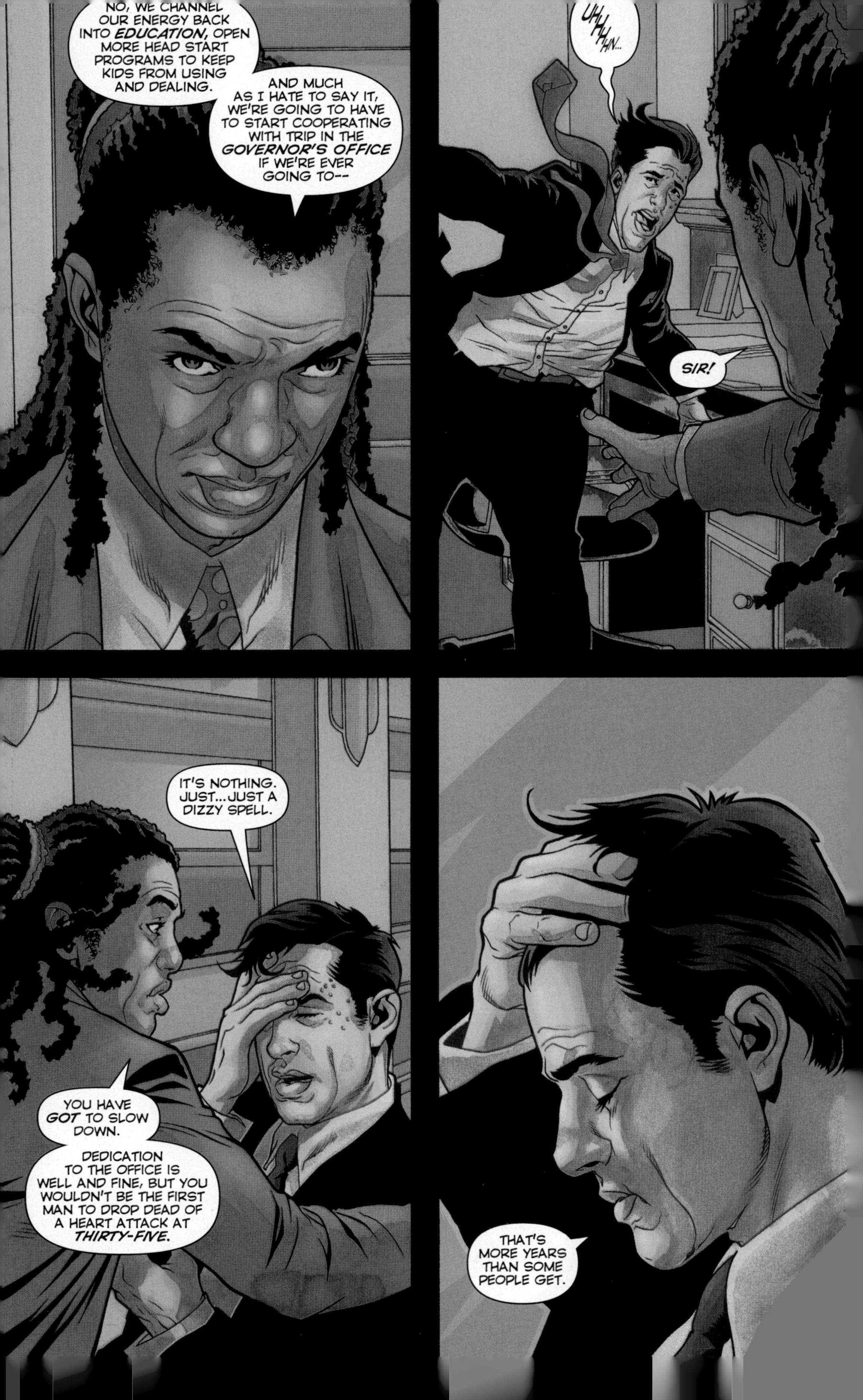
NO, WE CHANNEL OUR ENERGY BACK INTO *EDUCATION,* OPEN MORE HEAD START PROGRAMS TO KEEP KIDS FROM USING AND DEALING.
AND MUCH AS I HATE TO SAY IT, WE'RE GOING TO HAVE TO START COOPERATING WITH TRIP IN THE *GOVERNOR'S OFFICE* IF WE'RE EVER GOING TO--
UHHHHN...
SIR!
IT'S NOTHING. JUST...JUST A DIZZY SPELL.
YOU HAVE *GOT* TO SLOW DOWN.
DEDICATION TO THE OFFICE IS WELL AND FINE, BUT YOU WOULDN'T BE THE FIRST MAN TO DROP DEAD OF A HEART ATTACK AT *THIRTY-FIVE.*
THAT'S MORE YEARS THAN SOME PEOPLE GET.

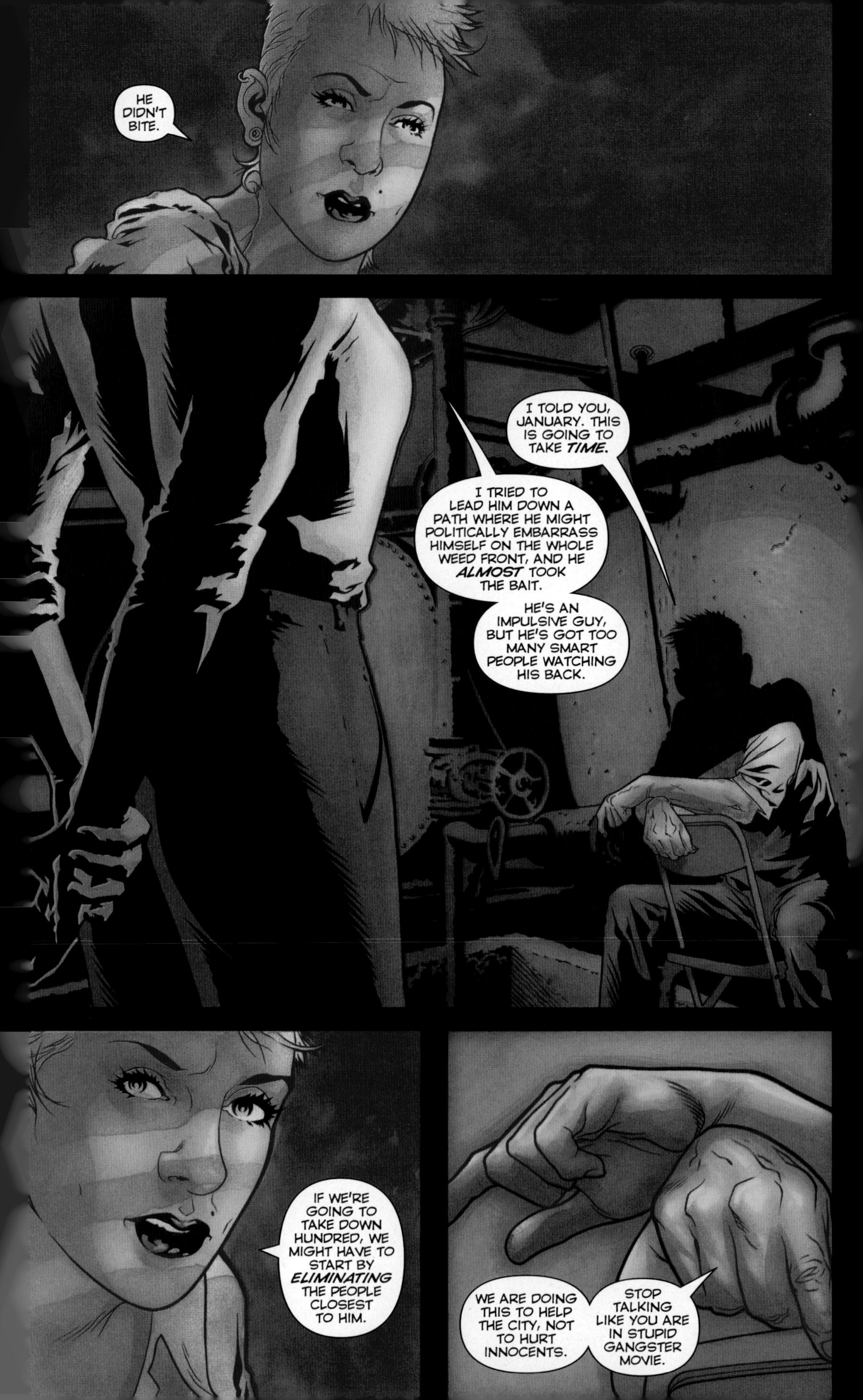
HE DIDN'T BITE.
I TOLD YOU, JANUARY. THIS IS GOING TO TAKE *TIME*.
I TRIED TO LEAD HIM DOWN A PATH WHERE HE MIGHT POLITICALLY EMBARRASS HIMSELF ON THE WHOLE WEED FRONT, AND HE *ALMOST* TOOK THE BAIT.
HE'S AN IMPULSIVE GUY, BUT HE'S GOT TOO MANY SMART PEOPLE WATCHING HIS BACK.
IF WE'RE GOING TO TAKE DOWN HUNDRED, WE MIGHT HAVE TO START BY *ELIMINATING* THE PEOPLE CLOSEST TO HIM.
STOP TALKING LIKE YOU ARE IN STUPID GANGSTER MOVIE.
WE ARE DOING THIS TO HELP THE CITY, NOT TO HURT INNOCENTS.

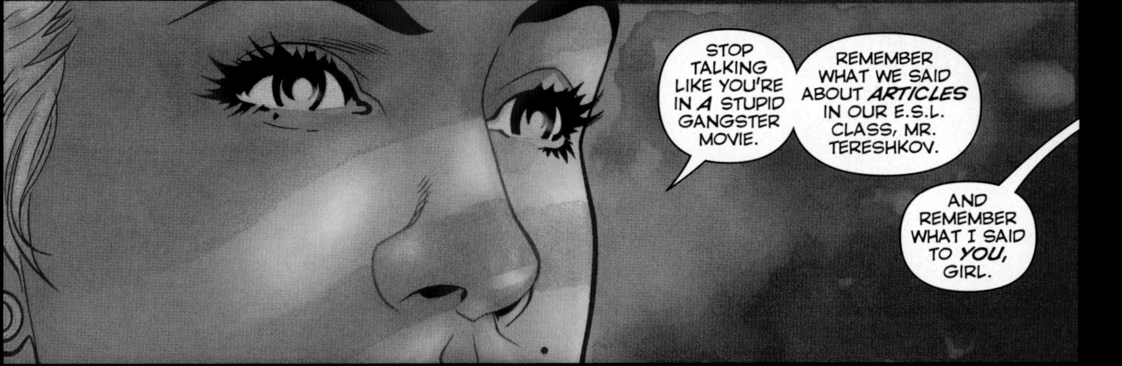
STOP TALKING LIKE YOU'RE IN A STUPID GANGSTER MOVIE.
REMEMBER WHAT WE SAID ABOUT ARTICLES IN OUR E.S.L. CLASS, MR. TERESHKOV.
AND REMEMBER WHAT I SAID TO YOU, GIRL.

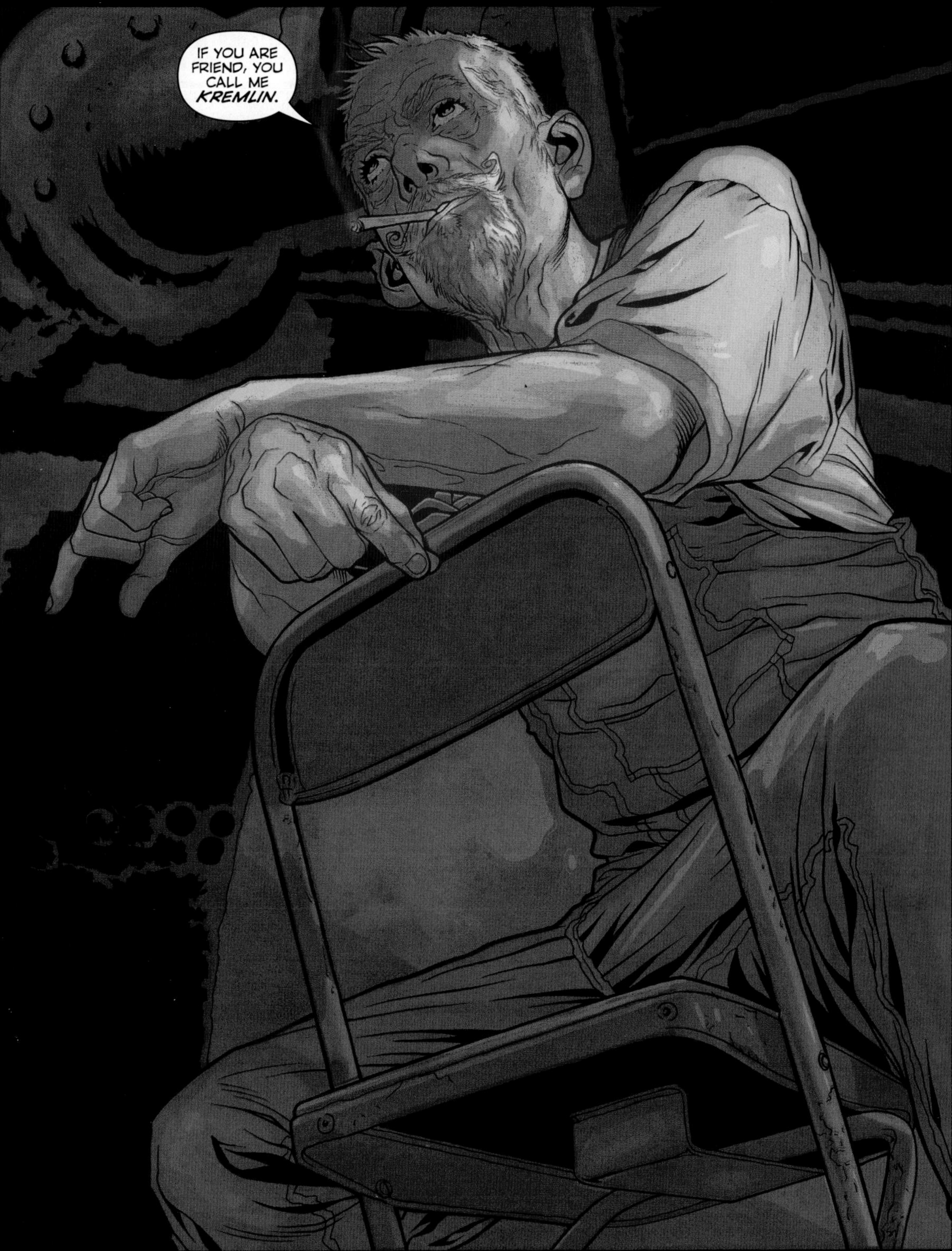
IF YOU ARE FRIEND, YOU CALL ME KREMLIN.

LANDMARKS OF NEW YORK

GRACIE MANSION

BUILT ABOUT 1799 ON THE SITE OF A
REVOLUTIONARY FORT AS THE COUNTRY
HOUSE OF ARCHIBALD GRACIE, SCOTTISH
MERCHANT, THIS COLONIAL STRUCTURE WAS

SECURITY SYSTEM REACTIVATED BY HUNDRED.

TIVO HAS RECORDED "IN THE PAPERS" ON NY1. TIVO HAS RECORDED "NBC NIGHTLY NEWS" ON NBC. TIVO HAS--

ANSWERING MACHINE FLASHES TWELVE MESSAGES. ANSWERING MACHINE FLASHES TWELVE MESSAGES.

HUNDRED TURNS HALLWAY LIGHT TO ON.

CLIMATE CONTROL SET TO SEVENTY-NINE DEGREES. FAN ON.

11:56 P.M. AND FIFTEEN SECONDS. 11:56 P.M. AND SIXTEEN SECONDS.

DESK LAMP IS OFF.

11:56 P.M. AND TWENTY SECONDS. 11:56 P.M. AND TWENTY-ONE SECONDS.

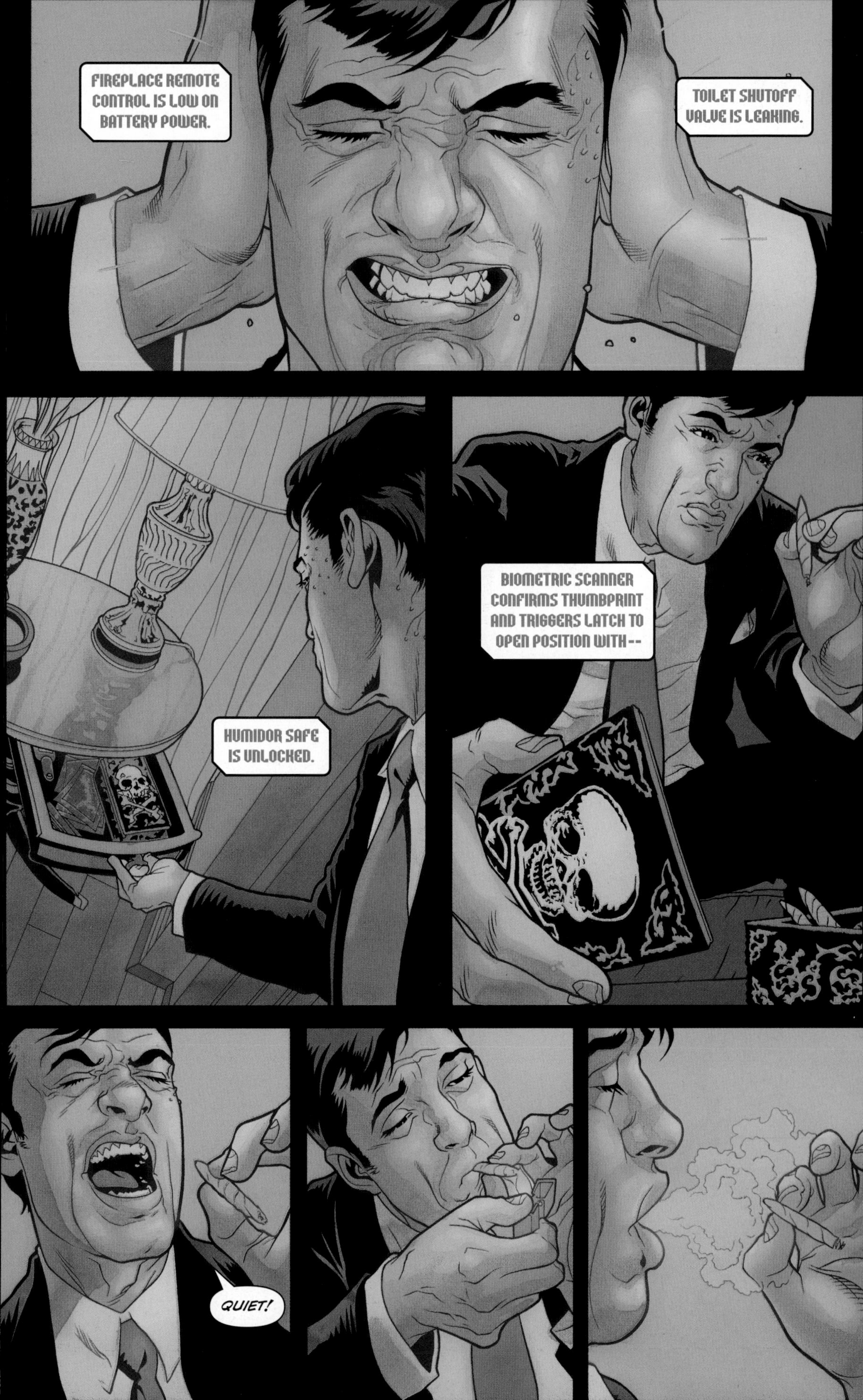
FIREPLACE REMOTE CONTROL IS LOW ON BATTERY POWER.
TOILET SHUTOFF VALVE IS LEAKING.
HUMIDOR SAFE IS UNLOCKED.
BIOMETRIC SCANNER CONFIRMS THUMBPRINT AND TRIGGERS LATCH TO OPEN POSITION WITH--
QUIET!

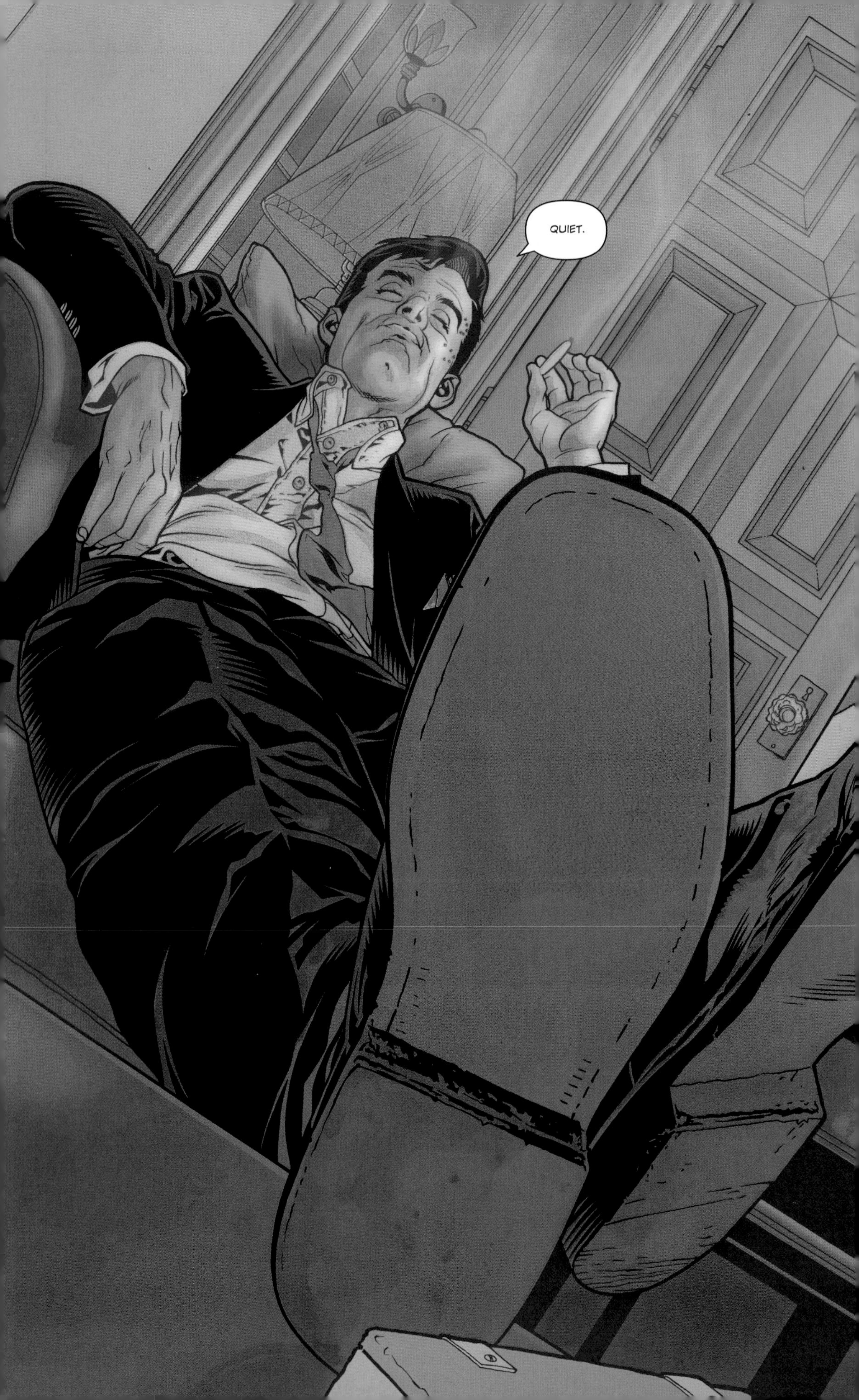
QUIET.

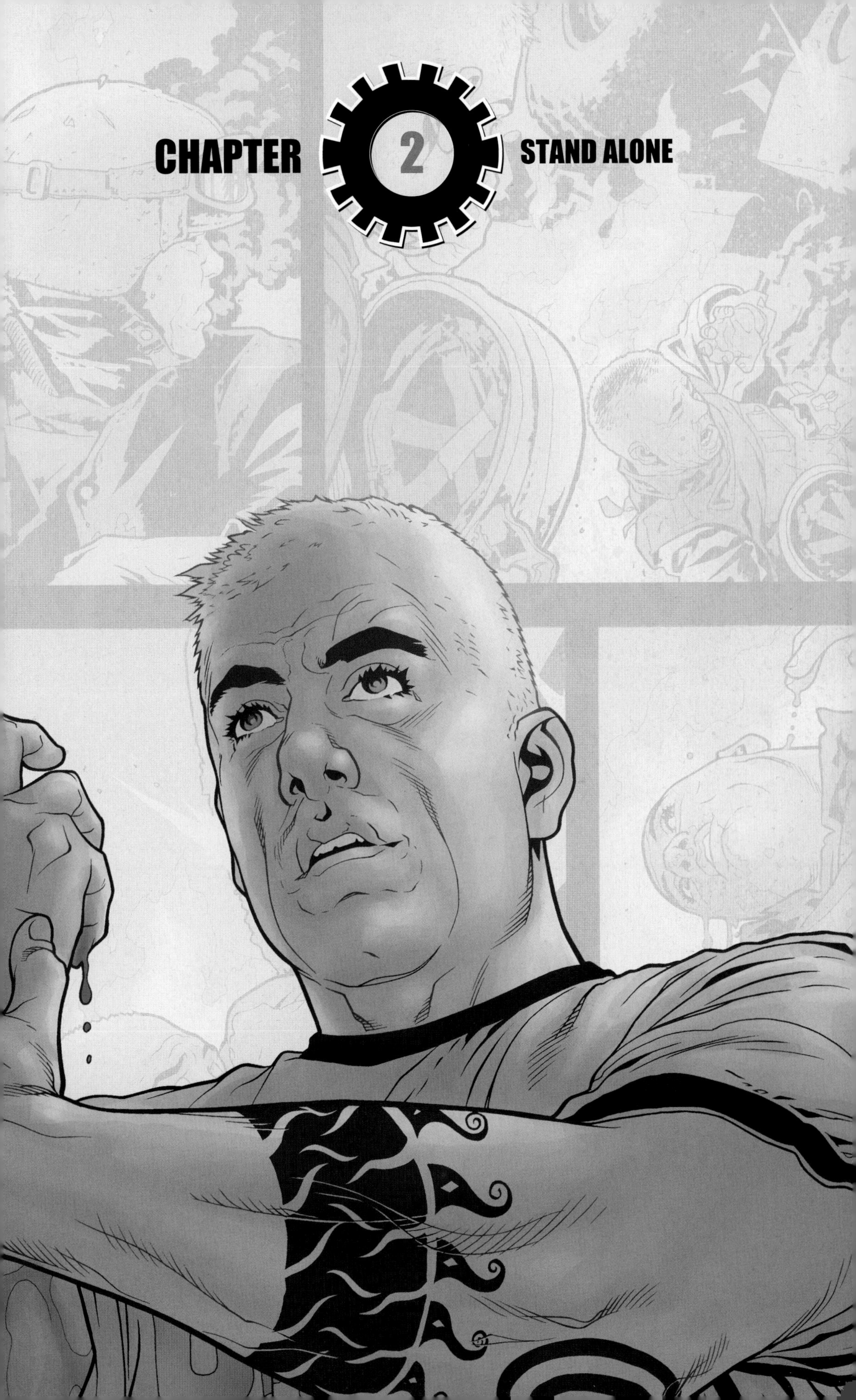
CHAPTER 2 STAND ALONE

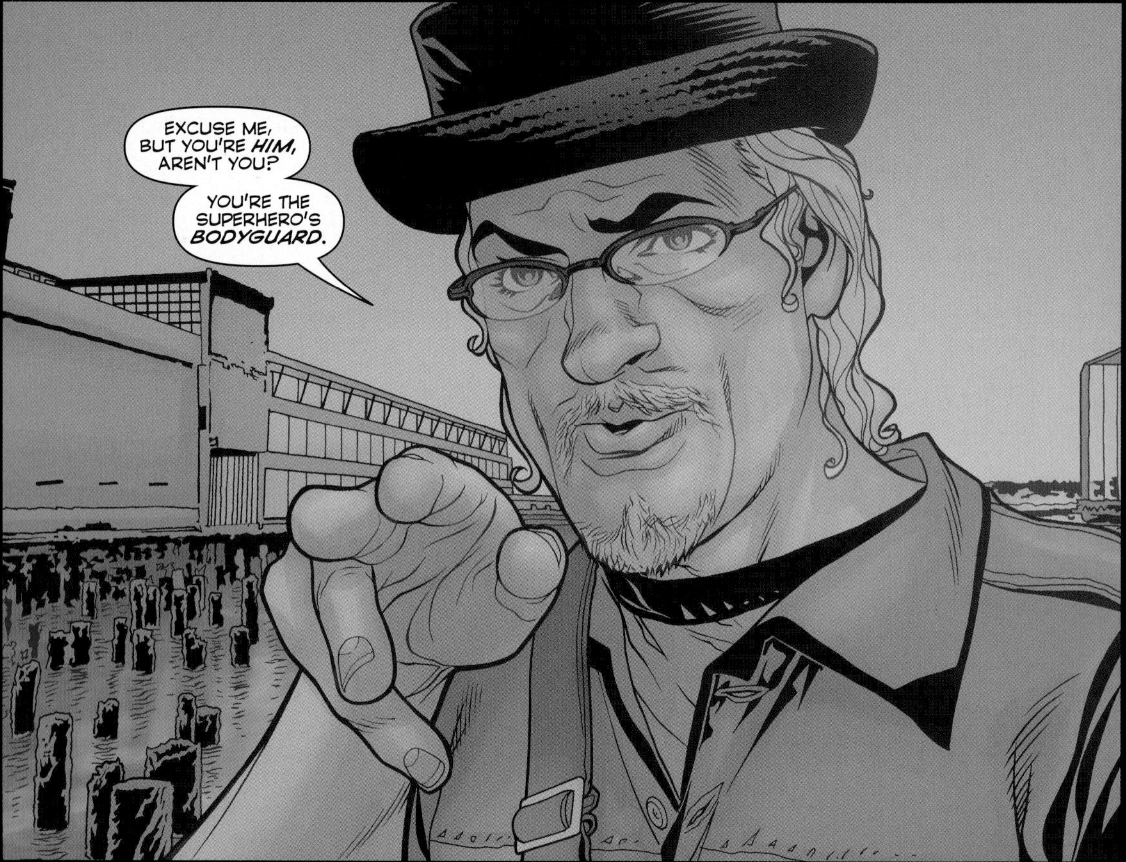
EXCUSE ME, BUT YOU'RE *HIM,* AREN'T YOU?
YOU'RE THE SUPERHERO'S *BODYGUARD.*

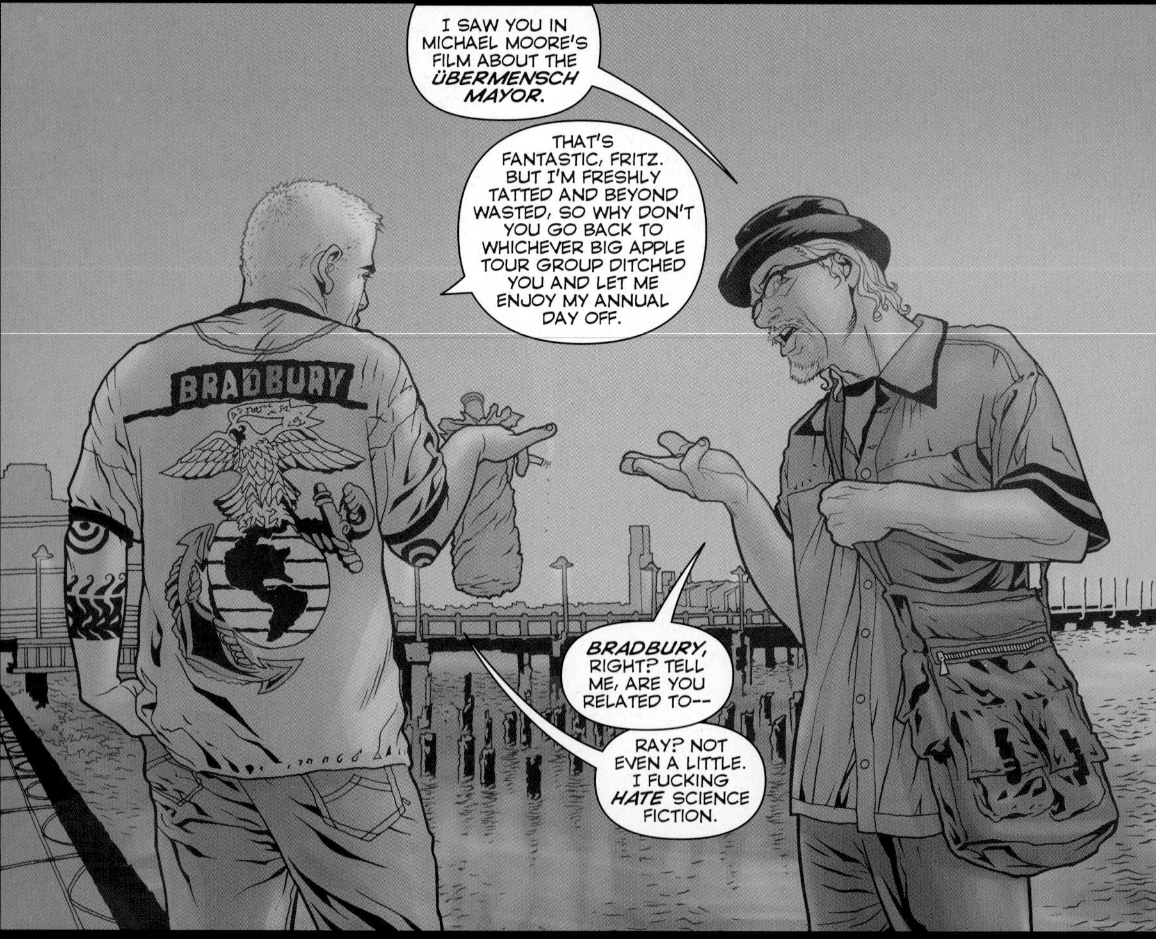
I SAW YOU IN MICHAEL MOORE'S FILM ABOUT THE *ÜBERMENSCH MAYOR.*
THAT'S FANTASTIC, FRITZ. BUT I'M FRESHLY TATTED AND BEYOND WASTED, SO WHY DON'T YOU GO BACK TO WHICHEVER BIG APPLE TOUR GROUP DITCHED YOU AND LET ME ENJOY MY ANNUAL DAY OFF.
BRADBURY
BRADBURY, RIGHT? TELL ME, ARE YOU RELATED TO--
RAY? NOT EVEN A LITTLE. I FUCKING *HATE* SCIENCE FICTION.

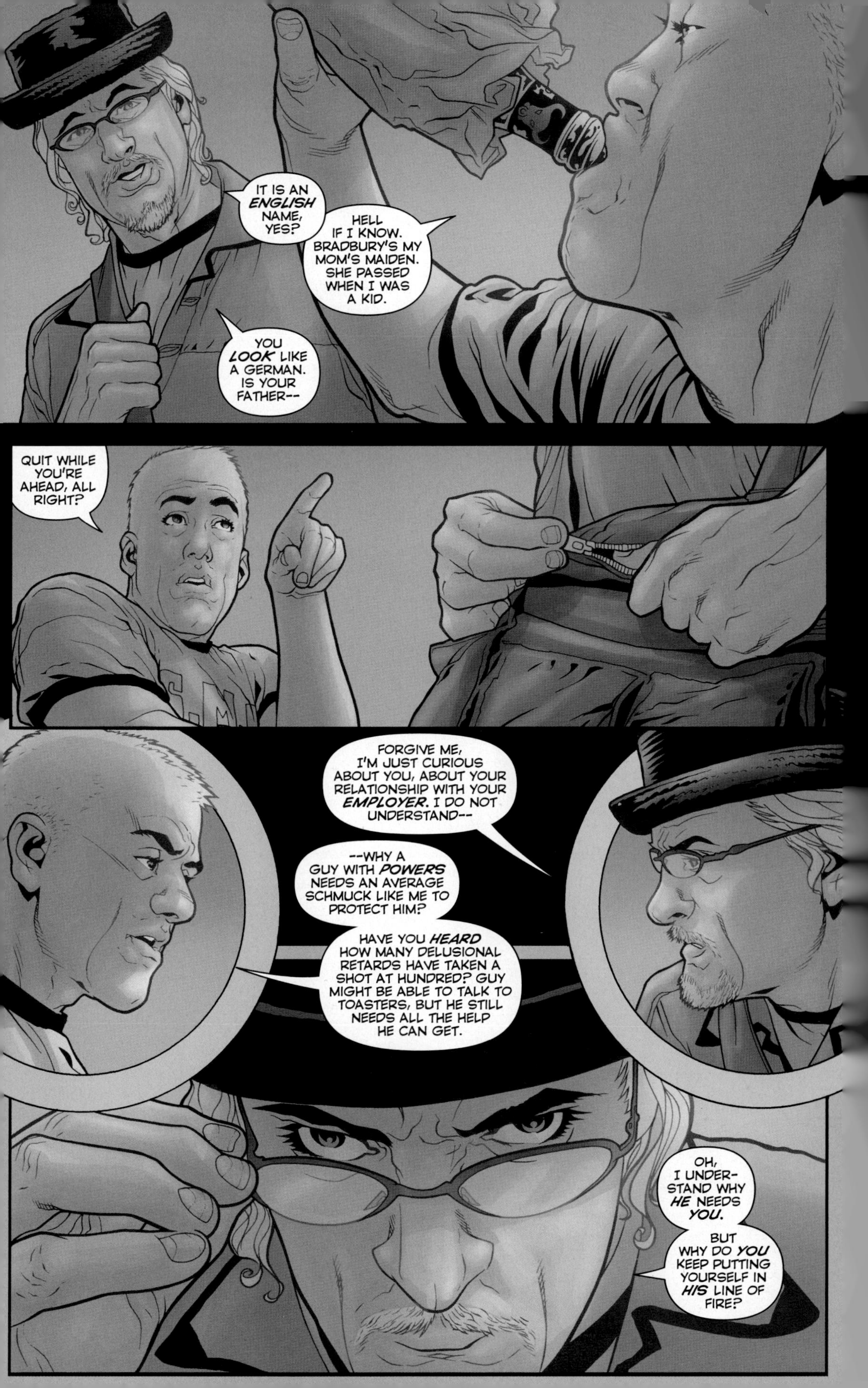
IT IS AN *ENGLISH* NAME, YES?
HELL IF I KNOW. BRADBURY'S MY MOM'S MAIDEN. SHE PASSED WHEN I WAS A KID.
YOU *LOOK* LIKE A GERMAN. IS YOUR FATHER--
QUIT WHILE YOU'RE AHEAD, ALL RIGHT?
FORGIVE ME, I'M JUST CURIOUS ABOUT YOU, ABOUT YOUR RELATIONSHIP WITH YOUR *EMPLOYER*. I DO NOT UNDERSTAND--
--WHY A GUY WITH *POWERS* NEEDS AN AVERAGE SCHMUCK LIKE ME TO PROTECT HIM?
HAVE YOU *HEARD* HOW MANY DELUSIONAL RETARDS HAVE TAKEN A SHOT AT HUNDRED? GUY MIGHT BE ABLE TO TALK TO TOASTERS, BUT HE STILL NEEDS ALL THE HELP HE CAN GET.
OH, I UNDER-STAND WHY *HE* NEEDS *YOU*.
BUT WHY DO *YOU* KEEP PUTTING YOURSELF IN *HIS* LINE OF FIRE?

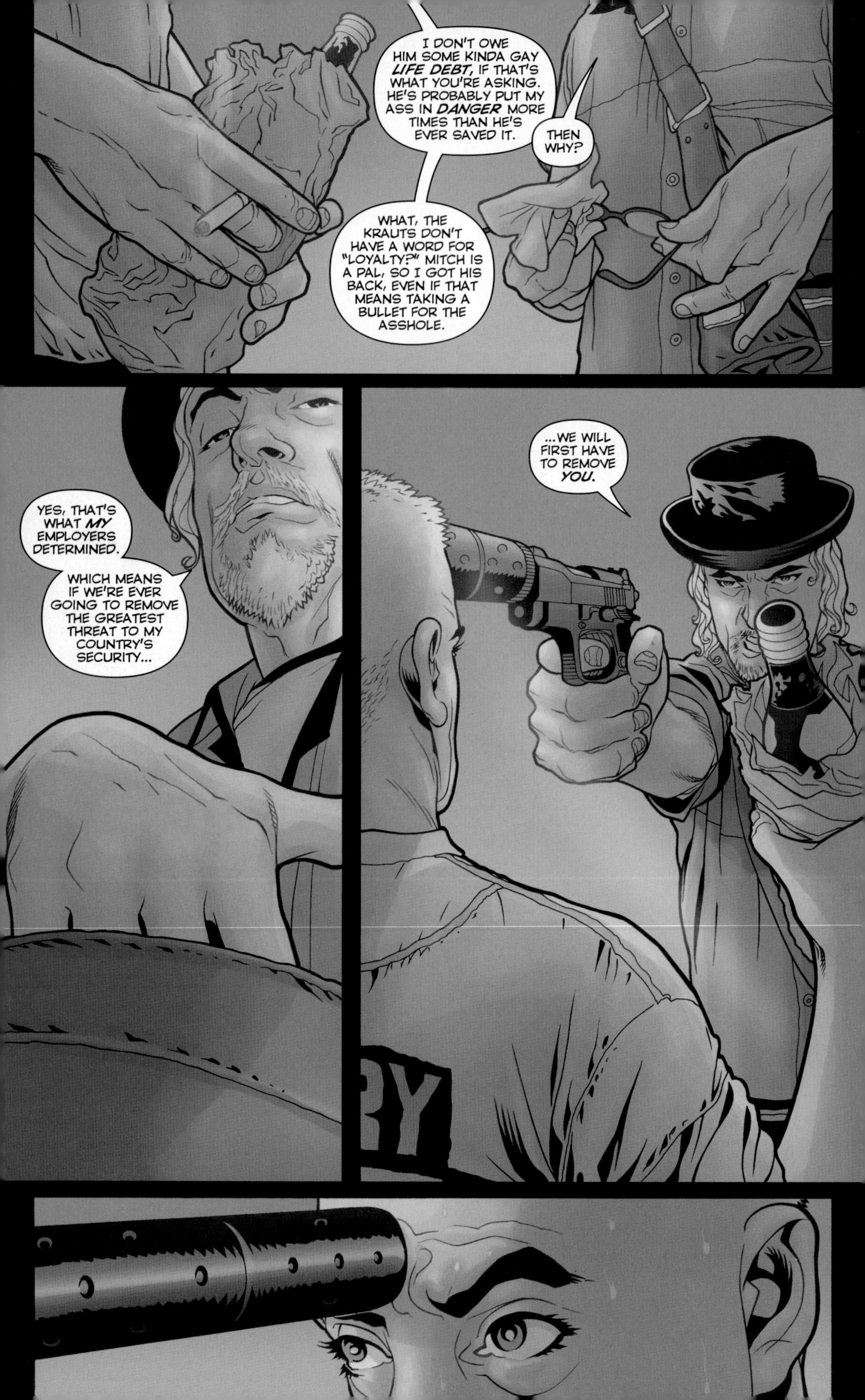
I DON'T OWE HIM SOME KINDA GAY LIFE DEBT, IF THAT'S WHAT YOU'RE ASKING. HE'S PROBABLY PUT MY ASS IN DANGER MORE TIMES THAN HE'S EVER SAVED IT.
THEN WHY?
WHAT, THE KRAUTS DON'T HAVE A WORD FOR "LOYALTY?" MITCH IS A PAL, SO I GOT HIS BACK, EVEN IF THAT MEANS TAKING A BULLET FOR THE ASSHOLE.
YES, THAT'S WHAT MY EMPLOYERS DETERMINED.
WHICH MEANS IF WE'RE EVER GOING TO REMOVE THE GREATEST THREAT TO MY COUNTRY'S SECURITY...
...WE WILL FIRST HAVE TO REMOVE YOU.
RY

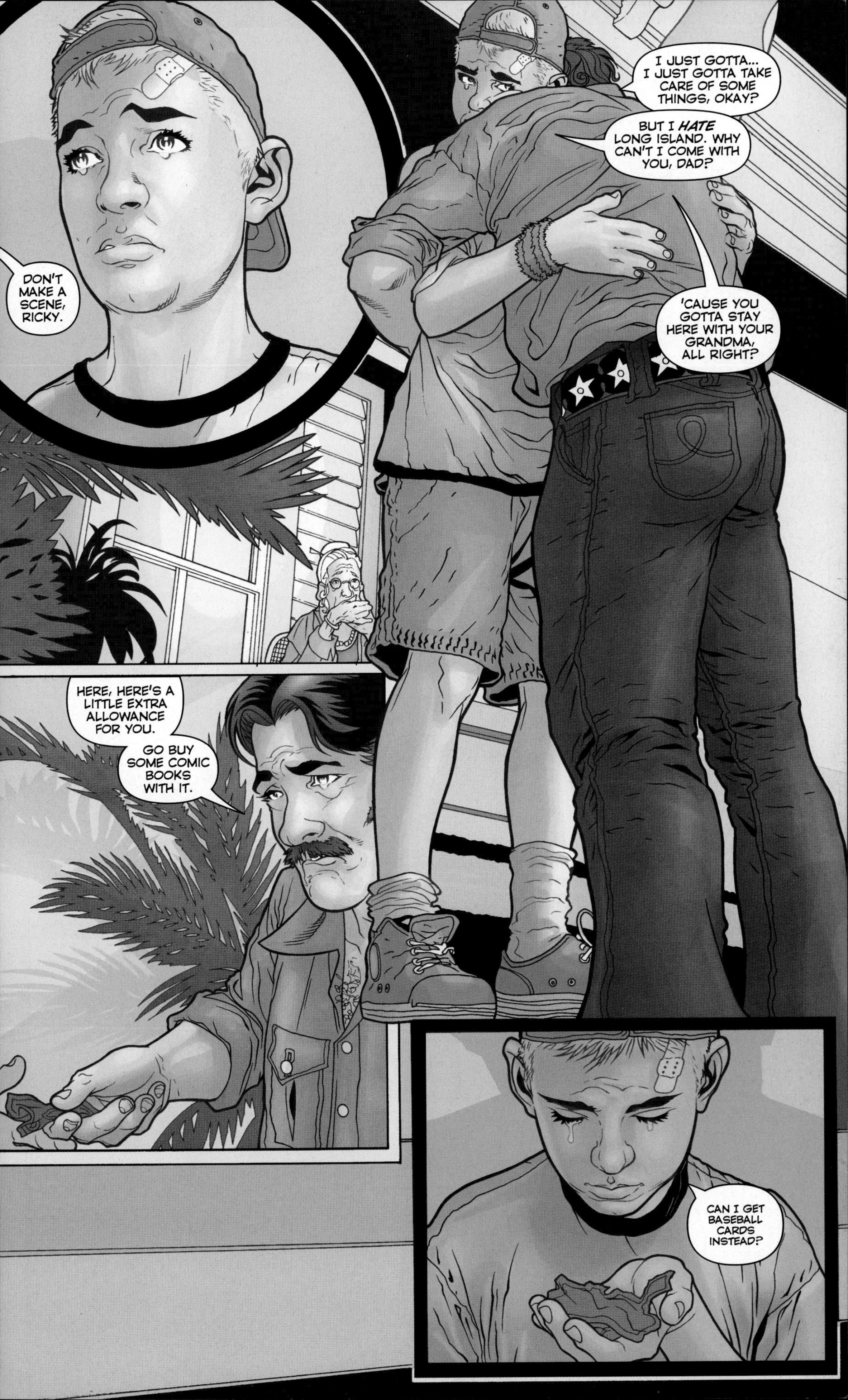
I JUST GOTTA... I JUST GOTTA TAKE CARE OF SOME THINGS, OKAY?
BUT I HATE LONG ISLAND. WHY CAN'T I COME WITH YOU, DAD?
DON'T MAKE A SCENE, RICKY.
'CAUSE YOU GOTTA STAY HERE WITH YOUR GRANDMA, ALL RIGHT?
HERE, HERE'S A LITTLE EXTRA ALLOWANCE FOR YOU.
GO BUY SOME COMIC BOOKS WITH IT.
CAN I GET BASEBALL CARDS INSTEAD?

LOOK, I'M...I'M JUST NOT CUT OUT TO DO THIS SOLO. YOU UNDERSTAND THAT, RIGHT?

BUT IF I'M GOOD, YOU'LL COME BACK SOON?

THERE'S NO *IFS*, LITTLE MAN.

YOU ALWAYS *BE* GOOD, NO MATTER WHAT.

SCREEEECH

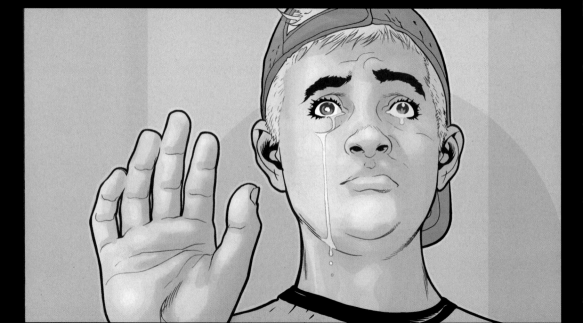

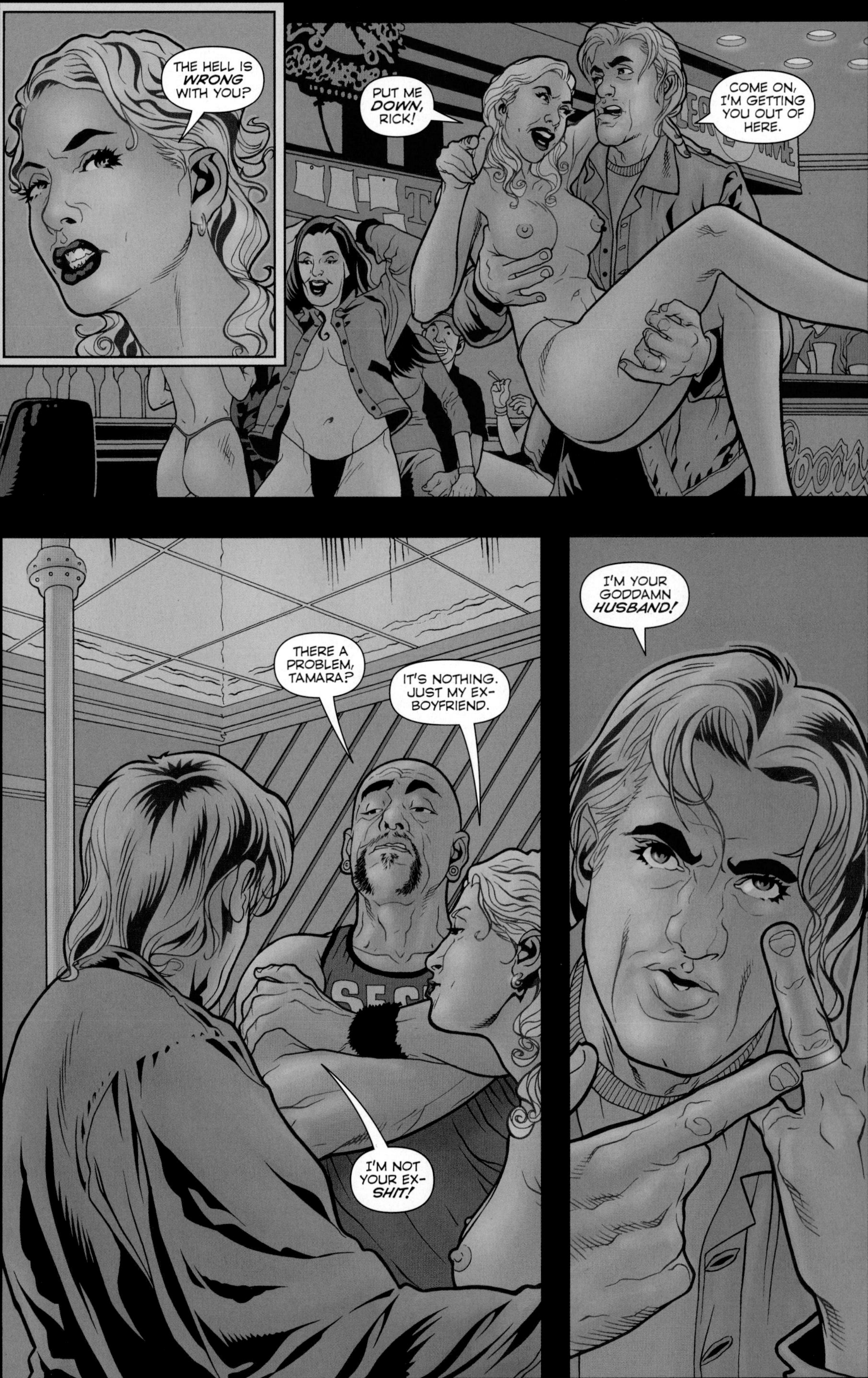
THE HELL IS *WRONG* WITH YOU?
PUT ME *DOWN*, RICK!
COME ON, I'M GETTING YOU OUT OF HERE.
THERE A PROBLEM, TAMARA?
IT'S NOTHING. JUST MY EX-BOYFRIEND.
I'M NOT YOUR EX-*SHIT!*
I'M YOUR GODDAMN *HUSBAND!*

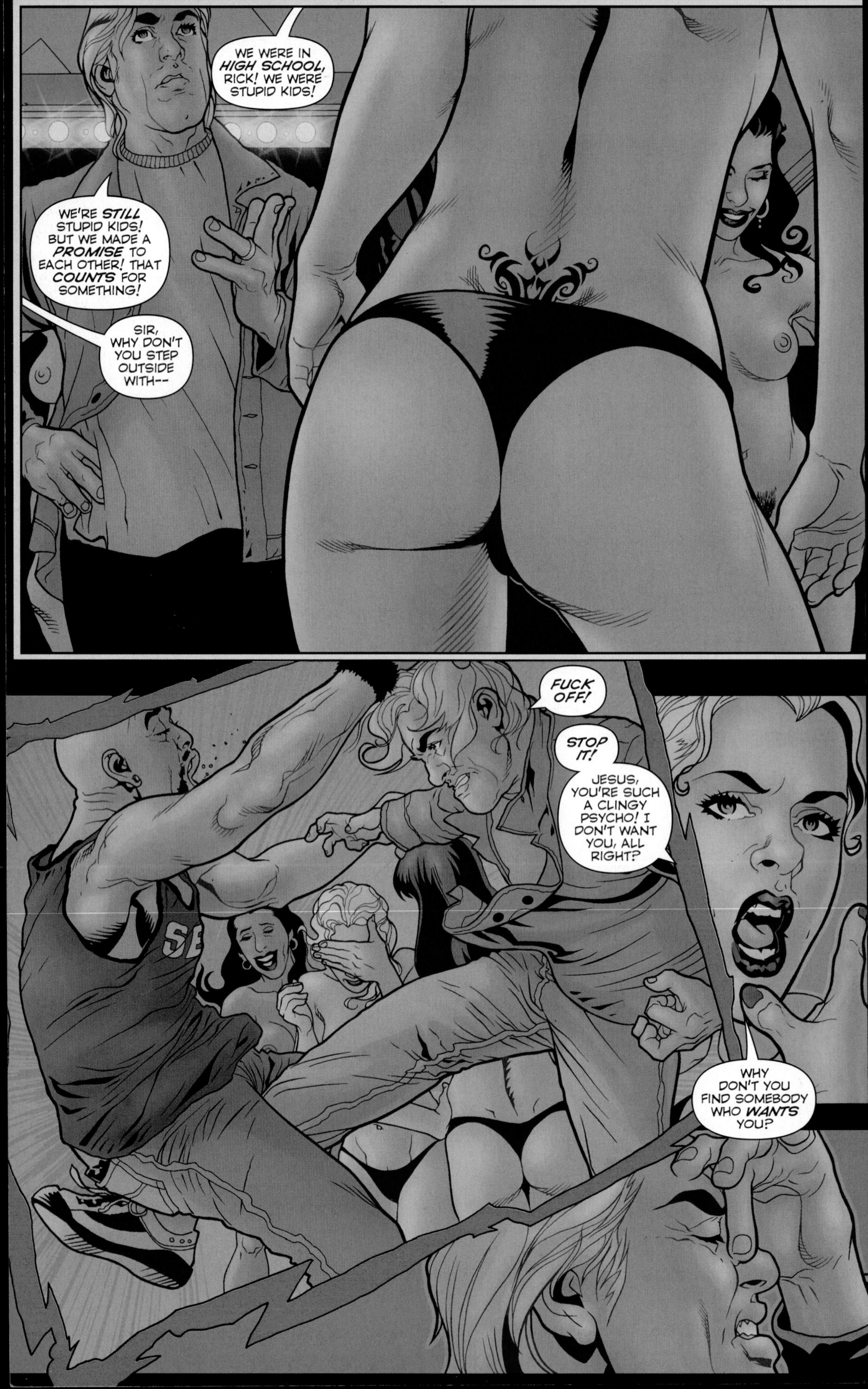
WE WERE IN *HIGH SCHOOL,* RICK! WE WERE STUPID KIDS!
WE'RE ***STILL*** STUPID KIDS! BUT WE MADE A ***PROMISE*** TO EACH OTHER! THAT ***COUNTS*** FOR SOMETHING!
SIR, WHY DON'T YOU STEP OUTSIDE WITH--
FUCK OFF!
STOP IT!
JESUS, YOU'RE SUCH A CLINGY PSYCHO! I DON'T WANT YOU, ALL RIGHT?
WHY DON'T YOU FIND SOMEBODY WHO ***WANTS*** YOU?

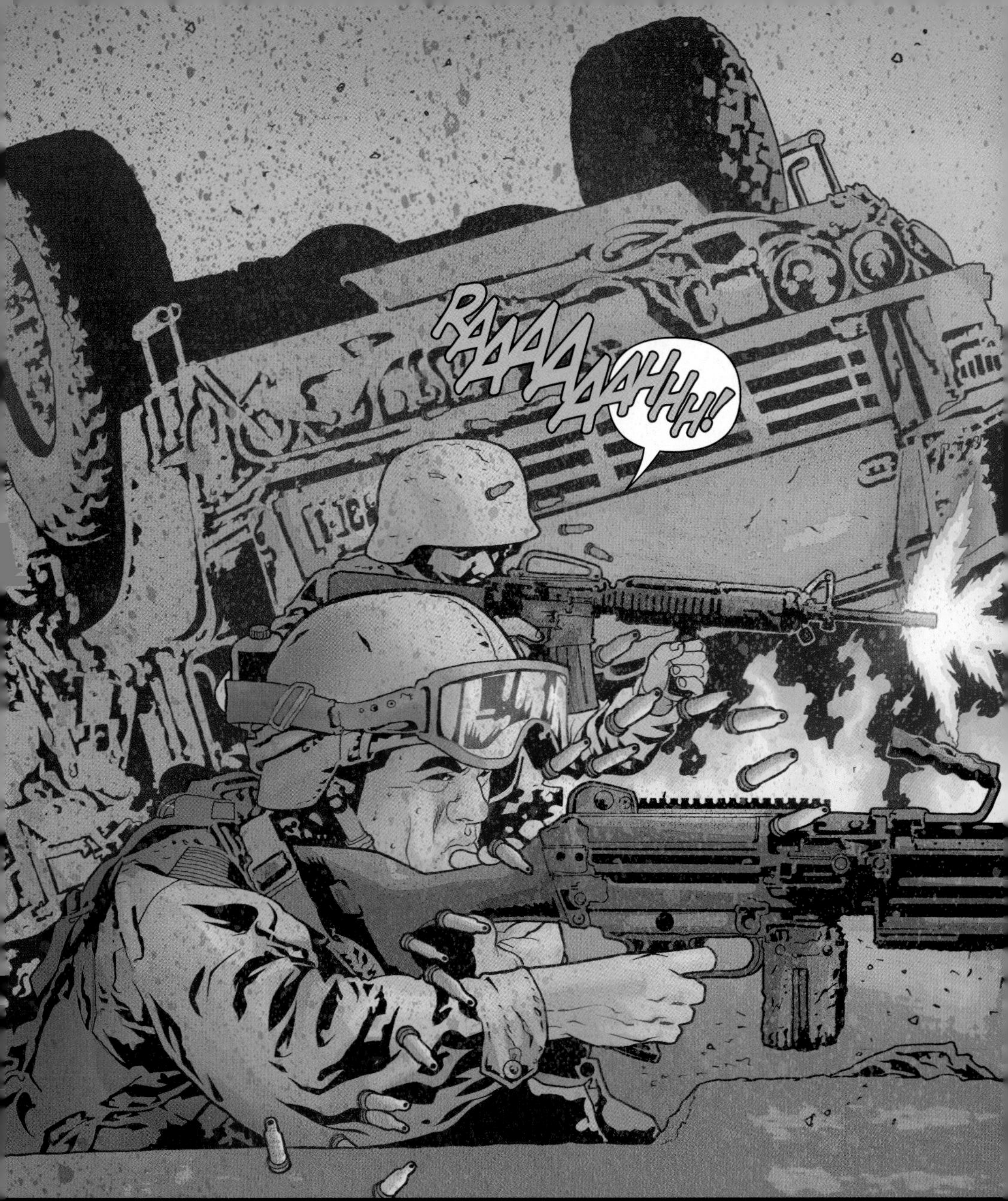
RAAAAAAAHHH!

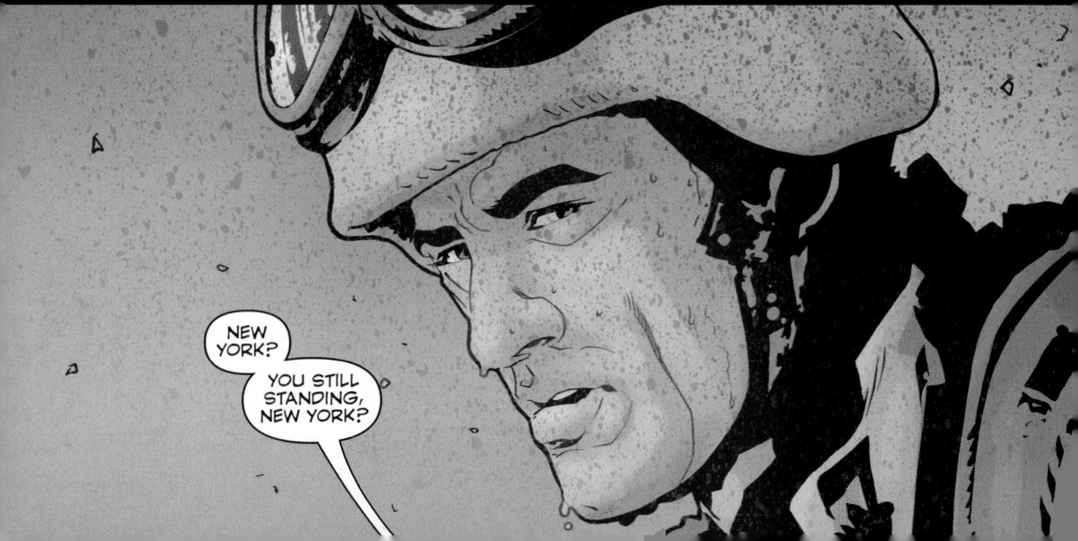
NEW YORK?
YOU STILL STANDING, NEW YORK?

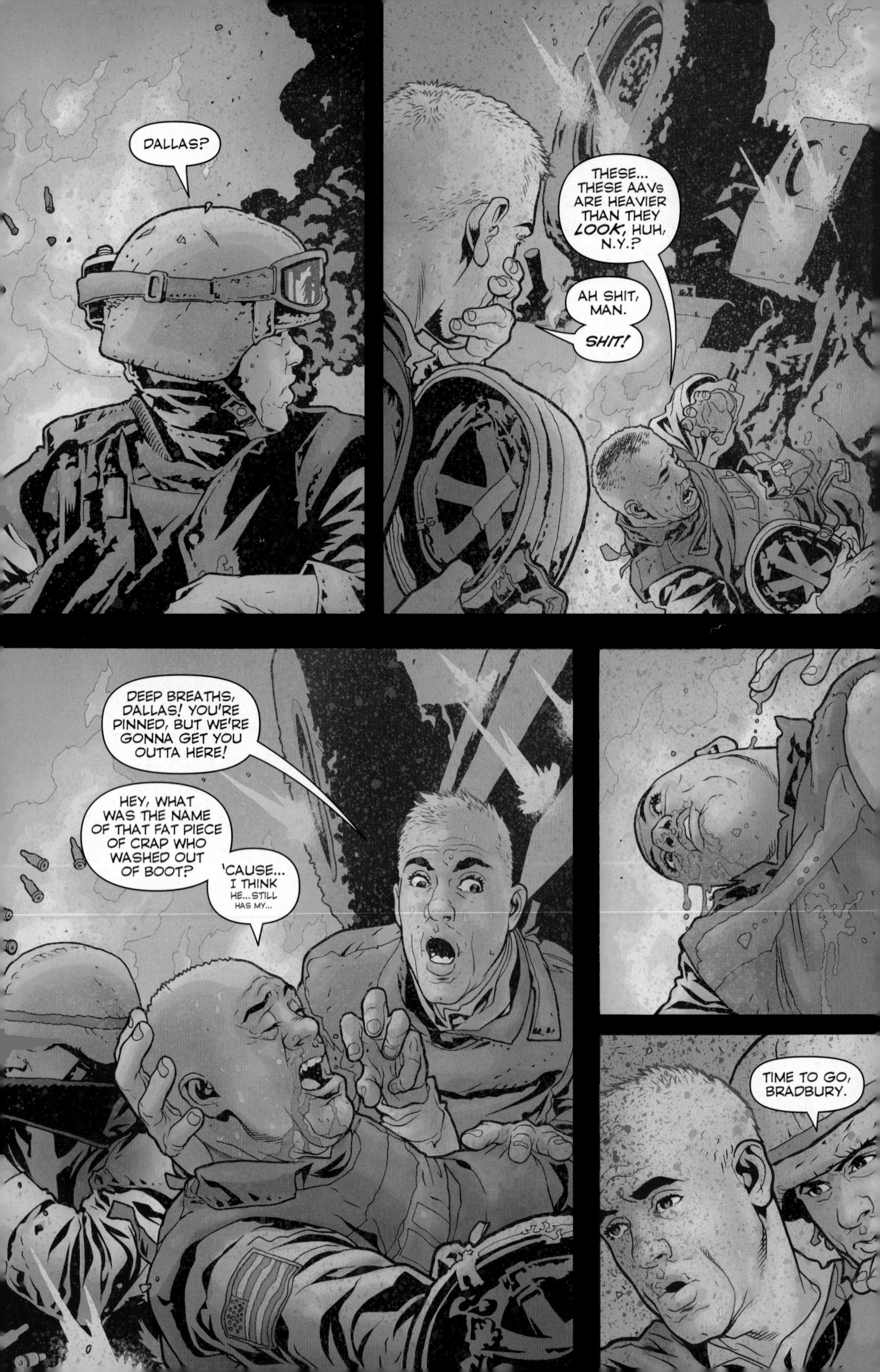
DALLAS?
THESE... THESE AAVs ARE HEAVIER THAN THEY LOOK, HUH, N.Y.?
AH SHIT, MAN.
SHIT!
DEEP BREATHS, DALLAS! YOU'RE PINNED, BUT WE'RE GONNA GET YOU OUTTA HERE!
HEY, WHAT WAS THE NAME OF THAT FAT PIECE OF CRAP WHO WASHED OUT OF BOOT?
'CAUSE... I THINK HE...STILL HAS MY...
TIME TO GO, BRADBURY.

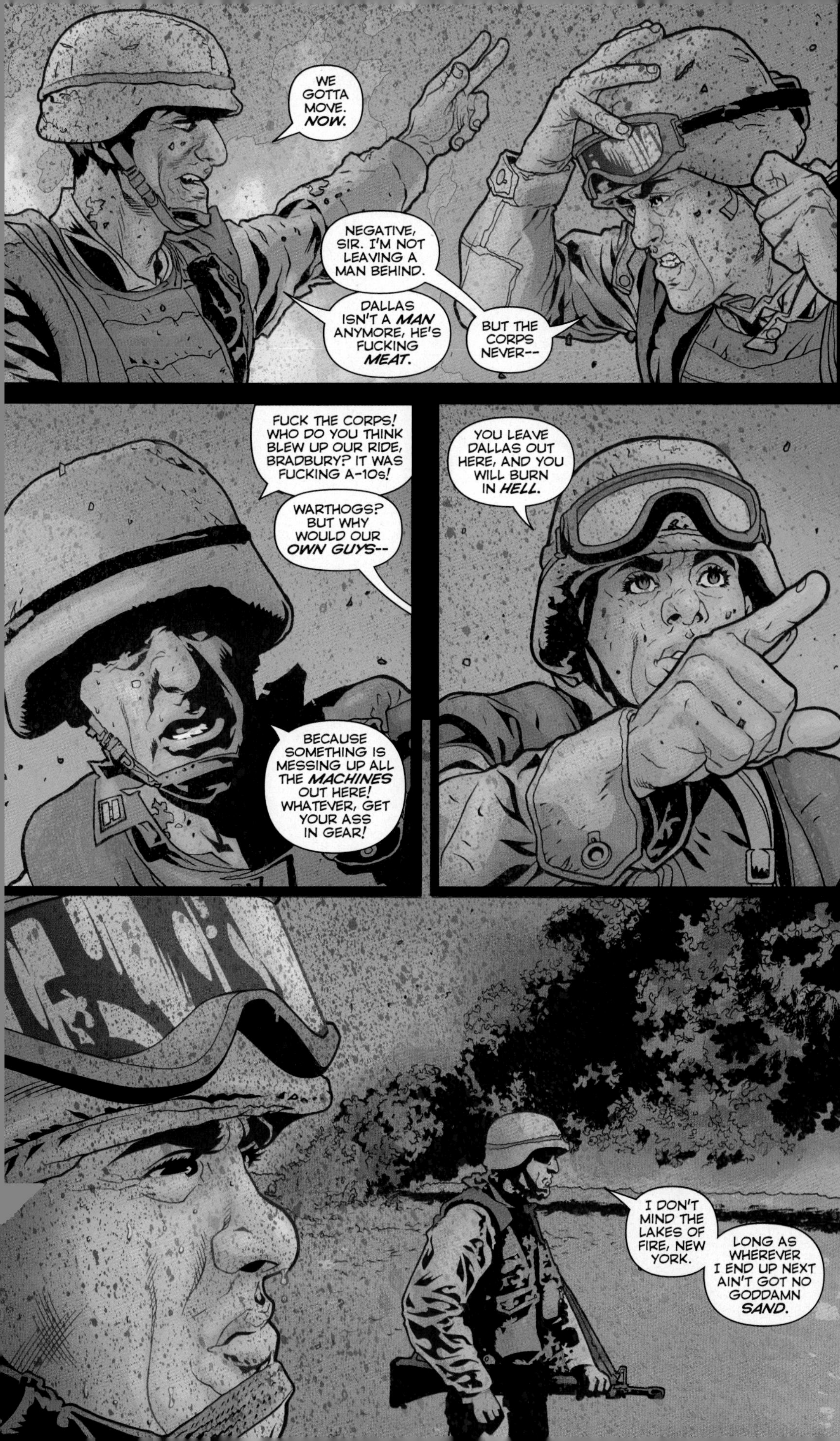
WE GOTTA MOVE. NOW.
NEGATIVE, SIR. I'M NOT LEAVING A MAN BEHIND.
DALLAS ISN'T A MAN ANYMORE, HE'S FUCKING MEAT.
BUT THE CORPS NEVER--
FUCK THE CORPS! WHO DO YOU THINK BLEW UP OUR RIDE, BRADBURY? IT WAS FUCKING A-10s!
WARTHOGS? BUT WHY WOULD OUR OWN GUYS--
BECAUSE SOMETHING IS MESSING UP ALL THE MACHINES OUT HERE! WHATEVER, GET YOUR ASS IN GEAR!
YOU LEAVE DALLAS OUT HERE, AND YOU WILL BURN IN HELL.
I DON'T MIND THE LAKES OF FIRE, NEW YORK.
LONG AS WHEREVER I END UP NEXT AIN'T GOT NO GODDAMN SAND.

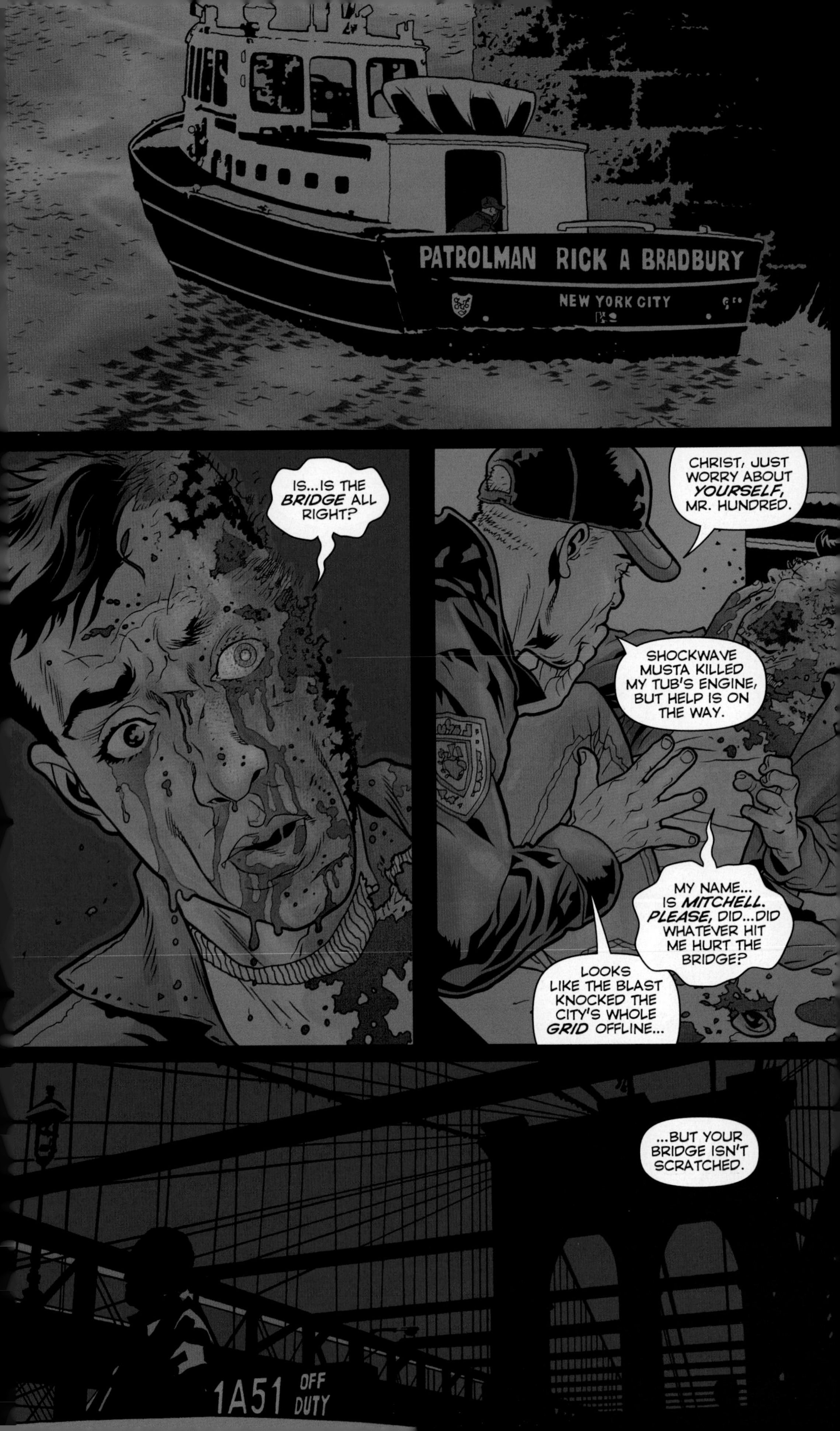
PATROLMAN RICK A BRADBURY
NEW YORK CITY
IS...IS THE BRIDGE ALL RIGHT?
CHRIST, JUST WORRY ABOUT YOURSELF, MR. HUNDRED.
SHOCKWAVE MUSTA KILLED MY TUB'S ENGINE, BUT HELP IS ON THE WAY.
MY NAME... IS MITCHELL. PLEASE, DID...DID WHATEVER HIT ME HURT THE BRIDGE?
LOOKS LIKE THE BLAST KNOCKED THE CITY'S WHOLE GRID OFFLINE...
...BUT YOUR BRIDGE ISN'T SCRATCHED.
1A51 OFF DUTY

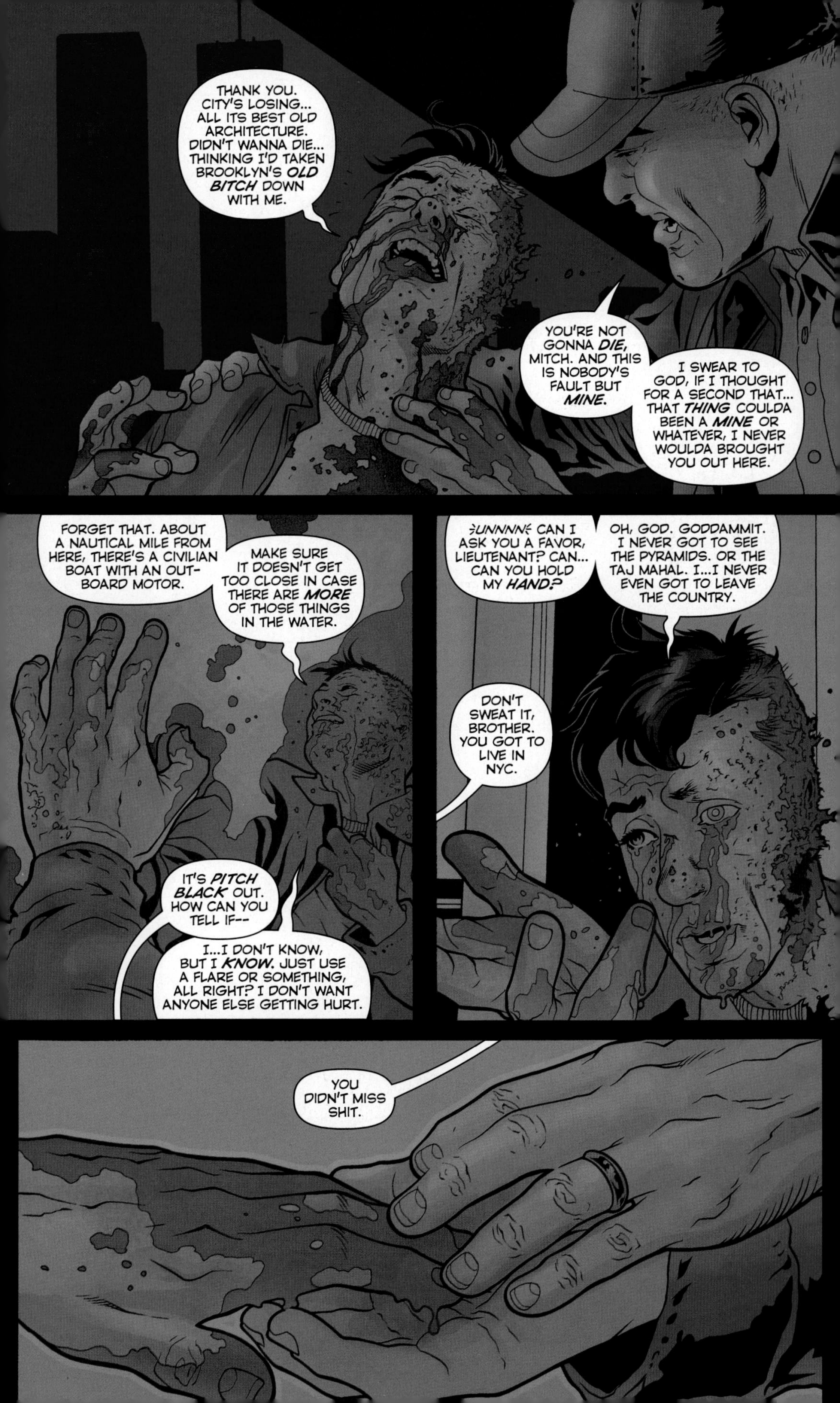
THANK YOU. CITY'S LOSING... ALL ITS BEST OLD ARCHITECTURE. DIDN'T WANNA DIE... THINKING I'D TAKEN BROOKLYN'S OLD BITCH DOWN WITH ME.
YOU'RE NOT GONNA DIE, MITCH. AND THIS IS NOBODY'S FAULT BUT MINE.
I SWEAR TO GOD, IF I THOUGHT FOR A SECOND THAT... THAT THING COULDA BEEN A MINE OR WHATEVER, I NEVER WOULDA BROUGHT YOU OUT HERE.
FORGET THAT. ABOUT A NAUTICAL MILE FROM HERE, THERE'S A CIVILIAN BOAT WITH AN OUT-BOARD MOTOR.
MAKE SURE IT DOESN'T GET TOO CLOSE IN CASE THERE ARE MORE OF THOSE THINGS IN THE WATER.
IT'S PITCH BLACK OUT. HOW CAN YOU TELL IF--
I...I DON'T KNOW, BUT I KNOW. JUST USE A FLARE OR SOMETHING, ALL RIGHT? I DON'T WANT ANYONE ELSE GETTING HURT.
UNNNN CAN I ASK YOU A FAVOR, LIEUTENANT? CAN... CAN YOU HOLD MY HAND?
OH, GOD. GODDAMMIT. I NEVER GOT TO SEE THE PYRAMIDS. OR THE TAJ MAHAL. I...I NEVER EVEN GOT TO LEAVE THE COUNTRY.
DON'T SWEAT IT, BROTHER. YOU GOT TO LIVE IN NYC.
YOU DIDN'T MISS SHIT.

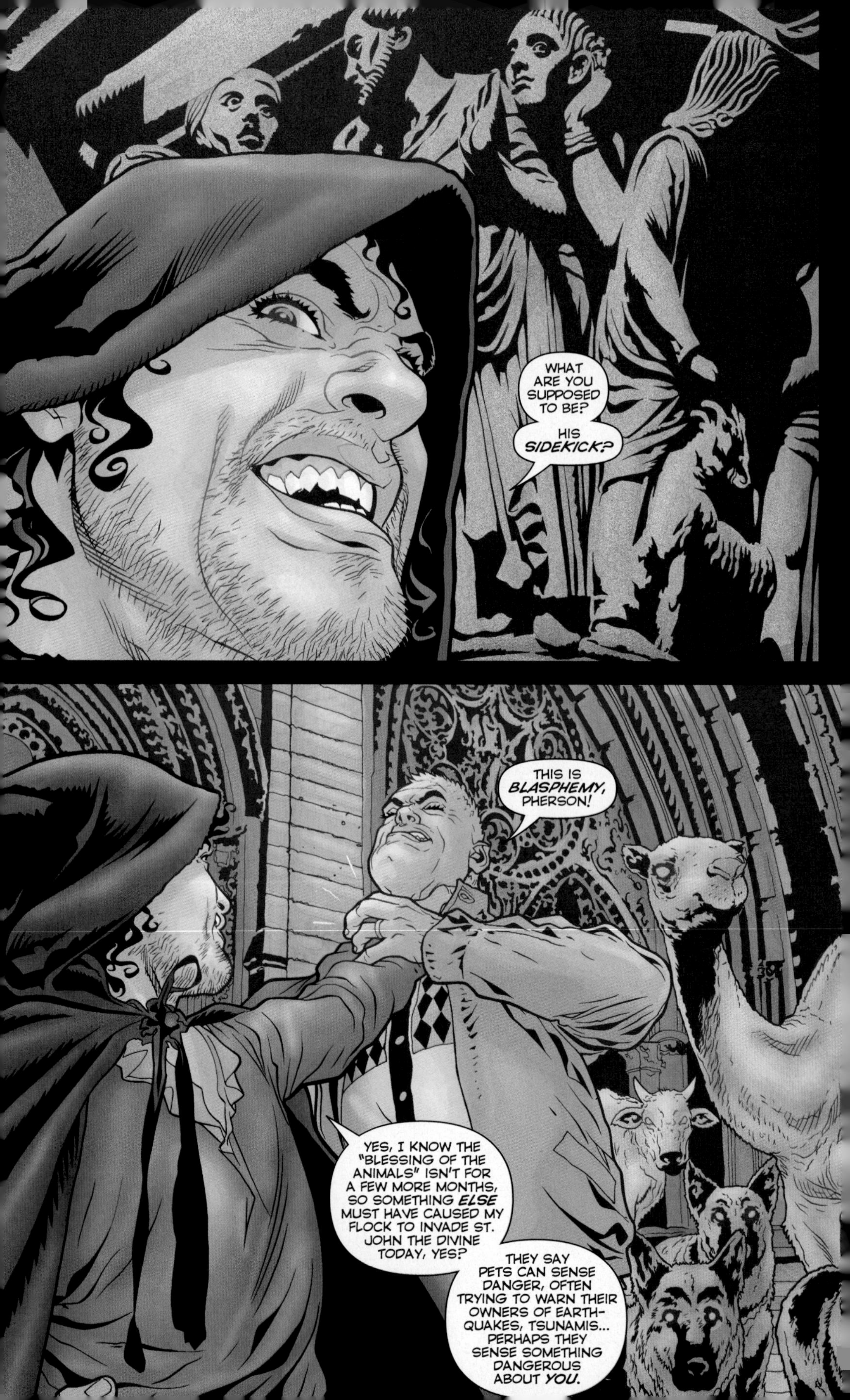
WHAT ARE YOU SUPPOSED TO BE?
HIS SIDEKICK?
THIS IS BLASPHEMY, PHERSON!
YES, I KNOW THE "BLESSING OF THE ANIMALS" ISN'T FOR A FEW MORE MONTHS, SO SOMETHING ELSE MUST HAVE CAUSED MY FLOCK TO INVADE ST. JOHN THE DIVINE TODAY, YES?
THEY SAY PETS CAN SENSE DANGER, OFTEN TRYING TO WARN THEIR OWNERS OF EARTH-QUAKES, TSUNAMIS... PERHAPS THEY SENSE SOMETHING DANGEROUS ABOUT YOU.

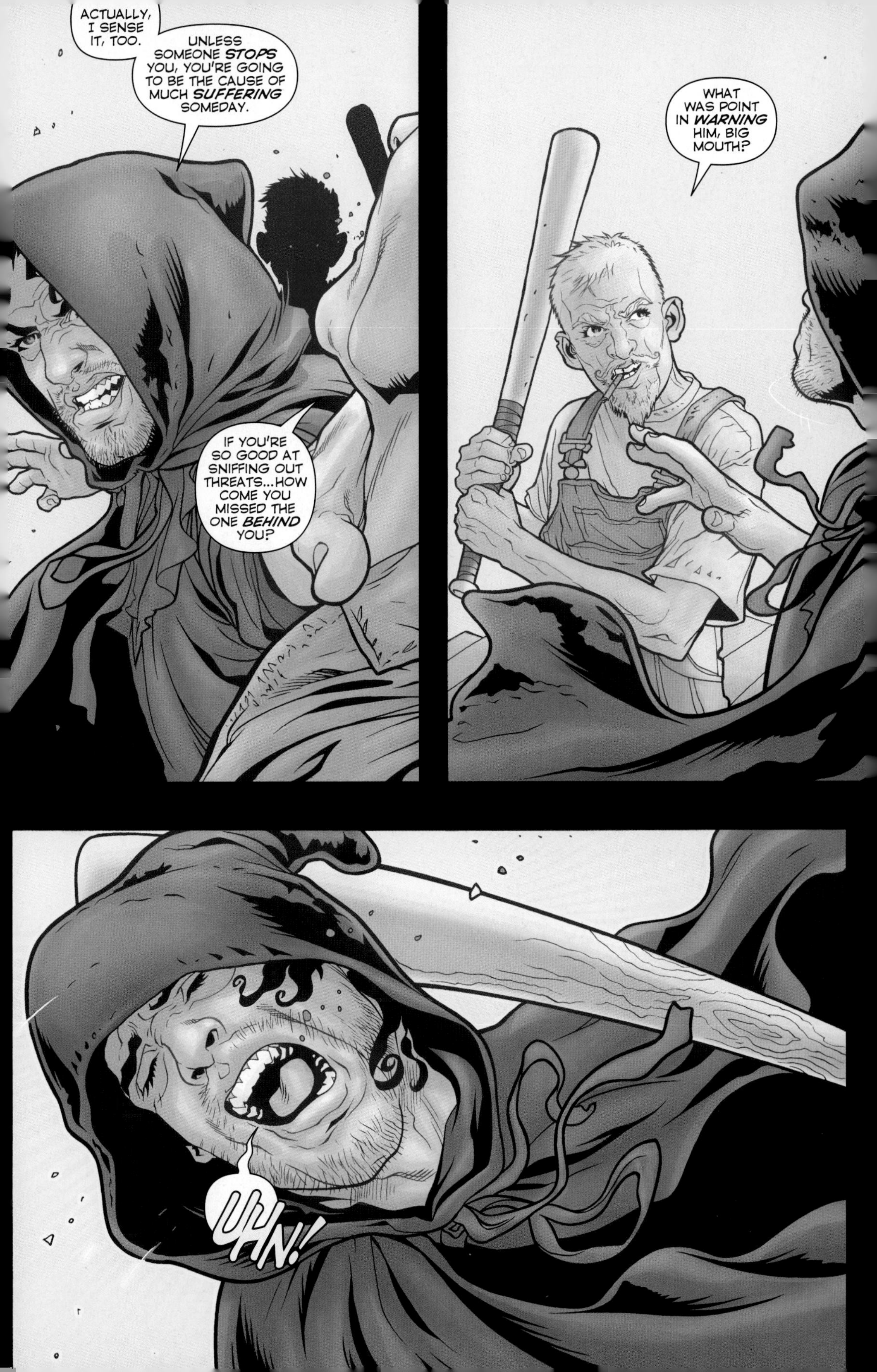
ACTUALLY, I SENSE IT, TOO.
UNLESS SOMEONE STOPS YOU, YOU'RE GOING TO BE THE CAUSE OF MUCH SUFFERING SOMEDAY.
IF YOU'RE SO GOOD AT SNIFFING OUT THREATS...HOW COME YOU MISSED THE ONE BEHIND YOU?
WHAT WAS POINT IN WARNING HIM, BIG MOUTH?
UHN!

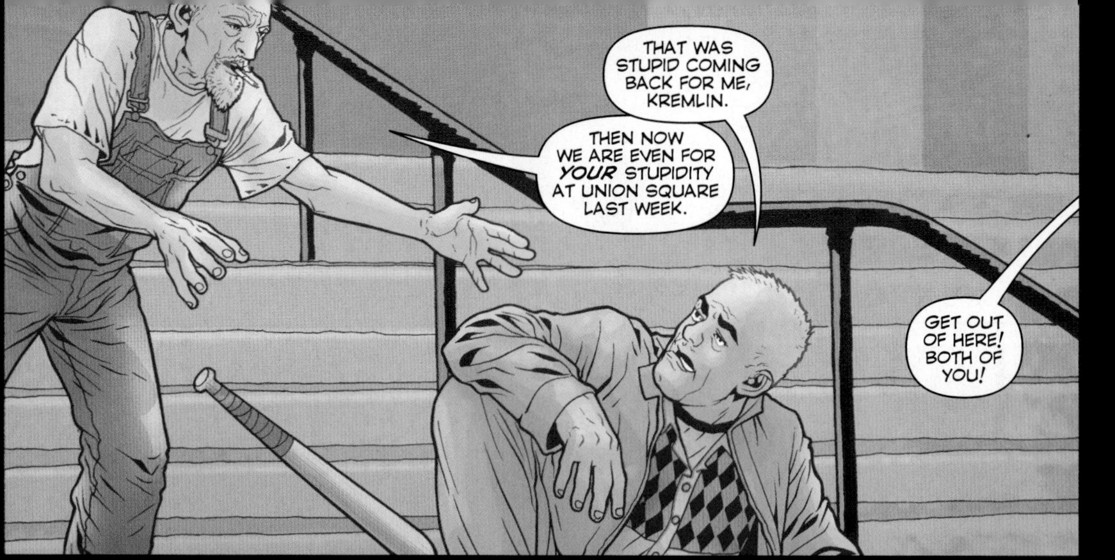
THAT WAS STUPID COMING BACK FOR ME, KREMLIN.
THEN NOW WE ARE EVEN FOR YOUR STUPIDITY AT UNION SQUARE LAST WEEK.
GET OUT OF HERE! BOTH OF YOU!

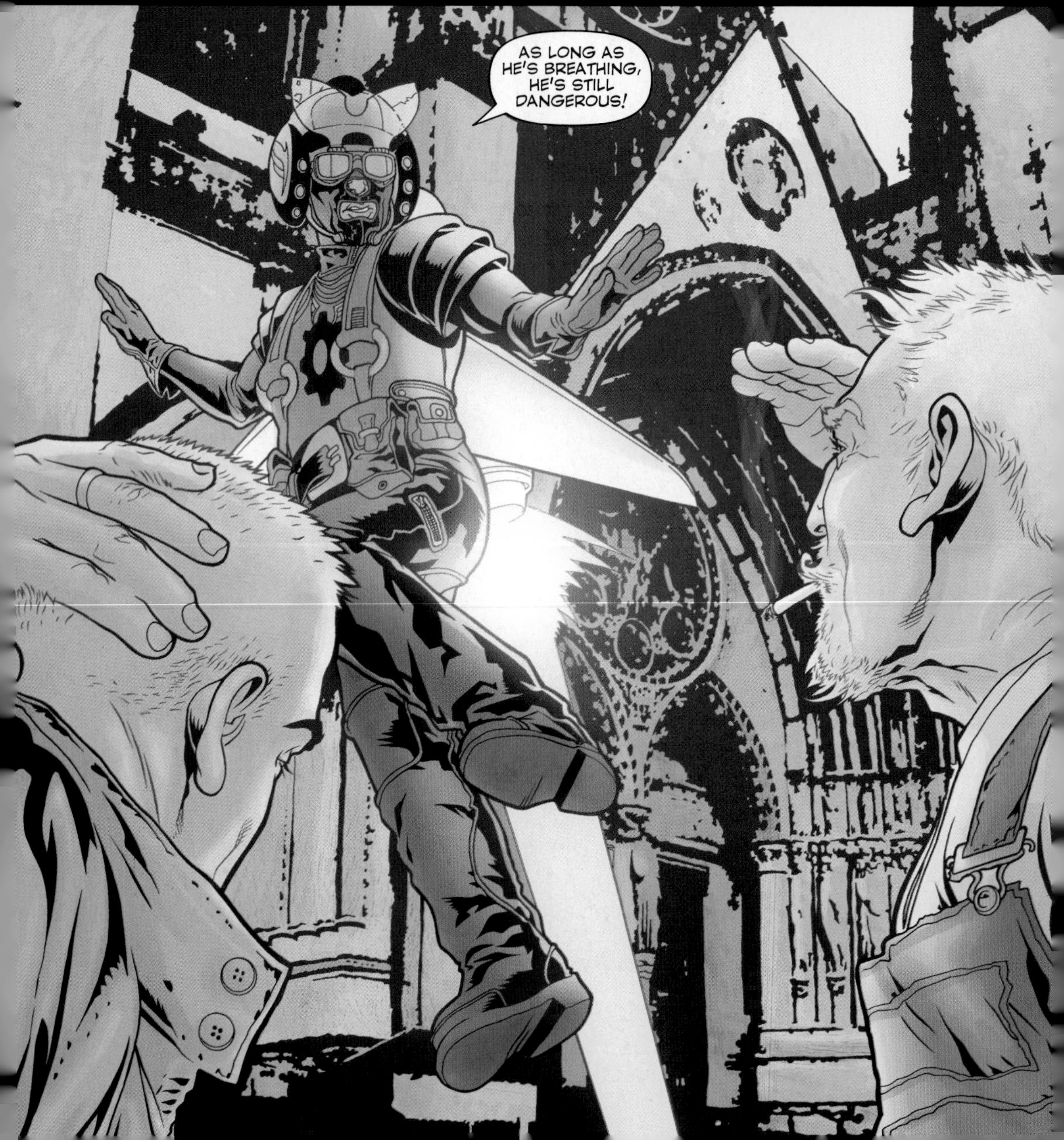
AS LONG AS HE'S BREATHING, HE'S STILL DANGEROUS!

ALL TRAFFIC CAMERAS ON THIS BLOCK, KINDLY DELETE ANY FOOTAGE OF MY PARTNERS, WOULD YOU?

I'M GONNA TRY TO GET PHERSON TO THE *DEPRIVATION TANK* I BUILT BEFORE HIS *BATS* CATCH UP WITH ME!

KREM, TRACK ME ON G.P.S. AND KEEP ME APPRISED OF MY FUEL SITCH!

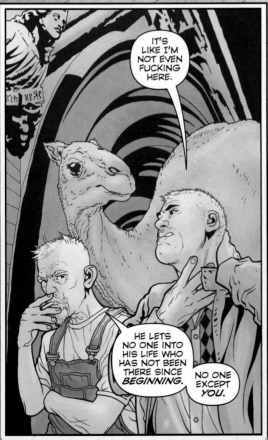

IT'S LIKE I'M NOT EVEN FUCKING HERE.

HE LETS NO ONE INTO HIS LIFE WHO HAS NOT BEEN THERE SINCE *BEGINNING*.

NO ONE EXCEPT *YOU*.

YEAH? WHY? YOU THINK HE SEES A BIT OF HIMSELF IN ME?

NO, DUMMY, IN YOU HE SEES *CHAUFFEUR*.

HE MIGHT BE ABLE TO HAVE CONVERSATIONS WITH CARS, BUT MITCHELL STILL DRIVES FOR *SHIT*.

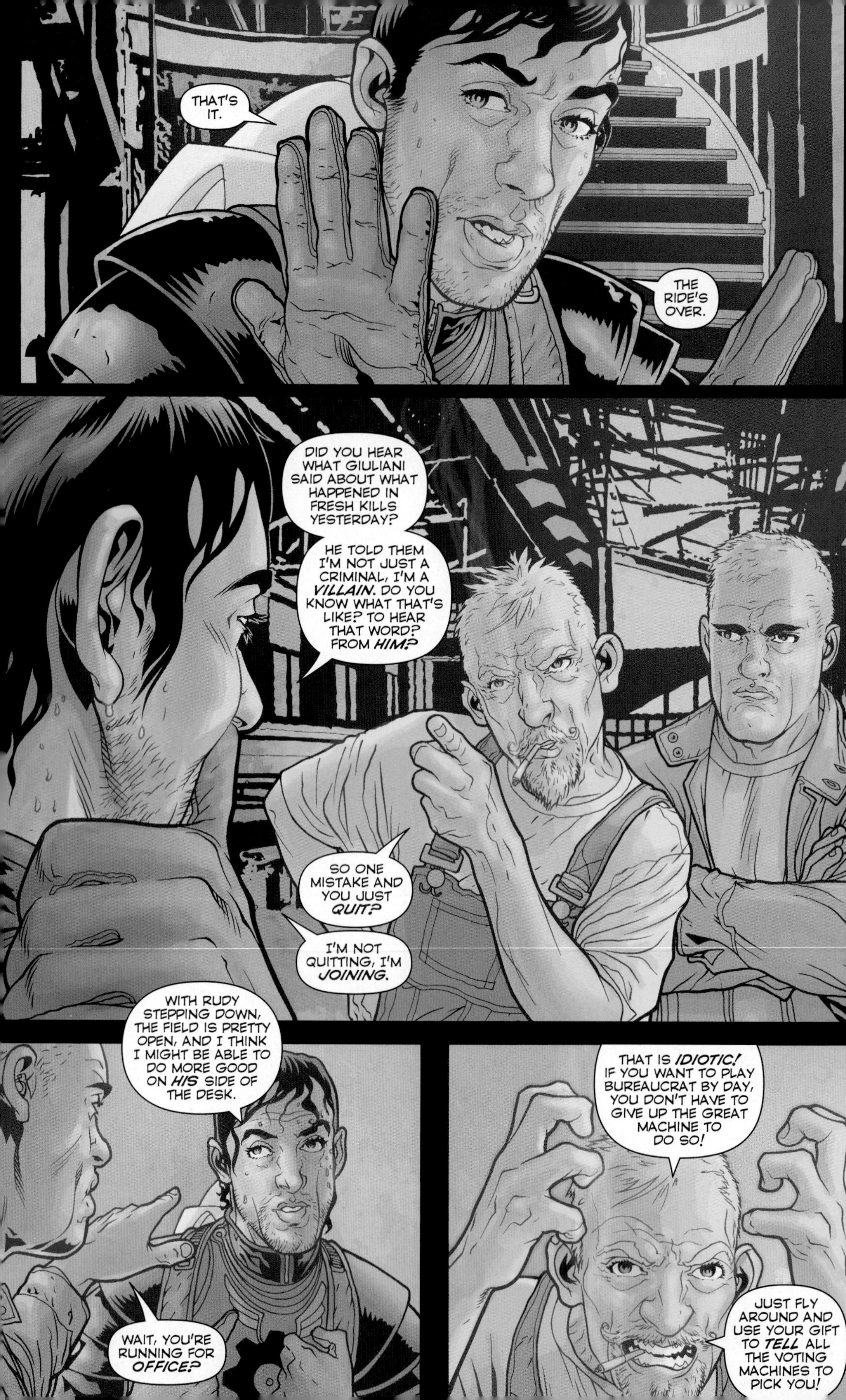
THAT'S IT.
THE RIDE'S OVER.
DID YOU HEAR WHAT GIULIANI SAID ABOUT WHAT HAPPENED IN FRESH KILLS YESTERDAY?
HE TOLD THEM I'M NOT JUST A CRIMINAL, I'M A VILLAIN. DO YOU KNOW WHAT THAT'S LIKE? TO HEAR THAT WORD? FROM HIM?
SO ONE MISTAKE AND YOU JUST QUIT?
I'M NOT QUITTING, I'M JOINING.
WITH RUDY STEPPING DOWN, THE FIELD IS PRETTY OPEN, AND I THINK I MIGHT BE ABLE TO DO MORE GOOD ON HIS SIDE OF THE DESK.
WAIT, YOU'RE RUNNING FOR OFFICE?
THAT IS IDIOTIC! IF YOU WANT TO PLAY BUREAUCRAT BY DAY, YOU DON'T HAVE TO GIVE UP THE GREAT MACHINE TO DO SO!
JUST FLY AROUND AND USE YOUR GIFT TO TELL ALL THE VOTING MACHINES TO PICK YOU!

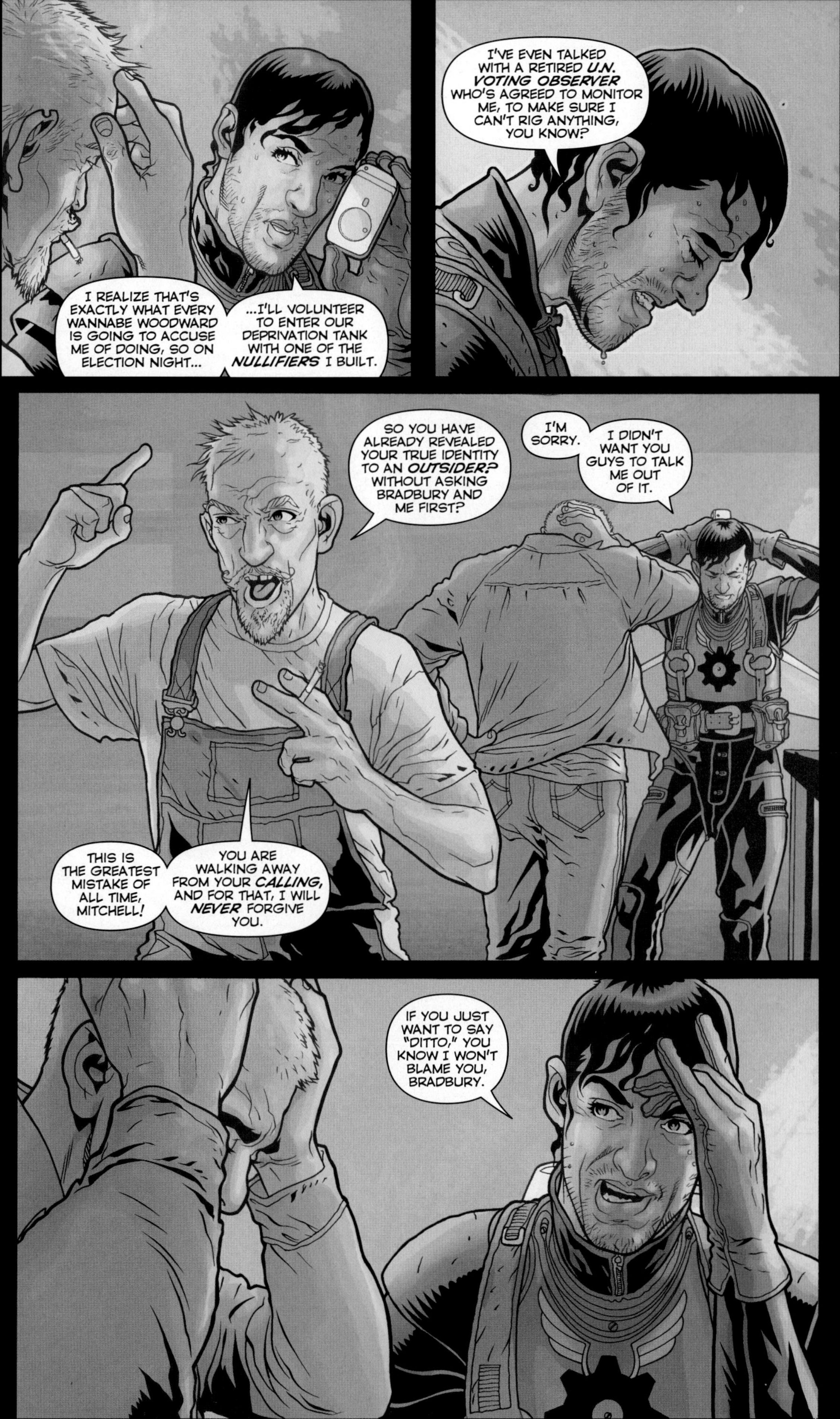
I REALIZE THAT'S EXACTLY WHAT EVERY WANNABE WOODWARD IS GOING TO ACCUSE ME OF DOING, SO ON ELECTION NIGHT...
...I'LL VOLUNTEER TO ENTER OUR DEPRIVATION TANK WITH ONE OF THE NULLIFIERS I BUILT.
I'VE EVEN TALKED WITH A RETIRED U.N. VOTING OBSERVER WHO'S AGREED TO MONITOR ME, TO MAKE SURE I CAN'T RIG ANYTHING, YOU KNOW?
SO YOU HAVE ALREADY REVEALED YOUR TRUE IDENTITY TO AN OUTSIDER? WITHOUT ASKING BRADBURY AND ME FIRST?
I'M SORRY.
I DIDN'T WANT YOU GUYS TO TALK ME OUT OF IT.
THIS IS THE GREATEST MISTAKE OF ALL TIME, MITCHELL!
YOU ARE WALKING AWAY FROM YOUR CALLING, AND FOR THAT, I WILL NEVER FORGIVE YOU.
IF YOU JUST WANT TO SAY "DITTO," YOU KNOW I WON'T BLAME YOU, BRADBURY.

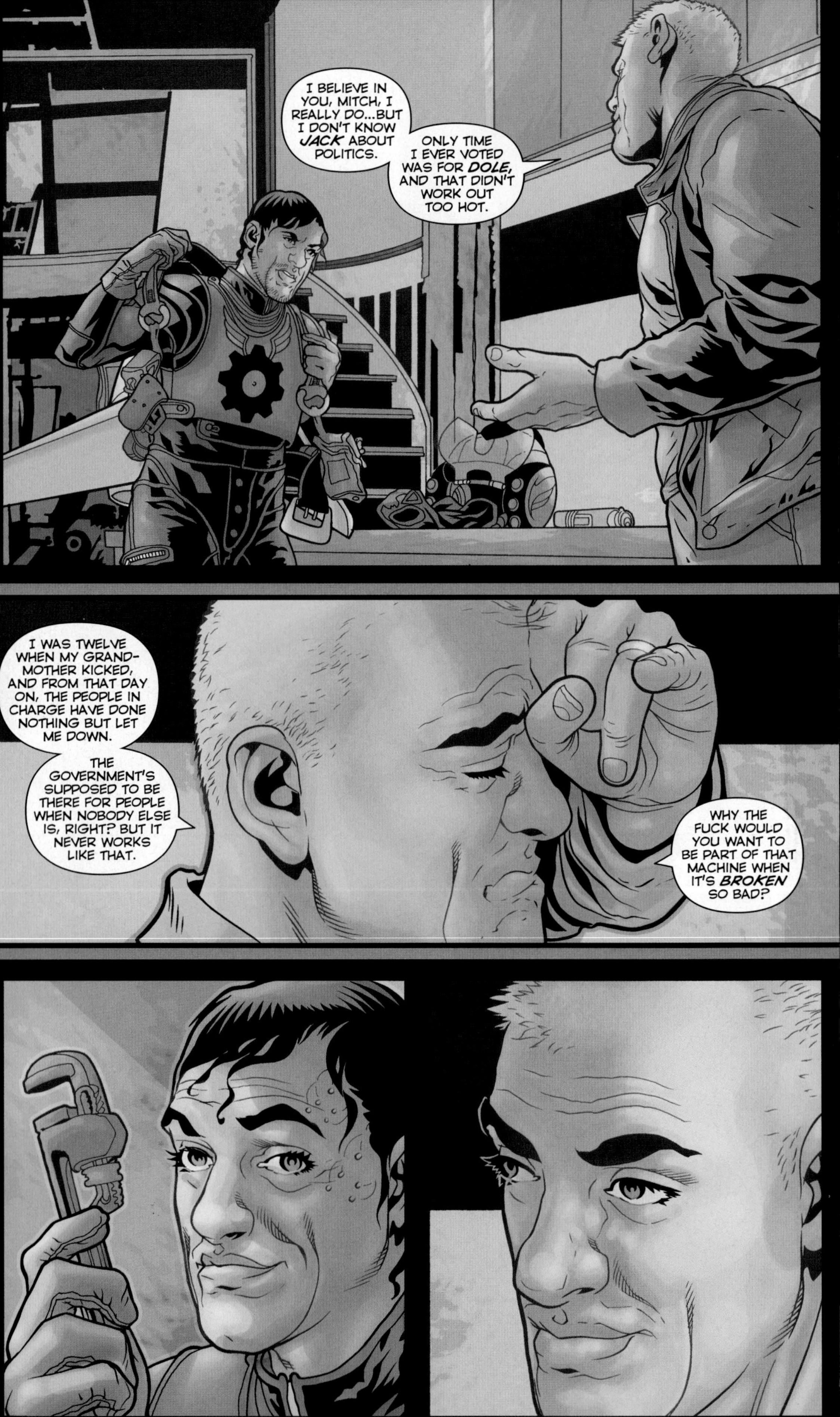
I BELIEVE IN YOU, MITCH, I REALLY DO...BUT I DON'T KNOW *JACK* ABOUT POLITICS.
ONLY TIME I EVER VOTED WAS FOR *DOLE*, AND THAT DIDN'T WORK OUT TOO HOT.
I WAS TWELVE WHEN MY GRAND-MOTHER KICKED, AND FROM THAT DAY ON, THE PEOPLE IN CHARGE HAVE DONE NOTHING BUT LET ME DOWN.
THE GOVERNMENT'S SUPPOSED TO BE THERE FOR PEOPLE WHEN NOBODY ELSE IS, RIGHT? BUT IT NEVER WORKS LIKE THAT.
WHY THE FUCK WOULD YOU WANT TO BE PART OF THAT MACHINE WHEN IT'S *BROKEN* SO BAD?

DON'T DO IT, MAN.

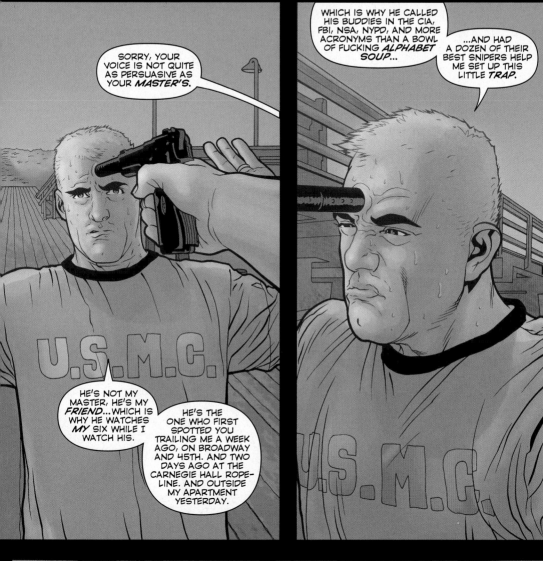

SORRY, YOUR VOICE IS NOT QUITE AS PERSUASIVE AS YOUR *MASTER'S*.

WHICH IS WHY HE CALLED HIS BUDDIES IN THE CIA, FBI, NSA, NYPD, AND MORE ACRONYMS THAN A BOWL OF FUCKING *ALPHABET SOUP*...

...AND HAD A DOZEN OF THEIR BEST SNIPERS HELP ME SET UP THIS LITTLE *TRAP*.

HE'S NOT MY *FRIEND*...WHICH IS WHY HE WATCHES *MY* SIX WHILE I WATCH HIS.

HE'S THE ONE WHO FIRST SPOTTED YOU TRAILING ME A WEEK AGO, ON BROADWAY AND 45TH. AND TWO DAYS AGO AT THE CARNEGIE HALL ROPE-LINE. AND OUTSIDE MY APARTMENT YESTERDAY.

...

BULLSHIT.

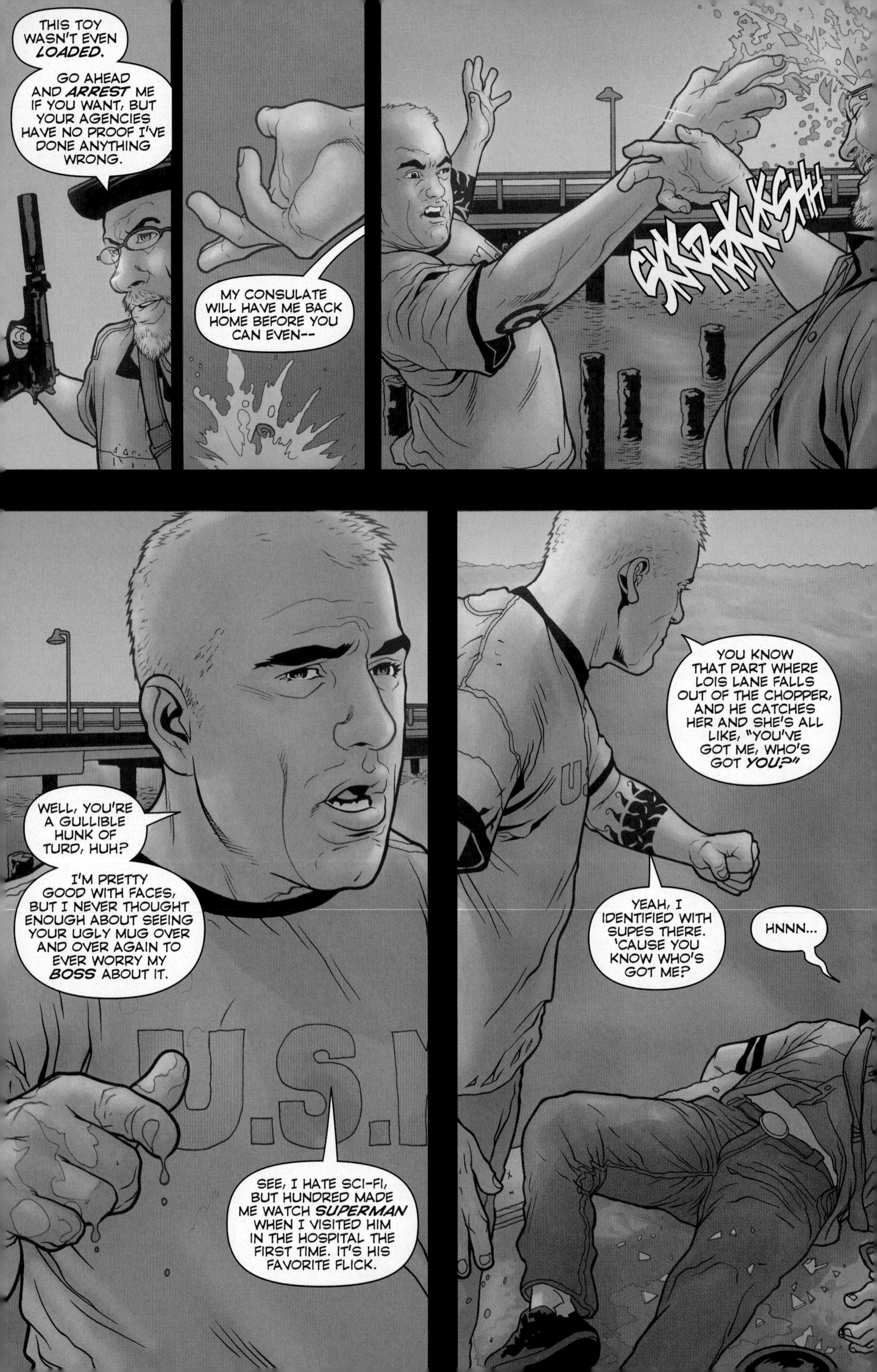
THIS TOY WASN'T EVEN *LOADED*.
GO AHEAD AND *ARREST* ME IF YOU WANT, BUT YOUR AGENCIES HAVE NO PROOF I'VE DONE ANYTHING WRONG.
MY CONSULATE WILL HAVE ME BACK HOME BEFORE YOU CAN EVEN--
SKRAKKSHH
WELL, YOU'RE A GULLIBLE HUNK OF TURD, HUH?
I'M PRETTY GOOD WITH FACES, BUT I NEVER THOUGHT ENOUGH ABOUT SEEING YOUR UGLY MUG OVER AND OVER AGAIN TO EVER WORRY MY *BOSS* ABOUT IT.
SEE, I HATE SCI-FI, BUT HUNDRED MADE ME WATCH *SUPERMAN* WHEN I VISITED HIM IN THE HOSPITAL THE FIRST TIME. IT'S HIS FAVORITE FLICK.
YOU KNOW THAT PART WHERE LOIS LANE FALLS OUT OF THE CHOPPER, AND HE CATCHES HER AND SHE'S ALL LIKE, "YOU'VE GOT ME, WHO'S GOT *YOU?*"
YEAH, I IDENTIFIED WITH SUPES THERE. 'CAUSE YOU KNOW WHO'S GOT ME?
HNNN...

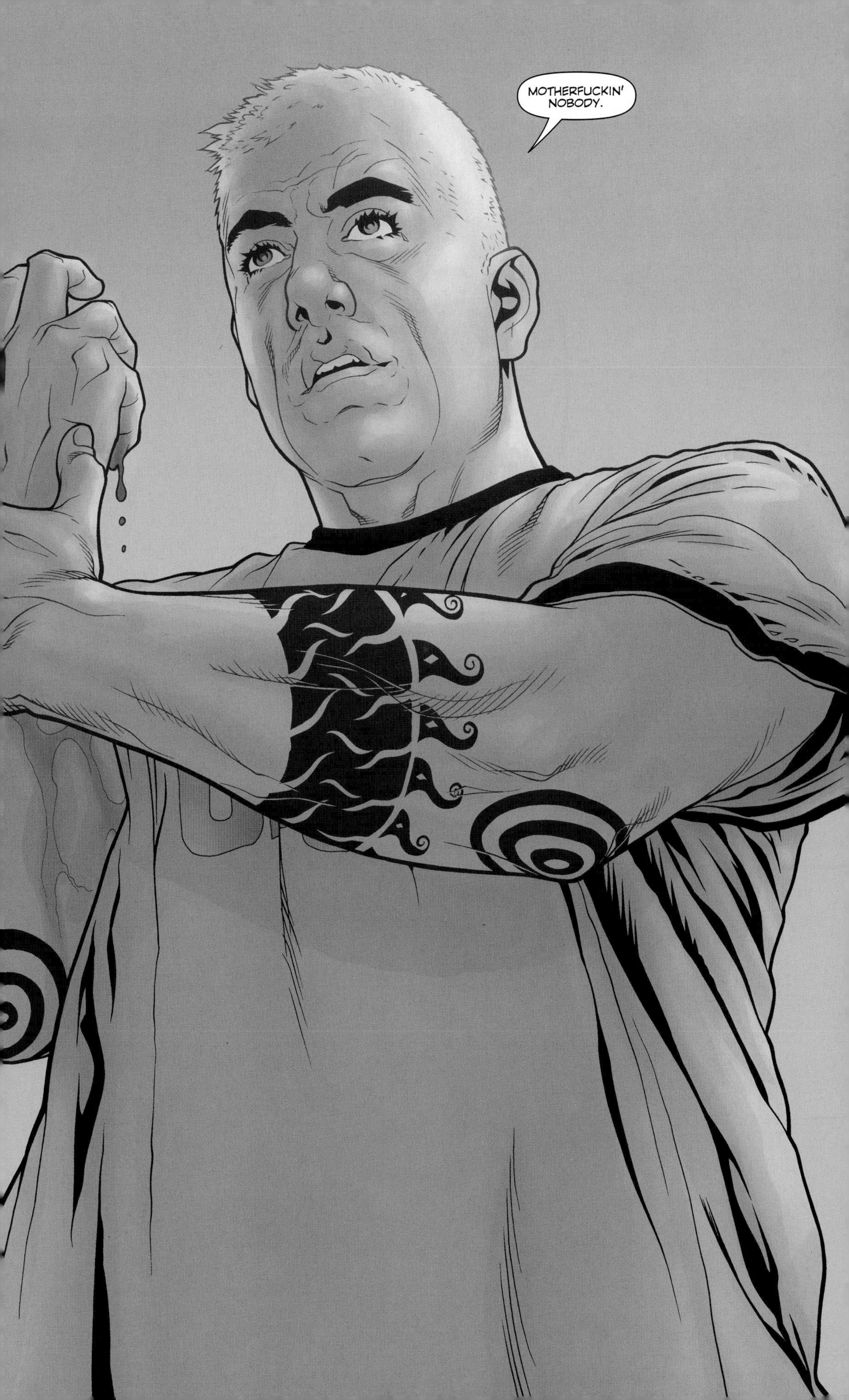
MOTHERFUCKIN' NOBODY.

CHAPTER 3 POWER DOWN

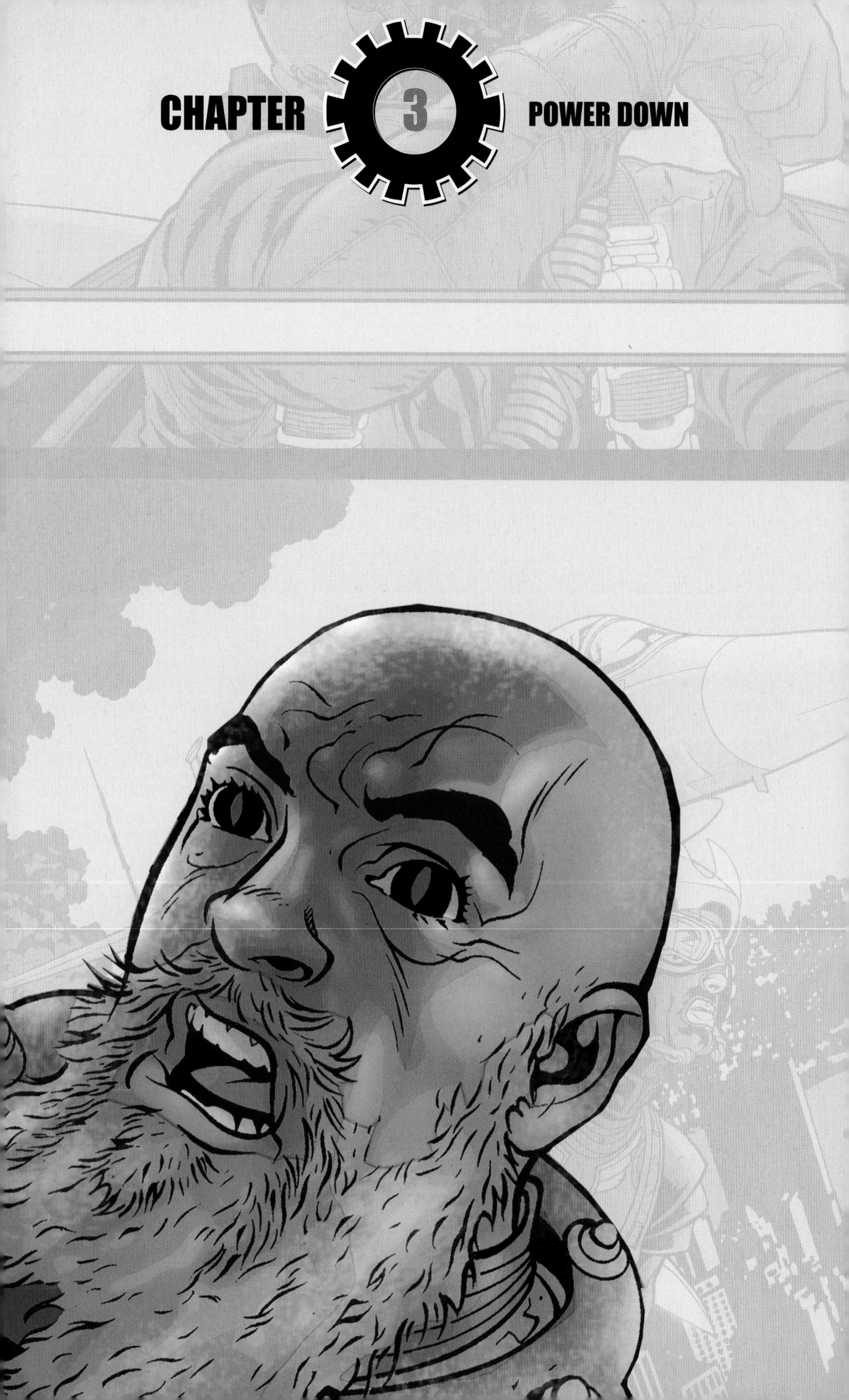

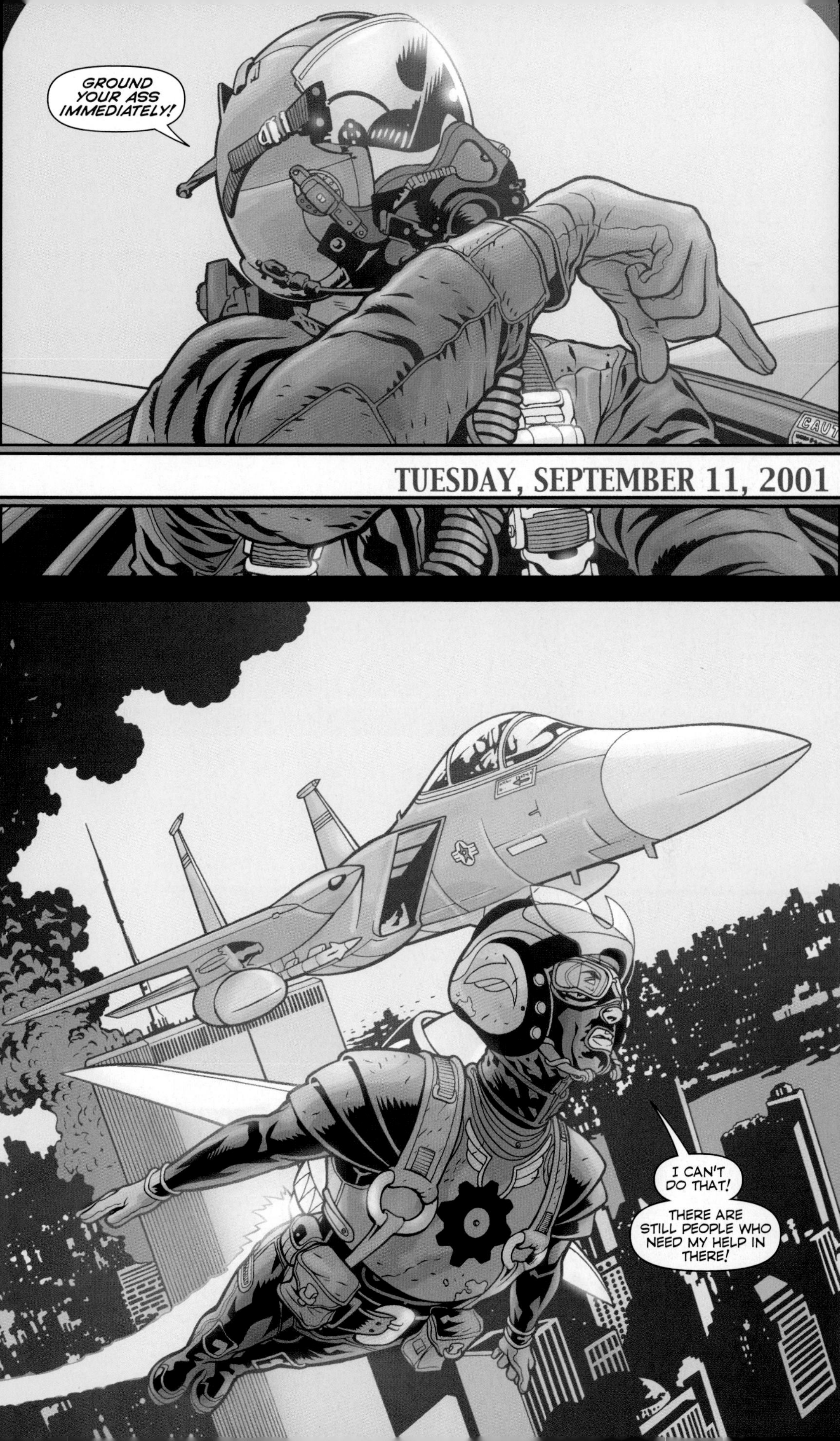
GROUND YOUR ASS IMMEDIATELY!
TUESDAY, SEPTEMBER 11, 2001
I CAN'T DO THAT!
THERE ARE STILL PEOPLE WHO NEED MY HELP IN THERE!

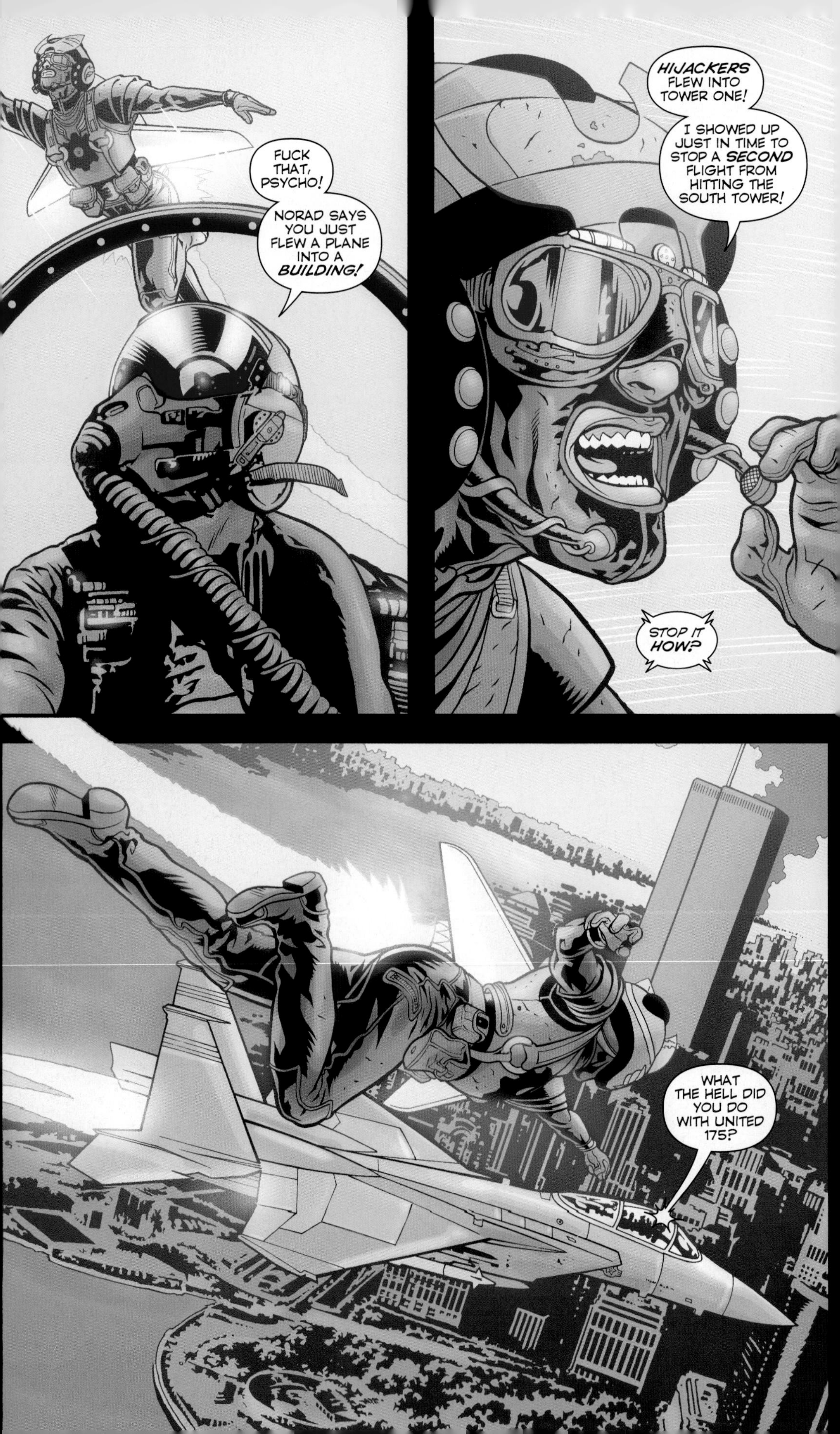
FUCK THAT, PSYCHO!
NORAD SAYS YOU JUST FLEW A PLANE INTO A BUILDING!
HIJACKERS FLEW INTO TOWER ONE!
I SHOWED UP JUST IN TIME TO STOP A SECOND FLIGHT FROM HITTING THE SOUTH TOWER!
STOP IT HOW?
WHAT THE HELL DID YOU DO WITH UNITED 175?

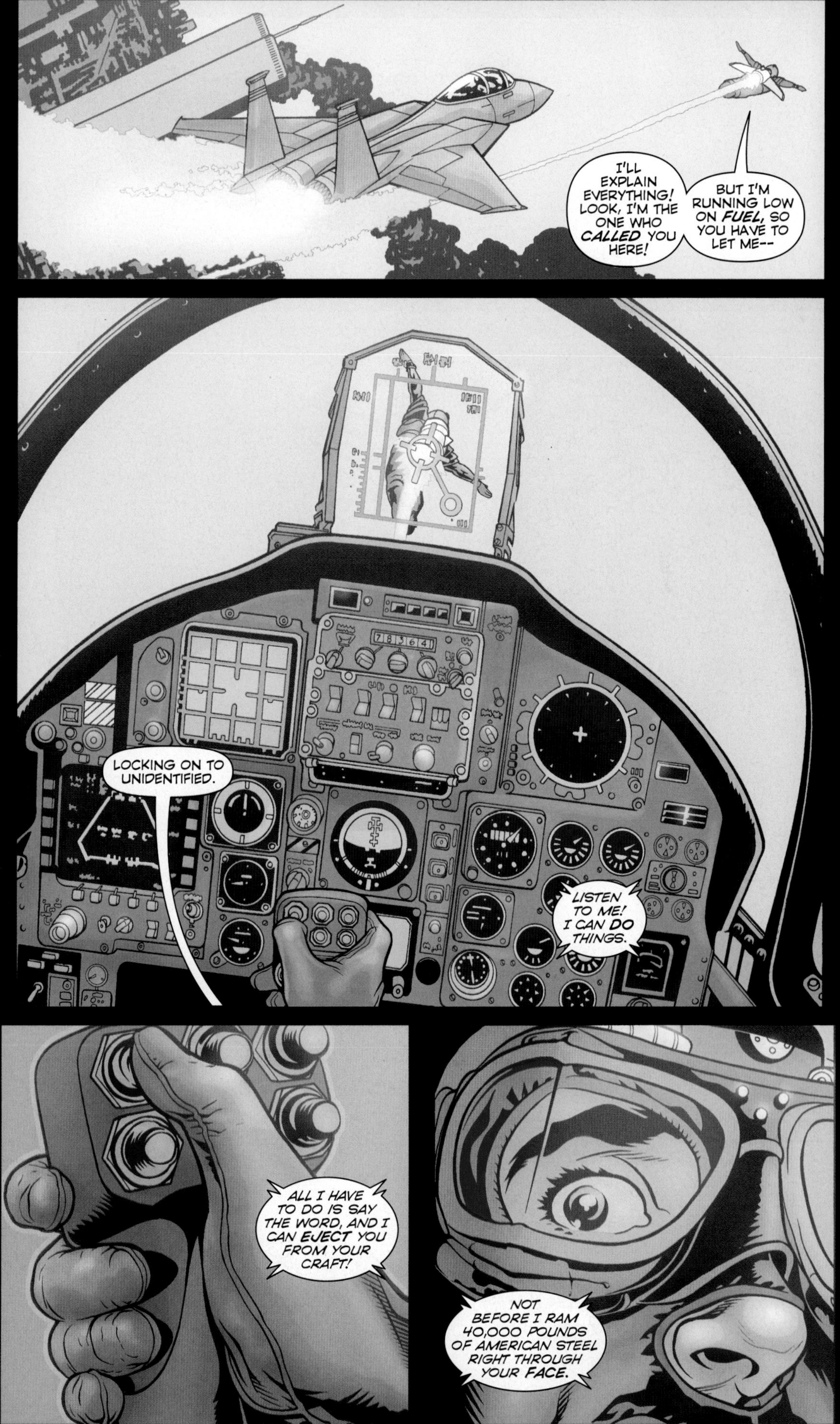
I'LL EXPLAIN EVERYTHING! LOOK, I'M THE ONE WHO CALLED YOU HERE!
BUT I'M RUNNING LOW ON FUEL, SO YOU HAVE TO LET ME--
LOCKING ON TO UNIDENTIFIED.
LISTEN TO ME! I CAN DO THINGS.
ALL I HAVE TO DO IS SAY THE WORD, AND I CAN EJECT YOU FROM YOUR CRAFT!
NOT BEFORE I RAM 40,000 POUNDS OF AMERICAN STEEL RIGHT THROUGH YOUR FACE.

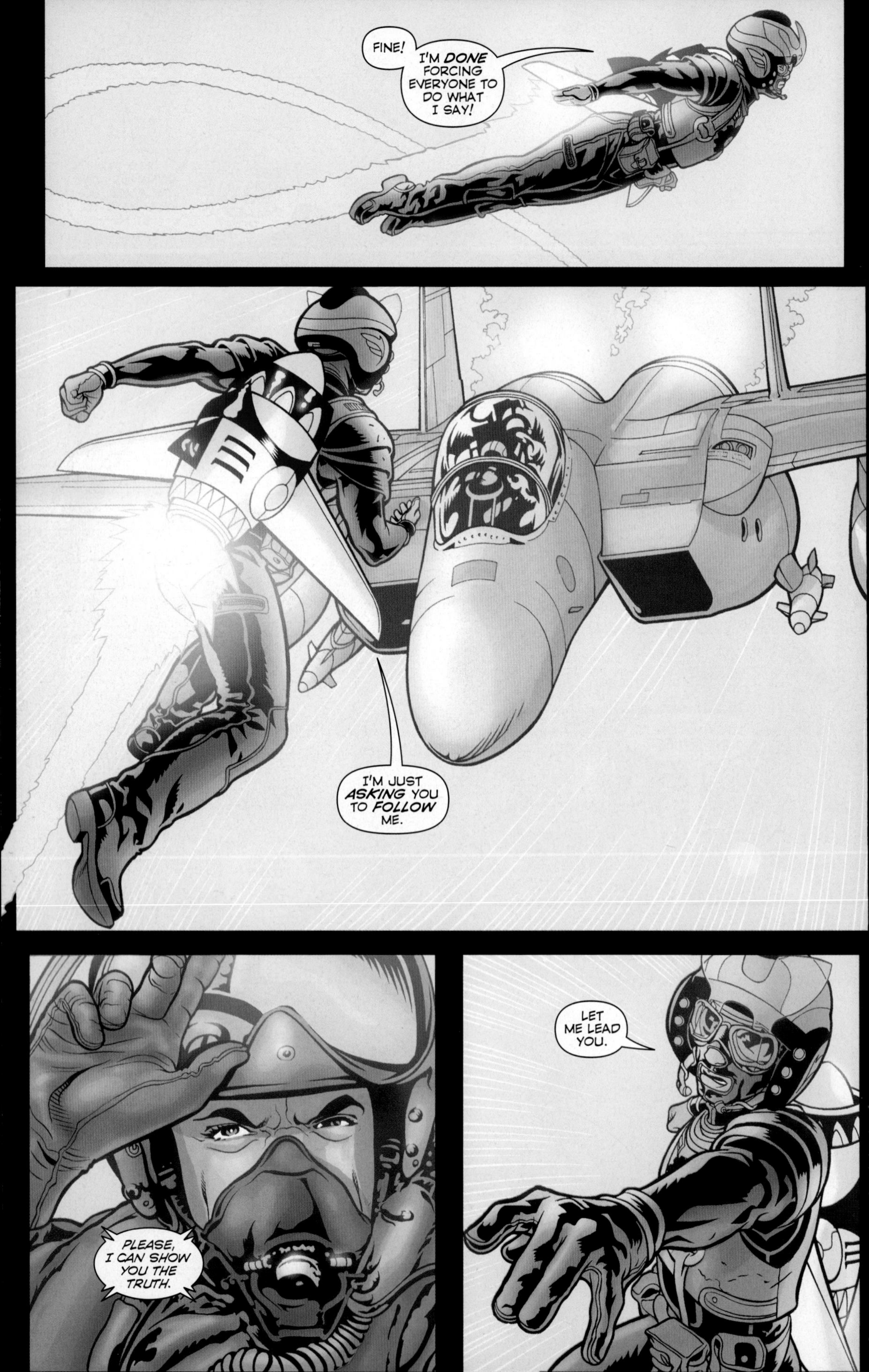
FINE!
I'M DONE FORCING EVERYONE TO DO WHAT I SAY!
I'M JUST ASKING YOU TO FOLLOW ME.
PLEASE, I CAN SHOW YOU THE TRUTH.
LET ME LEAD YOU.

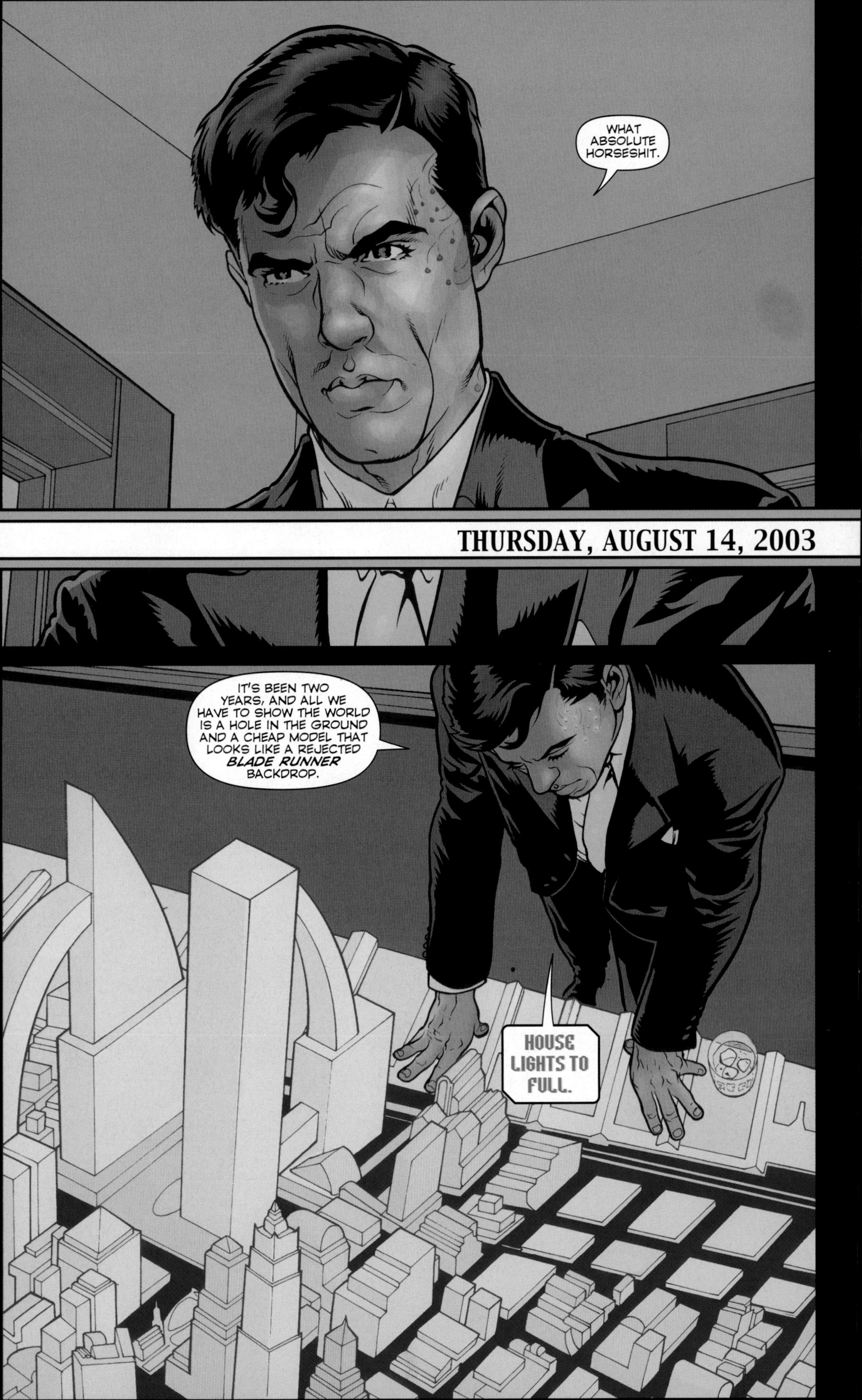
WHAT ABSOLUTE HORSESHIT.
THURSDAY, AUGUST 14, 2003
IT'S BEEN TWO YEARS, AND ALL WE HAVE TO SHOW THE WORLD IS A HOLE IN THE GROUND AND A CHEAP MODEL THAT LOOKS LIKE A REJECTED *BLADE RUNNER* BACKDROP.
HOUSE LIGHTS TO FULL.

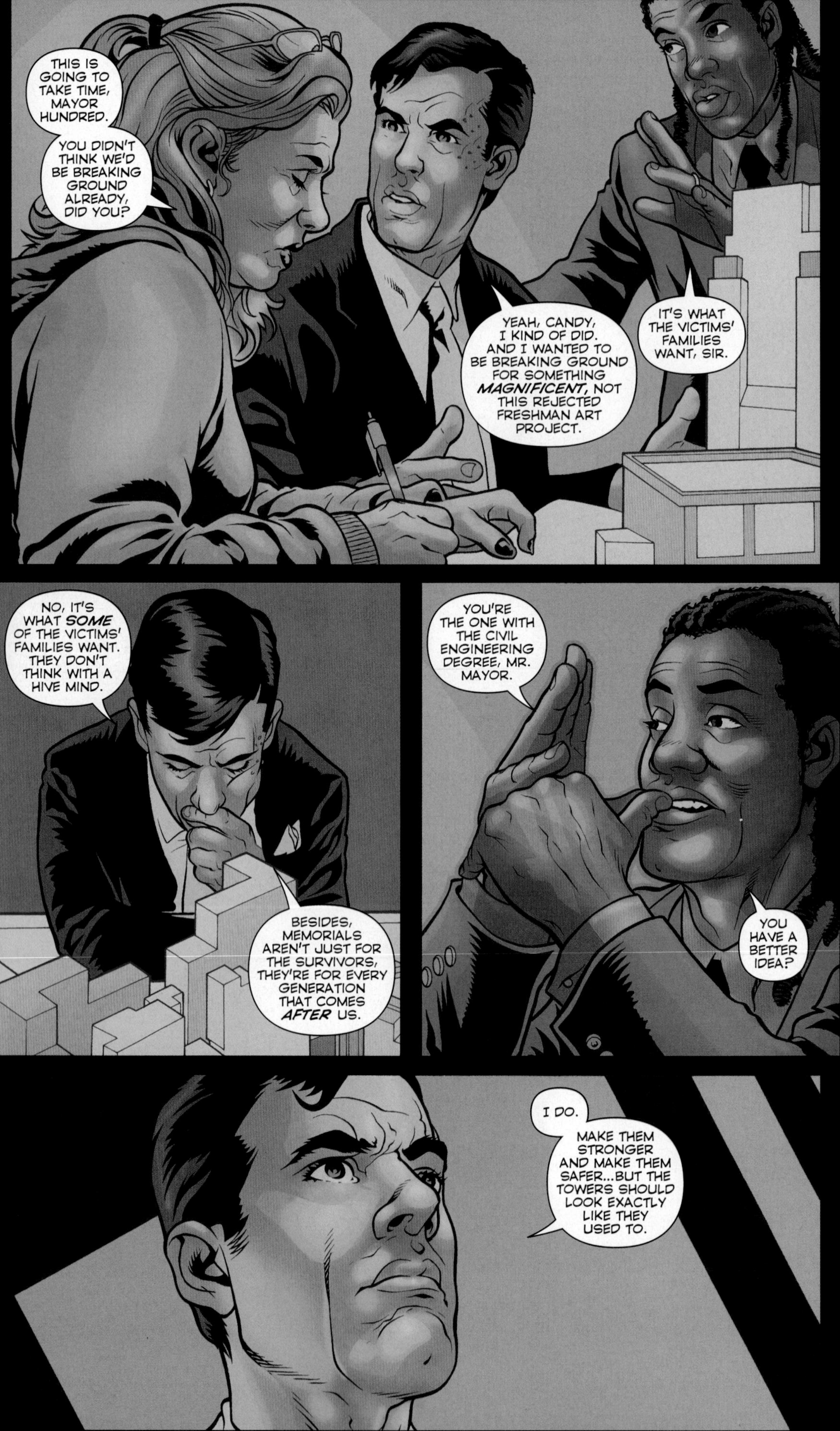
THIS IS GOING TO TAKE TIME, MAYOR HUNDRED.
YOU DIDN'T THINK WE'D BE BREAKING GROUND ALREADY, DID YOU?
YEAH, CANDY, I KIND OF DID. AND I WANTED TO BE BREAKING GROUND FOR SOMETHING *MAGNIFICENT,* NOT THIS REJECTED FRESHMAN ART PROJECT.
IT'S WHAT THE VICTIMS' FAMILIES WANT, SIR.
NO, IT'S WHAT *SOME* OF THE VICTIMS' FAMILIES WANT. THEY DON'T THINK WITH A HIVE MIND.
BESIDES, MEMORIALS AREN'T JUST FOR THE SURVIVORS, THEY'RE FOR EVERY GENERATION THAT COMES *AFTER* US.
YOU'RE THE ONE WITH THE CIVIL ENGINEERING DEGREE, MR. MAYOR.
YOU HAVE A BETTER IDEA?
I DO.
MAKE THEM STRONGER AND MAKE THEM SAFER...BUT THE TOWERS SHOULD LOOK EXACTLY LIKE THEY USED TO.

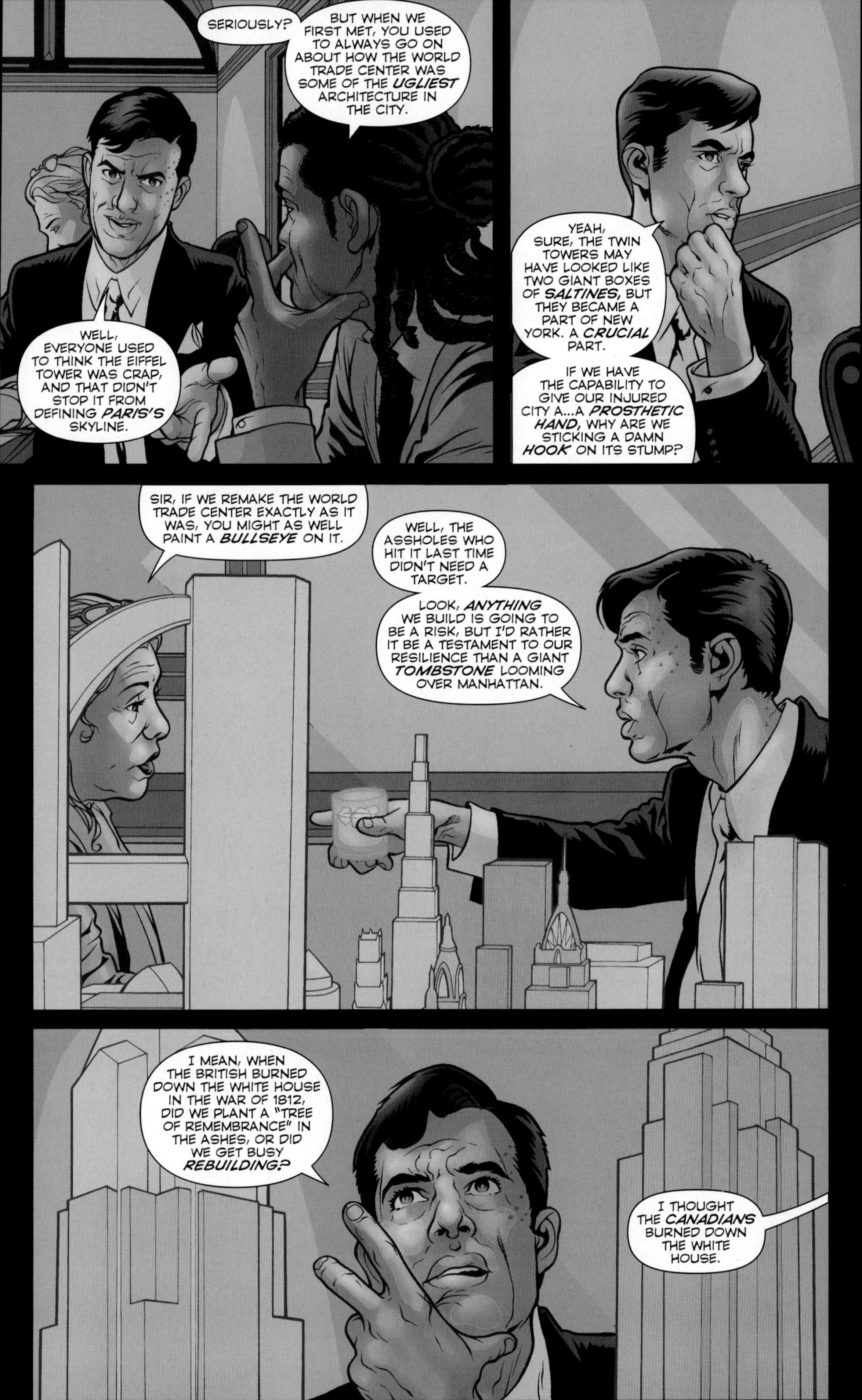

SERIOUSLY?
BUT WHEN WE FIRST MET, YOU USED TO ALWAYS GO ON ABOUT HOW THE WORLD TRADE CENTER WAS SOME OF THE UGLIEST ARCHITECTURE IN THE CITY.
WELL, EVERYONE USED TO THINK THE EIFFEL TOWER WAS CRAP, AND THAT DIDN'T STOP IT FROM DEFINING PARIS'S SKYLINE.
YEAH, SURE, THE TWIN TOWERS MAY HAVE LOOKED LIKE TWO GIANT BOXES OF SALTINES, BUT THEY BECAME A PART OF NEW YORK. A CRUCIAL PART.
IF WE HAVE THE CAPABILITY TO GIVE OUR INJURED CITY A...A PROSTHETIC HAND, WHY ARE WE STICKING A DAMN HOOK ON ITS STUMP?
SIR, IF WE REMAKE THE WORLD TRADE CENTER EXACTLY AS IT WAS, YOU MIGHT AS WELL PAINT A BULLSEYE ON IT.
WELL, THE ASSHOLES WHO HIT IT LAST TIME DIDN'T NEED A TARGET.
LOOK, ANYTHING WE BUILD IS GOING TO BE A RISK, BUT I'D RATHER IT BE A TESTAMENT TO OUR RESILIENCE THAN A GIANT TOMBSTONE LOOMING OVER MANHATTAN.
I MEAN, WHEN THE BRITISH BURNED DOWN THE WHITE HOUSE IN THE WAR OF 1812, DID WE PLANT A "TREE OF REMEMBRANCE" IN THE ASHES, OR DID WE GET BUSY REBUILDING?
I THOUGHT THE CANADIANS BURNED DOWN THE WHITE HOUSE.

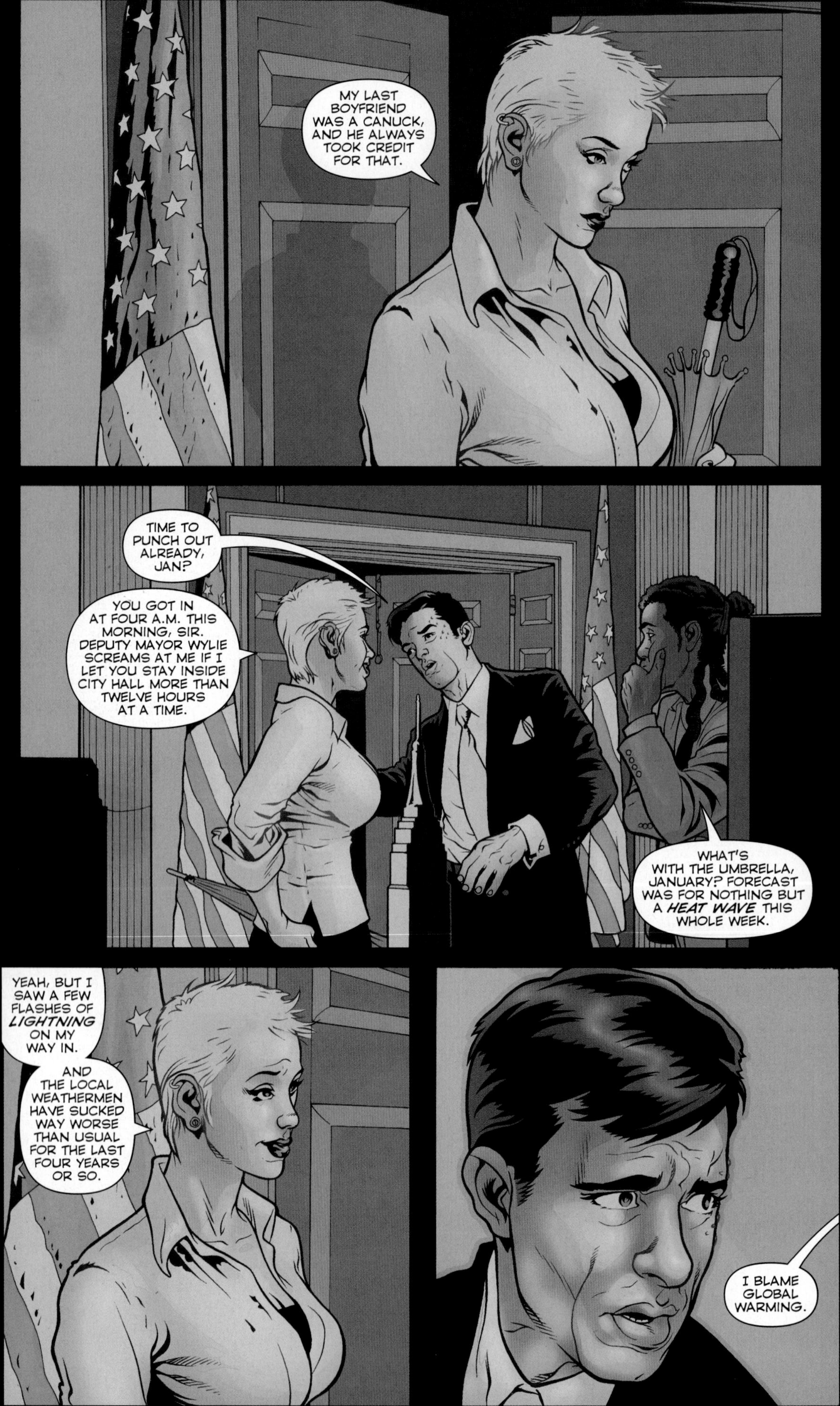
MY LAST BOYFRIEND WAS A CANUCK, AND HE ALWAYS TOOK CREDIT FOR THAT.
TIME TO PUNCH OUT ALREADY, JAN?
YOU GOT IN AT FOUR A.M. THIS MORNING, SIR. DEPUTY MAYOR WYLIE SCREAMS AT ME IF I LET YOU STAY INSIDE CITY HALL MORE THAN TWELVE HOURS AT A TIME.
WHAT'S WITH THE UMBRELLA, JANUARY? FORECAST WAS FOR NOTHING BUT A *HEAT WAVE* THIS WHOLE WEEK.
YEAH, BUT I SAW A FEW FLASHES OF *LIGHTNING* ON MY WAY IN.
AND THE LOCAL WEATHERMEN HAVE SUCKED WAY WORSE THAN USUAL FOR THE LAST FOUR YEARS OR SO.
I BLAME GLOBAL WARMING.

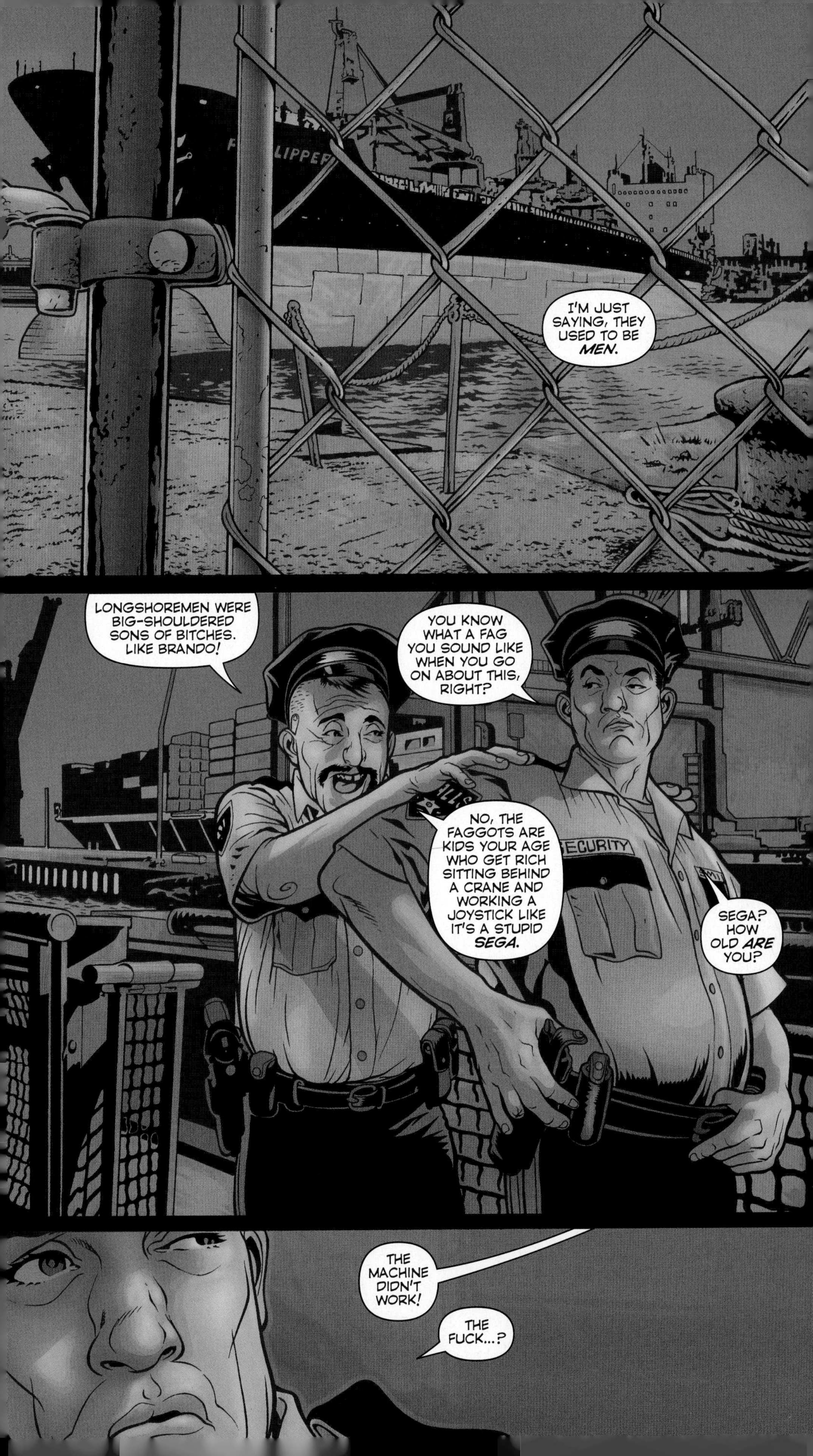
I'M JUST SAYING, THEY USED TO BE *MEN*.
LONGSHOREMEN WERE BIG-SHOULDERED SONS OF BITCHES. LIKE BRANDO!
YOU KNOW WHAT A FAG YOU SOUND LIKE WHEN YOU GO ON ABOUT THIS, RIGHT?
NO, THE FAGGOTS ARE KIDS YOUR AGE WHO GET RICH SITTING BEHIND A CRANE AND WORKING A JOYSTICK LIKE IT'S A STUPID *SEGA*.
SECURITY
SEGA? HOW OLD *ARE* YOU?
THE MACHINE DIDN'T WORK!
THE FUCK...?

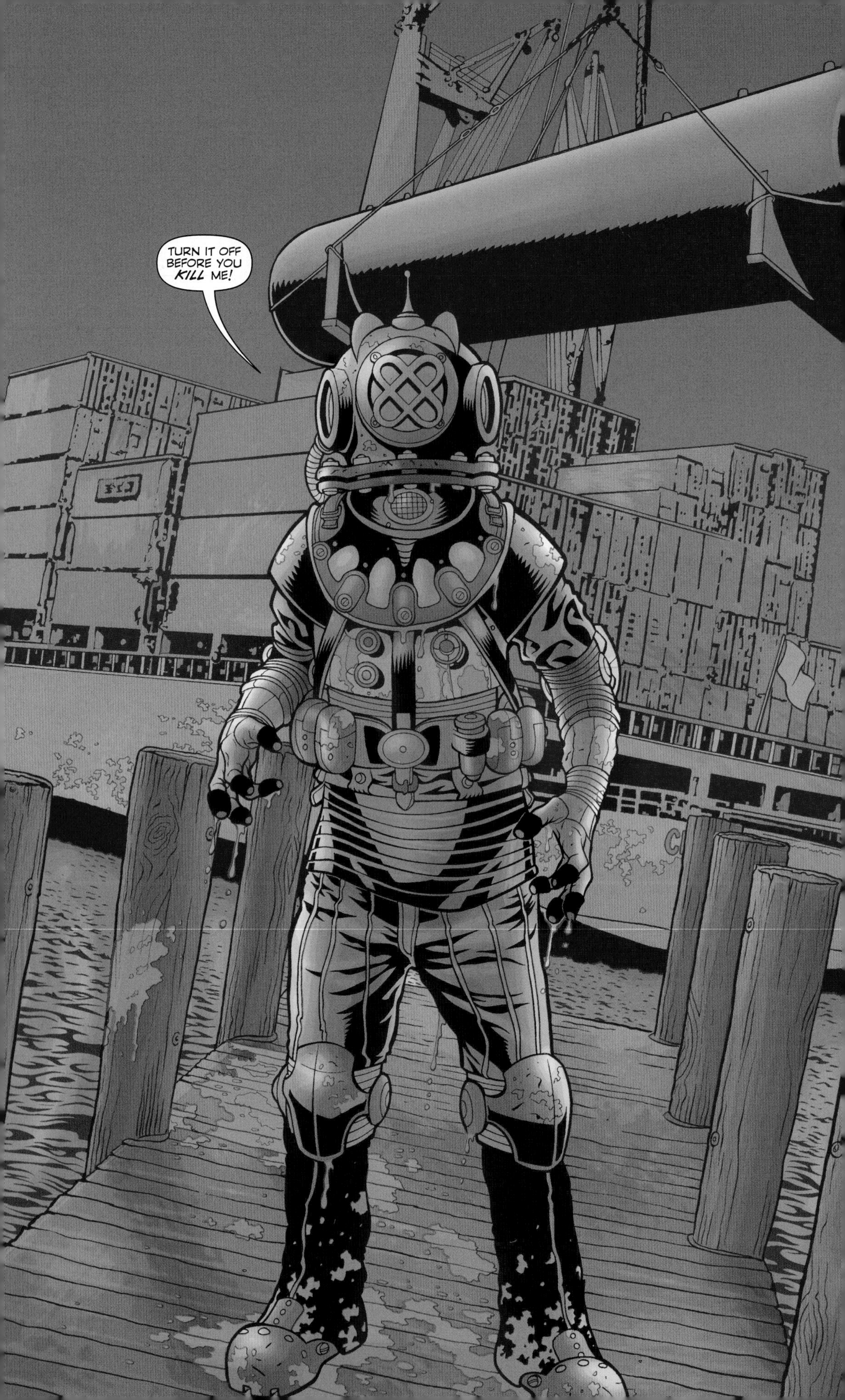
TURN IT OFF BEFORE YOU KILL ME!

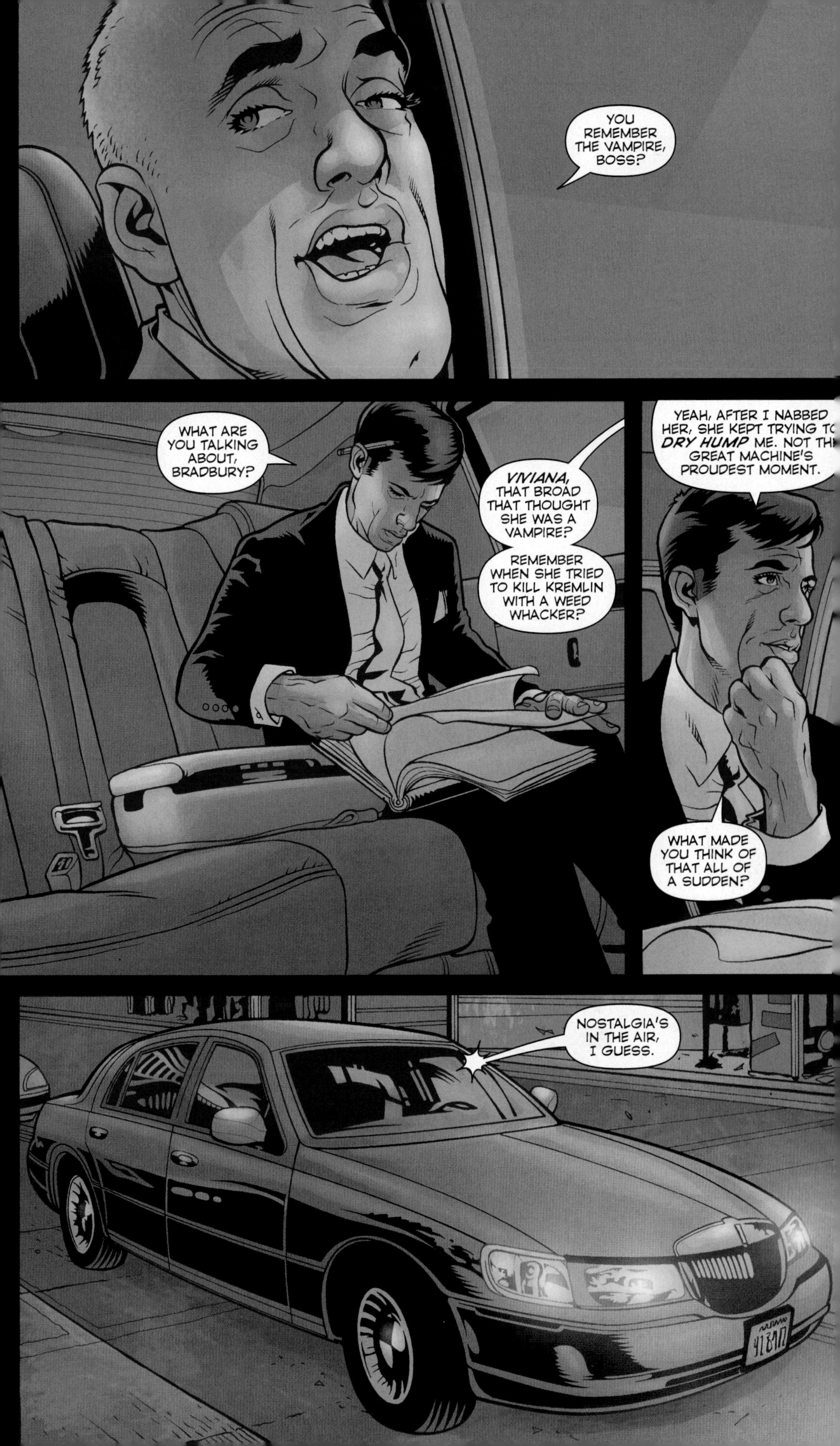
YOU REMEMBER THE VAMPIRE, BOSS?
WHAT ARE YOU TALKING ABOUT, BRADBURY?
VIVIANA, THAT BROAD THAT THOUGHT SHE WAS A VAMPIRE?
REMEMBER WHEN SHE TRIED TO KILL KREMLIN WITH A WEED WHACKER?
YEAH, AFTER I NABBED HER, SHE KEPT TRYING TO *DRY HUMP* ME. NOT THE GREAT MACHINE'S PROUDEST MOMENT.
WHAT MADE YOU THINK OF THAT ALL OF A SUDDEN?
NOSTALGIA'S IN THE AIR, I GUESS.

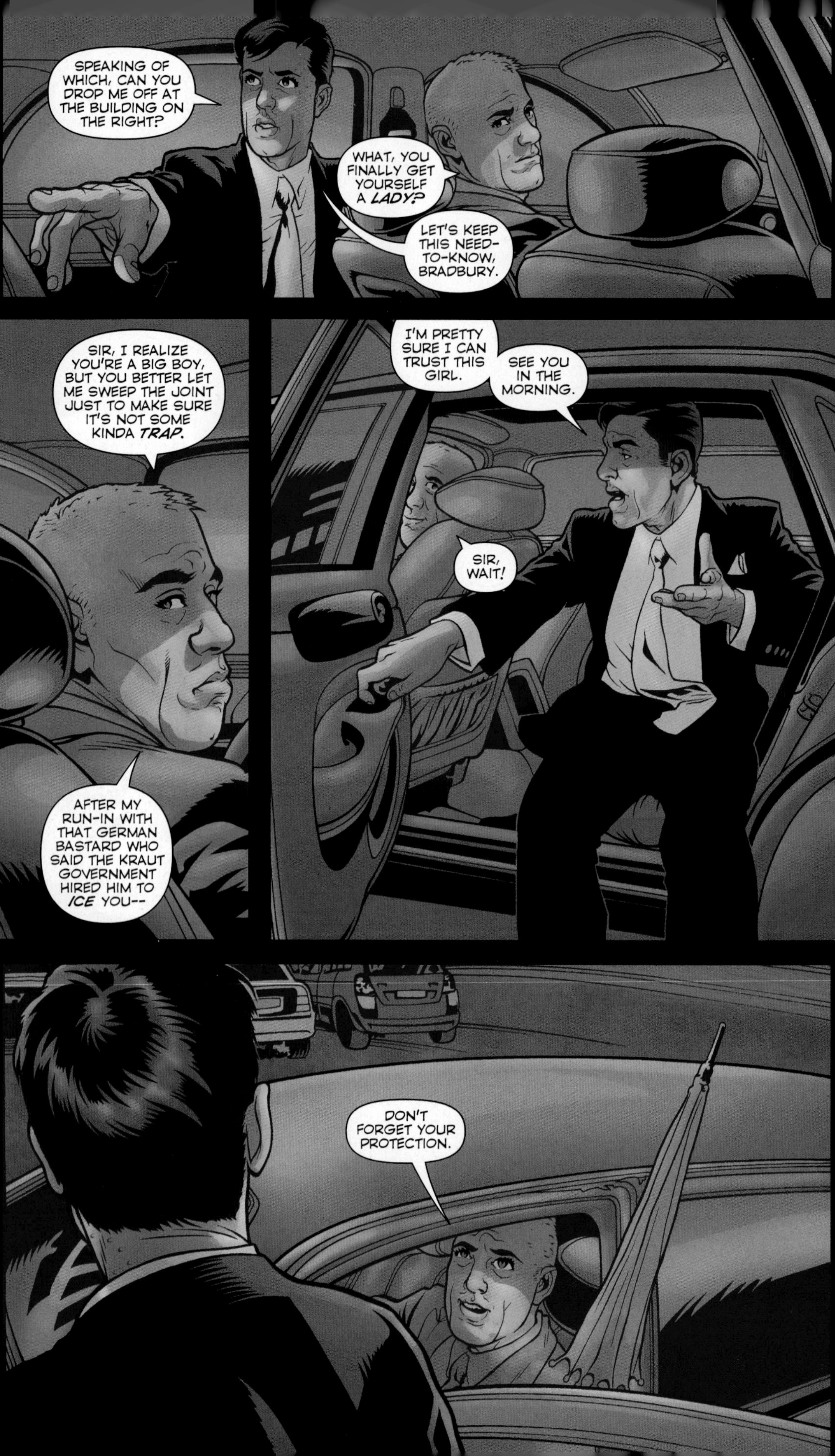
SPEAKING OF WHICH, CAN YOU DROP ME OFF AT THE BUILDING ON THE RIGHT?
WHAT, YOU FINALLY GET YOURSELF A LADY?
LET'S KEEP THIS NEED-TO-KNOW, BRADBURY.
SIR, I REALIZE YOU'RE A BIG BOY, BUT YOU BETTER LET ME SWEEP THE JOINT JUST TO MAKE SURE IT'S NOT SOME KINDA TRAP.
AFTER MY RUN-IN WITH THAT GERMAN BASTARD WHO SAID THE KRAUT GOVERNMENT HIRED HIM TO ICE YOU--
I'M PRETTY SURE I CAN TRUST THIS GIRL.
SEE YOU IN THE MORNING.
SIR, WAIT!
DON'T FORGET YOUR PROTECTION.

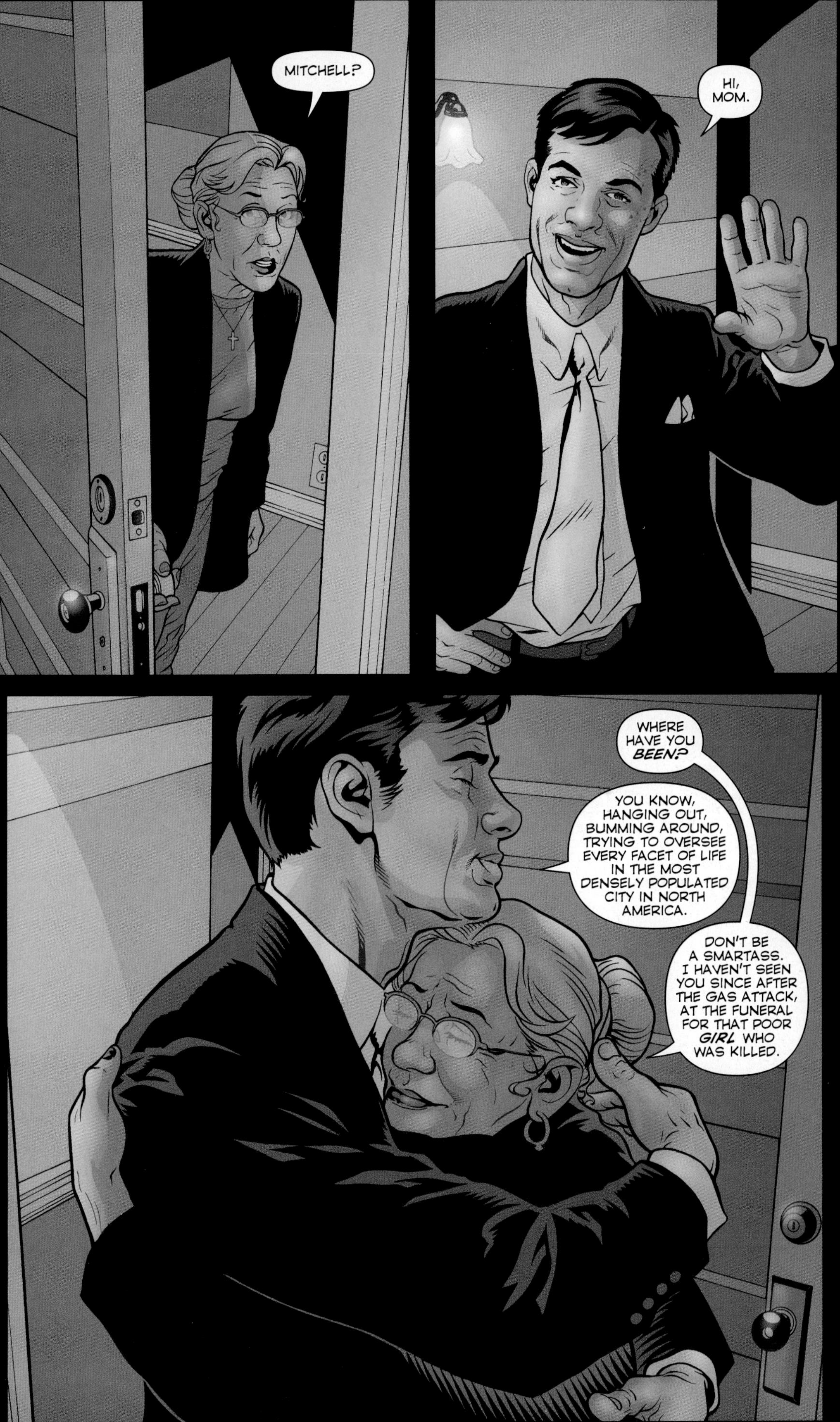
MITCHELL?
HI, MOM.
WHERE HAVE YOU *BEEN?*
YOU KNOW, HANGING OUT, BUMMING AROUND, TRYING TO OVERSEE EVERY FACET OF LIFE IN THE MOST DENSELY POPULATED CITY IN NORTH AMERICA.
DON'T BE A SMARTASS. I HAVEN'T SEEN YOU SINCE AFTER THE GAS ATTACK, AT THE FUNERAL FOR THAT POOR *GIRL* WHO WAS KILLED.

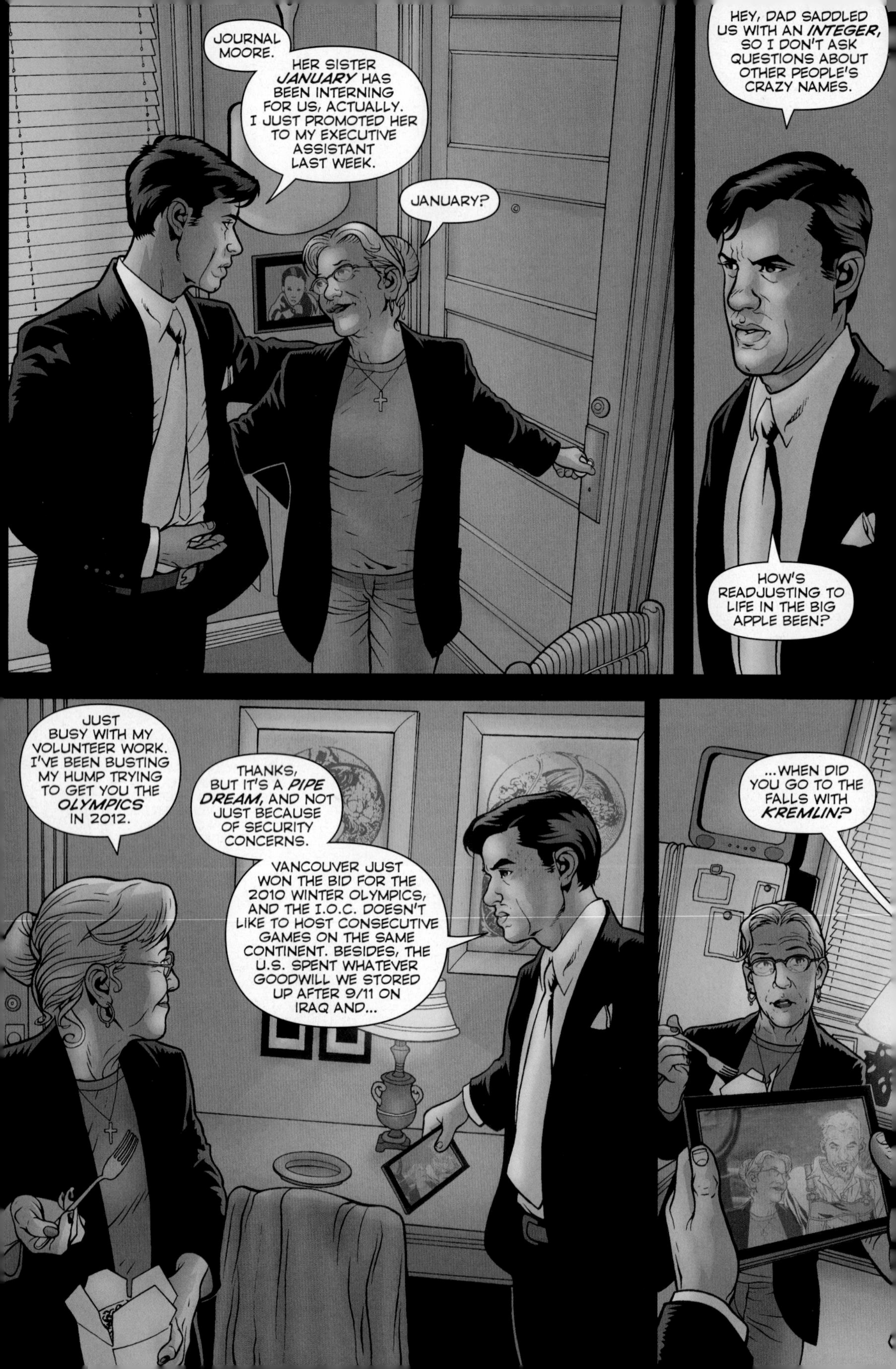
JOURNAL MOORE.
HER SISTER *JANUARY* HAS BEEN INTERNING FOR US, ACTUALLY. I JUST PROMOTED HER TO MY EXECUTIVE ASSISTANT LAST WEEK.
JANUARY?
HEY, DAD SADDLED US WITH AN *INTEGER,* SO I DON'T ASK QUESTIONS ABOUT OTHER PEOPLE'S CRAZY NAMES.
HOW'S READJUSTING TO LIFE IN THE BIG APPLE BEEN?
JUST BUSY WITH MY VOLUNTEER WORK. I'VE BEEN BUSTING MY HUMP TRYING TO GET YOU THE *OLYMPICS* IN 2012.
THANKS, BUT IT'S A *PIPE DREAM,* AND NOT JUST BECAUSE OF SECURITY CONCERNS.
VANCOUVER JUST WON THE BID FOR THE 2010 WINTER OLYMPICS, AND THE I.O.C. DOESN'T LIKE TO HOST CONSECUTIVE GAMES ON THE SAME CONTINENT. BESIDES, THE U.S. SPENT WHATEVER GOODWILL WE STORED UP AFTER 9/11 ON IRAQ AND...
...WHEN DID YOU GO TO THE FALLS WITH *KREMLIN?*

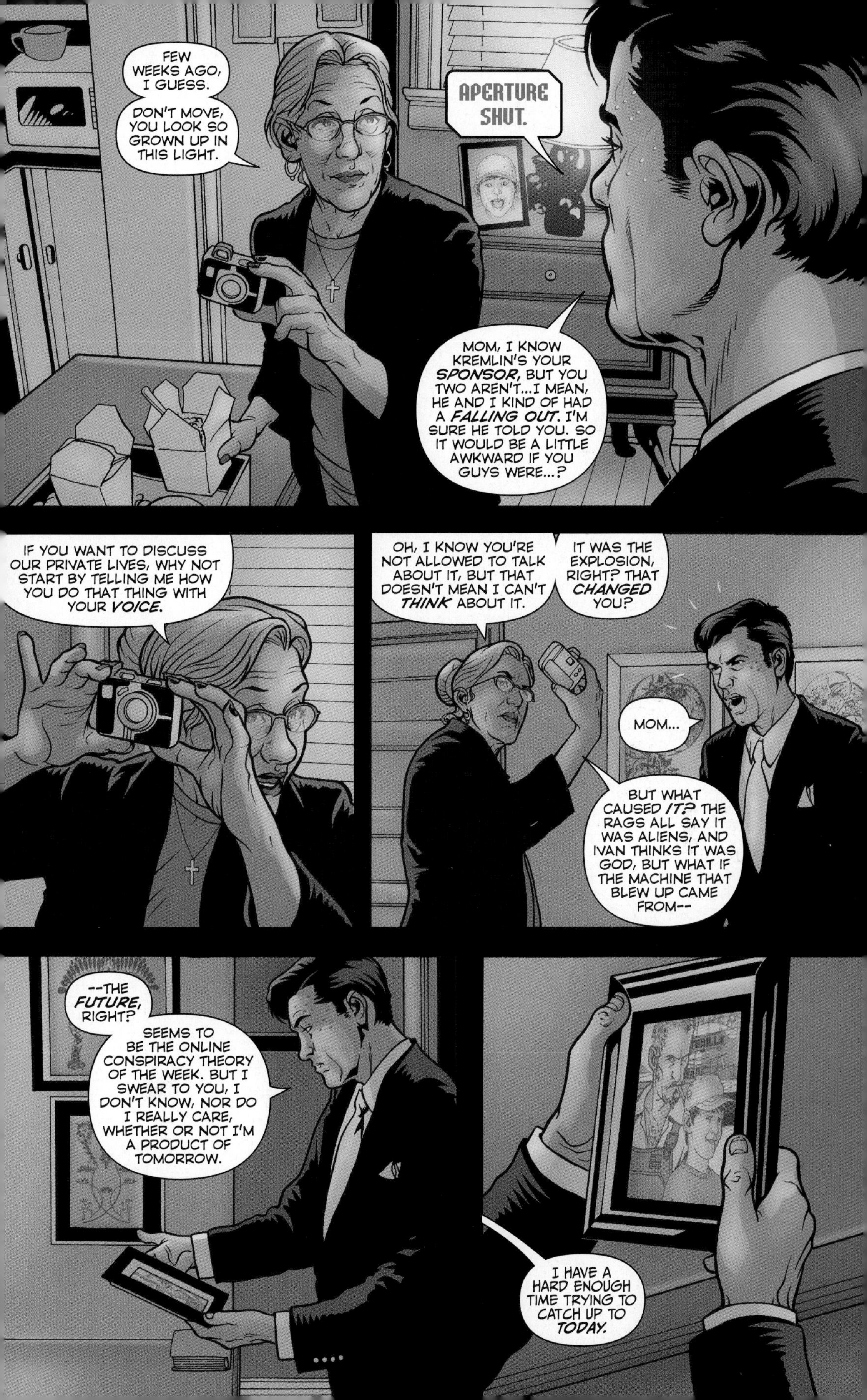

FEW WEEKS AGO, I GUESS.
DON'T MOVE, YOU LOOK SO GROWN UP IN THIS LIGHT.
APERTURE SHUT.
MOM, I KNOW KREMLIN'S YOUR SPONSOR, BUT YOU TWO AREN'T...I MEAN, HE AND I KIND OF HAD A FALLING OUT. I'M SURE HE TOLD YOU. SO IT WOULD BE A LITTLE AWKWARD IF YOU GUYS WERE...?
IF YOU WANT TO DISCUSS OUR PRIVATE LIVES, WHY NOT START BY TELLING ME HOW YOU DO THAT THING WITH YOUR VOICE.
OH, I KNOW YOU'RE NOT ALLOWED TO TALK ABOUT IT, BUT THAT DOESN'T MEAN I CAN'T THINK ABOUT IT.
IT WAS THE EXPLOSION, RIGHT? THAT CHANGED YOU?
MOM...
BUT WHAT CAUSED IT? THE RAGS ALL SAY IT WAS ALIENS, AND IVAN THINKS IT WAS GOD, BUT WHAT IF THE MACHINE THAT BLEW UP CAME FROM--
--THE FUTURE, RIGHT?
SEEMS TO BE THE ONLINE CONSPIRACY THEORY OF THE WEEK. BUT I SWEAR TO YOU, I DON'T KNOW, NOR DO I REALLY CARE, WHETHER OR NOT I'M A PRODUCT OF TOMORROW.
I HAVE A HARD ENOUGH TIME TRYING TO CATCH UP TO TODAY.

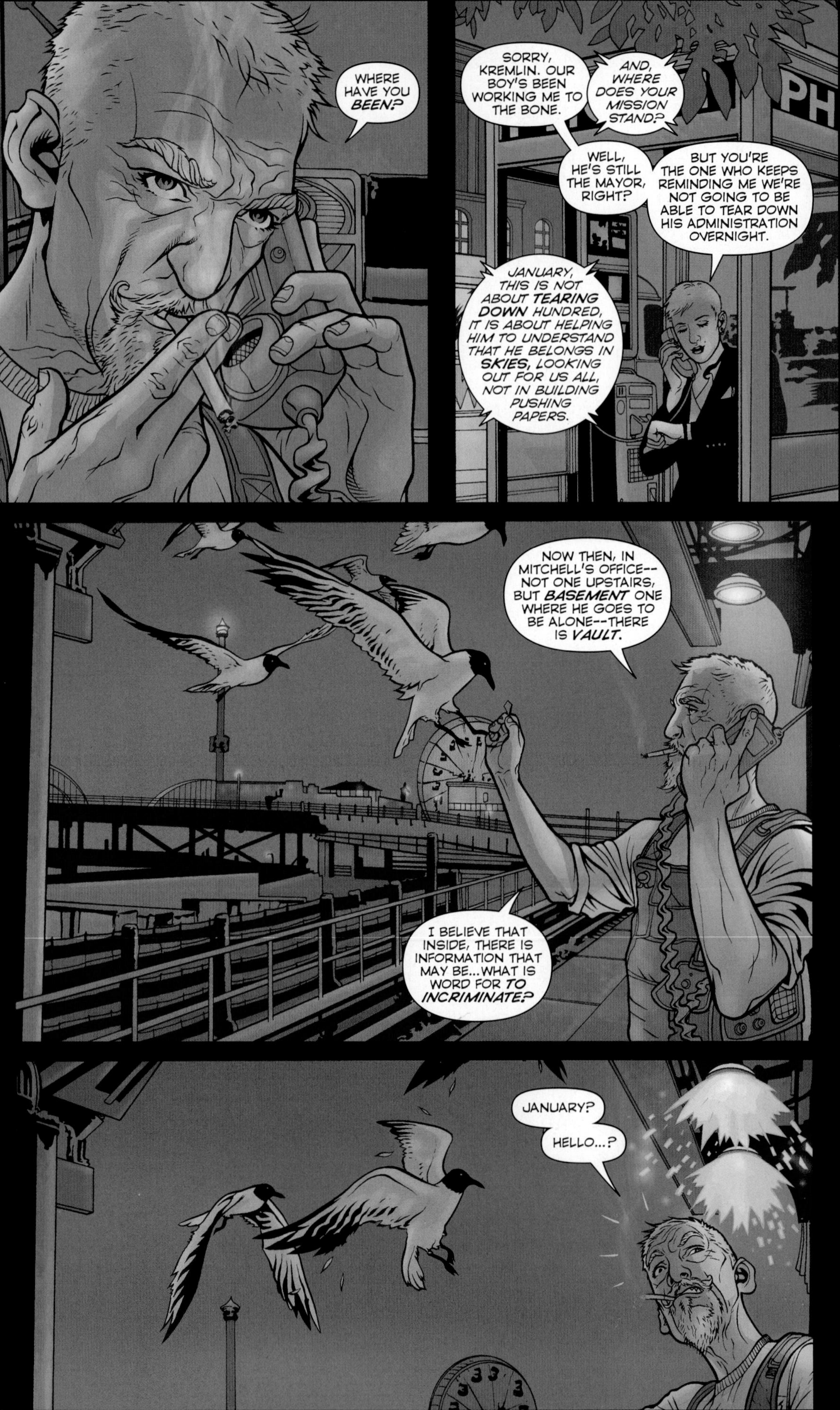
WHERE HAVE YOU BEEN?
SORRY, KREMLIN. OUR BOY'S BEEN WORKING ME TO THE BONE.
AND, WHERE DOES YOUR MISSION STAND?
WELL, HE'S STILL THE MAYOR, RIGHT?
BUT YOU'RE THE ONE WHO KEEPS REMINDING ME WE'RE NOT GOING TO BE ABLE TO TEAR DOWN HIS ADMINISTRATION OVERNIGHT.
JANUARY, THIS IS NOT ABOUT TEARING DOWN HUNDRED, IT IS ABOUT HELPING HIM TO UNDERSTAND THAT HE BELONGS IN SKIES, LOOKING OUT FOR US ALL, NOT IN BUILDING PUSHING PAPERS.
NOW THEN, IN MITCHELL'S OFFICE--NOT ONE UPSTAIRS, BUT BASEMENT ONE WHERE HE GOES TO BE ALONE--THERE IS VAULT.
I BELIEVE THAT INSIDE, THERE IS INFORMATION THAT MAY BE...WHAT IS WORD FOR TO INCRIMINATE?
JANUARY?
HELLO...?

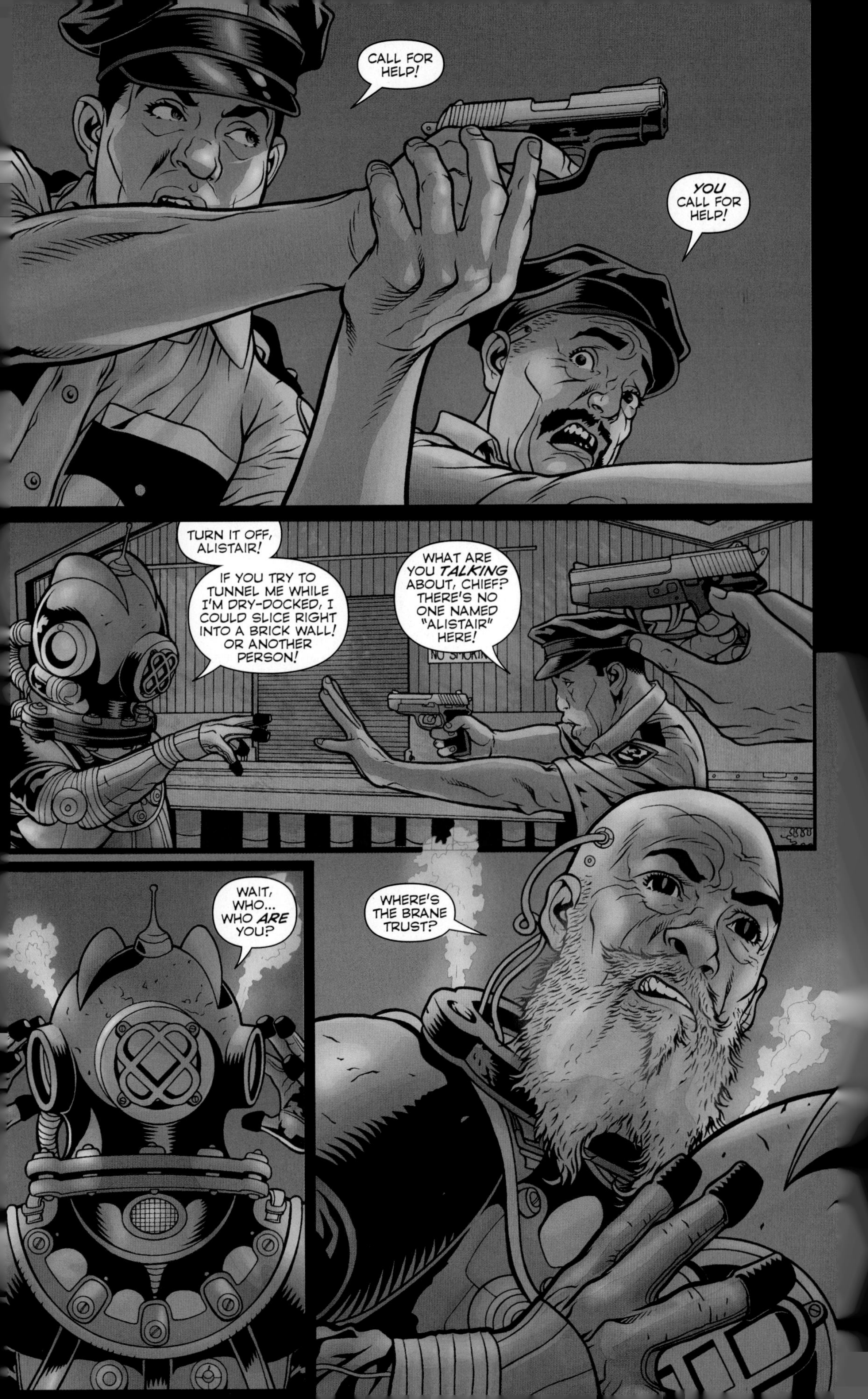

CALL FOR HELP!
YOU CALL FOR HELP!
TURN IT OFF, ALISTAIR!
IF YOU TRY TO TUNNEL ME WHILE I'M DRY-DOCKED, I COULD SLICE RIGHT INTO A BRICK WALL! OR ANOTHER PERSON!
WHAT ARE YOU TALKING ABOUT, CHIEF? THERE'S NO ONE NAMED "ALISTAIR" HERE!
NO SMOKIN
WAIT, WHO... WHO ARE YOU?
WHERE'S THE BRANE TRUST?

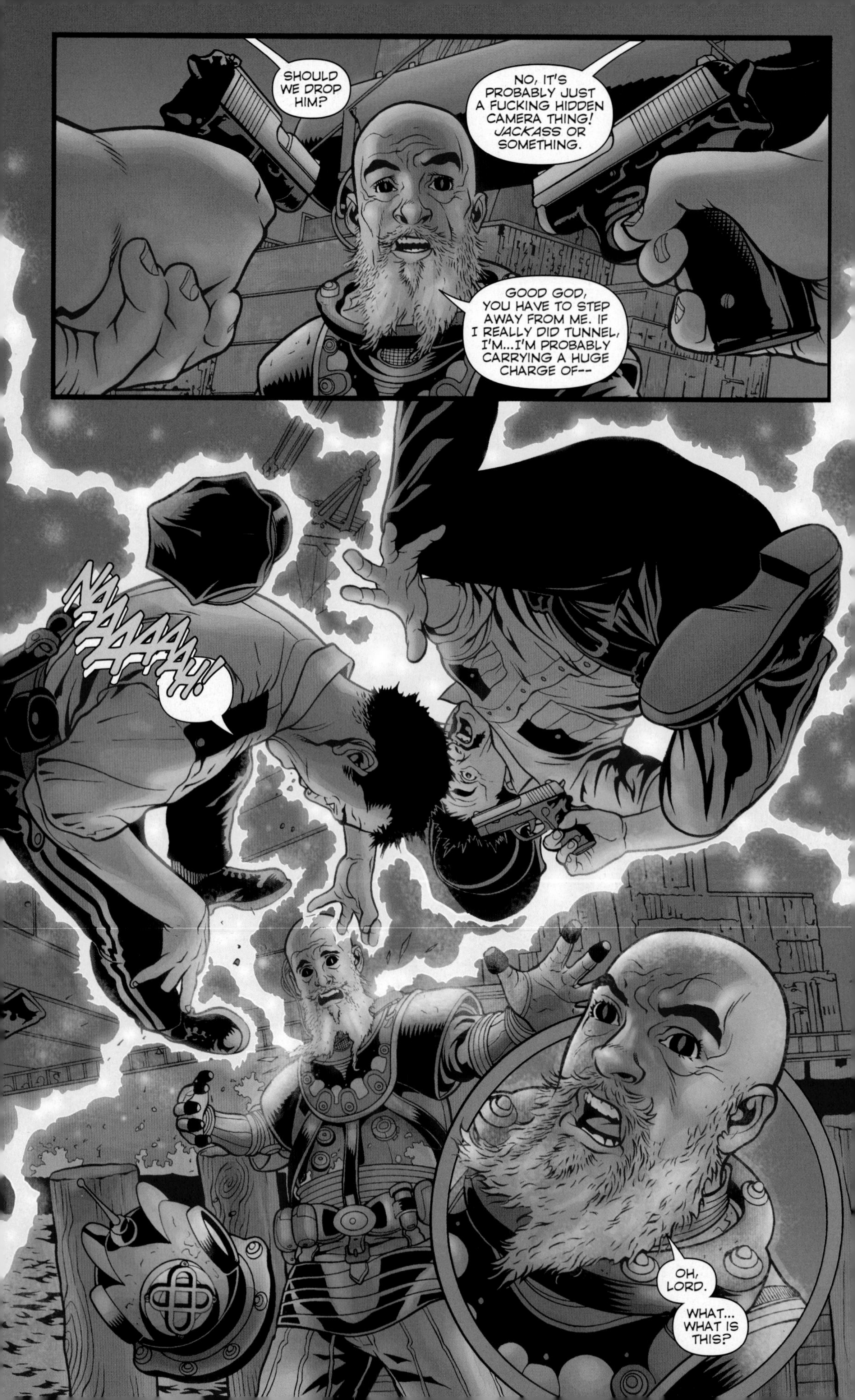

SHOULD WE DROP HIM?
NO, IT'S PROBABLY JUST A FUCKING HIDDEN CAMERA THING! JACKASS OR SOMETHING.
GOOD GOD, YOU HAVE TO STEP AWAY FROM ME. IF I REALLY DID TUNNEL, I'M...I'M PROBABLY CARRYING A HUGE CHARGE OF--
NAAAAAAAH!
OH, LORD.
WHAT... WHAT IS THIS?

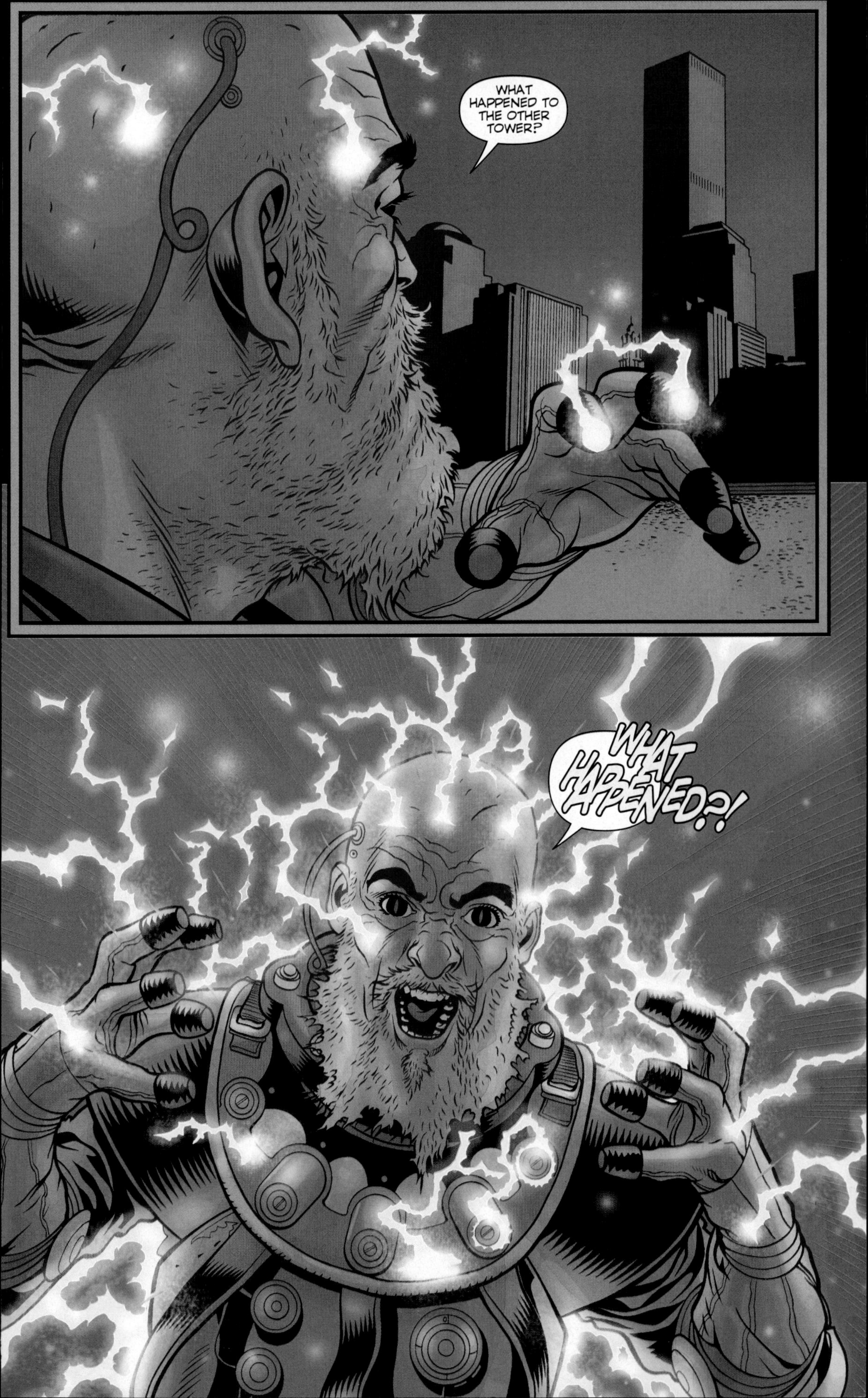
WHAT HAPPENED TO THE OTHER TOWER?
WHAT HAPPENED?!

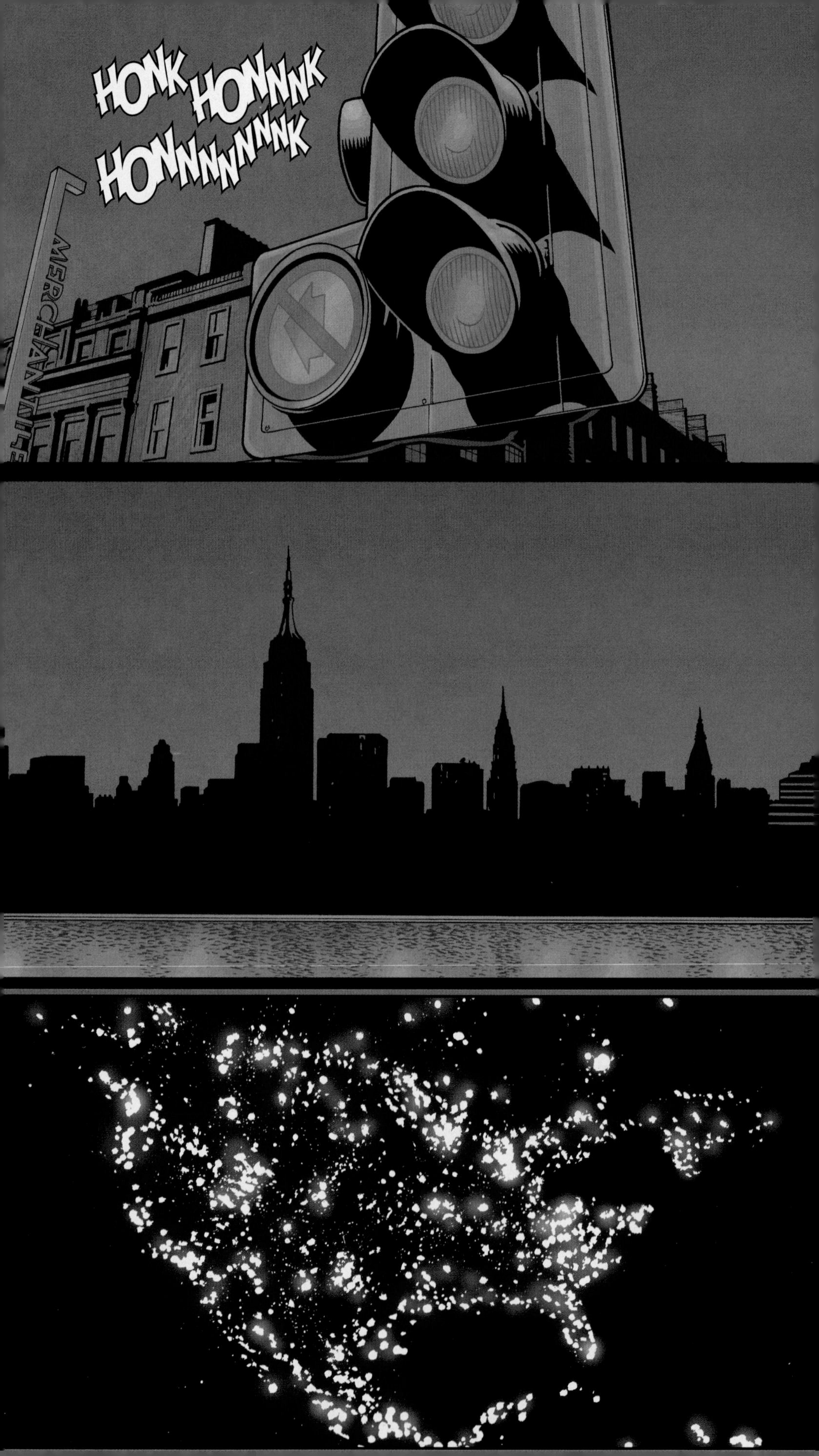
HONK HONNNK
HONNNNNNNK

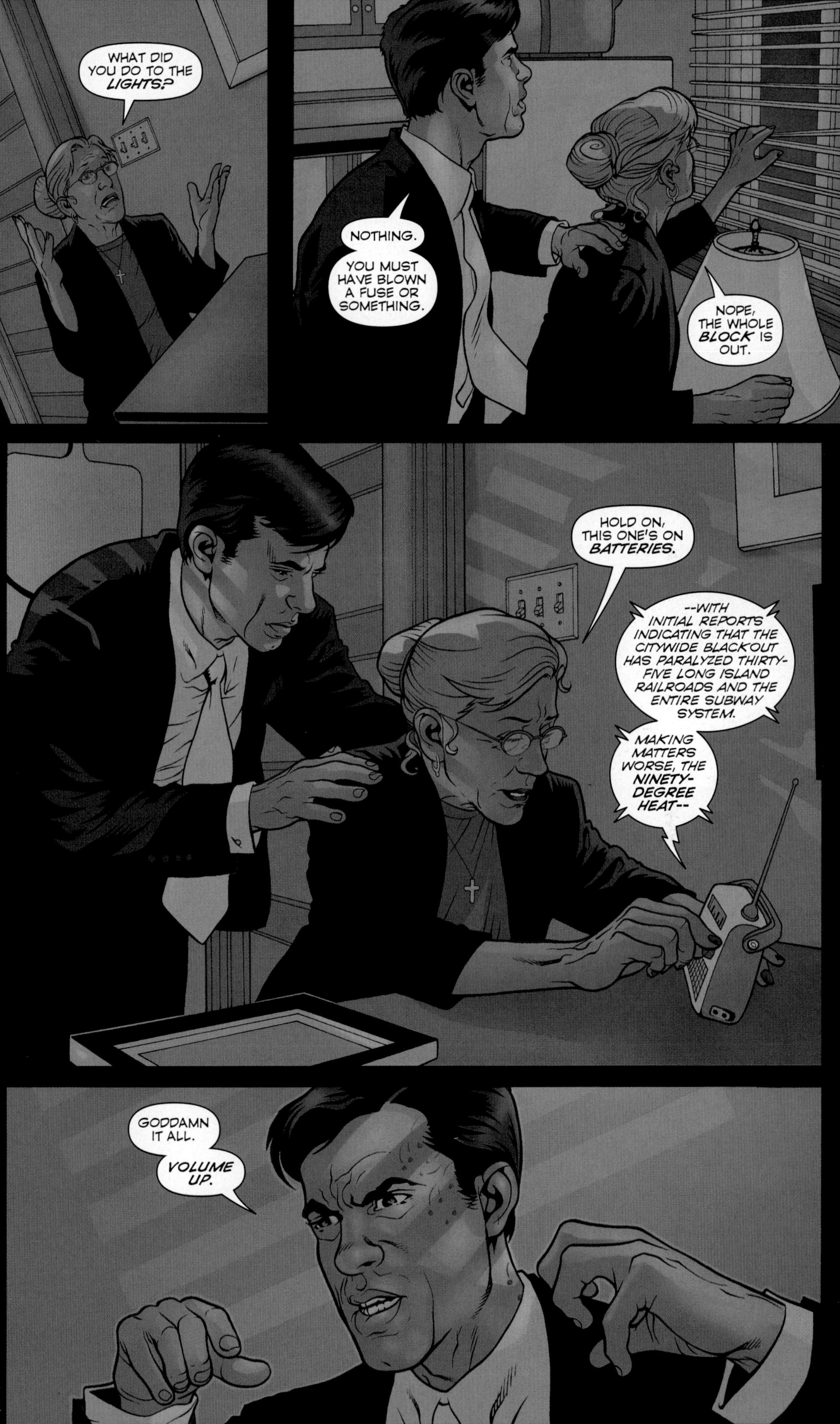
WHAT DID YOU DO TO THE *LIGHTS?*
NOTHING.
YOU MUST HAVE BLOWN A FUSE OR SOMETHING.
NOPE, THE WHOLE *BLOCK* IS OUT.
HOLD ON, THIS ONE'S ON ***BATTERIES.***
--WITH INITIAL REPORTS INDICATING THAT THE CITYWIDE BLACKOUT HAS PARALYZED THIRTY-FIVE LONG ISLAND RAILROADS AND THE ENTIRE SUBWAY SYSTEM.
MAKING MATTERS WORSE, THE ***NINETY-DEGREE HEAT--***
GODDAMN IT ALL.
VOLUME UP.

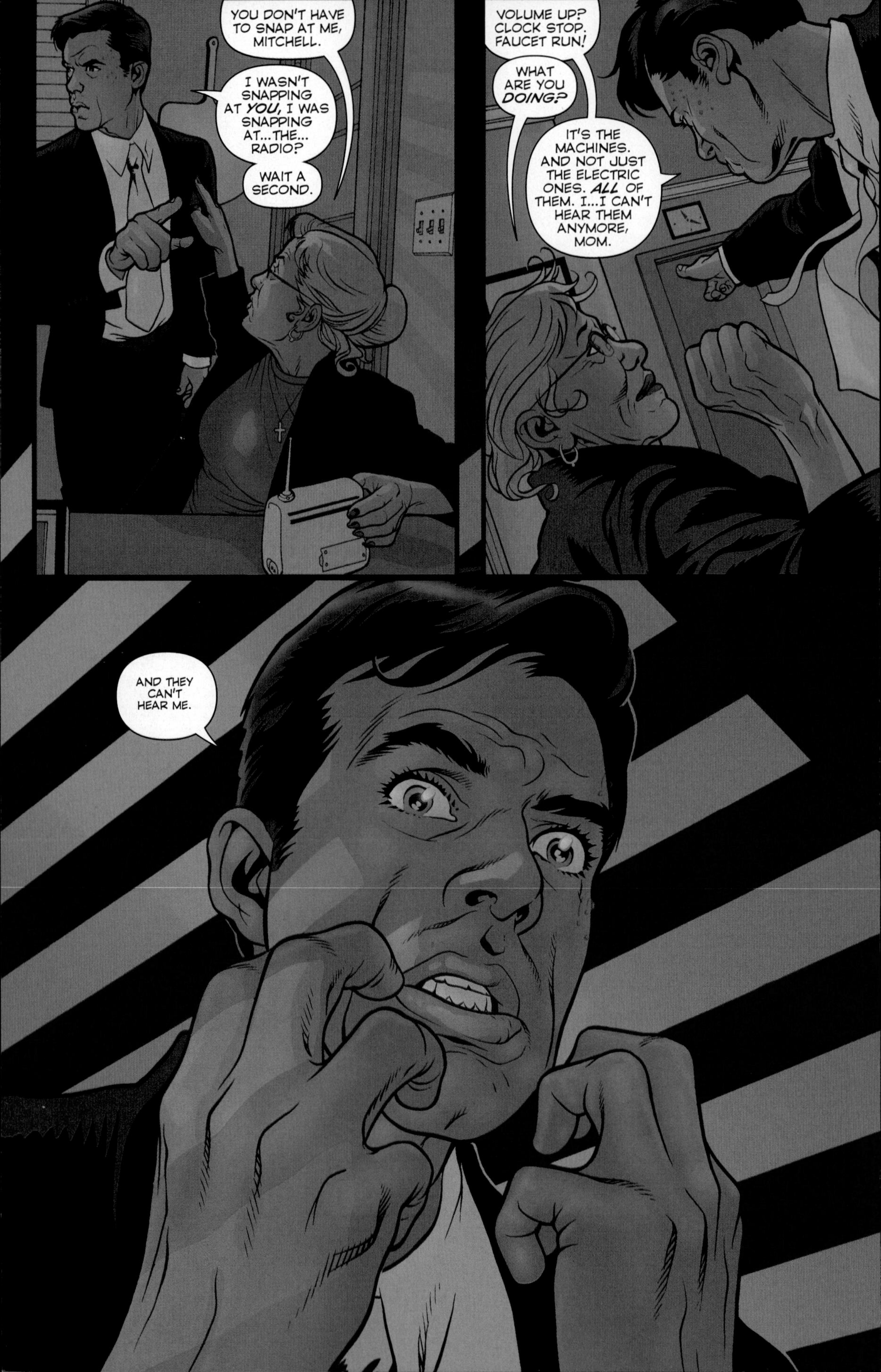
YOU DON'T HAVE TO SNAP AT ME, MITCHELL.
I WASN'T SNAPPING AT *YOU,* I WAS SNAPPING AT...THE... RADIO?
WAIT A SECOND.
VOLUME UP? CLOCK STOP. FAUCET RUN!
WHAT ARE YOU *DOING?*
IT'S THE MACHINES. AND NOT JUST THE ELECTRIC ONES. *ALL* OF THEM. I...I CAN'T HEAR THEM ANYMORE, MOM.
AND THEY CAN'T HEAR ME.

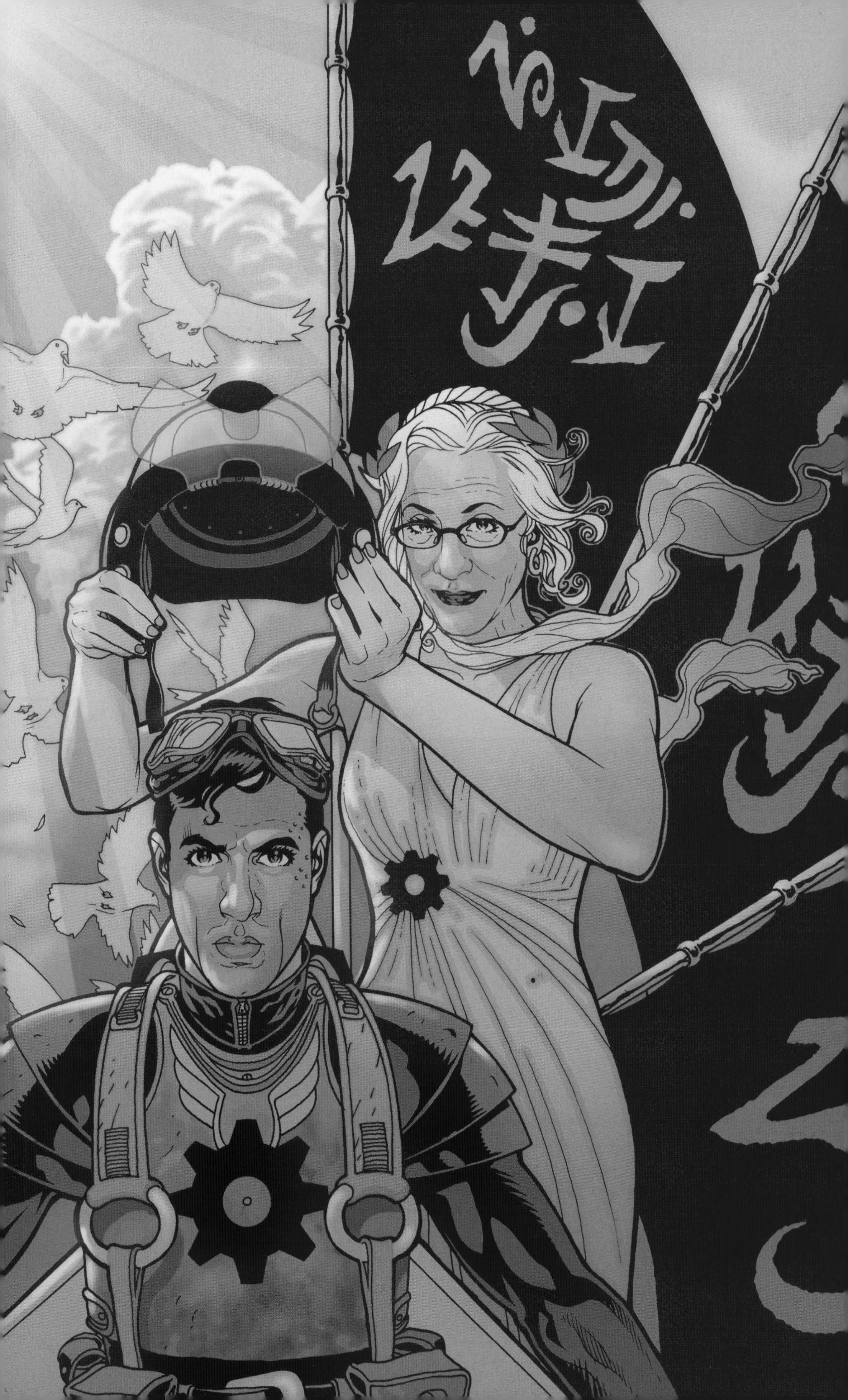

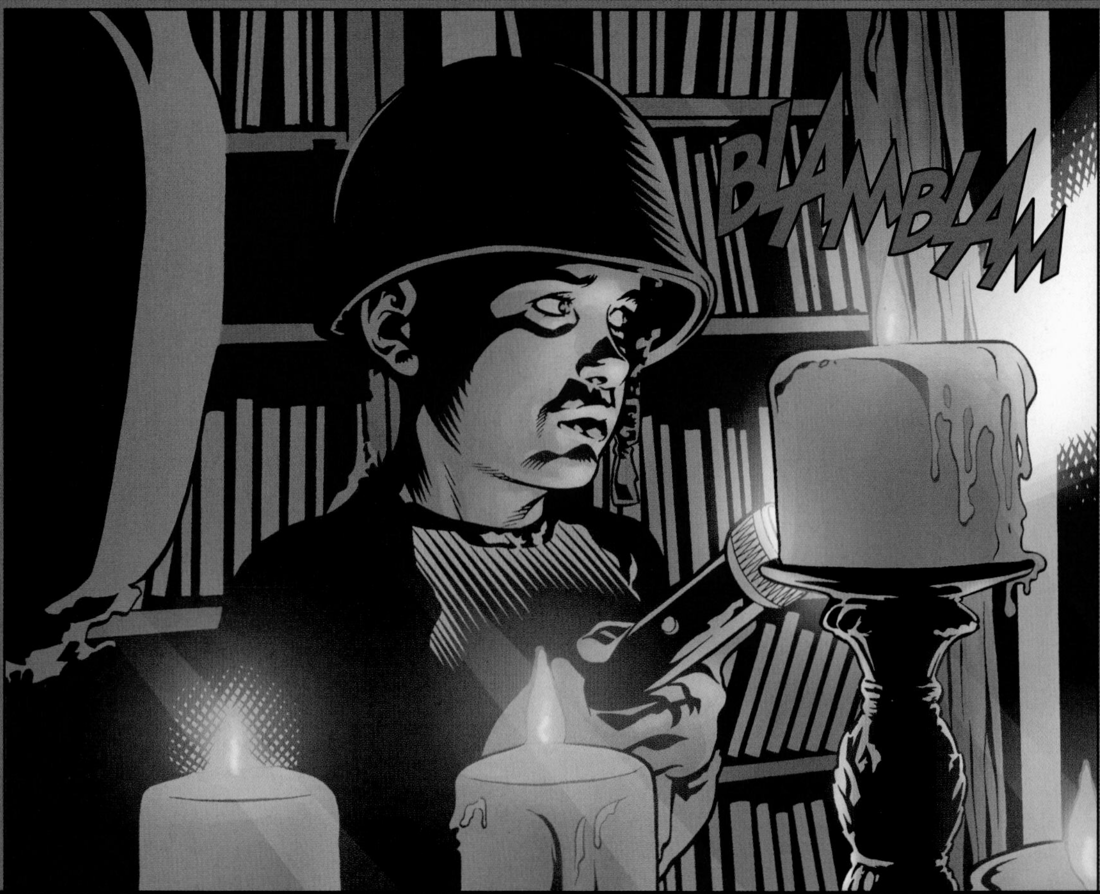
BLAMBLAM

WEDNESDAY, JULY 13, 1977

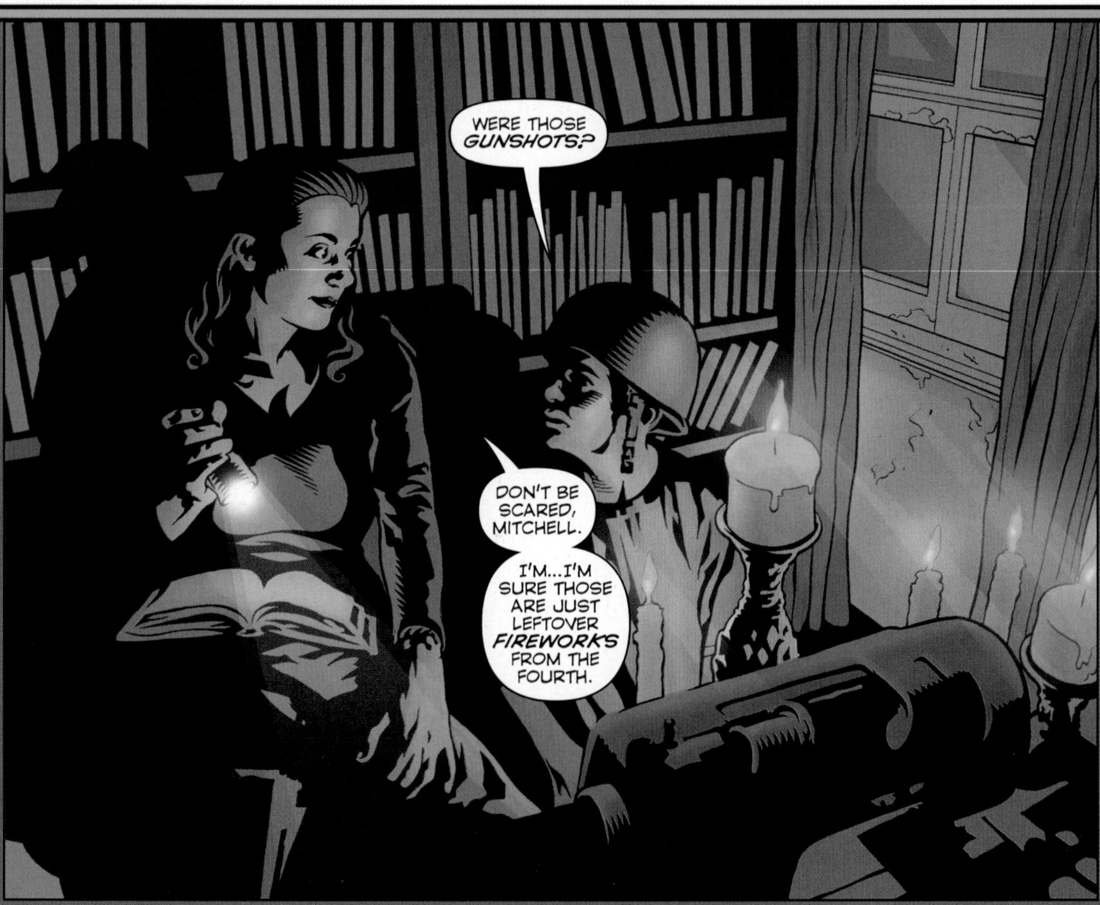
WERE THOSE GUNSHOTS?
DON'T BE SCARED, MITCHELL.
I'M...I'M SURE THOSE ARE JUST LEFTOVER FIREWORKS FROM THE FOURTH.

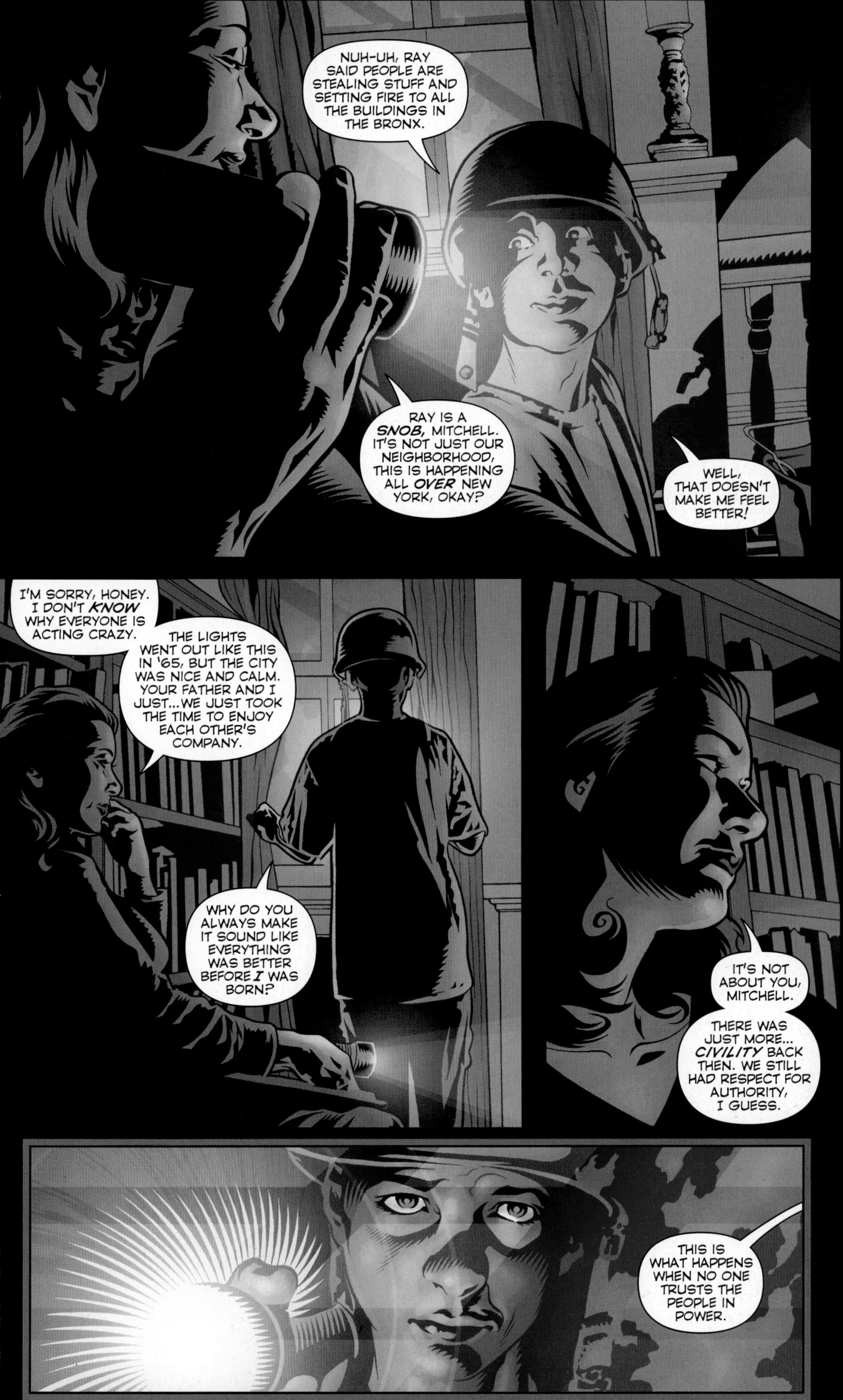
NUH-UH, RAY SAID PEOPLE ARE STEALING STUFF AND SETTING FIRE TO ALL THE BUILDINGS IN THE BRONX.
RAY IS A *SNOB,* MITCHELL. IT'S NOT JUST OUR NEIGHBORHOOD, THIS IS HAPPENING ALL *OVER* NEW YORK, OKAY?
WELL, THAT DOESN'T MAKE ME FEEL BETTER!
I'M SORRY, HONEY. I DON'T *KNOW* WHY EVERYONE IS ACTING CRAZY.
THE LIGHTS WENT OUT LIKE THIS IN '65, BUT THE CITY WAS NICE AND CALM. YOUR FATHER AND I JUST...WE JUST TOOK THE TIME TO ENJOY EACH OTHER'S COMPANY.
WHY DO YOU ALWAYS MAKE IT SOUND LIKE EVERYTHING WAS BETTER BEFORE *I* WAS BORN?
IT'S NOT ABOUT YOU, MITCHELL.
THERE WAS JUST MORE... *CIVILITY* BACK THEN. WE STILL HAD RESPECT FOR AUTHORITY, I GUESS.
THIS IS WHAT HAPPENS WHEN NO ONE TRUSTS THE PEOPLE IN POWER.

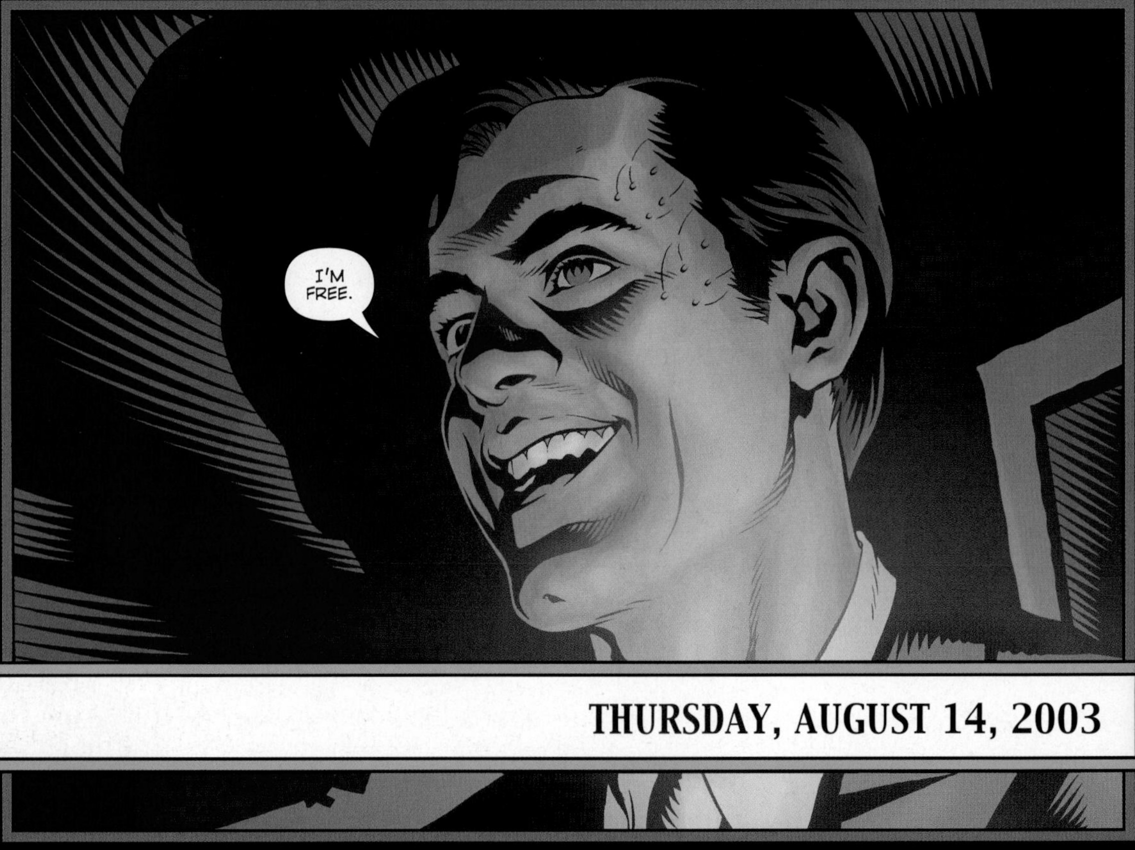
I'M FREE.

THURSDAY, AUGUST 14, 2003

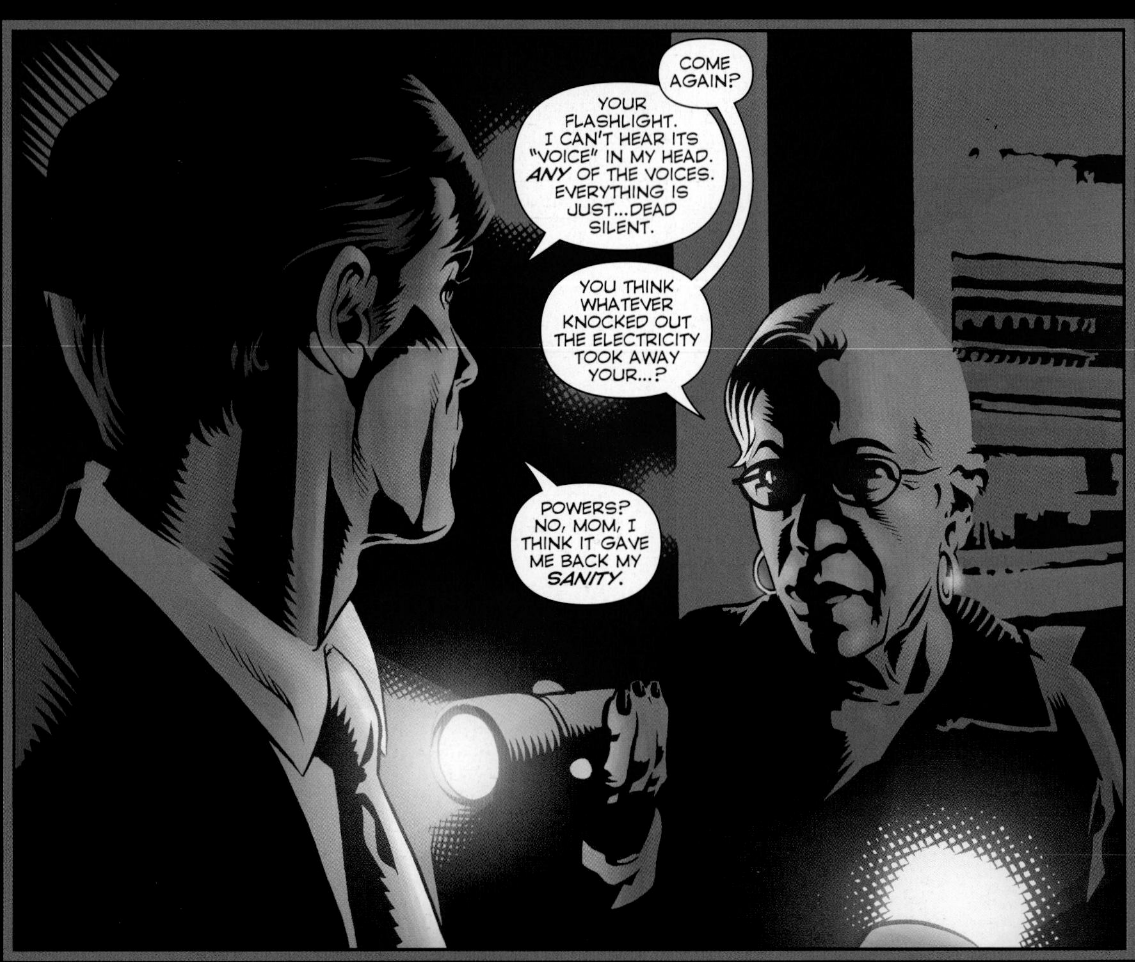
COME AGAIN?
YOUR FLASHLIGHT. I CAN'T HEAR ITS "VOICE" IN MY HEAD. ANY OF THE VOICES. EVERYTHING IS JUST...DEAD SILENT.
YOU THINK WHATEVER KNOCKED OUT THE ELECTRICITY TOOK AWAY YOUR...?
POWERS? NO, MOM, I THINK IT GAVE ME BACK MY SANITY.

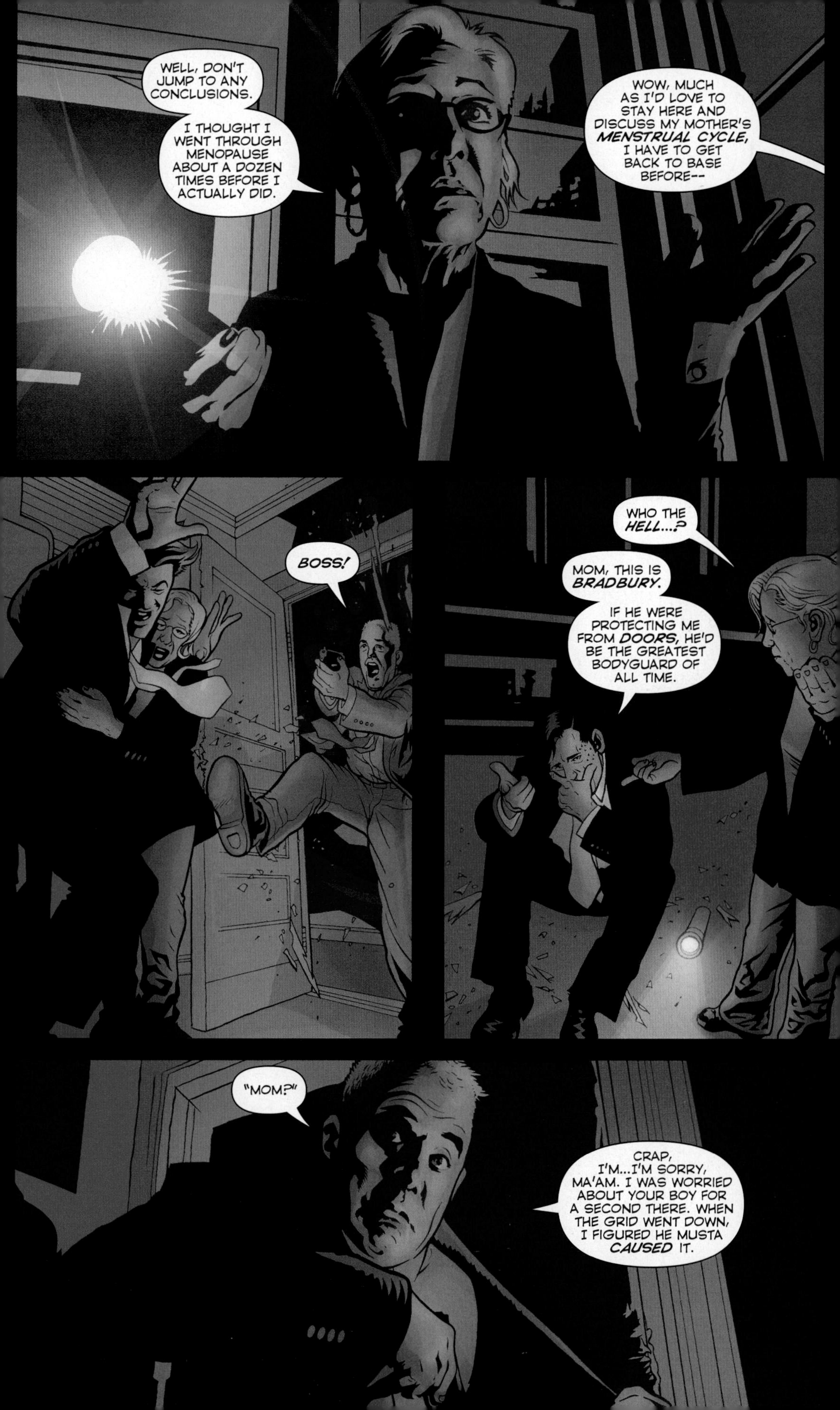
WELL, DON'T JUMP TO ANY CONCLUSIONS.
I THOUGHT I WENT THROUGH MENOPAUSE ABOUT A DOZEN TIMES BEFORE I ACTUALLY DID.
WOW, MUCH AS I'D LOVE TO STAY HERE AND DISCUSS MY MOTHER'S *MENSTRUAL CYCLE,* I HAVE TO GET BACK TO BASE BEFORE--
BOSS!
WHO THE *HELL...?*
MOM, THIS IS *BRADBURY.*
IF HE WERE PROTECTING ME FROM *DOORS,* HE'D BE THE GREATEST BODYGUARD OF ALL TIME.
"MOM?"
CRAP, I'M...I'M SORRY, MA'AM. I WAS WORRIED ABOUT YOUR BOY FOR A SECOND THERE. WHEN THE GRID WENT DOWN, I FIGURED HE MUSTA *CAUSED* IT.

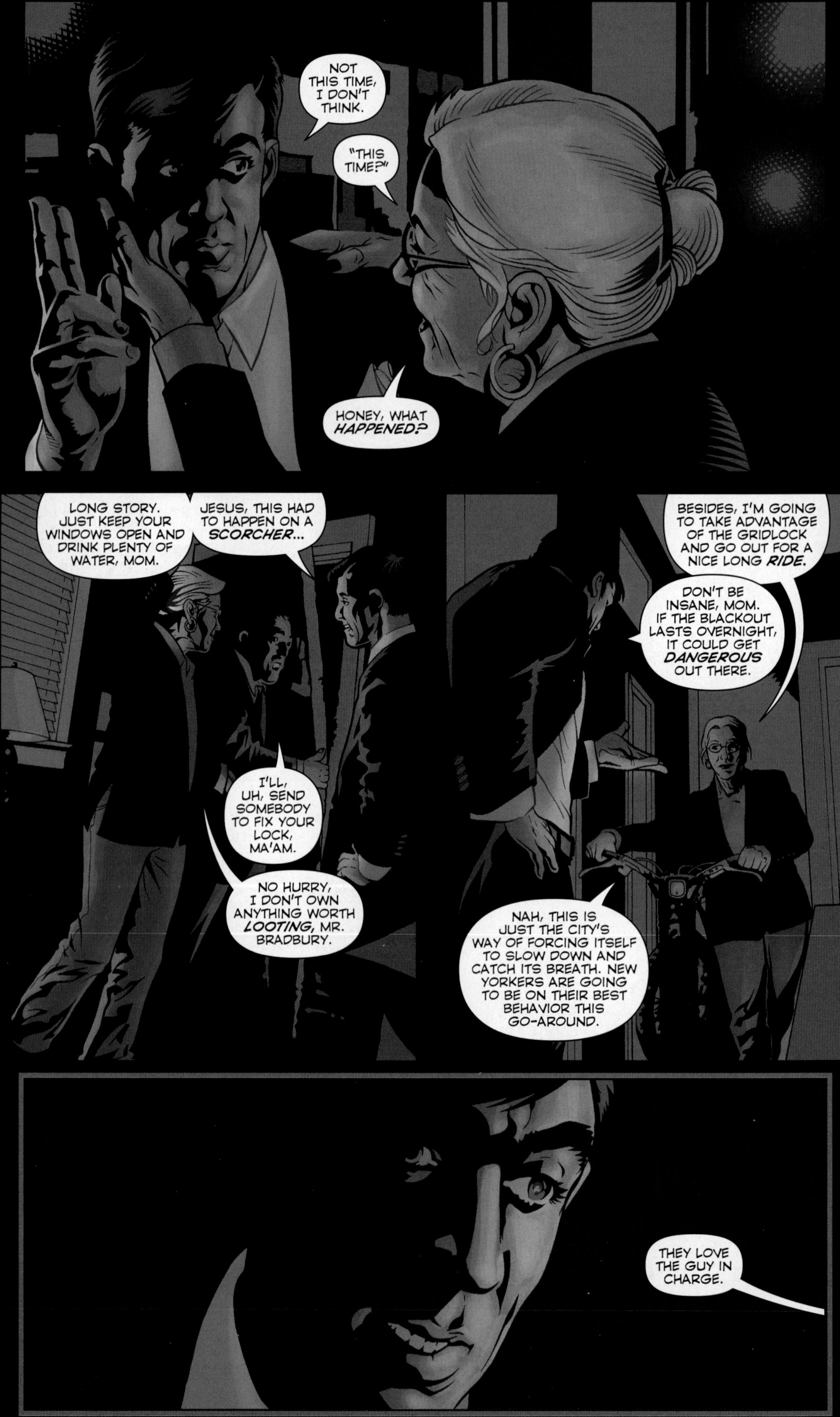
NOT THIS TIME, I DON'T THINK.
"THIS TIME?"
HONEY, WHAT *HAPPENED?*
LONG STORY. JUST KEEP YOUR WINDOWS OPEN AND DRINK PLENTY OF WATER, MOM.
JESUS, THIS HAD TO HAPPEN ON A *SCORCHER...*
I'LL, UH, SEND SOMEBODY TO FIX YOUR LOCK, MA'AM.
NO HURRY, I DON'T OWN ANYTHING WORTH *LOOTING,* MR. BRADBURY.
BESIDES, I'M GOING TO TAKE ADVANTAGE OF THE GRIDLOCK AND GO OUT FOR A NICE LONG *RIDE.*
DON'T BE INSANE, MOM. IF THE BLACKOUT LASTS OVERNIGHT, IT COULD GET *DANGEROUS* OUT THERE.
NAH, THIS IS JUST THE CITY'S WAY OF FORCING ITSELF TO SLOW DOWN AND CATCH ITS BREATH. NEW YORKERS ARE GOING TO BE ON THEIR BEST BEHAVIOR THIS GO-AROUND.
THEY LOVE THE GUY IN CHARGE.

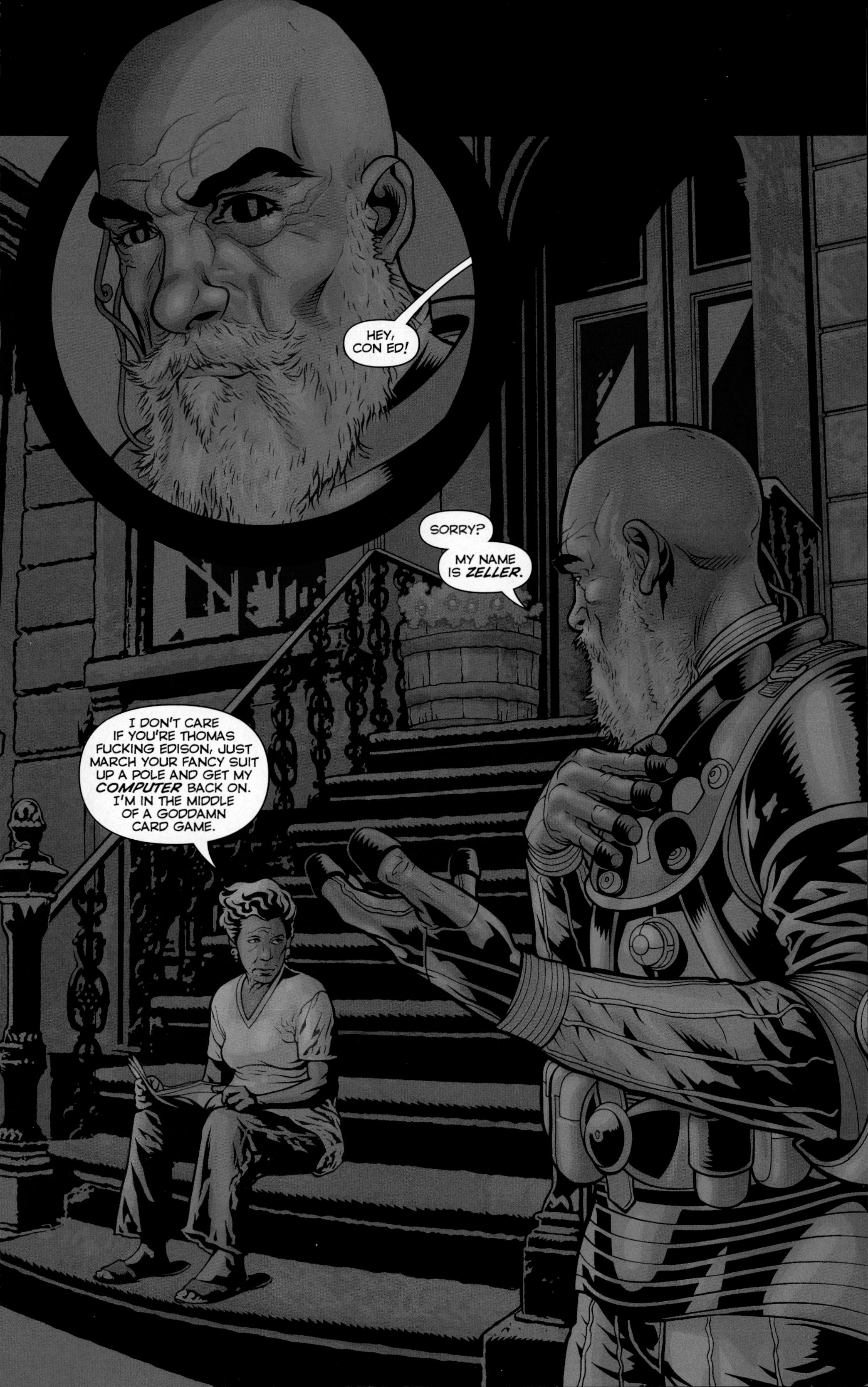
HEY, CON ED!
SORRY?
MY NAME IS ZELLER.
I DON'T CARE IF YOU'RE THOMAS FUCKING EDISON, JUST MARCH YOUR FANCY SUIT UP A POLE AND GET MY COMPUTER BACK ON. I'M IN THE MIDDLE OF A GODDAMN CARD GAME.

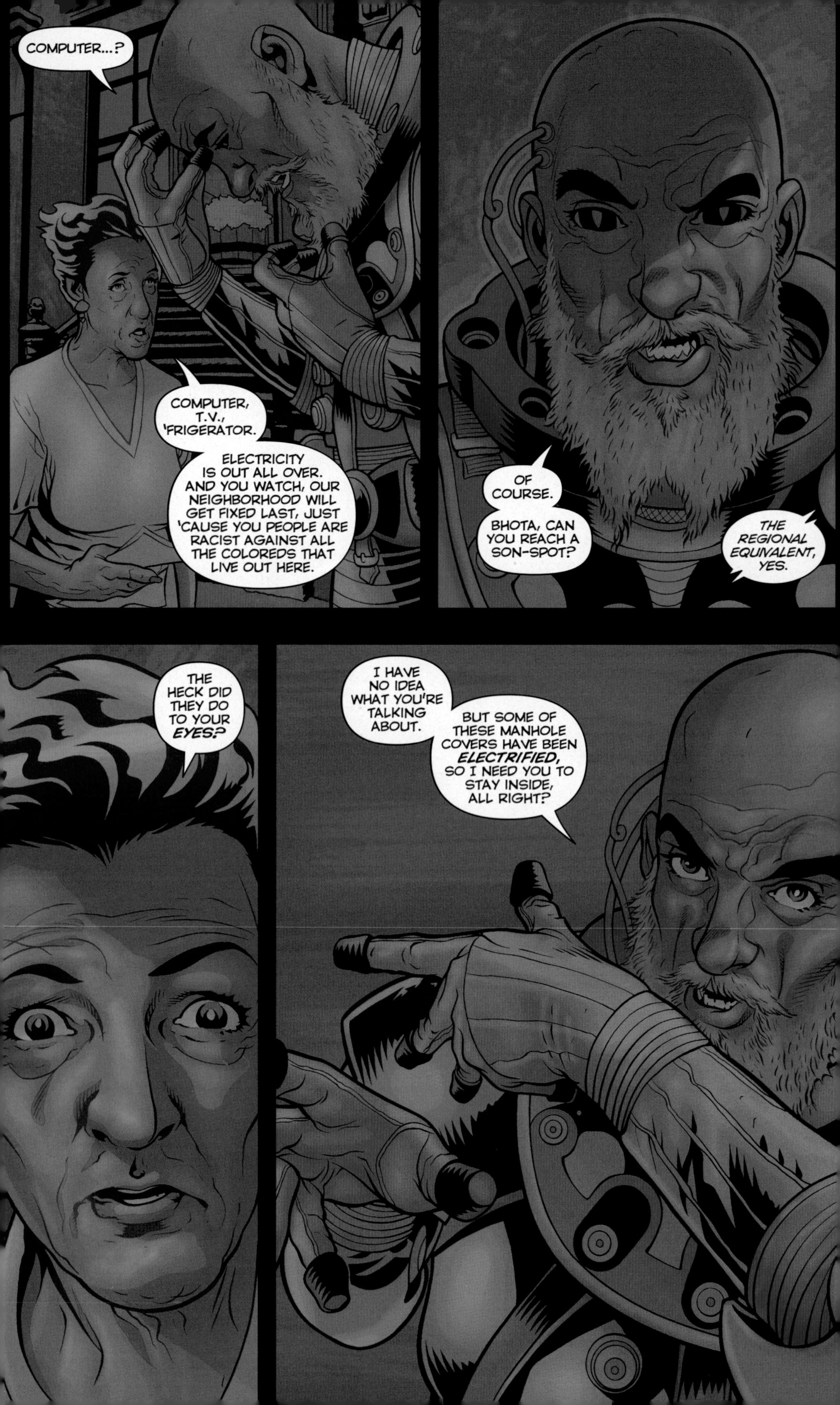
COMPUTER...?
COMPUTER, T.V., 'FRIGERATOR.
ELECTRICITY IS OUT ALL OVER. AND YOU WATCH, OUR NEIGHBORHOOD WILL GET FIXED LAST, JUST 'CAUSE YOU PEOPLE ARE RACIST AGAINST ALL THE COLOREDS THAT LIVE OUT HERE.
OF COURSE.
BHOTA, CAN YOU REACH A SON-SPOT?
THE REGIONAL EQUIVALENT, YES.
THE HECK DID THEY DO TO YOUR *EYES?*
I HAVE NO IDEA WHAT YOU'RE TALKING ABOUT.
BUT SOME OF THESE MANHOLE COVERS HAVE BEEN *ELECTRIFIED,* SO I NEED YOU TO STAY INSIDE, ALL RIGHT?

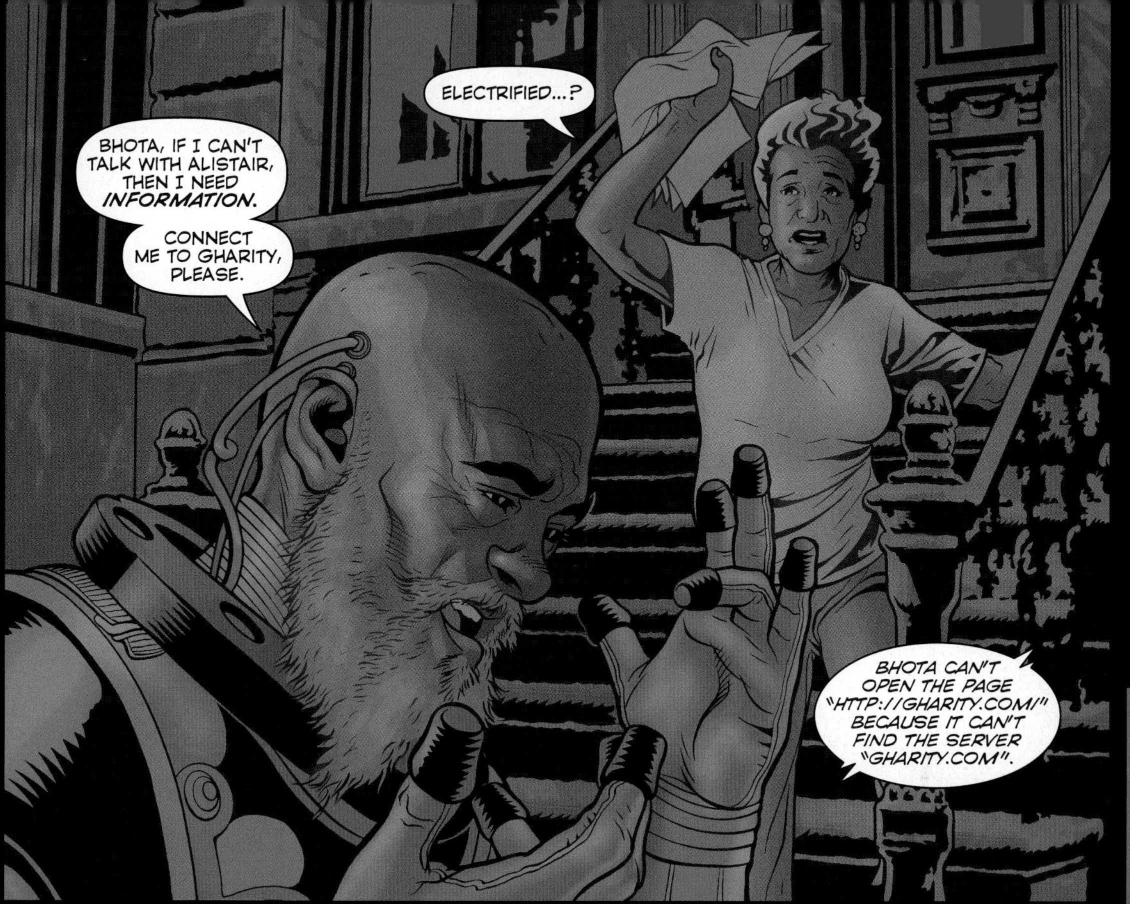
ELECTRIFIED...?
BHOTA, IF I CAN'T TALK WITH ALISTAIR, THEN I NEED *INFORMATION.*
CONNECT ME TO GHARITY, PLEASE.
BHOTA CAN'T OPEN THE PAGE "HTTP://GHARITY.COM/" BECAUSE IT CAN'T FIND THE SERVER "GHARITY.COM".

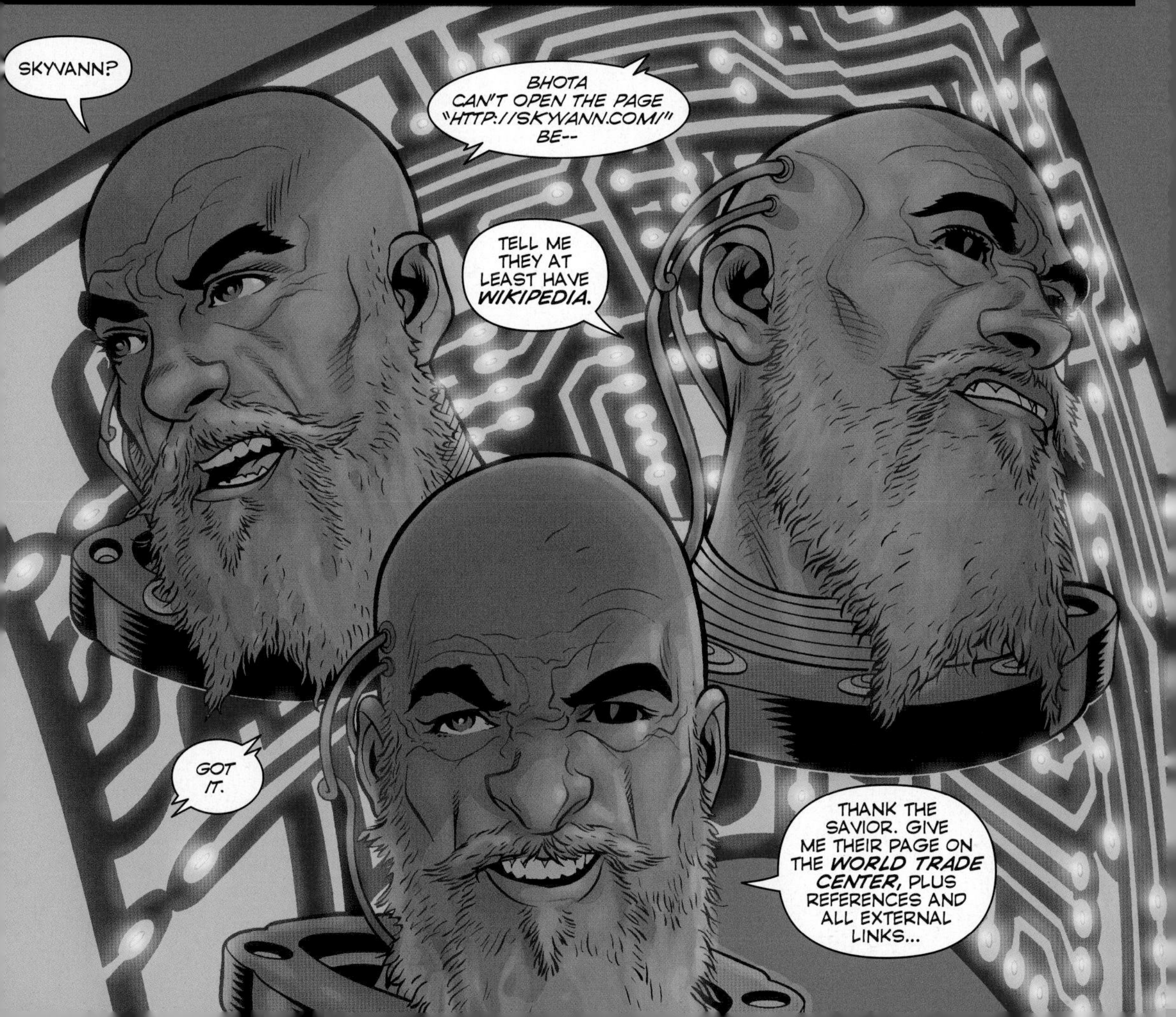
SKYVANN?
BHOTA CAN'T OPEN THE PAGE "HTTP://SKYVANN.COM/" BE--
TELL ME THEY AT LEAST HAVE *WIKIPEDIA.*
GOT IT.
THANK THE SAVIOR. GIVE ME THEIR PAGE ON THE *WORLD TRADE CENTER,* PLUS REFERENCES AND ALL EXTERNAL LINKS...

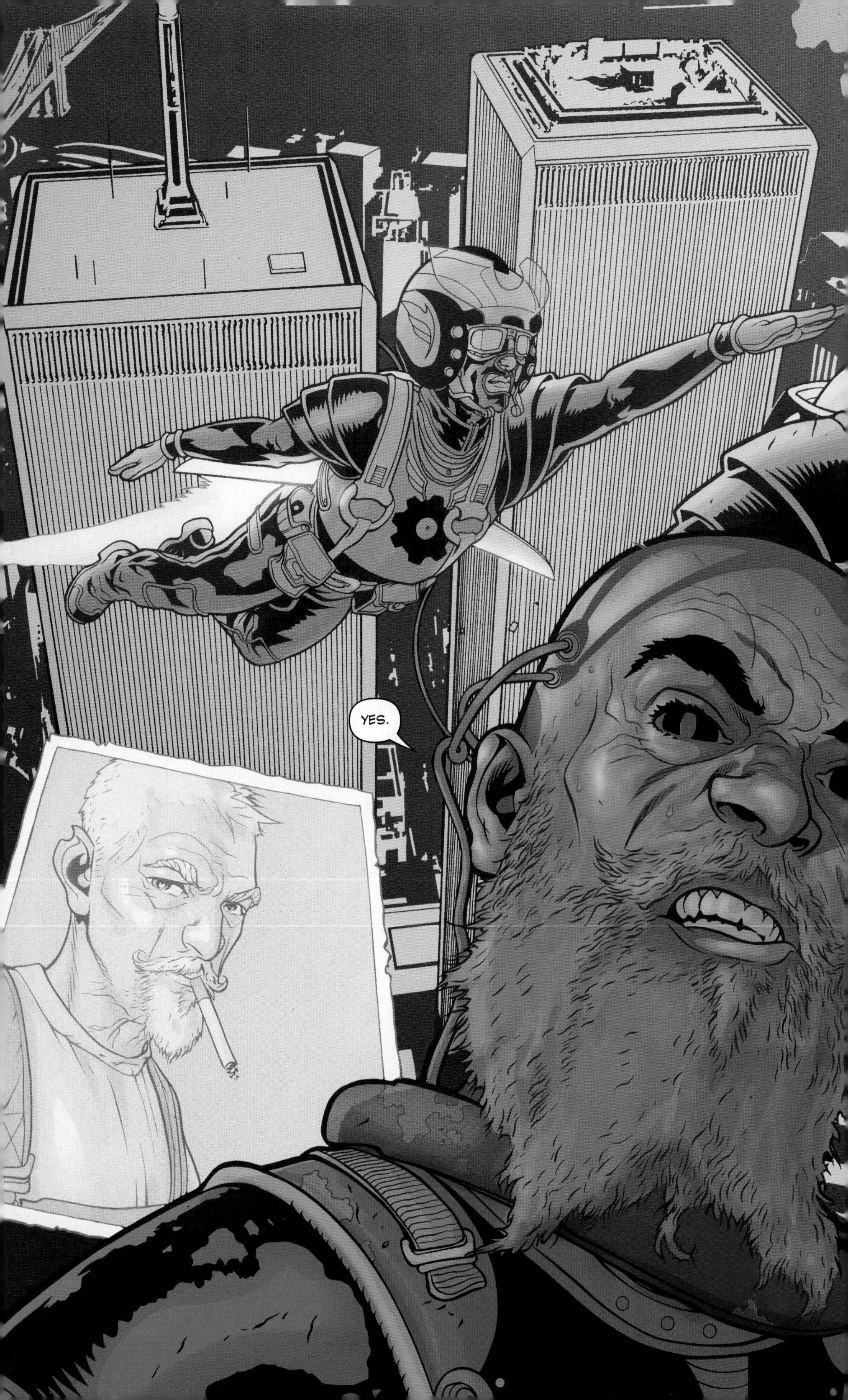
YES.

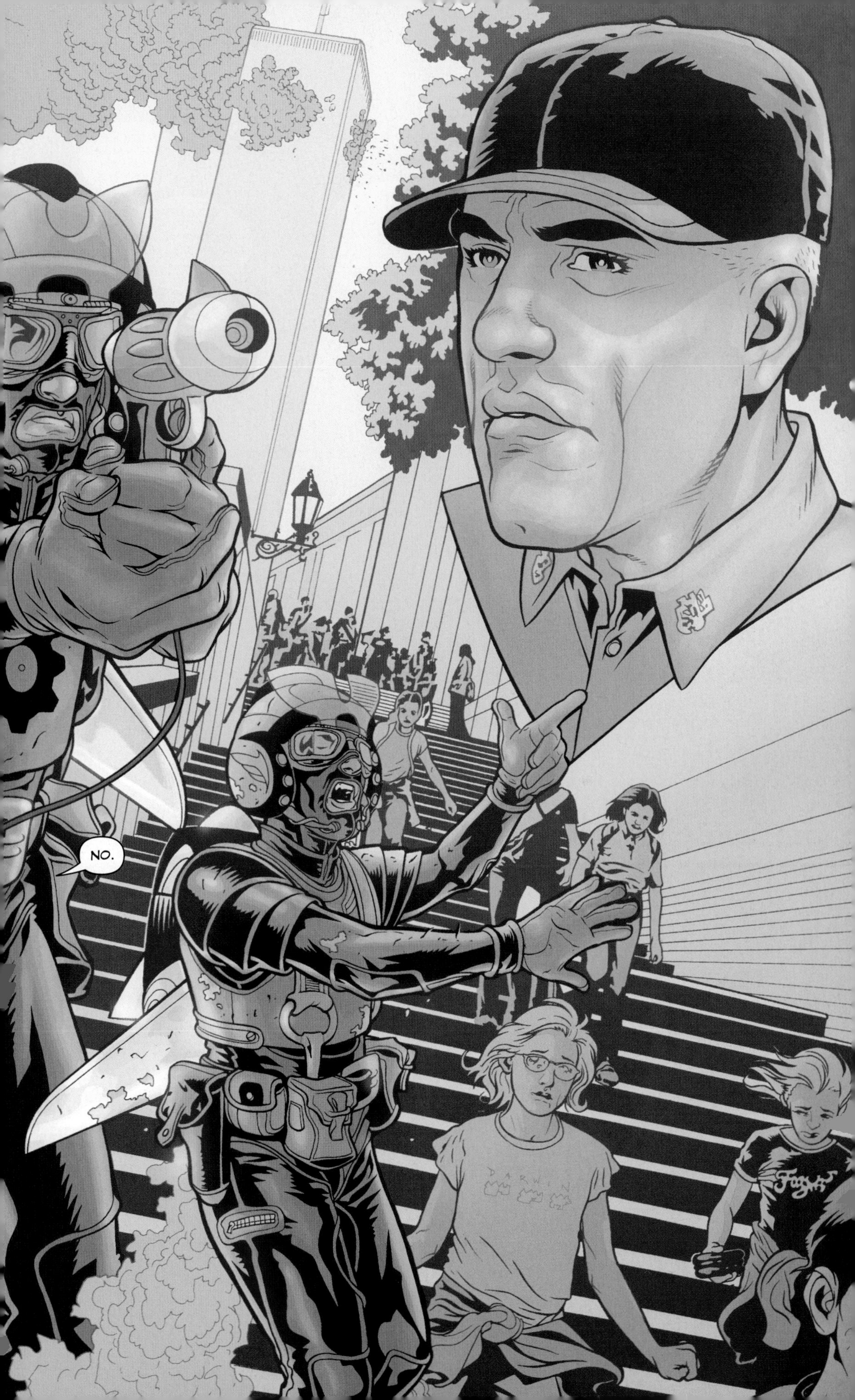
NO.

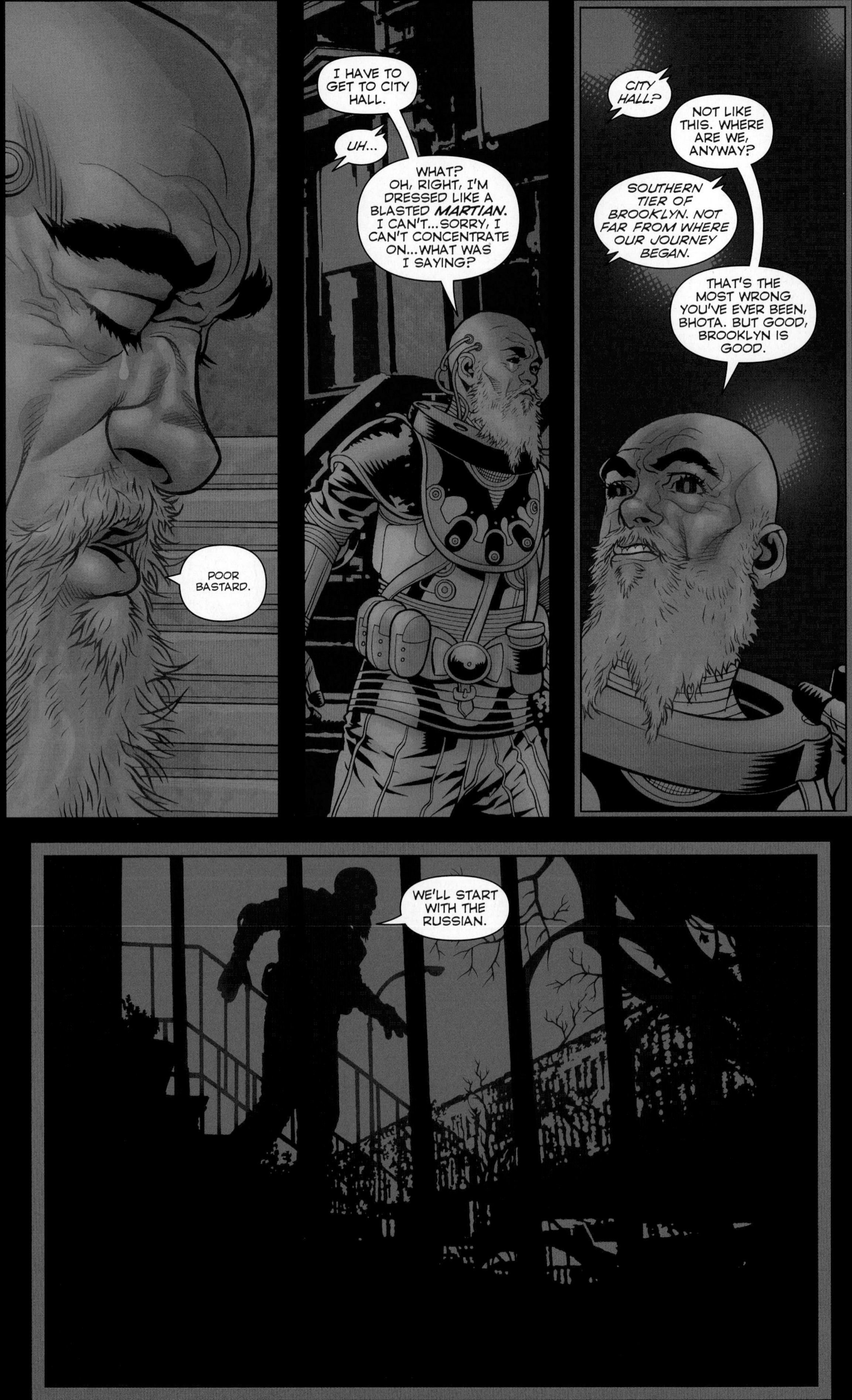
POOR BASTARD.
I HAVE TO GET TO CITY HALL.
UH...
WHAT? OH, RIGHT, I'M DRESSED LIKE A BLASTED MARTIAN. I CAN'T...SORRY, I CAN'T CONCENTRATE ON...WHAT WAS I SAYING?
CITY HALL?
NOT LIKE THIS. WHERE ARE WE, ANYWAY?
SOUTHERN TIER OF BROOKLYN. NOT FAR FROM WHERE OUR JOURNEY BEGAN.
THAT'S THE MOST WRONG YOU'VE EVER BEEN, BHOTA. BUT GOOD, BROOKLYN IS GOOD.
WE'LL START WITH THE RUSSIAN.

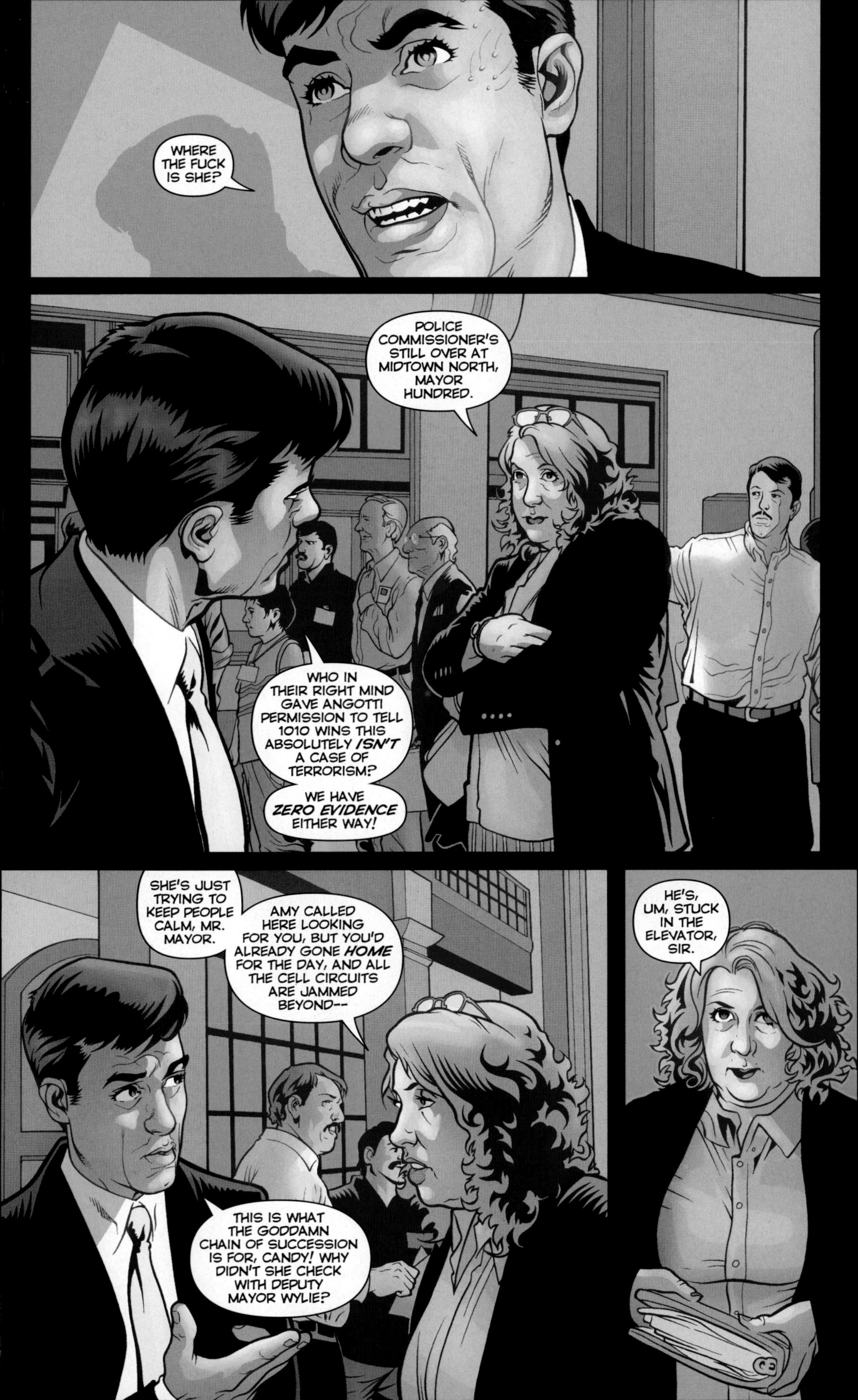
WHERE THE FUCK IS SHE?
POLICE COMMISSIONER'S STILL OVER AT MIDTOWN NORTH, MAYOR HUNDRED.
WHO IN THEIR RIGHT MIND GAVE ANGOTTI PERMISSION TO TELL 1010 WINS THIS ABSOLUTELY *ISN'T* A CASE OF TERRORISM?
WE HAVE *ZERO EVIDENCE* EITHER WAY!
SHE'S JUST TRYING TO KEEP PEOPLE CALM, MR. MAYOR.
AMY CALLED HERE LOOKING FOR YOU, BUT YOU'D ALREADY GONE *HOME* FOR THE DAY, AND ALL THE CELL CIRCUITS ARE JAMMED BEYOND--
THIS IS WHAT THE GODDAMN CHAIN OF SUCCESSION IS FOR, CANDY! WHY DIDN'T SHE CHECK WITH DEPUTY MAYOR WYLIE?
HE'S, UM, STUCK IN THE ELEVATOR, SIR.

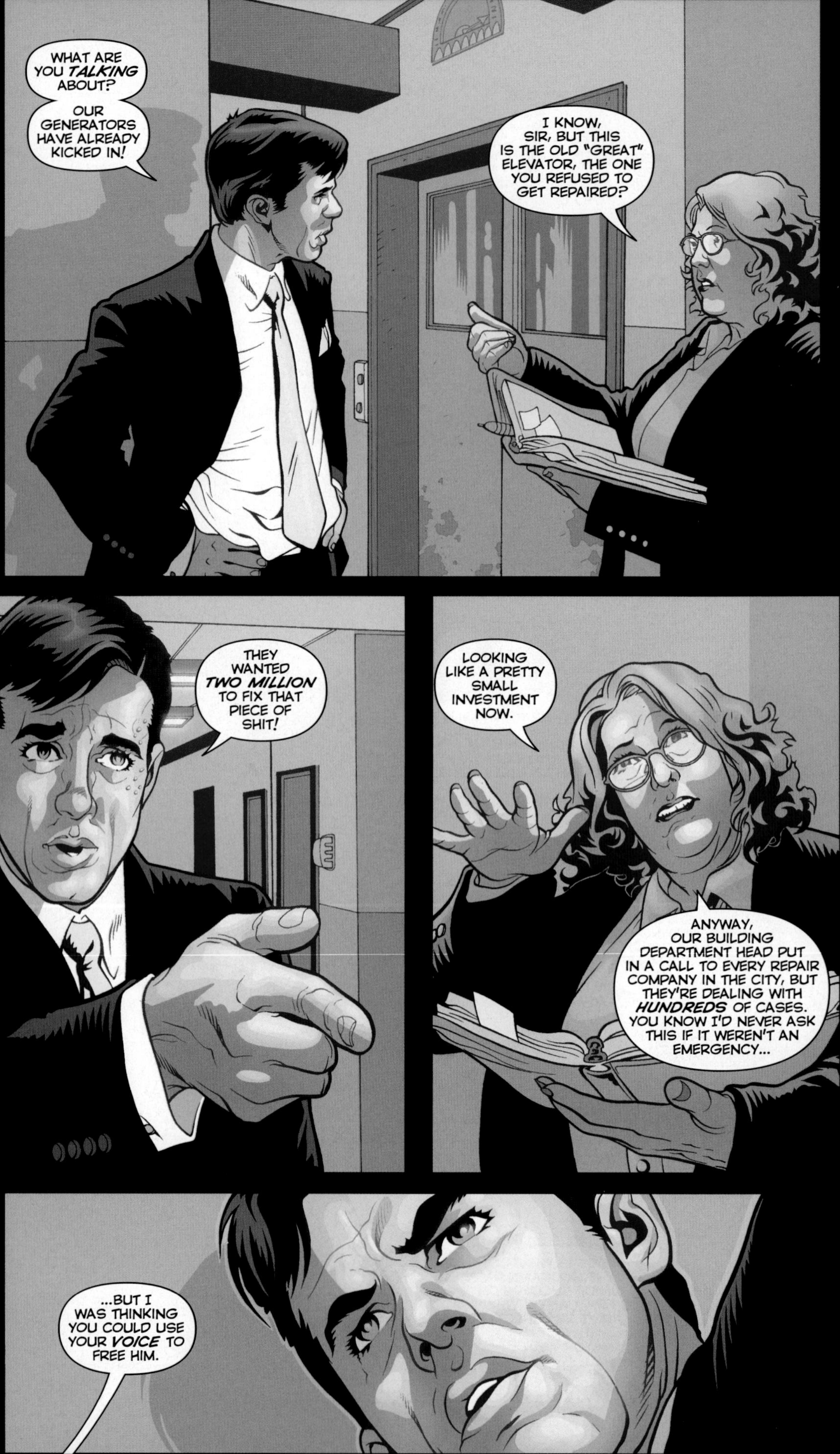
WHAT ARE YOU *TALKING* ABOUT?
OUR GENERATORS HAVE ALREADY KICKED IN!
I KNOW, SIR, BUT THIS IS THE OLD "GREAT" ELEVATOR, THE ONE YOU REFUSED TO GET REPAIRED?
THEY WANTED *TWO MILLION* TO FIX THAT PIECE OF SHIT!
LOOKING LIKE A PRETTY SMALL INVESTMENT NOW.
ANYWAY, OUR BUILDING DEPARTMENT HEAD PUT IN A CALL TO EVERY REPAIR COMPANY IN THE CITY, BUT THEY'RE DEALING WITH *HUNDREDS* OF CASES. YOU KNOW I'D NEVER ASK THIS IF IT WEREN'T AN EMERGENCY...
...BUT I WAS THINKING YOU COULD USE YOUR *VOICE* TO FREE HIM.

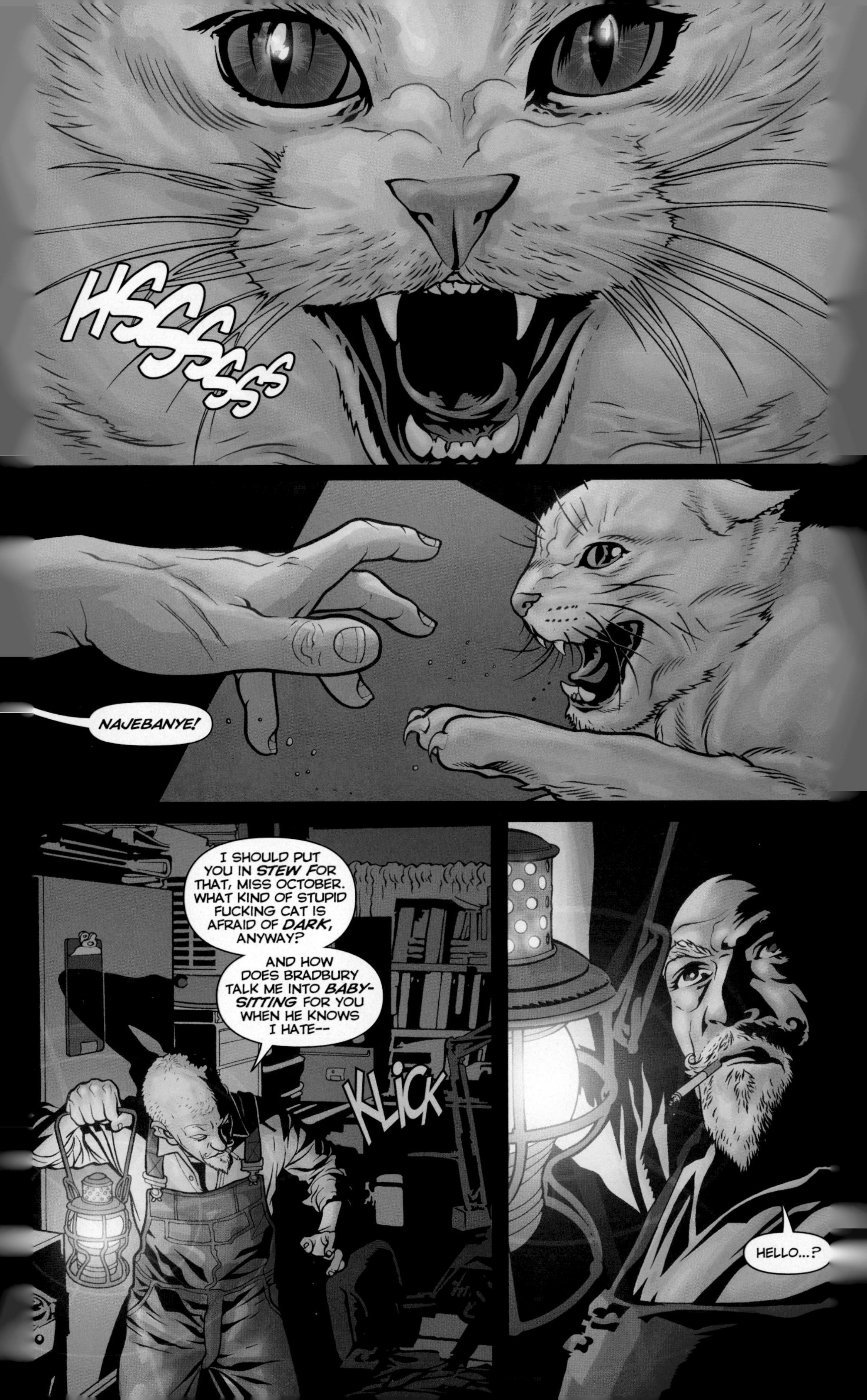
HSSSSSS
NAJEBANYE!
I SHOULD PUT YOU IN STEW FOR THAT, MISS OCTOBER. WHAT KIND OF STUPID FUCKING CAT IS AFRAID OF DARK, ANYWAY?
AND HOW DOES BRADBURY TALK ME INTO BABY-SITTING FOR YOU WHEN HE KNOWS I HATE--
KLICK
HELLO...?

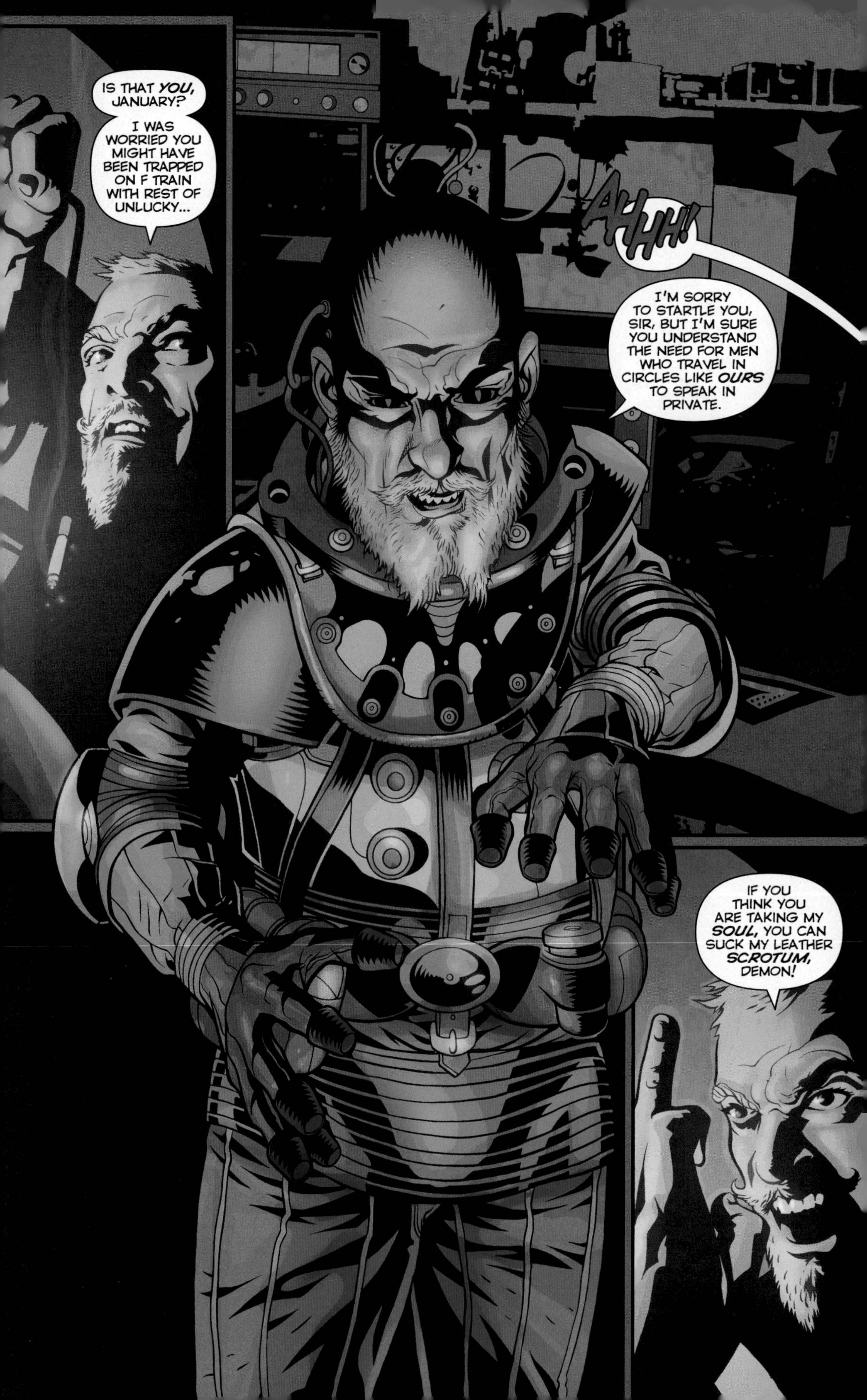
IS THAT *YOU*, JANUARY?
I WAS WORRIED YOU MIGHT HAVE BEEN TRAPPED ON F TRAIN WITH REST OF UNLUCKY...
AHHH!
I'M SORRY TO STARTLE YOU, SIR, BUT I'M SURE YOU UNDERSTAND THE NEED FOR MEN WHO TRAVEL IN CIRCLES LIKE *OURS* TO SPEAK IN PRIVATE.
IF YOU THINK YOU ARE TAKING MY ***SOUL,*** YOU CAN SUCK MY LEATHER ***SCROTUM,*** DEMON!

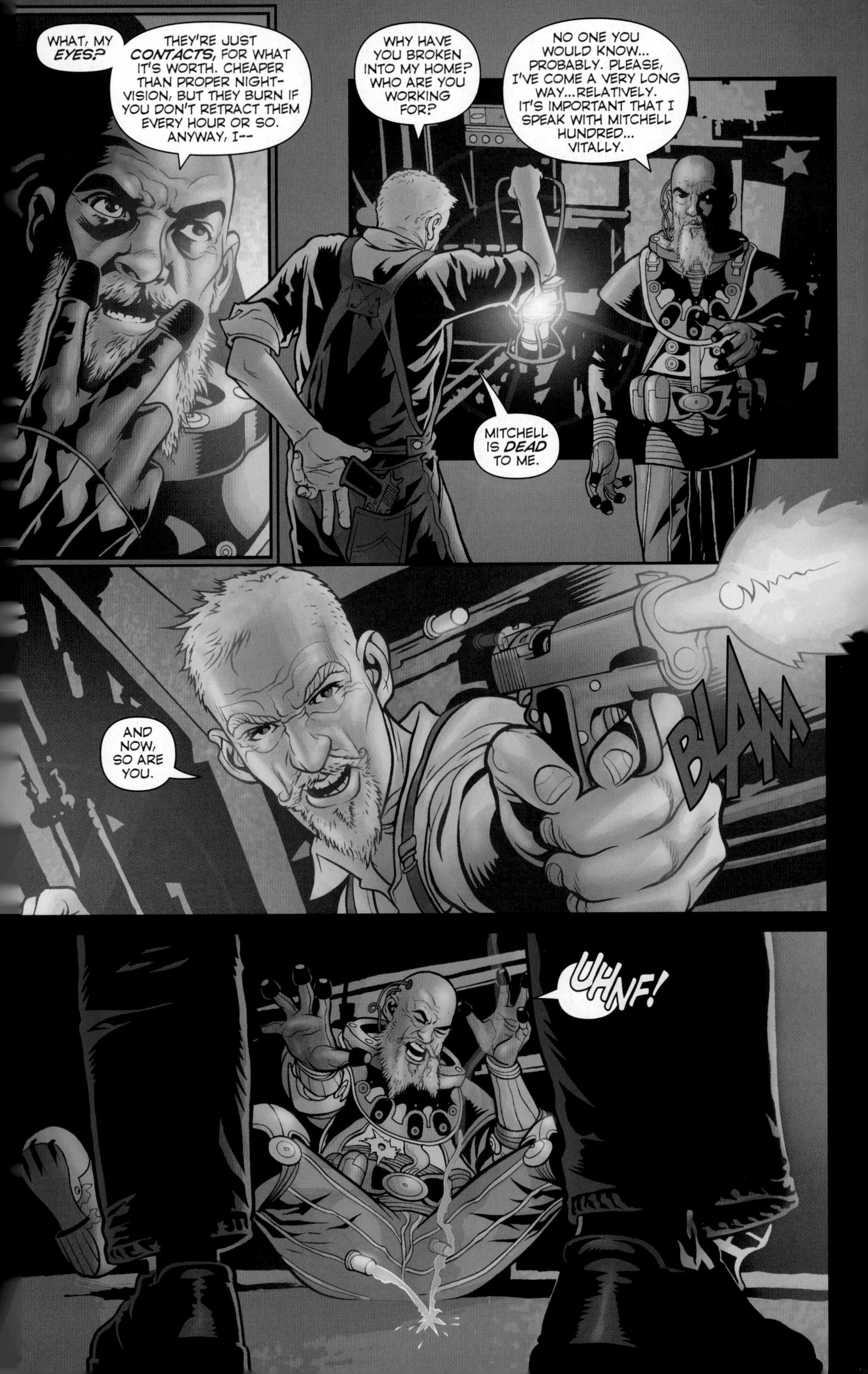
WHAT, MY *EYES?*
THEY'RE JUST *CONTACTS,* FOR WHAT IT'S WORTH. CHEAPER THAN PROPER NIGHT-VISION, BUT THEY BURN IF YOU DON'T RETRACT THEM EVERY HOUR OR SO. ANYWAY, I--
WHY HAVE YOU BROKEN INTO MY HOME? WHO ARE YOU WORKING FOR?
NO ONE YOU WOULD KNOW... PROBABLY. PLEASE, I'VE COME A VERY LONG WAY...RELATIVELY. IT'S IMPORTANT THAT I SPEAK WITH MITCHELL HUNDRED... VITALLY.
MITCHELL IS *DEAD* TO ME.
AND NOW, SO ARE YOU.
BLAM
UHNF!

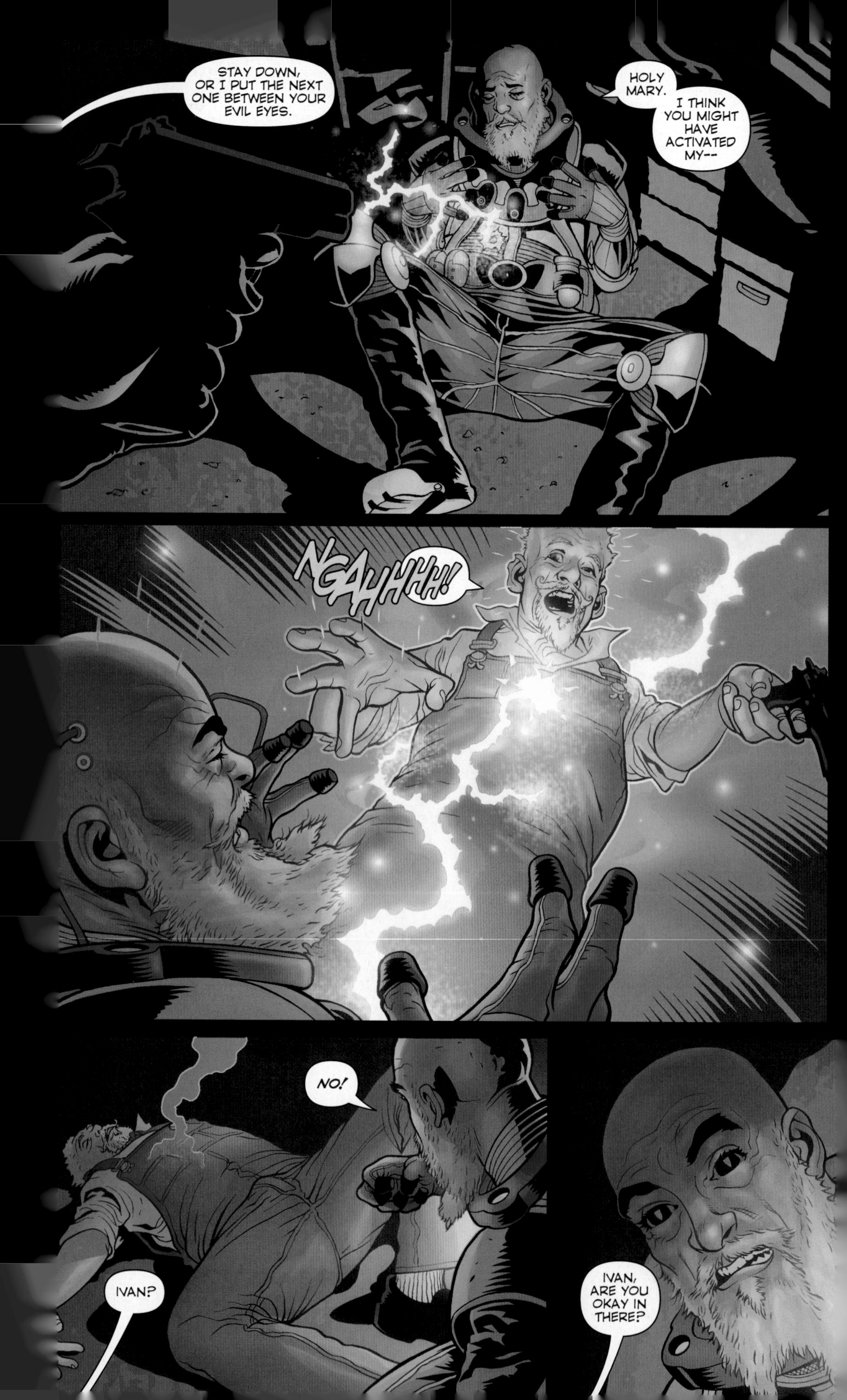
STAY DOWN, OR I PUT THE NEXT ONE BETWEEN YOUR EVIL EYES.
HOLY MARY.
I THINK YOU MIGHT HAVE ACTIVATED MY--
NGAHHHH!
NO!
IVAN?
IVAN, ARE YOU OKAY IN THERE?

I ALWAYS KNEW THIS PLACE WOULD BE THE DEATH OF ME.

JUST HANG TIGHT, DAVE. I'D USE MY "ABILITIES," BUT, UH...

...IT WOULDN'T BE FAIR TO OUR *CONSTITUENTS* IN THE SAME SITUATION. I UNDERSTAND COMPLETELY, SIR.

SCOOT AND I WILL BE FINE.

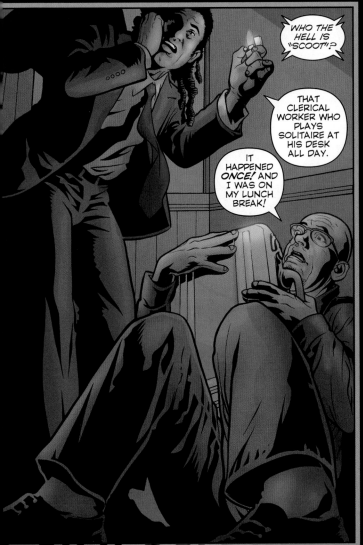

WHO THE HELL IS "SCOOT"?

THAT CLERICAL WORKER WHO PLAYS SOLITAIRE AT HIS DESK ALL DAY.

IT HAPPENED *ONCE!* AND I WAS ON MY LUNCH BREAK!

WELL, MAYBE YOU'VE MADE A LOVE CONNECTION.

YOU KNOW WHAT HAPPENED NINE MONTHS AFTER THE *LAST* BLACKOUT.

ACTUALLY, THE BIRTH RATE WENT *DOWN* THAT YEAR, SIR.

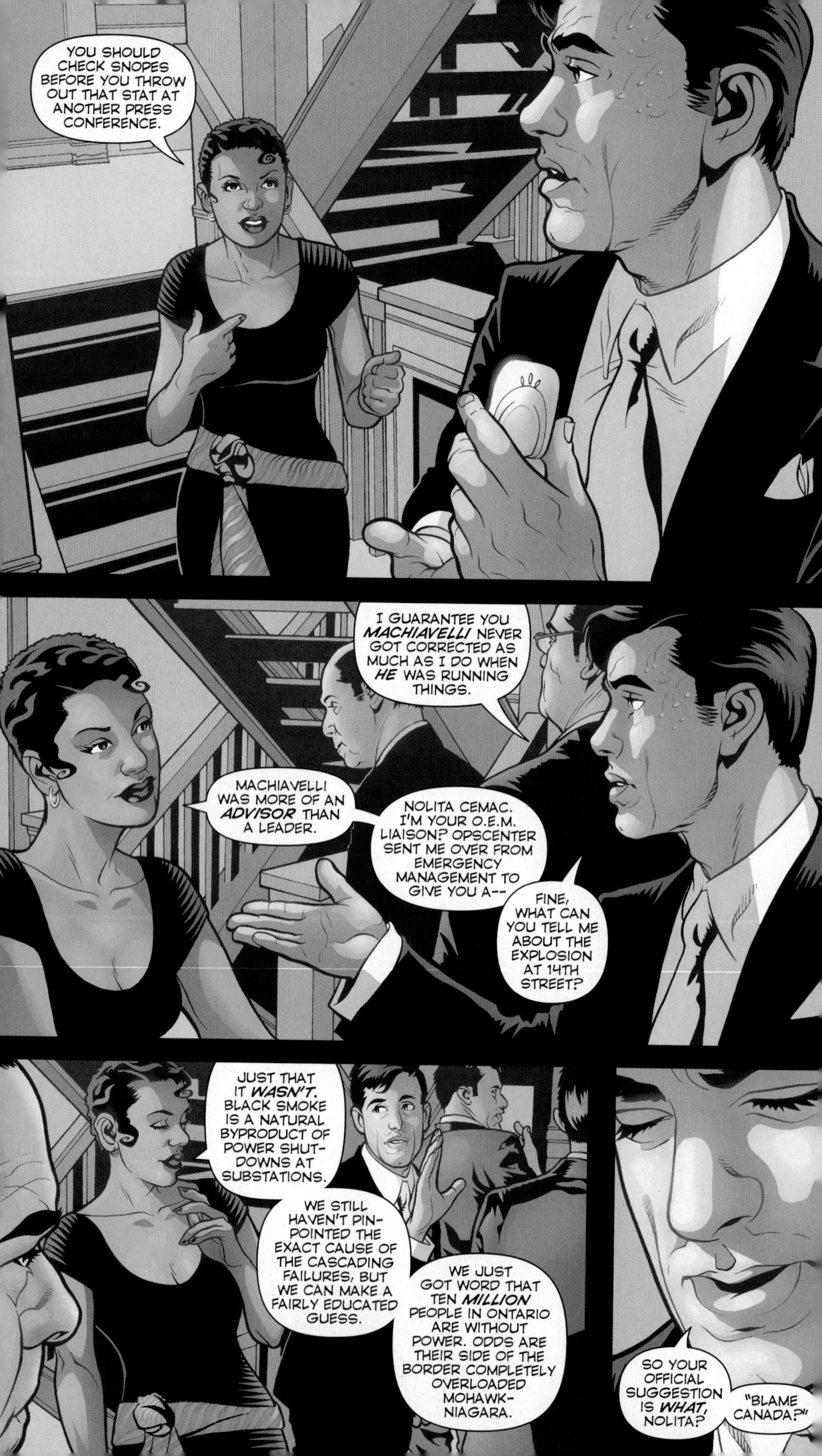
YOU SHOULD CHECK SNOPES BEFORE YOU THROW OUT THAT STAT AT ANOTHER PRESS CONFERENCE.
I GUARANTEE YOU MACHIAVELLI NEVER GOT CORRECTED AS MUCH AS I DO WHEN HE WAS RUNNING THINGS.
MACHIAVELLI WAS MORE OF AN ADVISOR THAN A LEADER.
NOLITA CEMAC. I'M YOUR O.E.M. LIAISON? OPSCENTER SENT ME OVER FROM EMERGENCY MANAGEMENT TO GIVE YOU A--
FINE, WHAT CAN YOU TELL ME ABOUT THE EXPLOSION AT 14TH STREET?
JUST THAT IT WASN'T. BLACK SMOKE IS A NATURAL BYPRODUCT OF POWER SHUT-DOWNS AT SUBSTATIONS.
WE STILL HAVEN'T PIN-POINTED THE EXACT CAUSE OF THE CASCADING FAILURES, BUT WE CAN MAKE A FAIRLY EDUCATED GUESS.
WE JUST GOT WORD THAT TEN MILLION PEOPLE IN ONTARIO ARE WITHOUT POWER. ODDS ARE THEIR SIDE OF THE BORDER COMPLETELY OVERLOADED MOHAWK-NIAGARA.
SO YOUR OFFICIAL SUGGESTION IS WHAT, NOLITA?
"BLAME CANADA?"

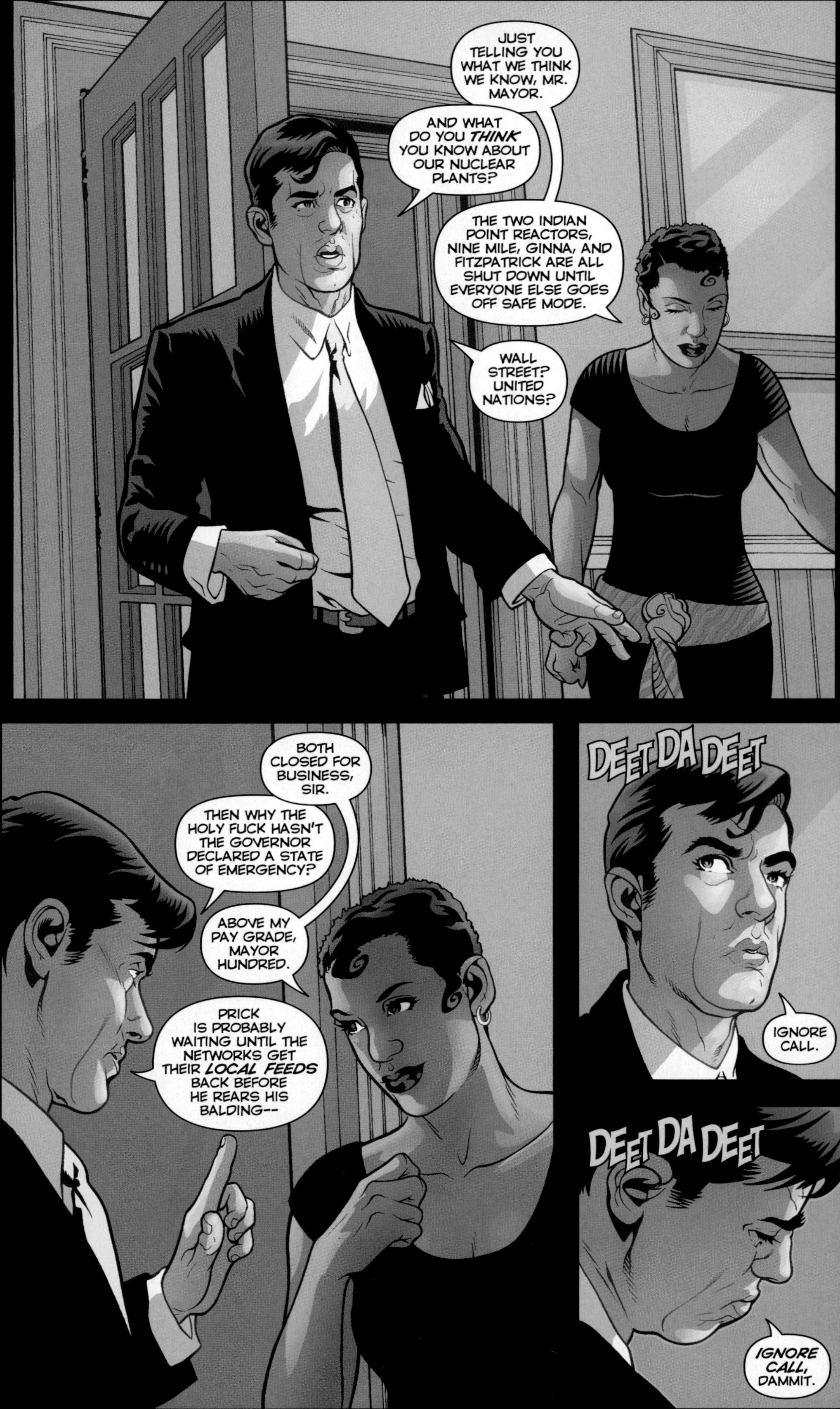
JUST TELLING YOU WHAT WE THINK WE KNOW, MR. MAYOR.
AND WHAT DO YOU *THINK* YOU KNOW ABOUT OUR NUCLEAR PLANTS?
THE TWO INDIAN POINT REACTORS, NINE MILE, GINNA, AND FITZPATRICK ARE ALL SHUT DOWN UNTIL EVERYONE ELSE GOES OFF SAFE MODE.
WALL STREET? UNITED NATIONS?
BOTH CLOSED FOR BUSINESS, SIR.
THEN WHY THE HOLY FUCK HASN'T THE GOVERNOR DECLARED A STATE OF EMERGENCY?
ABOVE MY PAY GRADE, MAYOR HUNDRED.
PRICK IS PROBABLY WAITING UNTIL THE NETWORKS GET THEIR *LOCAL FEEDS* BACK BEFORE HE REARS HIS BALDING--
DEET DA DEET
IGNORE CALL.
DEET DA DEET
IGNORE CALL, DAMMIT.

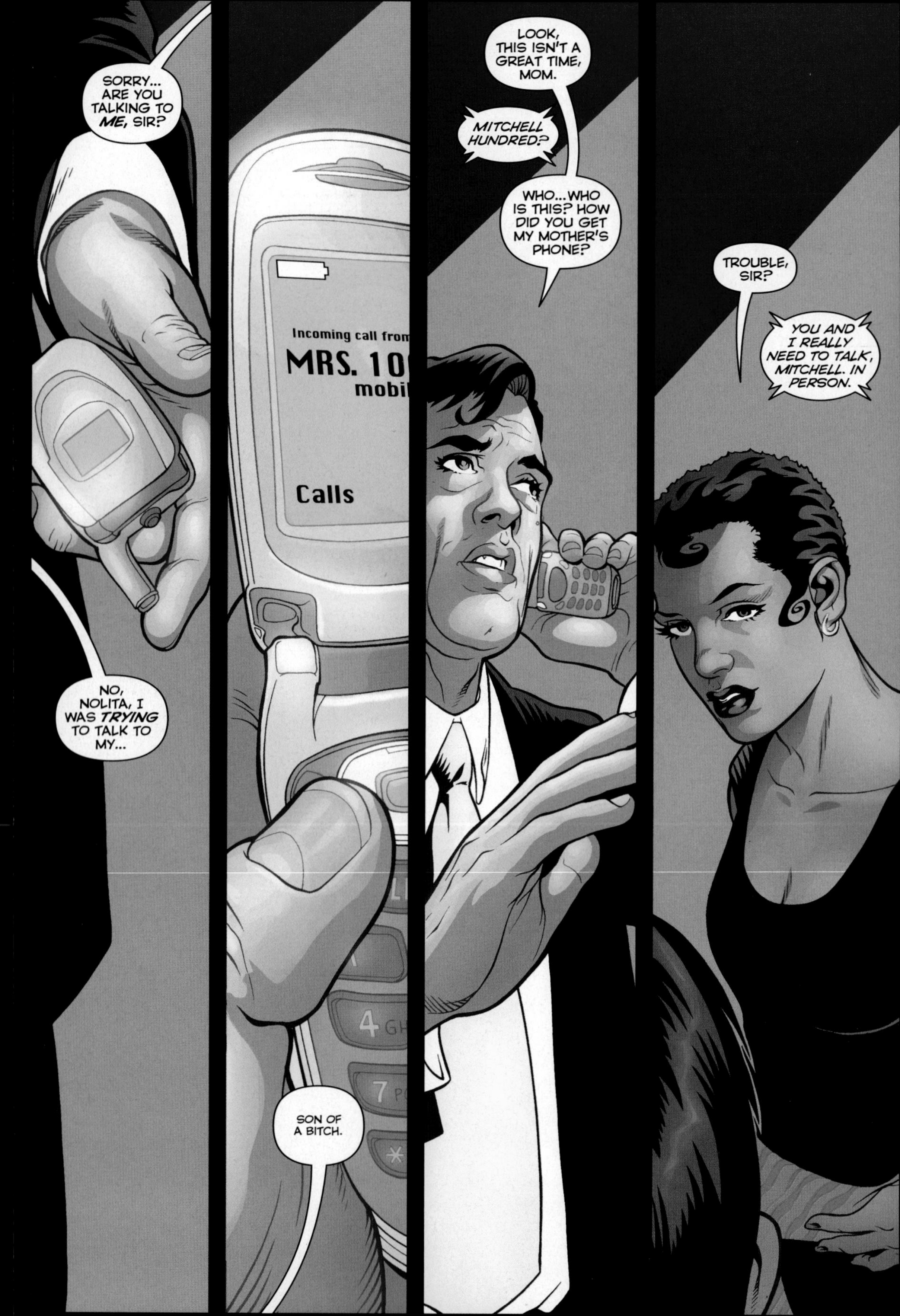
SORRY... ARE YOU TALKING TO *ME*, SIR?
NO, NOLITA, I WAS *TRYING* TO TALK TO MY...
Incoming call from
MRS. 10
mobil
Calls
SON OF A BITCH.
LOOK, THIS ISN'T A GREAT TIME, MOM.
MITCHELL HUNDRED?
WHO...WHO IS THIS? HOW DID YOU GET MY MOTHER'S PHONE?
TROUBLE, SIR?
YOU AND I REALLY NEED TO TALK, MITCHELL. IN PERSON.

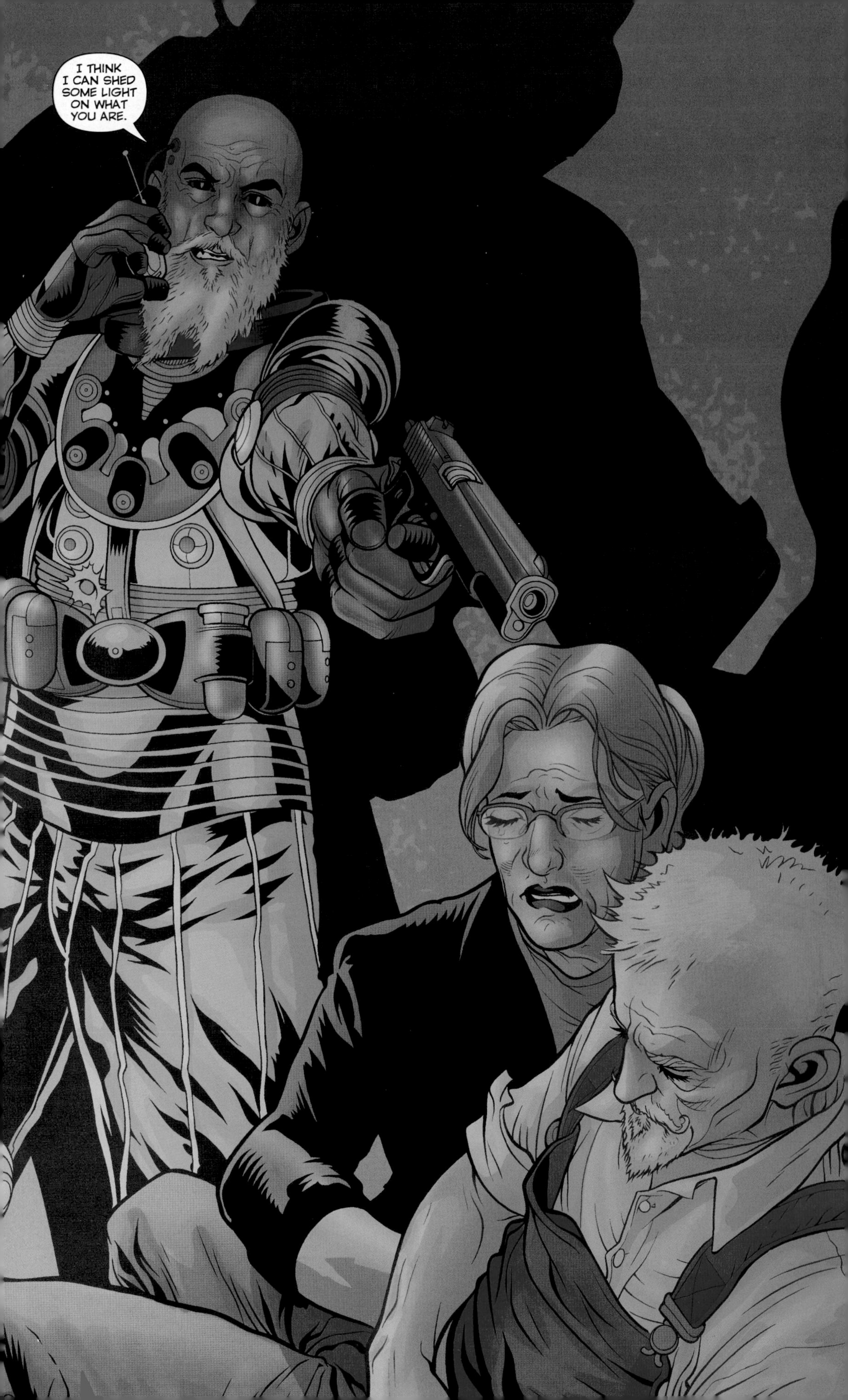
I THINK I CAN SHED SOME LIGHT ON WHAT YOU ARE.

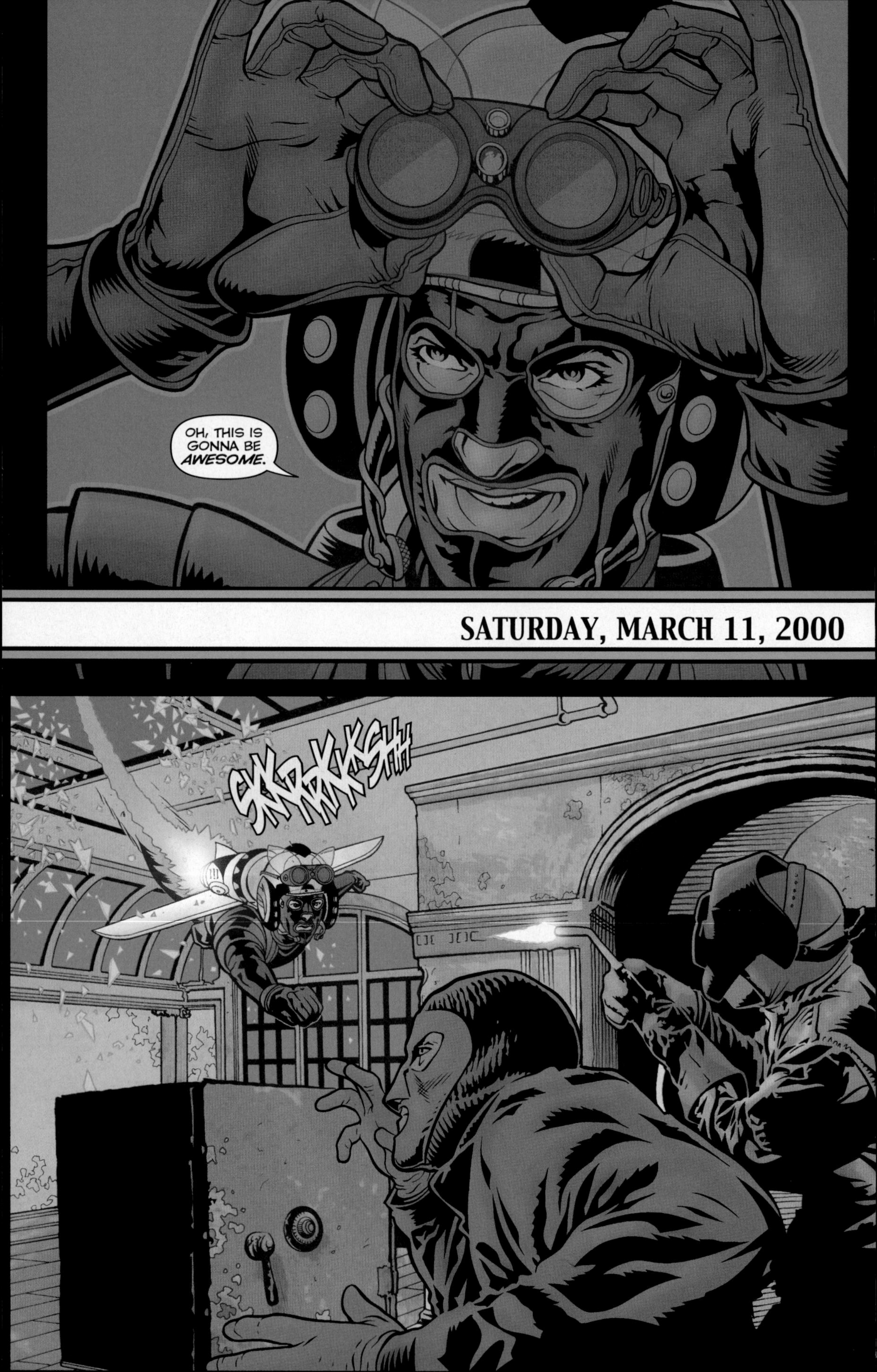
OH, THIS IS GONNA BE *AWESOME*.
SATURDAY, MARCH 11, 2000

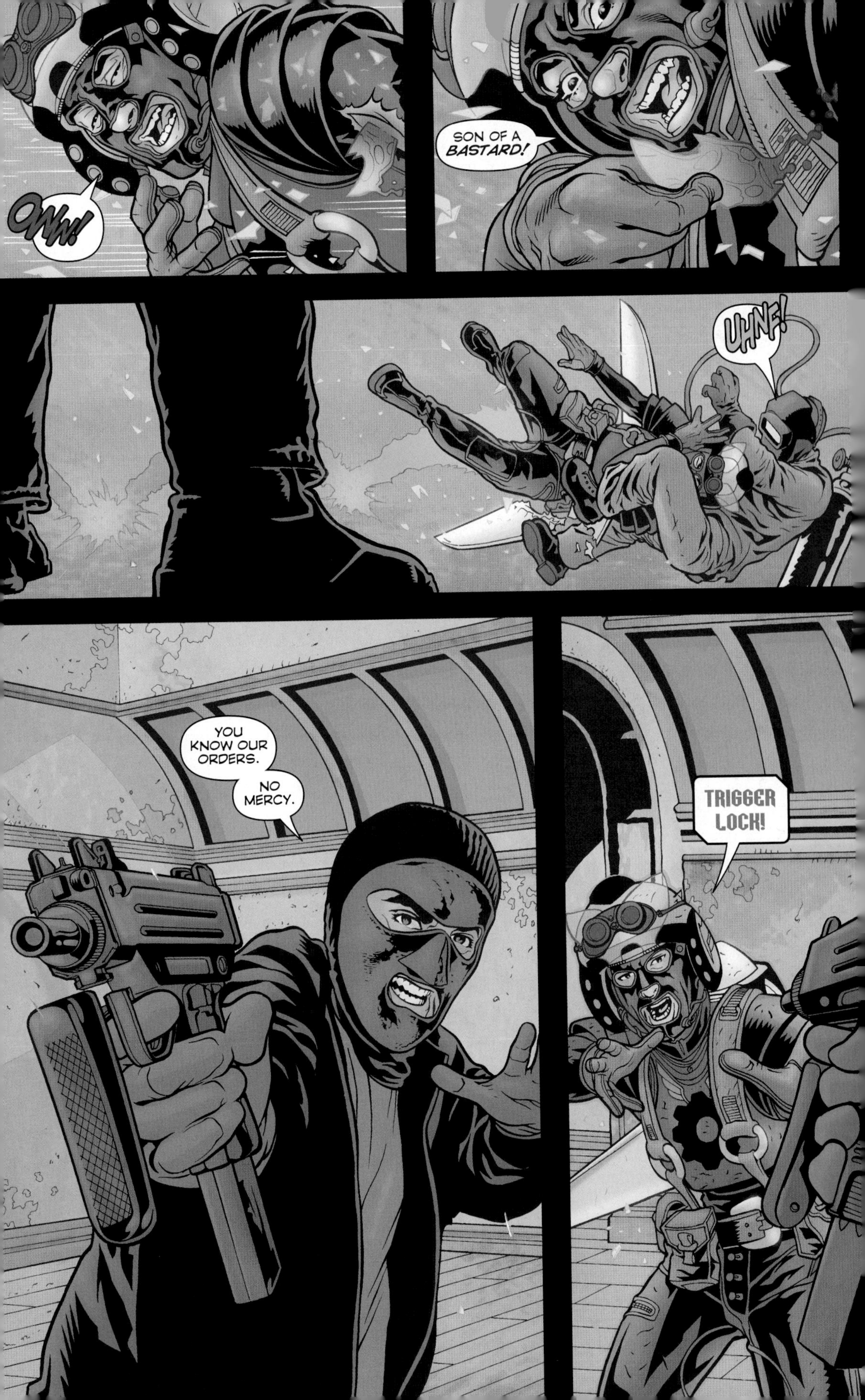

OWW!
SON OF A BASTARD!
UHNF!
YOU KNOW OUR ORDERS.
NO MERCY.
TRIGGER LOCK!

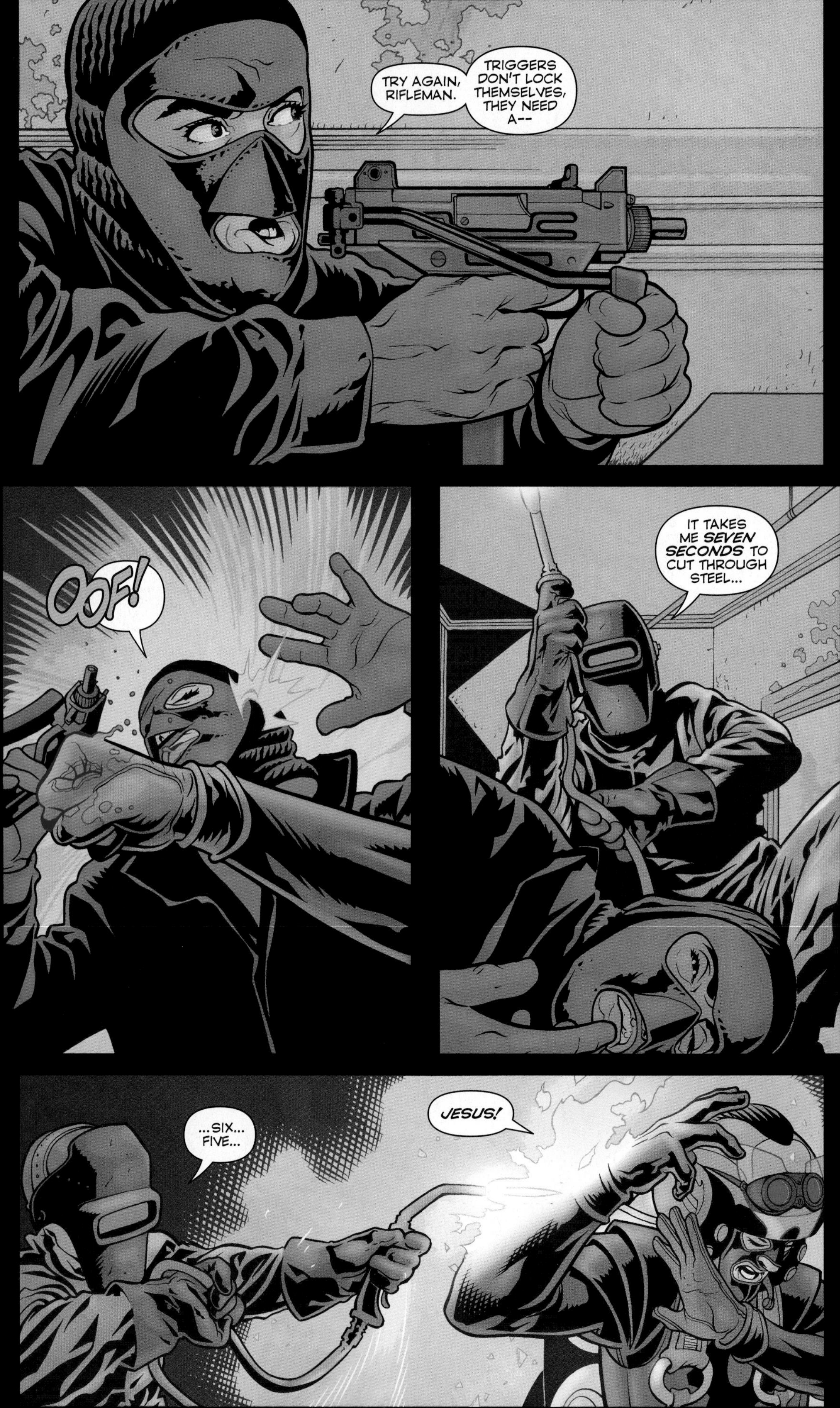
TRY AGAIN, RIFLEMAN.
TRIGGERS DON'T LOCK THEMSELVES, THEY NEED A--
OOF!
IT TAKES ME SEVEN SECONDS TO CUT THROUGH STEEL...
...SIX... FIVE...
JESUS!

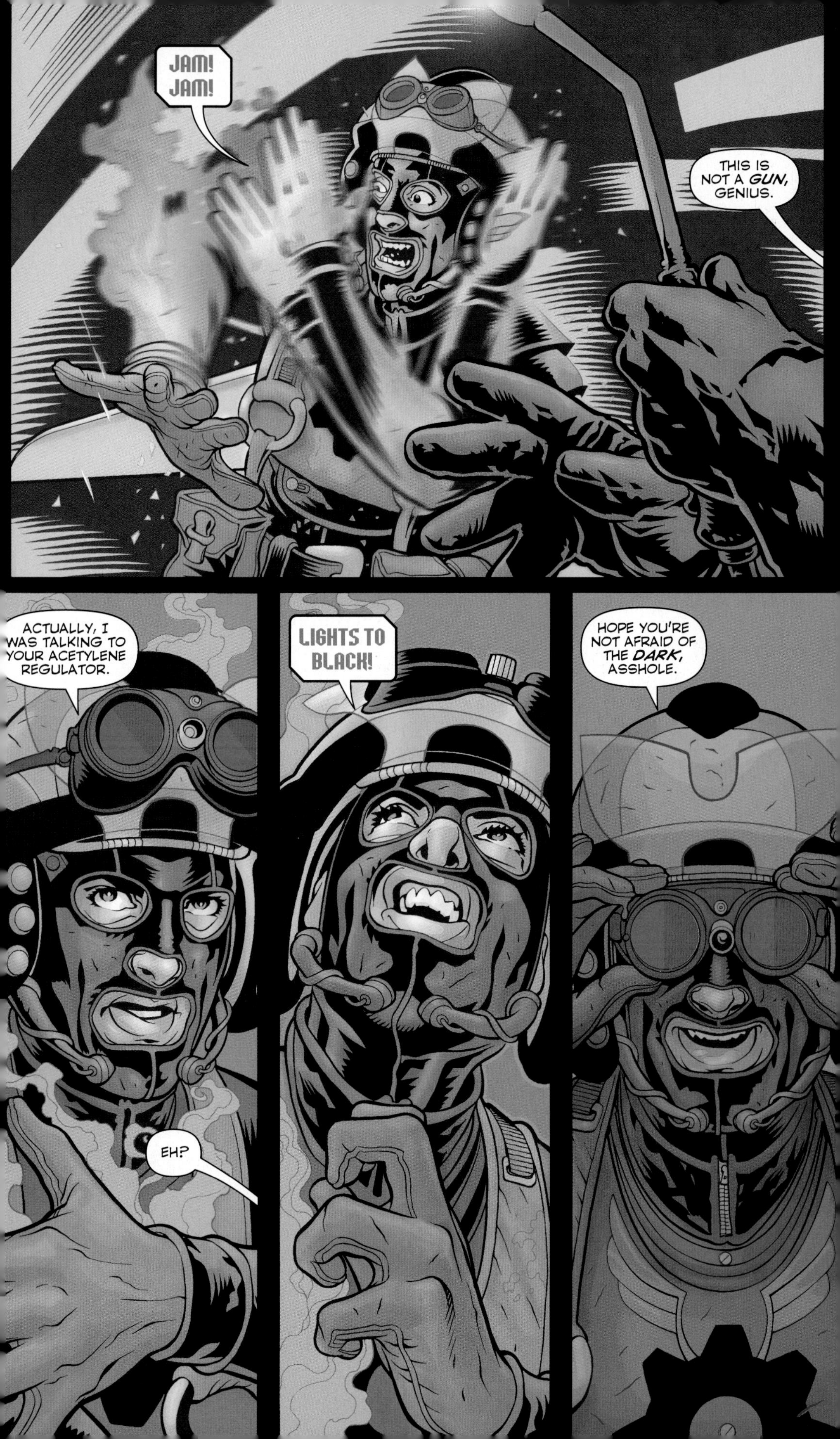
JAM! JAM!
THIS IS NOT A *GUN,* GENIUS.
ACTUALLY, I WAS TALKING TO YOUR ACETYLENE REGULATOR.
EH?
LIGHTS TO BLACK!
HOPE YOU'RE NOT AFRAID OF THE *DARK,* ASSHOLE.

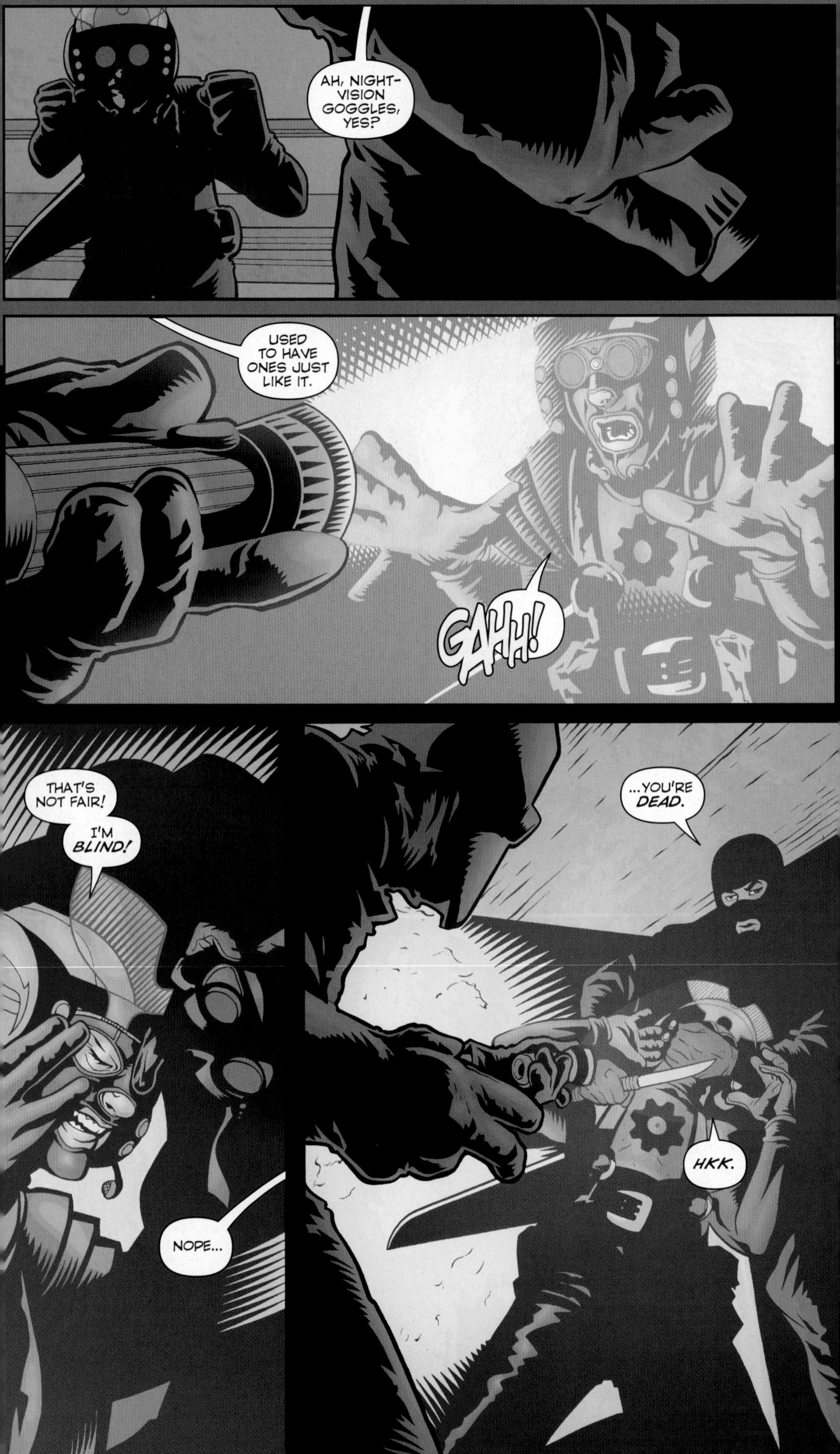
AH, NIGHT-VISION GOGGLES, YES?
USED TO HAVE ONES JUST LIKE IT.
GAHH!
THAT'S NOT FAIR!
I'M *BLIND!*
NOPE...
...YOU'RE *DEAD.*
HKK.

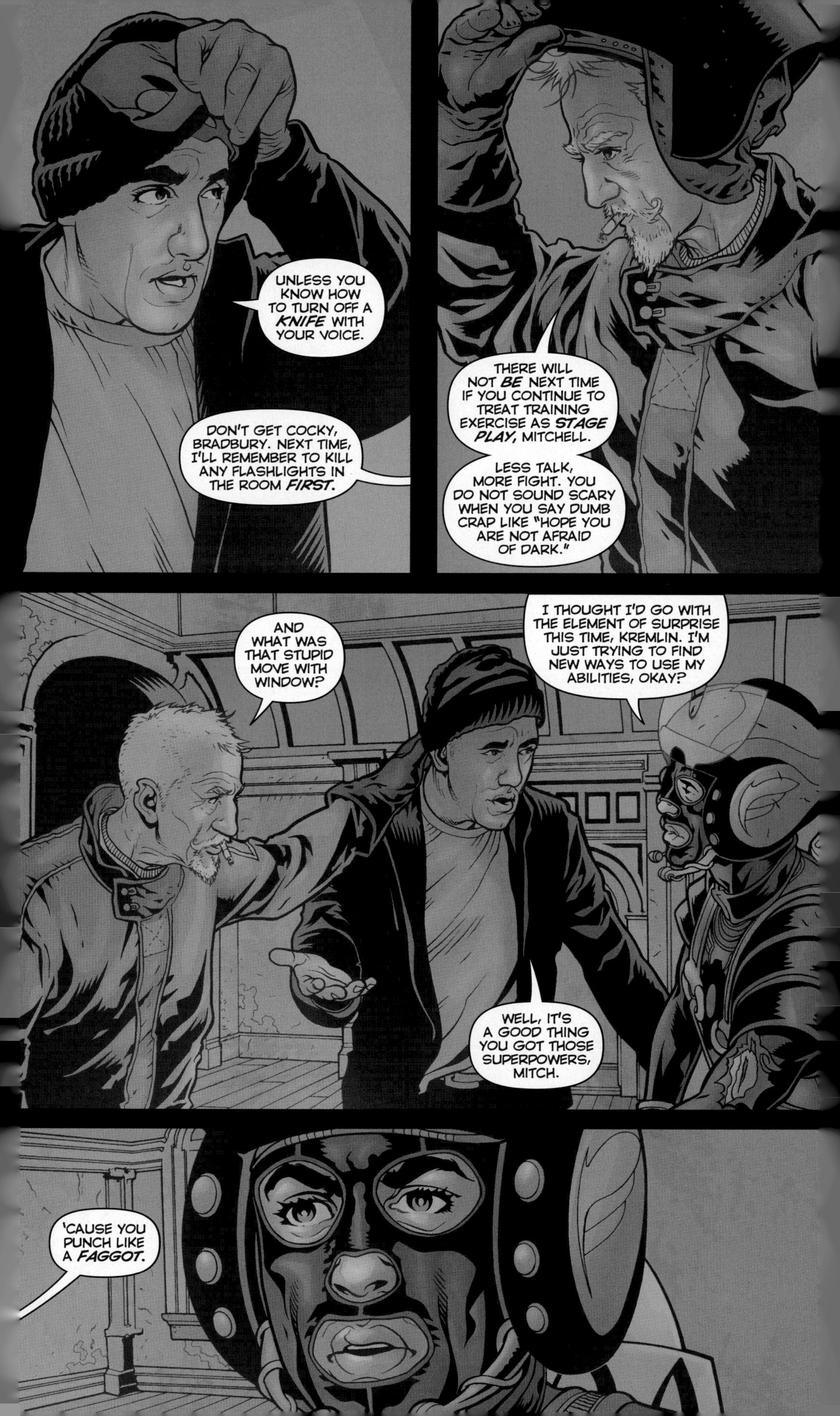
UNLESS YOU KNOW HOW TO TURN OFF A KNIFE WITH YOUR VOICE.
THERE WILL NOT BE NEXT TIME IF YOU CONTINUE TO TREAT TRAINING EXERCISE AS STAGE PLAY, MITCHELL.
DON'T GET COCKY, BRADBURY. NEXT TIME, I'LL REMEMBER TO KILL ANY FLASHLIGHTS IN THE ROOM FIRST.
LESS TALK, MORE FIGHT. YOU DO NOT SOUND SCARY WHEN YOU SAY DUMB CRAP LIKE "HOPE YOU ARE NOT AFRAID OF DARK."
AND WHAT WAS THAT STUPID MOVE WITH WINDOW?
I THOUGHT I'D GO WITH THE ELEMENT OF SURPRISE THIS TIME, KREMLIN. I'M JUST TRYING TO FIND NEW WAYS TO USE MY ABILITIES, OKAY?
WELL, IT'S A GOOD THING YOU GOT THOSE SUPERPOWERS, MITCH.
'CAUSE YOU PUNCH LIKE A FAGGOT.

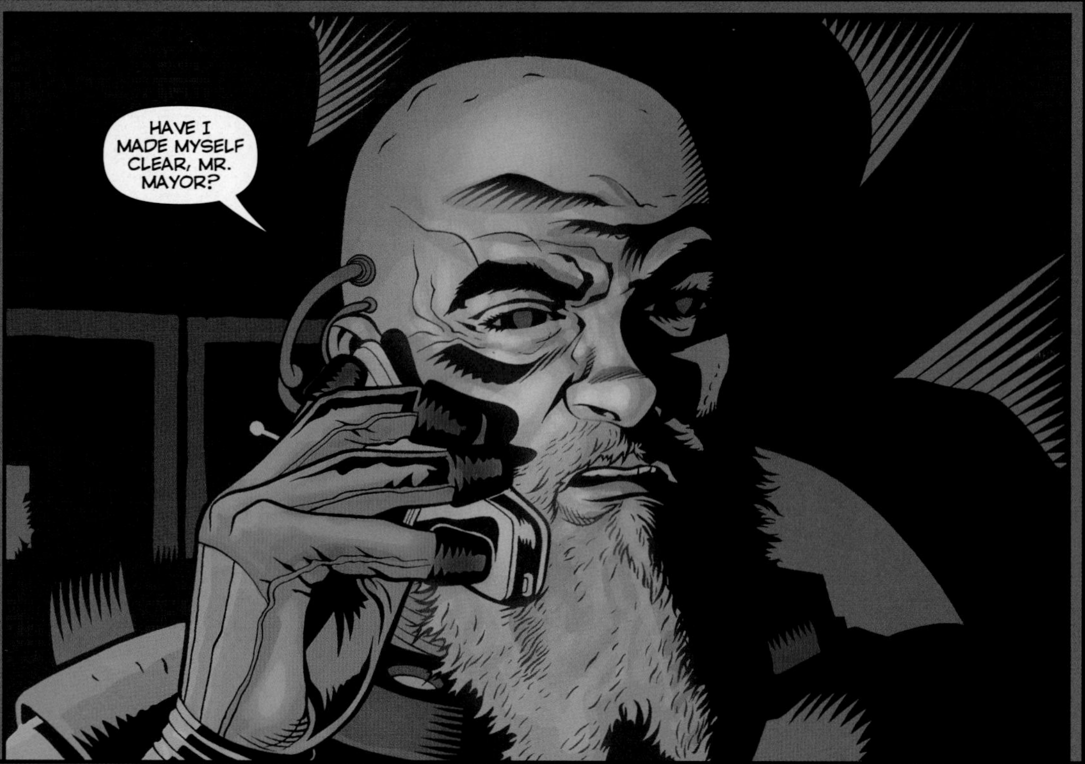
HAVE I MADE MYSELF CLEAR, MR. MAYOR?

THURSDAY, AUGUST 14, 2003

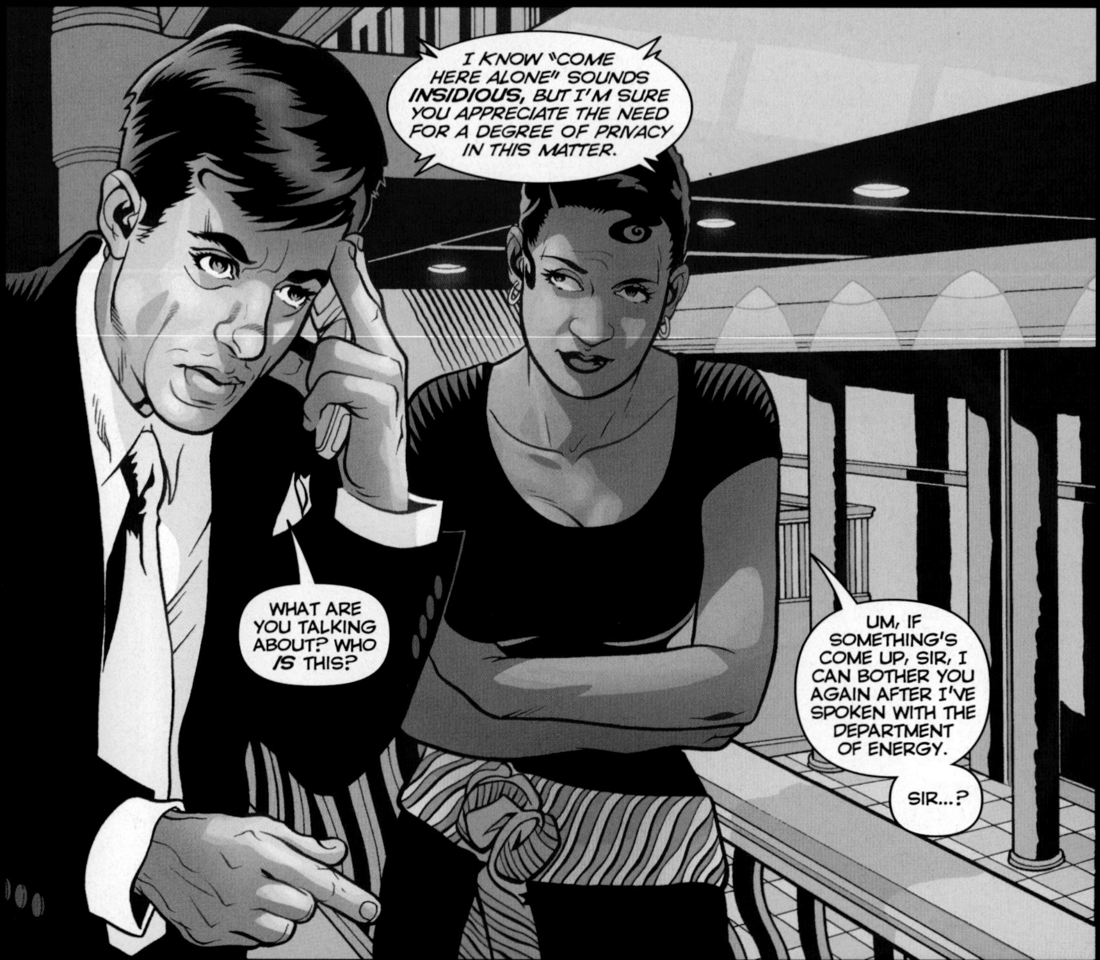
I KNOW "COME HERE ALONE" SOUNDS *INSIDIOUS*, BUT I'M SURE YOU APPRECIATE THE NEED FOR A DEGREE OF PRIVACY IN THIS MATTER.
WHAT ARE YOU TALKING ABOUT? WHO *IS* THIS?
UM, IF SOMETHING'S COME UP, SIR, I CAN BOTHER YOU AGAIN AFTER I'VE SPOKEN WITH THE DEPARTMENT OF ENERGY.
SIR...?

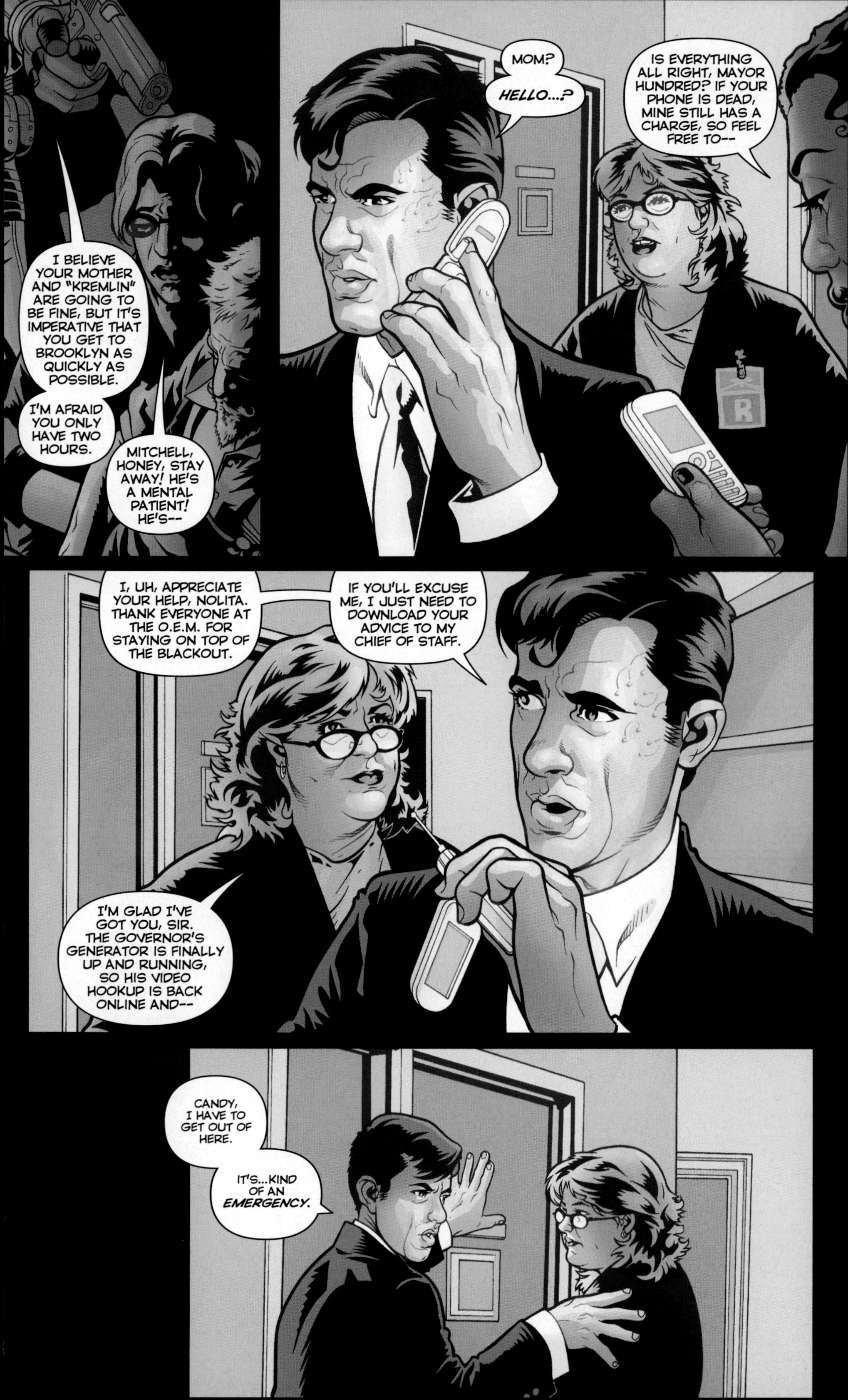
MOM?
HELLO...?
IS EVERYTHING ALL RIGHT, MAYOR HUNDRED? IF YOUR PHONE IS DEAD, MINE STILL HAS A CHARGE, SO FEEL FREE TO--
I BELIEVE YOUR MOTHER AND "KREMLIN" ARE GOING TO BE FINE, BUT IT'S IMPERATIVE THAT YOU GET TO BROOKLYN AS QUICKLY AS POSSIBLE.
I'M AFRAID YOU ONLY HAVE TWO HOURS.
MITCHELL, HONEY, STAY AWAY! HE'S A MENTAL PATIENT! HE'S--
I, UH, APPRECIATE YOUR HELP, NOLITA. THANK EVERYONE AT THE O.E.M. FOR STAYING ON TOP OF THE BLACKOUT.
IF YOU'LL EXCUSE ME, I JUST NEED TO DOWNLOAD YOUR ADVICE TO MY CHIEF OF STAFF.
I'M GLAD I'VE GOT YOU, SIR. THE GOVERNOR'S GENERATOR IS FINALLY UP AND RUNNING, SO HIS VIDEO HOOKUP IS BACK ONLINE AND--
CANDY, I HAVE TO GET OUT OF HERE.
IT'S...KIND OF AN EMERGENCY.

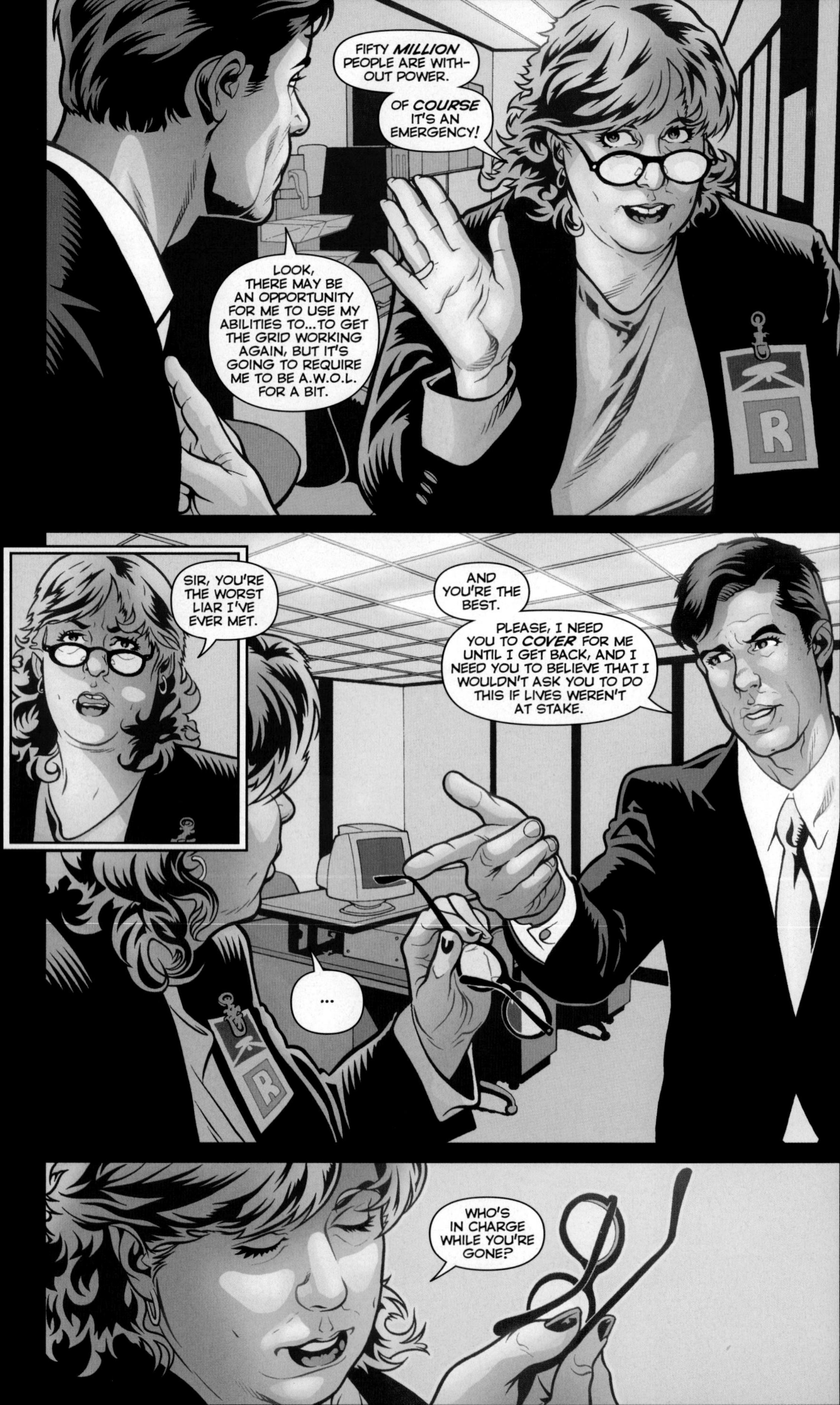
FIFTY *MILLION* PEOPLE ARE WITH-OUT POWER.
OF *COURSE* IT'S AN EMERGENCY!
LOOK, THERE MAY BE AN OPPORTUNITY FOR ME TO USE MY ABILITIES TO...TO GET THE GRID WORKING AGAIN, BUT IT'S GOING TO REQUIRE ME TO BE A.W.O.L. FOR A BIT.
SIR, YOU'RE THE WORST LIAR I'VE EVER MET.
AND YOU'RE THE BEST.
PLEASE, I NEED YOU TO *COVER* FOR ME UNTIL I GET BACK, AND I NEED YOU TO BELIEVE THAT I WOULDN'T ASK YOU TO DO THIS IF LIVES WEREN'T AT STAKE.
...
WHO'S IN CHARGE WHILE YOU'RE GONE?

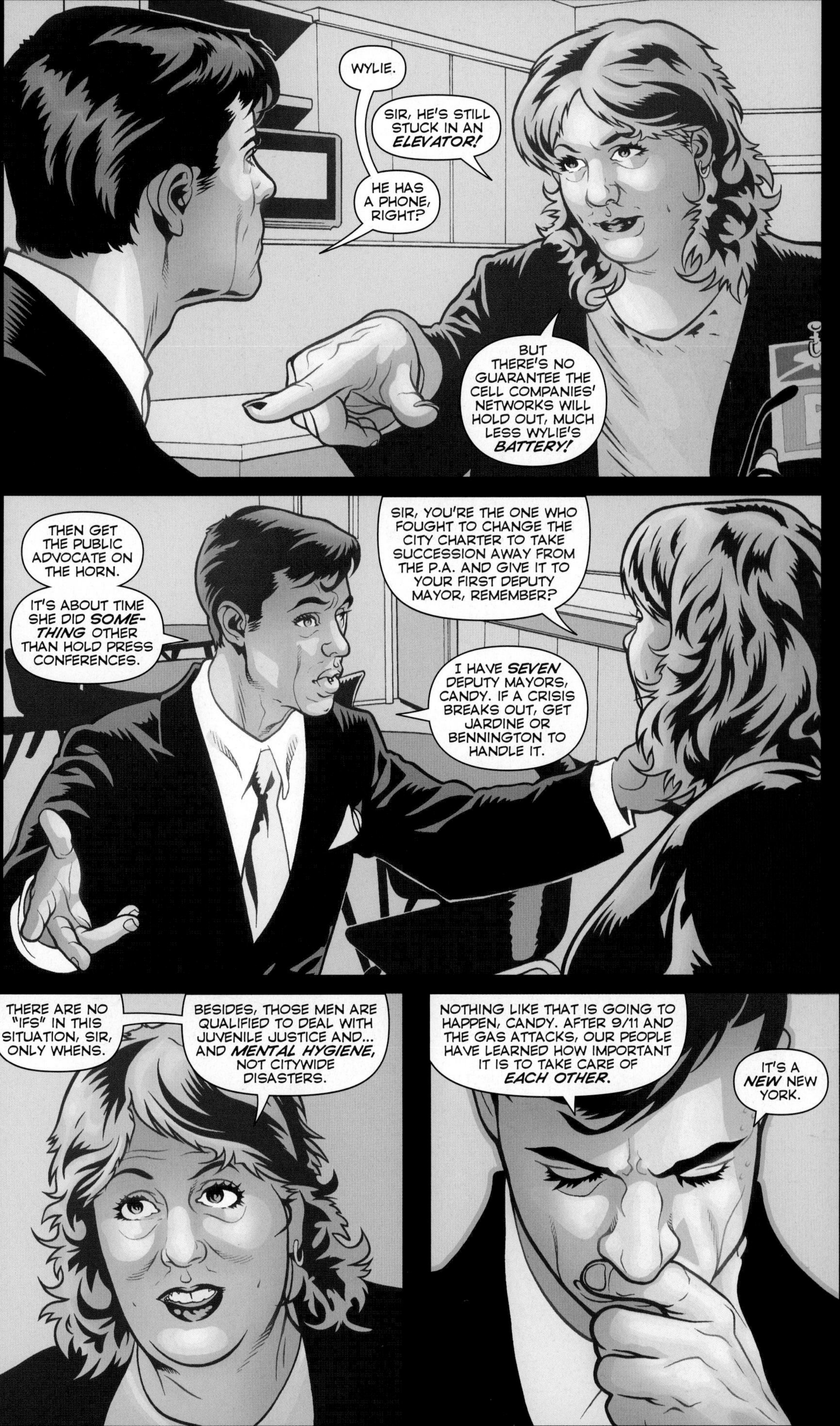
WYLIE.
SIR, HE'S STILL STUCK IN AN ELEVATOR!
HE HAS A PHONE, RIGHT?
BUT THERE'S NO GUARANTEE THE CELL COMPANIES' NETWORKS WILL HOLD OUT, MUCH LESS WYLIE'S BATTERY!
THEN GET THE PUBLIC ADVOCATE ON THE HORN.
IT'S ABOUT TIME SHE DID SOME-THING OTHER THAN HOLD PRESS CONFERENCES.
SIR, YOU'RE THE ONE WHO FOUGHT TO CHANGE THE CITY CHARTER TO TAKE SUCCESSION AWAY FROM THE P.A. AND GIVE IT TO YOUR FIRST DEPUTY MAYOR, REMEMBER?
I HAVE SEVEN DEPUTY MAYORS, CANDY. IF A CRISIS BREAKS OUT, GET JARDINE OR BENNINGTON TO HANDLE IT.
THERE ARE NO "IFS" IN THIS SITUATION, SIR, ONLY WHENS.
BESIDES, THOSE MEN ARE QUALIFIED TO DEAL WITH JUVENILE JUSTICE AND... AND MENTAL HYGIENE, NOT CITYWIDE DISASTERS.
NOTHING LIKE THAT IS GOING TO HAPPEN, CANDY. AFTER 9/11 AND THE GAS ATTACKS, OUR PEOPLE HAVE LEARNED HOW IMPORTANT IT IS TO TAKE CARE OF EACH OTHER.
IT'S A NEW NEW YORK.

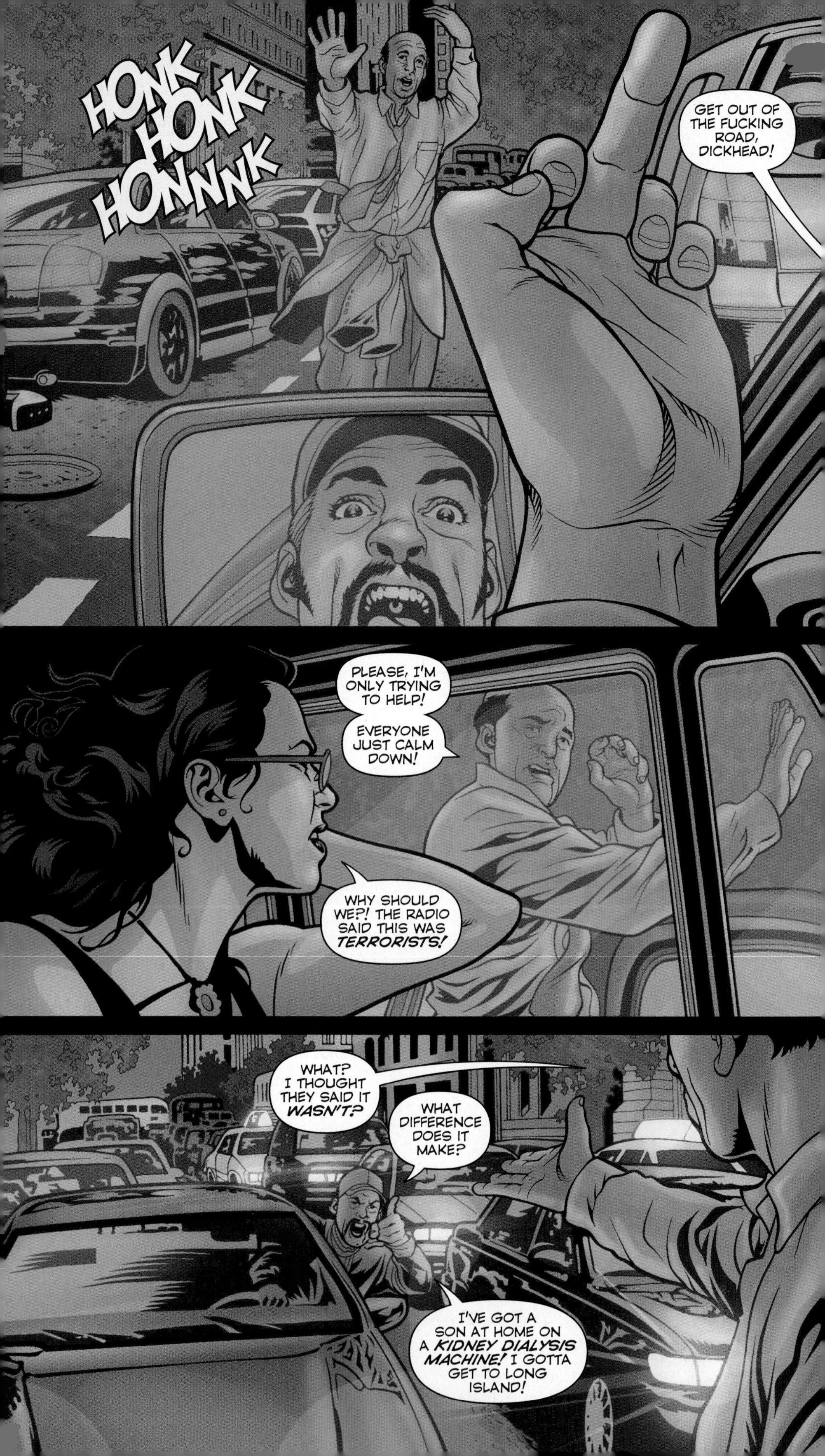

HONK HONK HONNNK
GET OUT OF THE FUCKING ROAD, DICKHEAD!
PLEASE, I'M ONLY TRYING TO HELP!
EVERYONE JUST CALM DOWN!
WHY SHOULD WE?! THE RADIO SAID THIS WAS TERRORISTS!
WHAT? I THOUGHT THEY SAID IT WASN'T?
WHAT DIFFERENCE DOES IT MAKE?
I'VE GOT A SON AT HOME ON A KIDNEY DIALYSIS MACHINE! I GOTTA GET TO LONG ISLAND!

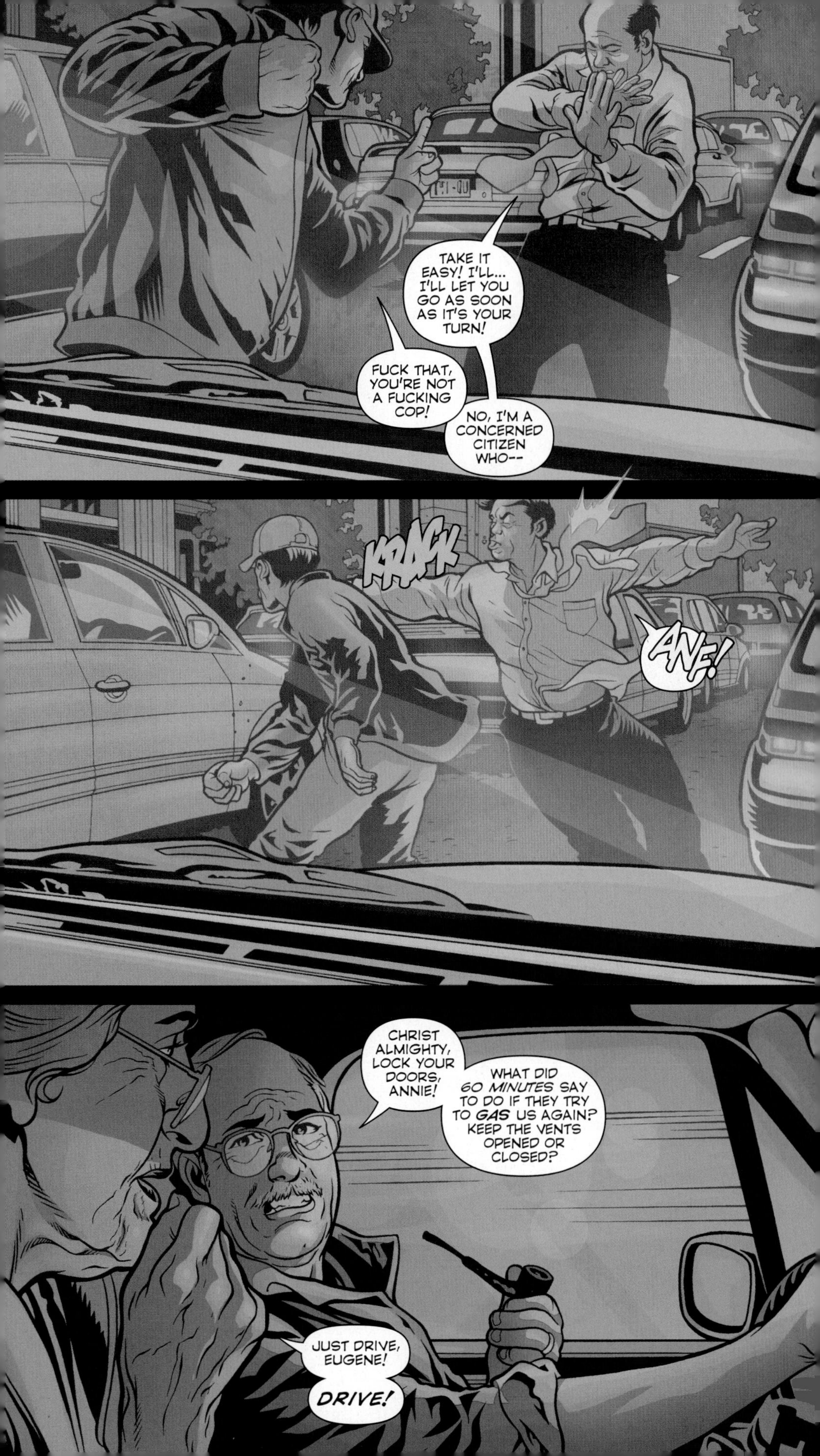
TAKE IT EASY! I'LL... I'LL LET YOU GO AS SOON AS IT'S YOUR TURN!
FUCK THAT, YOU'RE NOT A FUCKING COP!
NO, I'M A CONCERNED CITIZEN WHO--
KRACK
AWF!
CHRIST ALMIGHTY, LOCK YOUR DOORS, ANNIE!
WHAT DID 60 MINUTES SAY TO DO IF THEY TRY TO GAS US AGAIN? KEEP THE VENTS OPENED OR CLOSED?
JUST DRIVE, EUGENE!
DRIVE!

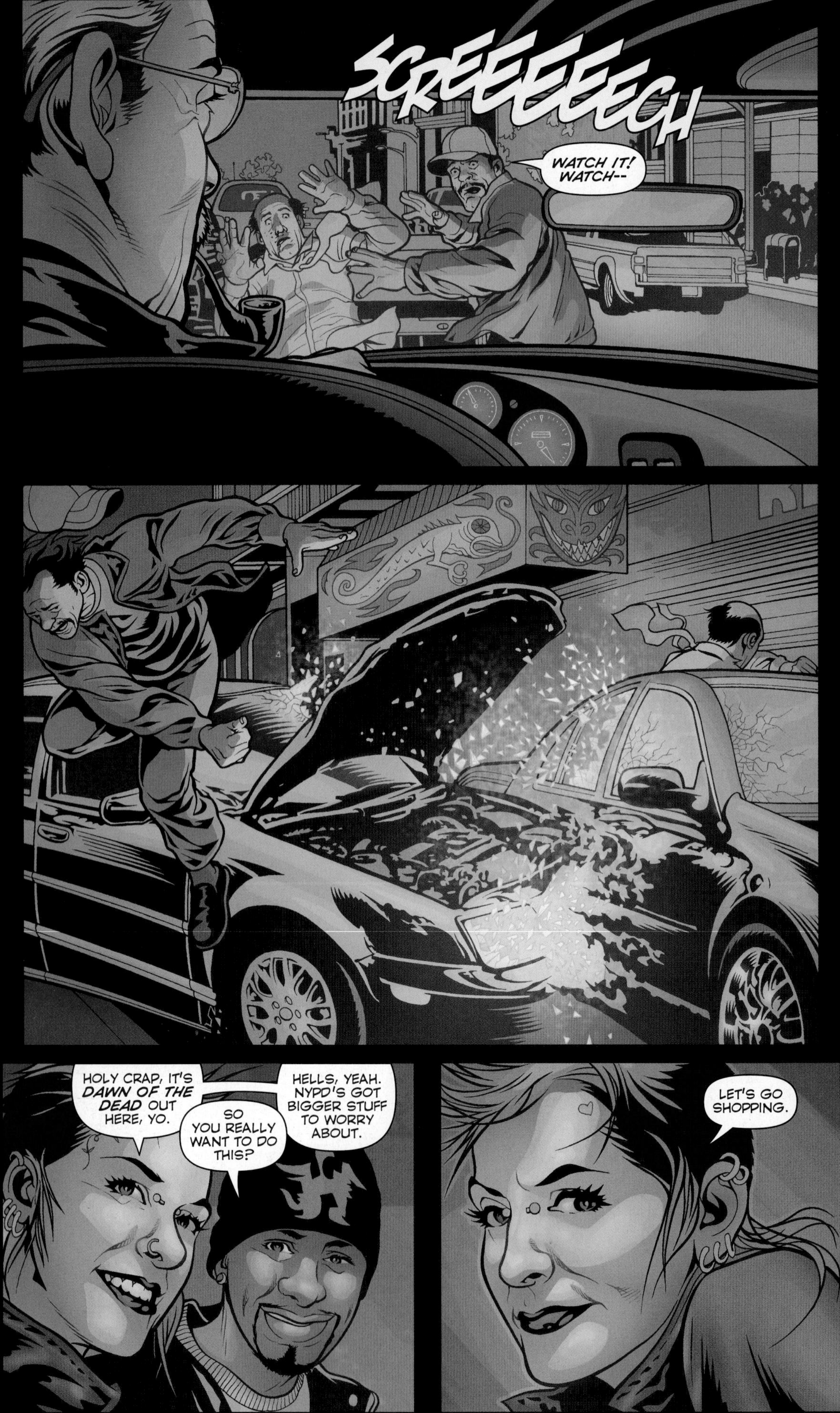
SCREEEEEECH
WATCH IT! WATCH--
HOLY CRAP, IT'S *DAWN OF THE DEAD* OUT HERE, YO.
SO YOU REALLY WANT TO DO THIS?
HELLS, YEAH. NYPD'S GOT BIGGER STUFF TO WORRY ABOUT.
LET'S GO SHOPPING.

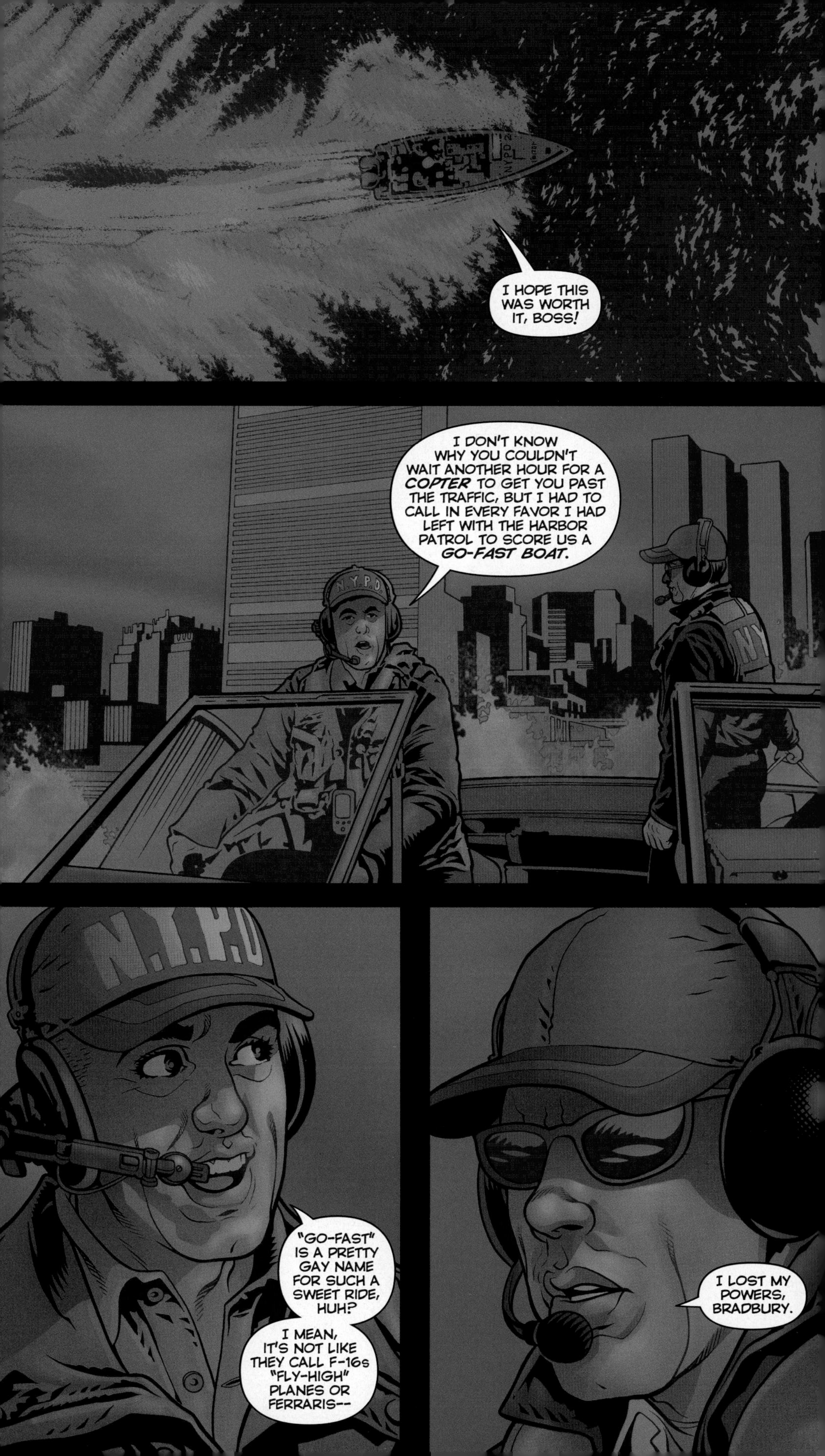
I HOPE THIS WAS WORTH IT, BOSS!
I DON'T KNOW WHY YOU COULDN'T WAIT ANOTHER HOUR FOR A *COPTER* TO GET YOU PAST THE TRAFFIC, BUT I HAD TO CALL IN EVERY FAVOR I HAD LEFT WITH THE HARBOR PATROL TO SCORE US A *GO-FAST BOAT*.
"GO-FAST" IS A PRETTY GAY NAME FOR SUCH A SWEET RIDE, HUH?
I MEAN, IT'S NOT LIKE THEY CALL F-16s "FLY-HIGH" PLANES OR FERRARIS--
I LOST MY POWERS, BRADBURY.

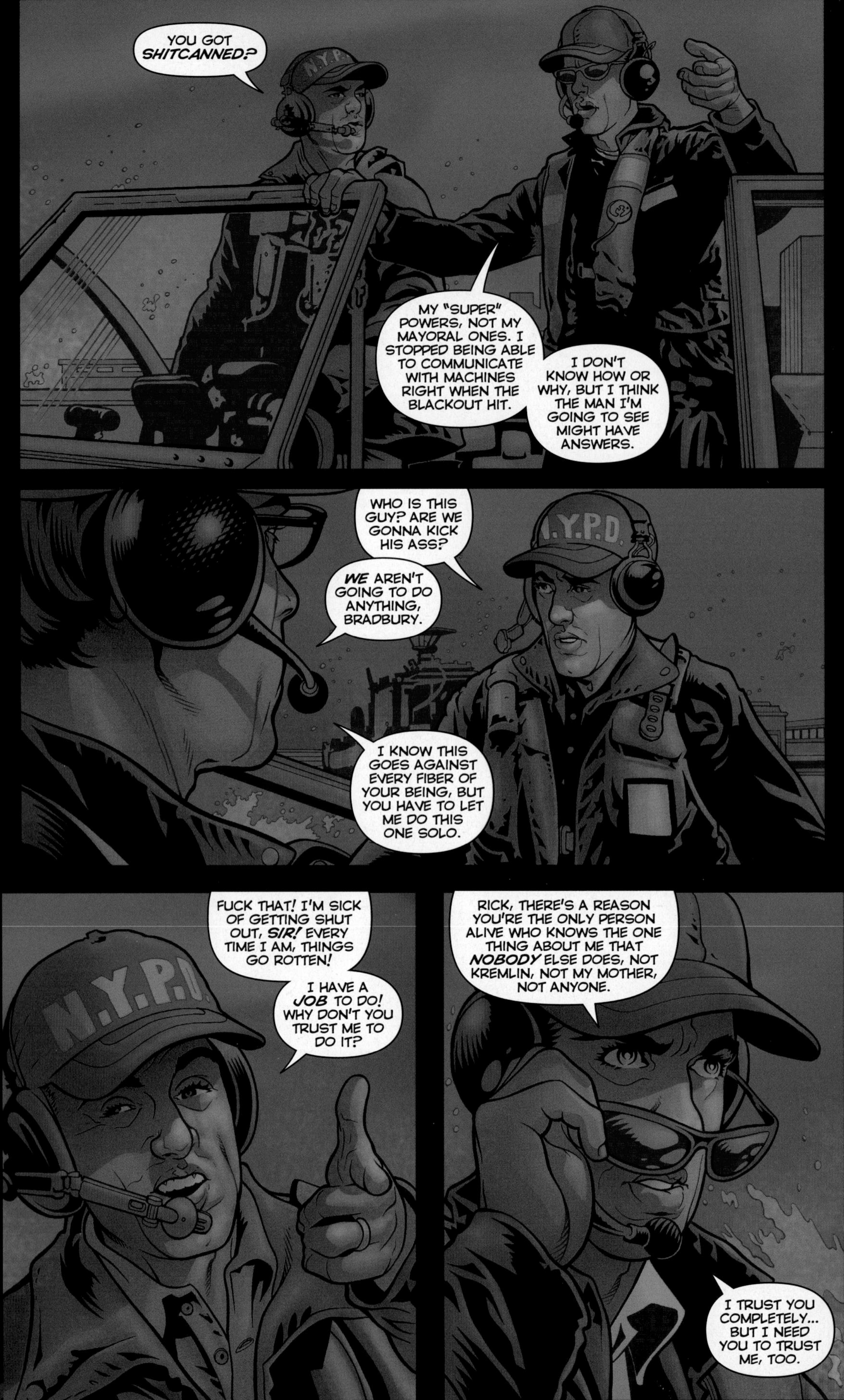
YOU GOT SHITCANNED?
MY "SUPER" POWERS, NOT MY MAYORAL ONES. I STOPPED BEING ABLE TO COMMUNICATE WITH MACHINES RIGHT WHEN THE BLACKOUT HIT.
I DON'T KNOW HOW OR WHY, BUT I THINK THE MAN I'M GOING TO SEE MIGHT HAVE ANSWERS.
N.Y.P.D.
WHO IS THIS GUY? ARE WE GONNA KICK HIS ASS?
WE AREN'T GOING TO DO ANYTHING, BRADBURY.
I KNOW THIS GOES AGAINST EVERY FIBER OF YOUR BEING, BUT YOU HAVE TO LET ME DO THIS ONE SOLO.
FUCK THAT! I'M SICK OF GETTING SHUT OUT, SIR! EVERY TIME I AM, THINGS GO ROTTEN!
I HAVE A JOB TO DO! WHY DON'T YOU TRUST ME TO DO IT?
N.Y.P.D.
RICK, THERE'S A REASON YOU'RE THE ONLY PERSON ALIVE WHO KNOWS THE ONE THING ABOUT ME THAT NOBODY ELSE DOES, NOT KREMLIN, NOT MY MOTHER, NOT ANYONE.
I TRUST YOU COMPLETELY... BUT I NEED YOU TO TRUST ME, TOO.

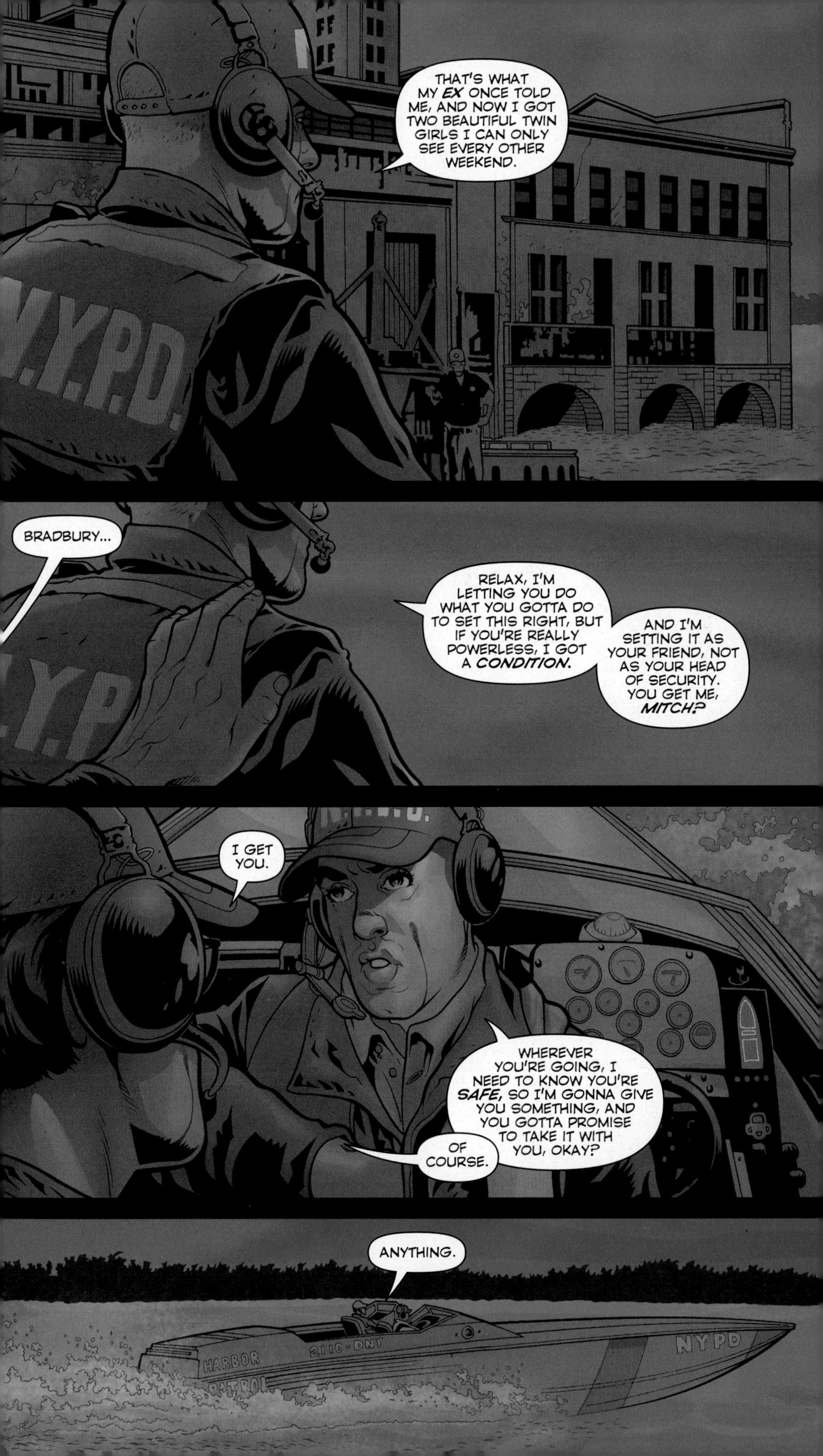
THAT'S WHAT MY EX ONCE TOLD ME, AND NOW I GOT TWO BEAUTIFUL TWIN GIRLS I CAN ONLY SEE EVERY OTHER WEEKEND.
N.Y.P.D.
BRADBURY...
RELAX, I'M LETTING YOU DO WHAT YOU GOTTA DO TO SET THIS RIGHT, BUT IF YOU'RE REALLY POWERLESS, I GOT A CONDITION.
AND I'M SETTING IT AS YOUR FRIEND, NOT AS YOUR HEAD OF SECURITY. YOU GET ME, MITCH?
I GET YOU.
WHEREVER YOU'RE GOING, I NEED TO KNOW YOU'RE SAFE, SO I'M GONNA GIVE YOU SOMETHING, AND YOU GOTTA PROMISE TO TAKE IT WITH YOU, OKAY?
OF COURSE.
ANYTHING.
2110-DNY
HARBOR
NYPD

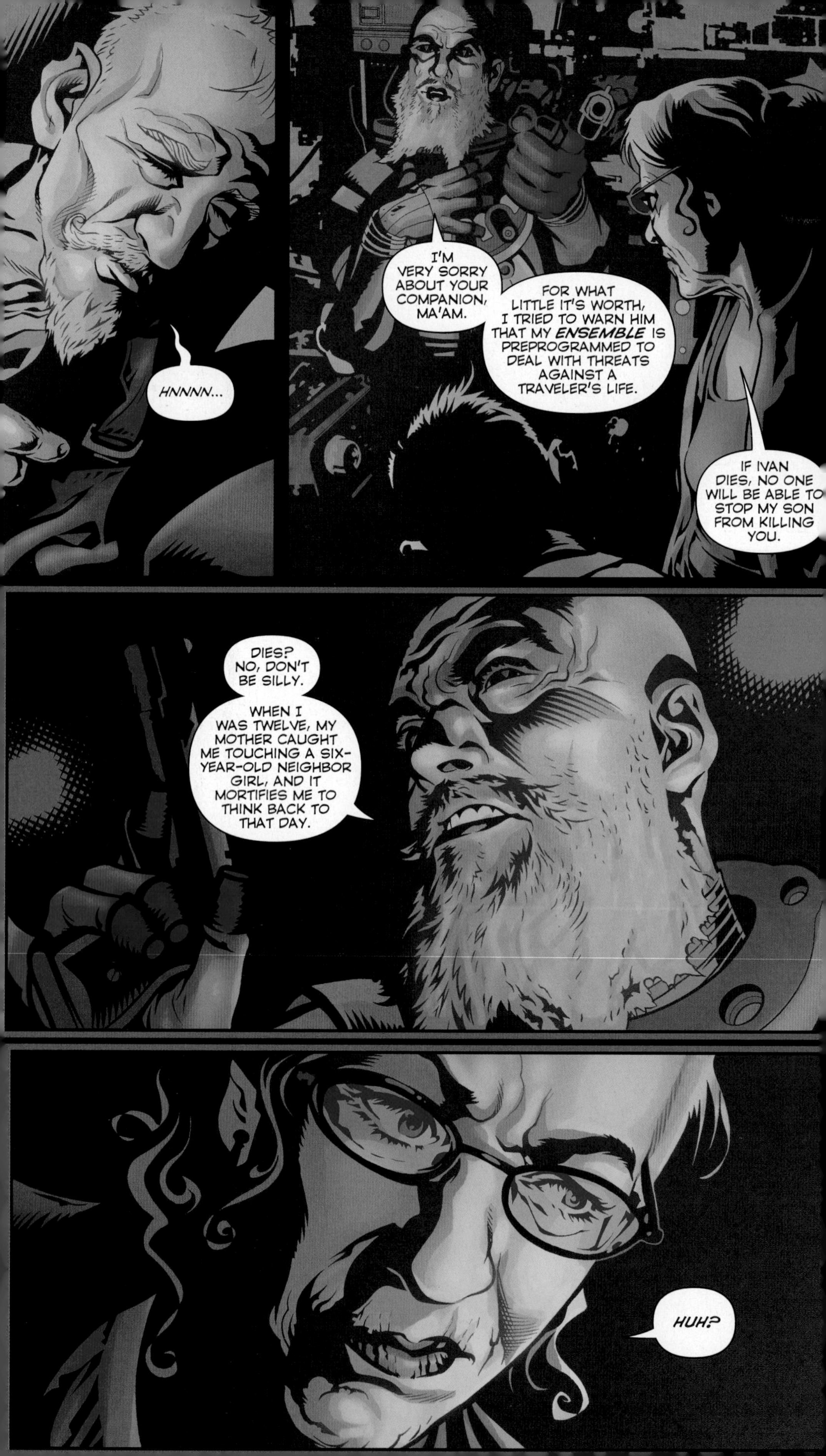
HNNNN...
I'M VERY SORRY ABOUT YOUR COMPANION, MA'AM.
FOR WHAT LITTLE IT'S WORTH, I TRIED TO WARN HIM THAT MY *ENSEMBLE* IS PREPROGRAMMED TO DEAL WITH THREATS AGAINST A TRAVELER'S LIFE.
IF IVAN DIES, NO ONE WILL BE ABLE TO STOP MY SON FROM KILLING YOU.
DIES? NO, DON'T BE SILLY.
WHEN I WAS TWELVE, MY MOTHER CAUGHT ME TOUCHING A SIX-YEAR-OLD NEIGHBOR GIRL, AND IT MORTIFIES ME TO THINK BACK TO THAT DAY.
HUH?

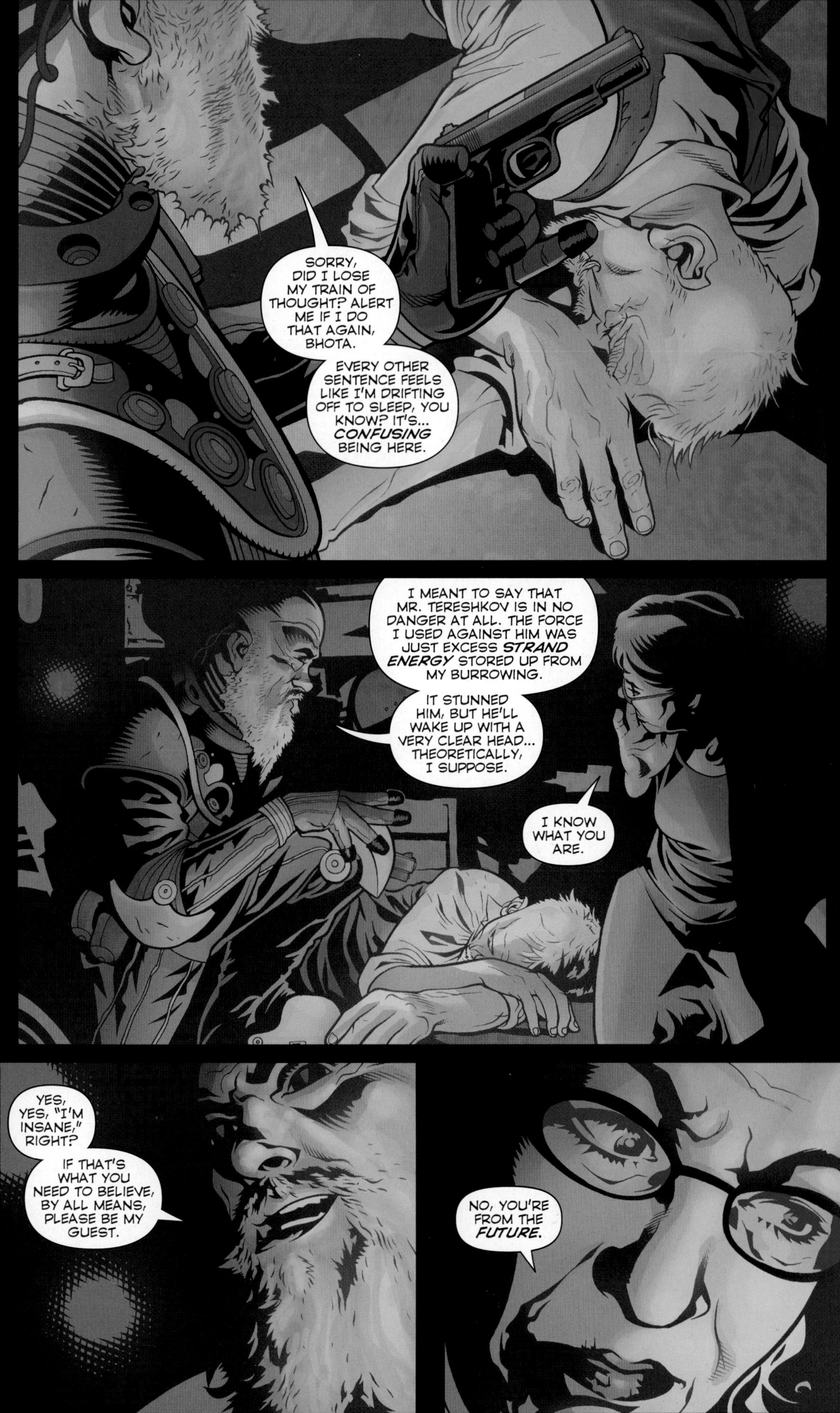
SORRY, DID I LOSE MY TRAIN OF THOUGHT? ALERT ME IF I DO THAT AGAIN, BHOTA.
EVERY OTHER SENTENCE FEELS LIKE I'M DRIFTING OFF TO SLEEP, YOU KNOW? IT'S... CONFUSING BEING HERE.
I MEANT TO SAY THAT MR. TERESHKOV IS IN NO DANGER AT ALL. THE FORCE I USED AGAINST HIM WAS JUST EXCESS STRAND ENERGY STORED UP FROM MY BURROWING.
IT STUNNED HIM, BUT HE'LL WAKE UP WITH A VERY CLEAR HEAD... THEORETICALLY, I SUPPOSE.
I KNOW WHAT YOU ARE.
YES, YES, "I'M INSANE," RIGHT?
IF THAT'S WHAT YOU NEED TO BELIEVE, BY ALL MEANS, PLEASE BE MY GUEST.
NO, YOU'RE FROM THE FUTURE.

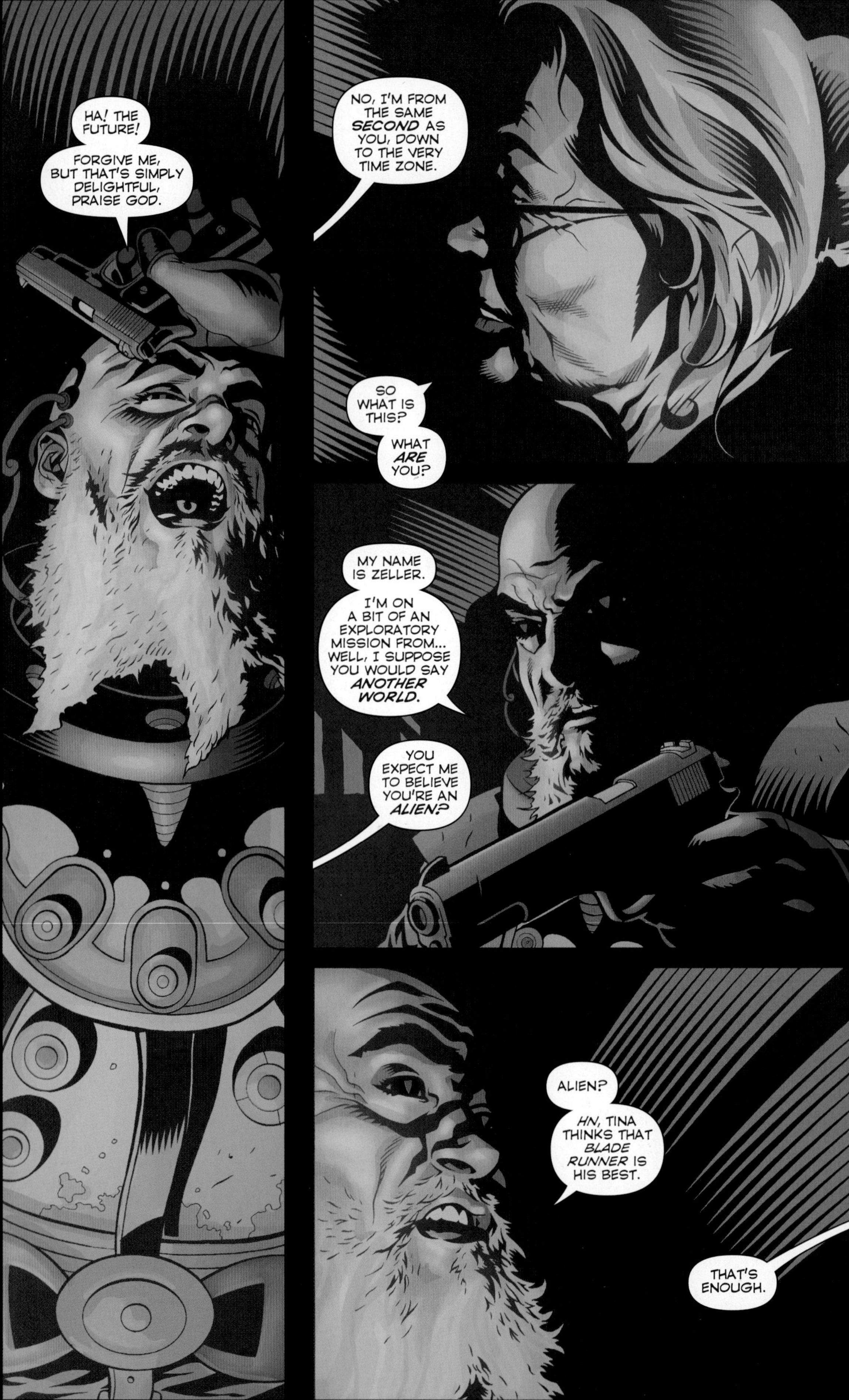
HA! THE FUTURE!
FORGIVE ME, BUT THAT'S SIMPLY DELIGHTFUL, PRAISE GOD.
NO, I'M FROM THE SAME *SECOND* AS YOU, DOWN TO THE VERY TIME ZONE.
SO WHAT IS THIS?
WHAT *ARE* YOU?
MY NAME IS ZELLER.
I'M ON A BIT OF AN EXPLORATORY MISSION FROM... WELL, I SUPPOSE YOU WOULD SAY *ANOTHER WORLD.*
YOU EXPECT ME TO BELIEVE YOU'RE AN *ALIEN?*
ALIEN?
HN, TINA THINKS THAT *BLADE RUNNER* IS HIS BEST.
THAT'S ENOUGH.

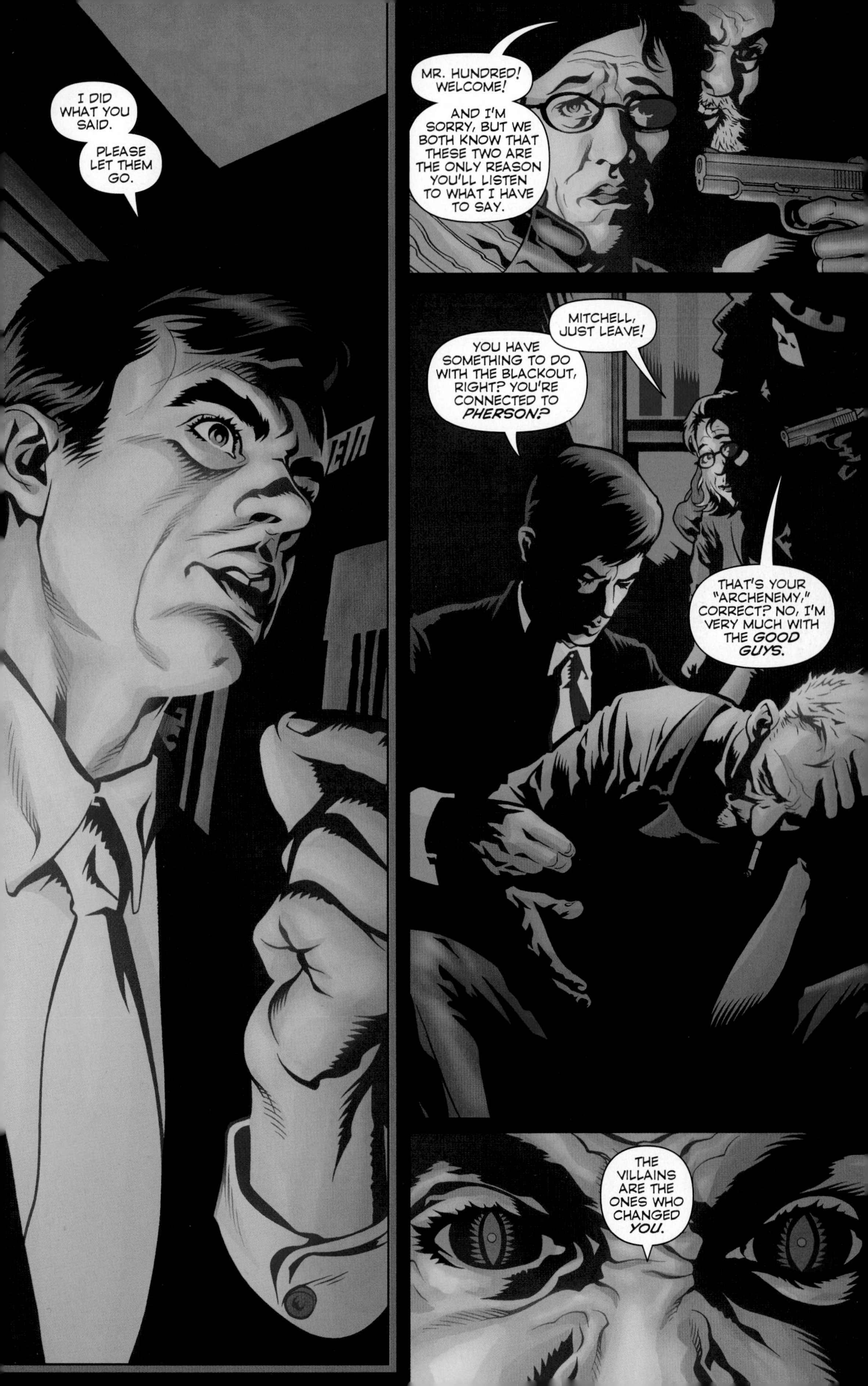
I DID WHAT YOU SAID.
PLEASE LET THEM GO.
MR. HUNDRED! WELCOME!
AND I'M SORRY, BUT WE BOTH KNOW THAT THESE TWO ARE THE ONLY REASON YOU'LL LISTEN TO WHAT I HAVE TO SAY.
MITCHELL, JUST LEAVE!
YOU HAVE SOMETHING TO DO WITH THE BLACKOUT, RIGHT? YOU'RE CONNECTED TO *PHERSON?*
THAT'S YOUR "ARCHENEMY," CORRECT? NO, I'M VERY MUCH WITH THE *GOOD GUYS.*
THE VILLAINS ARE THE ONES WHO CHANGED *YOU.*

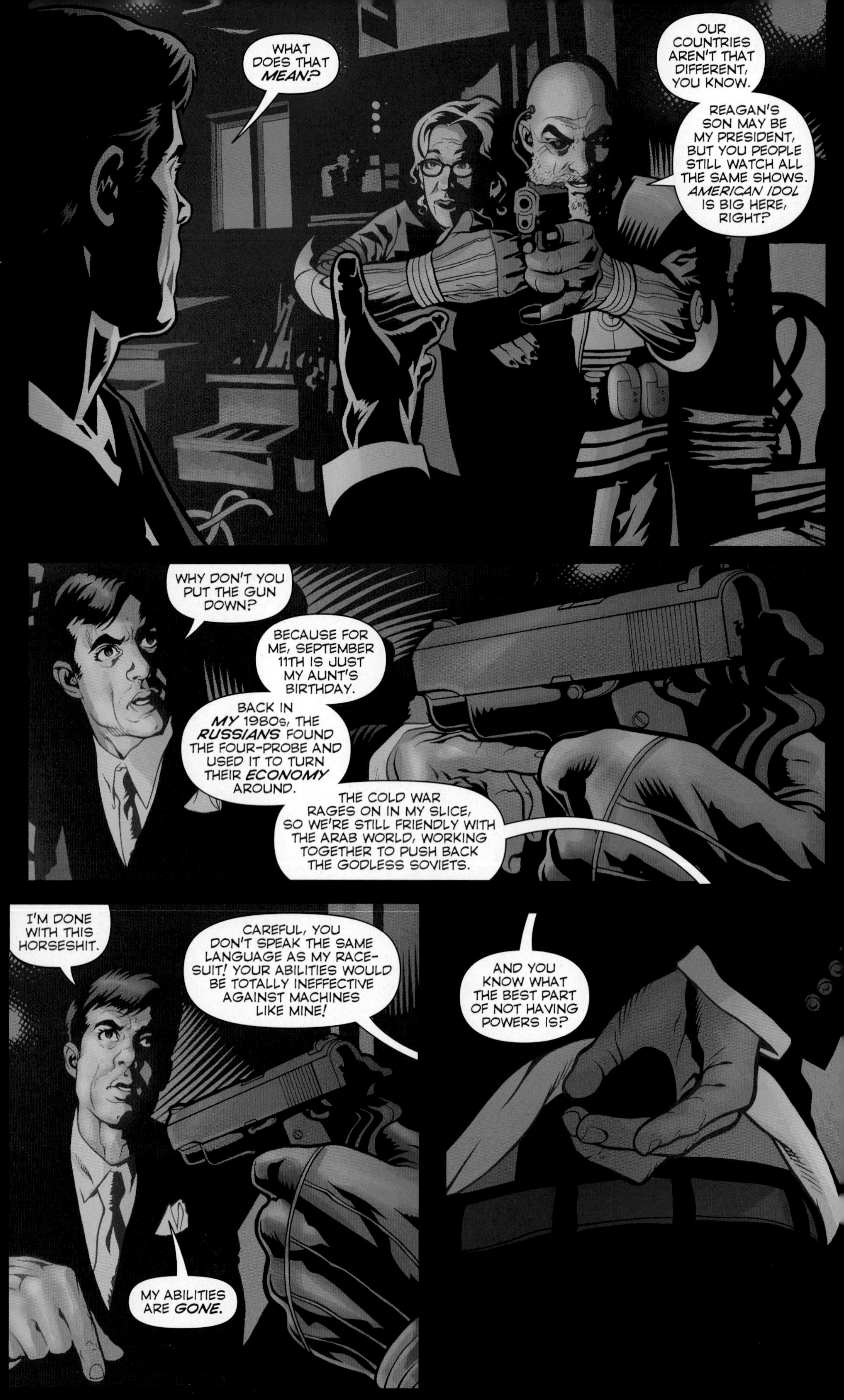
WHAT DOES THAT *MEAN?*
OUR COUNTRIES AREN'T THAT DIFFERENT, YOU KNOW.
REAGAN'S SON MAY BE MY PRESIDENT, BUT YOU PEOPLE STILL WATCH ALL THE SAME SHOWS. *AMERICAN IDOL* IS BIG HERE, RIGHT?
WHY DON'T YOU PUT THE GUN DOWN?
BECAUSE FOR ME, SEPTEMBER 11TH IS JUST MY AUNT'S BIRTHDAY.
BACK IN *MY* 1980s, THE *RUSSIANS* FOUND THE FOUR-PROBE AND USED IT TO TURN THEIR *ECONOMY* AROUND.
THE COLD WAR RAGES ON IN MY SLICE, SO WE'RE STILL FRIENDLY WITH THE ARAB WORLD, WORKING TOGETHER TO PUSH BACK THE GODLESS SOVIETS.
I'M DONE WITH THIS HORSESHIT.
CAREFUL, YOU DON'T SPEAK THE SAME LANGUAGE AS MY RACE-SUIT! YOUR ABILITIES WOULD BE TOTALLY INEFFECTIVE AGAINST MACHINES LIKE MINE!
MY ABILITIES ARE *GONE.*
AND YOU KNOW WHAT THE BEST PART OF NOT HAVING POWERS IS?

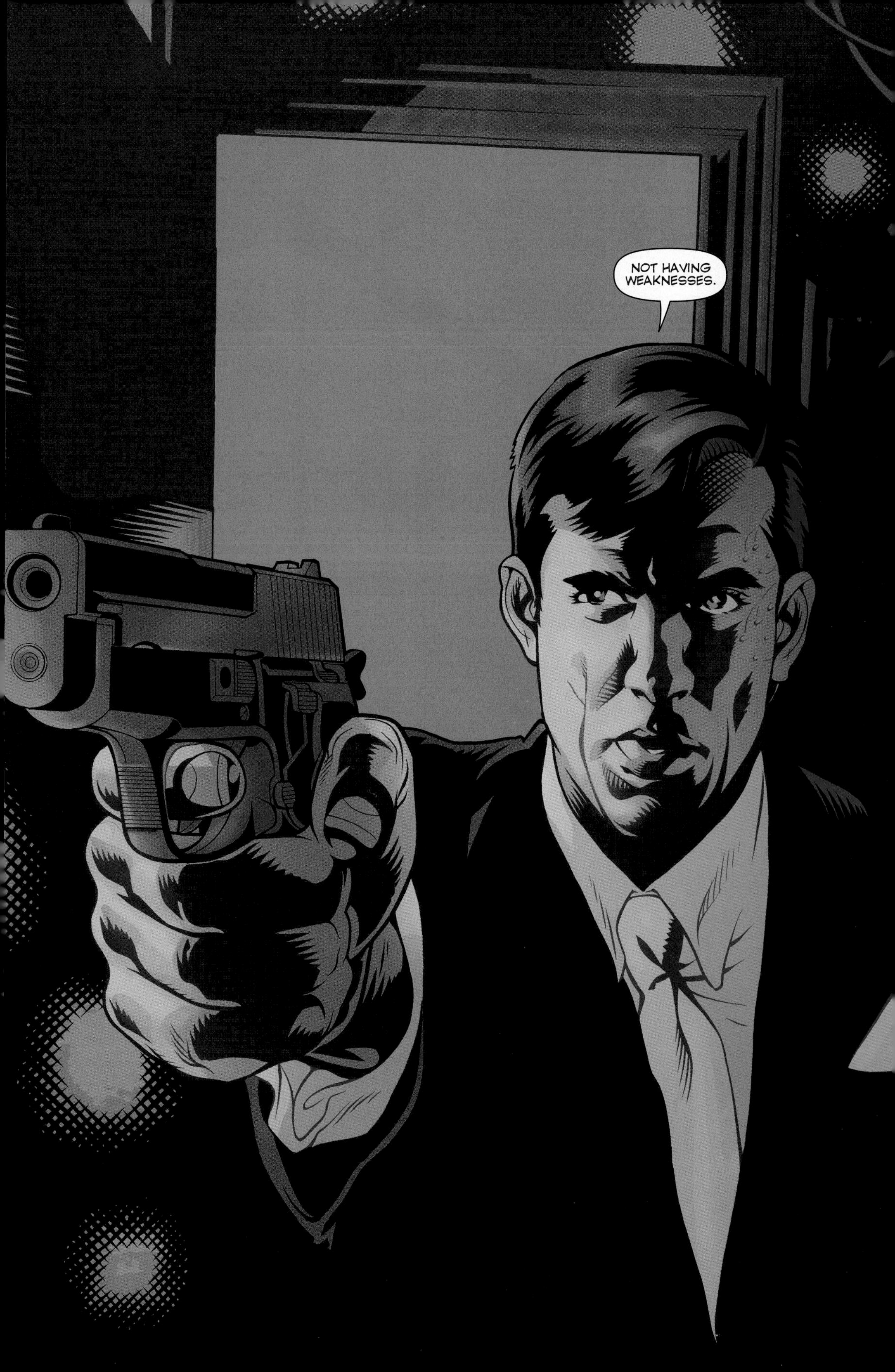
NOT HAVING WEAKNESSES.

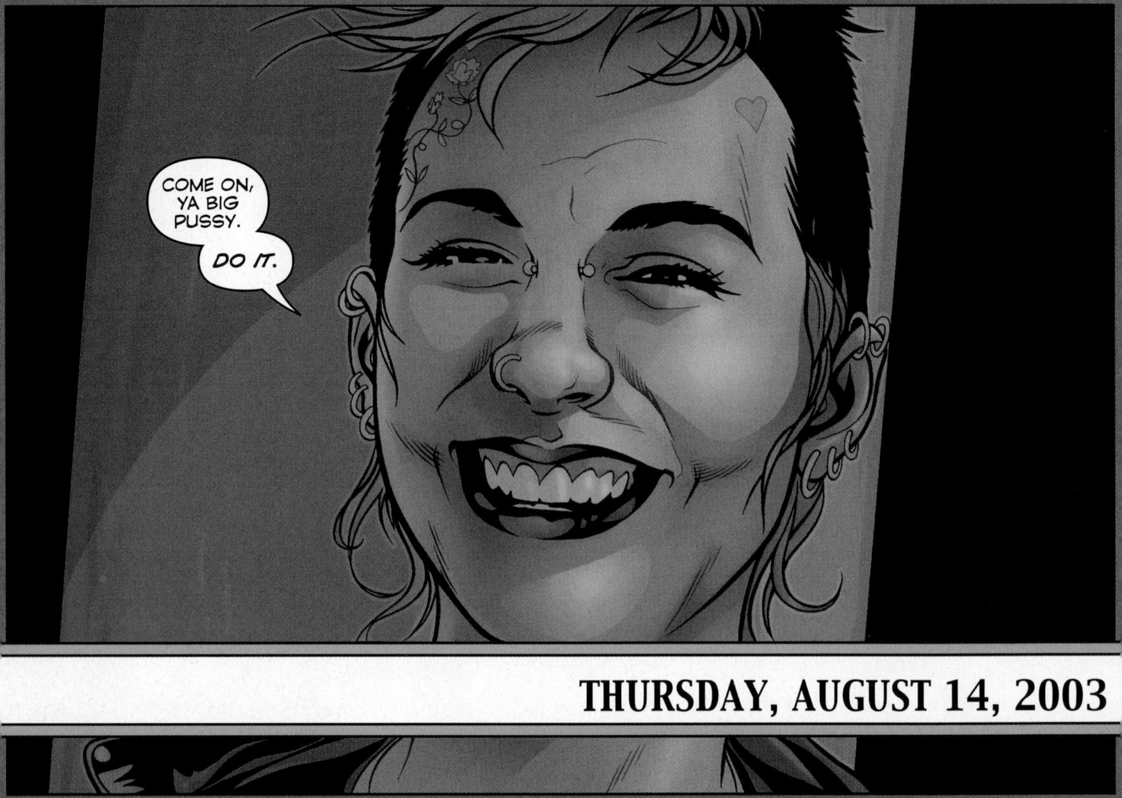
COME ON, YA BIG PUSSY.
DO IT.
THURSDAY, AUGUST 14, 2003

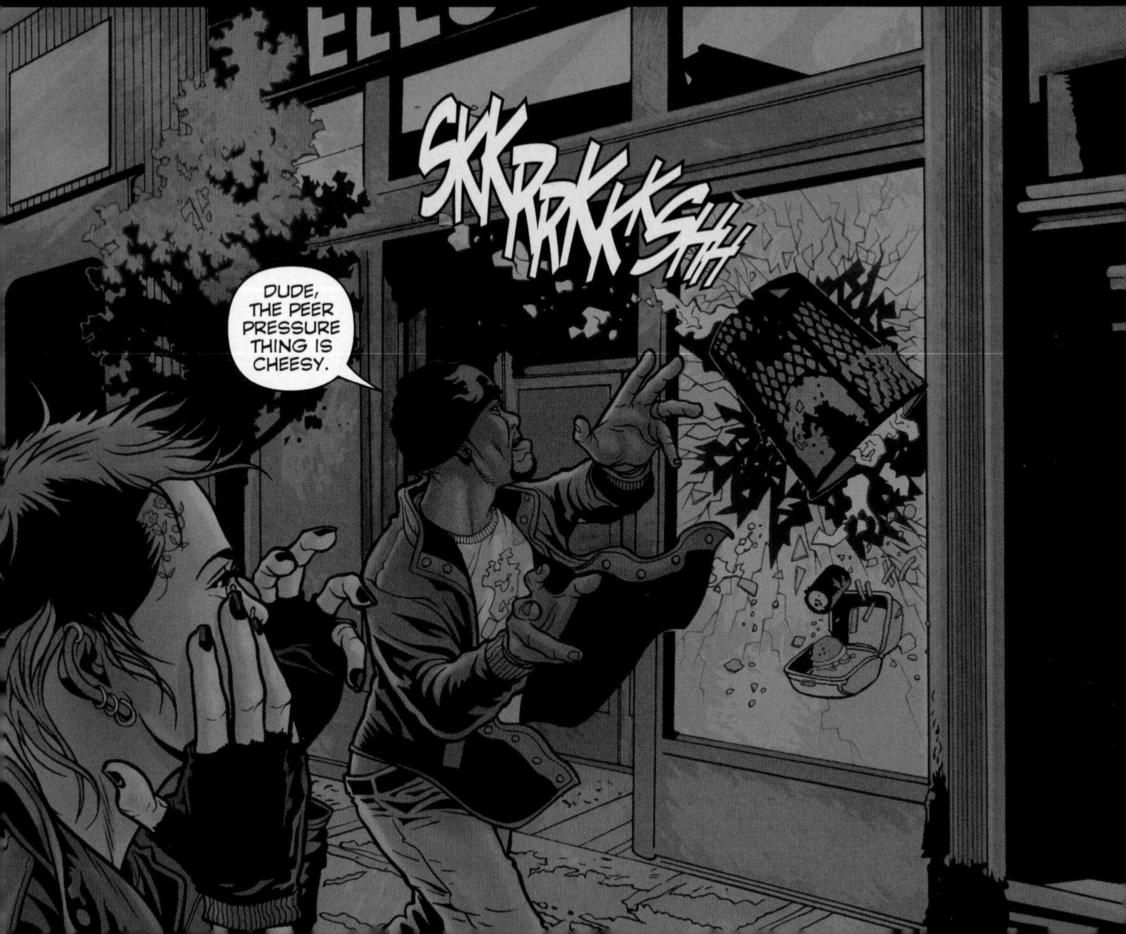
SKKRRKKKSHH
DUDE, THE PEER PRESSURE THING IS CHEESY.

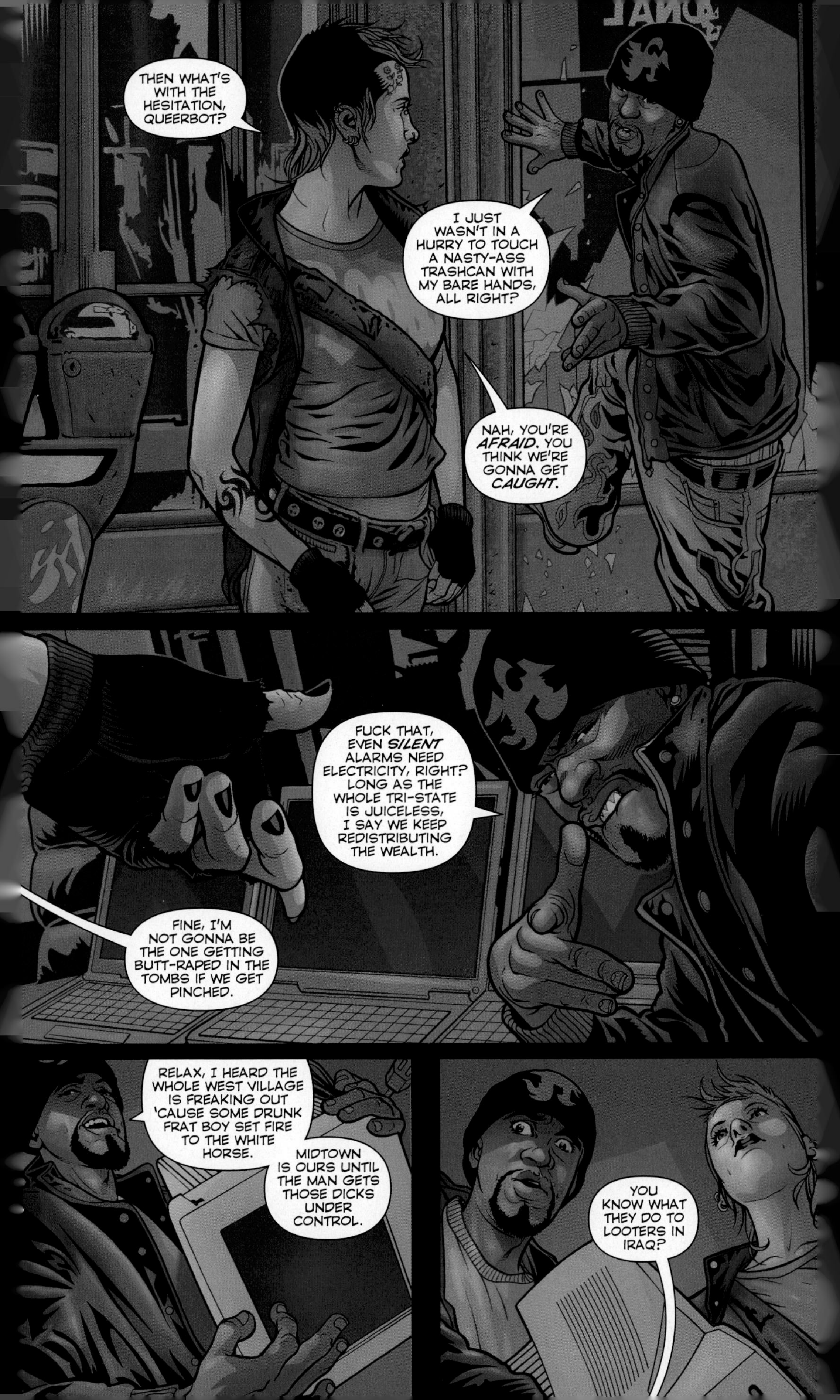

THEN WHAT'S WITH THE HESITATION, QUEERBOT?
I JUST WASN'T IN A HURRY TO TOUCH A NASTY-ASS TRASHCAN WITH MY BARE HANDS, ALL RIGHT?
NAH, YOU'RE *AFRAID*. YOU THINK WE'RE GONNA GET *CAUGHT*.
FUCK THAT, EVEN *SILENT* ALARMS NEED ELECTRICITY, RIGHT? LONG AS THE WHOLE TRI-STATE IS JUICELESS, I SAY WE KEEP REDISTRIBUTING THE WEALTH.
FINE, I'M NOT GONNA BE THE ONE GETTING BUTT-RAPED IN THE TOMBS IF WE GET PINCHED.
RELAX, I HEARD THE WHOLE WEST VILLAGE IS FREAKING OUT 'CAUSE SOME DRUNK FRAT BOY SET FIRE TO THE WHITE HORSE.
MIDTOWN IS OURS UNTIL THE MAN GETS THOSE DICKS UNDER CONTROL.
YOU KNOW WHAT THEY DO TO LOOTERS IN IRAQ?

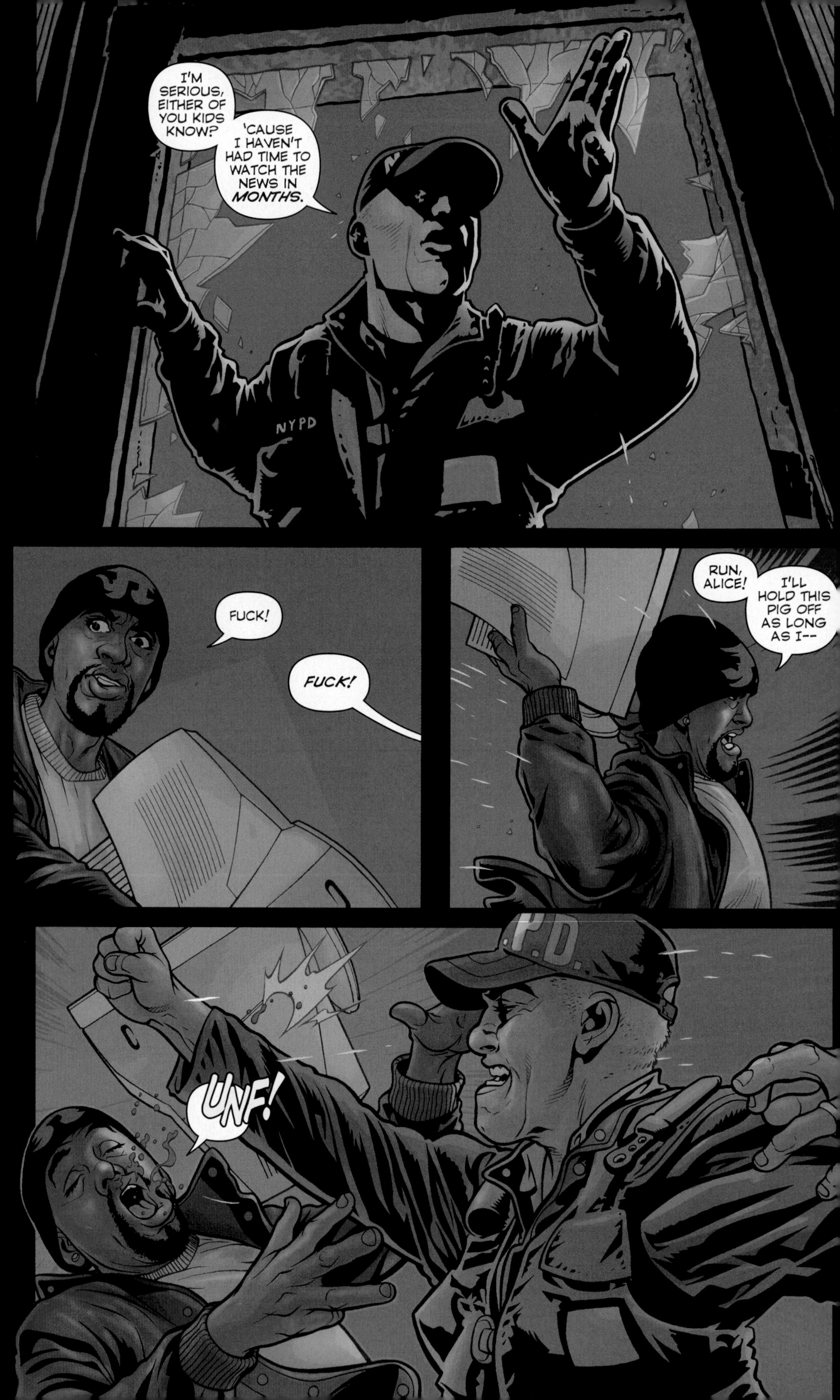
I'M SERIOUS, EITHER OF YOU KIDS KNOW?
'CAUSE I HAVEN'T HAD TIME TO WATCH THE NEWS IN *MONTHS*.
NYPD
FUCK!
FUCK!
RUN, ALICE!
I'LL HOLD THIS PIG OFF AS LONG AS I--
P.D.
UNF!

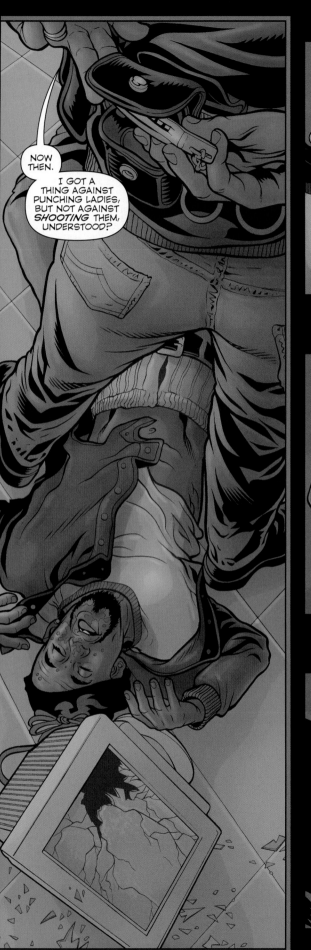

NOW THEN.

I GOT A THING AGAINST PUNCHING LADIES, BUT NOT AGAINST *SHOOTING* THEM, UNDERSTOOD?

IT WAS *HIS* IDEA! I'M A GOOD GIRL, SIR!

HE MADE ME USE DRUGS AND...AND HAVE SEX!

THANKS FOR COOPERATING, SEEING HOW I LEFT MY PIECE WITH A *FRIEND.* NAME'S BRADBURY. YOU'RE UNDER CITIZEN'S ARREST, BY THE WAY.

THAT'S BULLSHIT! YOU'RE NOT EVEN A REAL *COP?*

NOT ANYMORE.

THEN WHO THE HELL *DO* YOU WORK FOR?

THE POOR BASTARD WHO'S GONNA HAVE TO CLEAN THIS MESS UP.

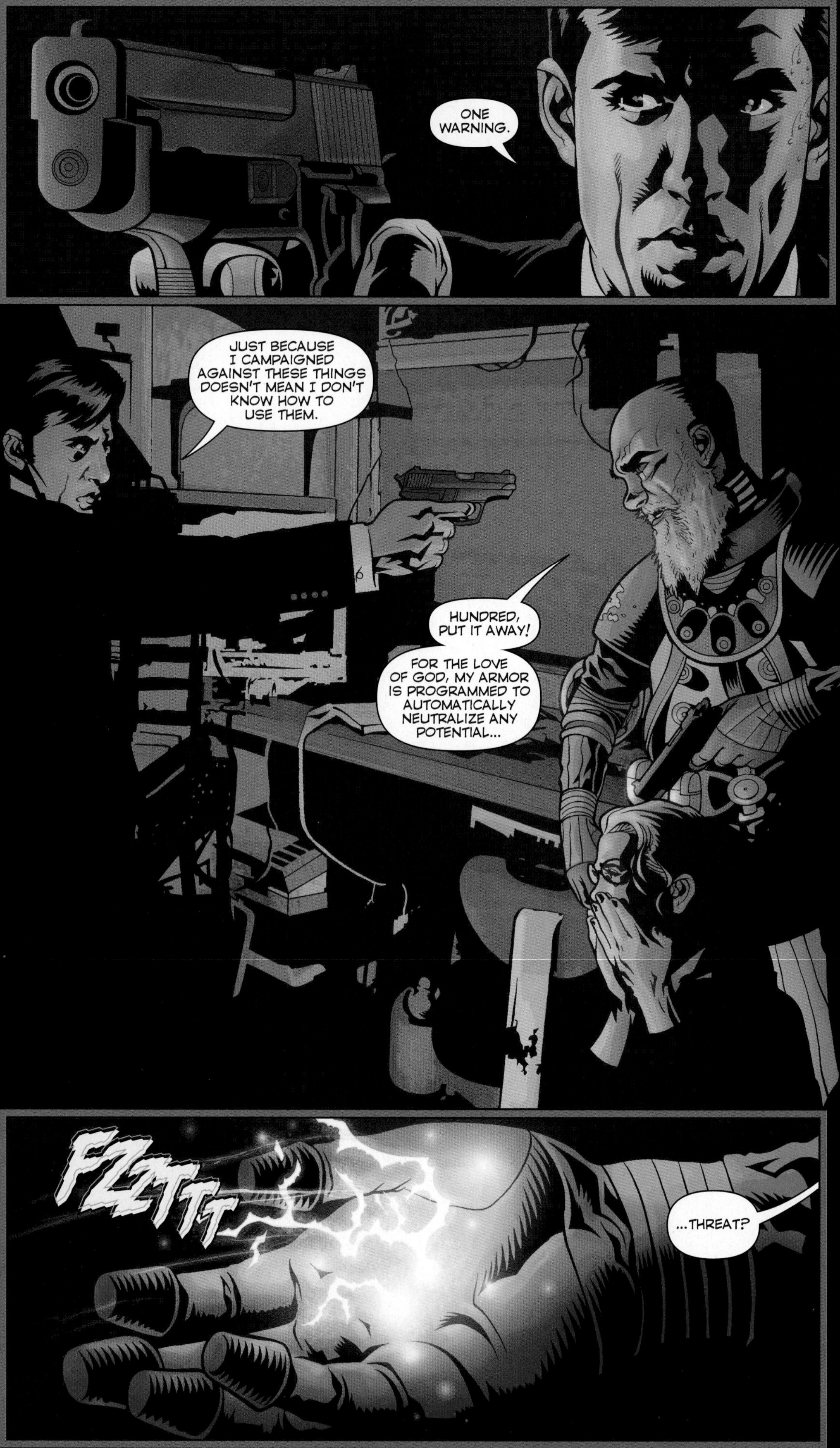
ONE WARNING.
JUST BECAUSE I CAMPAIGNED AGAINST THESE THINGS DOESN'T MEAN I DON'T KNOW HOW TO USE THEM.
HUNDRED, PUT IT AWAY!
FOR THE LOVE OF GOD, MY ARMOR IS PROGRAMMED TO AUTOMATICALLY NEUTRALIZE ANY POTENTIAL...
FZZTTTT
...THREAT?

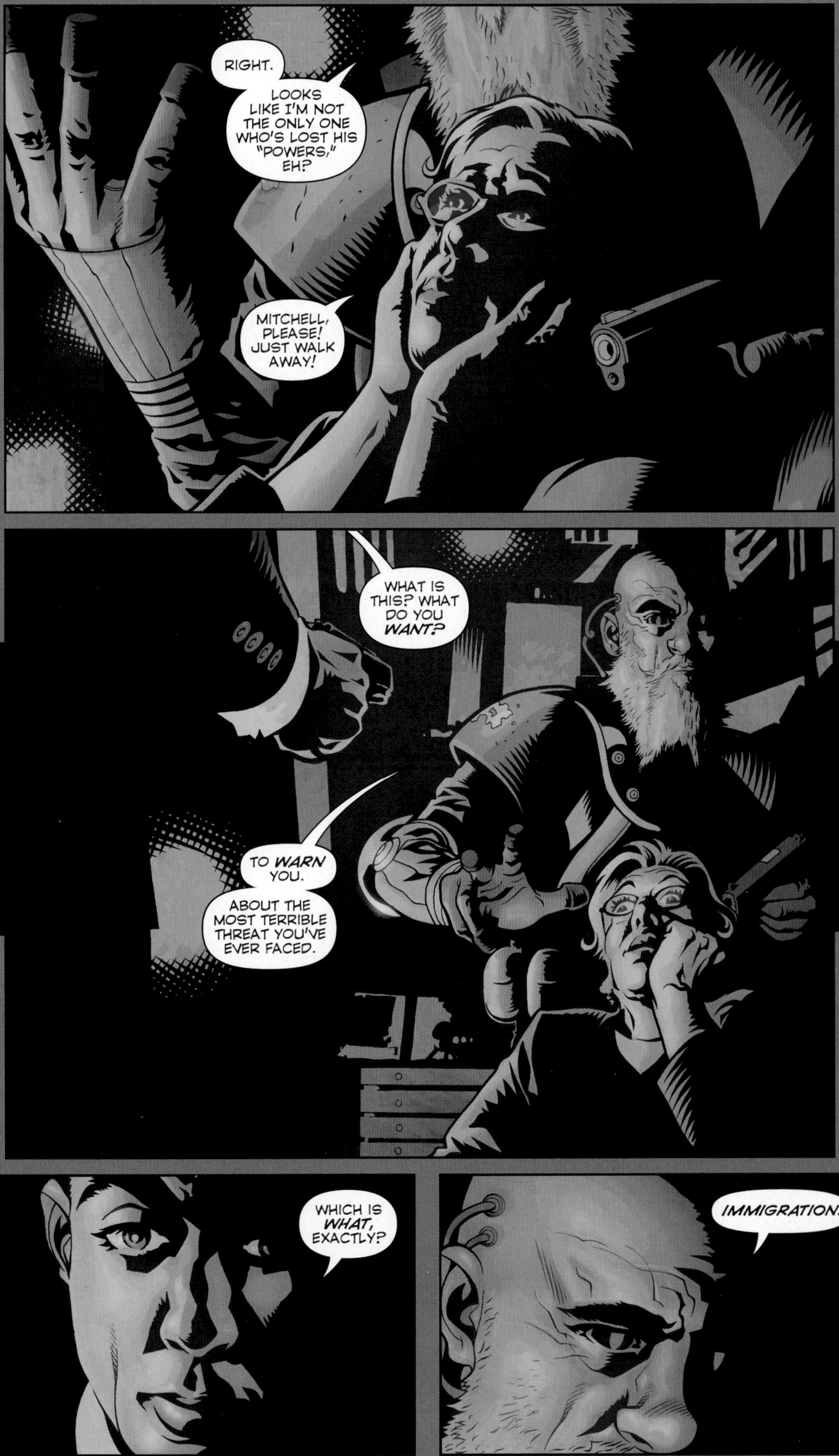
RIGHT.
LOOKS LIKE I'M NOT THE ONLY ONE WHO'S LOST HIS "POWERS," EH?
MITCHELL, PLEASE! JUST WALK AWAY!
WHAT IS THIS? WHAT DO YOU *WANT?*
TO *WARN* YOU.
ABOUT THE MOST TERRIBLE THREAT YOU'VE EVER FACED.
WHICH IS *WHAT,* EXACTLY?
IMMIGRATION.

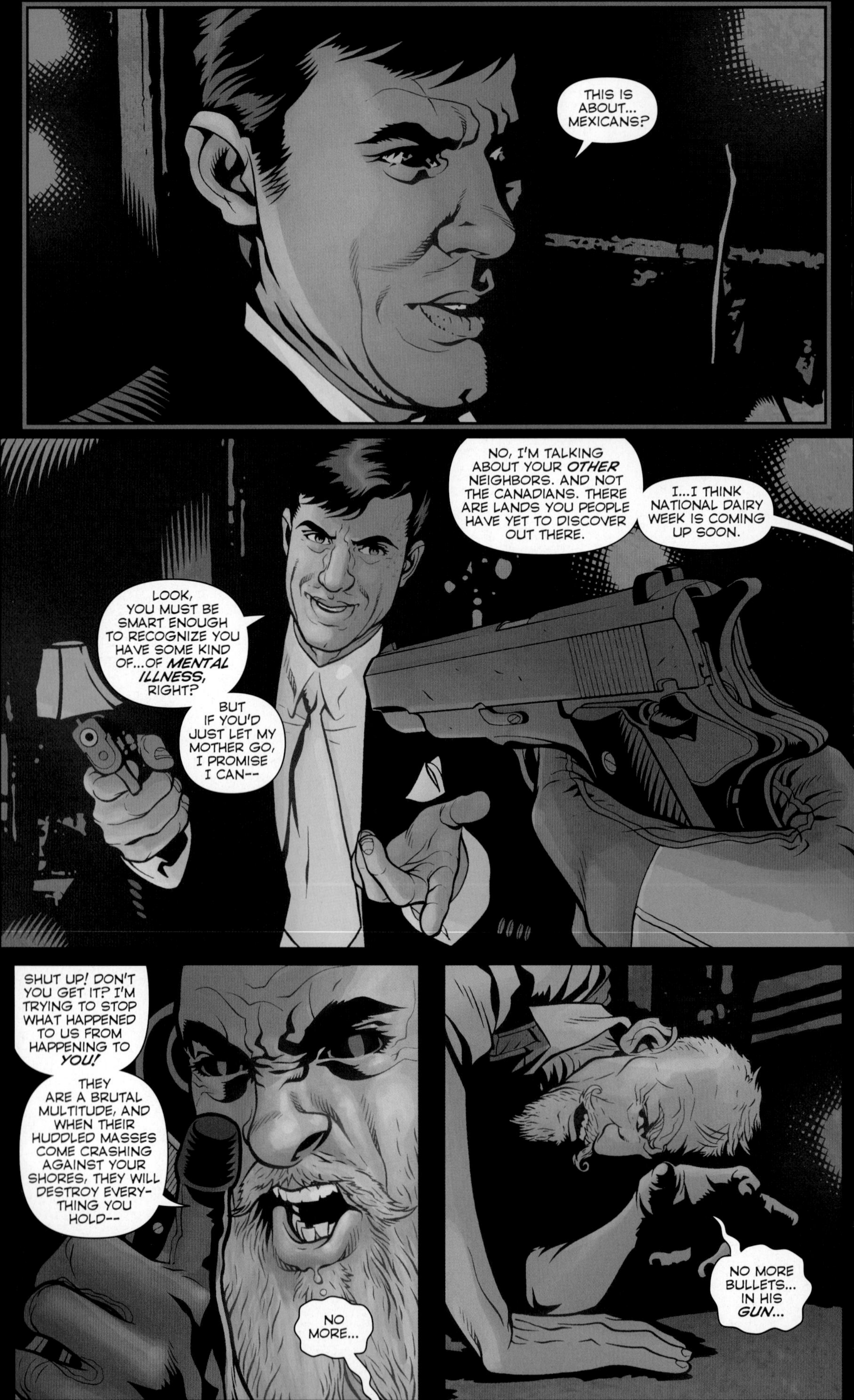
THIS IS ABOUT... MEXICANS?
NO, I'M TALKING ABOUT YOUR *OTHER* NEIGHBORS. AND NOT THE CANADIANS. THERE ARE LANDS YOU PEOPLE HAVE YET TO DISCOVER OUT THERE.
I...I THINK NATIONAL DAIRY WEEK IS COMING UP SOON.
LOOK, YOU MUST BE SMART ENOUGH TO RECOGNIZE YOU HAVE SOME KIND OF...OF *MENTAL ILLNESS*, RIGHT?
BUT IF YOU'D JUST LET MY MOTHER GO, I PROMISE I CAN--
SHUT UP! DON'T YOU GET IT? I'M TRYING TO STOP WHAT HAPPENED TO US FROM HAPPENING TO *YOU!*
THEY ARE A BRUTAL MULTITUDE, AND WHEN THEIR HUDDLED MASSES COME CRASHING AGAINST YOUR SHORES, THEY WILL DESTROY EVERYTHING YOU HOLD--
NO MORE...
NO MORE BULLETS... IN HIS *GUN*...

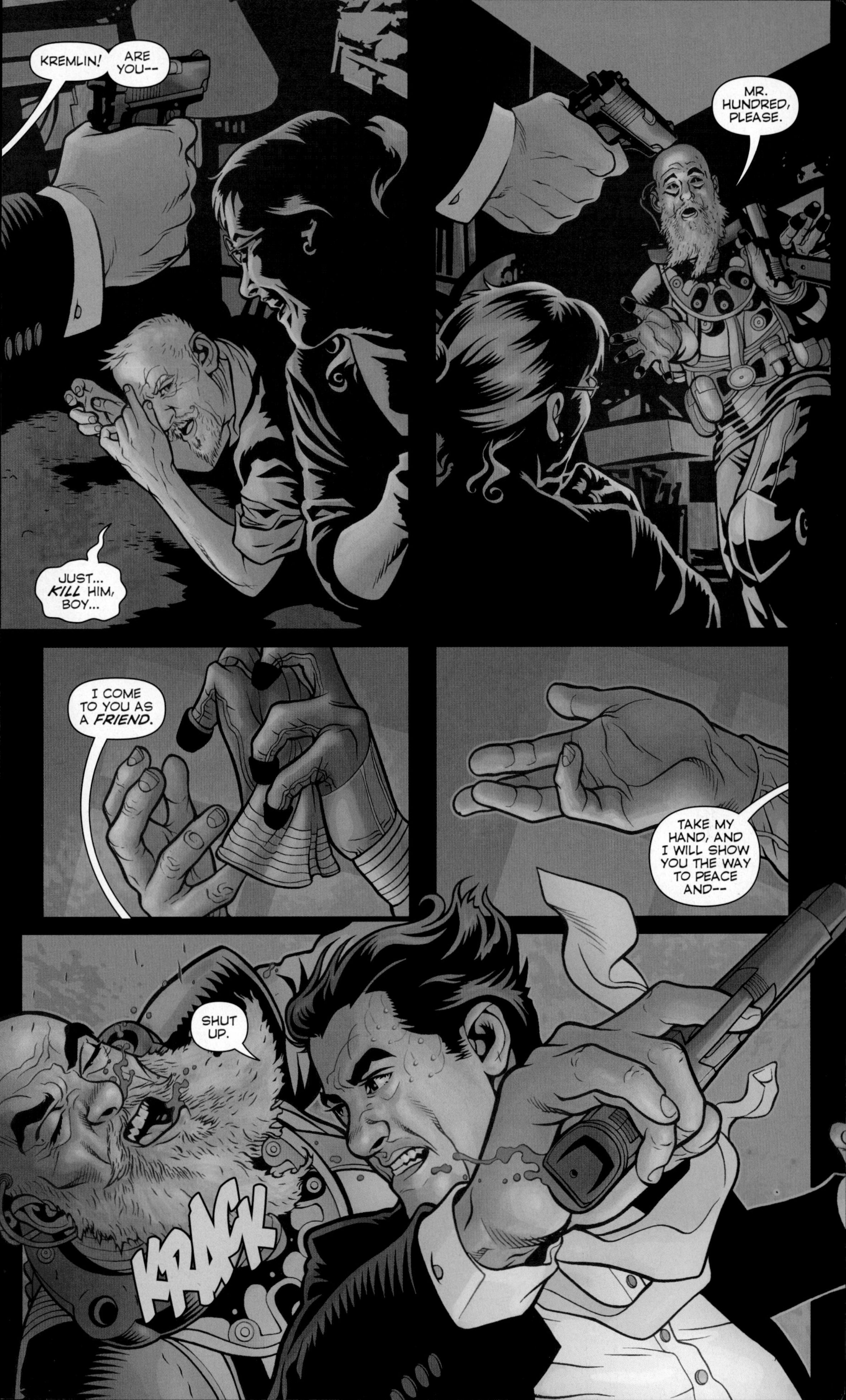
KREMLIN!
ARE YOU--
MR. HUNDRED, PLEASE.
JUST... *KILL* HIM, BOY...
I COME TO YOU AS A *FRIEND*.
TAKE MY HAND, AND I WILL SHOW YOU THE WAY TO PEACE AND--
SHUT UP.
KRACK

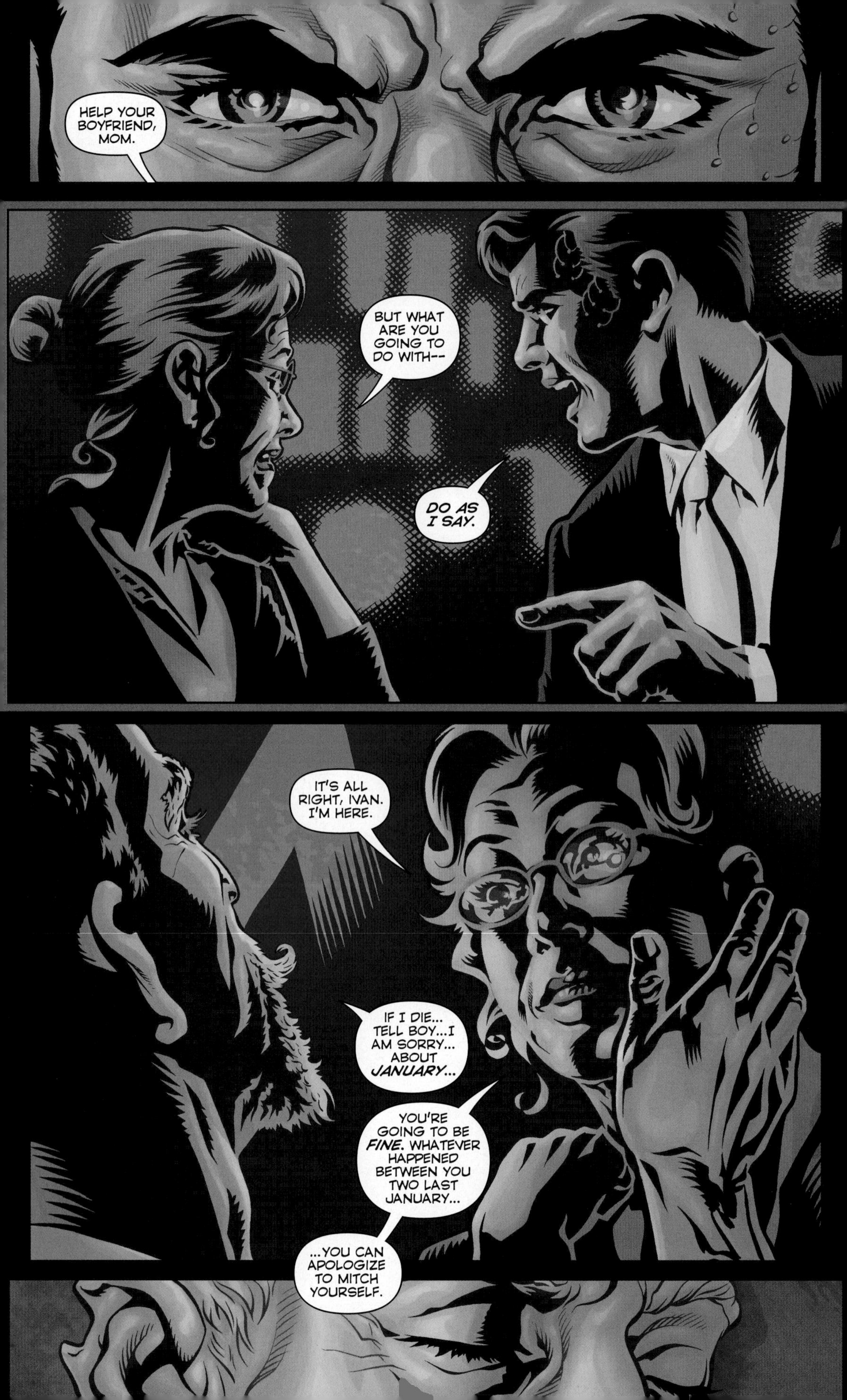
HELP YOUR BOYFRIEND, MOM.
BUT WHAT ARE YOU GOING TO DO WITH--
DO AS I SAY.
IT'S ALL RIGHT, IVAN. I'M HERE.
IF I DIE... TELL BOY...I AM SORRY... ABOUT JANUARY...
YOU'RE GOING TO BE FINE. WHATEVER HAPPENED BETWEEN YOU TWO LAST JANUARY...
...YOU CAN APOLOGIZE TO MITCH YOURSELF.

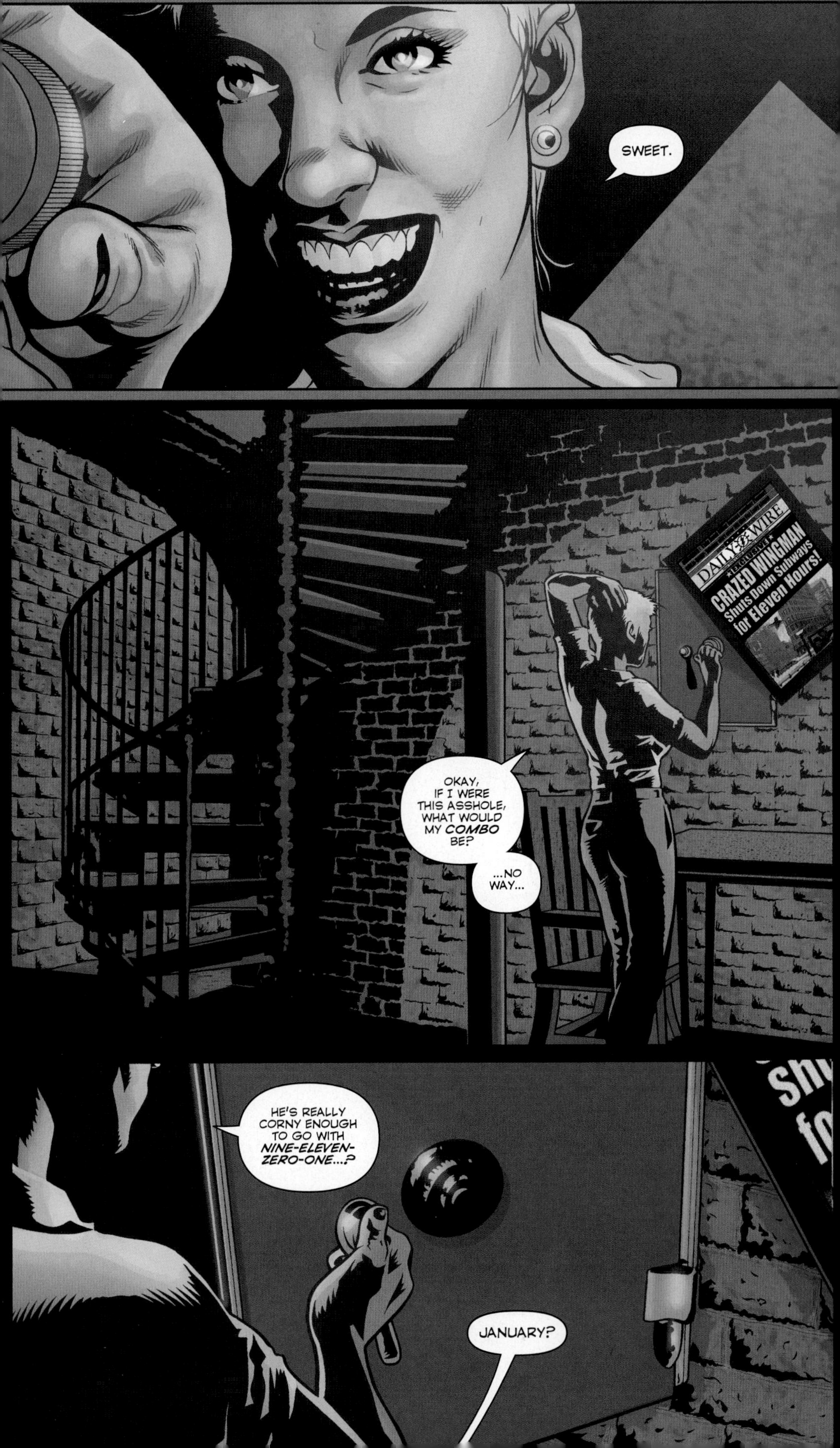
SWEET.
DAILY WIRE
EXCLUSIVE
CRAZED WINGMAN Shuts Down Subways for Eleven Hours!
OKAY, IF I WERE THIS ASSHOLE, WHAT WOULD MY *COMBO* BE?
...NO WAY...
HE'S REALLY CORNY ENOUGH TO GO WITH *NINE-ELEVEN-ZERO-ONE...?*
JANUARY?

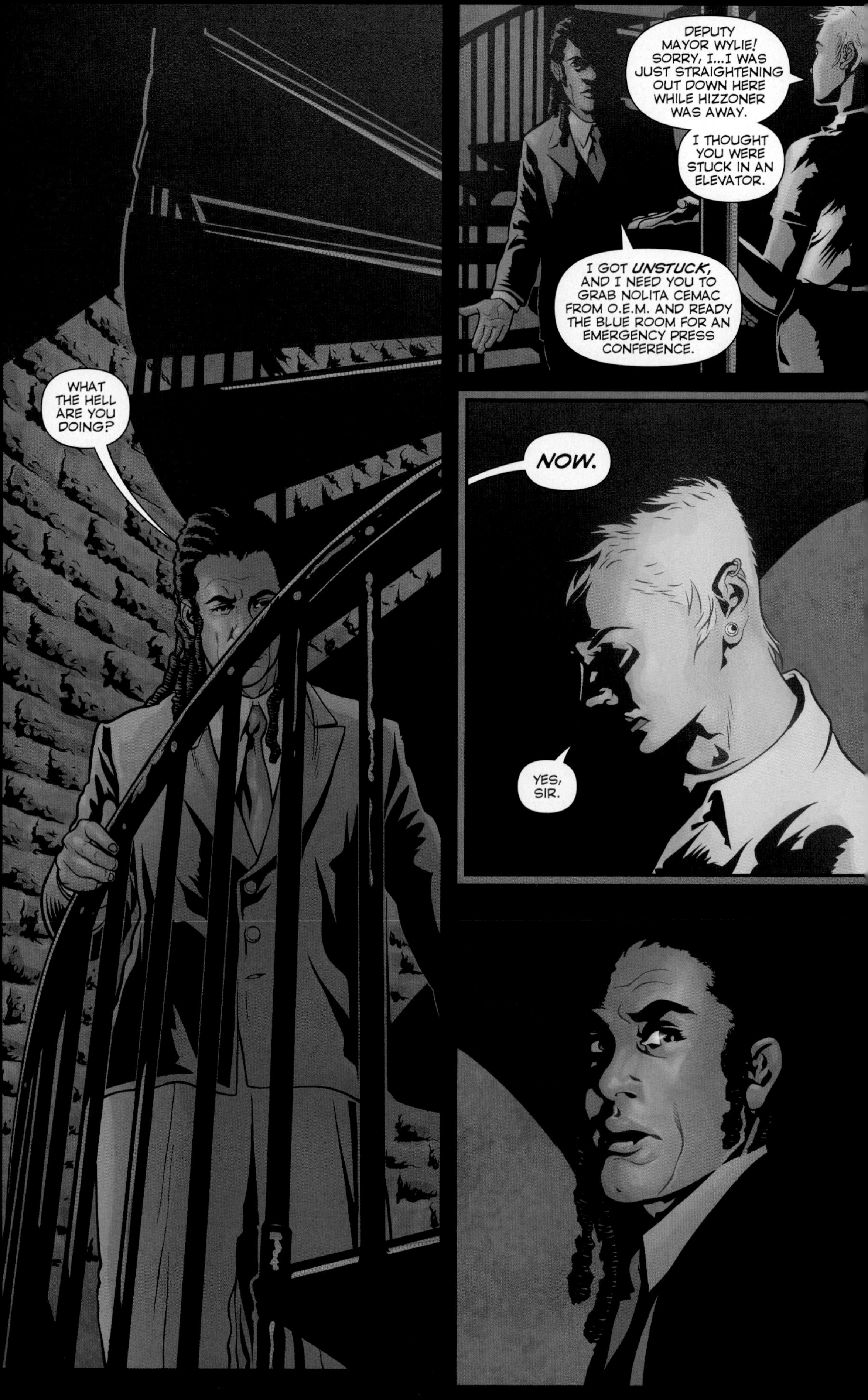
WHAT THE HELL ARE YOU DOING?
DEPUTY MAYOR WYLIE! SORRY, I...I WAS JUST STRAIGHTENING OUT DOWN HERE WHILE HIZZONER WAS AWAY.
I THOUGHT YOU WERE STUCK IN AN ELEVATOR.
I GOT UNSTUCK, AND I NEED YOU TO GRAB NOLITA CEMAC FROM O.E.M. AND READY THE BLUE ROOM FOR AN EMERGENCY PRESS CONFERENCE.
NOW.
YES, SIR.

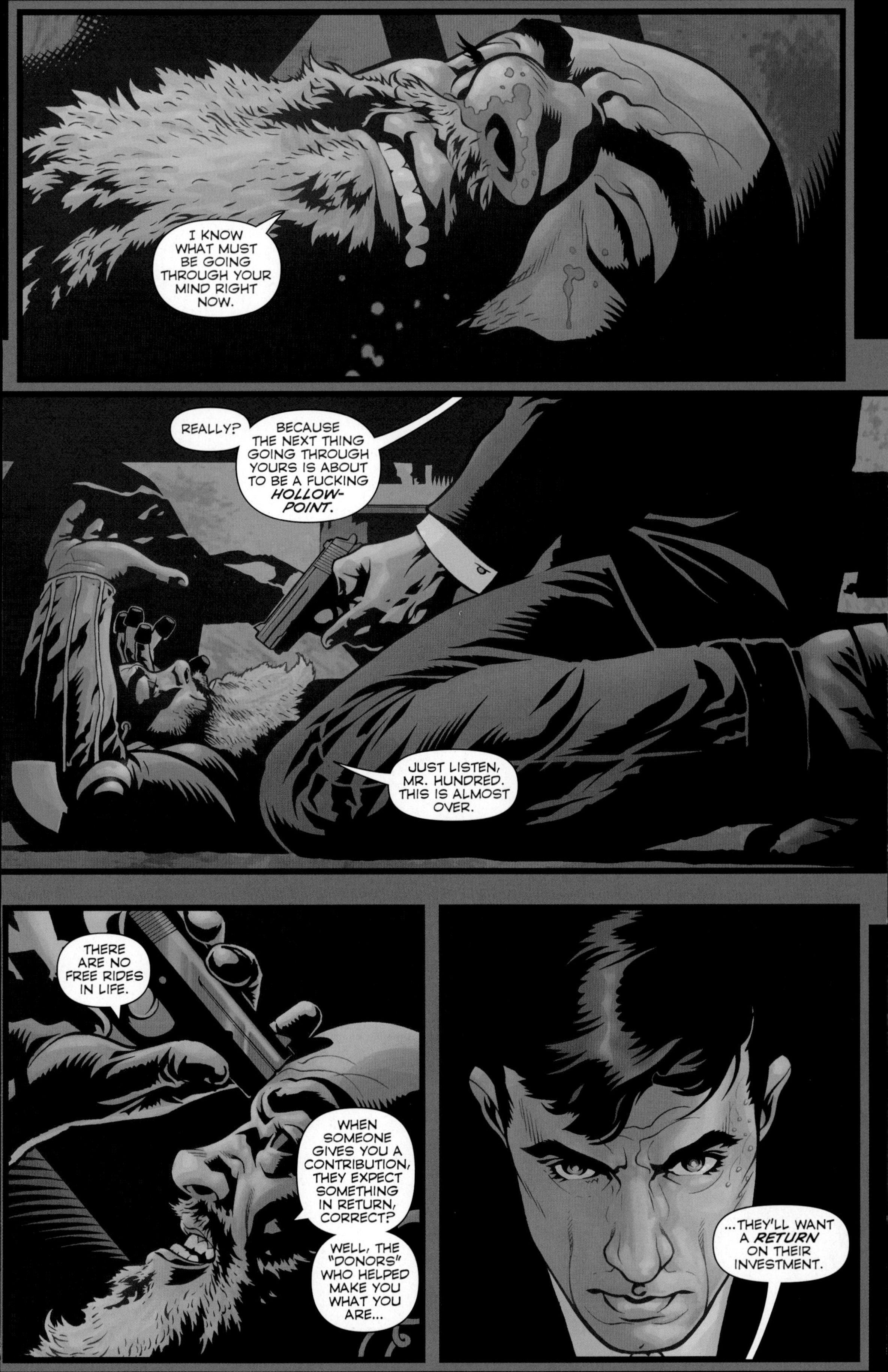
I KNOW WHAT MUST BE GOING THROUGH YOUR MIND RIGHT NOW.
REALLY?
BECAUSE THE NEXT THING GOING THROUGH YOURS IS ABOUT TO BE A FUCKING *HOLLOW-POINT*.
JUST LISTEN, MR. HUNDRED. THIS IS ALMOST OVER.
THERE ARE NO FREE RIDES IN LIFE.
WHEN SOMEONE GIVES YOU A CONTRIBUTION, THEY EXPECT SOMETHING IN RETURN, CORRECT?
WELL, THE "DONORS" WHO HELPED MAKE YOU WHAT YOU ARE...
...THEY'LL WANT A *RETURN* ON THEIR INVESTMENT.

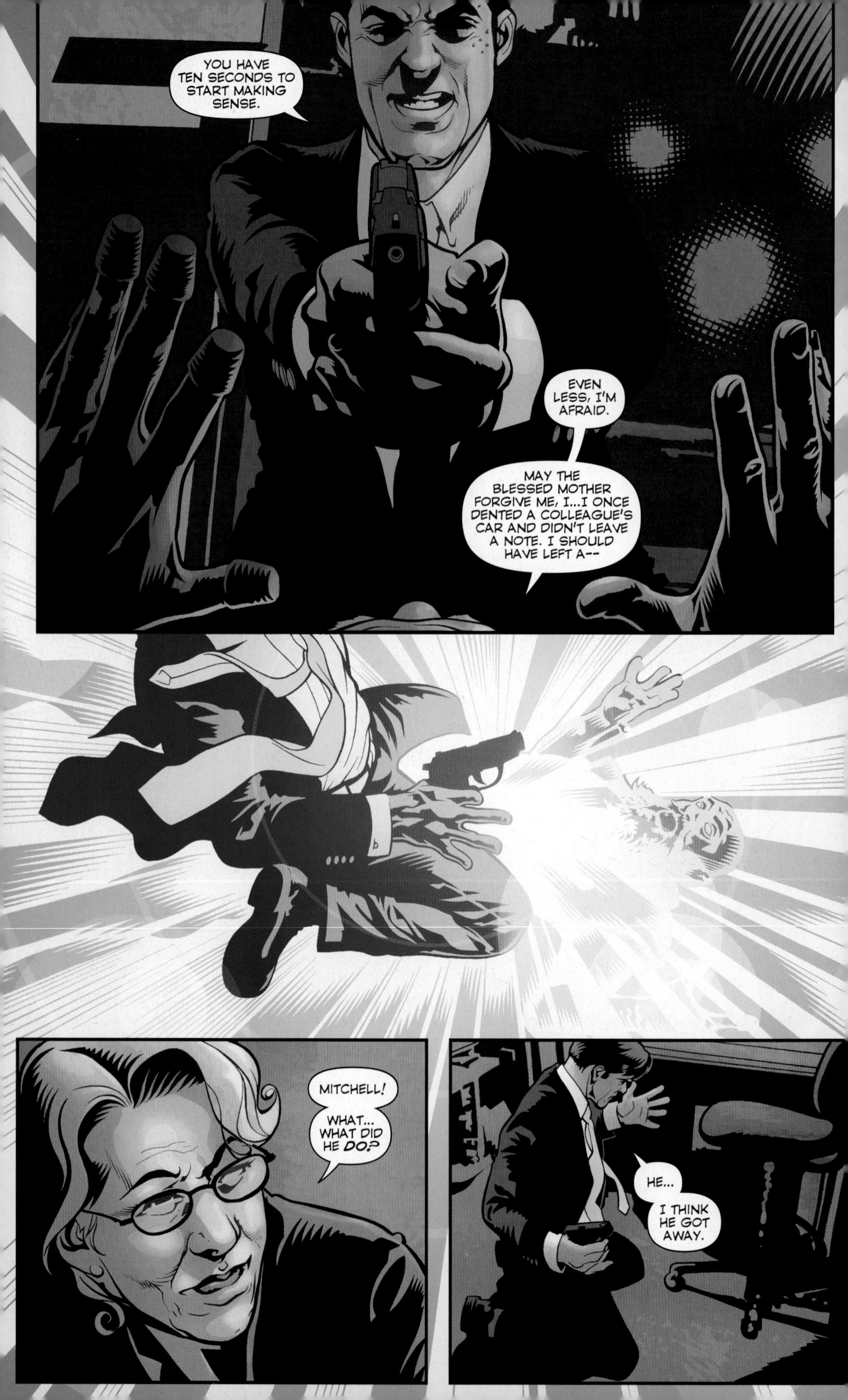
YOU HAVE TEN SECONDS TO START MAKING SENSE.
EVEN LESS, I'M AFRAID.
MAY THE BLESSED MOTHER FORGIVE ME, I...I ONCE DENTED A COLLEAGUE'S CAR AND DIDN'T LEAVE A NOTE. I SHOULD HAVE LEFT A--
MITCHELL!
WHAT... WHAT DID HE *DO?*
HE...
I THINK HE GOT AWAY.

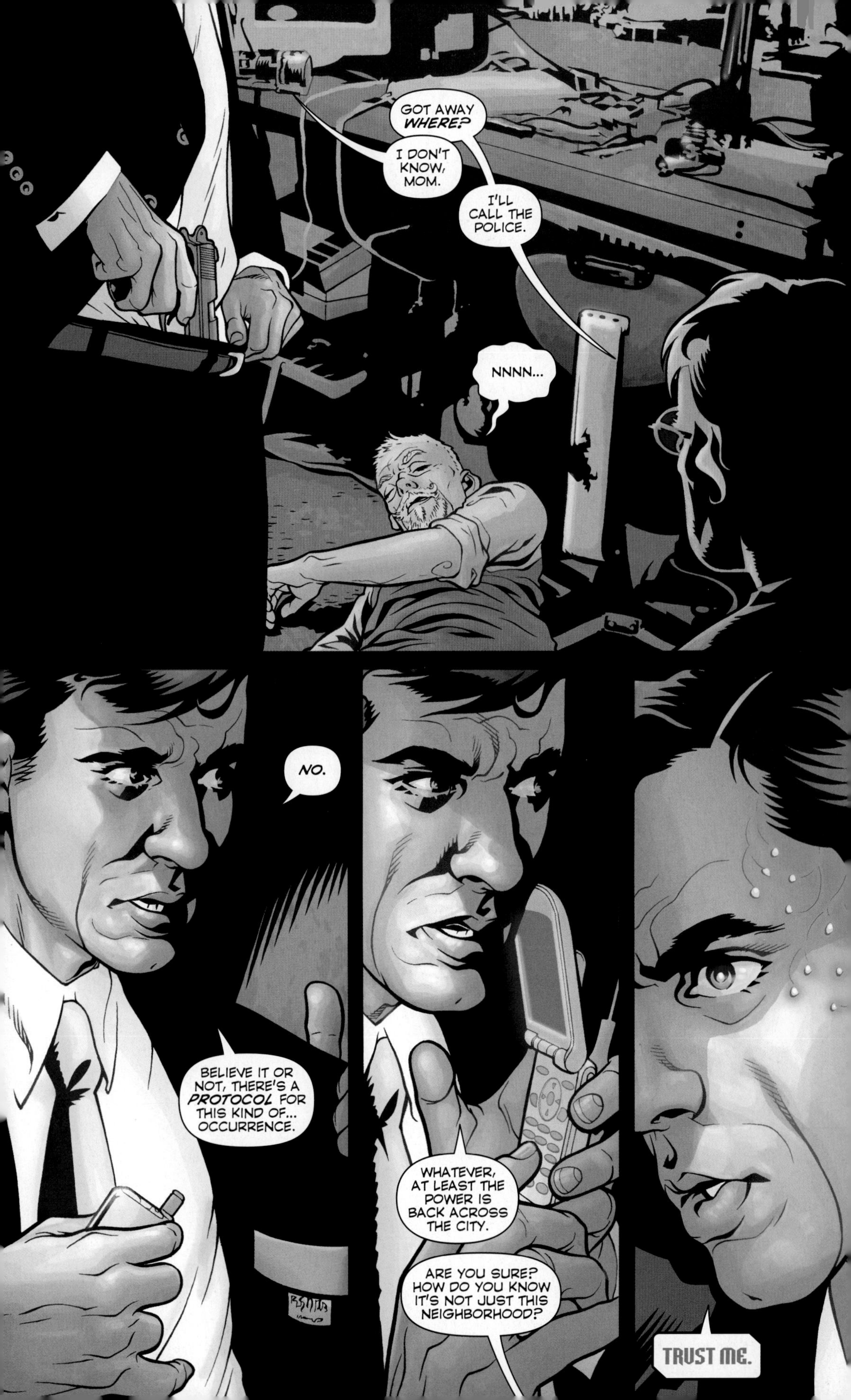

GOT AWAY *WHERE?*
I DON'T KNOW, MOM.
I'LL CALL THE POLICE.
NNNN...
NO.
BELIEVE IT OR NOT, THERE'S A *PROTOCOL* FOR THIS KIND OF... OCCURRENCE.
WHATEVER, AT LEAST THE POWER IS BACK ACROSS THE CITY.
ARE YOU SURE? HOW DO YOU KNOW IT'S NOT JUST THIS NEIGHBORHOOD?
TRUST ME.

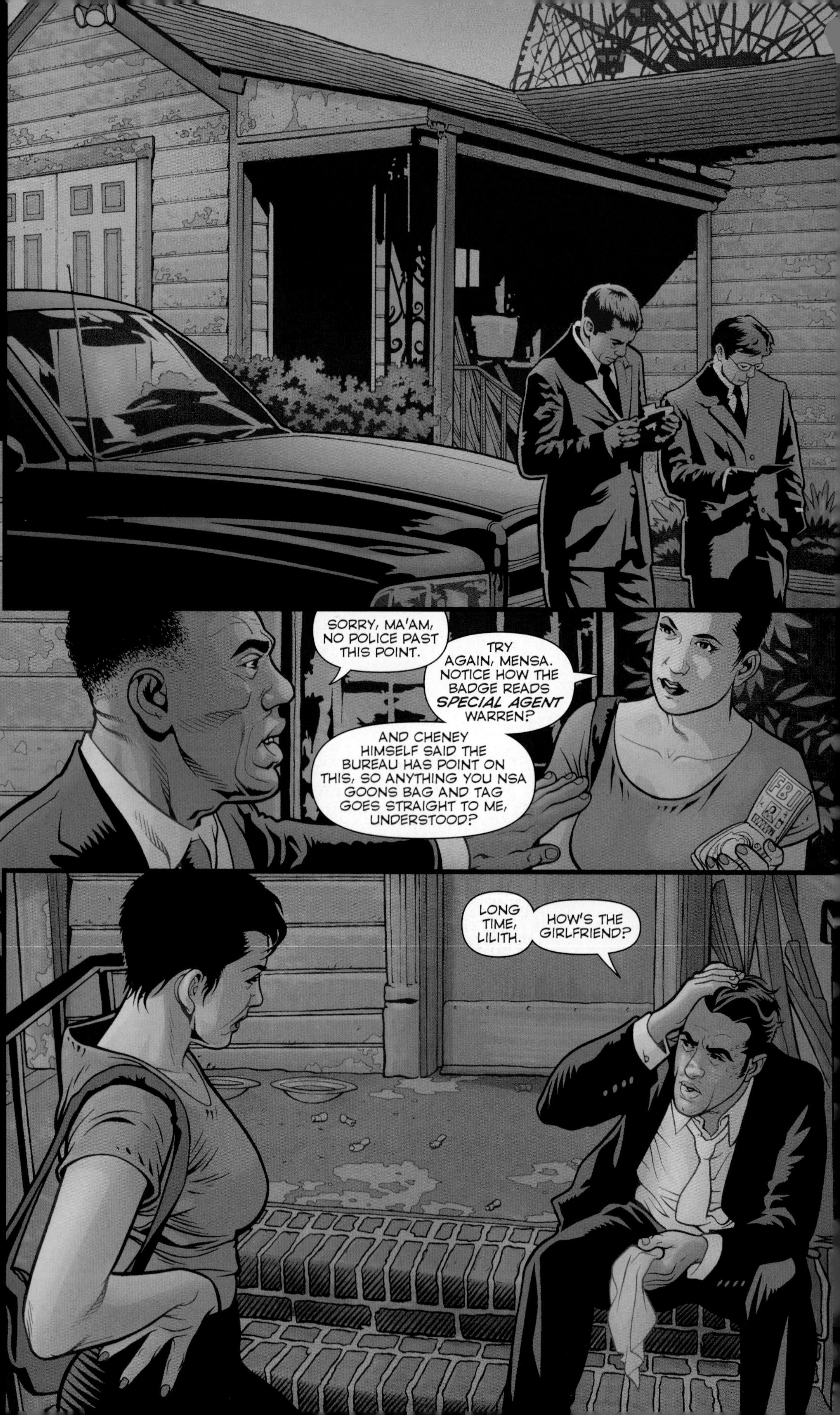
SORRY, MA'AM, NO POLICE PAST THIS POINT.
TRY AGAIN, MENSA. NOTICE HOW THE BADGE READS *SPECIAL AGENT* WARREN?
AND CHENEY HIMSELF SAID THE BUREAU HAS POINT ON THIS, SO ANYTHING YOU NSA GOONS BAG AND TAG GOES STRAIGHT TO ME, UNDERSTOOD?
FBI
LONG TIME, LILITH.
HOW'S THE GIRLFRIEND?

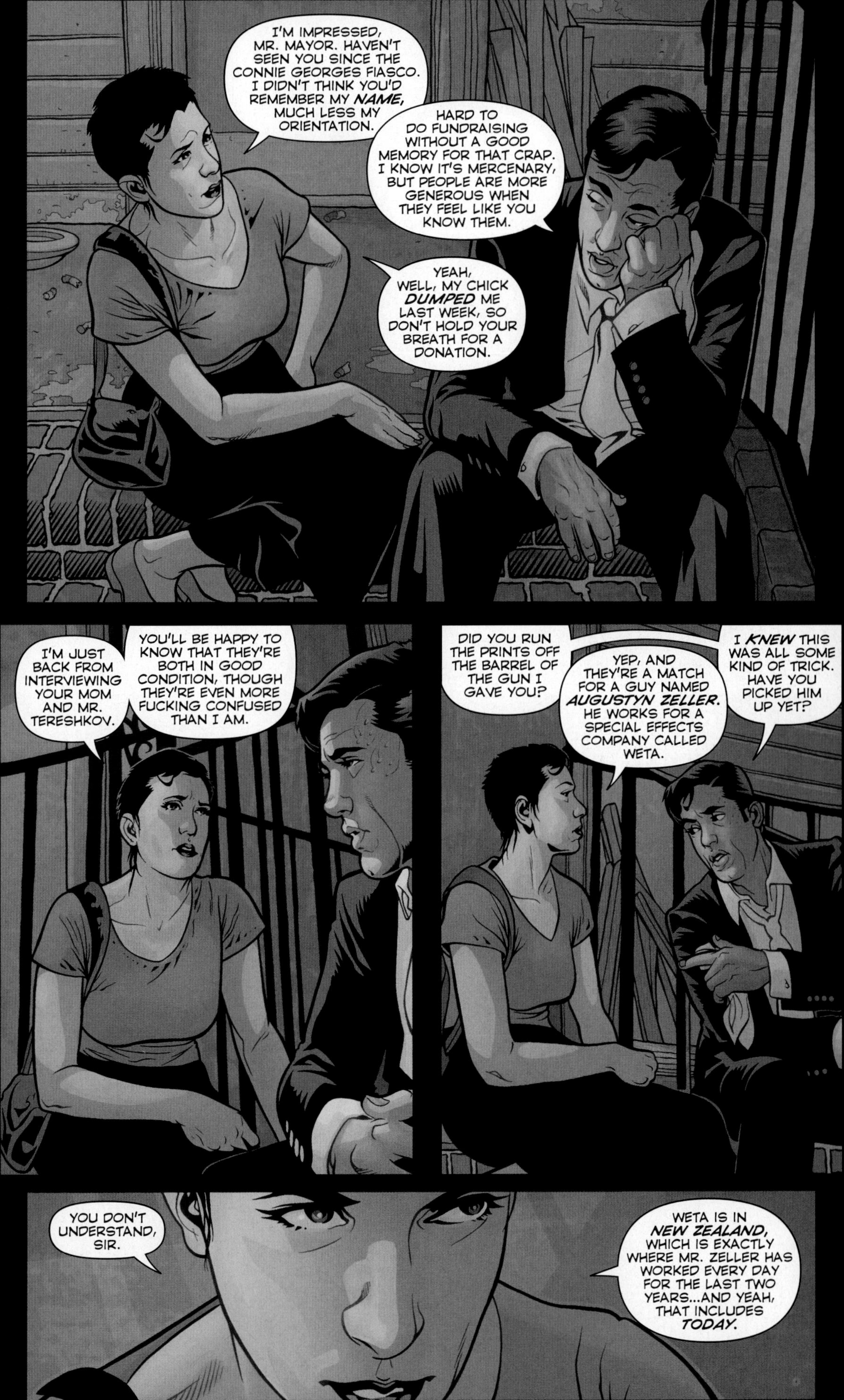

I'M IMPRESSED, MR. MAYOR. HAVEN'T SEEN YOU SINCE THE CONNIE GEORGES FIASCO. I DIDN'T THINK YOU'D REMEMBER MY NAME, MUCH LESS MY ORIENTATION.
HARD TO DO FUNDRAISING WITHOUT A GOOD MEMORY FOR THAT CRAP. I KNOW IT'S MERCENARY, BUT PEOPLE ARE MORE GENEROUS WHEN THEY FEEL LIKE YOU KNOW THEM.
YEAH, WELL, MY CHICK DUMPED ME LAST WEEK, SO DON'T HOLD YOUR BREATH FOR A DONATION.
I'M JUST BACK FROM INTERVIEWING YOUR MOM AND MR. TERESHKOV.
YOU'LL BE HAPPY TO KNOW THAT THEY'RE BOTH IN GOOD CONDITION, THOUGH THEY'RE EVEN MORE FUCKING CONFUSED THAN I AM.
DID YOU RUN THE PRINTS OFF THE BARREL OF THE GUN I GAVE YOU?
YEP, AND THEY'RE A MATCH FOR A GUY NAMED AUGUSTYN ZELLER. HE WORKS FOR A SPECIAL EFFECTS COMPANY CALLED WETA.
I KNEW THIS WAS ALL SOME KIND OF TRICK. HAVE YOU PICKED HIM UP YET?
YOU DON'T UNDERSTAND, SIR.
WETA IS IN NEW ZEALAND, WHICH IS EXACTLY WHERE MR. ZELLER HAS WORKED EVERY DAY FOR THE LAST TWO YEARS...AND YEAH, THAT INCLUDES TODAY.

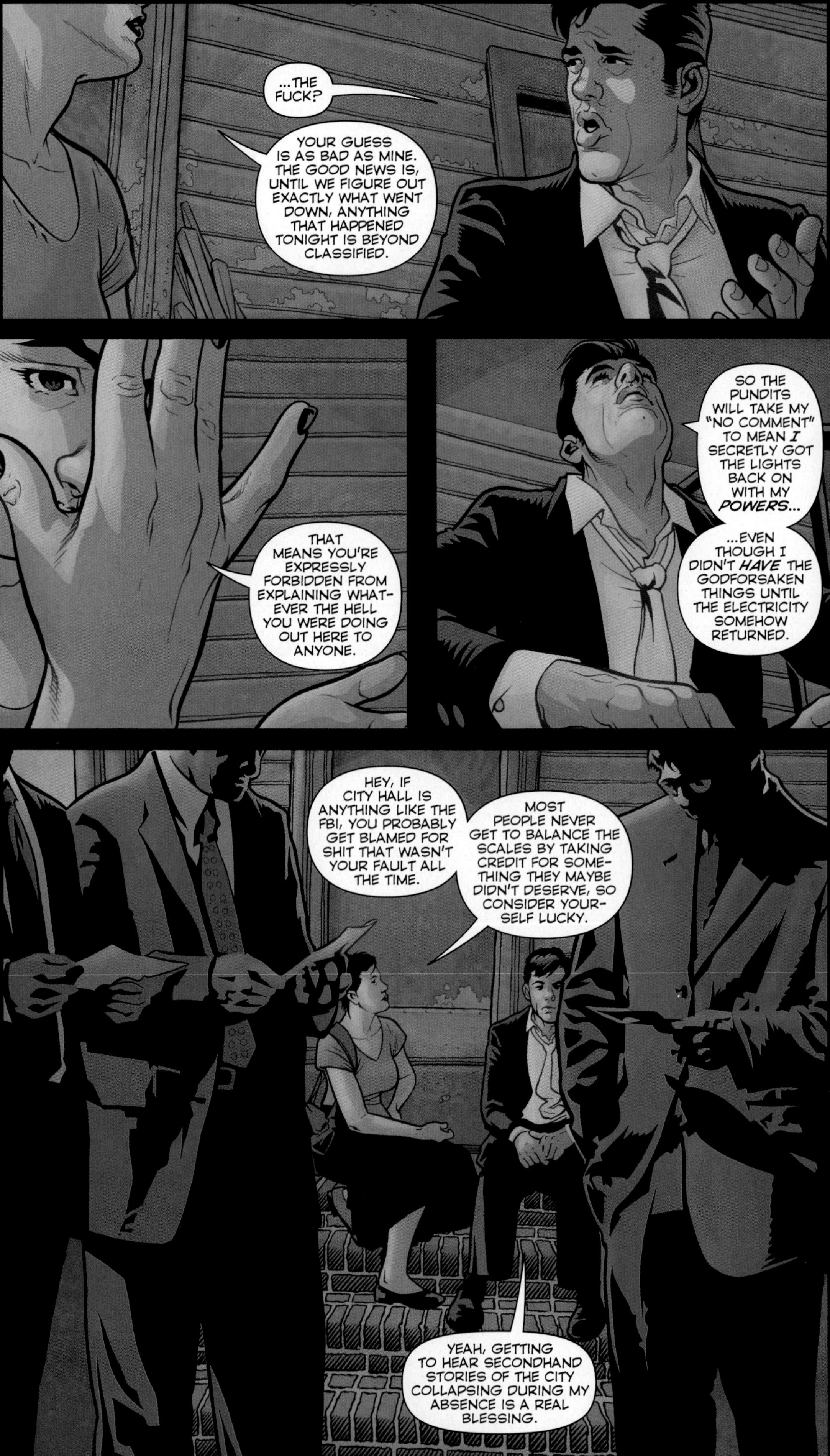
...THE FUCK?
YOUR GUESS IS AS BAD AS MINE. THE GOOD NEWS IS, UNTIL WE FIGURE OUT EXACTLY WHAT WENT DOWN, ANYTHING THAT HAPPENED TONIGHT IS BEYOND CLASSIFIED.
THAT MEANS YOU'RE EXPRESSLY FORBIDDEN FROM EXPLAINING WHATEVER THE HELL YOU WERE DOING OUT HERE TO ANYONE.
SO THE PUNDITS WILL TAKE MY "NO COMMENT" TO MEAN *I* SECRETLY GOT THE LIGHTS BACK ON WITH MY *POWERS*...
...EVEN THOUGH I DIDN'T *HAVE* THE GODFORSAKEN THINGS UNTIL THE ELECTRICITY SOMEHOW RETURNED.
HEY, IF CITY HALL IS ANYTHING LIKE THE FBI, YOU PROBABLY GET BLAMED FOR SHIT THAT WASN'T YOUR FAULT ALL THE TIME.
MOST PEOPLE NEVER GET TO BALANCE THE SCALES BY TAKING CREDIT FOR SOMETHING THEY MAYBE DIDN'T DESERVE, SO CONSIDER YOURSELF LUCKY.
YEAH, GETTING TO HEAR SECONDHAND STORIES OF THE CITY COLLAPSING DURING MY ABSENCE IS A REAL BLESSING.

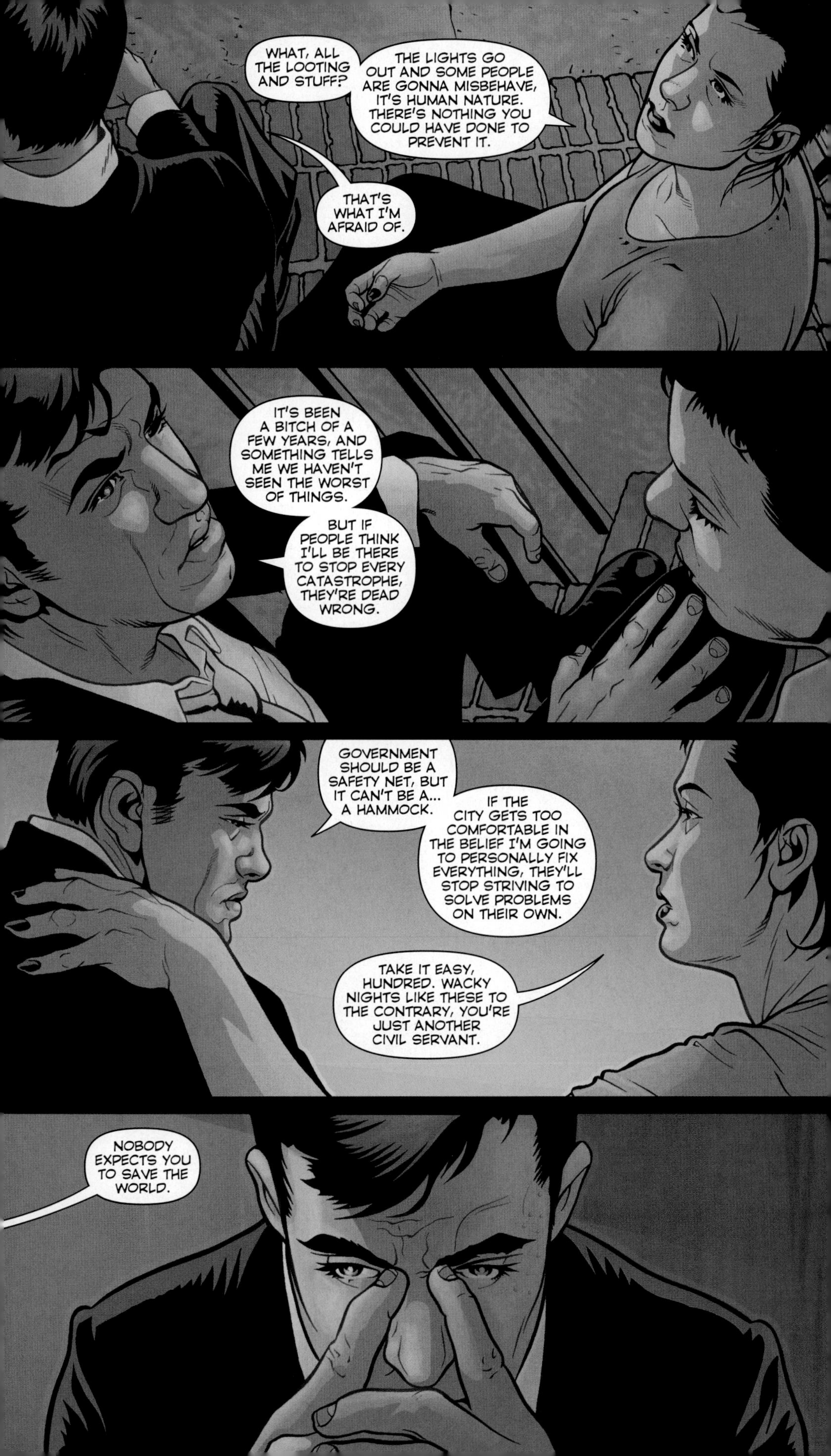
WHAT, ALL THE LOOTING AND STUFF?
THE LIGHTS GO OUT AND SOME PEOPLE ARE GONNA MISBEHAVE, IT'S HUMAN NATURE. THERE'S NOTHING YOU COULD HAVE DONE TO PREVENT IT.
THAT'S WHAT I'M AFRAID OF.
IT'S BEEN A BITCH OF A FEW YEARS, AND SOMETHING TELLS ME WE HAVEN'T SEEN THE WORST OF THINGS.
BUT IF PEOPLE THINK I'LL BE THERE TO STOP EVERY CATASTROPHE, THEY'RE DEAD WRONG.
GOVERNMENT SHOULD BE A SAFETY NET, BUT IT CAN'T BE A... A HAMMOCK.
IF THE CITY GETS TOO COMFORTABLE IN THE BELIEF I'M GOING TO PERSONALLY FIX EVERYTHING, THEY'LL STOP STRIVING TO SOLVE PROBLEMS ON THEIR OWN.
TAKE IT EASY, HUNDRED. WACKY NIGHTS LIKE THESE TO THE CONTRARY, YOU'RE JUST ANOTHER CIVIL SERVANT.
NOBODY EXPECTS YOU TO SAVE THE WORLD.

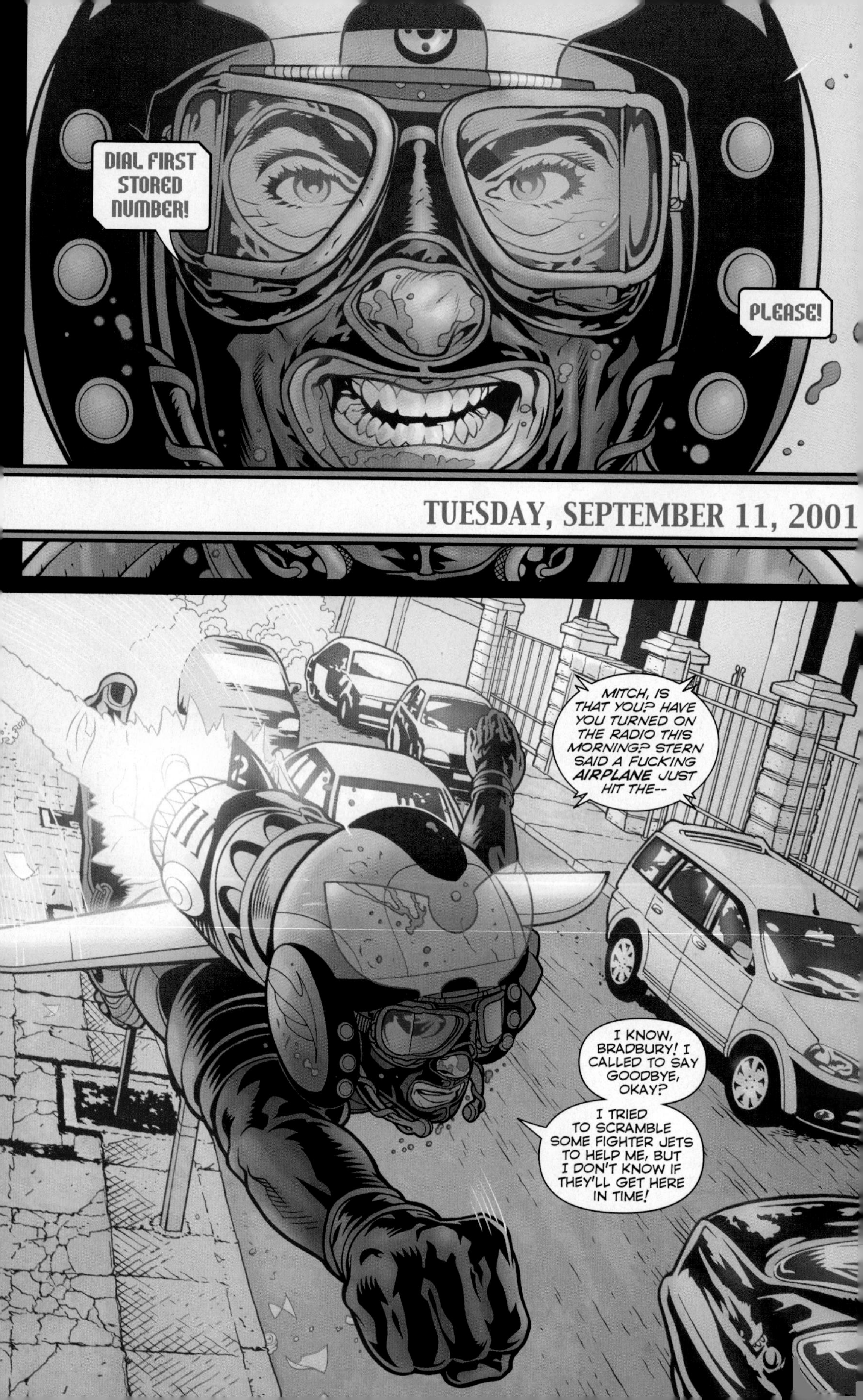
DIAL FIRST STORED NUMBER!
PLEASE!
TUESDAY, SEPTEMBER 11, 2001
MITCH, IS THAT YOU? HAVE YOU TURNED ON THE RADIO THIS MORNING? STERN SAID A FUCKING AIRPLANE JUST HIT THE--
I KNOW, BRADBURY! I CALLED TO SAY GOODBYE, OKAY?
I TRIED TO SCRAMBLE SOME FIGHTER JETS TO HELP ME, BUT I DON'T KNOW IF THEY'LL GET HERE IN TIME!

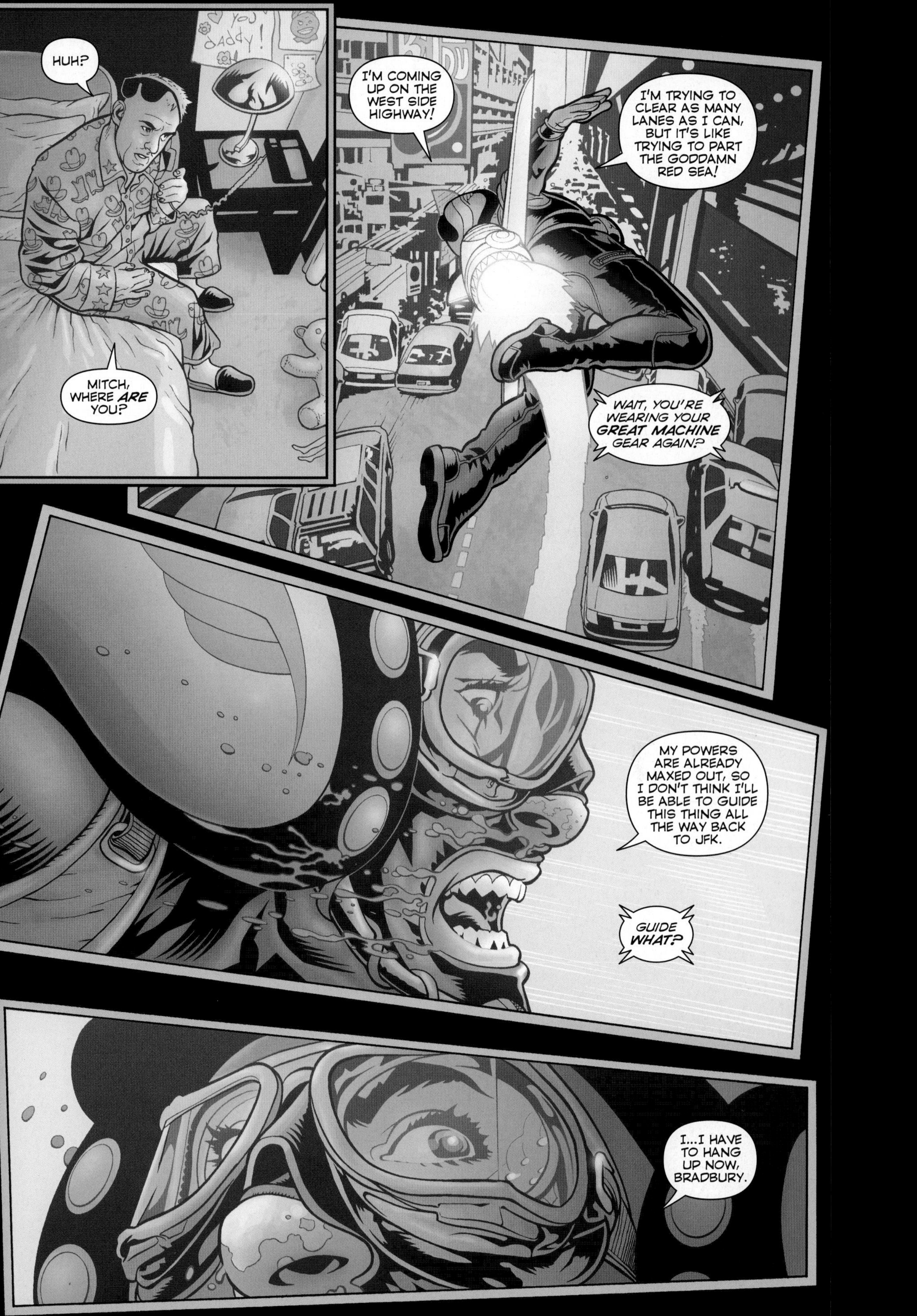
HUH?
MITCH, WHERE ARE YOU?
I'M COMING UP ON THE WEST SIDE HIGHWAY!
I'M TRYING TO CLEAR AS MANY LANES AS I CAN, BUT IT'S LIKE TRYING TO PART THE GODDAMN RED SEA!
WAIT, YOU'RE WEARING YOUR GREAT MACHINE GEAR AGAIN?
MY POWERS ARE ALREADY MAXED OUT, SO I DON'T THINK I'LL BE ABLE TO GUIDE THIS THING ALL THE WAY BACK TO JFK.
GUIDE WHAT?
I...I HAVE TO HANG UP NOW, BRADBURY.

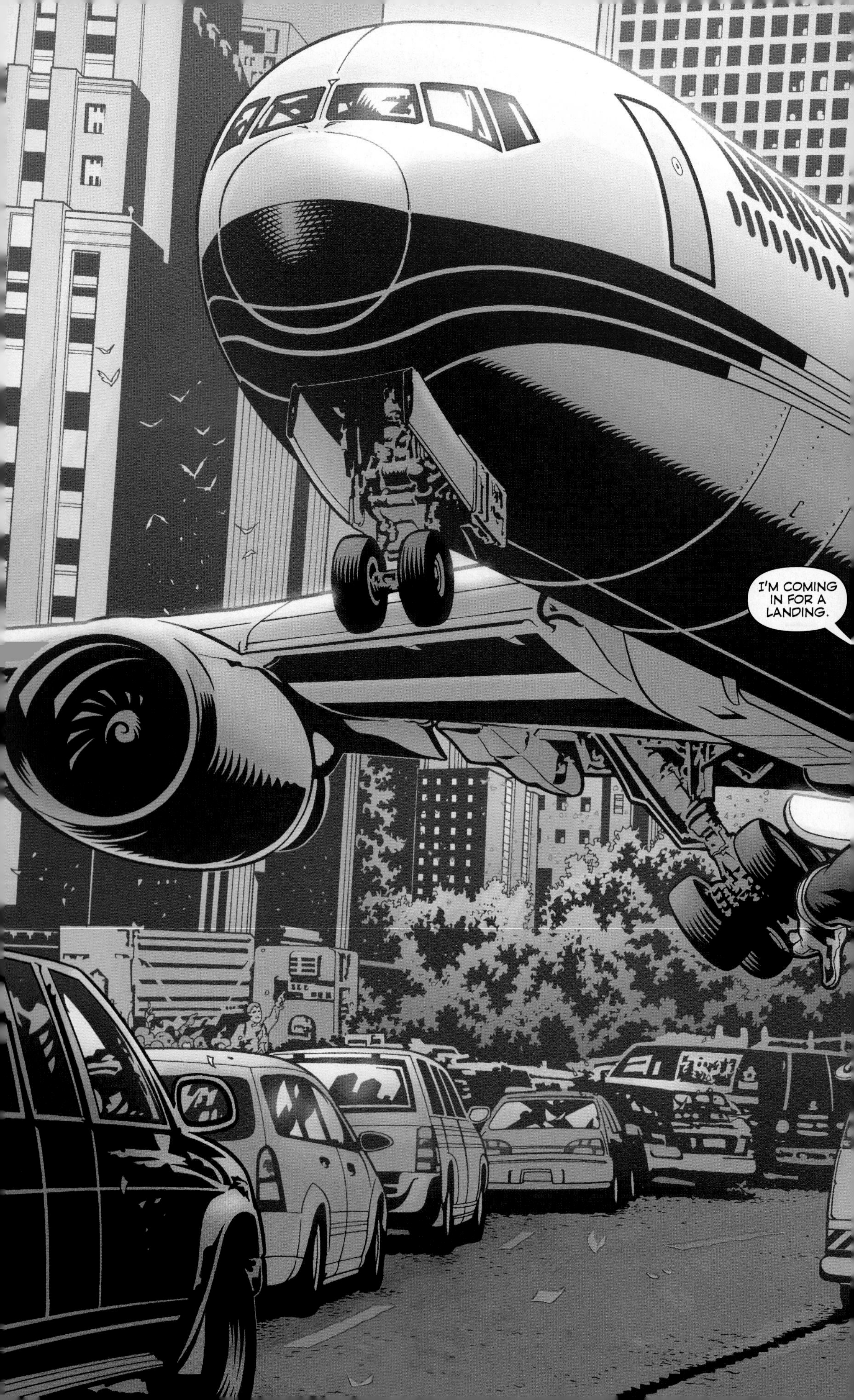
I'M COMING IN FOR A LANDING.

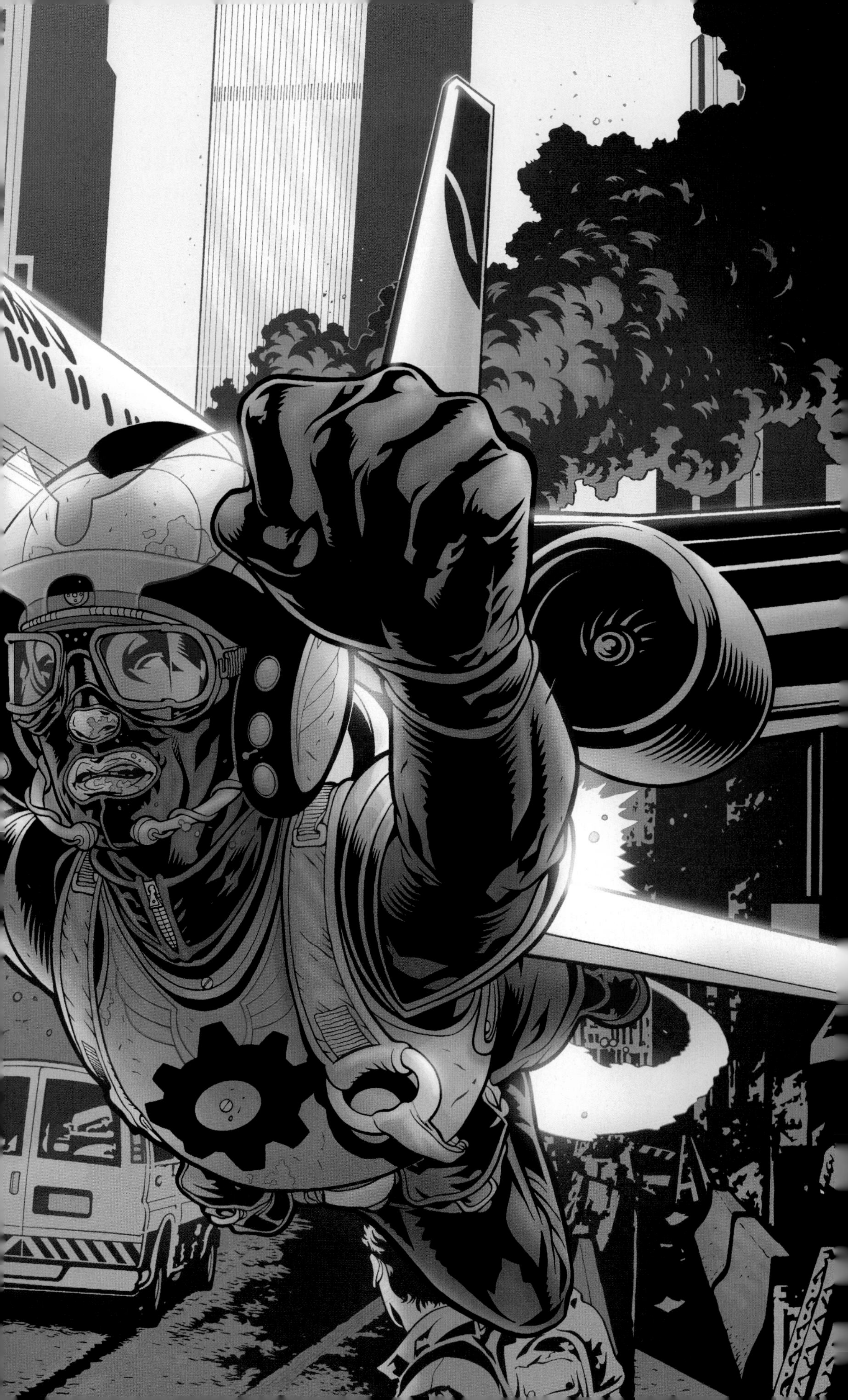

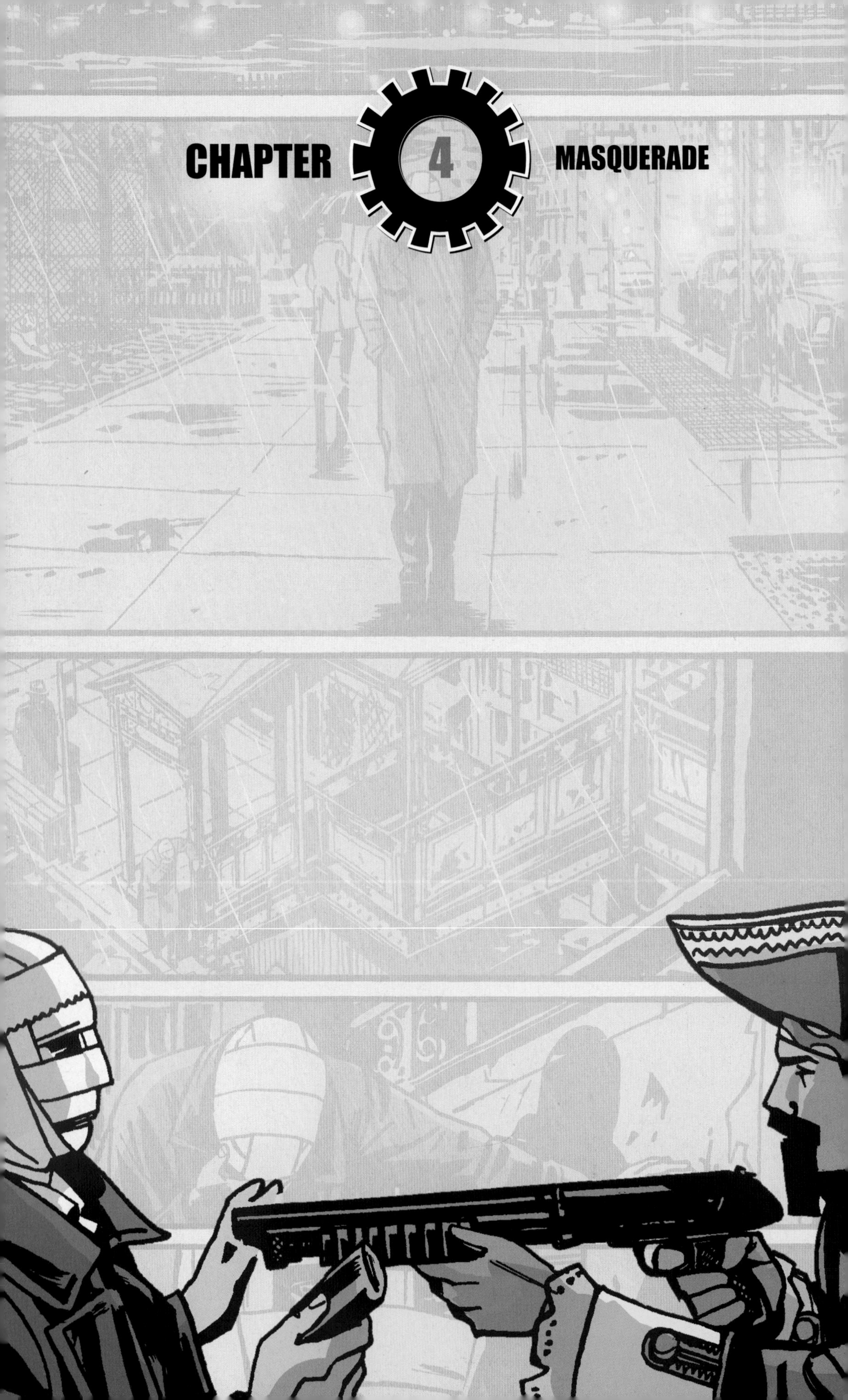
CHAPTER 4 MASQUERADE

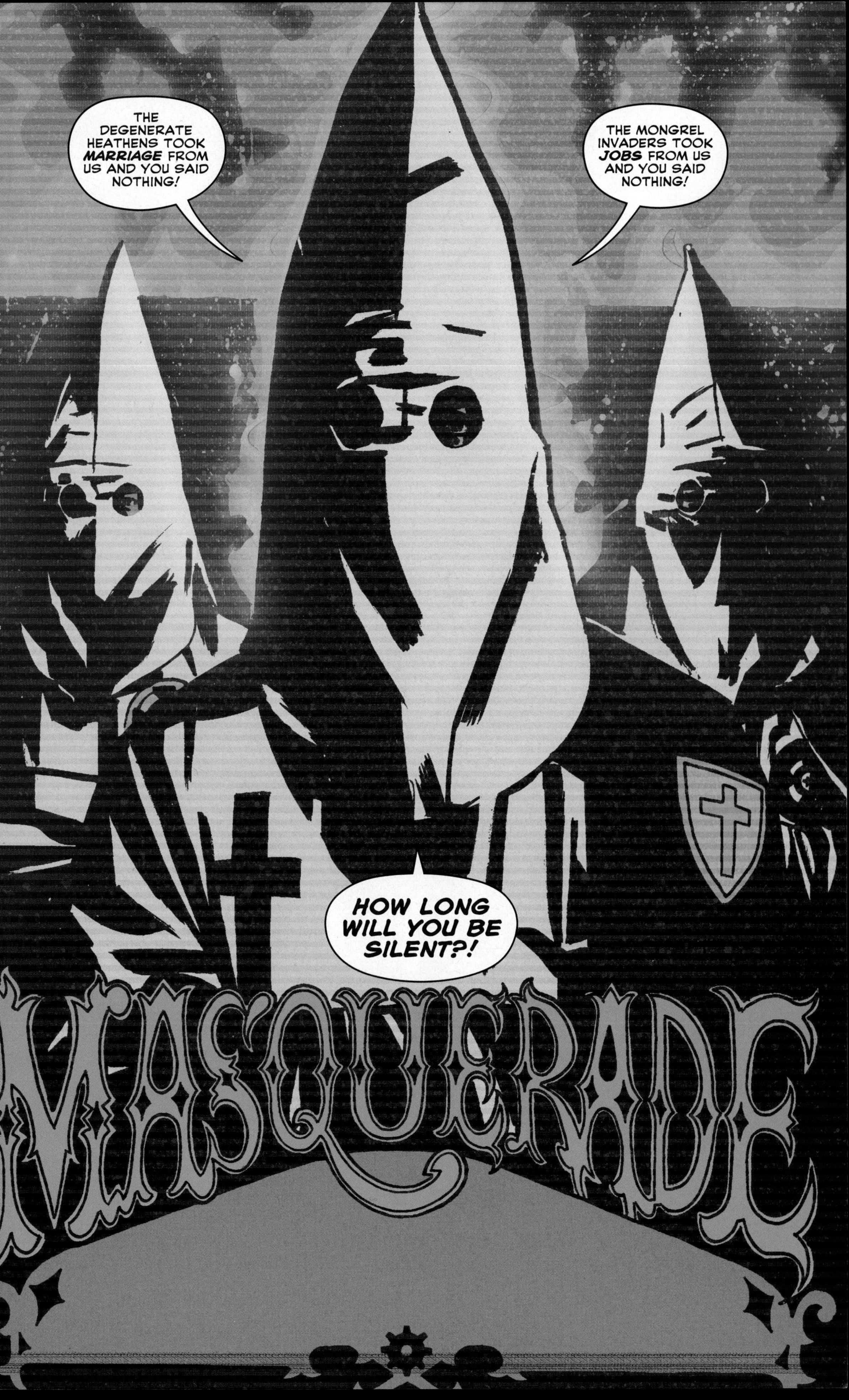
THE DEGENERATE HEATHENS TOOK MARRIAGE FROM US AND YOU SAID NOTHING!
THE MONGREL INVADERS TOOK JOBS FROM US AND YOU SAID NOTHING!
HOW LONG WILL YOU BE SILENT?!
MASQUERADE

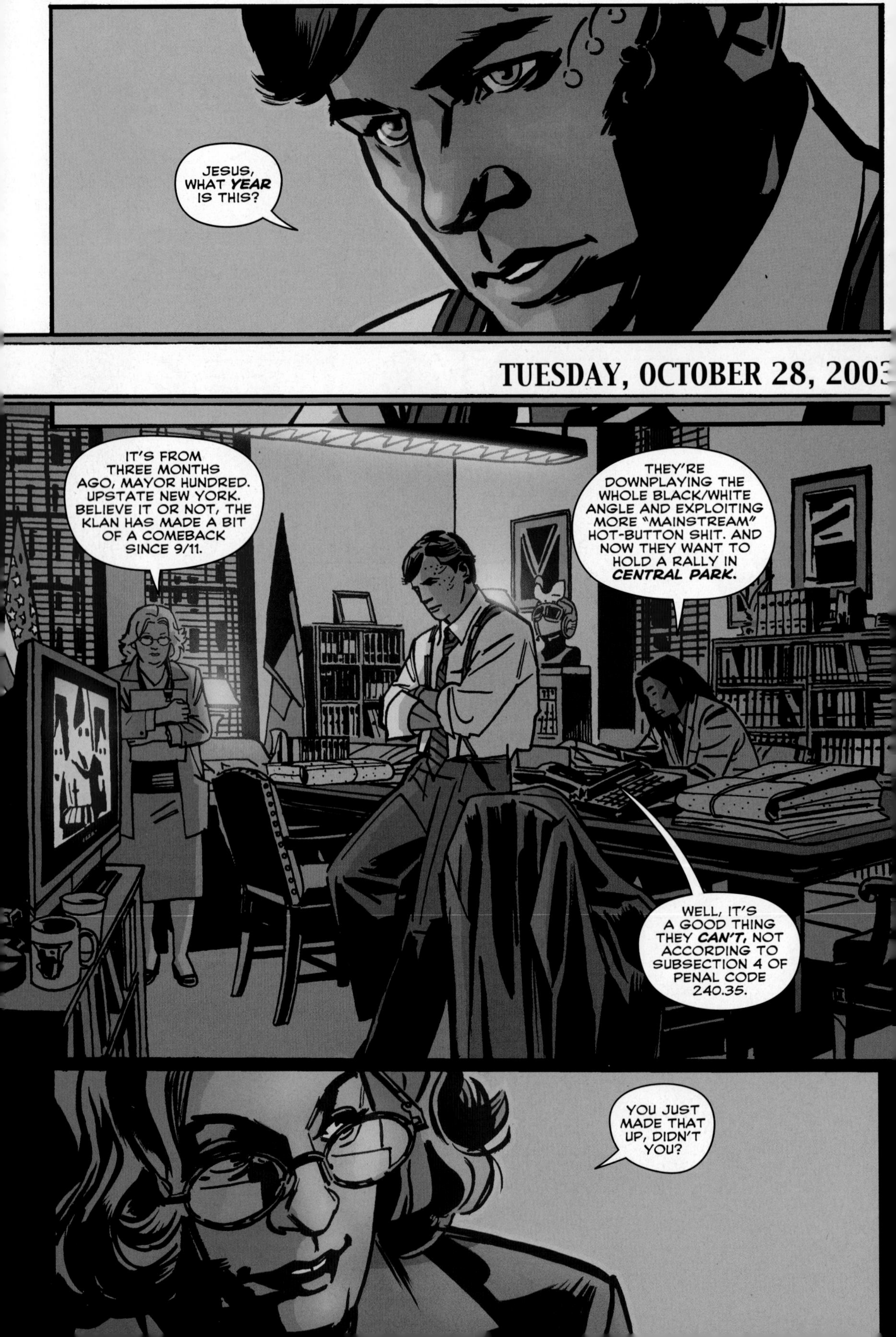
JESUS, WHAT YEAR IS THIS?
TUESDAY, OCTOBER 28, 2003
IT'S FROM THREE MONTHS AGO, MAYOR HUNDRED. UPSTATE NEW YORK. BELIEVE IT OR NOT, THE KLAN HAS MADE A BIT OF A COMEBACK SINCE 9/11.
THEY'RE DOWNPLAYING THE WHOLE BLACK/WHITE ANGLE AND EXPLOITING MORE "MAINSTREAM" HOT-BUTTON SHIT. AND NOW THEY WANT TO HOLD A RALLY IN CENTRAL PARK.
WELL, IT'S A GOOD THING THEY CAN'T, NOT ACCORDING TO SUBSECTION 4 OF PENAL CODE 240.35.
YOU JUST MADE THAT UP, DIDN'T YOU?

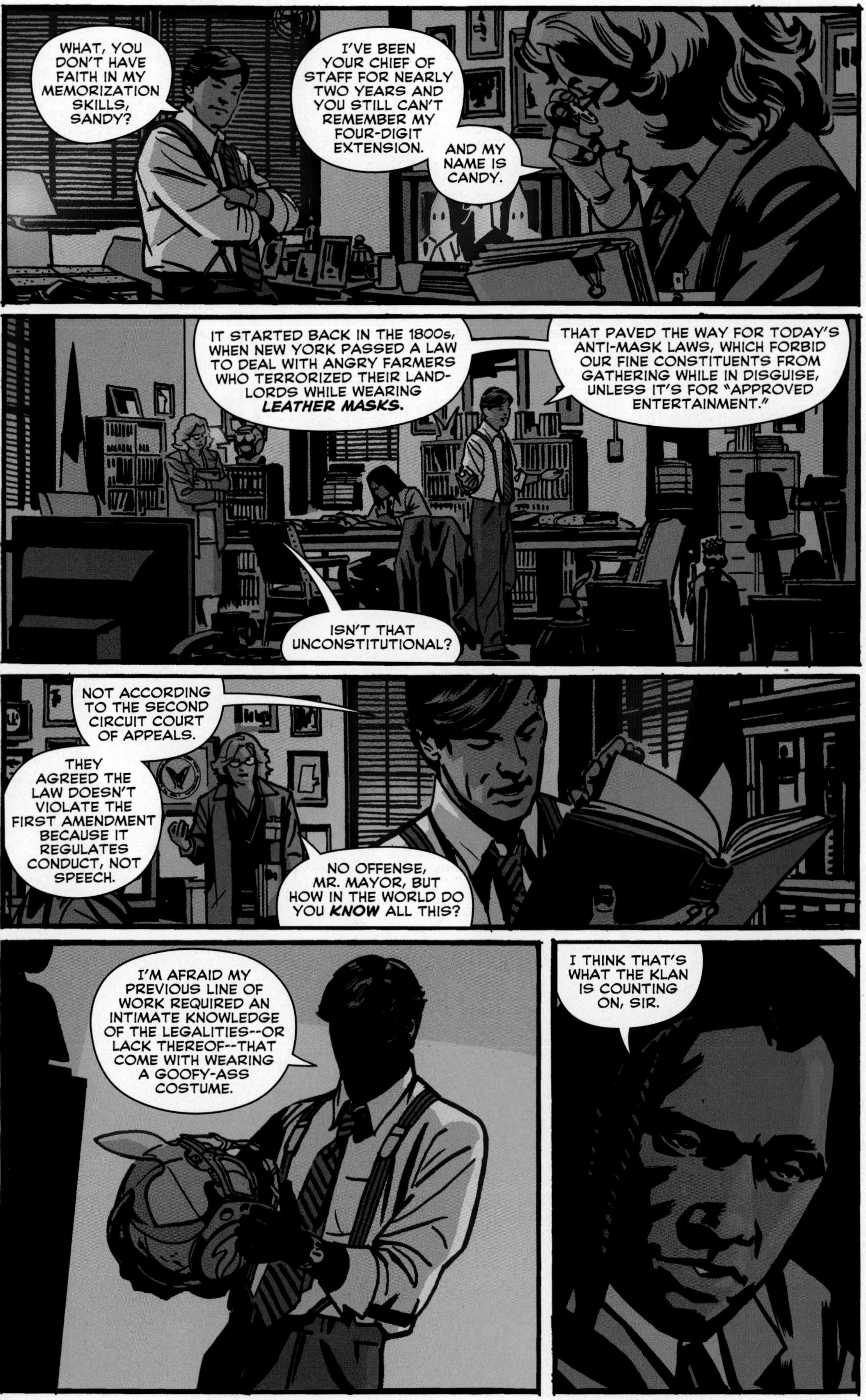
WHAT, YOU DON'T HAVE FAITH IN MY MEMORIZATION SKILLS, SANDY?
I'VE BEEN YOUR CHIEF OF STAFF FOR NEARLY TWO YEARS AND YOU STILL CAN'T REMEMBER MY FOUR-DIGIT EXTENSION.
AND MY NAME IS CANDY.
IT STARTED BACK IN THE 1800s, WHEN NEW YORK PASSED A LAW TO DEAL WITH ANGRY FARMERS WHO TERRORIZED THEIR LANDLORDS WHILE WEARING ***LEATHER MASKS.***
THAT PAVED THE WAY FOR TODAY'S ANTI-MASK LAWS, WHICH FORBID OUR FINE CONSTITUENTS FROM GATHERING WHILE IN DISGUISE, UNLESS IT'S FOR "APPROVED ENTERTAINMENT."
ISN'T THAT UNCONSTITUTIONAL?
NOT ACCORDING TO THE SECOND CIRCUIT COURT OF APPEALS.
THEY AGREED THE LAW DOESN'T VIOLATE THE FIRST AMENDMENT BECAUSE IT REGULATES CONDUCT, NOT SPEECH.
NO OFFENSE, MR. MAYOR, BUT HOW IN THE WORLD DO YOU ***KNOW*** ALL THIS?
I'M AFRAID MY PREVIOUS LINE OF WORK REQUIRED AN INTIMATE KNOWLEDGE OF THE LEGALITIES--OR LACK THEREOF--THAT COME WITH WEARING A GOOFY-ASS COSTUME.
I THINK THAT'S WHAT THE KLAN IS COUNTING ON, SIR.

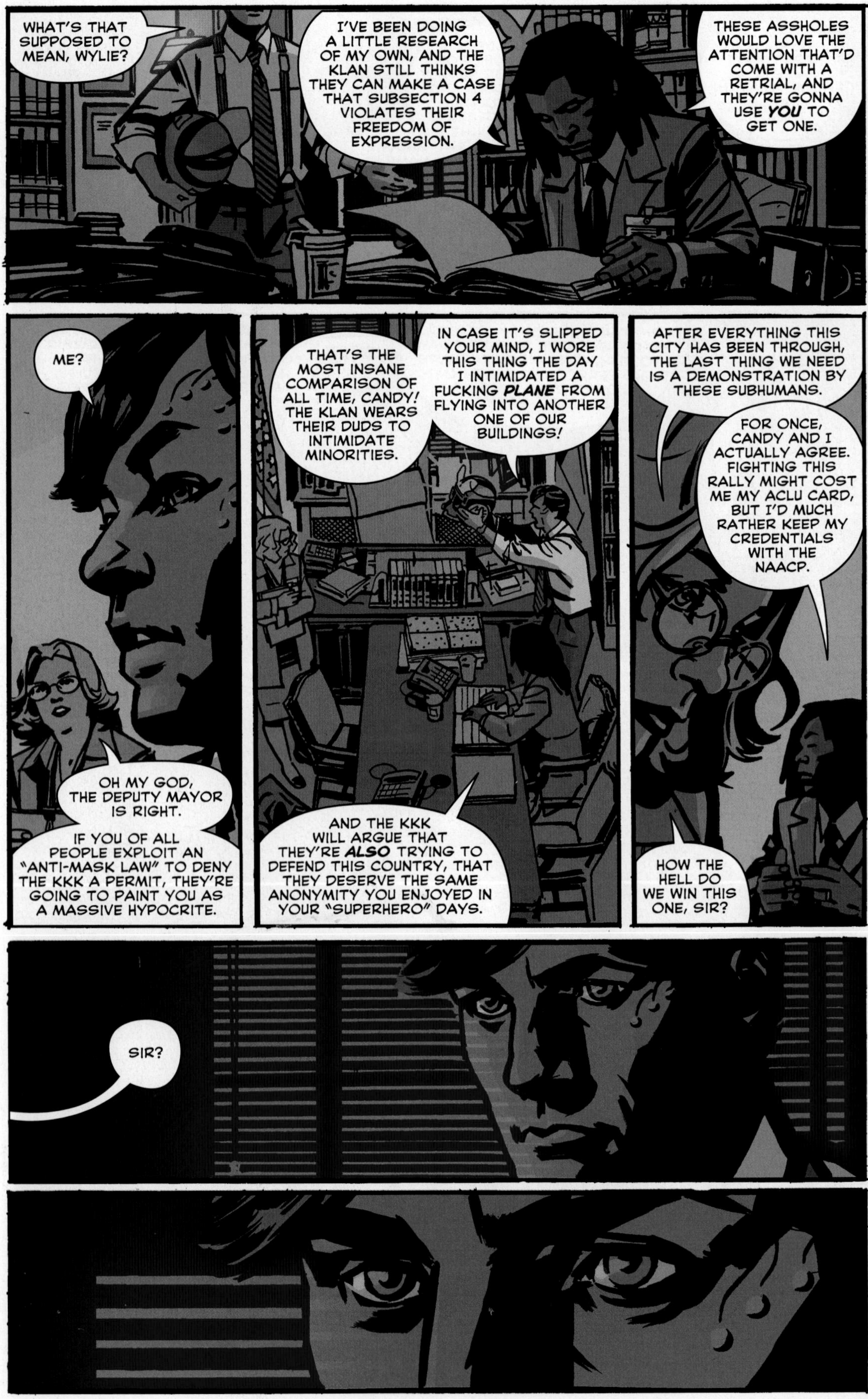
WHAT'S THAT SUPPOSED TO MEAN, WYLIE?
I'VE BEEN DOING A LITTLE RESEARCH OF MY OWN, AND THE KLAN STILL THINKS THEY CAN MAKE A CASE THAT SUBSECTION 4 VIOLATES THEIR FREEDOM OF EXPRESSION.
THESE ASSHOLES WOULD LOVE THE ATTENTION THAT'D COME WITH A RETRIAL, AND THEY'RE GONNA USE *YOU* TO GET ONE.
ME?
OH MY GOD, THE DEPUTY MAYOR IS RIGHT.
IF YOU OF ALL PEOPLE EXPLOIT AN "ANTI-MASK LAW" TO DENY THE KKK A PERMIT, THEY'RE GOING TO PAINT YOU AS A MASSIVE HYPOCRITE.
THAT'S THE MOST INSANE COMPARISON OF ALL TIME, CANDY! THE KLAN WEARS THEIR DUDS TO INTIMIDATE MINORITIES.
IN CASE IT'S SLIPPED YOUR MIND, I WORE THIS THING THE DAY I INTIMIDATED A FUCKING *PLANE* FROM FLYING INTO ANOTHER ONE OF OUR BUILDINGS!
AND THE KKK WILL ARGUE THAT THEY'RE *ALSO* TRYING TO DEFEND THIS COUNTRY, THAT THEY DESERVE THE SAME ANONYMITY YOU ENJOYED IN YOUR "SUPERHERO" DAYS.
AFTER EVERYTHING THIS CITY HAS BEEN THROUGH, THE LAST THING WE NEED IS A DEMONSTRATION BY THESE SUBHUMANS.
FOR ONCE, CANDY AND I ACTUALLY AGREE. FIGHTING THIS RALLY MIGHT COST ME MY ACLU CARD, BUT I'D MUCH RATHER KEEP MY CREDENTIALS WITH THE NAACP.
HOW THE HELL DO WE WIN THIS ONE, SIR?
SIR?

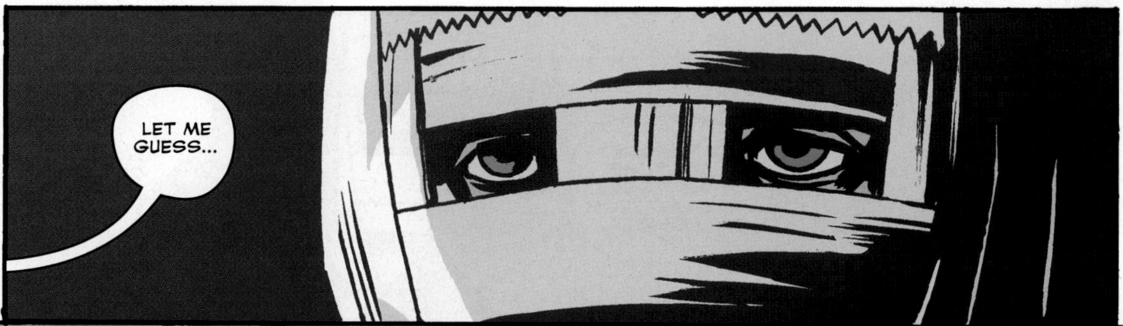
LET ME GUESS...

SUNDAY, OCTOBER 31, 1999

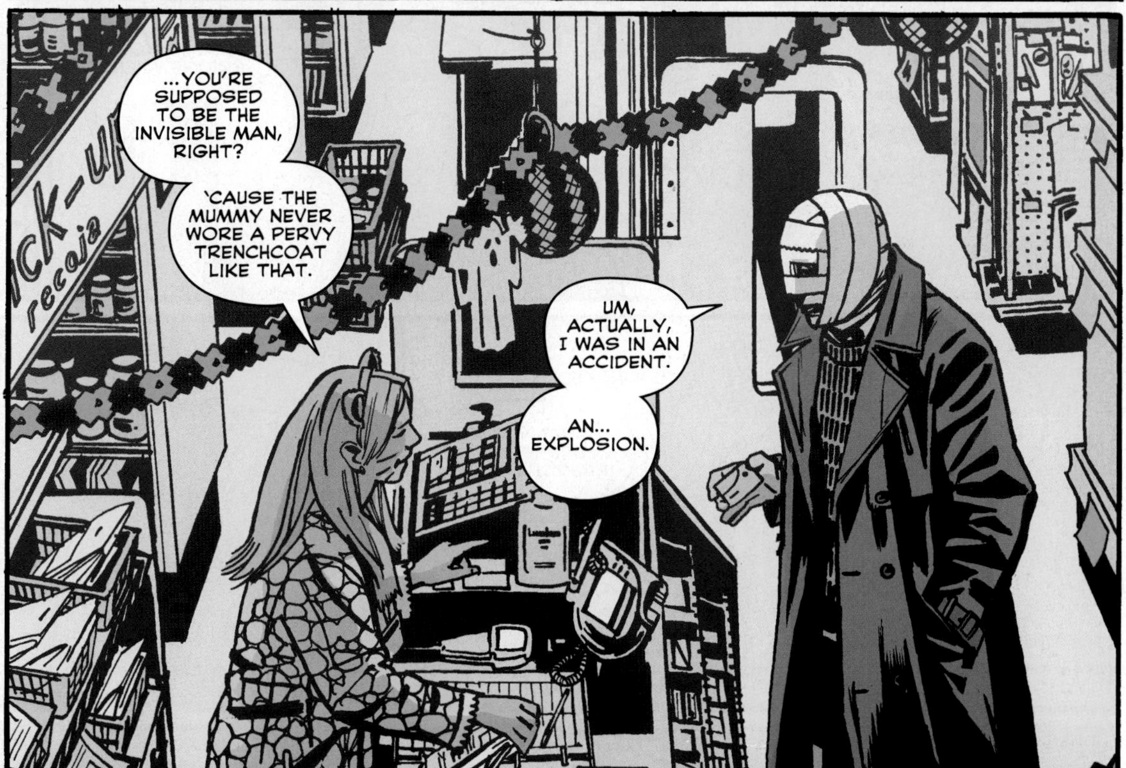
...YOU'RE SUPPOSED TO BE THE INVISIBLE MAN, RIGHT?
'CAUSE THE MUMMY NEVER WORE A PERVY TRENCHCOAT LIKE THAT.
UM, ACTUALLY, I WAS IN AN ACCIDENT.
AN... EXPLOSION.

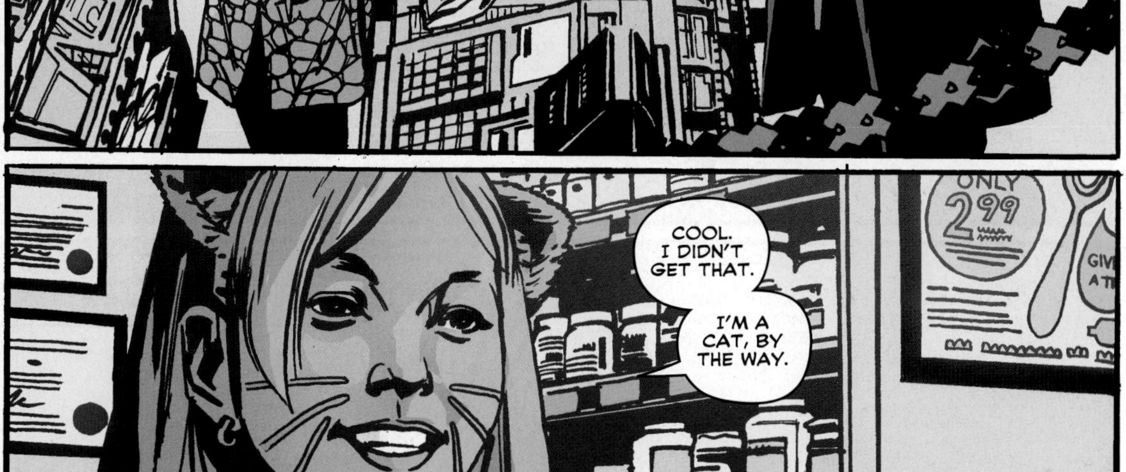
COOL. I DIDN'T GET THAT.
I'M A CAT, BY THE WAY.

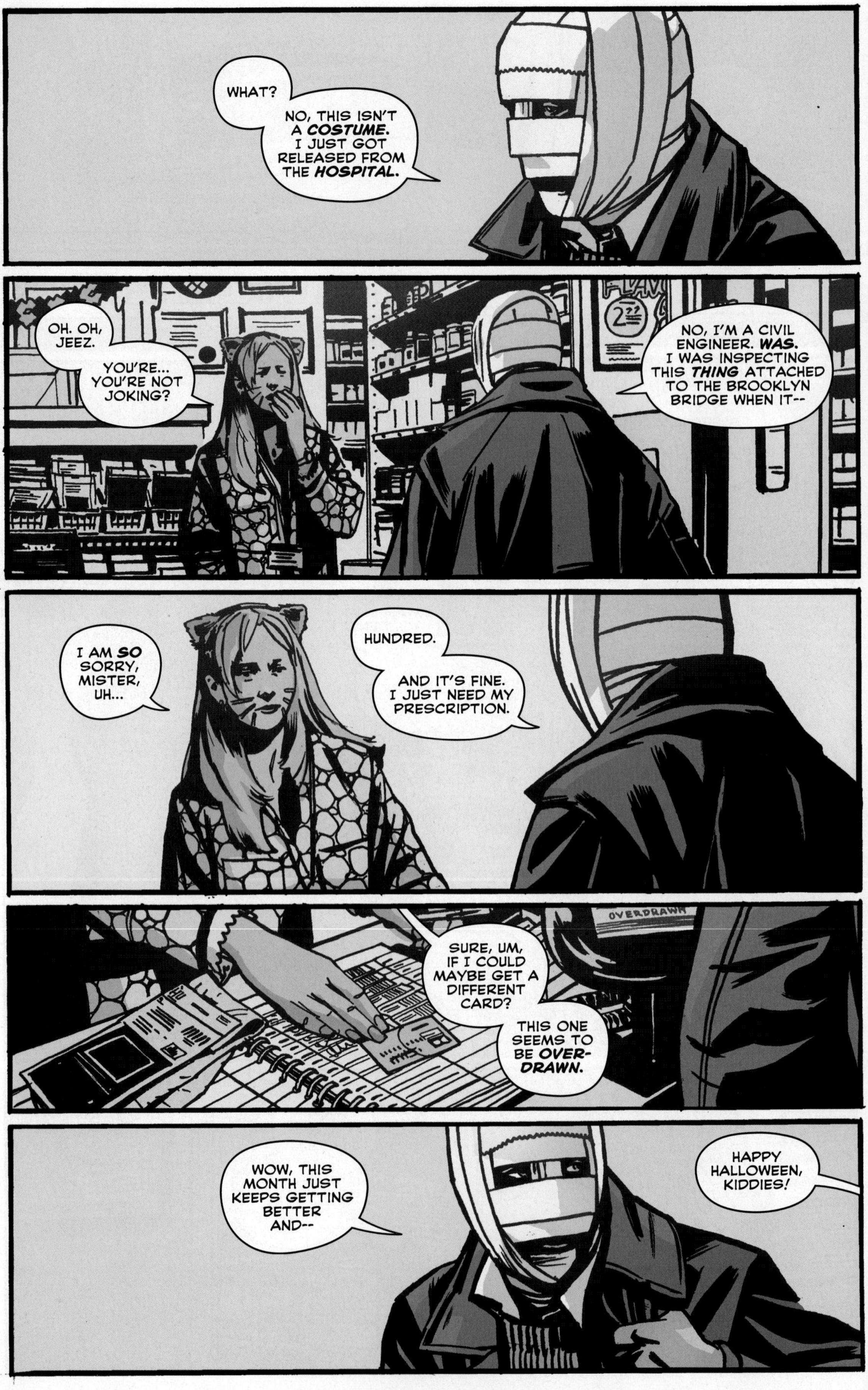
WHAT?
NO, THIS ISN'T A **COSTUME.** I JUST GOT RELEASED FROM THE **HOSPITAL.**
OH. OH, JEEZ.
YOU'RE... YOU'RE NOT JOKING?
NO, I'M A CIVIL ENGINEER. **WAS.** I WAS INSPECTING THIS **THING** ATTACHED TO THE BROOKLYN BRIDGE WHEN IT--
I AM **SO** SORRY, MISTER, UH...
HUNDRED.
AND IT'S FINE. I JUST NEED MY PRESCRIPTION.
OVERDRAWN
SURE, UM, IF I COULD MAYBE GET A DIFFERENT CARD?
THIS ONE SEEMS TO BE **OVER-DRAWN.**
WOW, THIS MONTH JUST KEEPS GETTING BETTER AND--
HAPPY HALLOWEEN, KIDDIES!

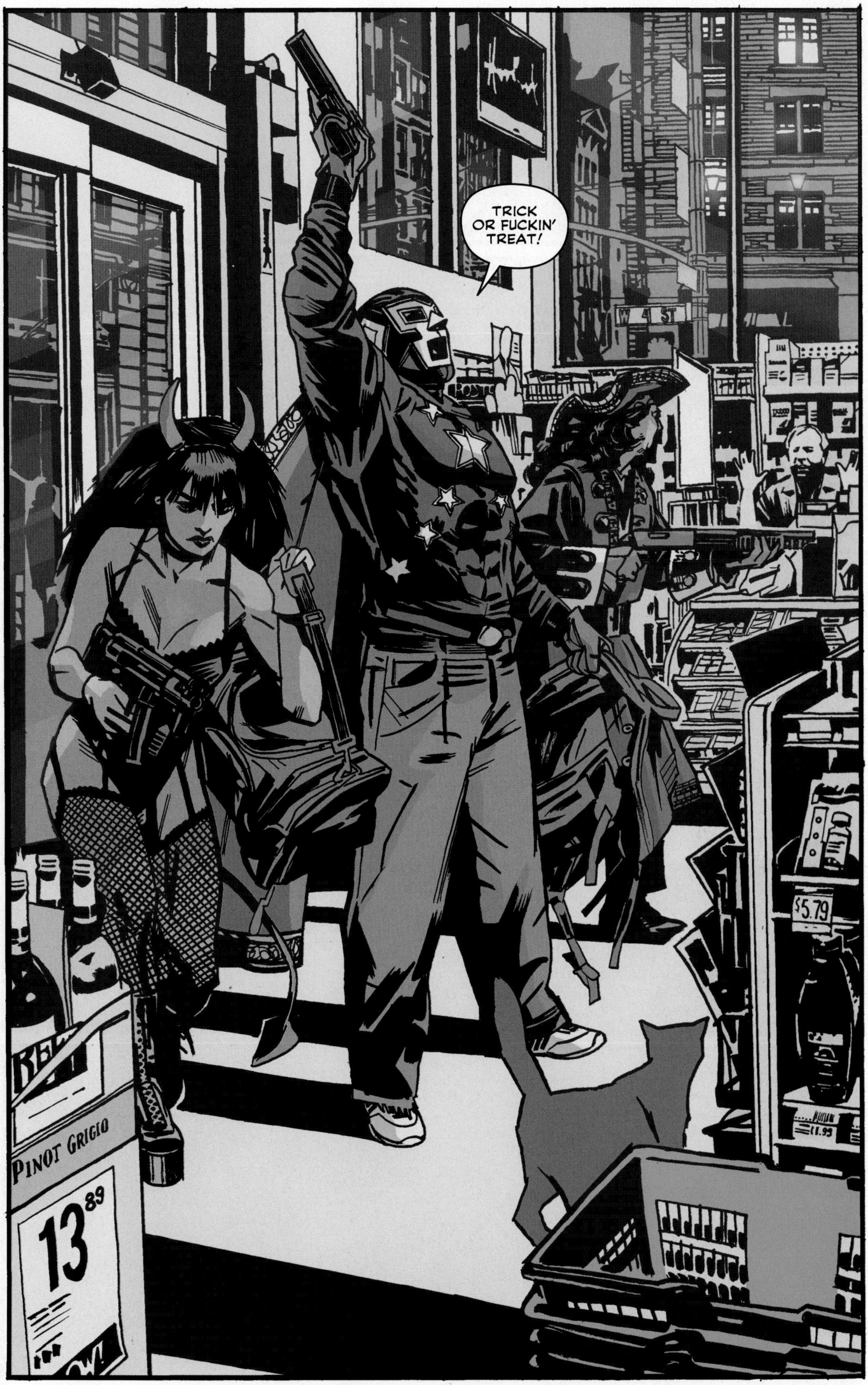
TRICK OR FUCKIN' TREAT!
W 4 ST
$5.79
PINOT GRIGIO
13.89

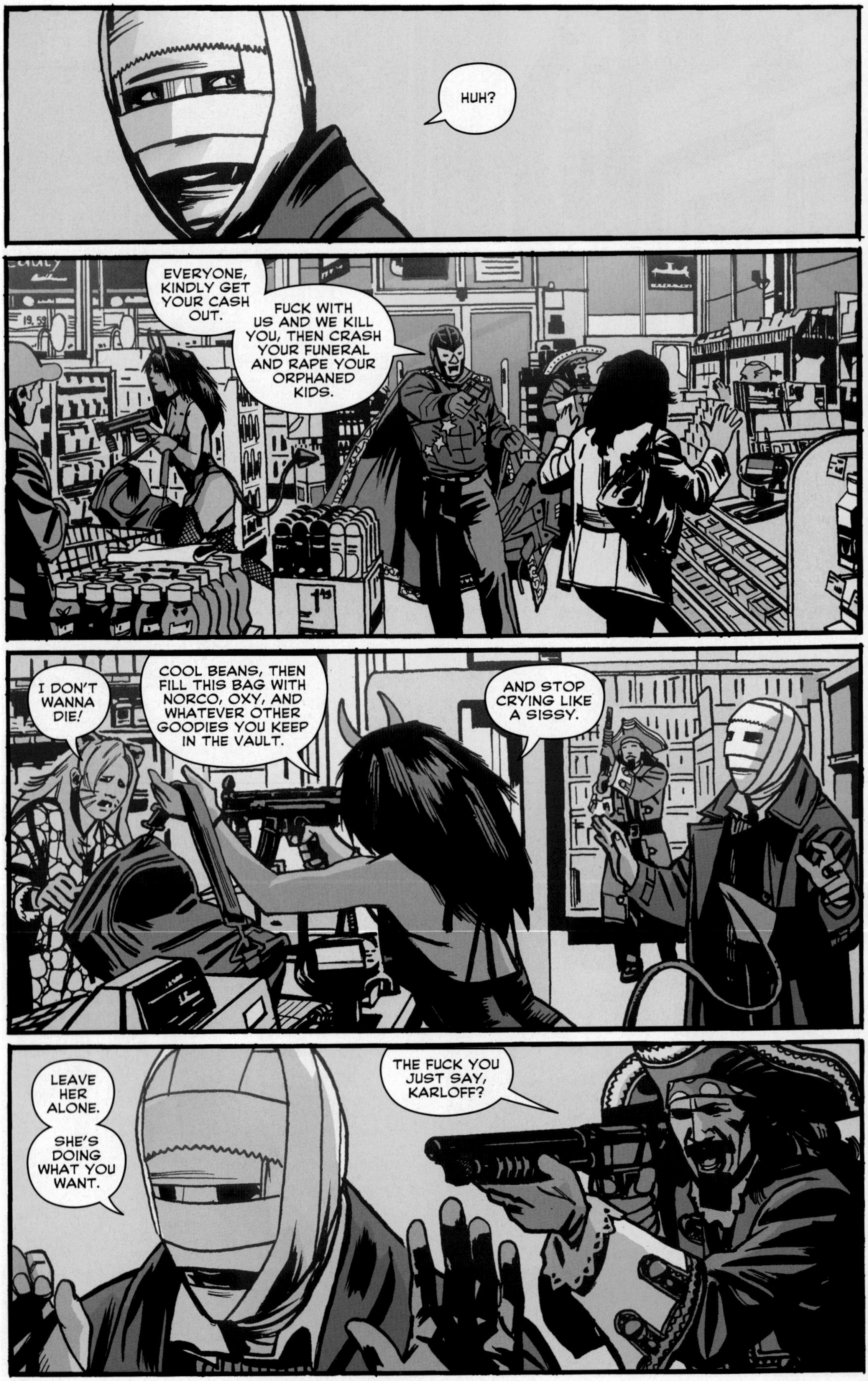
HUH?
EVERYONE, KINDLY GET YOUR CASH OUT.
FUCK WITH US AND WE KILL YOU, THEN CRASH YOUR FUNERAL AND RAPE YOUR ORPHANED KIDS.
I DON'T WANNA DIE!
COOL BEANS, THEN FILL THIS BAG WITH NORCO, OXY, AND WHATEVER OTHER GOODIES YOU KEEP IN THE VAULT.
AND STOP CRYING LIKE A SISSY.
LEAVE HER ALONE.
SHE'S DOING WHAT YOU WANT.
THE FUCK YOU JUST SAY, KARLOFF?

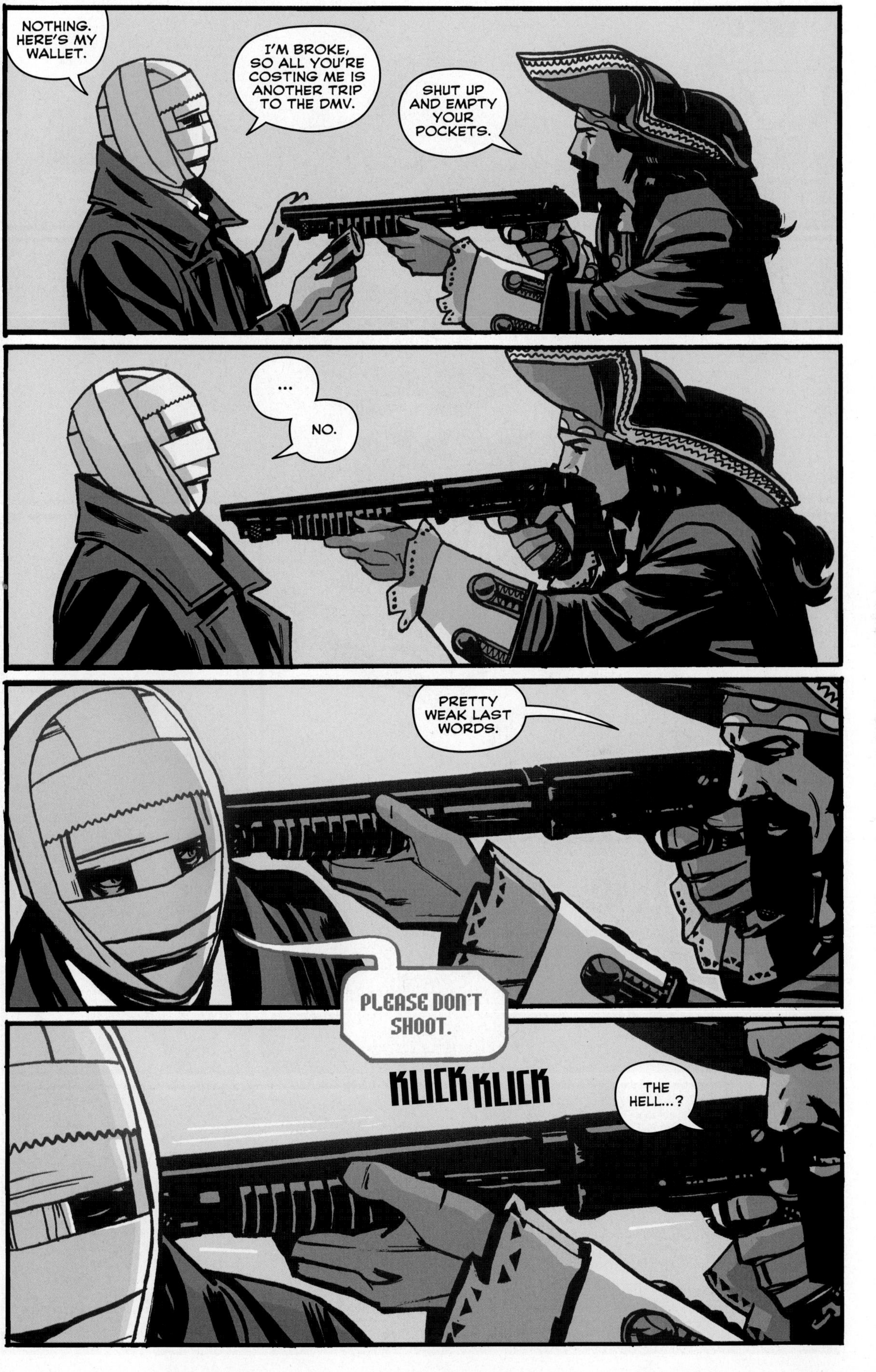
NOTHING. HERE'S MY WALLET.
I'M BROKE, SO ALL YOU'RE COSTING ME IS ANOTHER TRIP TO THE DMV.
SHUT UP AND EMPTY YOUR POCKETS.
...
NO.
PRETTY WEAK LAST WORDS.
PLEASE DON'T SHOOT.
KLICK KLICK
THE HELL...?

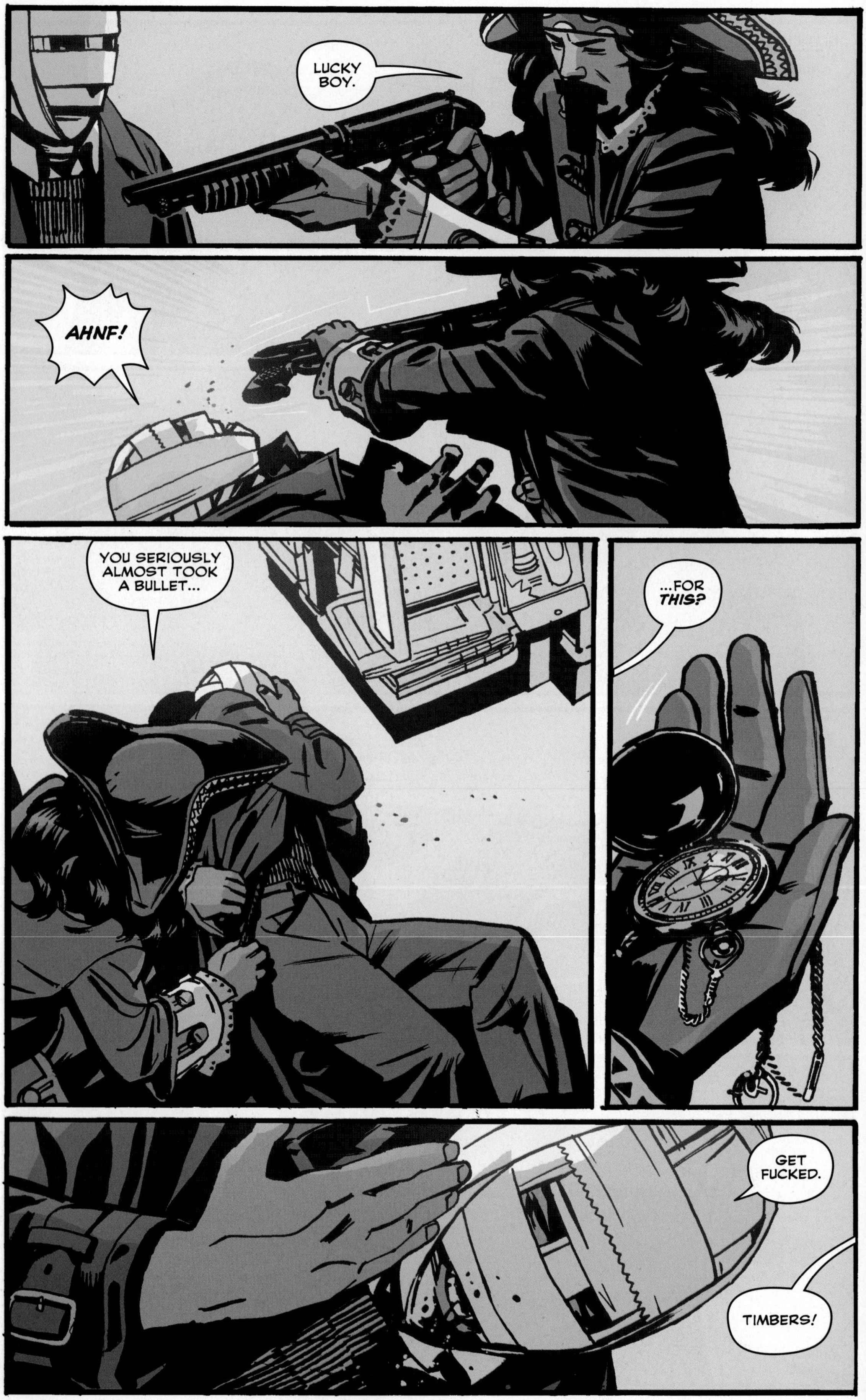
LUCKY BOY.
AHNF!
YOU SERIOUSLY ALMOST TOOK A BULLET...
...FOR THIS?
GET FUCKED.
TIMBERS!

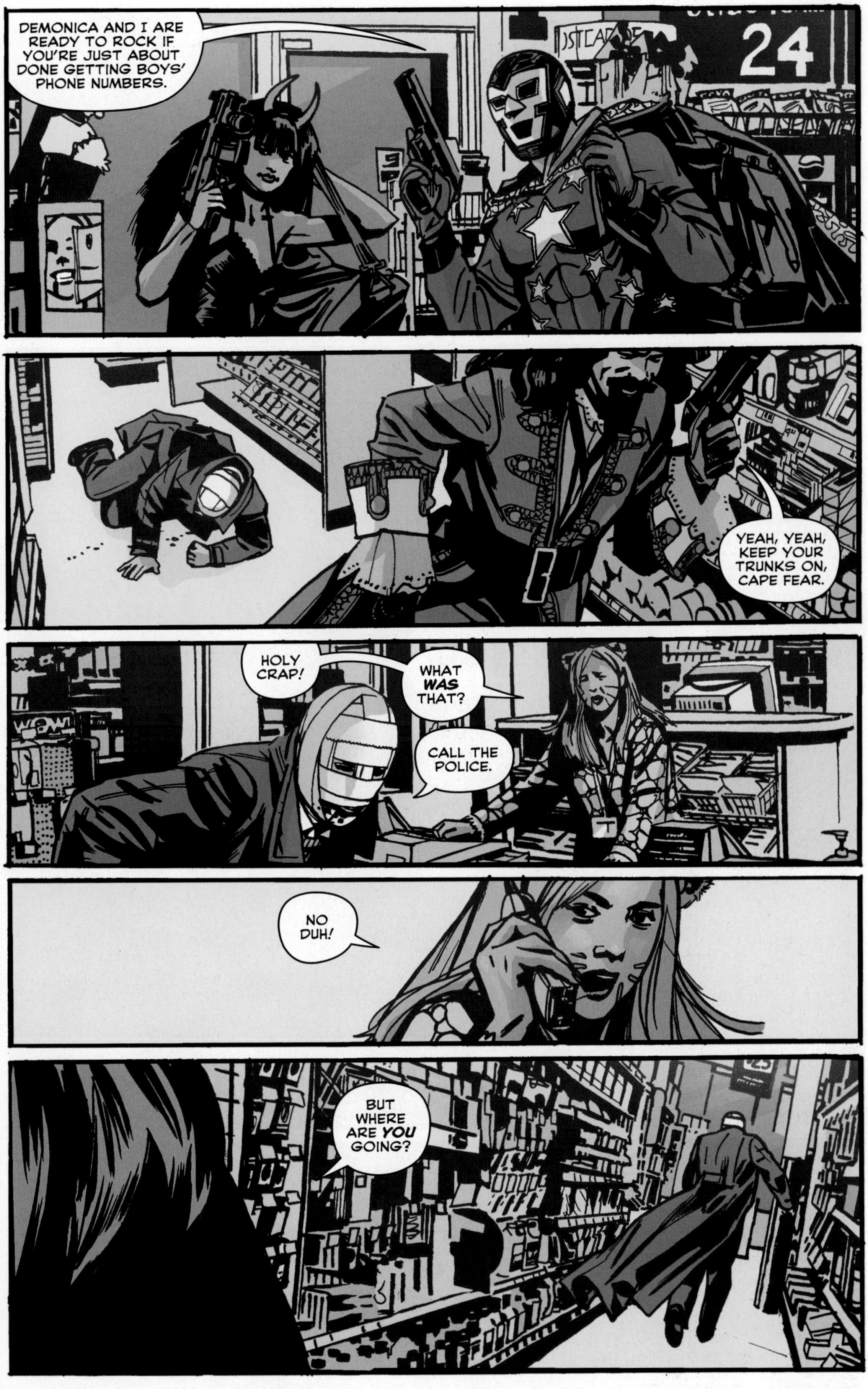
DEMONICA AND I ARE READY TO ROCK IF YOU'RE JUST ABOUT DONE GETTING BOYS' PHONE NUMBERS.
24
YEAH, YEAH, KEEP YOUR TRUNKS ON, CAPE FEAR.
HOLY CRAP!
WHAT *WAS* THAT?
CALL THE POLICE.
NO DUH!
BUT WHERE ARE *YOU* GOING?

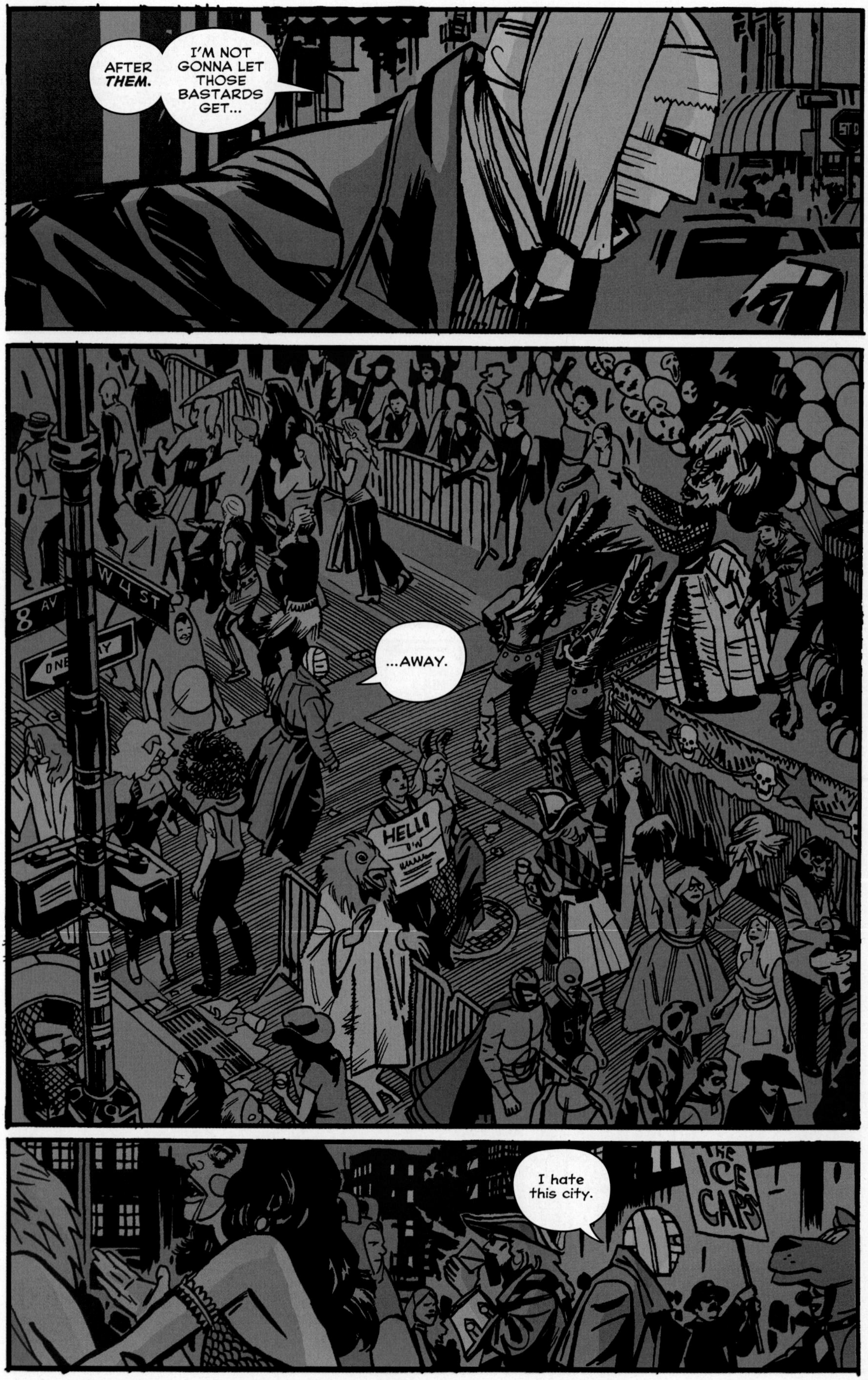
AFTER *THEM.*
I'M NOT GONNA LET THOSE BASTARDS GET...
W 4 ST
8 AV
...AWAY.
HELLO
I hate this city.
THE ICE CAPS

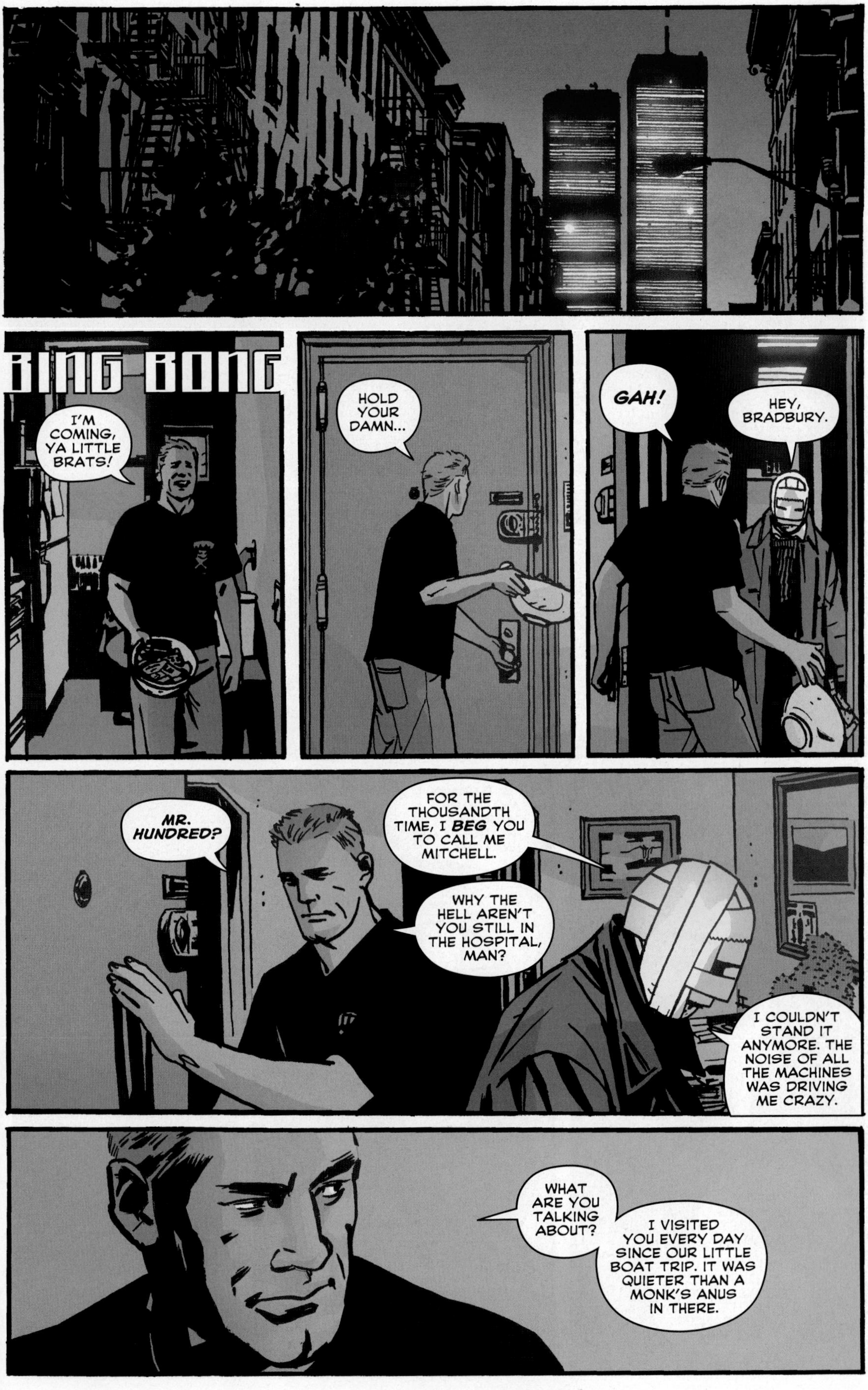
BING BONG
I'M COMING, YA LITTLE BRATS!
HOLD YOUR DAMN...
GAH!
HEY, BRADBURY.
MR. HUNDRED?
FOR THE THOUSANDTH TIME, I BEG YOU TO CALL ME MITCHELL.
WHY THE HELL AREN'T YOU STILL IN THE HOSPITAL, MAN?
I COULDN'T STAND IT ANYMORE. THE NOISE OF ALL THE MACHINES WAS DRIVING ME CRAZY.
WHAT ARE YOU TALKING ABOUT?
I VISITED YOU EVERY DAY SINCE OUR LITTLE BOAT TRIP. IT WAS QUIETER THAN A MONK'S ANUS IN THERE.

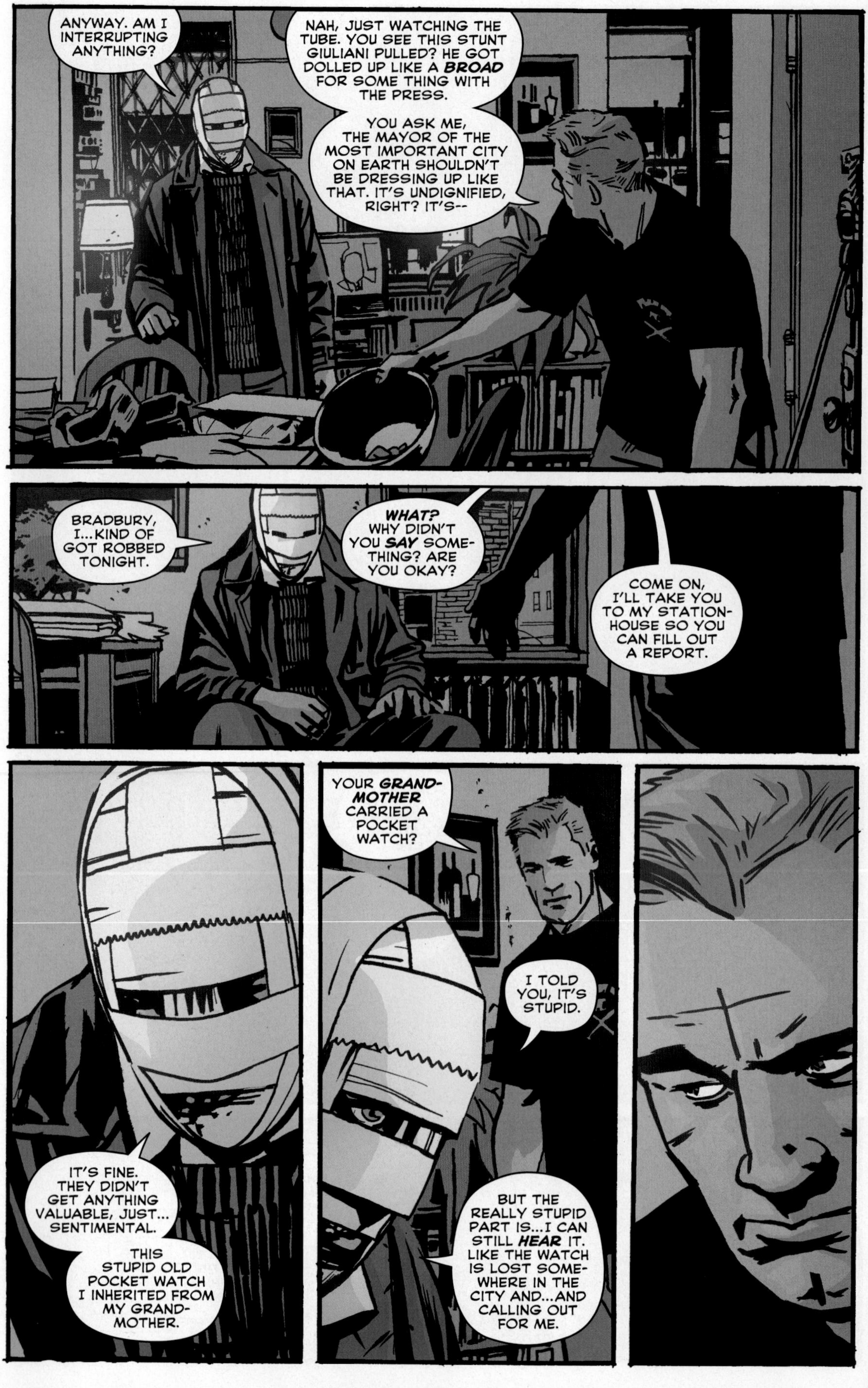
ANYWAY. AM I INTERRUPTING ANYTHING?
NAH, JUST WATCHING THE TUBE. YOU SEE THIS STUNT GIULIANI PULLED? HE GOT DOLLED UP LIKE A **BROAD** FOR SOME THING WITH THE PRESS.
YOU ASK ME, THE MAYOR OF THE MOST IMPORTANT CITY ON EARTH SHOULDN'T BE DRESSING UP LIKE THAT. IT'S UNDIGNIFIED, RIGHT? IT'S--
BRADBURY, I...KIND OF GOT ROBBED TONIGHT.
WHAT? WHY DIDN'T YOU **SAY** SOMETHING? ARE YOU OKAY?
COME ON, I'LL TAKE YOU TO MY STATIONHOUSE SO YOU CAN FILL OUT A REPORT.
IT'S FINE. THEY DIDN'T GET ANYTHING VALUABLE, JUST... SENTIMENTAL.
THIS STUPID OLD POCKET WATCH I INHERITED FROM MY GRANDMOTHER.
YOUR **GRANDMOTHER** CARRIED A POCKET WATCH?
I TOLD YOU, IT'S STUPID.
BUT THE REALLY STUPID PART IS...I CAN STILL **HEAR** IT. LIKE THE WATCH IS LOST SOMEWHERE IN THE CITY AND...AND CALLING OUT FOR ME.

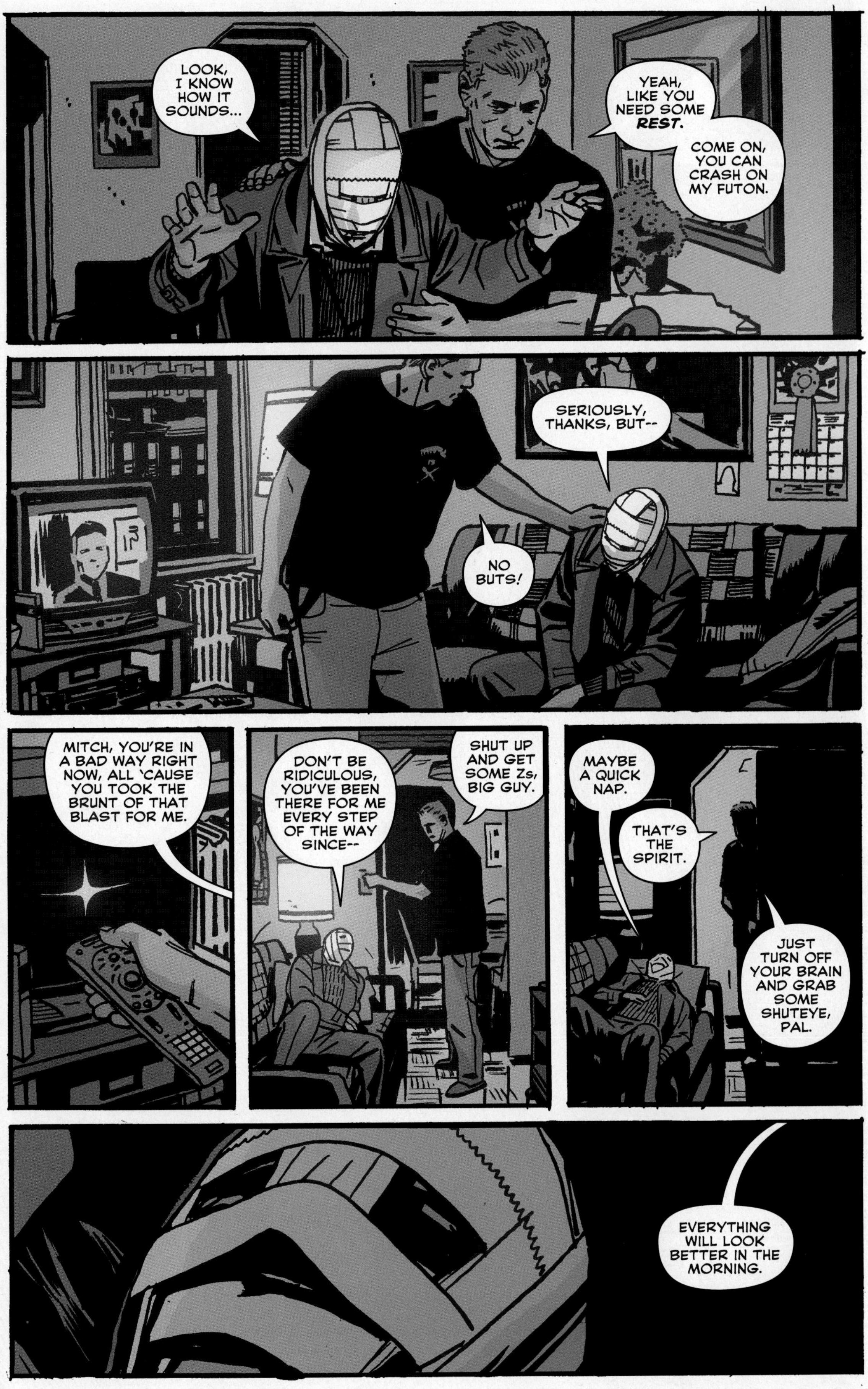
LOOK, I KNOW HOW IT SOUNDS...
YEAH, LIKE YOU NEED SOME REST.
COME ON, YOU CAN CRASH ON MY FUTON.
SERIOUSLY, THANKS, BUT--
NO BUTS!
MITCH, YOU'RE IN A BAD WAY RIGHT NOW, ALL 'CAUSE YOU TOOK THE BRUNT OF THAT BLAST FOR ME.
DON'T BE RIDICULOUS, YOU'VE BEEN THERE FOR ME EVERY STEP OF THE WAY SINCE--
SHUT UP AND GET SOME Zs, BIG GUY.
MAYBE A QUICK NAP.
THAT'S THE SPIRIT.
JUST TURN OFF YOUR BRAIN AND GRAB SOME SHUTEYE, PAL.
EVERYTHING WILL LOOK BETTER IN THE MORNING.

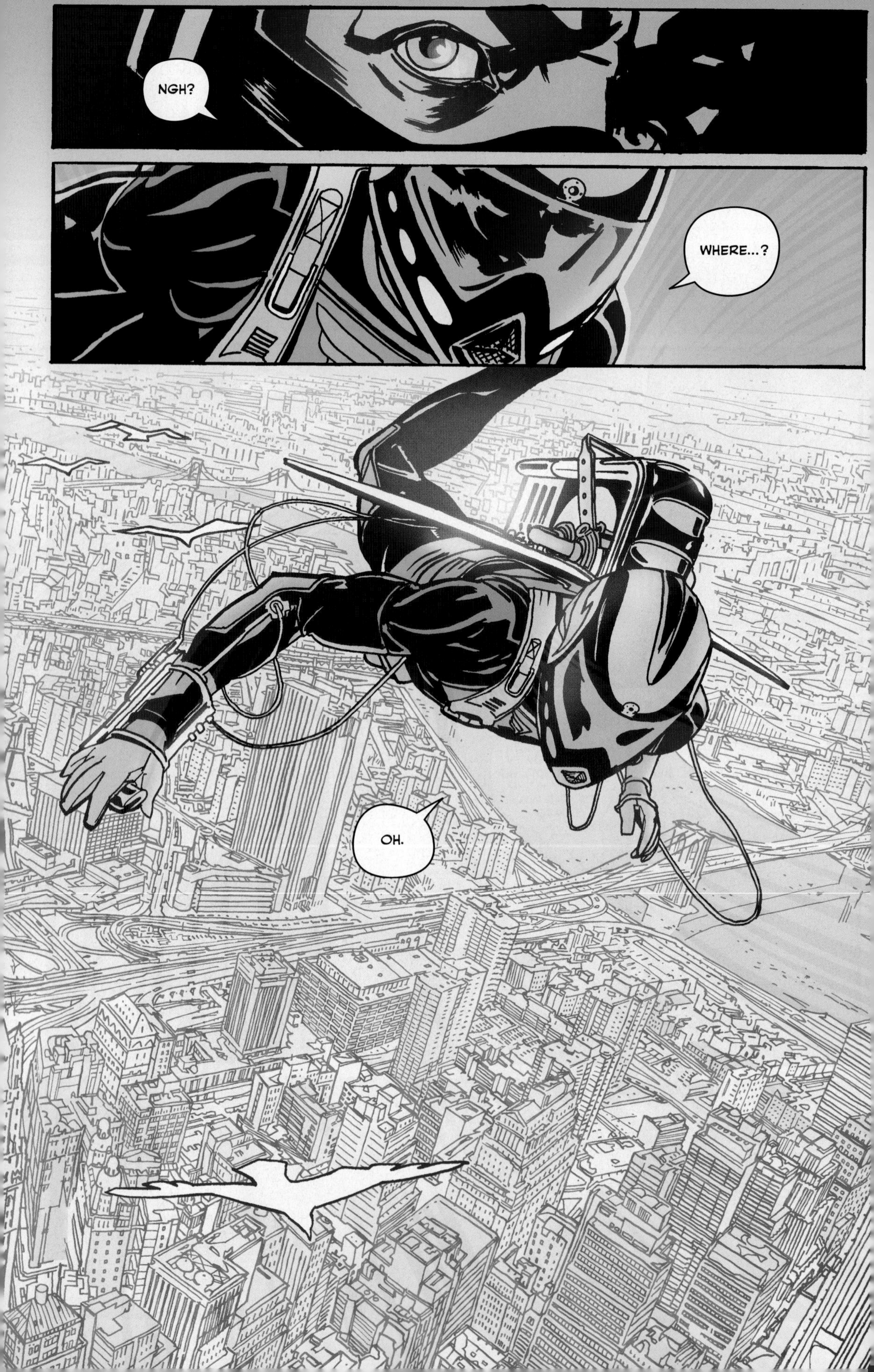
NGH?
WHERE...?
OH.

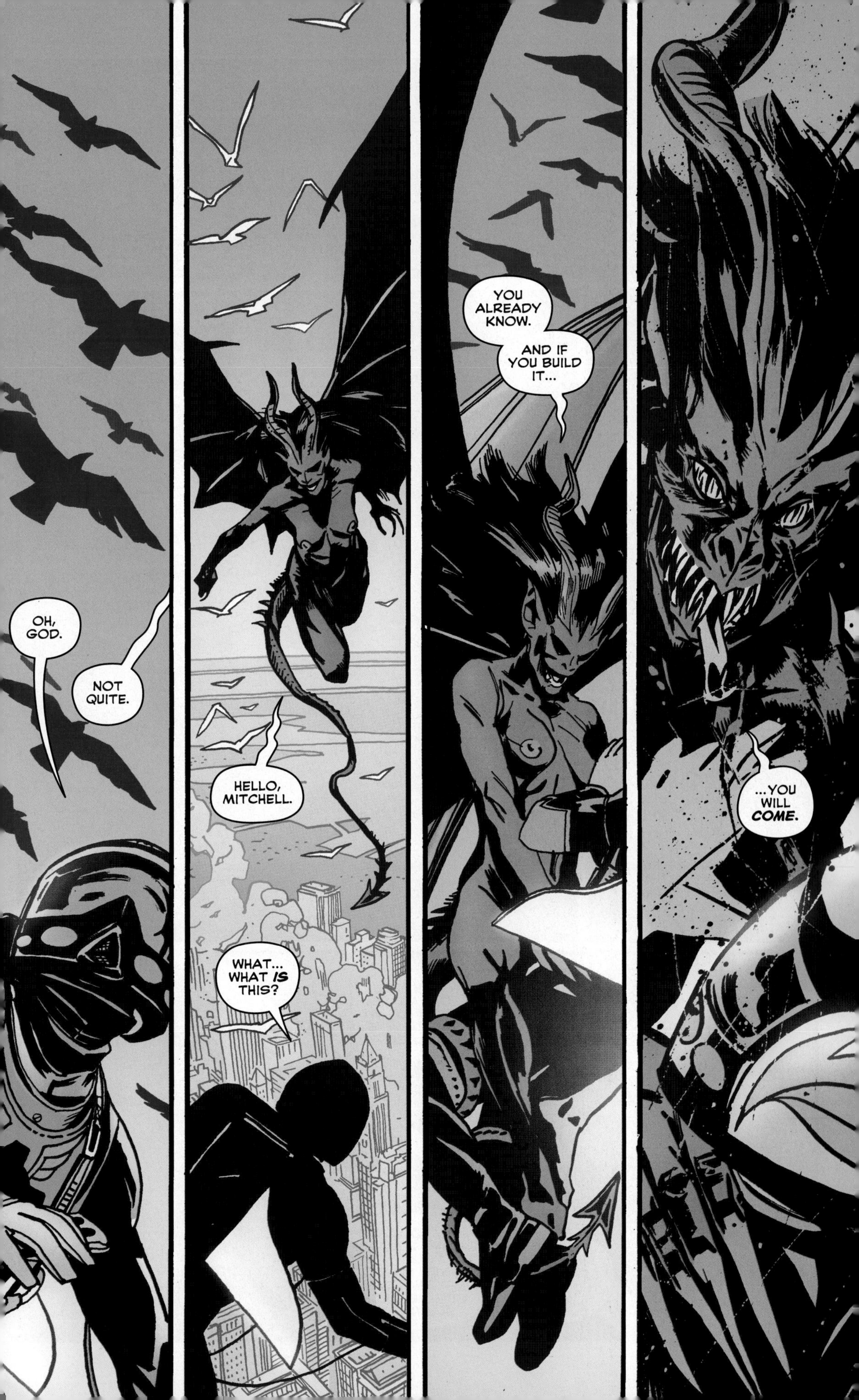
OH, GOD.
NOT QUITE.
HELLO, MITCHELL.
WHAT... WHAT *IS* THIS?
YOU ALREADY KNOW.
AND IF YOU BUILD IT...
...YOU WILL ***COME.***

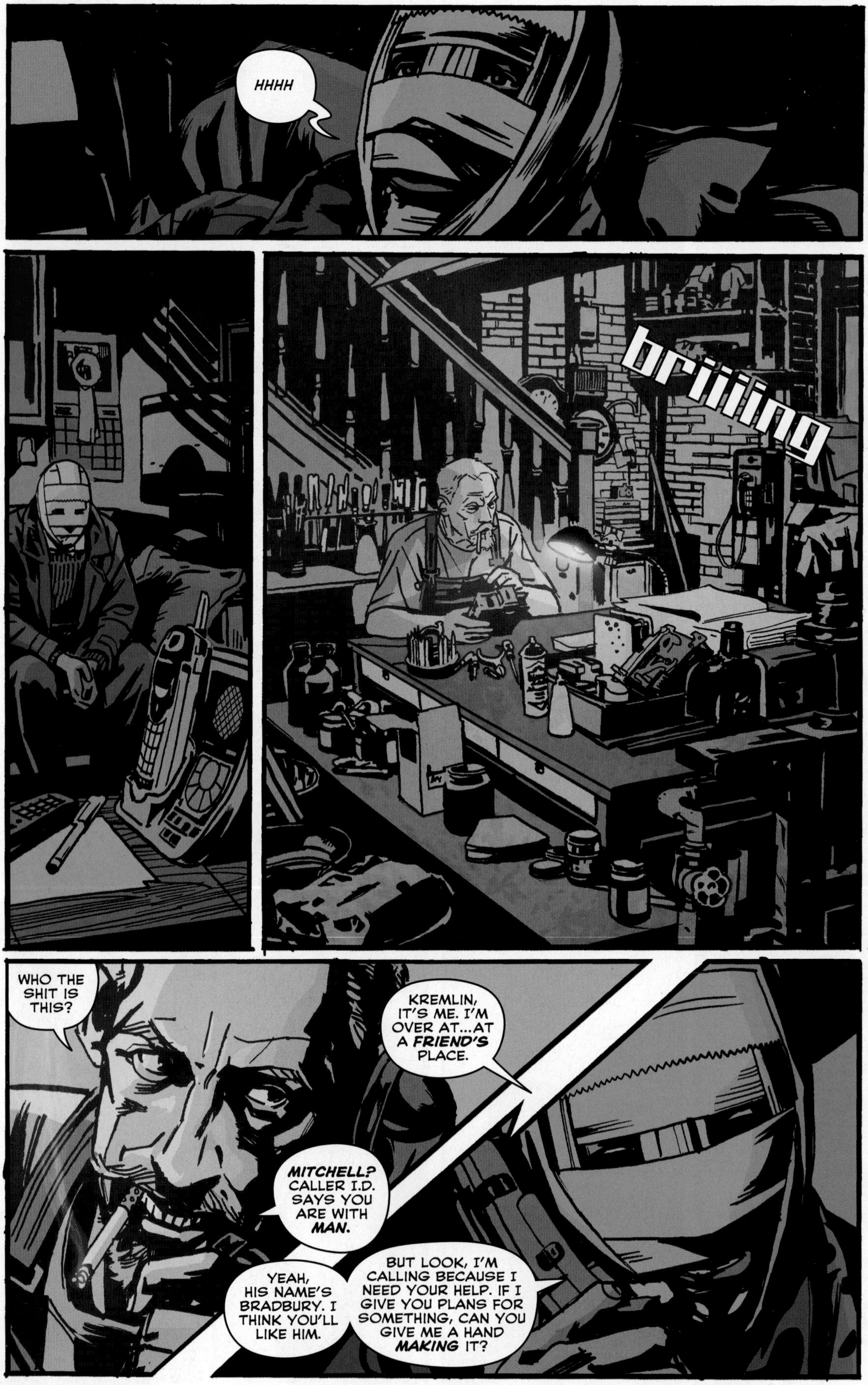

HHHH
briiiing
WHO THE SHIT IS THIS?
KREMLIN, IT'S ME. I'M OVER AT...AT A *FRIEND'S* PLACE.
MITCHELL? CALLER I.D. SAYS YOU ARE WITH *MAN.*
YEAH, HIS NAME'S BRADBURY. I THINK YOU'LL LIKE HIM.
BUT LOOK, I'M CALLING BECAUSE I NEED YOUR HELP. IF I GIVE YOU PLANS FOR SOMETHING, CAN YOU GIVE ME A HAND *MAKING* IT?

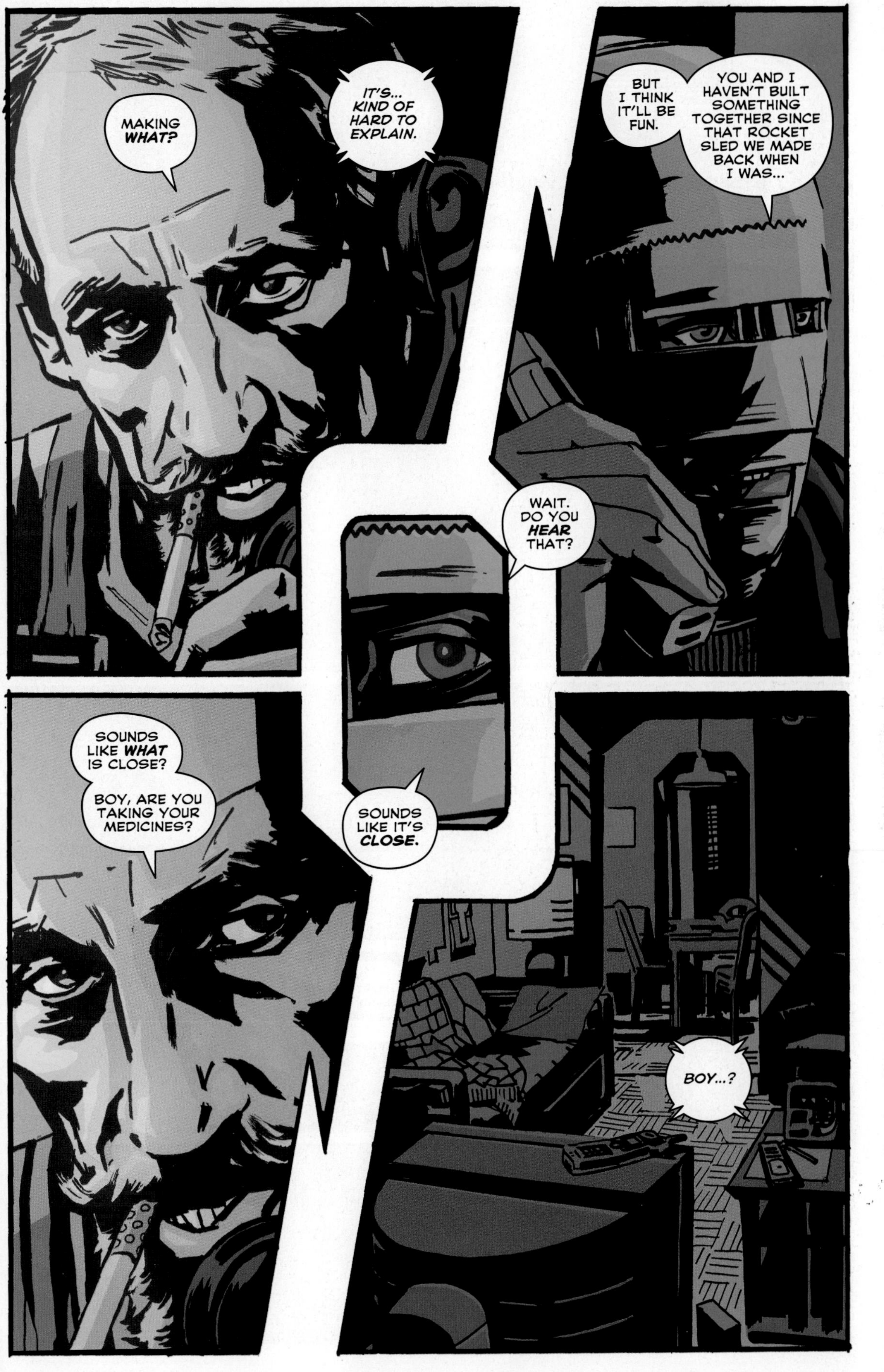
MAKING *WHAT?*
IT'S... KIND OF HARD TO EXPLAIN.
BUT I THINK IT'LL BE FUN.
YOU AND I HAVEN'T BUILT SOMETHING TOGETHER SINCE THAT ROCKET SLED WE MADE BACK WHEN I WAS...
WAIT. DO YOU *HEAR* THAT?
SOUNDS LIKE IT'S *CLOSE.*
SOUNDS LIKE *WHAT* IS CLOSE?
BOY, ARE YOU TAKING YOUR MEDICINES?
BOY...?

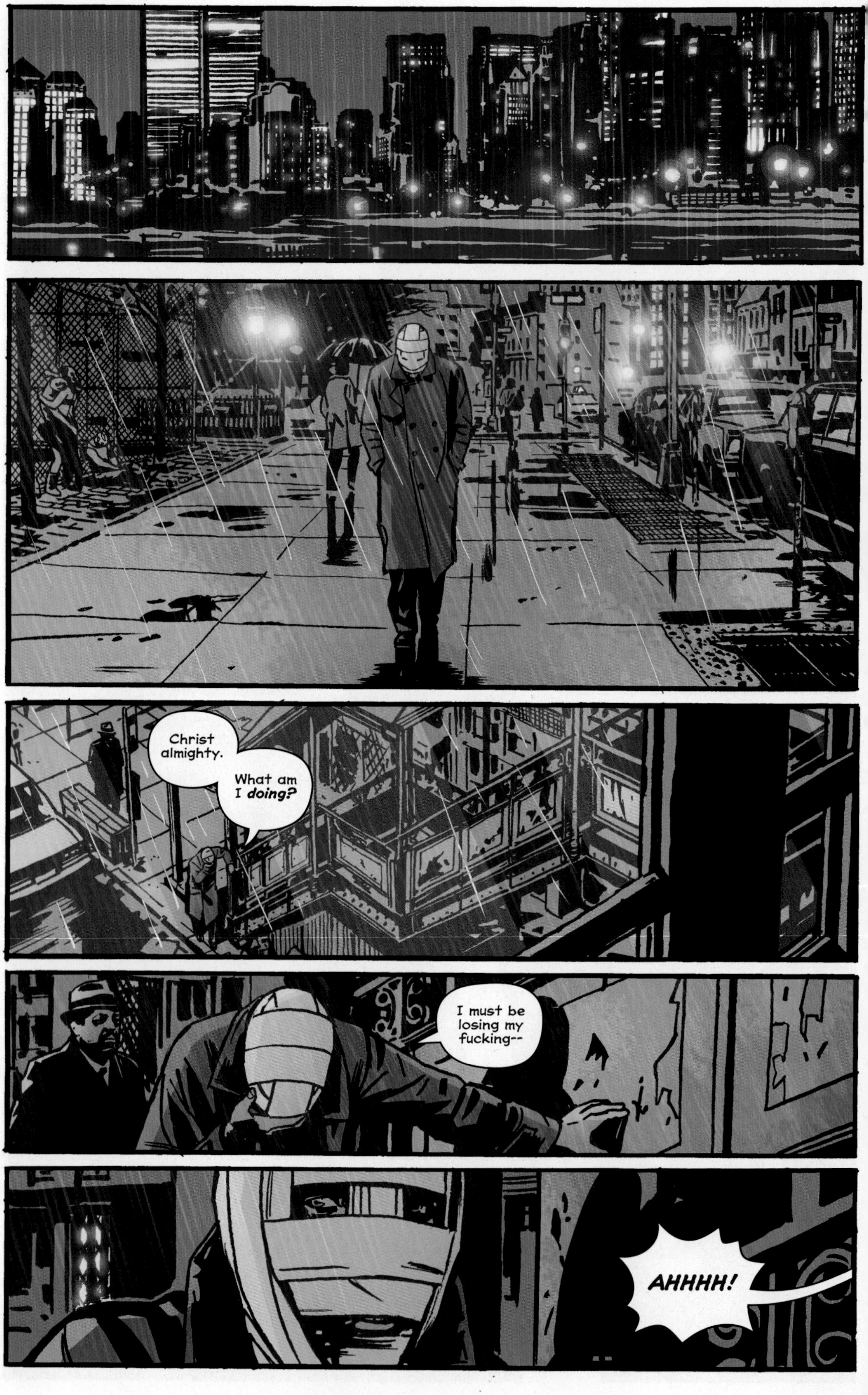
Christ almighty.
What am I *doing?*
I must be losing my fucking--
AHHHH!

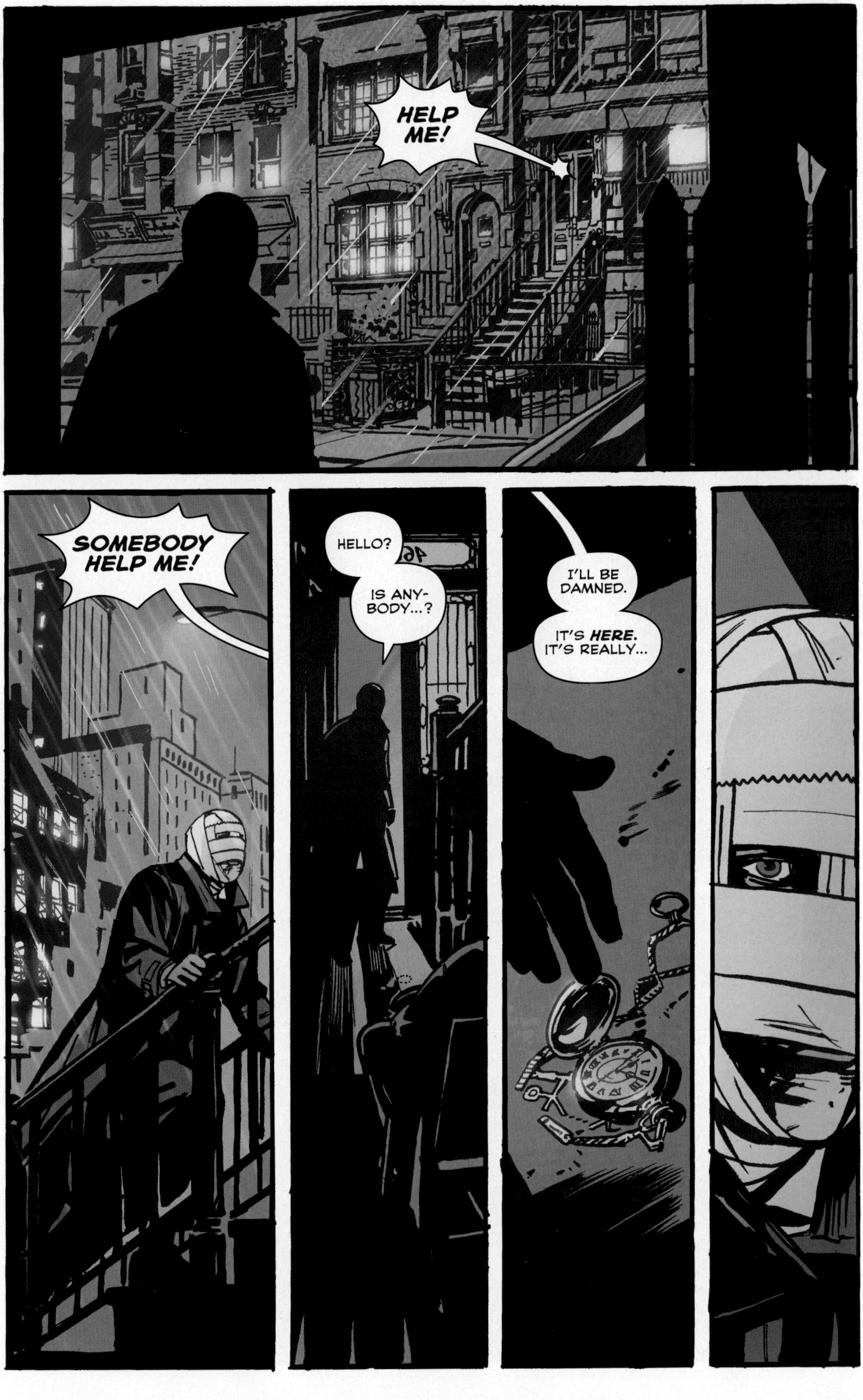
HELP ME!
SOMEBODY HELP ME!
HELLO?
IS ANYBODY...?
I'LL BE DAMNED.
IT'S **HERE.** IT'S REALLY...

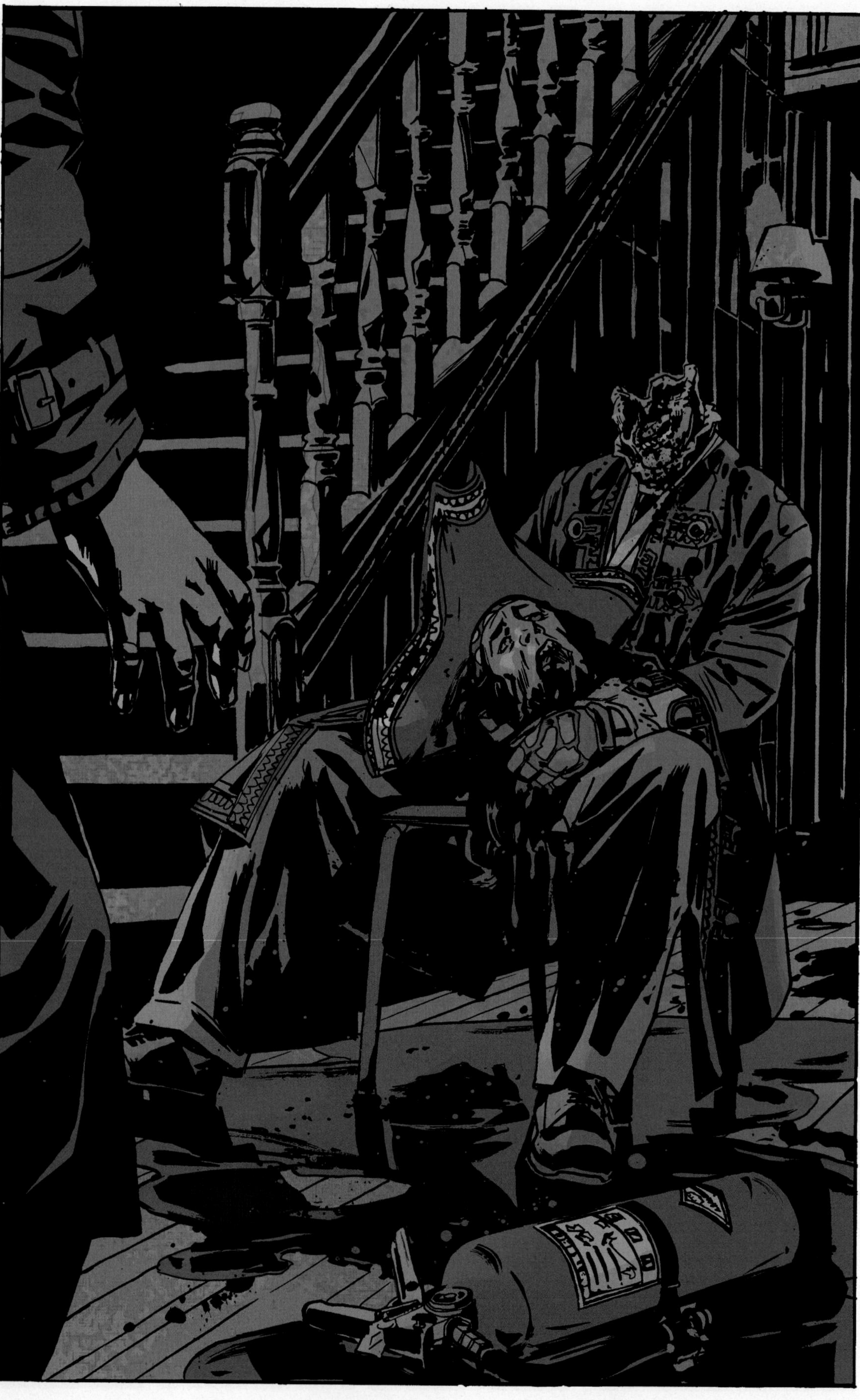

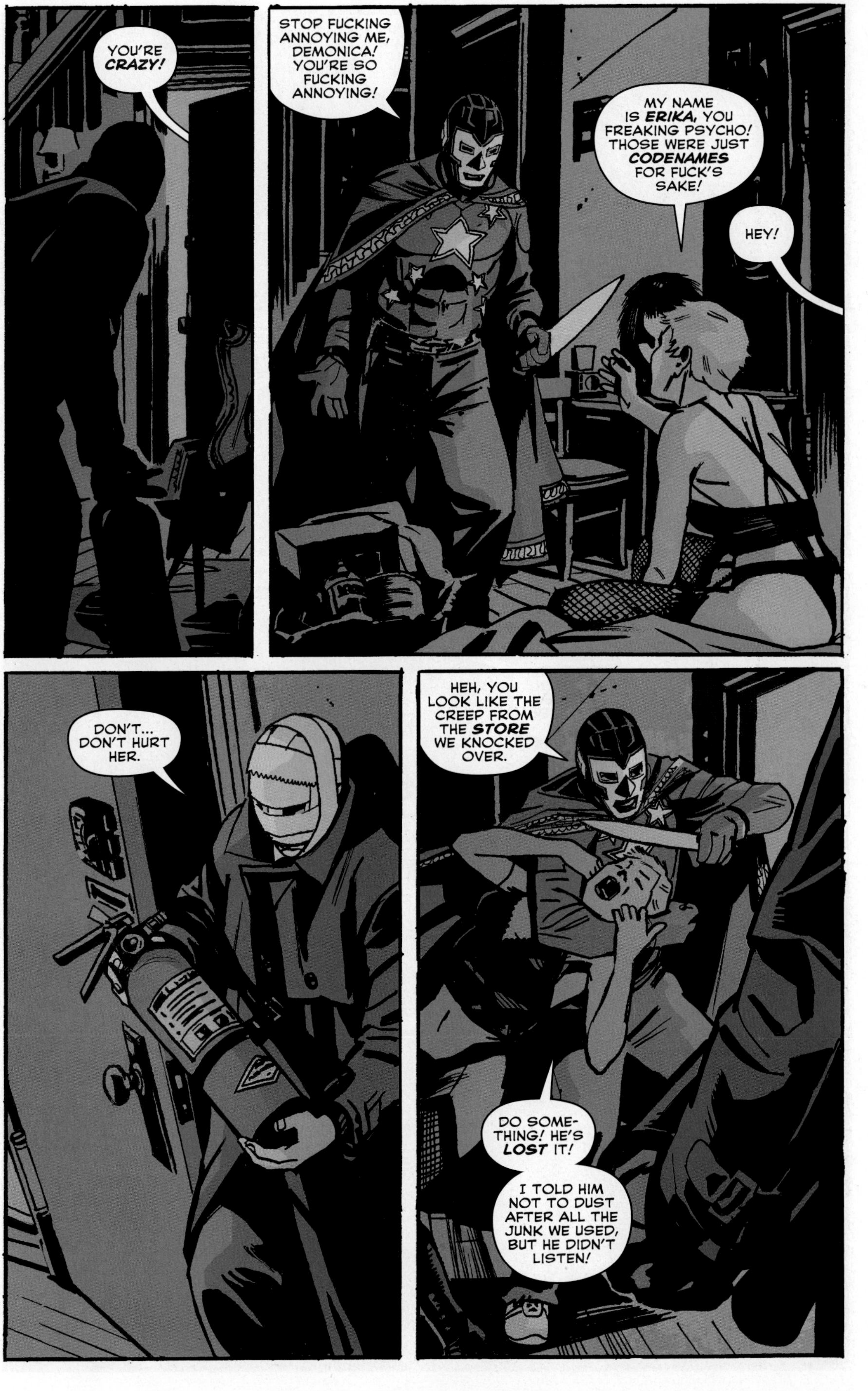
YOU'RE CRAZY!
STOP FUCKING ANNOYING ME, DEMONICA! YOU'RE SO FUCKING ANNOYING!
MY NAME IS ERIKA, YOU FREAKING PSYCHO! THOSE WERE JUST CODENAMES FOR FUCK'S SAKE!
HEY!
DON'T... DON'T HURT HER.
HEH, YOU LOOK LIKE THE CREEP FROM THE STORE WE KNOCKED OVER.
DO SOME-THING! HE'S LOST IT!
I TOLD HIM NOT TO DUST AFTER ALL THE JUNK WE USED, BUT HE DIDN'T LISTEN!

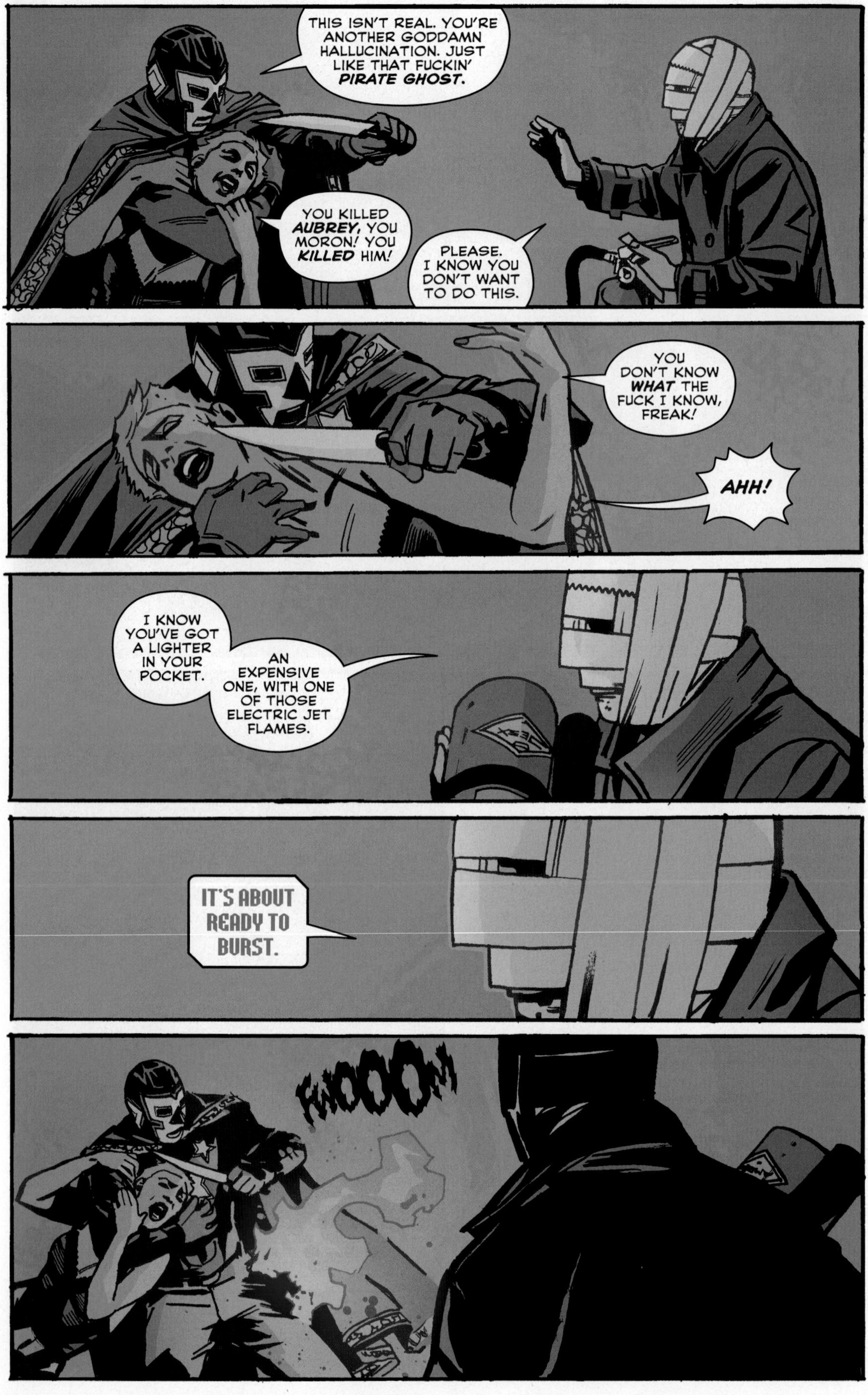
THIS ISN'T REAL. YOU'RE ANOTHER GODDAMN HALLUCINATION. JUST LIKE THAT FUCKIN' PIRATE GHOST.
YOU KILLED AUBREY, YOU MORON! YOU KILLED HIM!
PLEASE. I KNOW YOU DON'T WANT TO DO THIS.
YOU DON'T KNOW WHAT THE FUCK I KNOW, FREAK!
AHH!
I KNOW YOU'VE GOT A LIGHTER IN YOUR POCKET.
AN EXPENSIVE ONE, WITH ONE OF THOSE ELECTRIC JET FLAMES.
IT'S ABOUT READY TO BURST.
FWOOOM

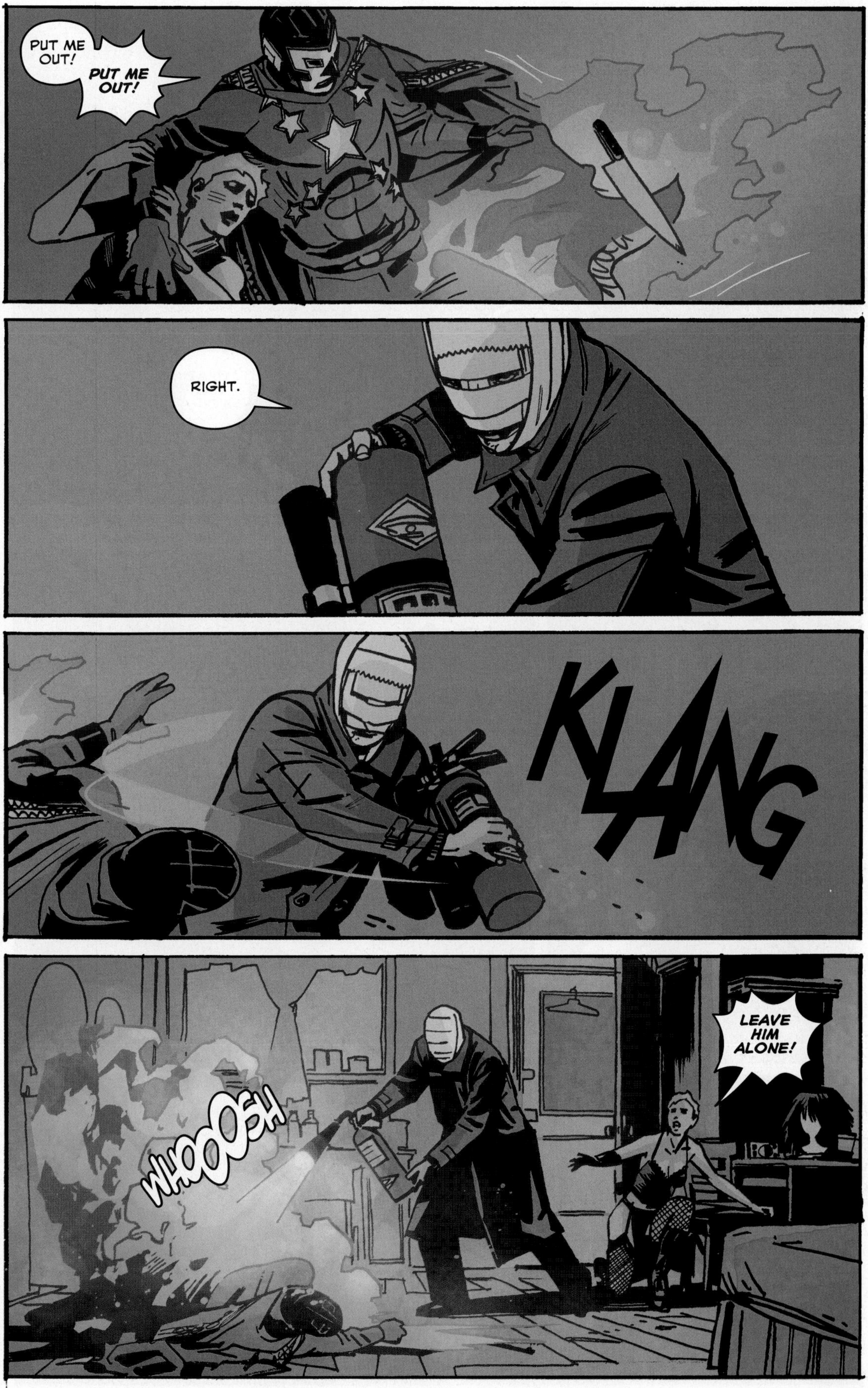
PUT ME OUT!
PUT ME OUT!
RIGHT.
KLANG
WHOOOSH
LEAVE HIM ALONE!

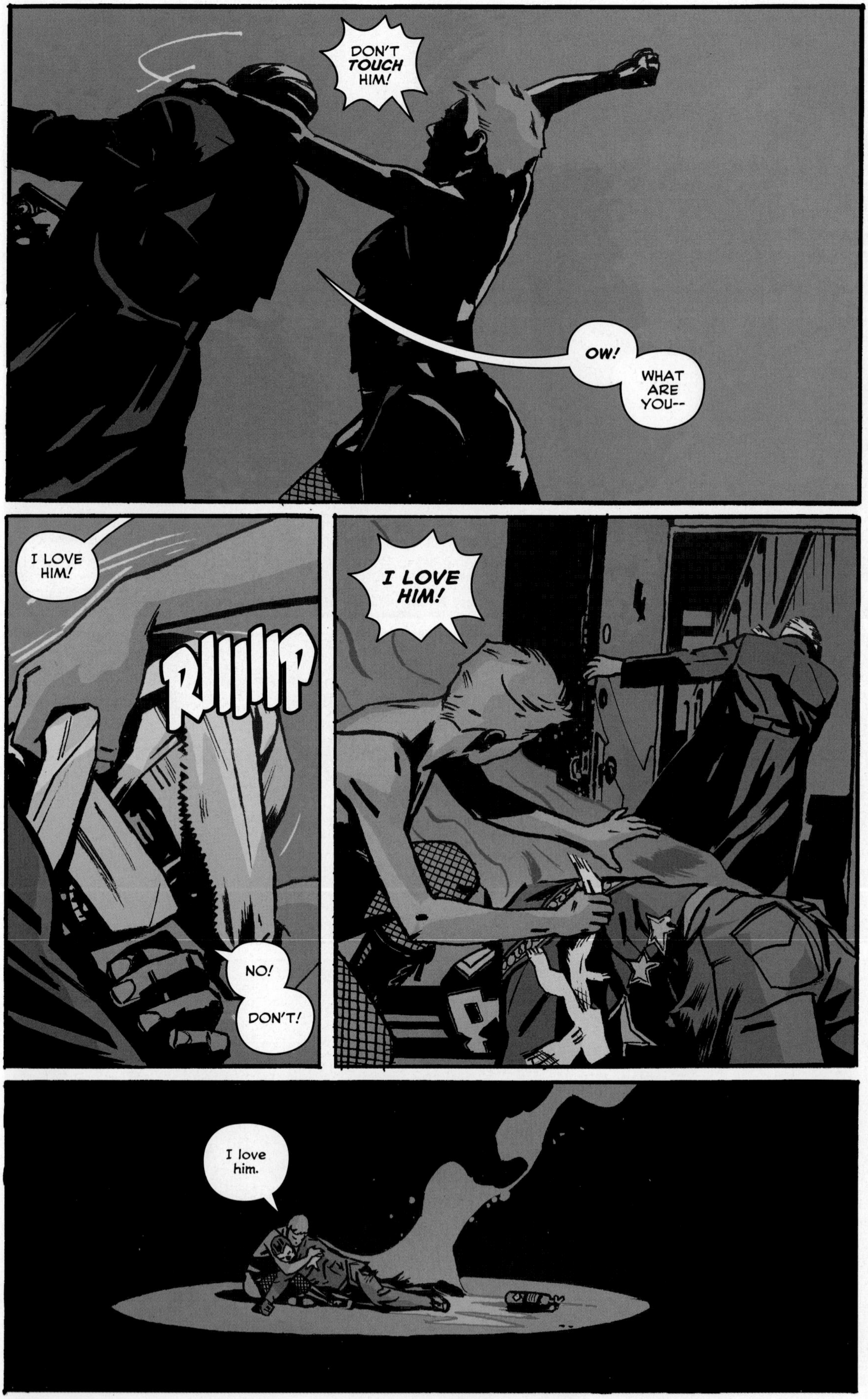
DON'T TOUCH HIM!
OW!
WHAT ARE YOU--
I LOVE HIM!
RIIIIP
NO!
DON'T!
I LOVE HIM!
I love him.

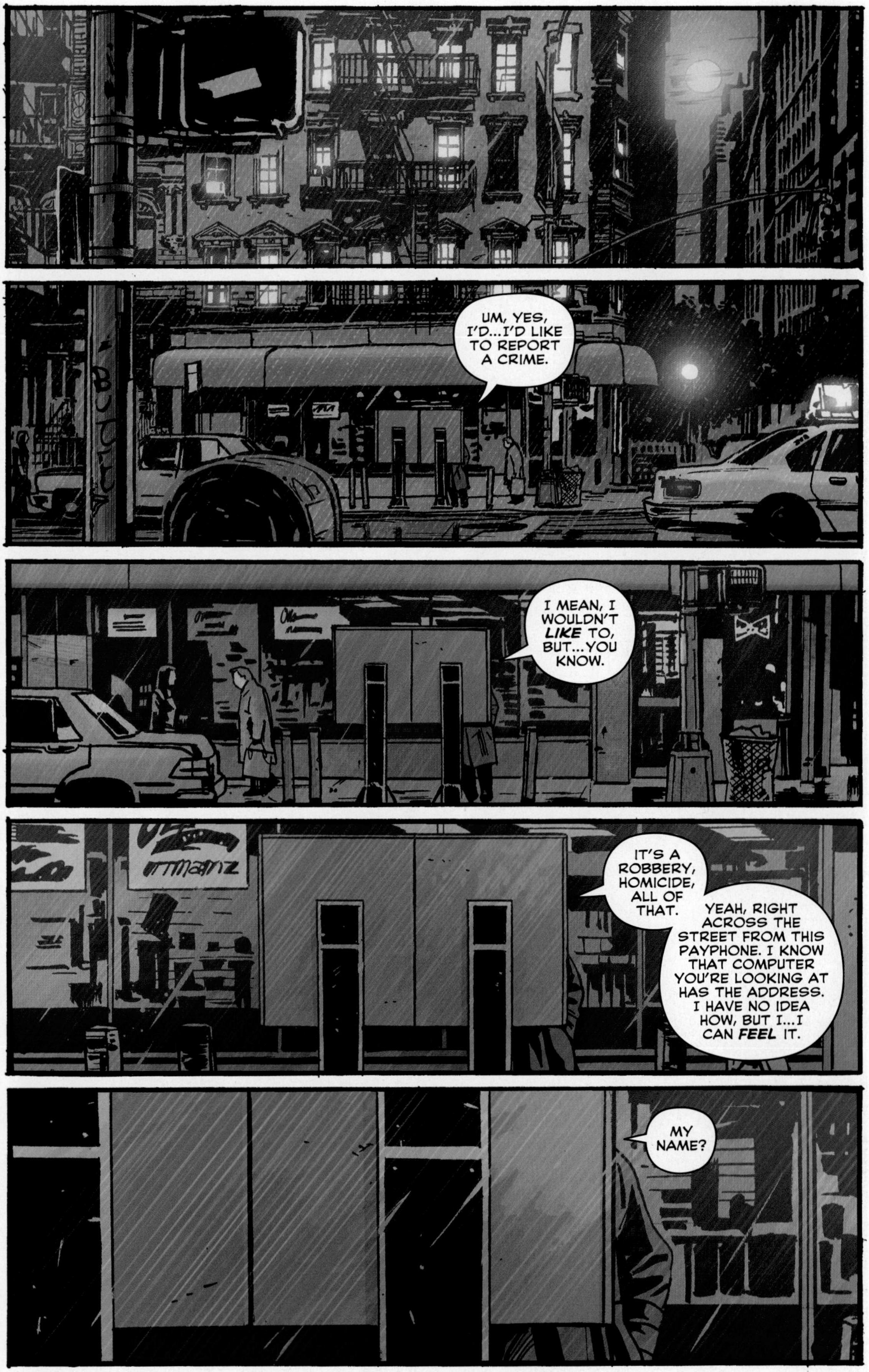
UM, YES, I'D...I'D LIKE TO REPORT A CRIME.
I MEAN, I WOULDN'T *LIKE* TO, BUT...YOU KNOW.
IT'S A ROBBERY, HOMICIDE, ALL OF THAT.
YEAH, RIGHT ACROSS THE STREET FROM THIS PAYPHONE. I KNOW THAT COMPUTER YOU'RE LOOKING AT HAS THE ADDRESS. I HAVE NO IDEA HOW, BUT I...I CAN *FEEL* IT.
MY NAME?

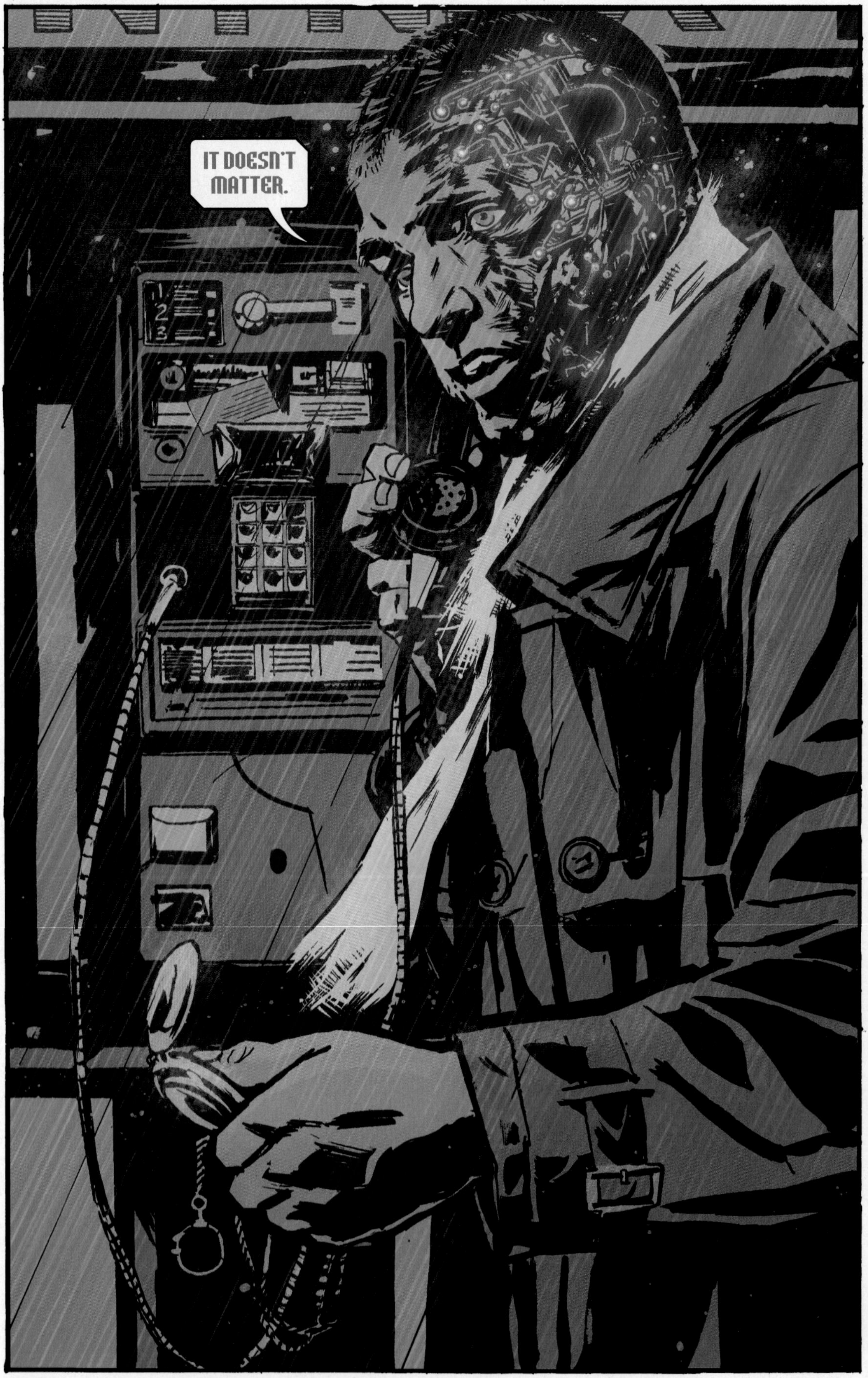
IT DOESN'T MATTER.

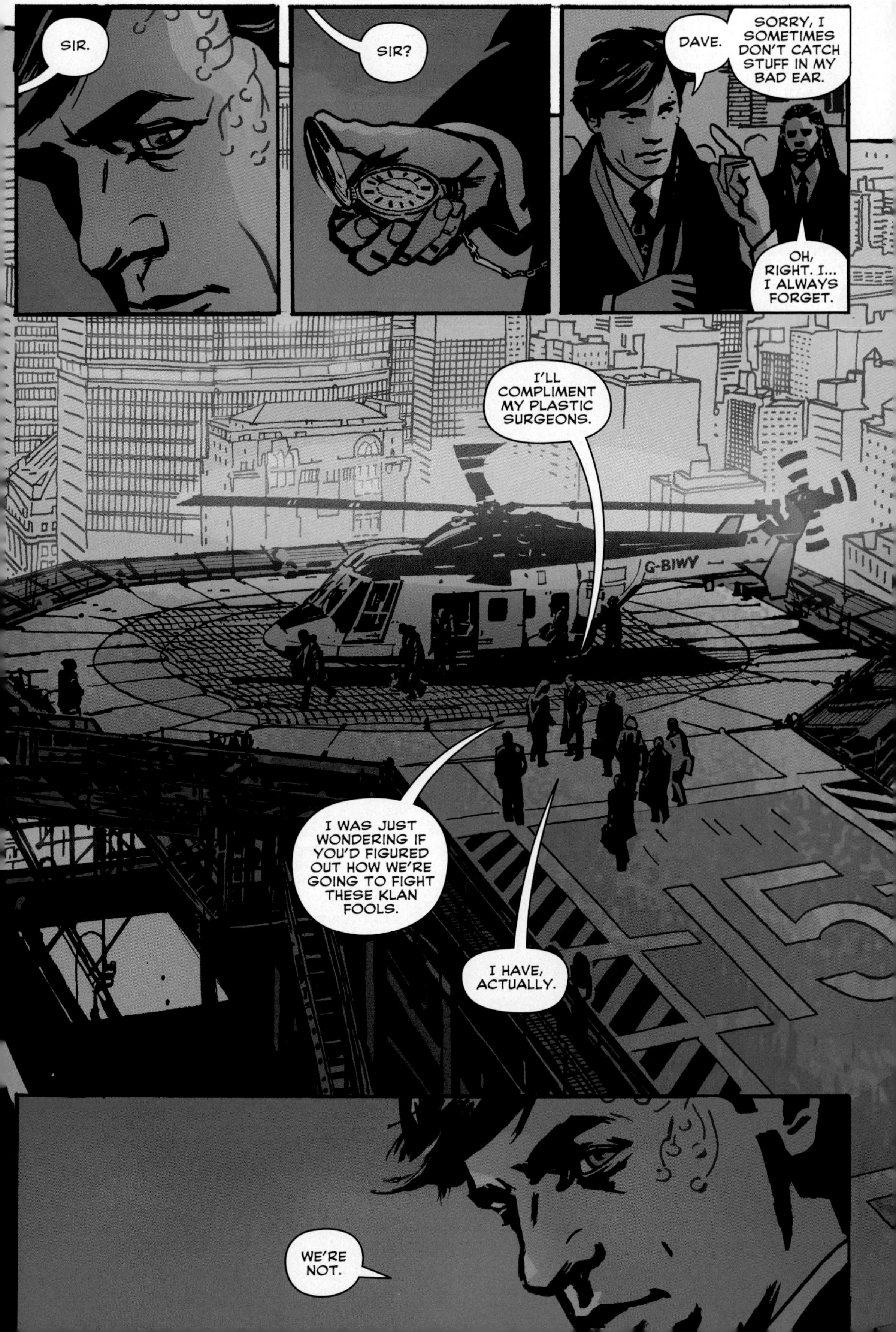
SIR.
SIR?
DAVE.
SORRY, I SOMETIMES DON'T CATCH STUFF IN MY BAD EAR.
OH, RIGHT. I... I ALWAYS FORGET.
I'LL COMPLIMENT MY PLASTIC SURGEONS.
G-BIWY
I WAS JUST WONDERING IF YOU'D FIGURED OUT HOW WE'RE GOING TO FIGHT THESE KLAN FOOLS.
I HAVE, ACTUALLY.
WE'RE NOT.

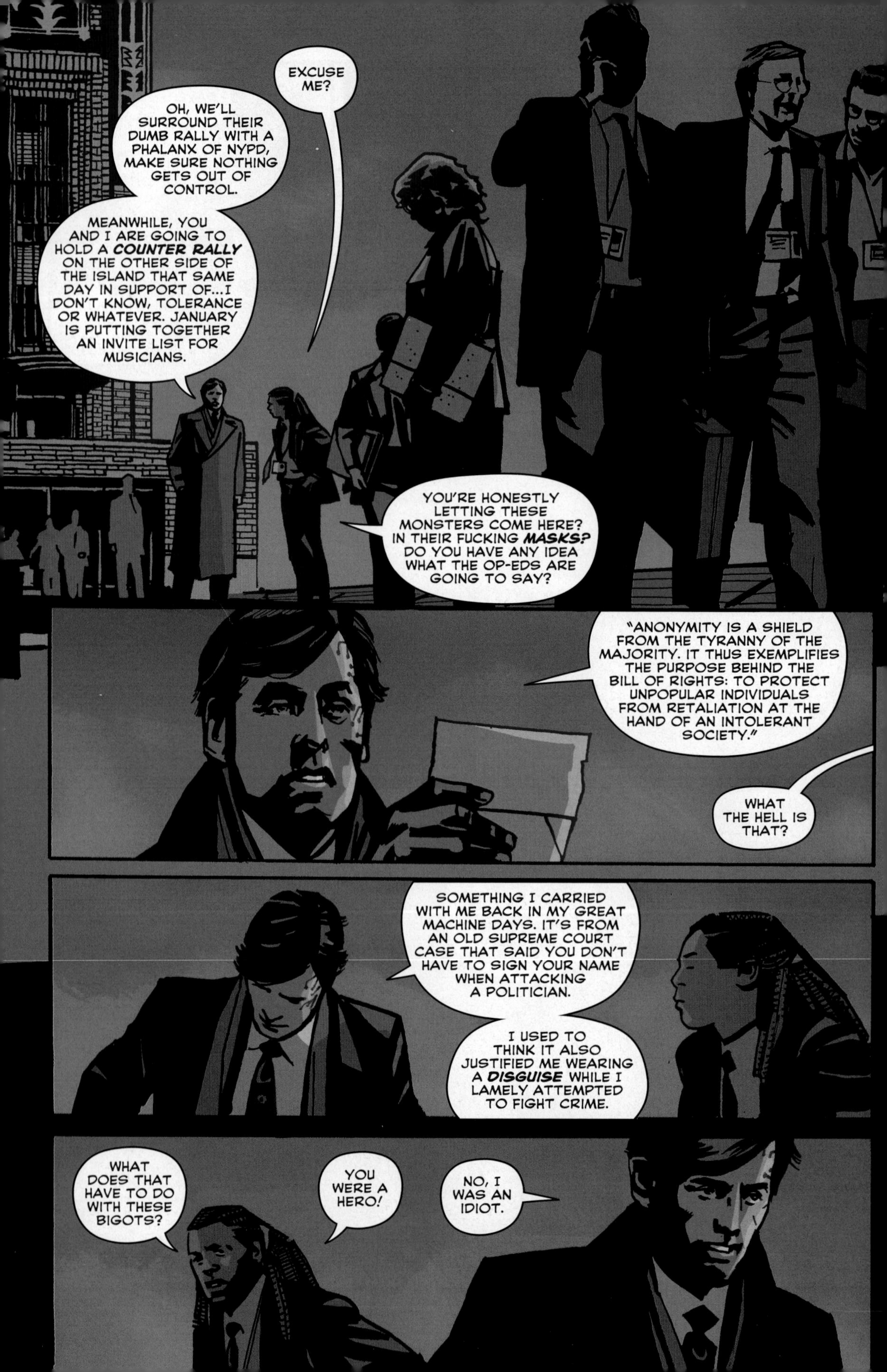
OH, WE'LL SURROUND THEIR DUMB RALLY WITH A PHALANX OF NYPD, MAKE SURE NOTHING GETS OUT OF CONTROL.
EXCUSE ME?
MEANWHILE, YOU AND I ARE GOING TO HOLD A COUNTER RALLY ON THE OTHER SIDE OF THE ISLAND THAT SAME DAY IN SUPPORT OF...I DON'T KNOW, TOLERANCE OR WHATEVER. JANUARY IS PUTTING TOGETHER AN INVITE LIST FOR MUSICIANS.
YOU'RE HONESTLY LETTING THESE MONSTERS COME HERE? IN THEIR FUCKING MASKS? DO YOU HAVE ANY IDEA WHAT THE OP-EDS ARE GOING TO SAY?
"ANONYMITY IS A SHIELD FROM THE TYRANNY OF THE MAJORITY. IT THUS EXEMPLIFIES THE PURPOSE BEHIND THE BILL OF RIGHTS: TO PROTECT UNPOPULAR INDIVIDUALS FROM RETALIATION AT THE HAND OF AN INTOLERANT SOCIETY."
WHAT THE HELL IS THAT?
SOMETHING I CARRIED WITH ME BACK IN MY GREAT MACHINE DAYS. IT'S FROM AN OLD SUPREME COURT CASE THAT SAID YOU DON'T HAVE TO SIGN YOUR NAME WHEN ATTACKING A POLITICIAN.
I USED TO THINK IT ALSO JUSTIFIED ME WEARING A DISGUISE WHILE I LAMELY ATTEMPTED TO FIGHT CRIME.
WHAT DOES THAT HAVE TO DO WITH THESE BIGOTS?
YOU WERE A HERO!
NO, I WAS AN IDIOT.

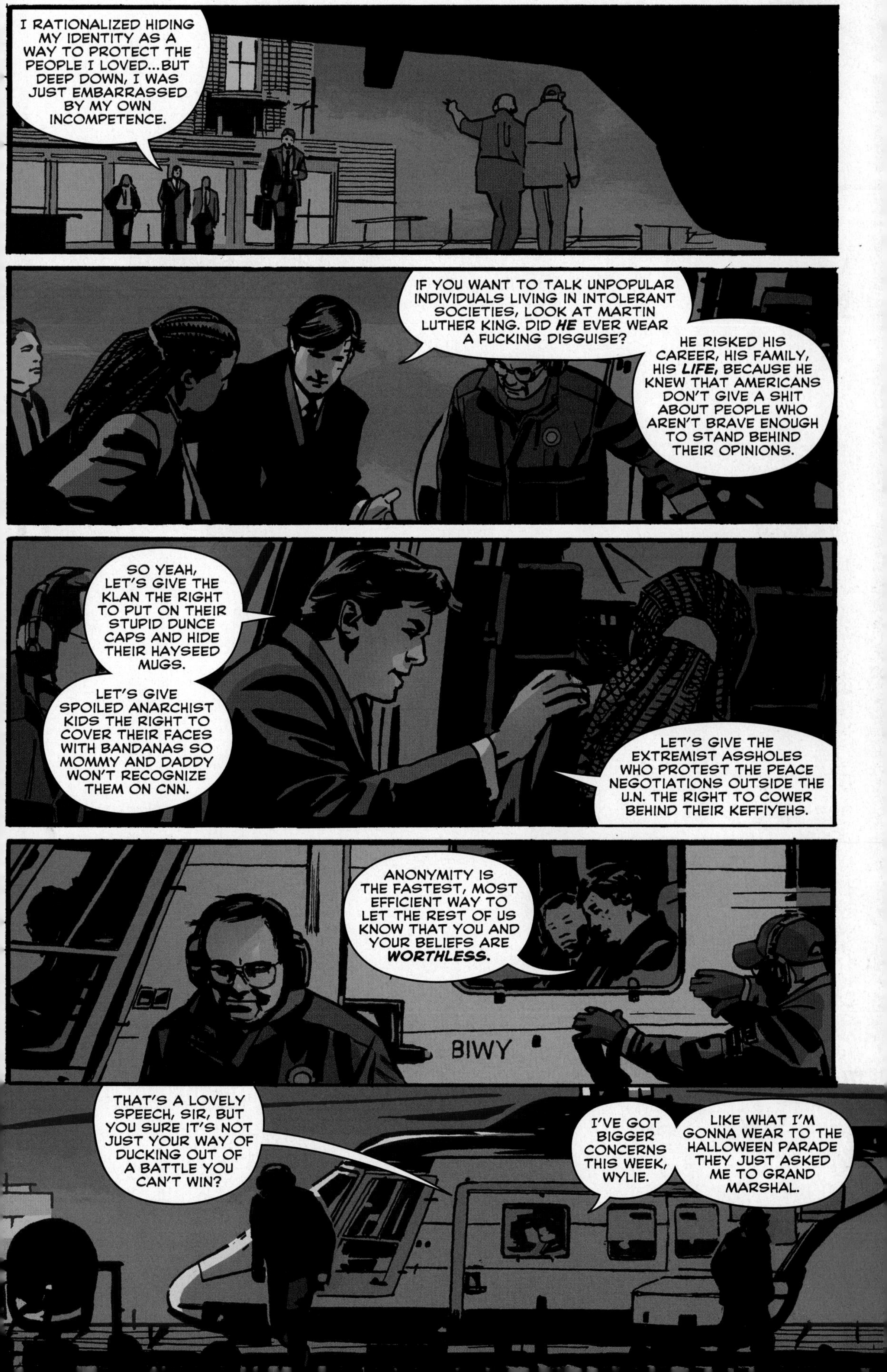
I RATIONALIZED HIDING MY IDENTITY AS A WAY TO PROTECT THE PEOPLE I LOVED...BUT DEEP DOWN, I WAS JUST EMBARRASSED BY MY OWN INCOMPETENCE.
IF YOU WANT TO TALK UNPOPULAR INDIVIDUALS LIVING IN INTOLERANT SOCIETIES, LOOK AT MARTIN LUTHER KING. DID HE EVER WEAR A FUCKING DISGUISE?
HE RISKED HIS CAREER, HIS FAMILY, HIS LIFE, BECAUSE HE KNEW THAT AMERICANS DON'T GIVE A SHIT ABOUT PEOPLE WHO AREN'T BRAVE ENOUGH TO STAND BEHIND THEIR OPINIONS.
SO YEAH, LET'S GIVE THE KLAN THE RIGHT TO PUT ON THEIR STUPID DUNCE CAPS AND HIDE THEIR HAYSEED MUGS.
LET'S GIVE SPOILED ANARCHIST KIDS THE RIGHT TO COVER THEIR FACES WITH BANDANAS SO MOMMY AND DADDY WON'T RECOGNIZE THEM ON CNN.
LET'S GIVE THE EXTREMIST ASSHOLES WHO PROTEST THE PEACE NEGOTIATIONS OUTSIDE THE U.N. THE RIGHT TO COWER BEHIND THEIR KEFFIYEHS.
ANONYMITY IS THE FASTEST, MOST EFFICIENT WAY TO LET THE REST OF US KNOW THAT YOU AND YOUR BELIEFS ARE WORTHLESS.
BIWY
THAT'S A LOVELY SPEECH, SIR, BUT YOU SURE IT'S NOT JUST YOUR WAY OF DUCKING OUT OF A BATTLE YOU CAN'T WIN?
I'VE GOT BIGGER CONCERNS THIS WEEK, WYLIE.
LIKE WHAT I'M GONNA WEAR TO THE HALLOWEEN PARADE THEY JUST ASKED ME TO GRAND MARSHAL.

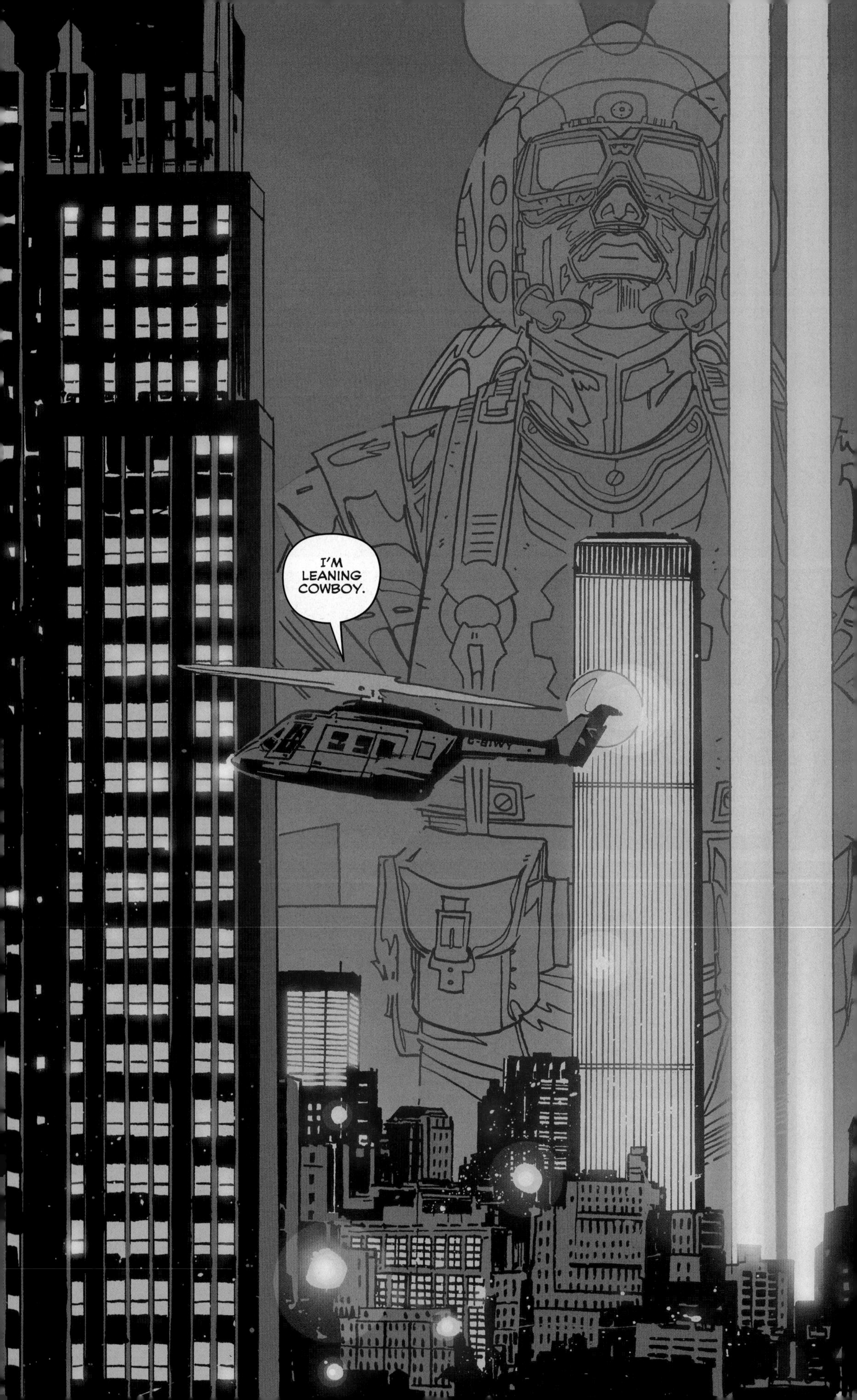
I'M LEANING COWBOY.

CHAPTER 5 INSIDE THE MACHINE

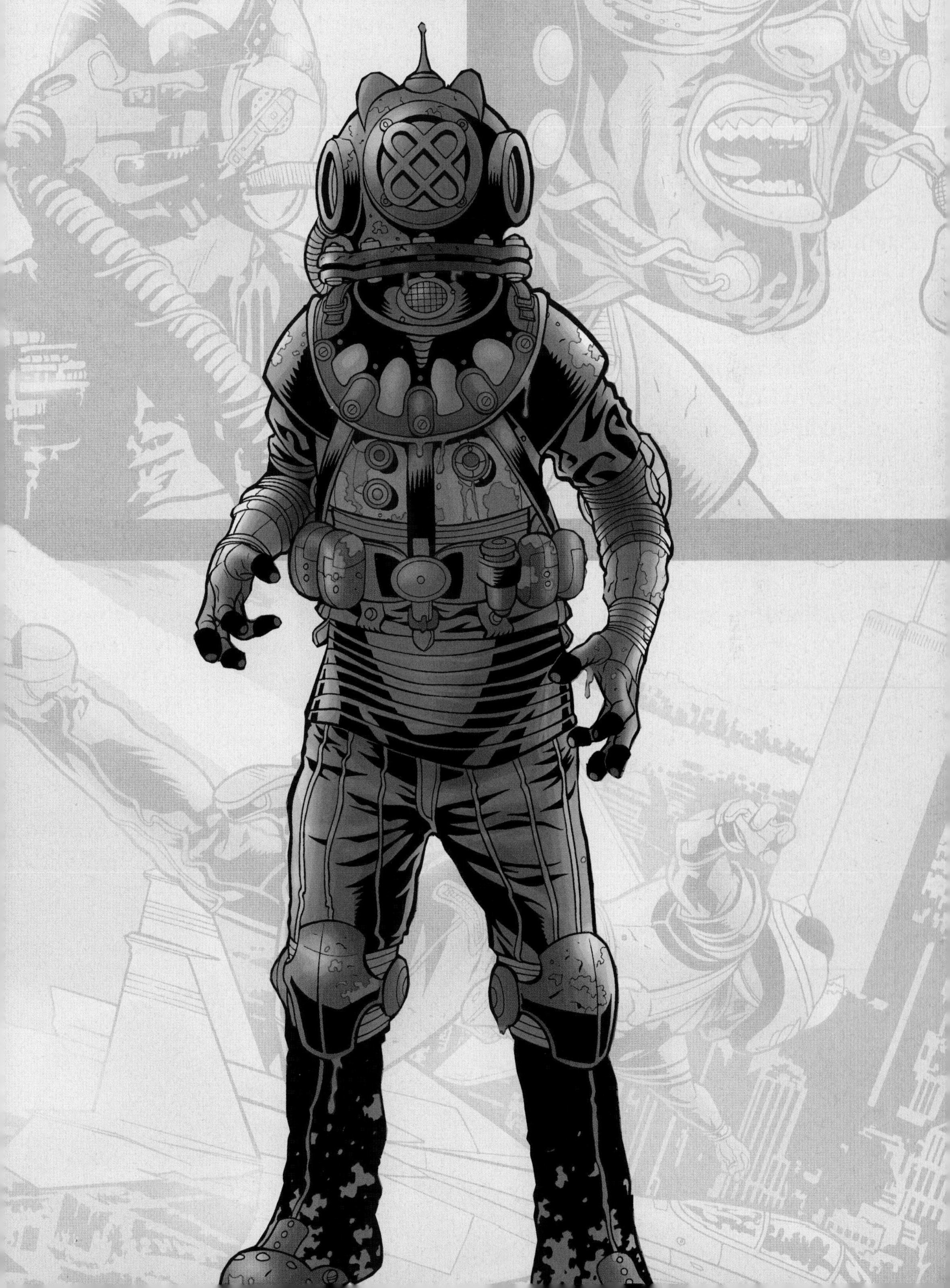

Introduction by Brian K. Vaughan

Comic books made by more than one creator are often derogatively referred to as "assembly-line books," implying that each stage of the work is dispassionately passed from one craftsman to the next in order to churn out product as quickly as possible. And while EX MACHINA does hit stands with shocking regularity, the above description doesn't capture our process in the least.

All of the artists behind this series are close friends, and it's sometimes hard to tell where one person's job starts and another's ends. My scripts often begin with a brilliant visual idea suggested by penciller and co-creator Tony Harris during one of our regular phone calls. While Old Man Harris and I are gabbing, our inker (first the amazing Tom Feister, now the equally talented Jim Clark) might catch a small continuity error in one of the previous issue's unfinished pages, which I'll try to address in the dialogue with the help of letterer extraordinaire Jared K. Fletcher. Meanwhile, J.D. Mettler will be e-mailing all of us his incomparable colors, getting input about setting the mood for a particular scene with a specific palette. This complex cross-country network is constantly being guided from the WildStorm offices by the tireless Ben Abernathy and Kristy Quinn.

And those are just the names you see in the credit box. Each month, our team is ably assisted by countless more people, whether it's the dedicated cast of actors Tony shoots for photo reference or the government sources who are kind enough to supply me with the inside scoop on life in City Hall. Our production is bigger and more complicated than many independent films, but everyone involved feels a responsibility beyond our individual contributions to the series, and I think it makes for a unique kind of book that feels like the work of one unified vision.

EX MACHINA has always suggested that the behind-the-scenes story is infinitely more interesting than the one the public gets to see, so it's only fitting that we finally reveal the secret inner workings of our "machine."

I hope you agree it's a great one.

- Brian K. Vaughan
Los Angeles, 2007

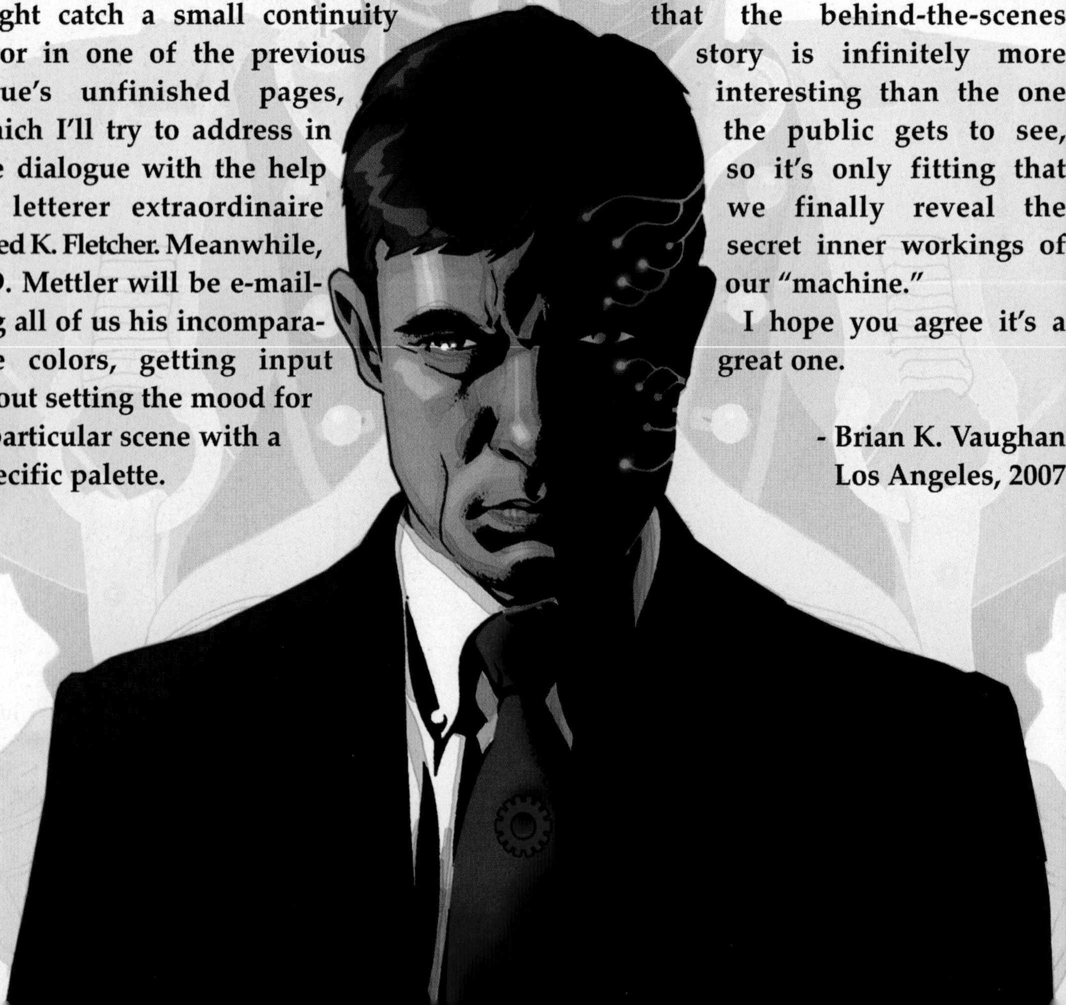

Inside Process: Interior page showcase

Tony Harris is always experimenting with different techniques to push himself as an artist and excel at his craft. On his covers, he typically adds a "graywash" layer to the board following the inking stage, to add a little more depth to the finished piece. For a few issues of EX MACHINA, he experimented with this technique on the interiors as well.

What follows are the opening six pages to EX MACHINA #23, featuring script, pencils, gray-washed inks and color stages.

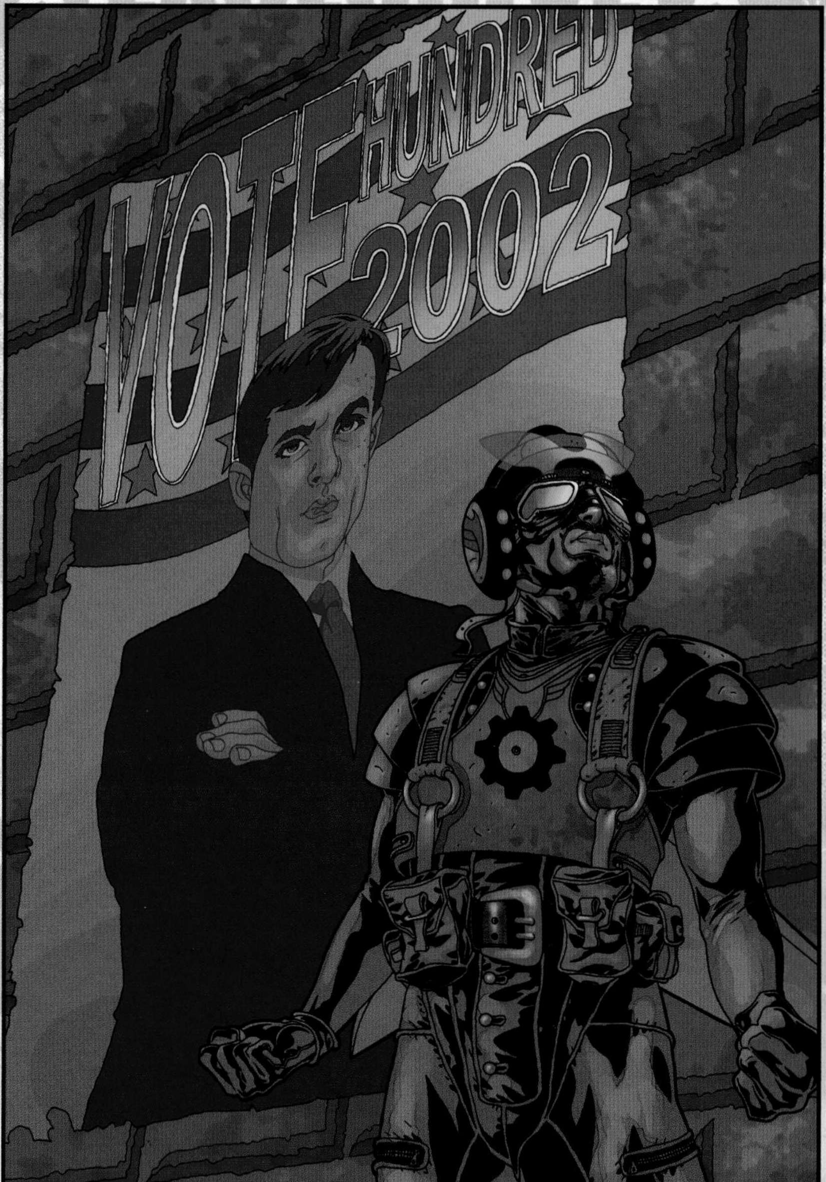

VOTE
HUNDRED
2002

This art was commissioned by *Wizard Magazine* for a piece they were doing on the Great Machine. When printed, they cropped out the background and just ran the free-floating figure.

The Full Script for
EX MACHINA #23
Prepared for Tony Harris
and WildStorm
June 27, 2006

Page One

Page One, Panel One

We open with this close-up of an African-American DOORMAN, wearing a uniform like this one:
[redacted]

1) Doorman: You can't come in here!

Page One, Panel Two

One of these things, same as always:

2) Date (in the style of a right-justified newspaper heading):

Monday, April 2, 2001

Page One, Panel Three

Pull out to the largest panel of the page, as CLEVELAND (the pot dealer from last issue) RUNS into the lobby of this quiet old apartment building and KNOCKS his way past the startled doorman.

3) Doorman: This is a private buil--
4) Doorman: OOF!

5) Cleveland: Help! He's trying to kill me!

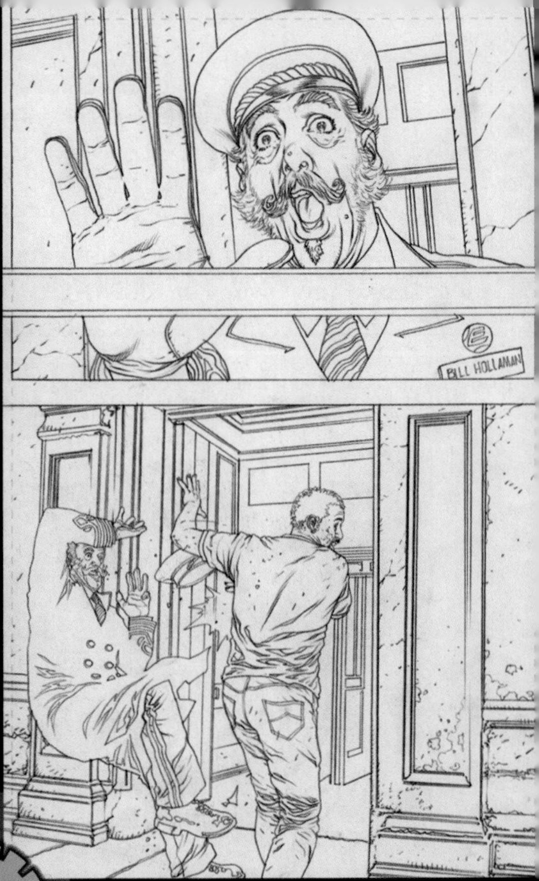
BILL HOLLAMAN

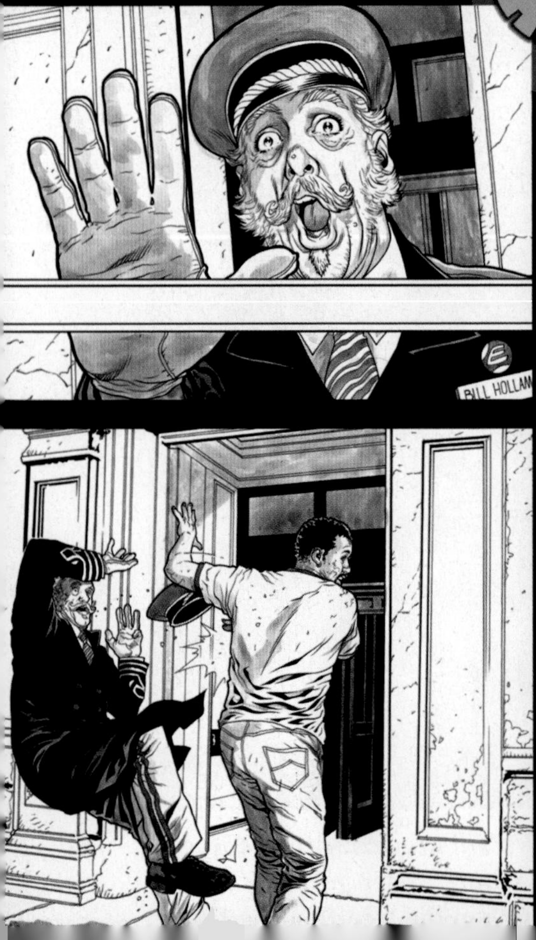
BILL HOLLAM

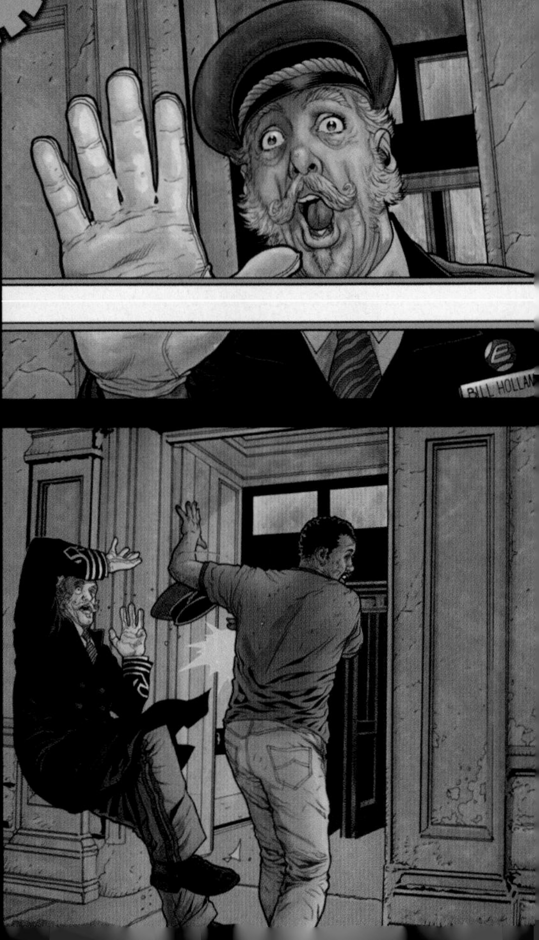
BILL HOLLAM

Page Two

Page Two, Panel One
Cut to the revolving door entrance to this old apartment building, as the helmeted GREAT MACHINE runs inside. He left his busted jetpack in the cab, so he's wingless here.

1) Great Machine (small font, whispering): Where did he go?

Page Two, Panel Two
Pull out to the largest panel of the page for a shot of the Great Machine and the doorman, as the floored doorman points at a nearby STAIRWELL DOOR.

2) Doorman: Say again?

3) Great Machine: Where the hell did he go?

4) Doorman: Stuh… stairwell.

Page Two, Panel Three
Change angles on the two men, as the Great Machine runs for an old elevator with an "OUT OF ORDER" sign on it.

5) Great Machine (small font, whispering): -koff- -koff- Thanks.

6) Doorman: Don't bother, man!
7) Doorman: That elevator hasn't worked in years!

Page Two, Panel Four
Push in on the Great Machine, as he gives a little half-smile.

8) Great Machine (GREEN FONT/BALLOON): I think I can coax her out of retirement.

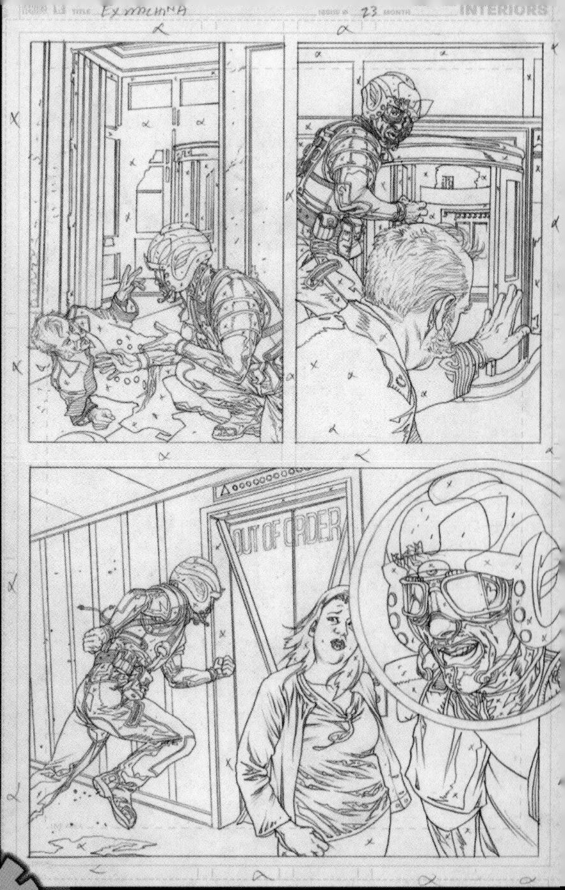

INTERIORS
OUT OF ORDER

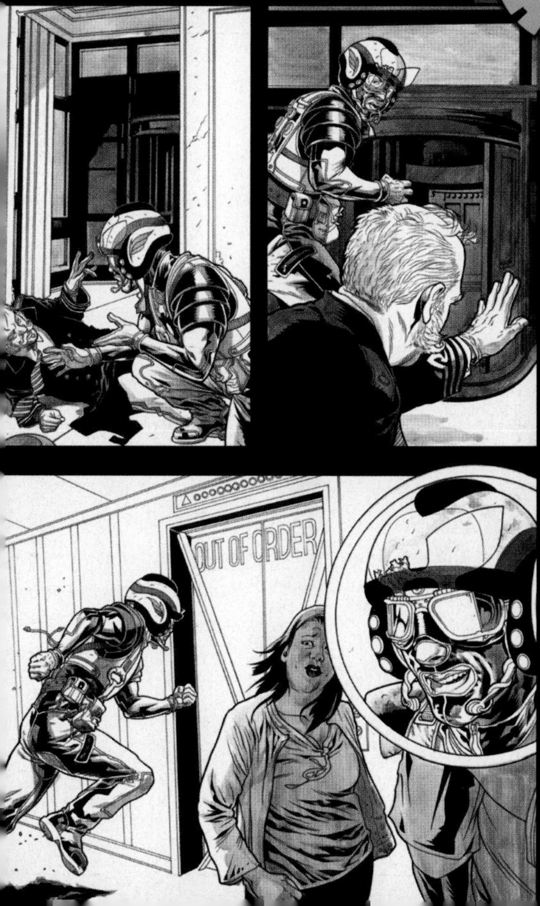

OUT OF ORDER

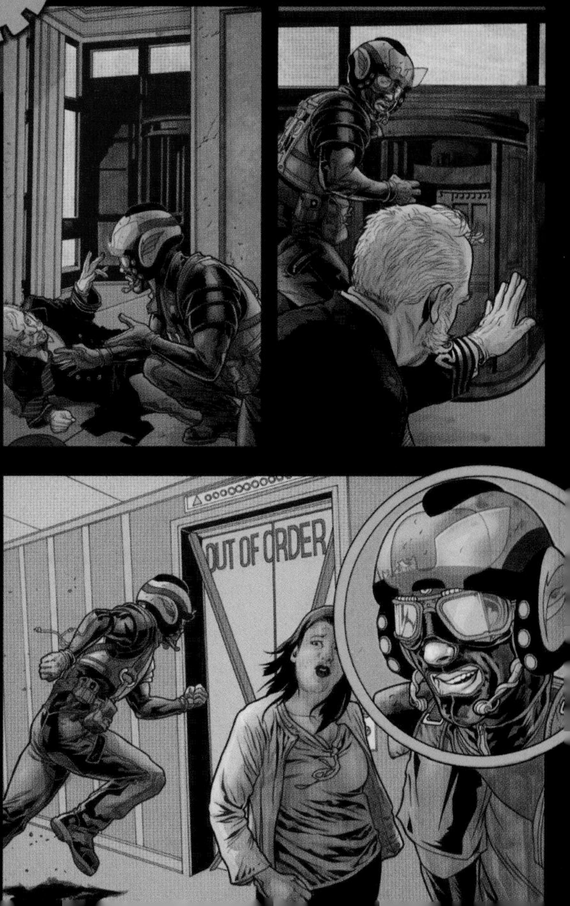

OUT OF ORDER

Page Three

Page Three, Panel One

Cut to the Great Machine's warehouse hideout (from Sprouse's special) where KREMLIN is talking into a microphone, while BRADBURY listens in behind him.

1) Kremlin: Mitchell, let him go!
2) Kremlin: No pusher boy is worth dying for!

Page Three, Panel Two

Cut onto the roof of the apartment building, where the Great Machine bursts out of a roof-access door.

3) Great Machine: You stick with a job until it's finished, Kremlin.

4) Electronic (tailless): But Bradbury says there is deli getting robbed two blocks from you! Those people need you more than--

Page Three, Panel Three

Pull out to the largest panel of the page. We're in the foreground with Cleveland, who is RUNNING at us, right for the EDGE of the five-story building's roof!

5) Great Machine: Cleveland, don't!

Page Three, Panel Four

Push in on the Great Machine, who yells:

6) Great Machine: You'll never make it!

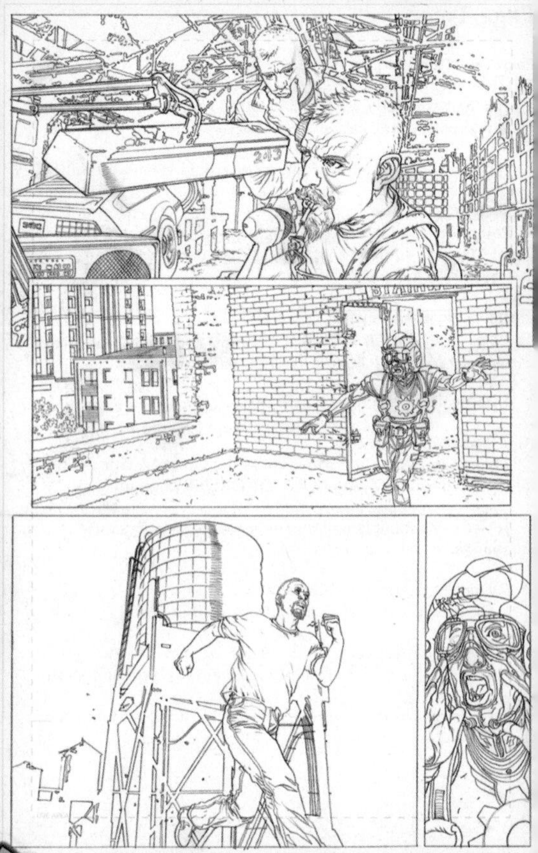

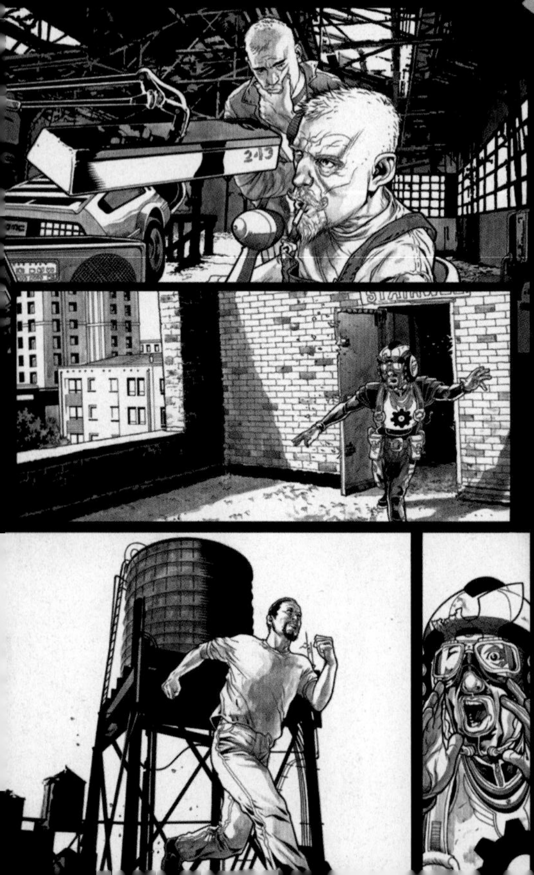

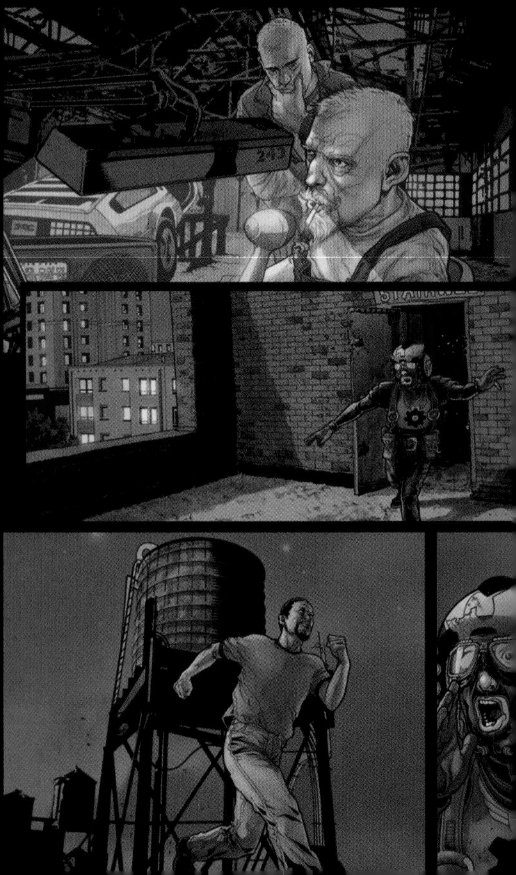

Page Four

Page Four, Panel One

Cut to Cleveland, who LEAPS over a wide alleyway towards another roof across the way.

1) Cleveland: Eat dick!

Page Four, Panel Two

We're behind the Great Machine, looking over his shoulder, as he watches Cleveland LAND safely on the other roof.

2) Great Machine: Son of a…

Page Four, Panel Three

Change angles on the Great Machine, as he RUNS as fast as he can, preparing to jump just like Cleveland did.

3) Great Machine (small font, whispering): My legs are machines, my legs are machines, my legs are…

Page Four, Panel Four

Change angles for this largest panel of the page, a cool-ass shot of the wingless Mitchell JUMPING across the wide alleyway. Maybe we're down in the alley, looking up at him as he makes the leap? Whatever looks coolest, man.

No Copy

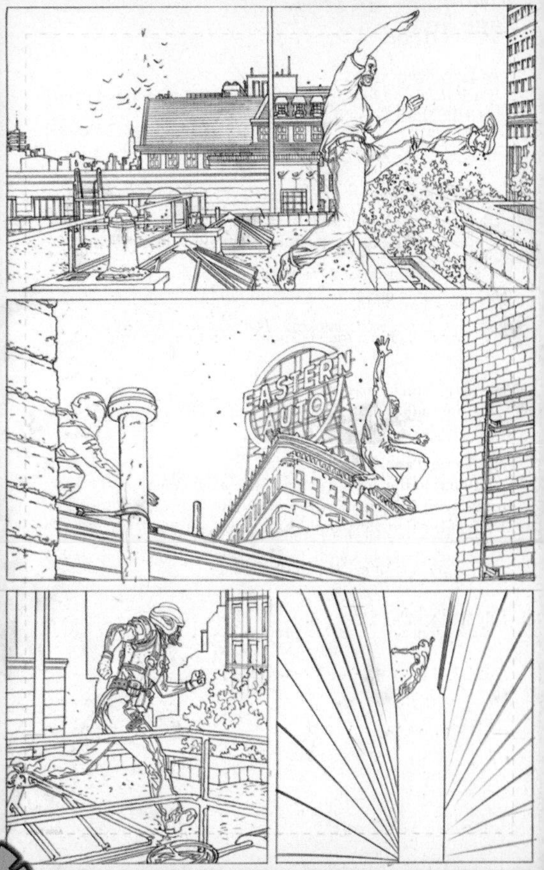
EASTERN
AUTO

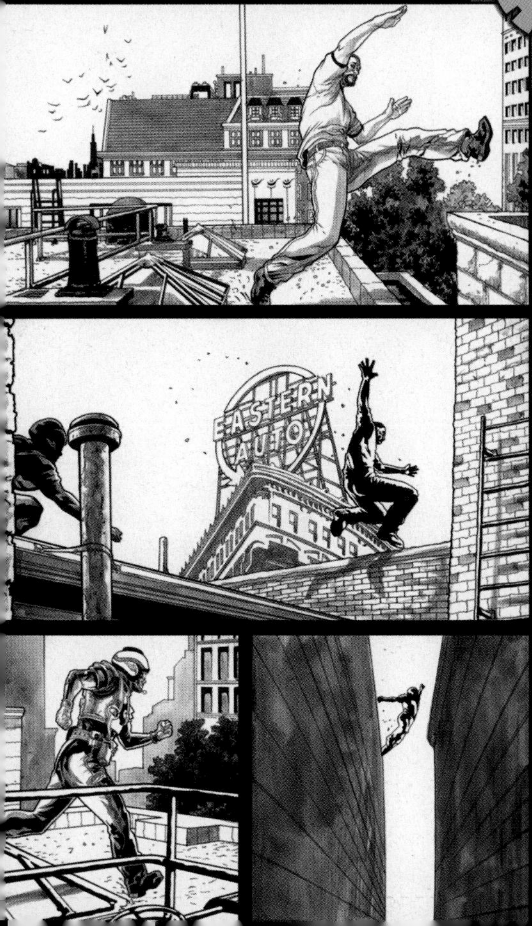
EASTERN
AUTO

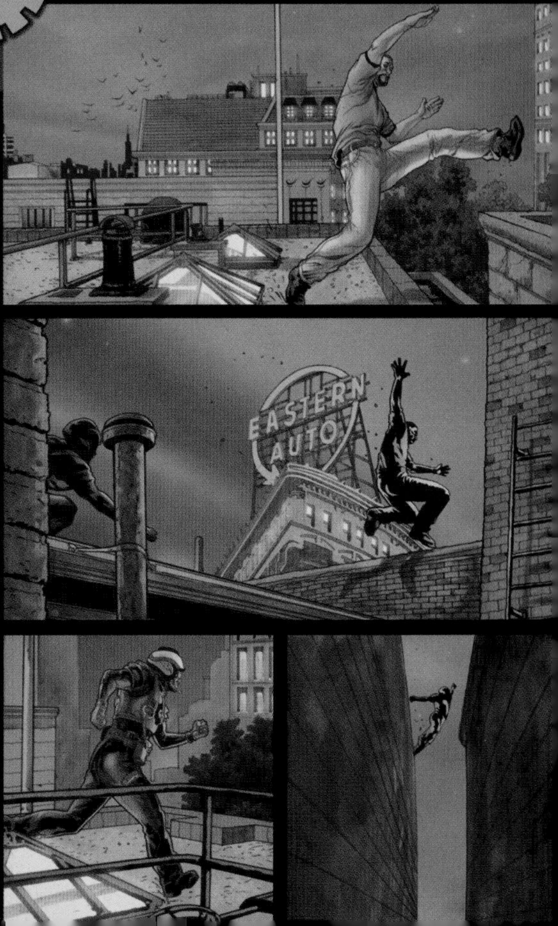
EASTERN
AUTO

Page Five

Page Five, Panel One
Push in, as the Machine just MISSES the roof, and narrowly CATCHES the edge of it with his arms.

1) Great Machine: UNF!

Page Five, Panel Two
Pull out to a shot of both men, as Cleveland looks down at the Machine (holding on for dear life), and aims the RAYGUN he stole at his face.

2) Cleveland: Dude.
3) Cleveland: Stop. Fucking. *FOLLOWING ME!*

Page Five, Panel Three
Push in tight on the Great Machine, as his scars begin to GLOW beneath his goggles.

4) Great Machine (GREEN FONT/BALLOON): Voltage spike.

Page Five, Panel Four
Pull out to the largest panel of the page, as the raygun in Cleveland's hand suddenly EXPLODES in a burst of sparks, electrocuting him..

5) SFX: KZZZAXXXX

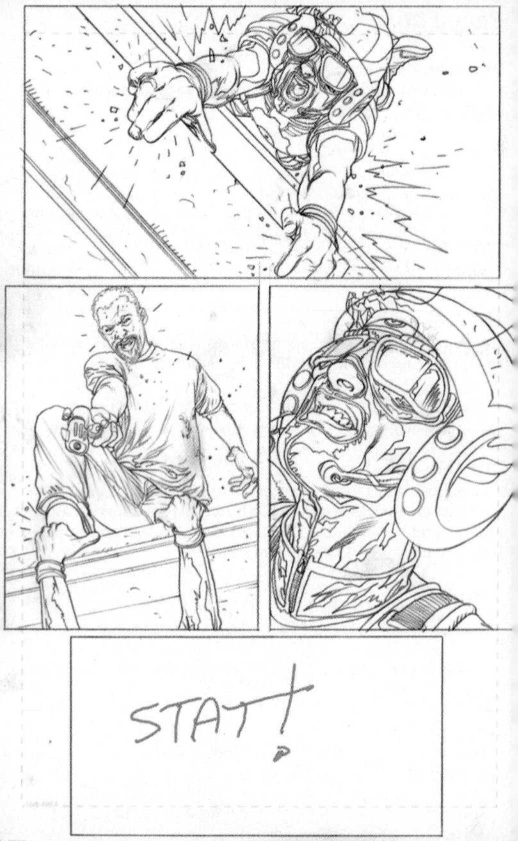
STAT!

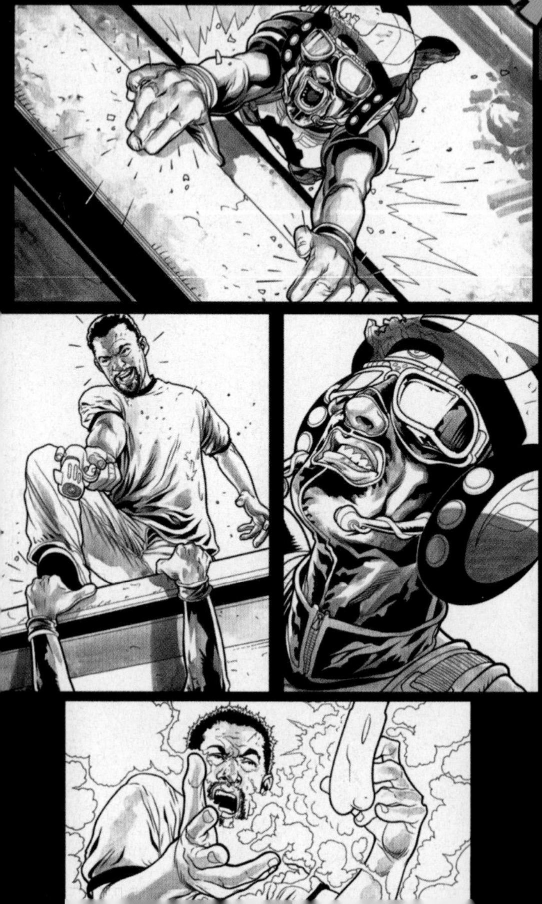

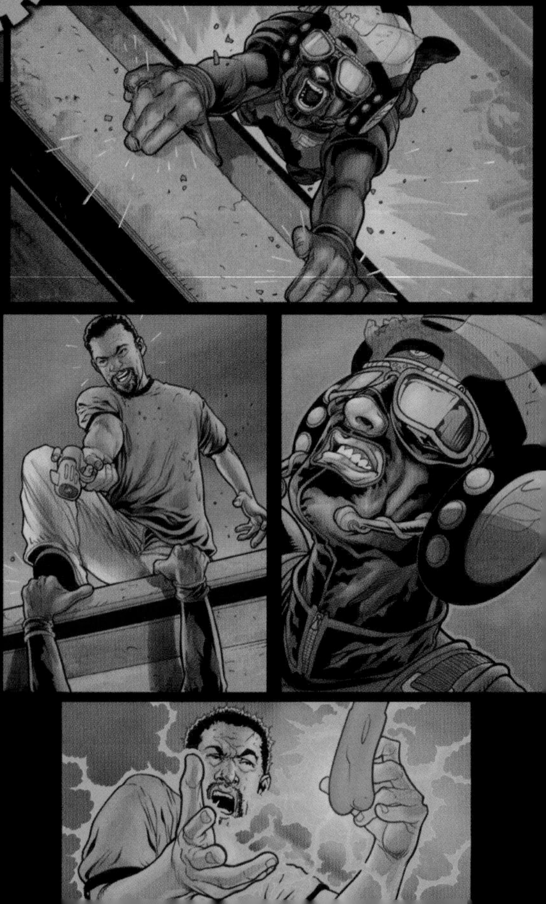

Page Six

Page Six, Panel One

We're with Cleveland's fallen body in the foreground of this shot. In the background, the Great Machine PULLS himself up onto the roof.

1) Cleveland: Nnn…!

Page Six, Panel Two

Pull out to the largest panel of the page for a shot of both men. The Great machine is standing over the groggy Cleveland, as Mitchell pulls out a pair of HANDCUFFS from one of his pouches.

2) Great Machine (small font, whispering): Cleveland Severtson, I'm placing you under citizen's arrest.

3) Cleveland: All this for a little grass?

4) Great Machine (small font, whispering): An apartment-full is hardly a little. Besides, you sell to children.

Page Six, Panel Three

Push in on the two men, as the Great Machine handcuffs Cleveland.

5) Cleveland: No, I sell to rich folk! I can't control who they give their shit to.
6) Cleveland: Look, I'm not a rapist! I've never murdered anybody! You can't send me to prison!

7) Great Machine (small font, whispering): I'm not. I'm sending you to the cops.

Page Six, Panel Four

This is just a shot of the exhausted Great Machine, as he matter-of-factly says:

8) Great Machine: I can't control who they give their shit to.
9) Great Machine: -koff- -koff-

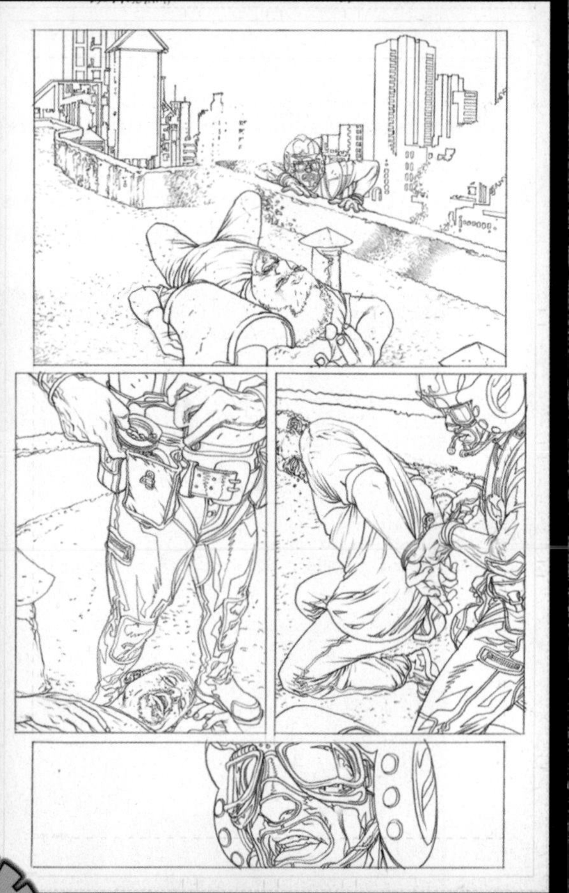

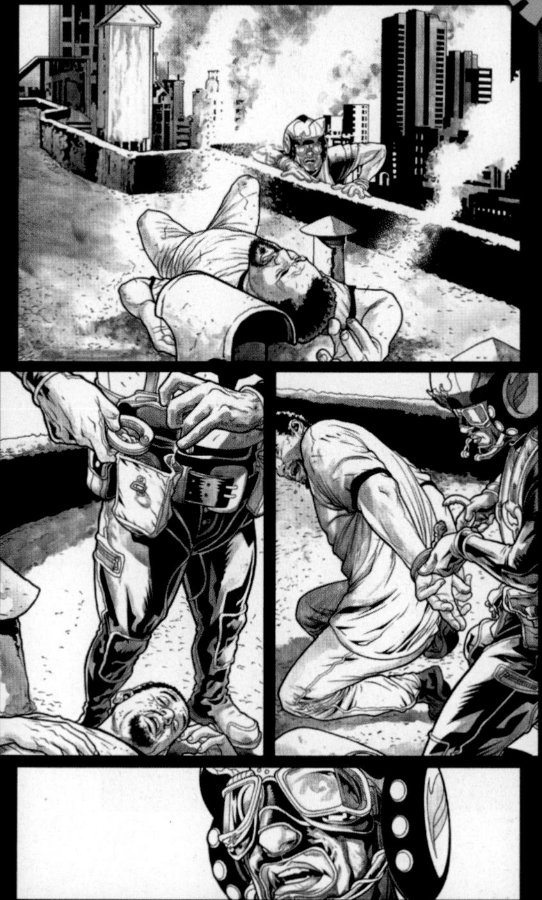

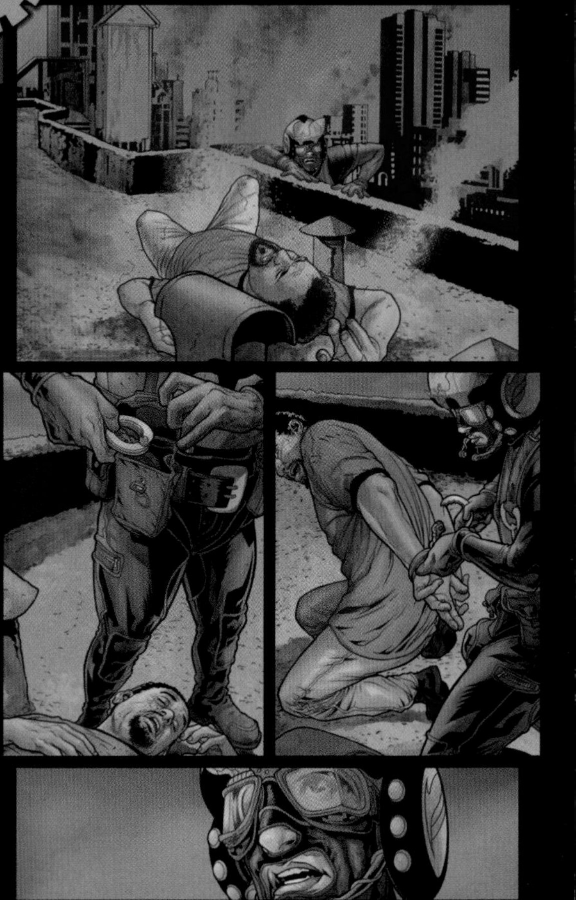

Inside the Covers

Tony Harris is an Eisner-winning cover artist from his STARMAN days—and in 2006, he was again nominated for "Best Cover Artist." What follows is an Inside look into Tony's cover creation process, as he pencils, inks and colors every cover on his own, with notes from the old man himself.

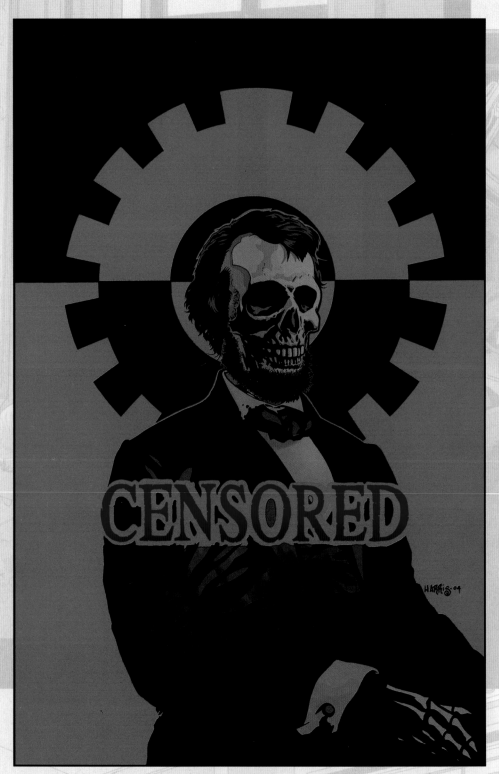

#1

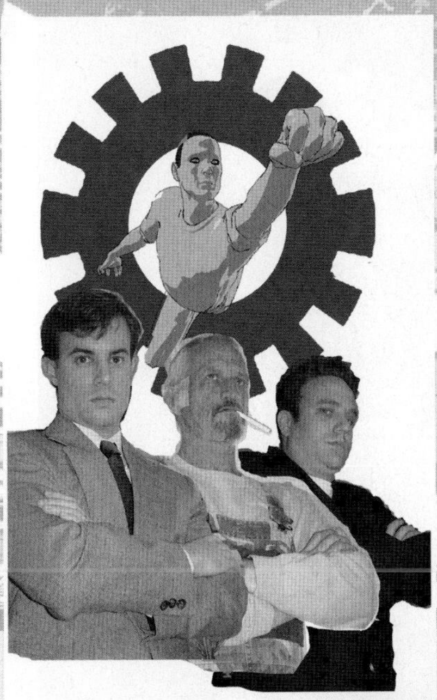

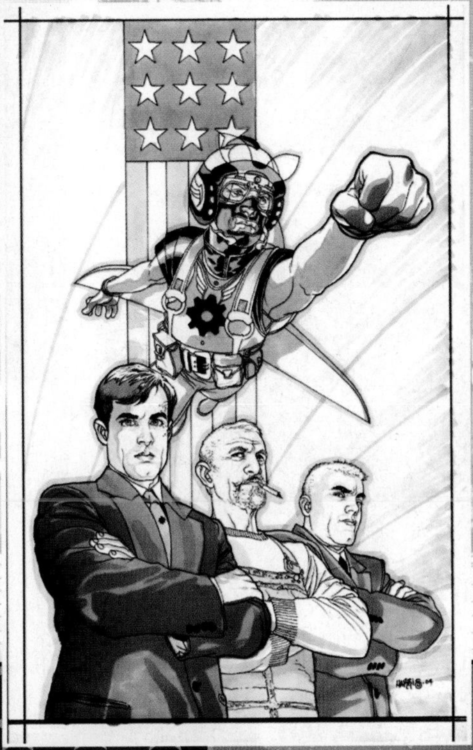

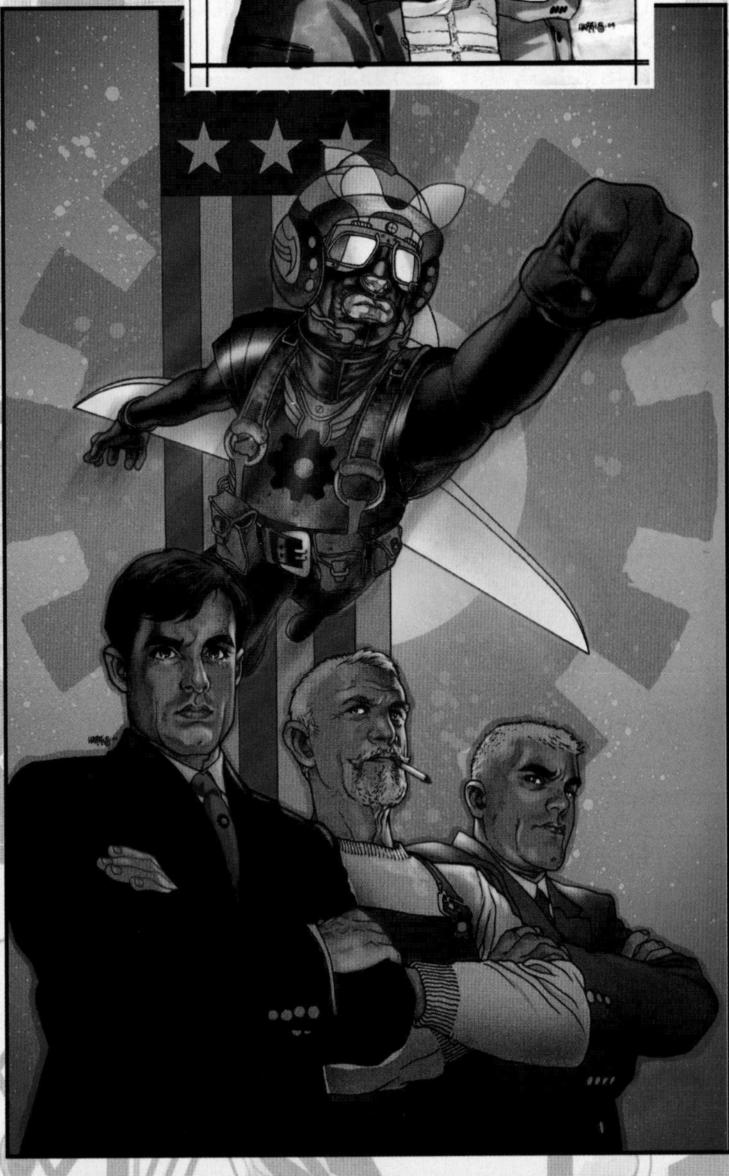

This was actually the second cover produced for the first issue. (More on that in a moment!) But the team felt the first version I did (which was eventually used as the cover to #4) wasn't powerful enough to be issue one's cover. I have to say, in hindsight, I agree.

#4

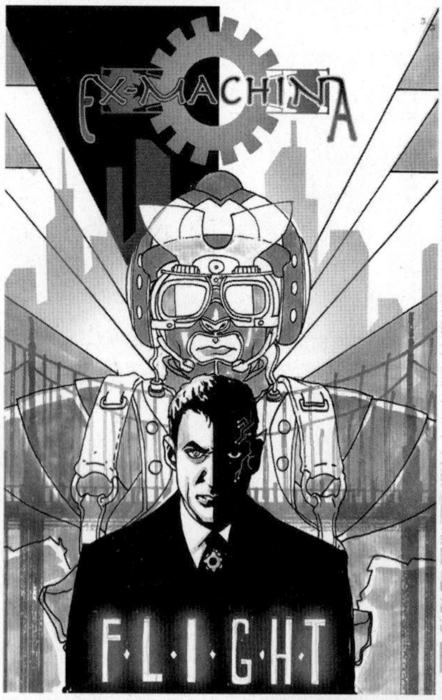
EX MACHINA
F·L·I·G·H·T

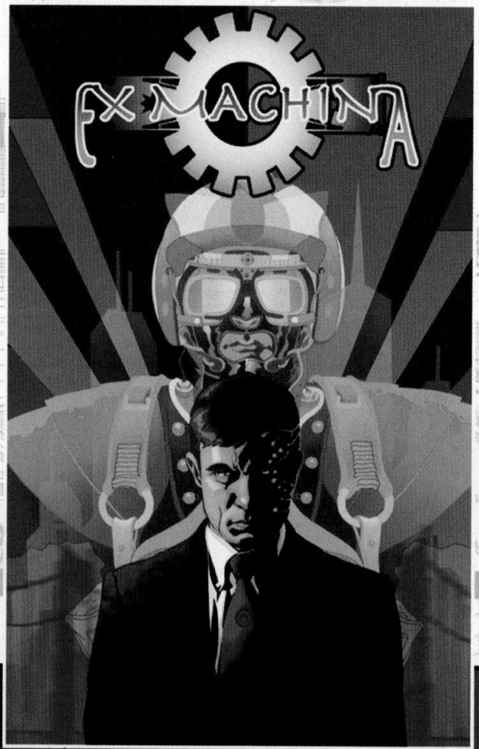
EX MACHINA

This is the final cover for issue #4. As mentioned, this was originally the first issue cover.

My initial thoughts were to include a single bold word that would encompass the story inside. Later, we decided not to do this because it would fight with the logo and cover copy. I did, however, get to do this with the Lincoln cover to issue #2—effectively, as can be seen on page 248!

The ghosted city here was done totally digital and does not appear on the original. Note the super-ghosted Brooklyn Bridge at the bottom.

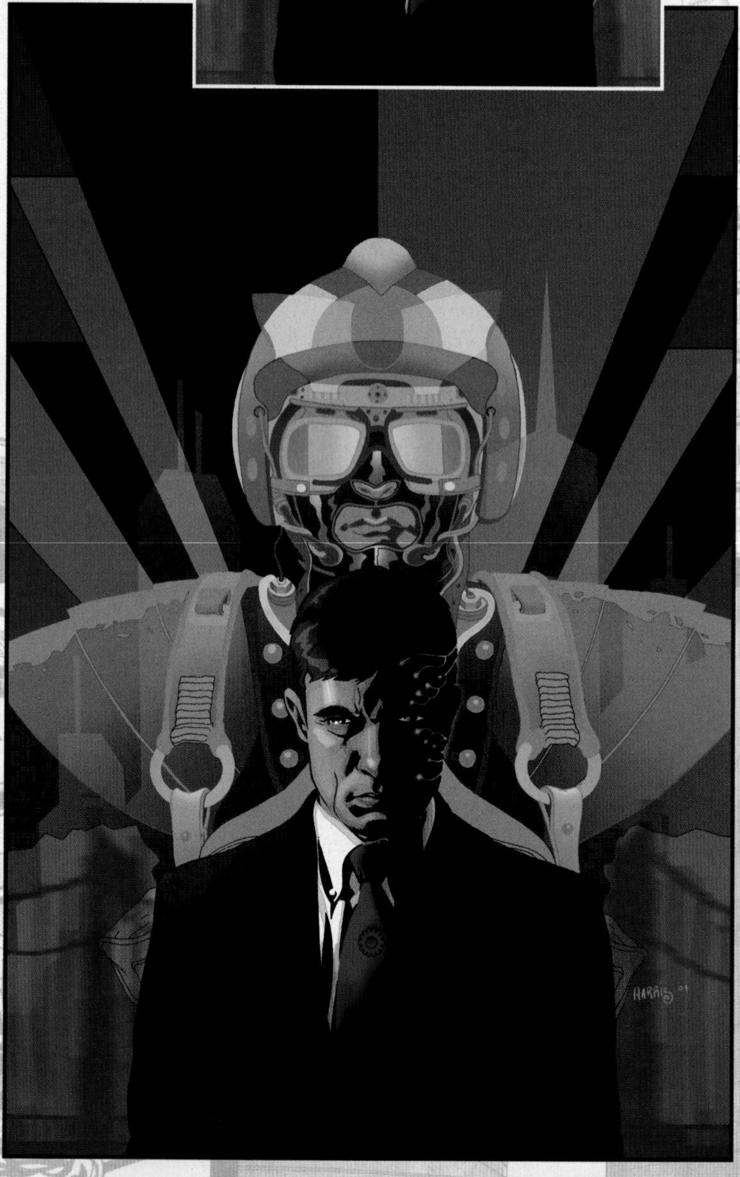

#5

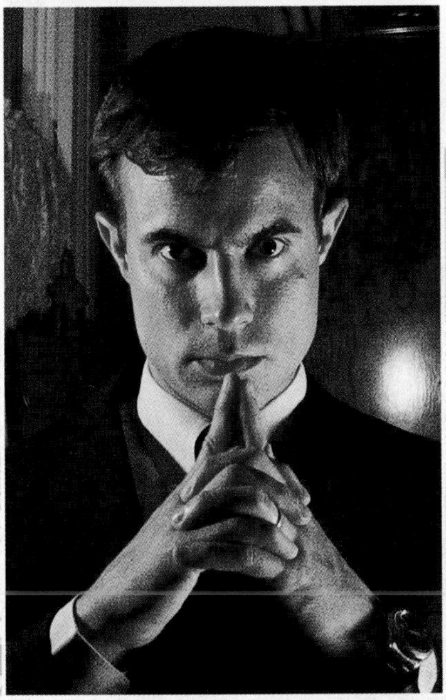

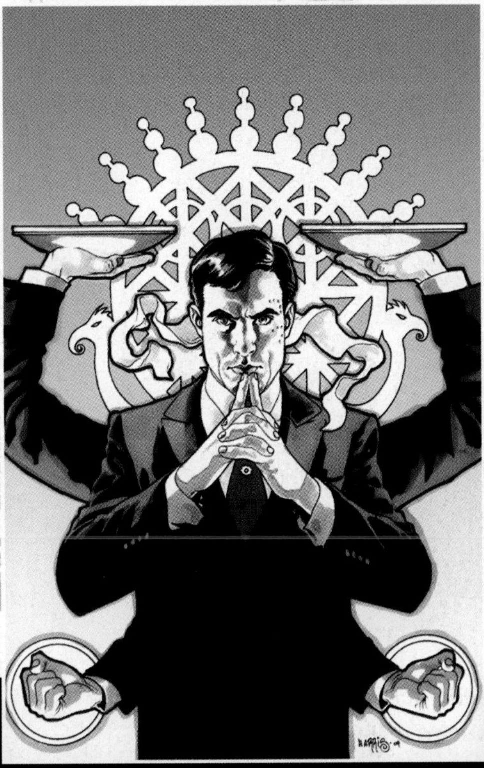

Here is my model for Mitchell Hundred, Jimmy Hill. He can have such an intense look when he's lit right. For this design I wanted to riff on Mitchell's multi-tasking as the Great Machine and the Mayor. So this cover represents the balance of Force (bottom pair of hands), Deliberation (middle pair), and the Scales of Justice (top pair).

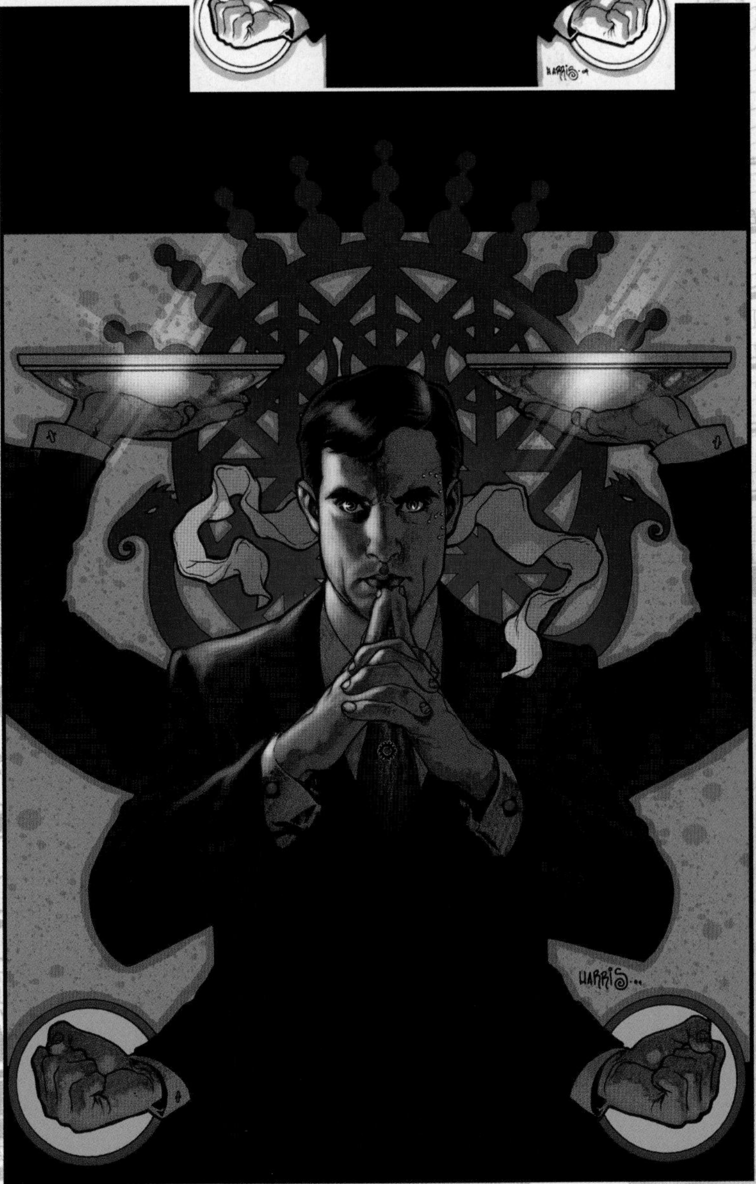

#12

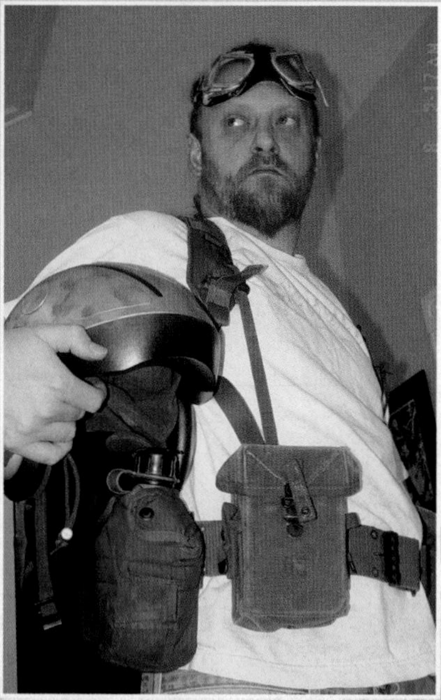

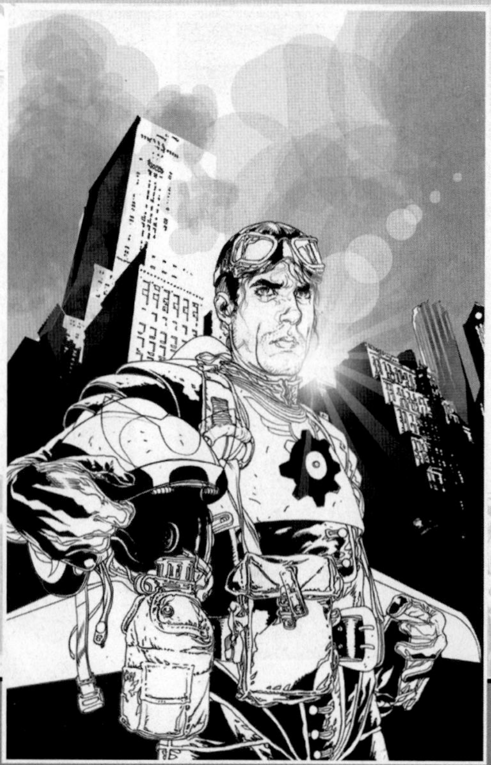

I used a shot of myself here because Jimmy wasn't available. I later shot his head and inserted it, then added the skyline as an afterthought. I really wanted to play with how matted down and sweaty his hair would be under that mask and helmet on a summer day. I thought it all worked out quite well.

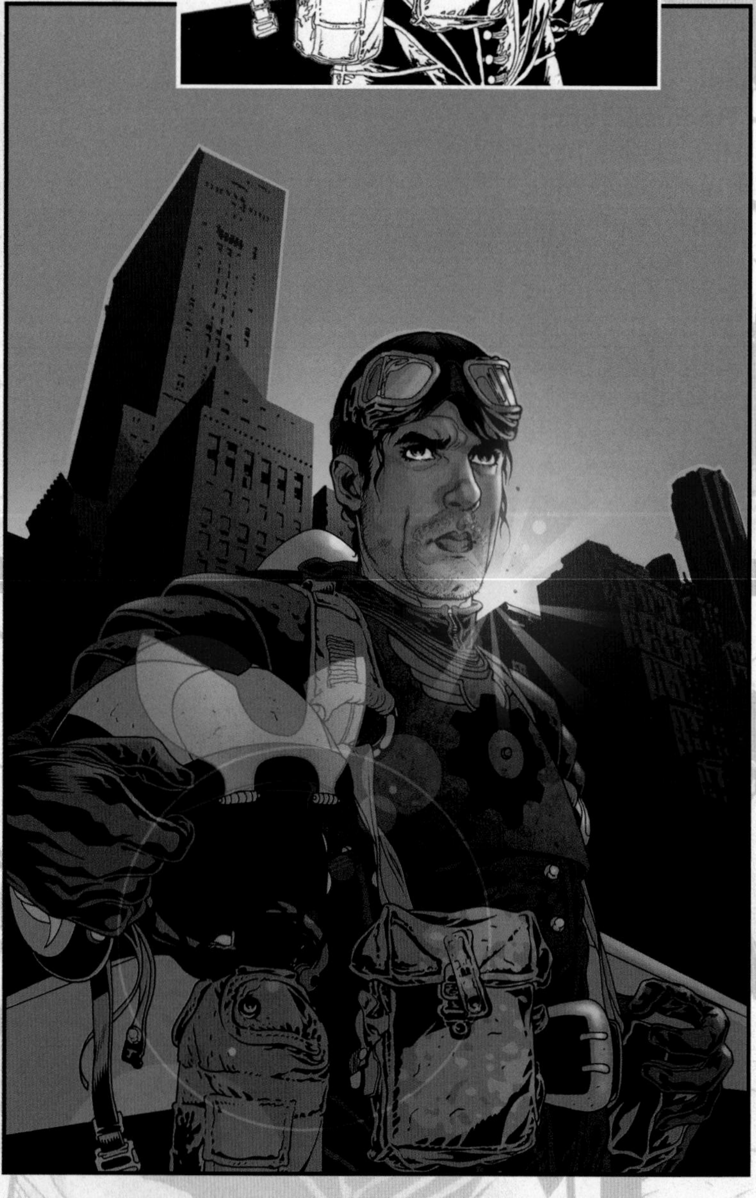

#29

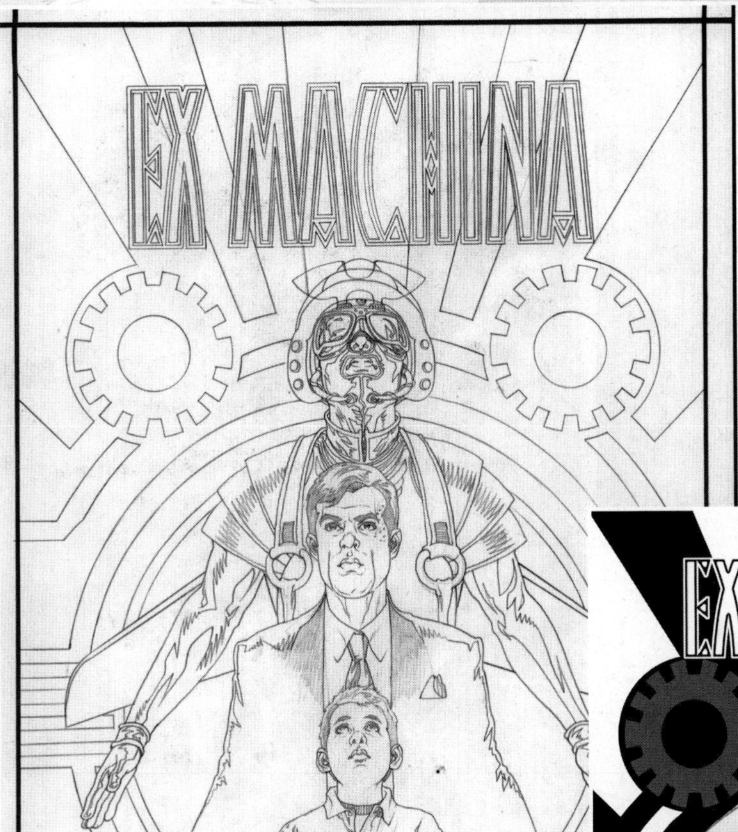
EX MACHINA

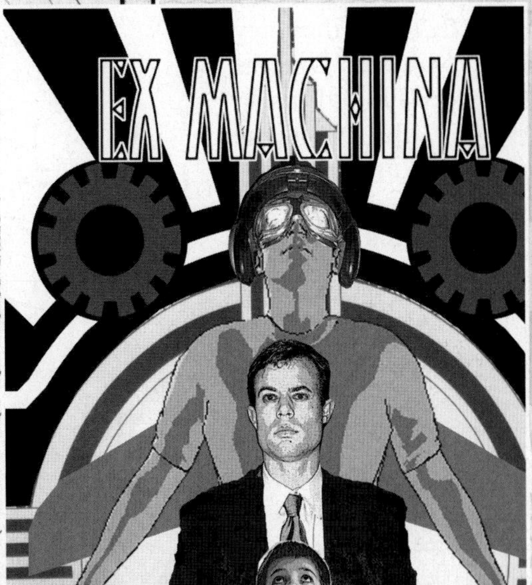
EX MACHINA

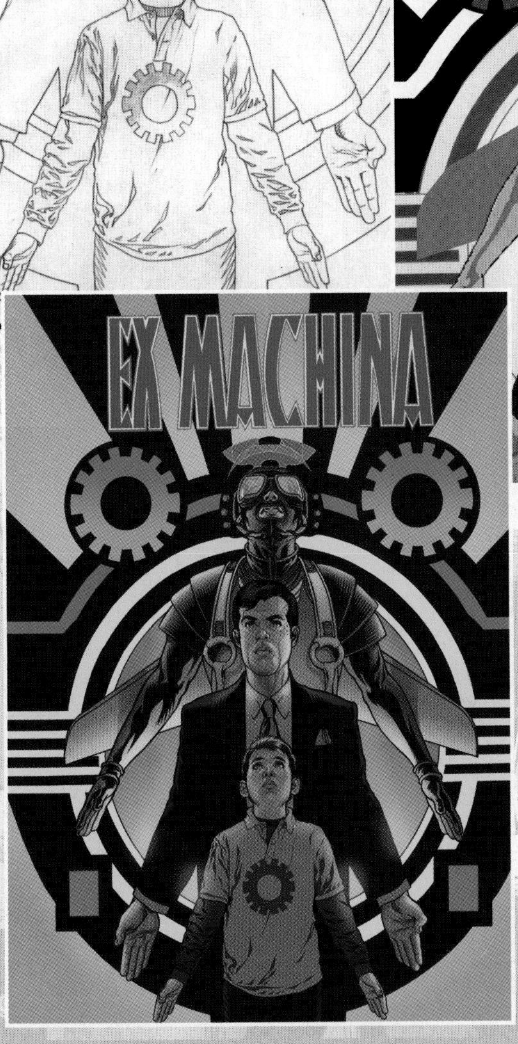
EX MACHINA

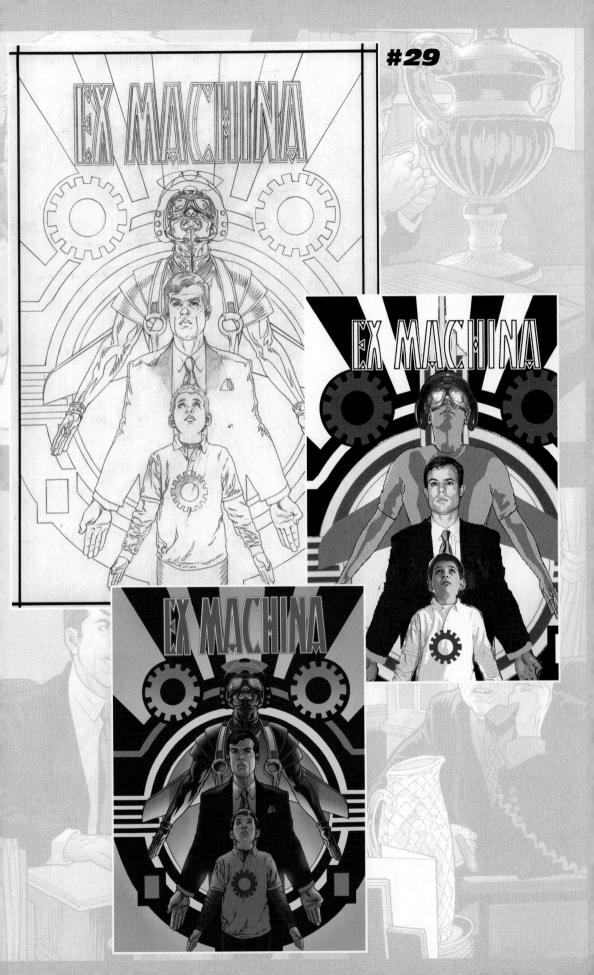

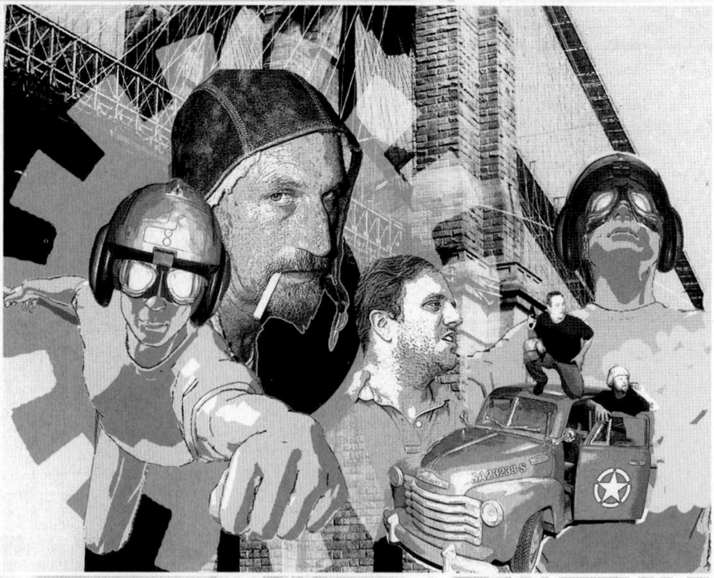

This might be my favorite EX MACHINA image to date. I got lucky with the design flowing properly.

I was worried when it was cut in two (to be the covers to the EX MACHINA SPECIALS) that they wouldn't work as well individually. But after some deliberation I removed the Brooklyn Bridge (pictured in the photo comp) and replaced it with the Statue of Liberty and the NYC skyline featuring the Twin Towers. Then it all came together with the addition of the field of stars.

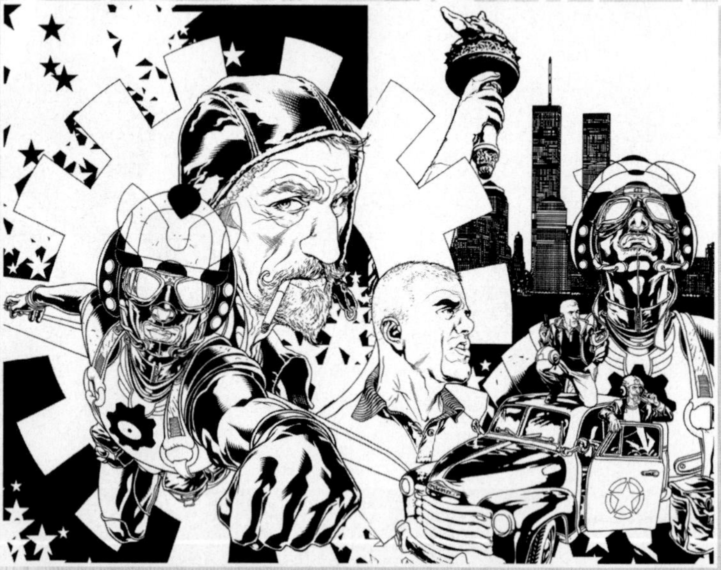

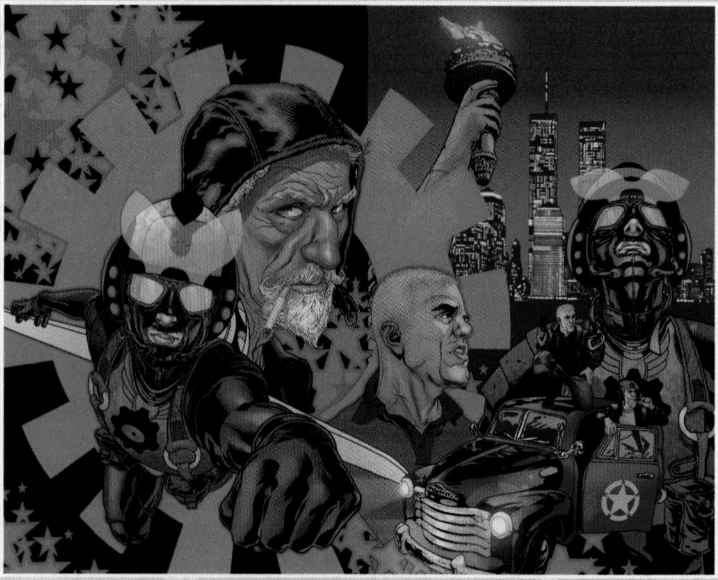

SPECIALS

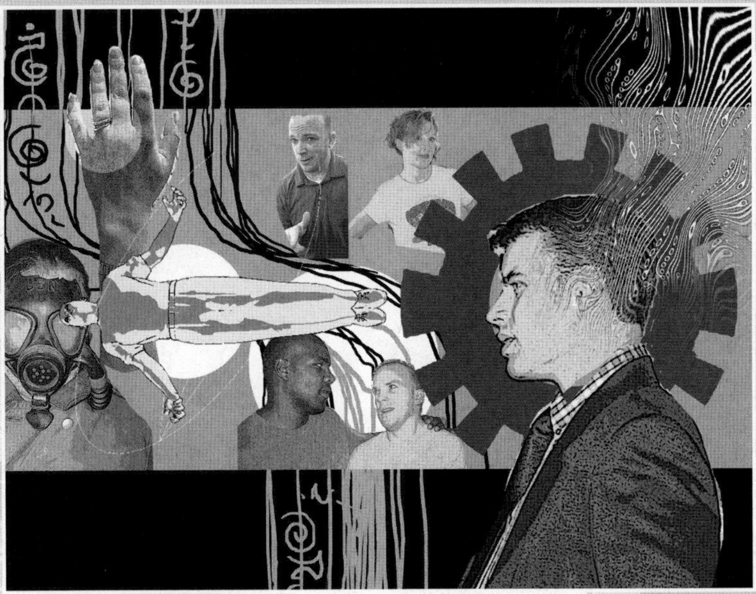

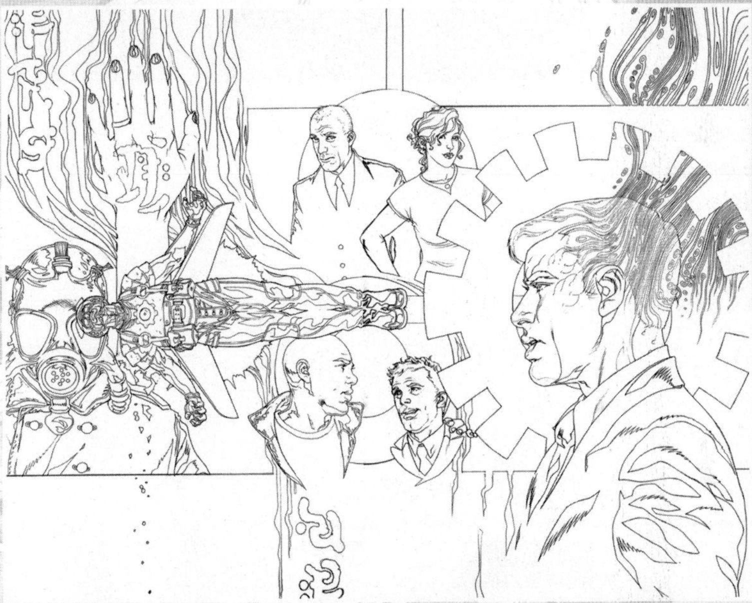

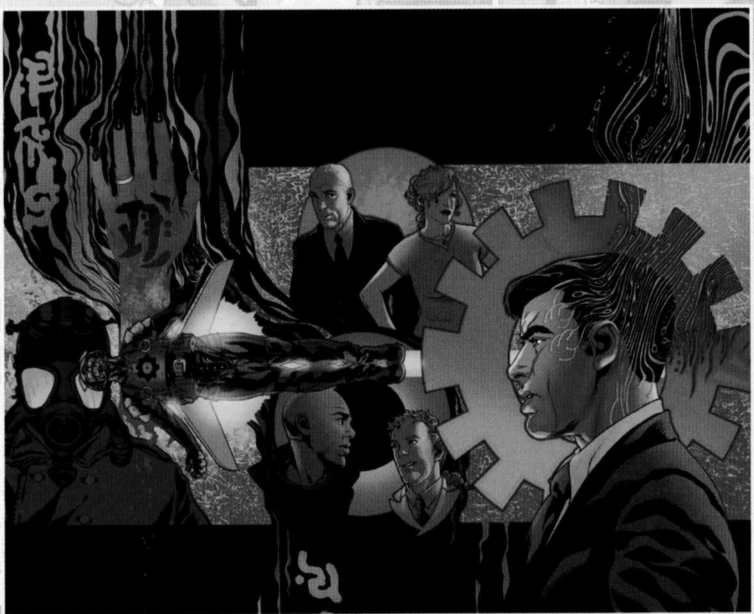

TAG

I used different Tarot Card titles to label the different characters and the issues dealt with in the story arc featured here.

The research and decision-making on this particular cover made it especially rewarding. Plus I got to play with my son's plastic rayguns I used as reference. The juxtaposition of hero and villain on the right side of the image was the cement that brought the whole design home for me.

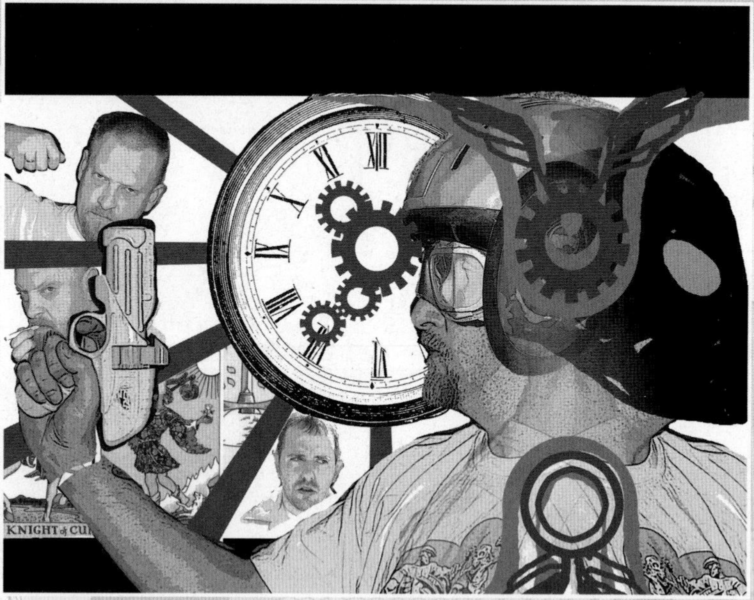

KNIGHT of CU

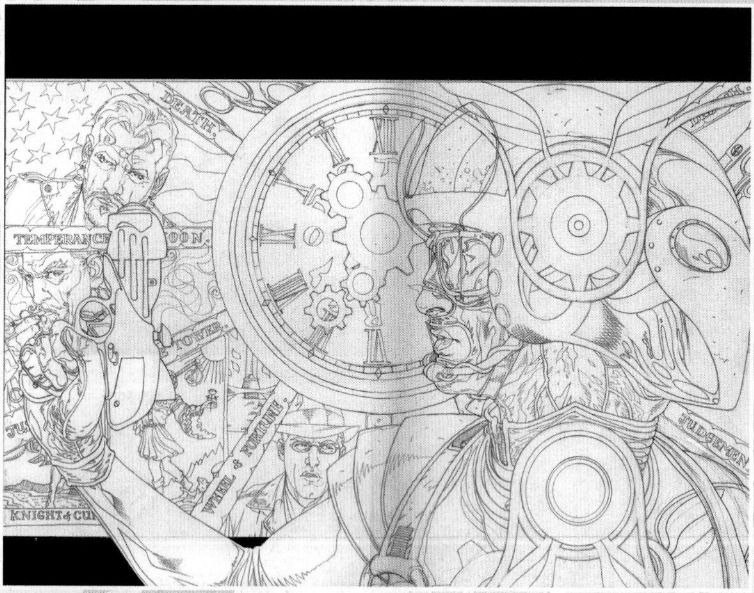

DEATH.
TEMPERANCE
OON.
TOWER.
WHEEL of FORTUNE
JUDGEMEN
KNIGHT of CU

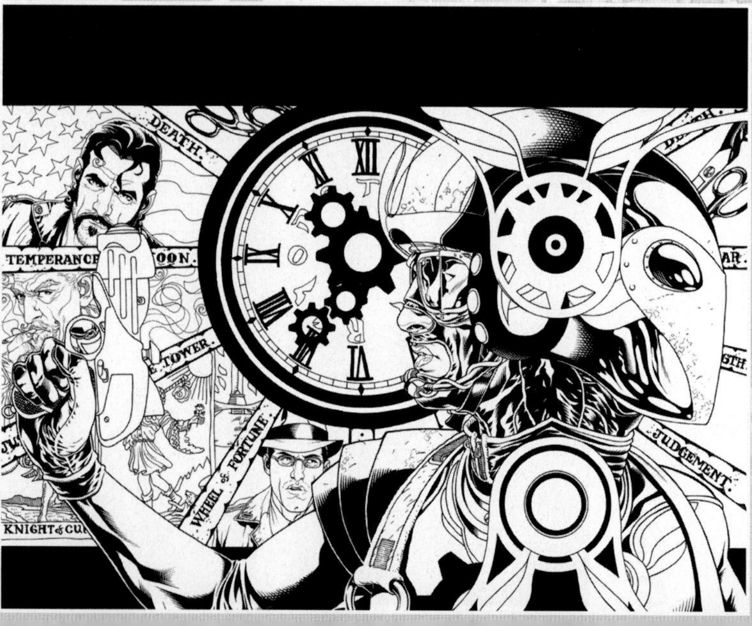

DEATH.
TEMPERANCE
OON.
TOWER.
WHEEL of FORTUNE
JUDGEMENT.
KNIGHT of CU

FACT V. FICTION

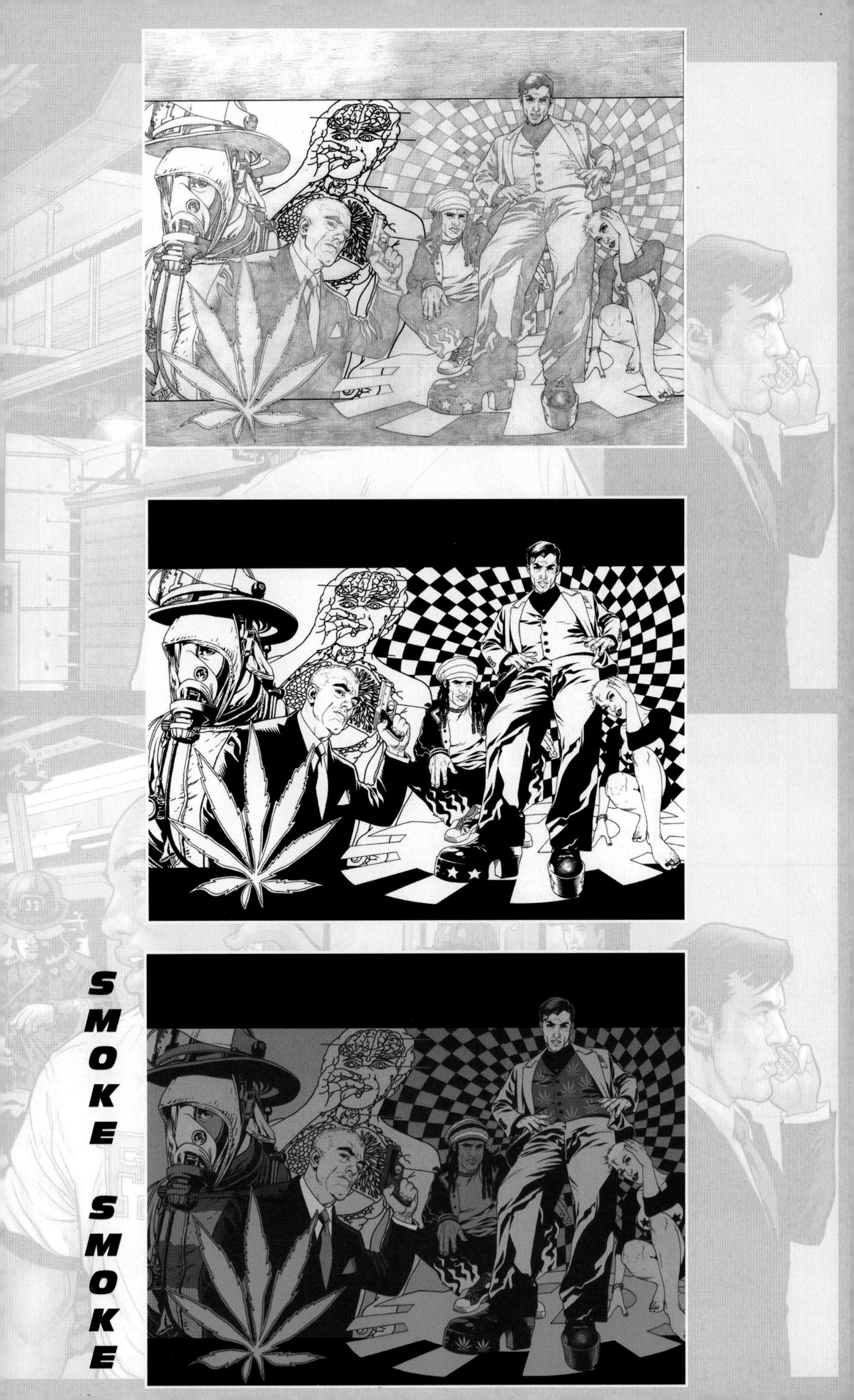
SMOKE SMOKE

Ex Machina: Concepts & Photos

These were some 3-D images of the jet pack Brian Frey built. Originally, I wanted these commissioned so that I could do full turnarounds for photo ref while drawing the Machine in action. It proved to be too time consuming, so it was easier to just keep hard copies laying around and draw the jet pack freehand whenever needed. I did, however, create the entire cover to issue #10 digitally, using one of these images with a "skin" painted on.

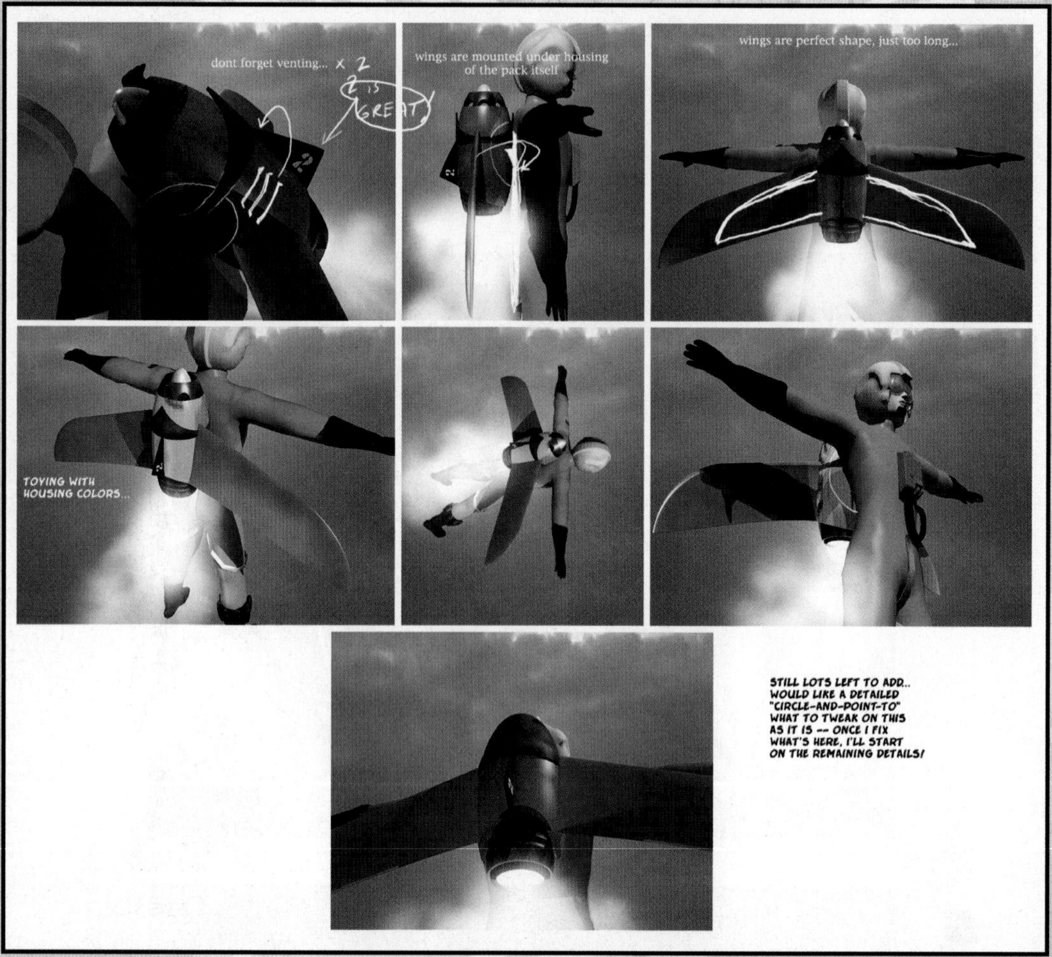
dont forget venting... x 2
2 is GREAT
wings are mounted under housing of the pack itself
wings are perfect shape, just too long...
TOYING WITH HOUSING COLORS...
STILL LOTS LEFT TO ADD.. WOULD LIKE A DETAILED "CIRCLE-AND-POINT-TO" WHAT TO TWEAK ON THIS AS IT IS -- ONCE I FIX WHAT'S HERE, I'LL START ON THE REMAINING DETAILS!

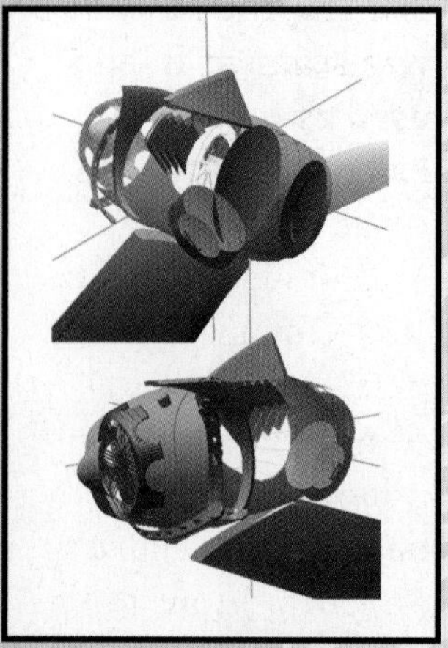

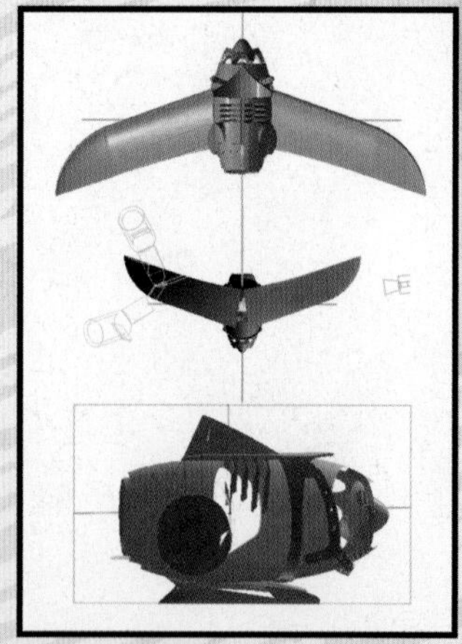

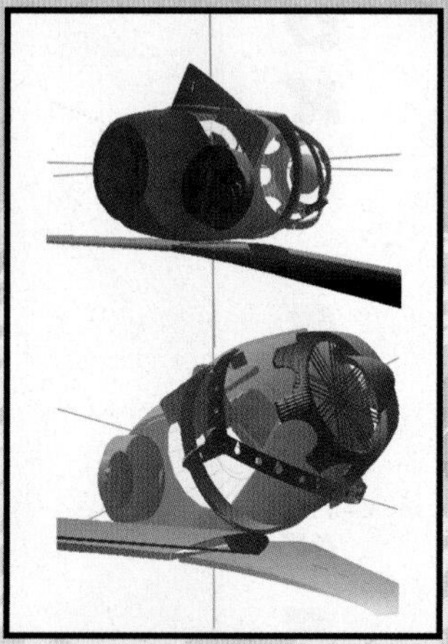

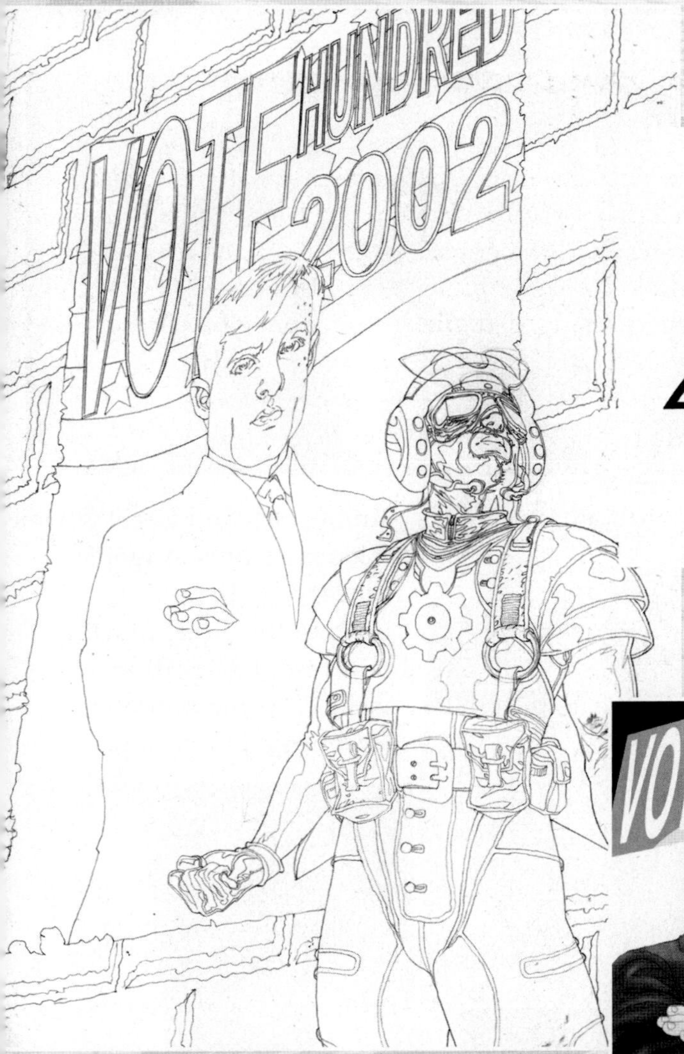
VOTE HUNDRED
2002

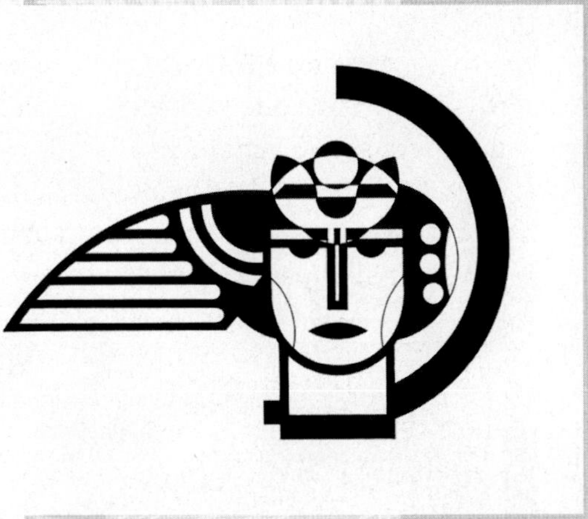

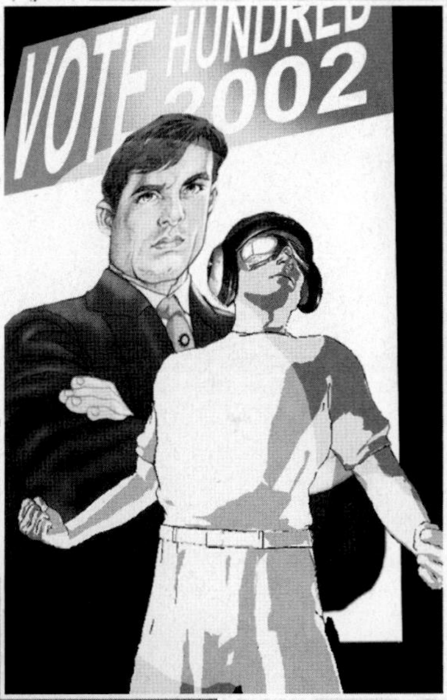
VOTE HUNDRED
2002

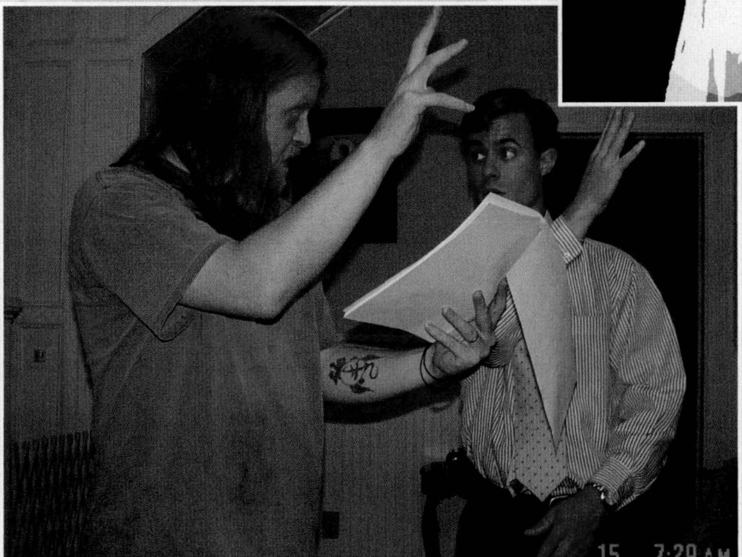
15 7:29 AM

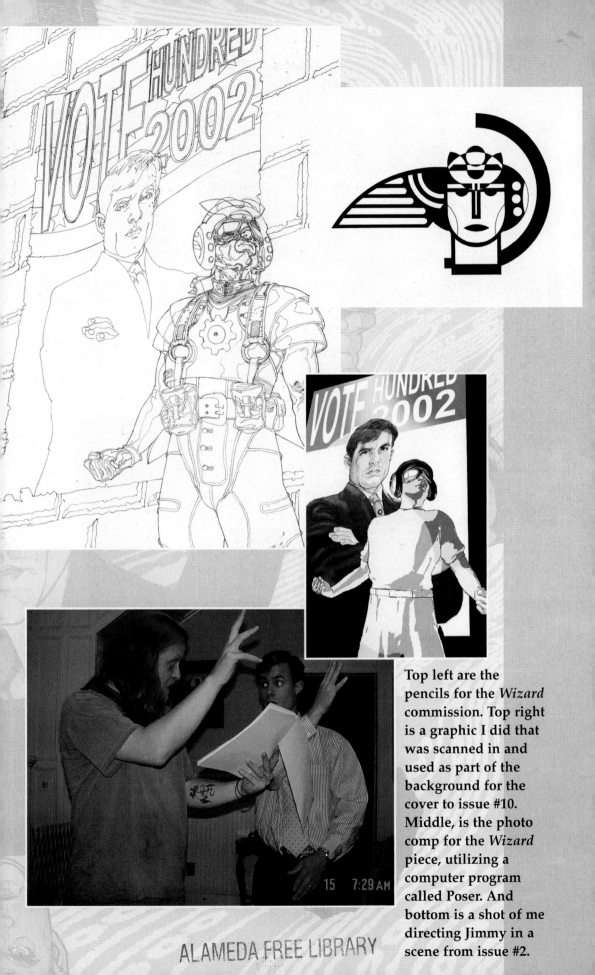

Top left are the pencils for the *Wizard* commission. Top right is a graphic I did that was scanned in and used as part of the background for the cover to issue #10. Middle, is the photo comp for the *Wizard* piece, utilizing a computer program called Poser. And bottom is a shot of me directing Jimmy in a scene from issue #2.

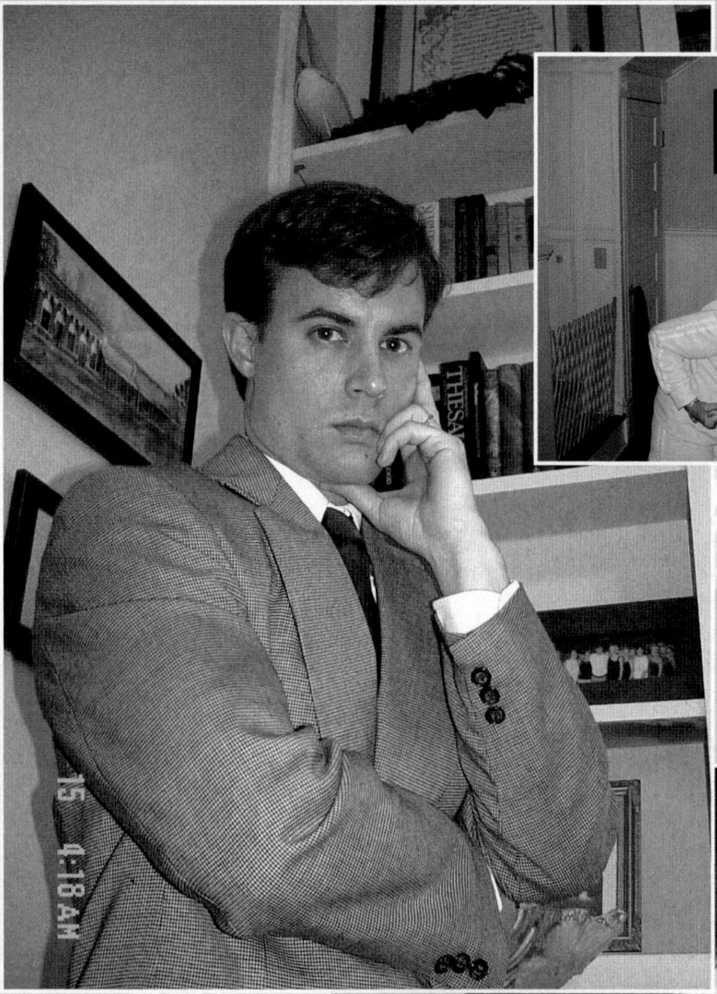

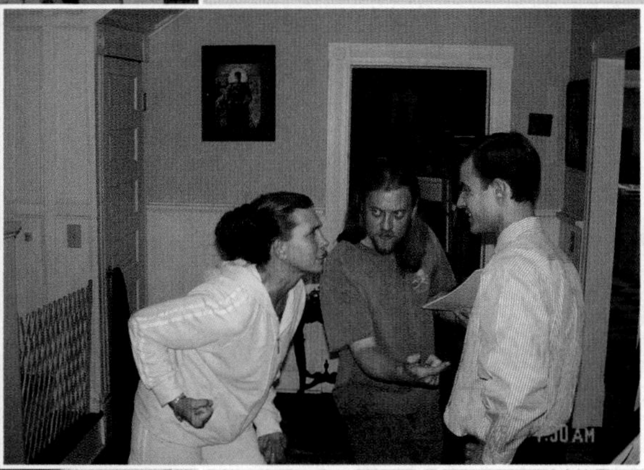

Jimmy Hill and Greta O'Dell (Commissioner Angotti) rehearsing the rooftop beating the Great Machine takes from Angotti in issue 2. At the bottom is Kremlin's aviator cap.

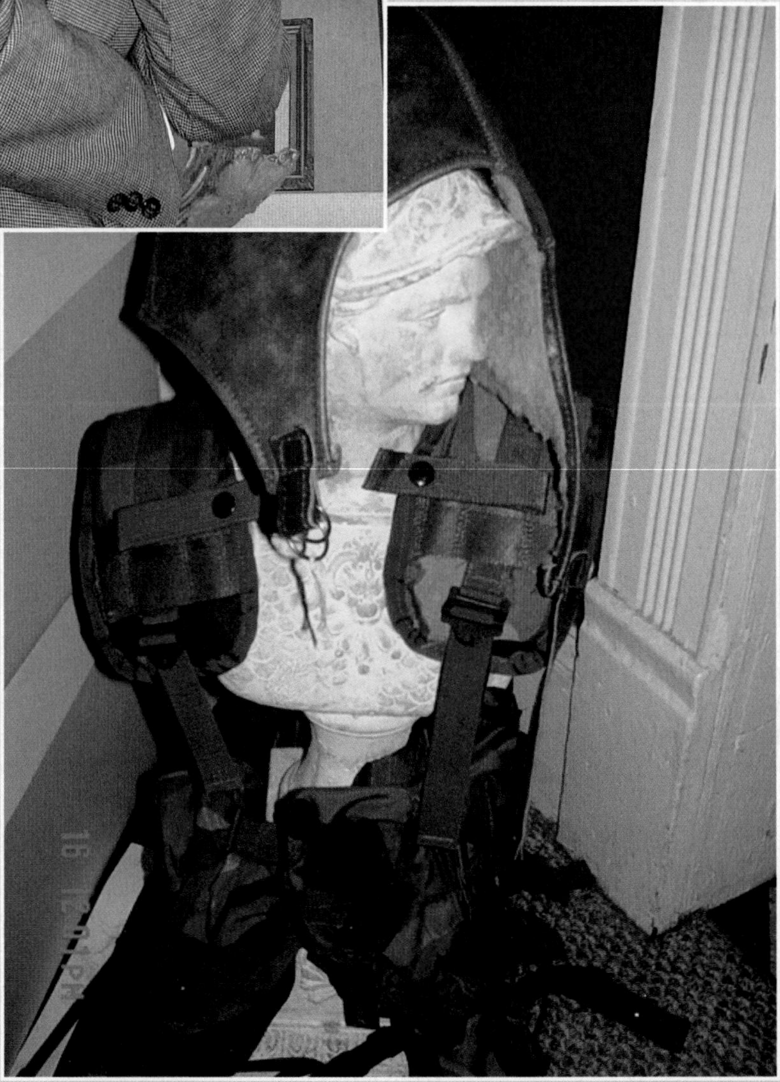

Afterword by Tony Harris

There's an old saying that goes, "I'm my own worst critic." That would totally be true in my case—except for the fact that I have a wife and two children. My wife and kids, specifically my son, are my worst critics. I wouldn't have it any other way. There is an honesty to their comments that makes them pure; the kind of honesty that you can only get from those closest to you.

Back when I was drawing STARMAN for DC Comics, my editor was the legendary Archie Goodwin. Aside from the honor of working for Archie, I also felt he was the single best editor I've ever worked for. He had the same honesty about my art that my wife has. Each month when it was time for me to do the painted cover on the book, I would submit anywhere from one to three sketches for approval. Generally I would try to let Archie know—in a roundabout way—which of the sketches I was leaning toward, without tempering his input. Now here's where it gets interesting. My wife sees everything I do before it goes out the door, in every stage from sketch to pencil, ink or paint. In the four years I worked for Archie, my wife always picked the sketch that Archie would ultimately choose. Every time.

Every single time.

As an artist, it is so important to trust in your ability, your skill. But equally important are the people you surround yourself with. Your confidants. Over the years I have shared studio space with other artists, writers, painters, and friends. They came and went, and sometimes I moved on. These days, my trusted friends, co-workers, and confidants are the guys I work with on EX MACHINA. I can honestly say this is the best collaboration I've experienced in 19 years of working in comics. And as much as I never thought it would happen again, I found in Ben Abernathy the same feeling of trust and comfort that I remember fondly from the years I spent working under Archie Goodwin.

Then there is Brian K. Vaughan. What can I say that everyone else already hasn't?

It's all been said so I won't repeat it. But I can speak to what it's like to work with him. I've been blessed to work with a lot of talented writers, but this working relationship is the truest collaboration I've experienced. I came to EX MACHINA on the back end of Brian's deal with WildStorm, so it was a shock and surprise that he was so open to what I had to say and what I had to show him. The Great Machine went from being a typical superhero with a cape to the leather clad, jetpack-wearing, helmeted gimp we all love today. And once I was on board, I had some other ideas, too. I went to Brian with them and much to my surprise he liked them. I gotta say I wasn't used to that from writers; a lot of them are very guarded when it comes to their scripts and they want drawn exactly what was written. Brian wants that to, but he also wants his script interpreted. He wants to collaborate. Lucky me.

Guess who else I trust? You. I really don't have a choice. Team Machina put a book about politics in your hands, and you all "got" it. You made it fly. And all of us on the team immediately got it, too. I think that's why we all signed on so quickly. A lot of people didn't think it would work, so I wonder: how's that working out for them now, do you think?

I had hoped to give you all a special treat with this book. An inside look at the Machine. How it works, and how we work. Hopefully we did that, and right now you are twice as excited about EX MACHINA as you were before you read this. The funny part is, we just arrived at the halfway point! I realized this the other day when I started working on issue 28. We have so much more to come—so many more great stories and hopefully some creative leaps in the art. My point is, we are just getting warmed up and the future looks bright. Thanks so much for making it possible to see my dreams come true on such a great project.

- Tony Harris, 2006

A NOTE FROM THE EDITOR:

We don't have enough room to show all of the script for the MASQUERADE special here, so the following pages excerpt the beginning and end. John Paul Leon's original pencils are presented to keep Brian's words company! As you can see, we had different versions of page one, and I wanted to find out why...

A NOTE FROM THE ARTIST:

On the first version I wanted to leave a frame on the splash to hint at the fact that it was a shot of a TV image. Ended up looking too "art nouveau" and frilly, so I redid it as a full bleed to emphasize the image and not the decorative quality of the lettering. In retrospect, the title lettering should have been bolder and more contemporary. This turn of the century, carnival look seemed right at the time.

It was a pleasure working with Brian and Tony, and I thank them for the opportunity to be part of such an original book.

-John Paul Leon

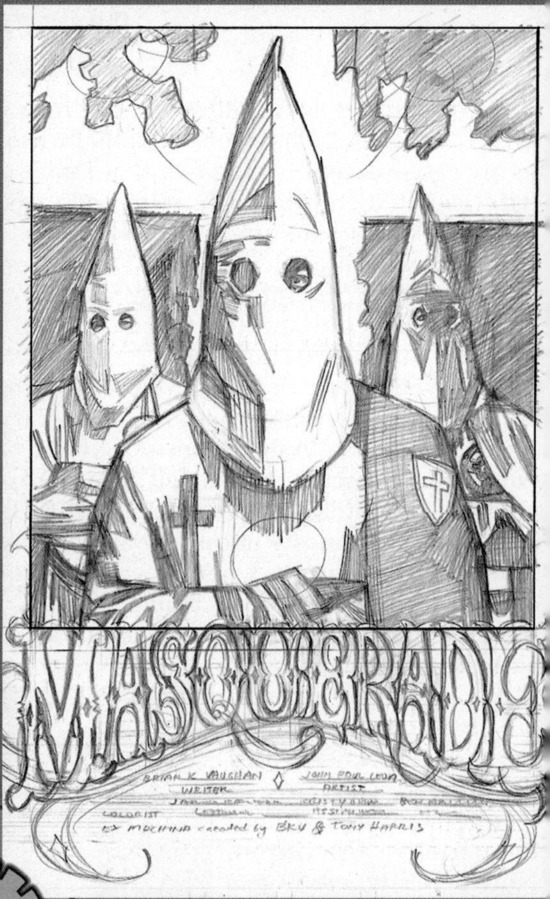
MASQUERADE
BRIAN K VAUGHAN
WRITER
JOHN PAUL LEON
ARTIST
EX MACHINA created by BKV & TONY HARRIS

The Full Script for
EX MACHINA
MASQUERADE SPECIAL
Prepared for WildStorm Comics

April 9, 2007 Brian K. Vaughan

John - Great to be working with you, man! I'm a HUGE fan of your artwork. Anyway, my scripts are pretty detailed (to help save you some time gathering reference, I'll occasionally throw in some annoying web links), but these panel descriptions are just suggestions. If you ever see a better way to layout a page or frame a shot, please go to town. I trust you completely. And feel free to drop me an email or give me a call with any questions. - BKV

Page One

Page One, SPLASH
Okay, we're gonna open with this unexpected shot of a GRAND WIZARD OF THE KU KLUX KLAN dressed in full robe and mask, maybe something like this: http://www.ferris.edu/jimcrow/question/kkk.jpg

He has his white fist raised in the air as he screams at the top of his voice. Please leave us some room somewhere in this shot for TITLE AND CREDITS:

1) Klansman: The degenerate heathens took marriage from us and you said nothing!

2) Klansman: The mongrel invaders took jobs from us and you said nothing!

3) Klansmen: HOW LONG WILL YOU BE SILENT?!

4) Title:

MASQUERADE

5) Credits:

Brian K. Vaughan - Writer John Paul Leon - Penciller
_________ - Inker
__________ - Colorist
Jared K Fletcher - Letterer
Kristy Quinn - Assistant Editor
Ben Abernathy - Editor

Ex Machina created by BKV & Tony Harris

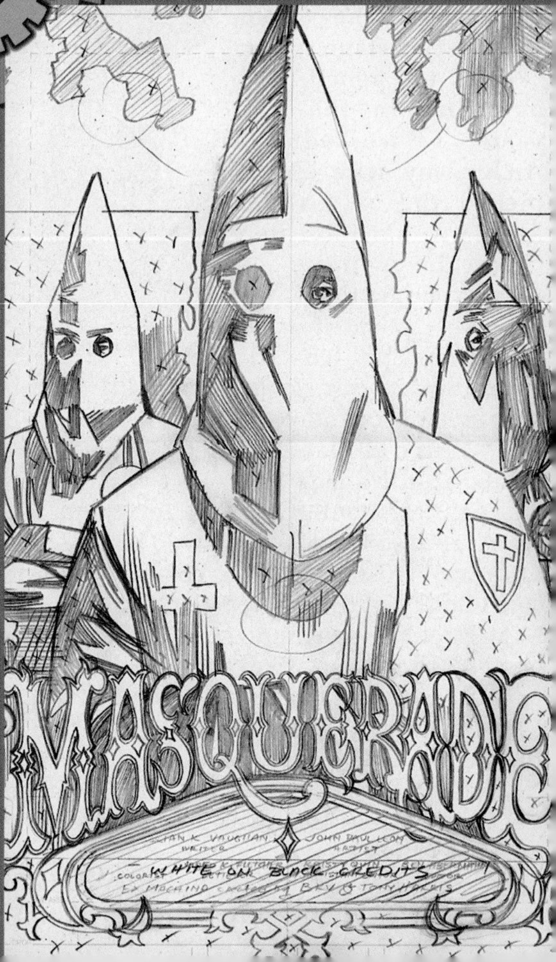
MASQUERADE
WHITE ON BLACK CREDITS

Page Two

Page Two, Panel One

Smash cut to our story's present (2003) for this close-up of MAYOR MITCHELL HUNDRED. Ben should be able to get you plenty of reference for all of these characters.

1) Mitchell: Jesus, what year is this?

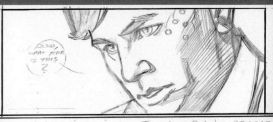

Page Two, Panel Two

Okay, this is a device we use in lieu of captions every so often, John. It's not so much a panel, as it is the thin, page-wide gutter between panels one and three. On the right of this strip of white newsprint will be a typewritten date that our letterer can handle. We're trying to simulate the look of the date that's in the corner of every page of most newspapers.

2) Date (in the style of a right-justified newspaper heading):

Tuesday, October 25, 2003

Page Two, Panel Three

Pull out to the largest panel of the page to reveal that we're inside the Mayor's UPSTAIRS OFFICE inside City Hall (see the end of the first chapter of "Tag" for reference, but feel free to use your imagination, since Mitch is always changing offices). Mitchell is watching that image of the Klansman from Page One on a FLATSCREEN TELEVISION, and the Mayor is joined by two other characters: DAVE WYLIE (our African-American Deputy Mayor) and CANDY (the mayor's heavyset female Chief of Staff).

3) Candy: It's from six months ago, Mayor Hundred. Upstate New York. Believe it or not, the Klan has made a bit of a comeback since 9/11.

4) Wylie: They're downplaying the whole black/white angle and exploiting more "mainstream" hot-button shit. And now they want to hold a rally in Central Park.

5) Mitchell: Well, it's a good thing they can't, not according to subsection 4 of Penal Code Section 240.35.

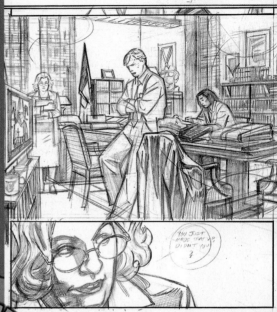

Page Two, Panel Four

Push in close on a skeptical Candy.

6) Candy: You just made that up, didn't you?

JESUS, WHAT YEAR IS THIS ?
Tuesday, October 25, 2003
YOU JUST MADE THAT UP, DIDN'T YOU ?

Page Three

Page Three, Panel One

Pull out for this shot of Mitchell and Candy.

1) Mitchell: What, you don't have faith in my memorization skills, Sandy?

2) Candy: I've been your Chief of Staff for nearly two years and you still can't remember my four-digit extension.

3) Candy: And my name is Candy.

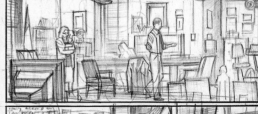

Page Three, Panel Two

Pull out to the largest panel of the page for a shot of all three characters, and please leave some room for Mitchell's talky-talk:

4) Mitchell: It started back in the 1800s, when New York passed a law to deal with destitute farmers who terrorized their landlords while wearing leather masks.

5) Mitchell: That paved the way for today's anti-mask laws, which forbid our fine constituents from gathering while in disguise, unless it's for "approved entertainment."

6) Candy: Isn't that unconstitutional?

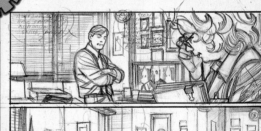

Page Three, Panel Three

Change angles on the duo, as Mitchell walks over to a nearby BOOKSHELF.

7) Mitchell: Not according to the Second Circuit Court of Appeals.

8) Mitchell: They agreed the law doesn't violate the First Amendment because it regulates conduct, not speech.

9) Candy: No offense, Mr. Mayor, but how in the world do you know all this?

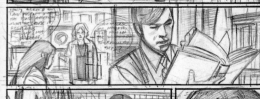

Page Three, Panel Four

Push in on Mitchell, as he picks up his old GREAT MACHINE HELMET, and holds it up to look at here.

10) Mitchell: I'm afraid my previous line of work required an intimate knowledge of the legalities--or lack thereof--that come with wearing a goofy-ass costume.

Page Three, Panel Five

Cut over to Wylie.

11) Wylie: I think that's what the Klan is counting on, sir.

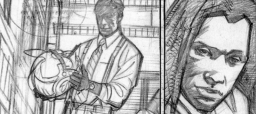

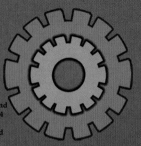

Page Four

Page Four, Panel One

Pull out, as Mitchell (who's holding the helmet under one of his arms here) turns to speak with Wylie.

1) Mitchell: What is that supposed to mean, Wylie?

2) Wylie: I've been doing a little research of my own, and the Klan still thinks they can make a case that Subsection 4 violates their freedom of expression.

3) Wylie: These assholes would love the attention that'd come with a retrial, and they're gonna use you to get one.

Page Four, Panel Two

Change angles for this shot of Candy and a confused Mitchell.

4) Mitchell: Me?

5) Candy: Oh my God, the Deputy Mayor is right.

6) Candy: If you of all people exploit an anti-mask law to deny the KKK a permit, they're going to paint you to be a massive hypocrite.

Page Four, Panel Three

Pull out to the largest panel of the page for a shot of all three characters, as Wylie watches Mitchell argue with Candy. Mitchell is holding up his helmet for them to look at here.

7) Mitchell: That's the most insane comparison of all time, Candy! The Klan wears their duds to intimidate minorities.

8) Mitchell: In case it's slipped your mind, I wore this thing the day I intimidated a fucking plane from flying into another one of our buildings!

9) Wylie: And the KKK will argue that they're also trying to defend this country, that they deserve the same anonymity you enjoyed in your "superhero" days.

Page Four, Panel Four

Push in on Candy and Wylie, both of whom look concerned.

10) Candy: After everything this city has been through, the last thing we need is a demonstration by these subhumans.

11) Wylie: For once, Candy and I actually agree. Fighting this rally might cost me my ACLU card, but I'd much rather keep my credentials with the NAACP.

12) Wylie: How the hell do we win this one, sir?

(CONTINUED ON NEXT PAGE...)

Page Four, Panel Five

Push in on Mitchell, who appears lost in thought.

13) Wylie (from off): Sir?

Page Four, Panel Six

Finally, push in even tighter for this extreme close-up of MITCHELL'S GREEN EYES.

No Copy

EX MACHINA
INTERIORS
SIR?

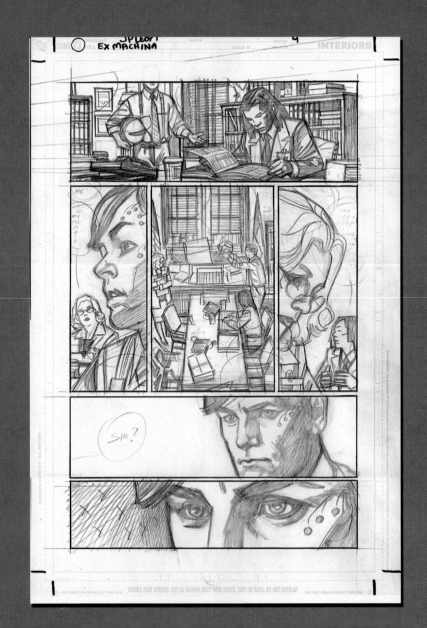

Page Five

Page Five, Panel One

Smash cut to a few years earlier for a similar "letterbox" page-wide panel that's a close-up of Mitchell's green eyes. But this time, they're framed by what appears to be some WHITE BANDAGES.

1) Pharmacist (from off): Let me guess…

Page Five, Panel Two

Once again, this is a thin, page-wide gutter between panels one and three. On the right of this strip of white newsprint will be a typewritten date that our letterer can handle.

2) Date (in the style of a right-justified newspaper heading):

Sunday, October 31, 1999

Page Five, Panel Three

Pull out to the largest panel of the page to reveal MITCHELL HUNDRED just a few weeks after the accident that gave him his powers. He's standing inside a PHARMACY, and he's wearing a trenchcoat and simple civilian clothes. Most importantly, his ENTIRE HEAD (except his eyes, nose, and mouth) is COVERED IN BANDAGES, a bit like this: http://www.movie-gazette.com/cinereviews/gallery.asp?id=1351&img=http://images.movie-gazette.com/albums/20050504/face-of-another-02.jpg

3) Pharmacist (from off): …you're supposed to be the Invisible Man, right?

Page Five, Panel Four

Pull out to reveal that Mitchell is the only person in line at this pharmacy, and he's speaking to a FEMALE PHARMACIST (in a white lab coat) who's wearing CAT EARS and has WHISKERS painted on her face. There can be some HALLOWEEN DECORATIONS around to help explain what the hell is going on for those who missed the date up above…

4) Pharmacist: 'Cause the Mummy never wore a pervy trenchcoat like that.

5) Mitchell: Um, actually, I was in an accident.
6) Mitchell: An… explosion.

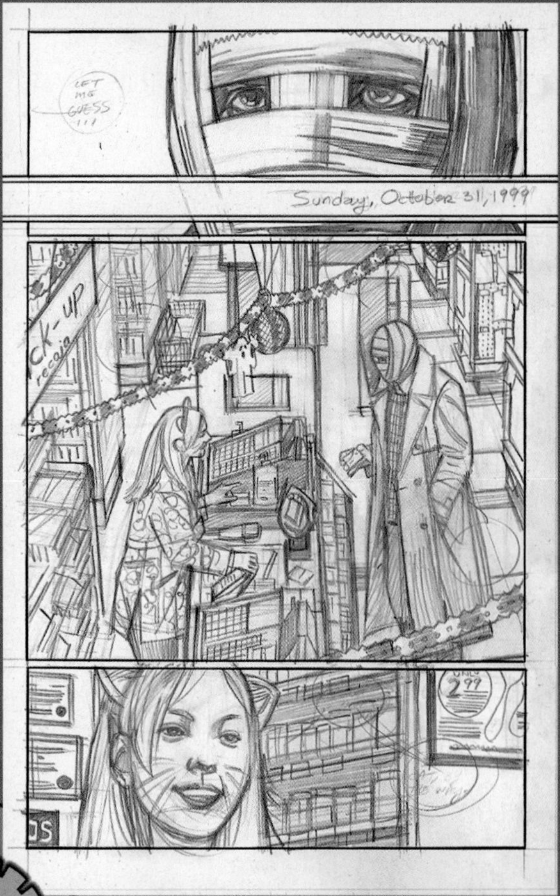
LET ME GUESS...
Sunday, October 31, 1999
ck-up

Page Six

Page Six, Panel One

Push in close on the woman, as she smiles at us stupidly.

1) Pharmacist: Cool. I didn't get that.
2) Pharmacist: I'm a cat, by the way.

Page Six, Panel Two

Cut back to the bandaged Mitchell.

3) Mitchell: What?
4) Mitchell: No, this isn't a costume. I just got released from the hospital.

Page Six, Panel Three

Pull out to the largest panel of the page for another shot of both characters, as the horrified woman suddenly covers her mouth in embarrassment.

5) Pharmacist: Oh. Oh, jeez.
6) Pharmacist: You're… you're not joking?

7) Mitchell: No, I'm a civil engineer. Was. I was inspecting this thing attached to the Brooklyn Bridge when it--

Page Six, Panel Four

Push in closer on the two.

8) Pharmacist: I am so sorry, Mister, uh…

9) Mitchell: Hundred.
10) Mitchell: And it's fine. I just need my prescription.

Page Six, Panel Five

This is just a shot of the woman, as she sheepishly holds up Mitchell's MasterCard.

11) Pharmacist: Sure, um, if I could maybe get a different card?
12) Pharmacist: This one seems to be overdrawn.

Page Six, Panel Six

Cut to an annoyed and depressed Mitchell, as he reaches into his trenchcoat for something.

13) Mitchell: Wow, this month just keeps getting better and--

14) Another Voice (from off): Happy Halloween, kiddies!

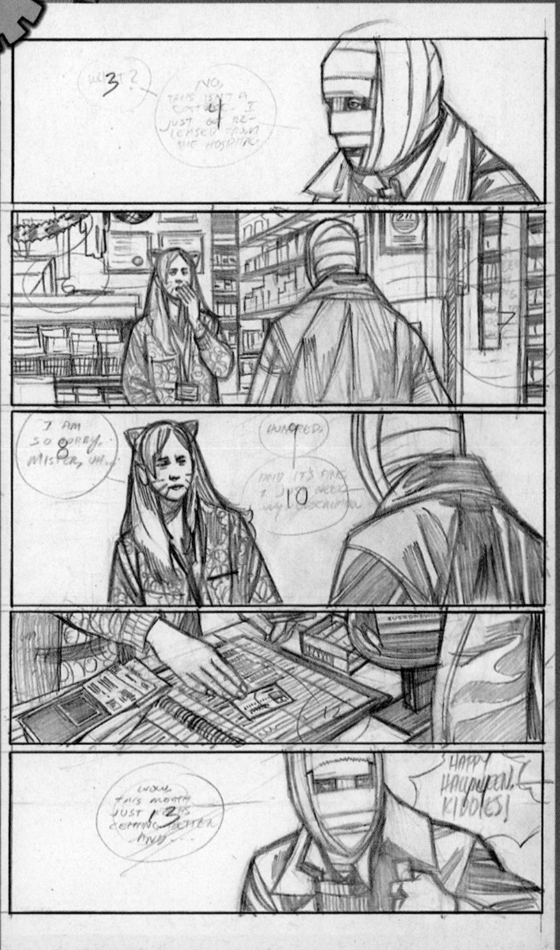
I AM SO SORRY, MISTER, UH...
HAPPY HALLOWEEN, KIDDIES!

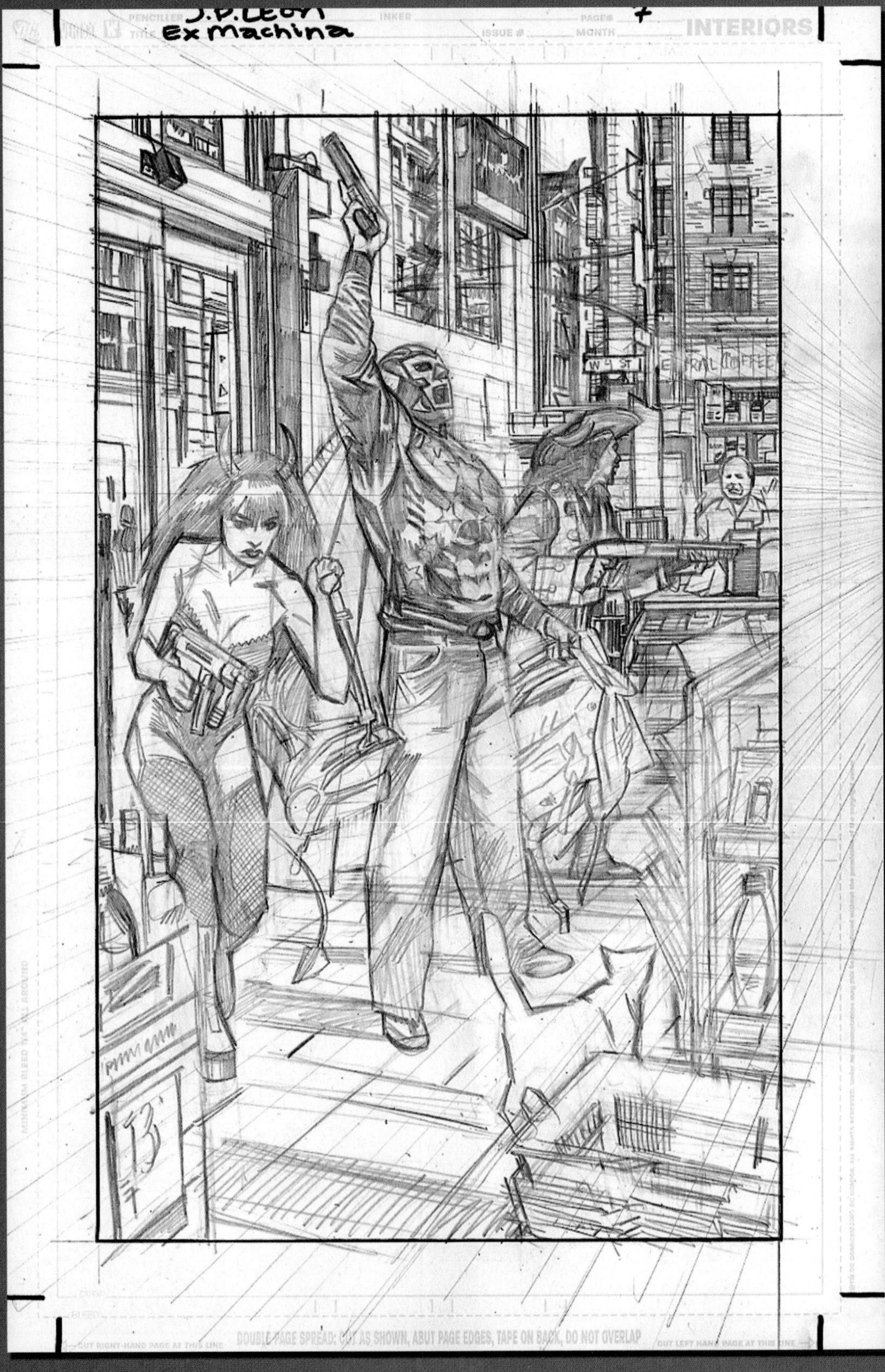
PENCILLER J.P. Leon
TITLE Ex Machina
INKER
PAGE# 7
ISSUE #
MONTH
INTERIORS
W 4 ST
COFFEE
13
DOUBLE PAGE SPREAD: CUT AS SHOWN, ABUT PAGE EDGES, TAPE ON BACK, DO NOT OVERLAP

A NOTE FROM THE EDITOR:

I couldn't resist showing this page a little bigger.

Page Seven

Page Seven, SPLASH
        Cut over to the entrance to the pharmacy for this bizarre SPLASH, where we find THREE GUN-TOTING ROBBERS dressed in Halloween costumes. There's a MALE PIRATE wearing a fake beard, and a painted-red FEMALE DEVIL wearing horns and sexy attire. Standing in front of these two is their leader, a guy dressed as a SUPERHERO, but not any existing heroes, please. I'm picturing a simple cape and cowl sort of like Space Ghost's, but a very different color scheme (yellow and purple, maybe?) to suggest that this is an entirely original character. The CUSTOMERS and OTHER EMPLOYEES in this shot all look SCARED and CONFUSED by these gun-toting thugs.

        1) Superhero: Trick or fuckin' treat.

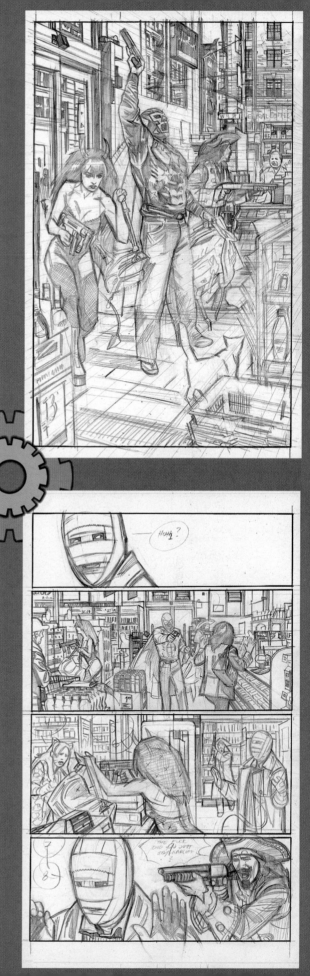

Page Eight

Page Eight, Panel One
        Cut to Mitchell, who's clearly not sure whether or not this is a JOKE.

        1) Mitchell: Huh?

Page Eight, Panel Two
        Cut to the "Superhero," as he starts aiming his gun at FRIGHTENED CUSTOMERS.

        2) Superhero: Everyone, kindly get your cash out.
        3) Superhero: Fuck with us and we kill you, then crash your funeral and rape your orphaned kids.

Page Eight, Panel Three
        Cut to the crying female pharmacist for this largest panel of the page, as the gun-toting Devil Girl hands her an empty DUFFEL BAG.

        4) Pharmacist: I don't wanna die!

        5) Devil Girl: Cool beans, then fill this bag with Norco, Oxy, and whatever other goodies you keep in the vault.
        6) Devil Girl: And stop crying like a sissy.

Page Eight, Panel Four
        Cut over to Mitchell (who's speaking to the off-panel Devil Girl), as the nearby "Pirate" angrily asks him a question.

        7) Mitchell: Leave her alone.
        8) Mitchell: She's doing what you want.

        9) Pirate: The fuck did you just say, Karloff?

Page Nine

Page Nine, Panel One

Pull out, as Mitchell takes out his wallet and hands it to the Pirate, who keeps his gun aimed at Mitchell's chest.

1) Mitchell: Nothing. Here's my wallet.

2) Mitchell: I'm broke, so all you're costing me is another trip to the DMV.

3) Pirate: Shut up and empty your pockets.

Page Nine, Panel Two

This is just a close-up of Mitch, deciding that he has nothing to lose, so why not make a stand?

4) Mitchell: …

5) Mitchell: No.

Page Nine, Panel Three

And this shot can be from Mitch's P.O.V., as the pissed-off pirate COCKS his gun and aims it right at our FACE.

6) Pirate: Idiot.

Page Nine, Panel Four

Cut to Mitchell, who FLINCHES in fear. He doesn't realize that he's using his powers to telepathically control machines, but we can see something GLOWING GREEN beneath the bandages on the left side of his face.

7) Mitchell (unique font, green): Please don't shoot.

Page Nine, Panel Five

Pull out to a shot of both men for this largest panel of the page. The pirate SQUEEZES his trigger… but much to Mitchell's relief, nothing seems to happen.

8) SFX (from gun): klick klick

9) Pirate: The hell…?

NOTHING. HERE'S MY WALLET.
I'M BROKE, SO ALL YOU'RE COSTING ME IS ANOTHER TRIP TO THE DMV.
SHUT UP AND EMPTY YOUR POCKETS.
... NO.
IDIOT
7
KLICK KLICK
THE HELL...?

Page Ten

Page Ten, Panel One

Push in on the pirate, as he looks at his malfunctioning gun.

1) Pirate: Lucky boy.

Page Ten, Panel Two

Pull out to the largest panel of the page, as the pirate then brutally PISTOL-WHIPS Mitchell with his gun, knocking our hero to the ground!

2) Mitchell: AHNF!

Page Ten, Panel Three

Change angles, as the Pirate begins callously going through the fallen Mitchell's pockets.

No Copy

Page Ten, Panel Four

Push in on the confused pirate, as he holds up an old-fashioned POCKET WATCH: http://upload.wikimedia.org/wikipedia/commons/thumb/4/45/MontreGousset001.jpg/250px-MontreGousset001.jpg

3) Pirate: You almost took a bullet… for this?

Page Ten, Panel Five

Cut down to Mitchell, as he looks up at us and HISSES something through bloody teeth.

4) Mitchell: Get fucked.

5) Superhero (from off): Timbers!

LUCKY BOY.
AHNF!
YOU ALMOST TOOK A BULLET ... FOR THIS?
GET FUCKED
TIMBERS!

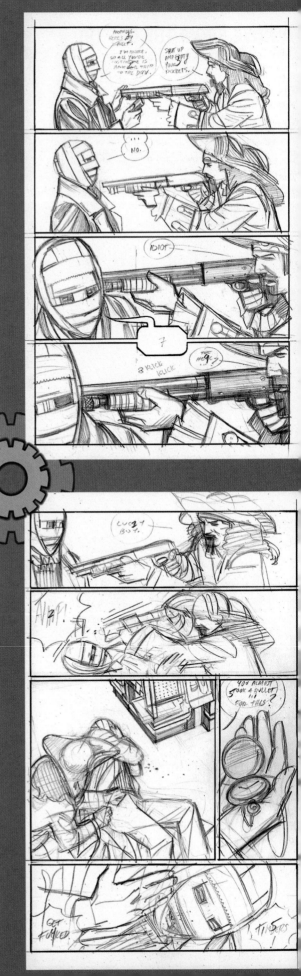

Page Eleven

Page Eleven, Panel One

Cut back to the entrance for the largest panel of the page, where the Superhero and Demon Girl are standing with overflowing duffel bags.

1) Superhero: Demonica and I are ready to rock if you're just about done getting boys' phone numbers.

Page Eleven, Panel Two

Cut back to the pirate, as he pockets Mitchell's watch and RUNS after his friends.

2) Pirate: Yeah, yeah, keep your trunks on, Cape Fear.

Page Eleven, Panel Three

Change angles, as Mitchell slowly gets to his feet. Behind him, the female pharmacist SCREAMS in disbelief.

3) Pharmacist: Holy crap!
4) Pharmacist: What was that?

5) Mitchell: Call the police.

Page Eleven, Panel Four

Push in on the pharmacist.

6) Pharmacist: No duh!
7) Pharmacist: But where are you going!

Page Eleven, Panel Five

Cut back to Mitchell, as he bravely RUNS for the exit.

8) Mitchell: After them.

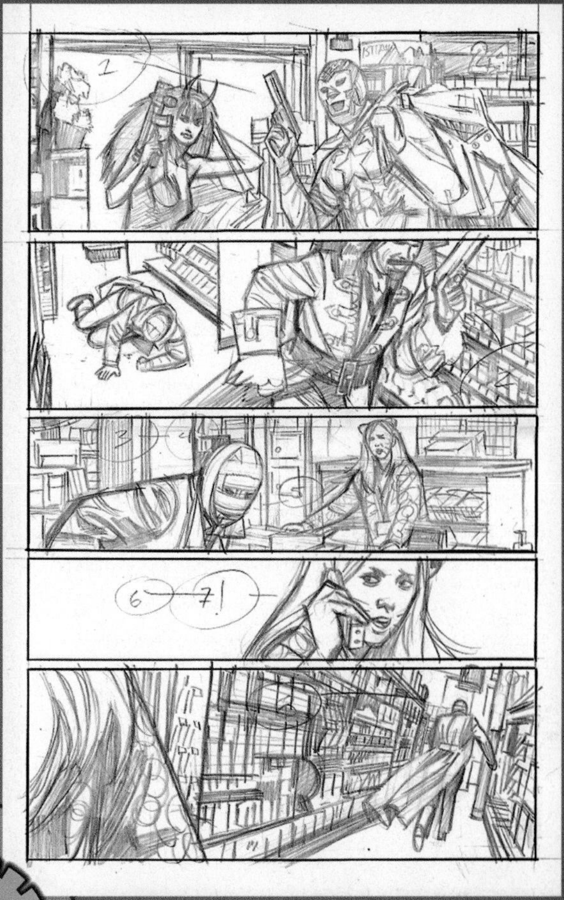

Page Twelve

Page Twelve, Panel One

Cut outside, as Mitchell runs out into the night.

1) Mitchell: I'm not gonna let those bastards get…

Pages Twelve, Panel Two

Finally, we're looking over Mitchell's shoulder in the foreground of this three-quarter SPLASH, as he stops in his tracks and we reveal that we're smack in the middle of the WEST VILLAGE HALLOWEEN PARADE, where Mitchell is confronted by HUNDREDS OF REVELERS IN COSTUMES (but nothing copyrighted, please!), including a few other pirates, superheroes, and sexy girls. But sadly, our robbers are NOWHERE TO BE SEEN, as they've completely blended into the crowded street.

Plenty of reference for the floats and shit here: http://www.halloween-nyc.com/index.php

2) Mitchell: …away.

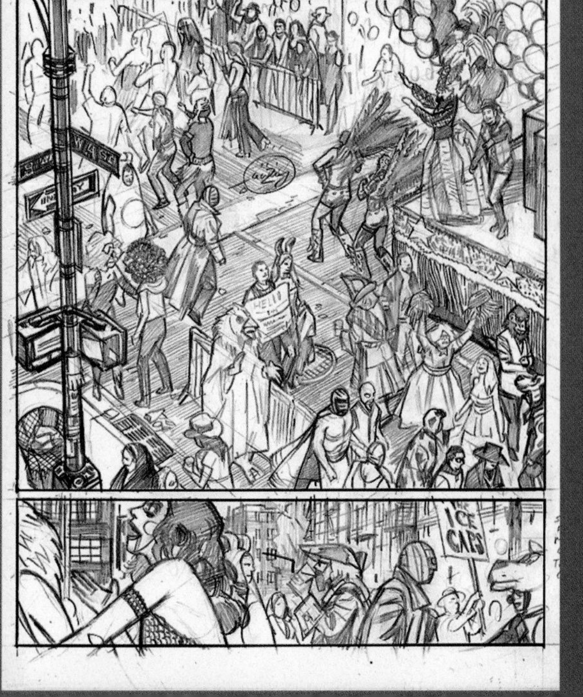

Page Twenty-seven

Page Twenty-seven, Panel One
Cut to a little later for this establishing shot of the MOON hanging in the night sky.

No Copy

Page Twenty-seven, Panel Two
These next four panels are letterbox shots of the same New York City PAY PHONE, something like this: http://www.supermanhomep-age.com/images/phonebooth/movie-phonebooth.jpg
To begin with, we're directly across the street from the phone, looking at the back of it. We can maybe see Mitchell's legs and feet as he talks on the other side of this half-booth, but we can't see his face at all yet.

1) Mitchell: Um, yes, I'd... I'd like to report a crime.

Page Twenty-seven, Panel Three
Move in closer on this same phone, like we're "dolly-ing" towards it.

2) Mitchell: I mean, I wouldn't like to, but... you know.

Page Twenty-seven, Panel Four
Move in even closer. We still can't see Mitch's face.

3) Mitchell: It's a robbery, homicide, all of that.
4) Mitchell: Yeah, right across the street from this payphone. I know that computer you're looking at has the address. I have no idea how, but I... I can feel it.

Page Twenty-seven, Panel Five
And move in even tighter on the back of this payphone.

5) Mitchell: My name?

Page Twenty-eight

Page Twenty-eight, SPLASH
Finally, change angles for this SPLASH of Mitchell, our first look at him without the bandages. He has the phone pressed to his right ear, and we're looking at his left side, which we can see is HIDEOUSLY DISFIGURED, as it was in the explosion from Issue #1. His left ear is missing almost entirely, and the rest of the left side of his face is a mess of STITCHES, EXPOSED MUSCLE AND SCAR TISSUE. But growing over these scars and stitches is a NETWORK OF CIRCUITRY that covers much of his face. It's much more elaborate than the few clean circuits Mitch has left on his reconstructed face in the present. This network of circuitry is again GLOWING brightly here, lighting the entire shot with its brightness. In his free hand, we can see that Mitch is holding his grandmother'S POCKET WATCH.

1) Mitchell (unique font, green): It doesn't matter.

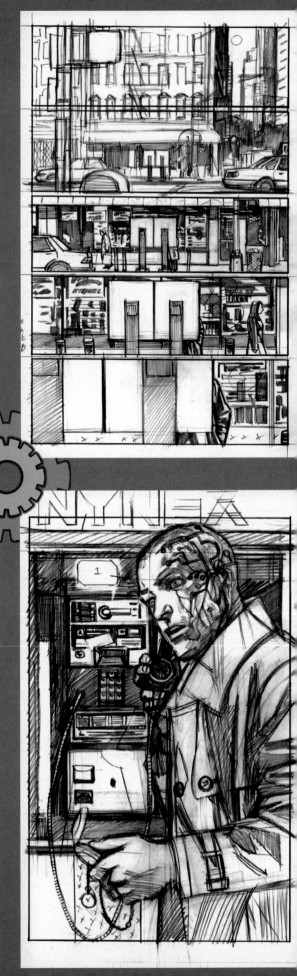

Page Twenty-nine

Page Twenty-nine, Panel One

Smash cut back to our story's present for one last close-up of Mitchell's EYES.

1) Wylie (from off): Sir.

Page Twenty-nine, Panel Two

Pull out to the largest panel of the page to reveal that we're now on the HELICOPTER PAD on top of City Hall (see Issue #3 for reference). We're with Mitchell in the foreground. He's looking down at the POCKET WATCH in his hand, oblivious to the fact that Deputy Mayor Wylie is standing just a few feet behind his left shoulder.

2) Wylie: Sir?

Page Twenty-nine, Panel Three

Push in on the two, as Mitch turns around and gestures at his prosthetic left ear.

3) Mitchell: Dave.
4) Mitchell: Sorry, don't always catch stuff in my bad ear.

5) Wylie: Oh, right. I… I always forget.

Page Twenty-nine, Panel Four

Change angles on the two men, as Mitch pockets his grandmother's watch.

6) Mitchell: I'll compliment my plastic surgeons.

7) Wylie: I was just wondering if you'd figured out how we're going to fight these Klan bitches.

8) Mitchell: I have, actually.

Page Twenty-nine, Panel Five

And this is just a dramatic shot of Mayor Hundred, as he looks right at us and says:

9) Mitchell: We're not.

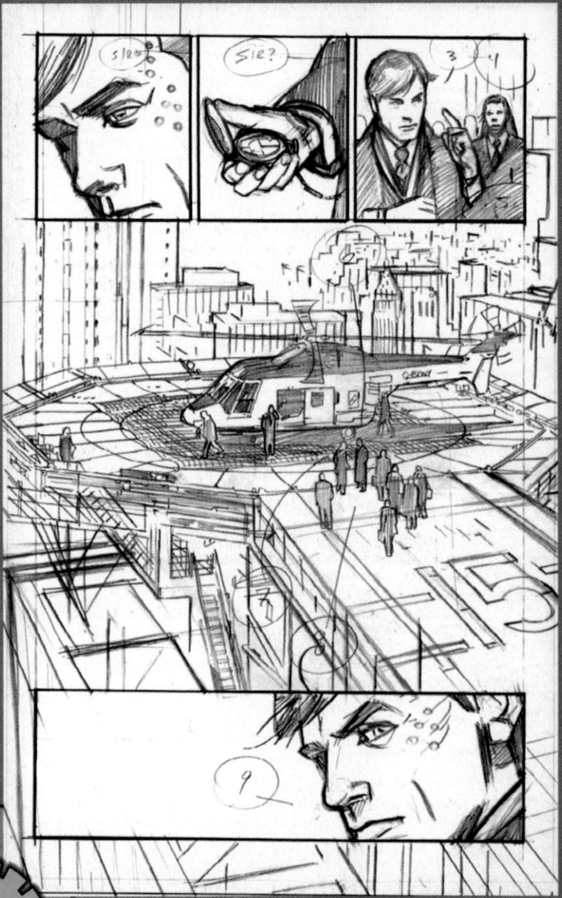
SIR?
SIR?

Page Thirty

Page Thirty, Panel One

Pull out to another shot of both men. Wylie looks confused.

1) Wylie: Excuse me?

2) Mitchell: Oh, we'll surround their dumb rally with a phalanx of NYPD, make sure nothing gets out of control.
3) Mitchell: Meanwhile, you and I are going to hold a counter rally on the other side of the island that same day in support of… I don't know, tolerance or whatever.

Page Thirty, Panel Two

Push in closer on the two, as Mitchell reaches into his pocket for something.

4) Mitchell: January is putting together an invite list for musicians. Everyone wants to be involved, so we'll get whoever the kids like these days.

5) Wylie: You're honestly letting these monsters come here?
6) Wylie: In their fucking masks?

Page Thirty, Panel Three

Push in on Mitchell, as he pulls out a small SCRAP OF PAPER. Please leave room for him to read all this out loud:

7) Mitchell: "Anonymity is a shield from the tyranny of the majority. It thus exemplifies the purpose behind the Bill of Rights: to protect unpopular individuals from retaliation--and their ideas from suppression--at the hand of an intolerant society."

Page Thirty, Panel Four

Pull out to another shot of both men.

8) Wylie: What the hell is that?

9) Mitchell: It's from an old Supreme Court case that said you can't prohibit the anonymous distribution of political junk.
10) Mitchell: I used to think it also justified me wearing a disguise while I lamely attempted to fight crime, so I carried a copy with me back in my Great Machine days.

Page Thirty, Panel Five

Change angles for this largest panel of the page, as Mitchell turns his back on an indignant Wylie.

11) Wylie: What does that have to do with these bigots? You were a hero!

12) Mitchell: No, I was an idiot.

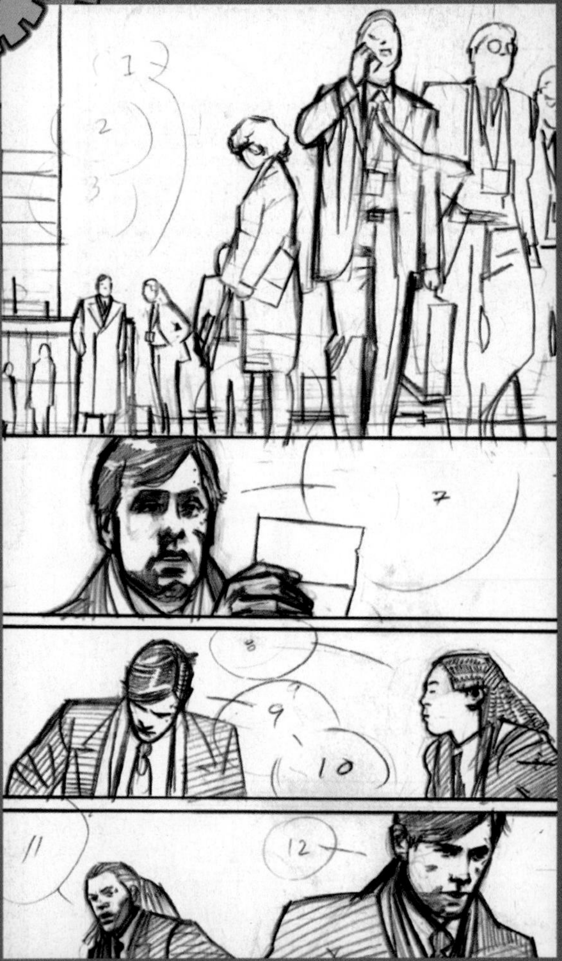

Page Thirty-one

Page Thirty-one, Panel One
          Push in on Mitchell, as he turns around to talk with us.

          1) Mitchell: I rationalized hiding my identity as a way to pro-
tect the people I loved… but deep down, I was just embarrassed by my own
incompetence.

Page Thirty-one, Panel Two
          Pull out to a shot of both men, as Wylie listens to Mitchell talk.

          2) Mitchell: If you want to talk unpopular individuals living in
intolerant societies, look at Martin Luther King. Did he ever wear a fucking
disguise?
          3) Mitchell: He risked his career, his family, his life, because he
knew that Americans don't give a shit about people who aren't brave enough
to put a name and a face to their opinions.

Page Thirty-one, Panel Three
          Push in on Mitchell for this largest panel of the page, and please
leave room for all of this word soup:

          4) Mitchell: So yeah, let's give the Klan the right to put on their
idiotic dunce caps and hide their hayseed mugs.
          5) Mitchell: Let's give spoiled anarchist kids the right to cover
their faces with bandanas so mommy and daddy won't recognize them on
CNN.
          6) Mitchell: Let's give the extremist assholes who protest the
peace negotiations outside the U.N. the right to cower behind their keffiyehs.

Page Thirty-one, Panel Four
          And this is just a nice shot of the Mayor, as he looks off at noth-
ing in particular.

          7) Mitchell: Anonymity is the fastest, most efficient way to let
the rest of us know that you and your beliefs are worthless.

Page Thirty-one, Panel Five
          Cut over to Wylie, who has his arms crossed. He doesn't look
totally convinced by his boss' words.

          8) Wylie: That's a lovely speech, sir, but you sure it's not just
your way of ducking out of a battle you can't win?
          9) Wylie: All due respect, everyone who hides behind a mask
might be a coward…

Page Thirty-two

Page Thirty-two, SPLASH
          Finally, we end on this SPLASH of a somber Mitchell, a nice
profile shot of the Mayor with his NECKTIE whipping in the Fall wind.
His scars GLOW faintly as he looks out at the city he controls. Large in the
sky above him, we can see an impressionistic shot of the jetpack-wearing
GREAT MACHINE (our classic clunky version!) SOARING through the
sky. The Great Machine should have muted coloring or something to make
it clear the hero isn't actually flying through the sky. This is just one of
Mitchell's fondest memories of the past.

          1) Wylie (from off): …but not every coward hides behind a
mask.

END OF BOOK 3